*Philosophy and the State
in France*

Philosophy and the State in France

THE RENAISSANCE TO THE ENLIGHTENMENT

Nannerl O. Keohane

PRINCETON UNIVERSITY PRESS, PRINCETON, NEW JERSEY

Copyright © 1980 by Princeton University Press
Published by Princeton University Press, Princeton, New Jersey
In the United Kingdom: Princeton University Press, Guildford, Surrey

All Rights Reserved

Library of Congress Cataloging in Publication Data will be found
on the last printed page of this book

This book has been composed in Linotype Janson

Clothbound editions of Princeton University Press books
are printed on acid-free paper, and binding materials are
chosen for strength and durability

Printed in the United States of America by Princeton
University Press, Princeton, New Jersey

Decorations throughout the book are from Guillaume de La Perrière,
Le Miroir politique (Paris, 1567).

Contents

PREFACE ix

INTRODUCTION 3

PART I. THE ORDER OF THE KINGDOM AND THE ORDER OF THE SOUL

ONE. Sixteenth-Century Constitutionalism 25
1. The Ancient Constitution 25
2. Philippe de Commynes and Medieval Constitutionalism 28
3. Claude de Seyssel and *La Monarchie de France* 32
4. Seyssel on the Orders of the Kingdom and the Ordering of the Will 38
5. Etienne Pasquier and the *Recherches de la France* 42
6. François Hotman and *Francogallia* 49

TWO. The Development of Absolutist Thought 54
1. Types of Monarchical Power 54
2. Guillaume Budé and Absolutist Rhetoric under Francis I 58
3. Michel de l'Hôpital on Justice and the Order of the State 61
4. Jean Bodin on the Commonwealth: The Theory of Sovereignty 67
5. Bodin on the Commonwealth: Patterns of Participation in Power 73
6. Justice and the Common Good 79

THREE. Individualism and Humanism 83
1. Civic Humanism in the Sixteenth Century 83
2. The Abbey of Thélème: Rabelais 87
3. On Voluntary Servitude: La Boétie 92
4. Montaigne's Individualism 98
5. Montaigne's Communities: Friendship and Authority 106
6. Public and Private Virtue 111

PART II. INTEREST AND PRUDENCE: THE STATE AND THE SAGE

FOUR. Two Moralities: The Philosopher and the *Patrie* — 119
  1. Separation from the State — 119
  2. The Absolutism of the Jurists — 124
  3. Justus Lipsius on Private Tranquillity and Public Profit — 129
  4. Pierre Charron's *Sagesse* — 135
  5. Charron's Politics — 139
  6. The Erudite Libertines and the Double Arcana — 144

FIVE. Public Utility Preferred to Private: Mercantilism and *Raison d'Etat* — 151
  1. The Passions and the Interests — 151
  2. Mercantilism and the Socialization of Avarice — 158
  3. Montchrétien's Political Economy — 163
  4. The Politics of Reason of State — 168
  5. Richelieu on the Interests of the Monarch and the Interests of the State — 174

SIX. A Variety of Loves and the Sovereignty of Will — 183
  1. Augustine and French Thought — 183
  2. Self-love from Sebond to Sénault — 188
  3. Balzac and the Glory of the Individual — 197
  4. Descartes' Provisional Morality — 202
  5. The Philosopher and the City — 208

SEVEN. The Politics of Interest in the Fronde — 213
  1. Rebellion in France and Europe — 213
  2. The Ormée in Bordeaux: The People's Fronde — 217
  3. Claude Joly on the Ancient Constitution: The Parlementary Fronde — 220
  4. Retz in Paris: The Noble Fronde — 223
  5. Saint-Evremond and Cyrano: The Libertines and the Fronde — 229

PART III. THE ZENITH AND DECLINE OF ABSOLUTE MONARCHY

EIGHT. Orthodox Absolutist Theory and the *Métier du Roi* — 241
  1. Absolutist Rhetoric in the Wake of the Fronde — 241
  2. Louis XIV and the Business of a King — 244

3. Bossuet: The Apogee of Absolutist Thought 251
4. Apollo at Noonday 258

NINE. Authority and Community in the Two Cities 262
1. Jansenism and Opposition 262
2. Pascal on Authority, Custom, Justice 266
3. Pascal on Concupiscence and *Amour-propre* 273
4. Unity in Diversity: The Community of the Saved 277

TEN. Self-Love and Society: Jansenism and the *Honnête Homme* 283
1. The Ideal of *l'Honnêteté* 283
2. The *Maxims* of La Rochefoucauld 289
3. The *Essays* of Pierre Nicole 293
4. Jean Domat and the "Esprit des Lois" 303
5. The Dispersion of Jansenist Ideas 307

ELEVEN. The Growth of Opposition to Absolute Monarchy in France 312
1. The Revocation of the Edict of Nantes 312
2. Denis Veiras and the Politics of Utopia 318
3. La Bruyère and the Characters of His Contemporaries 323
4. Vauban and the Self-knowledge of the "Grand Estat" 327

TWELVE. The Conduct of a Prince and a Program for Reform 332
1. The Duke of Burgundy's Circle 332
2. Fénelon's Utopias and the Ethic of *Pur Amour* 338
3. A Program for Reform 343
4. Boulainvilliers and the *Thèse Nobiliaire* 346
5. Boisguilbert and Laissez-faire 350

PART IV. APPROACHES TO A SYNTHESIS

THIRTEEN. A New Science of Politics in a Republic Protected by a King 361
1. Political Inquiry in the Regency 361
2. Evangelistic Utilitarianism 365
3. The Machine of State 369
4. The Marquis d'Argenson on Interest and *Amour-propre* 376
5. Liberty, Equality, and Order 383

FOURTEEN. Montesquieu: Constitutionalism and Civic Virtue 392
1. Political Science and the *Spirit of the Laws* 392
2. Social Physics and the Conservation of Complexity 395
3. Absolutism and Moderate Government 401
4. The Ancients and the Moderns 408
5. Virtue and Politics 415

FIFTEEN. Rousseau: The General Interest in the General Will 420
1. The Morals of the Age 420
2. The Masterpiece of Policy in Our Century 425
3. Rousseau's Alternative Moralities: *Emile* 432
4. Rousseau's Alternative Moralities: The *Social Contract* 435
5. Authority, Liberty, and Community 442

CONCLUSION 451
1. The Individual and the Polity 451
2. Public and Private Spheres 454
3. Subjects and Citizens 457
4. Interest and Community 461

BIBLIOGRAPHY 465

INDEX 489

Preface

In the liberal tradition closely associated with Anglo-American political experience, two principles are often taken to be fundamental: that power must be checked and divided if it is not to be abused, and that the rights of individuals are the basic elements to be safeguarded by the state. In France, from the sixteenth century until well into the eighteenth, the first of these principles was rejected outright and the second commonly ignored. Bodin's assertion that sovereignty is indivisible was taken as axiomatic by his countrymen; and Frenchmen were more concerned with interests than with rights. Careful political thinkers, no friends to tyranny, arrived at conclusions about the organization of power, and the status of individuals within the polity, at odds with those we sometimes regard as self-evident.

Yet the ideas of these thinkers are not alien to our beliefs about well-ordered states. Concepts of sovereignty and interest developed by French philosophers and jurists are important components of a stock of ideas and attitudes common to citizens of constitutionalist democracies today. By exploring the development and flourishing of these concepts in French political theory before the Revolution, we may hope for a clearer understanding of our principles. And the unfamiliar guise in which these concepts appear in their native settings can renew our awareness of the diverse solutions human beings can devise for durable political dilemmas.

This study is intended as a contribution to such understanding and awareness. It is a history of ideas, of traditions of discourse among a small number of literate and privileged Frenchmen who wrote about politics in the period between the full flowering of the Renaissance and that of the Enlightenment. Since most of these writers were self-conscious about the connection between their enterprise and that of authors from antiquity through the Middle Ages, the book is an account of one part of a lengthy dialogue in political philosophy. One prominent theme in this dialogue, particularly important during the era discussed here, is the juxtaposition of philosophy and the state. This juxtaposition marks the contrast between the contemplative life of the philosopher and the active life of rulers and men of affairs. It also attends the presentation of a new task for philosophers discoursing about politics, who are confronted with a new phenomenon: the modern state. The ideas I discuss were developed in response to contemporary events in the polity and society, and some notion of those events is necessary for a satisfactory grasp of those ideas. I have tried to provide enough historical narrative to make the period comprehensible to those unfamiliar with it, and enough discussion of economic and social issues to remind readers that these ideas are reflections upon facts. My major sources, however, are books and essays written by philosophers who helped shape the character of the new polity.

The book is meant to be useful to readers with disparate backgrounds and reasons for interest in the material. Since it is not intended solely for specialists in French life and letters, I have translated all quotations. Unless otherwise noted, the translations are my own. Many of the works have never been translated, and others are available only in unreliable or partial translations. Occasionally I have quoted directly from familiar translations that I did not think I could improve upon; in other instances I have consulted several translations as a check on my interpretation. I have modernized spelling and grammar in the few instances in which I used contemporary English versions of the texts.

One of the purposes of the book is to introduce readers to a rich and varied secondary literature. I have, therefore, provided a generous bibliography, but limited it to those works I found sufficiently pertinent to mention in the notes. A few books were specially important in determining the direction of my argument and suggesting sources. Lionel Rothkrug's work first revealed the richness of the seventeenth century, and stimulated the expansion of a book originally conceived as covering the period from 1685 to 1750. Books by W. F. Church, Julian Franklin, Donald Kelley, and Etienne Thuau were particularly valuable on the Renaissance and early seventeenth century. The importance of the individualist tradition became clear from reading A. J. Krailsheimer and Anthony Levi. Albert Hirschman's book helped focus several arguments in the final version. Quentin Skinner's study was published after mine was completed, but his approach to our craft as expressed in several earlier essays influenced me a good deal.

A number of scholars have read all or part of the manuscript and have made valuable suggestions. Donald Kelley and George Armstrong Kelly gave good advice on the organization of the whole study, as well as helpful reactions to each chapter. Others who read large portions of the book include Charles Drekmeier, Julian Franklin, Albert Hirschman, Bruce Kuklick, John Pocock, Melvin Richter, Judith Shklar, and Giovanni Sartori. Among the numerous colleagues who read a section or a chapter, I am particularly indebted to Paul Baltes, Roger Boesche, Blair Campbell, Paul David, Elisabeth Hansot, Roland Pennock, Molly Shanley, Peter Stillman, Richard Teichgraeber, and Gordon Wright. Peter Breiner, Martine Mont-Reynaud, Claude Fillet, and Catherine Stark assisted with specific research problems. Helen Morales and Lois Renner typed the early versions, and Kate Hughes the final draft. I am happy to acknowledge my debt to all of these.

Fellowship support for early stages of research and writing was provided by a grant from the American Association of University Women and a Summer Stipend from the National Endowment for the Humanities, plus sabbatical support from Swarthmore College. Research and leave funds from Stanford University, as well as grants from the National Endowment for the Humanities and the Rockefeller Foundation, administered through the Center for Advanced Study in the Behavioral Sciences, supported the last stages of the work. Like many another fortunate maker of books, I take special pleasure in recording my gratitude to the Center for months of blissful scholarly solitude interrupted only by stimulating conversations with colleagues. The Center bears a certain resemblance to Rabelais' abbey of Thélème. It is a utopian place to live and work; unlike most utopias, it proves better than its promise.

Sanford G. Thatcher and Margaret Case of Princeton University Press provided excellent editorial support and insight at all stages of publication. Among other institutions and their staffs, I am indebted to the libraries of Harvard, Yale, and Stanford Universities, the Bibliothèque de l'Arsenal and the Bibliothèque nationale. Parts of Chapter Three appeared in *Political Theory*, and I am grateful for permission to reprint those portions. Stanford University Press graciously allowed me to quote extensively from Donald Frame's translation of Montaigne's *Essays*. Parallel versions of Chapter One and Chapter Fifteen appeared as essays in *Constitutionalism* (NOMOS XX) and in *Political Theory*.

A final debt that I am happy to recognize is to my family, for support and encouragement of all kinds. My father taught me to love philosophy and history. My children accepted the long hours at the typewriter with good humor. My mother-in-law made many of those hours possible, and shared professionally in the excitement of writing. My husband Robert O. Keohane read, argued, nurtured, raised my confidence and my consciousness, and to him, above all, I am grateful.

There is one sense in which the entire book must be bracketed. There are few women on these pages—an occasional member of a salon or a utopia, a mother recognized for raising citizens for the *patrie*. For the most part, these are men writing about male pursuits.

As a woman, I take an ironic pleasure in writing about men who thought women incapable of participating in or discoursing about politics. This is a book in which masculine nouns and pronouns are used almost exclusively. To have done otherwise would suggest what is not true: that these writers believed politics to be a matter for both sexes. It is well to specify this exclusion at the outset; and I hope that readers who are forewarned will sometimes pause to reflect upon it.

Musing on such topics, I think of the contributions my mother made to the writing of this book. She exchanged her press card for an apron when she married, and taught us and tended us until we were all through college, when she went back to a promising career cut short by an early death. I am grateful for what she did, yet frustrated by the knowledge that she never had the opportunity to finish her own book. With these things in mind, I dedicate this one to her memory. Montesquieu said of his long treatise: *Prolem sine matre creatam.* The same could surely not be said of mine.

*Philosophy and the State
in France*

Introduction

ONE way of picturing the pattern of political development in France assumes a traditional constitutionalist monarchy enduring from medieval times, abruptly superseded by an absolutist regime in the seventeenth century. Contemporaries of Richelieu and subjects of the aging Louis XIV sometimes took this pattern for granted, contrasting their situation with the "good old days" of Henry IV, Francis I, or Saint Louis. Their nostalgia was not unfounded. The French monarchy did become more concentrated and powerful in the seventeenth century.[1] Dynastic and aggrandizing warfare dictated major changes in the state. A new administrative structure focused on the intendants in the provinces, and provided a greatly expanded place for government in the economy. A more or less successful policy of weakening old noble families and corporate institutions helped tip the balance of power in favor of the crown. But the differences between the seventeenth-century "absolutist" state and the "traditional" monarchy are not so great as has sometimes been supposed. The will to rationalization and centralization was present in the polity long before Richelieu came to power in the 1620s. Even at the height of Louis XIV's ascendancy, in the 1670s, pockets of privilege, custom, and exclusion flourished in France.

It is a commonplace, but one that bears repeating here, that no state is ever "absolute" in the sense of wielding power that is effectively unlimited. The structural conditions that dictate how power will be deployed beyond the monarch's throne or office, and the results of ordinary human frailty, set limits even when no institutions are responsible for doing so. The most "unlimited" tyranny may be most threatened with limitations of both sorts, and disciplined authority may find its reach extended by imposing limitations on itself. These insights were central to the arguments of French publicists who distinguished between absolute royal power and despotic power. At no time did the French monarchy claim power unlimited by considerations of the

[1] Richard Bonney concludes his careful study of *Political Change in France under Richelieu and Mazarin*, p. 441, by asserting that "in political terms, France in 1661 was scarcely recognizable as the same country that had survived the trauma of Henri IV's assassination and the troubles of Louis XIII's minority."

common good; and the moral purposes of Christianity were accepted as governing the ways a king's power should be used. Submission to divine laws, however vaguely formulated, and to some version of the fundamental constitutive laws of the French polity was part of what it meant to kings of France to exercise a *puissance absolue*.

What made their power "absolute" insofar as it ever was so, was their claim to act as the final interpreters of those laws, to reorganize the realm in accordance with their own vision of what the common good required, and to require from the French people whatever resources were needed in money and in arms to pursue their policies without waiting for the legitimating imprimatur of any other institution.[2] French monarchs of the seventeenth century, especially Louis XIV, managed to make good on these claims to a greater extent than their predecessors. In this sense, the regime was more "absolutist" than before. But the rhetoric accompanying the claims and the potential obstacles to the exercise of royal power remained very much the same.

As several historians have pointed out, the old regime rarely destroyed any institution.[3] New magistrates and officers were added to those whose powers they supplanted, whose claims and privileges to some extent remained intact. The practice of selling offices that became general in France after the fifteenth century encouraged the creation of new posts, and discouraged the disappearance of old ones. Judged purely as a political device, this policy illustrates the ambiguous character of a number of policies pursued by French monarchs. It demonstrates the flexibility of control available to an absolutist king, who could create offices at will. But such officers developed independence and corporate consciousness, which placed limits on that same flexibility in the future.[4] This pattern characterized the *ancien régime*: new practices were superimposed on old ways of doing things, new taxes added to the old. Yet the old practices, like the old taxes, continued as elements to be reckoned with.

The central dilemma faced by the French monarchy in the early

[2] The clearest discussion of "absolutism" is Fritz Hartung and Roland Mousnier, "Quelques problèmes concernant la monarchie absolue," in the Proceedings of the Tenth Congress of the International Committee for the Historical Sciences, IV, 1-55.

[3] "This regime did not suppress, it superimposed; it allowed old institutions and ancestral forces to become fossilized, or rather sleep, never dreaming that they might someday be resuscitated." Goubert, *L'Ancien Régime*, II, 16. See also Eugene L. Asher, *The Resistance to the Maritime Classes: The Survival of Feudalism in the France of Colbert*, and Robert R. Harding, *Anatomy of a Power Elite*, on the fortunes of the provincial governors.

[4] Roland Mousnier, *La Venalité des offices sous Henry IV et Louis XIII*, pp. 581-667.

modern period, the dilemma to which such practices were a response, was the consolidation of control over a territory peopled by subjects of diverse cultures and ancient customary expectations, dominated by numerous powerful lesser lords. The specter of petty seigneurial overlordship haunted French politics and political theory long after feudalism as a social and economic system had been weakened. Noble contentiousness against the crown was a recurrent threat, and some form of "bastard feudalism" characterized the society and polity right up to the end of the *ancien régime*.[5] Until the sixteenth century, French monarchs were also preoccupied with bringing into the kingdom rich duchies and provinces that had maintained a more or less independent status, areas such as Burgundy, Brittany, Provence, Navarre. Even when subjected to the crown of France, these provinces retained many of their traditional customs and privileges, including provincial and regional assemblies and a plethora of provisions for municipal government. Agents of the king were required to bargain for taxes with notables assembled in various institutions in areas where zealous particularism remained strong for centuries. In other areas corrupt oligarchies were relieved of their civic duties with little bother, and to general relief. The outcome was a bewildering variety of expectations and arrangements that offered rich material for a centralizing government to attack, as well as durable resistance to such efforts.[6]

The label "Renaissance monarch" has been coined to describe the kings throughout Europe in the fifteenth and sixteenth centuries who dealt with such challenges by focusing power in their own persons and their courts, promulgating the notion of a state radiating from the central figure of a brilliant individual, the prince.[7] Many Frenchmen welcomed the Renaissance monarchy as an alternative to local tyranny and civil strife. They assumed that the business of a king is to protect all his subjects equally in their several conditions, and that in order to do this effectively, he should enjoy a kind of power that they described as *absolue*. It seemed to them that the attempt to put barriers in the way of royal power was bound to have unsatisfactory consequences. It would frustrate a benevolent ruler unnecessarily, and ham-

[5] Joseph R. Strayer, *On the Medieval Origins of the Modern State*, pp. 57-88, discusses "bastard feudalism." On the fate of feudalism in early modern France, compare Robert Mandrou, *La France aux XVIIe et XVIIIe siècles*, pp. 64-80, and J.H.M. Salmon, *Society in Crisis: France in the Sixteenth Century*, ch. 2. Jerome Blum, *The End of the Old Order in Rural Europe*, places the French case in a European perspective.

[6] Wallace K. Ferguson, *Europe in Transition: 1300-1520*, pp. 177-181; Pierre Goubert, *L'Ancien Régime*, vol. II: *Les Pouvoirs*, ch. 4.

[7] J. Russell Major, *Representative Institutions in Renaissance France, 1421-1559*, ch. 1.

per his ability to benefit his people. It would provide dangerous alternative loci of power in the state to threaten the security of ordinary subjects. And it would open the way for invasion from abroad, in the form of English arms or papal domination of the church.

The most pressing threat to the consolidation of the French monarchy until the end of the fifteenth century had been English control of territories on the mainland, and the reiterated claim by English monarchs to the throne of France. This contributed to the enduring disinclination on the part of many Frenchmen to preach doctrines of resistance to the monarchy. The threat of English arms led to support for embattled kings, and doctrines of resistance were associated from the earliest times with the rebellious and cantankerous English, whose "regicidal proclivities" were contrasted with the loyalty, stability, and firm allegiances of the French.[8] Of equal importance to some Frenchmen was the integrity of the French church to control its own policies and offices. An absolutist monarch was an ally for Gallicanism against ultramontane domination.

For most Frenchmen of the sixteenth and seventeenth centuries, however, the real threat of tyranny came not from across the Channel or the Alps, and not from Paris, but from much closer to home. They worried more about overmighty subjects than about authoritative sovereigns. They looked to the concentrated power of the king as a bulwark against particularistic oppression in the polity. As Roland Mousnier put it, "there was no need to insist on the guarantee of the rights of individuals. The rights of the strong were sufficiently guaranteed by the nature of things. The rights of the others could only be guaranteed by the power of the King."[9] Power in the hands of kings meant protection against the abusive power of others, and Frenchmen expected kings to protect each of them against disproportionate power in the hands of their fellows. This attitude, which made it difficult for Frenchmen to cooperate in influencing or attempting to control the central government right up until the Revolution, can be discovered in late medieval times. In assessing the regime of his master Louis XI, who died in 1483, the memoirist Philippe de Commynes observed, "although some of his successors were a bit more compassionate toward the people and less quick to punish than he had been, this gives no cause for blaming him, nor grounds for saying that I have ever seen a better prince. It is true that he pressed his subjects hard; but

---

[8] P. S. Lewis, *Later Medieval France: The Polity*, pp. 91-93.

[9] "Comment les Français du XVIIe siècle voyaient la constitution," *XVIIe siècle* no. 25-26 (1955), p. 28.

he never allowed anyone else to do so, at home or abroad [*ny privé ne estrange*]."[10]

Frenchmen who welcomed consolidation of power in the monarchy were thus not unconcerned with the securities and liberties of subjects. They believed that concentrated power provides more effective protection for all members of a community than divided power; and they regarded the traditional complexities and deep-rooted interests that comprised the polity as sufficient warrants against abuse of power, rendering specific institutional barriers designed to prevent abuse unnecessary. Throughout the early modern era, however, two types of institutions offered some prospect of a more regularized limitation on the power of the central government, and spokesmen for these institutions discoursed about absolutism in different tones from those used by men who glorified the Renaissance prince.

The two types of institutions were the parlements, or superior courts of justice in the several provinces of France, led by the parlement of Paris; and the assemblies of the three orders of the kingdom, the Estates-General at the level of the whole nation, and the provincial estates that remained vigorous in several areas. The parlements were a recurrent focus for opposition to the program of the centralizing monarchy. They were a central factor in the civil war that occurred during the minority of Louis XIV, the Fronde. When the Sun King reached his majority, he bent his efforts fairly successfully to rendering the parlements incapable of offering effective opposition to this will. But the parlements revived in the early and middle decades of the eighteenth century as a force to be reckoned with by his successors. The doctrines developed by these magistrates to defend their role in law-making—their privilege to remonstrate with the king before they agreed to register his laws—are central to one of the traditions of argument that we will explore. The parlements never became a major counterforce to the absolutist monarchy, an independent locus of power in the state, however; and it was not part of their own conception of their role that they should be so.

The assemblies of the notables and estates of the kingdom were an outgrowth of the royal council of feudal times. They were created by late medieval monarchs to determine and shape public opinion on the eve of important national ventures requiring financial support. As a

[10] Philippe de Commynes, *Mémoires*, edited by Joseph Calmette, II, 324. Similar sentiments were frequently expressed by fifteenth-century Frenchmen, including Gerson; see the useful discussion of "Jean-Juvenal des Ursins and the Common Literary Attitude towards Tyranny in Fifteenth-Century France" by P. S. Lewis, *Medium Aevum* XXXIV (1965), 103-121.

prelude to negotiating with each province, locality, and group of notables when money was needed and ordinary revenues were insufficient, monarchs occasionally sought general support for their policies, and commitment in principle to a new tax, in central assemblies. The people resisted this innovation, partly because they were anxious to protect the privileges associated with local and provincial institutions, and were slow to recognize interests binding them to other parts of France; and partly because the difficulties of traveling made men unwilling to be delegates to such assemblies.[11] The notion that the Estates-General was a bold and vigorous popular institution suppressed by the absolutist kings does not withstand examination. In the fourteenth and fifteenth centuries, the monarchs tried to use the assemblies as instruments for their own purposes, and the people resisted. Once the kings managed to establish the convention that they could tax the people regularly without some national assembly granting its consent, they no longer had much need of such bodies. In periods of crisis for the polity in later centuries, when either prince or people felt that the convening of an Estates-General would be beneficial, it proved difficult to institutionalize such meetings. The old regional hostilities, the stubborn resistance to tax increases and to tax reforms, and the jealousies and suspicions among the three orders, blocked efforts to establish patterns of cooperative behavior that would make the estates effective participants in governance. No widely accepted tradition of argument would have justified such a course of action. The provincial estates continued as forces to be reckoned with in certain areas of the kingdom right up into the eighteenth century. But they worked more to differentiate one province from another, and to ensure the retention of special privileges or exemptions, than to deflect or modify the general intentions of a determined king and ministers.

Thus, instead of an abrupt replacement of limited monarchy by absolutism, there was a more complicated pattern. Old claims and privileges remained persistent, and the new institutions set up by the monarchy developed their own independent prerogatives. Yet from the late fifteenth century onwards, there was a trend toward concentrated power, marked by peaks and valleys—the alternation of *temps faibles* and *temps forts* in the power of the king.[12] The times of weakness occurred when the king was sickly or incompetent, and especially

[11] Joseph R. Strayer and Charles H. Taylor, *Studies in Early French Taxation*; Lewis, *Later Medieval France*, ch. 4.
[12] The terms *temps forts* and *temps faibles* are used by Denis Richet, *La France moderne: L'esprit des institutions*; an older description of this process of development that remains worth consulting is George Pagès, *La Monarchie d'Ancien Régime en France*.

when he was a child. Regencies for minor kings meant danger for the monarchy. The *temps forts* were the early decades of the reigns of mature and aggressive monarchs, particularly Francis I, Henry IV, and Louis XIII and XIV.

This view of the course of political development in early modern France, occurring through periods of monarchical advance succeeded by noble resurgence and monarchical retreat, is borne out in the researches of numerous historians. The social and economic changes that accompanied this political development have attracted increasing attention in recent years. There have been numerous analyses of the shifting configurations of orders and classes that provided the bases for the Renaissance monarchy and the absolutist state. Scholars dispute heatedly about whose interests were served by these regimes, and precisely what role they played in economic development and social change. From one perspective, the absolutist state appears as a "redeployed and recharged apparatus of feudal domination, . . . the new political carapace of a threatened nobility."[13] From another, the same regime is seen as hospitable to the interests of nascent capitalism, providing protection for the developing bourgeoisie against the self-protective instincts of the feudal aristocracy. From yet a third perspective, the absolutist state is regarded as an arbiter or neutral force, a transitional regime in which the interests of old aristocracy and rising bourgeoisie were neatly held in balance, a situation that allowed the monarchy itself to prosper.[14]

These arguments among modern scholars echo the substance, though not the phraseology, of disputes by Frenchmen of the *ancien régime*. Then as now, it was possible to see the monarchy as based in the middle class, as balancing off the new against the old, or as closely tied to the fortunes of the old aristocracy, depending on what one feared or hoped for. So many tenaciously held perspectives bespeak a complex situation. Nobles, townsmen, merchants, peasants, and officers of the crown all played their parts in supporting and opposing the cen-

[13] Perry Anderson, *Lineages of the Absolutist State*, p. 18; another version of this same position is taken by Boris Porchnev, *Les Soulèvements populaires en France de 1623 à 1648*, p. 43.

[14] Scholars who see the regime as hospitable to capitalism include Nicos Poulantzas, *Political Power and Social Classes*, and Immanuel Wallerstein, *The Modern World-System*. The third perspective is that of Roland Mousnier, *Les XVIe et XVIIe siècles*, and Jacques Ellul, *Histoire des institutions de l'époque Franque à la Révolution*. Mousnier is criticized by A. D. Lublinskaya, "The Contemporary Bourgeois Conception of Absolute Monarchy," *Economy and Society* 1 (1972), 65-92; in *French Absolutism: The Crucial Phase, 1620-1629*, Lublinskaya subjects various hypotheses to critical examination, and offers evidence for a position closer to that of Poulantzas or Wallerstein.

tralizing monarchy in France. One aspect of that support and opposition, the aspect that concerns us in this study, is the effort by such men to explain what they saw happening around them, and justify what they hoped would emerge from a situation they recognized as novel and uncertain.[15] Members of the aristocracy wrote to defend beleaguered privileges and bolster their influence in the polity. Jurists proud of their corporate independence and zealous of their craft mined treatises of Roman law and reinterpreted ancient practices to defend their courts against monarchical encroachment. Other jurists, equally proud of their position as ministers of the king, mined those same treatises and reformulated those same practices to demonstrate the sanctity of untrammeled sovereign power. Officers of the growing administrative bureaucracy developed theories explaining their own roles in the new governmental structure and bolstering the authority of the king who had created them. Kings and prime ministers themselves took up the task of defining and defending what they were doing.

Not all those affected by the centralizing monarchies spoke for themselves so eloquently, of course. The views of French merchants may or may not have been represented by those treatises we now recognize as liberal or constitutionalist in tone. Their interests were voiced in a few bold economic tracts, at first mercantilist and later laissez-faire in tone, written by members of the lesser nobility. But the merchants rarely spoke for themselves. And the great mass of the poorer people, the peasants and artisans, spoke quite another language than that of learned tracts in their recurrent and often desperate efforts to defend their lives and meager privileges against the ravages of war, seigneurial oppression, and monarchical taxation. Occasionally, as in the pamphlets issued by the men of the Ormée at the height of the Fronde, ordinary Frenchmen found their own voice in political argument; or else a particularly far-sighted and sensitive member of the upper classes, such as Vauban, would speak for them. For the most part, the political and economic interests of the middle and lower classes were expressed in other ways.

Still, a great number of Frenchmen did write about politics during these centuries. Not all of them wrote as partisans of some clear-cut

[15] Michael Oakeshott, *On Human Conduct*, part III, makes vivid the novelty of the task facing men who tried to understand "the character of a modern European state" in the early years of its formation. "Everything in this state . . . was vaguely familiar, but nothing was recognizably the same. Little had been lost on the way, little undeniably new had been added, but all had been changed." Furthermore, he adds, "the character of a state is not a model from which copies may be struck off; it is what the effort to understand this experience has made of it" (p. 198).

interest in the economy and polity. There were more detached observers of the passing scene, philosophers of politics, who sought some more transcendent vantage point on political reality. Such men were not disinterested; but their situation as men of leisure and principled bookishness allowed them to connect the struggles they saw taking place around them with other features of *la condition humaine*, as recorded by men of their sort in other times and places. They wanted to provide guidance for like-minded men on what is worth struggling for, what one is obliged to do as a member of a larger community, and how far one may be justified in cultivating the pleasures of a private and retiring life. Like those men more actively involved in the transformative events in society and polity, they tried, in their own way, to render a bewildering succession of events more manageable.

Their ideas were not developed in isolation, of course. In their thinking about politics, Frenchmen demonstrated a number of intellectual preferences and debts. They were familiar with the classics of Greek and Roman literature so dear to the humanists of the Renaissance: Plutarch and Seneca, Plato and Aristotle, Cicero and the Epicureans. They were for the most part jurists by training, and were steeped in Roman law. In wrestling with the problems of defining sovereignty and specifying areas in which the sovereign has no business intervening —in delimiting the public and the private realms—they relied heavily on Roman formulas. In providing guidance about the ends for which political power should be used, and in defining the good life for members of a political community, they depended on the philosophers of the polis, the sages of the Roman republic, and the fathers of the church.

Among contemporaries, Frenchmen were in regular correspondence with men of letters throughout Europe. Their ties with Italy, Holland, and England were particularly strong. Hobbesian ideas were taken more seriously by Frenchmen than they were at home, and it is worth recalling that they had been developed while Hobbes lived in France. Much of what we find novel in Mandeville and Adam Smith is rooted in the nascent utilitarianism of the Jansenists of Port-Royal, who were themselves Augustinians and Hobbists. The ideas of the Jansenists were transmitted by English visitors, including Locke, and by numerous Protestant exiles who left France in the 1680s for England and for Holland. The natural-law arguments of Locke and Pufendorf found their way into France through the translations and treatises of Barbeyrac and Burlamaqui in the early eighteenth century, but they did not come as alien imports. Many of the arguments central to that tradition had been developed by dissident Huguenots during the Wars of

Religion in sixteenth-century France, and then diffused throughout Europe, to find a place in the doctrines developed in the Netherlands and Germany in the seventeenth century, and a voice in the claims of the Puritan soldiers in the English civil war.[16] Despite these and many other fruitful borrowings, however, it is possible to isolate those political arguments that are most distinctly French in their origin and expression, and see how they are rooted in French political experience.

These were immensely fertile centuries for ideology, theory, and philosophy in politics. For the first time, the printing press made pamphleteering possible, and distributed learned treatises to a wide audience.[17] Men formed the habit of thinking historically, attempting to fit their own times into a spectrum of development over centuries, categorizing and interpreting the past. They tested themselves against the ancients in incessant disputes about the relative excellence of ancients and moderns.[18] They wondered about their own virtue and the virtues of their times; they longed for a better past, which they hoped to find in some remote present, in some far corner of the world yet unexplored. They were optimistic about the prospects for a science of man, and convinced themselves that a burgeoning of discoveries in what Francis Bacon called "civil knowledge" was just around the bend. In these and other ways, there were continuities in thinking about human beings, society, and politics that provided the durable context within which more specific discussions about kingly power and corporate and popular participation in the French polity were placed.

It is these continuities in argument that I want first of all to stress. Paul Hazard, introducing his excellent study of the dawning of the Enlightenment in France, asserted that "one day the French people almost to a man were thinking like Bossuet. The day after, they were thinking like Voltaire."[19] This memorable *mot* is misleading on both counts. Many Frenchmen long before 1680 had more in common with Voltaire than with Bossuet; and quite a few of them after 1715 found Bossuet's ideas more congenial than Voltaire's. This makes for difficulties for intellectual historians, who must post signs and fences along

[16] J.M.H. Salmon, *The French Religious Wars in English Political Thought*. On Mandeville's French background, Thomas A. Horne, *The Social Thought of Bernard Mandeville*, ch. 2.

[17] E. H. Kossmann, "The Singularity of Absolutism," in Ragnhild Hatton, ed., *Louis XIV and Absolutism*, pp. 3-17.

[18] Samuel Kinser, "Ideas of Temporal Change and Cultural Process in France, 1470-1535," in Anthony Molho and John A. Tedeschi, eds., *Renaissance Studies in Honor of Hans Baron*; Hans Baron, "The *Querelle* of Ancients and Moderns as a Problem for Renaissance Scholarship," *JHI* xx (1959), 3-22.

[19] *La Crise de la conscience européene*, translated by J. L. May as *The European Mind*, p. xv.

the routes that arguments have taken. Yet the indebtedness of Diderot and Voltaire to Bayle and Fontenelle and Malebranche, and of these in turn to Pascal, Descartes, Naudé, and Gassendi, and of all of them to Montaigne, Charron, Bacon, and Bodin, is clear. As Norman Hampson pointed out, the Enlightenment "looks like linking up with the Renaissance, itself receding in the direction of the twelfth century."[20] Beyond that there are the echoes of antiquity, the deep familiarity with the classics that permeates the *Essays* of Montaigne, or the formidable grounding in the *Politics* of Aristotle and the codebooks of Roman law that distinguishes Bodin's *République*.

Yet despite the continuities there were also changes. The differences between Bodin and Montaigne on the one hand, and Rousseau and Montesquieu on the other, are obvious enough. The point is that the changes took place within a basic continuity of arguments and preoccupations, and that the changes in political argument themselves tell us a good deal about developments in society and polity in the intervening centuries. Historians of political thought have tended to exaggerate the differences and to speak of ruptures or silences in French thought between the sixteenth and the eighteenth centuries, because they have regarded the seventeenth as a wasteland populated only by sterile and complacent supporters of the Bourbon kings.

The seventeenth century, far from being a wasteland in French political thought, was a pivotal and exciting period. This conviction determines the structure of my argument. The overall purpose of this book is to chart the development of ideas about philosophy and politics, monarchical power and popular participation, the sovereign and the subject in early modern France. This development spanned several centuries; but the names and central arguments from the sixteenth and eighteenth centuries are generally familiar to students of political thought. Although much work remains to be done, the Enlightenment has been studied from several points of view. If one wants to know more about the wars of religion, good books can be consulted. It is the seventeenth century that is still alien to us. This is the piece of the puzzle that most urgently requires putting into place if we are to understand the course of political argument in France. In this study, therefore, the discussion of the sixteenth and eighteenth centuries is governed by the desire to see how they provided the foundations and capstones for seventeenth-century arguments. Without some knowledge of sixteenth-century preoccupations, the seventeenth century cannot be understood; and the importance of seventeenth-century argu-

[20] *The Cultural History of the Enlightenment*, p. 15; see also Ira O. Wade, *The Intellectual Origins of the French Enlightenment*.

ments is more firmly established when it is apparent that they bore fruit in the political theories of the Enlightenment. The ideas expressed between the accession of Henry IV and the death of Louis XIV, however, are our primary concern.

In any study such as this, choices of topics and emphases must be made that will appear wrong-headed or eccentric to other scholars. Within the seventeenth century itself, the political ideas in the dramas of Racine and Molière are not treated. Little attention is given to the political theory of exiled Frenchmen after the revocation of the Edict of Nantes, including such important figures as Bayle and Jurieu. Arguments for popular sovereignty and natural liberty in the tracts produced by sixteenth-century Huguenots are slighted. This reflects my judgment that accounts already available do full justice to the Huguenots, and that because of this, scholars tend to exaggerate their role in French thought and overlook other traditions of argument.[21] I have paid less attention to arguments about religion and the state, and the Gallican tradition among jurists, than some readers will find warranted. But this book is not intended as a comprehensive survey. I have tried to identify the most important contributions to a fairly coherent set of arguments to which countless other Frenchmen contributed in less striking ways. And I have been particularly concerned with theorists who offered distinctive solutions to political dilemmas recognized as important by their contemporaries, and still of concern to us today.

A corollary preoccupation that has guided my choices from the outset has been the desire to shed light on the political theories of Montesquieu and Rousseau, by showing how their arguments are rooted in earlier French thought. One reason I (and presumably many of my readers) find this material worth pondering is that it helps us understand two great figures with whom we are already familiar. Many of these themes find a denouement in the ideas of other important thinkers of the Enlightenment—Voltaire and Diderot, Helvétius and the Physiocrats. To work out all these denouements, however, is a matter for another book.

To understand how political thinkers who shared basic premises about monarchy and its purposes could nonetheless disagree among themselves on important points, it is useful to think of three modes of

[21] For Jurieu, Guy H. Dodge, *The Political Theory of the Huguenots of the Dispersion* is the standard work; there are good discussions of Bayle in the works cited above by Wade and Hazard. More generally, the importance of natural law in French thought is brought out in studies as diverse as those of Robert Derathé, *Jean-Jacques Rousseau et la science-politique de son temps*, and Kingsley Martin, *French Liberal Thought in the Eighteenth Century*.

political argument in France: constitutionalism, absolutism, and individualism. The notion of traditions of argument, vocabularies, or modes of discourse has proved fruitful for several historians of political thought in recent years, and serves well in this enquiry.[22] The names that I have chosen for the three modes of argument have the defect of being somewhat shopworn, but they bring with them an initial cluster of connotations that will help clarify the traditions I describe. A first statement of the central themes in each of these three modes of argument will be made here and in the next three chapters. A full understanding of the differences and areas of congruence among them depends on seeing what happened to them as they developed along separate courses and then gradually converged.

In political theory, an alternation of periods analogous to the *temps faibles* and *temps forts* of the monarchy itself can be discerned: periods when constitutionalism was prominent in France, and periods dominated by energetic absolutist argument. These periods do not correspond exactly to the strong and weak periods of the monarchy, but the two were correlated. Absolutist arguments tended to dominate in the first decades of a period of strong kingship, and the last years of a period of weakness. Constitutionalist arguments were more often heard at the end of a strong reign, and the beginning of the *temps faibles*. The reasons for this pattern are fairly obvious: royalist rhetoric was evoked by the brilliant prospects and early achievements of a Francis I or Louis XIV, as well as by the deep longing for order and stability of a people worn out by civil war. Constitutionalist arguments were heard when long reigns began to be felt as a burden on the people, and alternatives to autocratic rule were worth exploring. This pattern was maintained, in broad outline, from the mid-sixteenth to the mid-eighteenth century.

There was also a secular trend toward absolutism in French political theory, underlying the peaks and valleys, from the fifteenth through the seventeenth centuries. But we should be careful not to exaggerate this trend, or assume a unilinear development. Propagandists for the late medieval Valois kings assiduously cultivated various myths associated with the sacred character of kingship. They stressed the christological aspects of the monarch's status as head of the *corpus mysticum*, his second, immortal, and unfleshly body—his realm.[23] An apologist for Charles VI, Jean de Terre-Vermeil, referred to his king as "God on

[22] See particularly Quentin Skinner, *The Foundations of Modern Political Thought*, and J.G.A. Pocock, *Politics, Language and Time*.
[23] Marc Bloch, *Les Rois thaumaturges*; Ernst Kantorowicz, *The King's Two Bodies: a Study in Medieval Political Theology*.

earth" nearly three centuries before Louis XIV established himself in godlike splendor at Versailles.[24] And some of the refulgent royalist rhetoric of the reign of Francis I or Henry IV matches anything produced by the Sun King's adulators. Beneath the myths and rhetoric, the juristic basis for absolutism was laid early on as well, in the principles of *la puissance absolue* drawn from the Roman law, and in the Gallican insistence on the freedom of the French king from control by any source.[25] Thus several elements of absolutist thought were available at the beginning of the sixteenth century.

Until the later part of that century, the elements distinctive of absolutist thought were used interchangeably with those we associate with constitutionalism. But by the end of the religious wars, two separate ways of conceiving the French monarchy began to be apparent. The constitutionalists remained faithful to the arguments of Renaissance jurists, as the absolutists moved toward the theory of the divine right of kings, and a fascination with *raison d'état*. Only after Bodin's theory of sovereignty was combined with ancient images linking monarchy and religion was a theory of divine right properly so-called produced in France. This step was taken during the reign of Henry IV, by publicists grateful for the blessings of strong government and anxious to secure them to posterity, as well as wishing to please their king. The final element in absolutist thought was added in the 1620s and 1630s under the auspices of cardinal de Richelieu, who saw to it that *raison d'état* became part of the political reason supporting the monarchy of France. Thus, in several stages, an absolutist dogma was forged that supported and justified the activities of Louis XIV.

Bodin's theory stands as one of the crucial junctures in the development of absolutist thought, even though Bodin himself retained many elements of the constitutionalist tradition. The major early source of constitutionalism was the political theory of Claude de Seyssel, a Renaissance civil servant and jurist who wrote a treatise for the edification of the young Francis I. French constitutionalism, from its medieval origins into the eighteenth century, was a distinctive blend of legalism, pluralism, and historicism. It was a theory of a complex polity, centered around a monarch whose power was formally absolute, but making room for effective sharing in power by other bodies in the state, especially the judges, the assemblies of the nobility, and the clergy.

[24] Lewis, *Later Medieval France*, pp. 81-85.
[25] As William J. Bouwsma points out, however, Gallicanism had, from the outset, important implications for constitutionalist thought as well; "Gallicanism and the nature of Christendom," in Molho and Tedeschi, *Renaissance Studies*, pp. 811-830.

Constitutionalist theory relied on a vague but durable conception of French fundamental law constitutive of the monarchy itself, law that the monarch did not devise and had no power to alter. It differed from English constitutionalism in depicting an harmonious tension of mutually connected authorities within the state, rather than a mechanical conception of checks and balances. During the period covered in this book, constitutionalist argument in France put increasing stress on French history as the source of evidence for, and legitimation of, its claims.

Whereas constitutionalist theory described a complex polity, absolutist theory depicted a regime organized by perfect unitary sovereignty. This tradition stressed the central role of the monarch himself as the ordering principle of all social life, the ultimate source of authority and energy within the state. References to the king as the image of God mark absolutist theorists, while constitutionalists were more likely to speak of the king as a paternal figure, or as the servant of his people. The absolutist king was sometimes depicted as the master of the lives and even the property of his subjects, superior to the fundamental laws of the polity, the source of all law and the embodiment of the law of nature. Absolutism required on the one hand an intense personalization of kingly power, an incarnation of pure authority in a single human individual to be adored and obeyed, and on the other abstraction from any human qualities in the intangible symbol of the state, pure authority and public purpose organized without human frailty. The tensions between these two requirements plagued absolutist theory throughout our period, and the former tended to give way to the latter over time.[26] But the king as individual remained important to absolutist politics—the single figure accountable to none but God himself and the image of God upon the earth.

The images and arguments of absolutism are so alien to our own ideas about the constitution of a satisfactory polity that we may find it hard to see how men could have accepted them. These images correspond to a type of political organization that historians describe as an exotic, ephemeral hybrid, "a strange and dangerous beast . . . an isolated, short-lived type of state that, with all its glitter and display of power, was largely unsuccessful."[27] The extraordinary hubris, the intellectual pride and isolation of absolutist monarchies make them

[26] J. H. Shennan, *The Origins of the Modern European State 1450-1725*; Heinz Eulau, "The Depersonalization of the Concept of Sovereignty," and more generally, Preston King, *The Ideology of Order*.
[27] Kossmann in Hatton, *Louis XIV and Absolutism*, p. 5; and Anderson, *Lineages*, p. 29.

18—Introduction

inaccessible to us. Yet some of these images and suppositions linger in the reification and deification of the state to which we are not immune. To understand how such images could have been so potent in the period of their full-blown splendor, it is important to set aside the notion of the state as one organization among others, one part of a complex social and economic structure existing side by side with other human institutions.[28] This concept of the state is common to liberalism, to Marxist theory, and to contemporary political science—not, of course, unrelated to one another. In sharp contrast to these views, absolutist theory makes the state constitutive of social order and unity in a very direct way. For absolutist theorists, the will and power of the king provide the cement and structure for society, just as God's will and power construct the universe. The ordering authority of the king literally holds the nation together; as Bodin describes it in a trenchant metaphor, such sovereignty is like the keel of a ship that makes the difference between a vessel and an "evil-favored hoop of wood."[29] When this is kept in mind, it is easier to see why apologists for absolute monarchy were so adulatory, and how they could praise absolute power while condemning tyranny and despotism in the same breath, as alien to the exercise of such godlike power.

Defenders of the French monarchy insisted that there was a profound difference between absolutism and tyranny. The distinction became increasingly difficult for many Frenchmen to discern. The constitutionalist arguments of sixteenth-century jurists and historians were somewhat self-consciously reiterated during the abortive rebellions of the mid-seventeenth century, without achieving enough novelty or ascendancy to provide a forceful ideology for those rebellions. Apart from that, constitutionalism was rather stagnant and peripheral throughout much of the seventeenth century, until it was revived and given new importance in the last decades of the Sun King's reign, as discontent with the activities of the monarchy began to grow. The old Seysselian notion of fruitful participation by corporate bodies in the state began to be revived, and the historical interests of late Renaissance jurists were renewed a century later. In this setting, and in conjunction with continental natural-law theories and the ideas of English Whigs, French constitutionalism began to develop once again. During this period, men such as Fénelon and his adherents in the circle of the

---

[28] Recent attempts to make absolutist argument more comprehensible include L. J. MacFarlane, "Absolutism, Tyranny and the Minimum Conditions of Constitutional Rule," *Government and Opposition* XII (1977), 212-233; and Alfred Stepan's discussion of "organic-statist" thought, *State and Society*.

[29] *The Six Bookes of a Commonweale*, edited by Kenneth McRae, 1, 2, ix.

duke of Burgundy put forth the rudiments of what was later called the *thèse nobiliaire*, an offshoot of the constitutionalist tradition that attempted to give a revitalized hereditary aristocracy an institutional role in the French polity, based on the councils discovered in the mists of the French past. This "noble thesis" was set over against the durable *thèse royale*, the thesis of absolutist politics that found its own novel expression in the eighteenth century in the arguments we now associate with enlightened despotism. At this time the two modes of argument that had originally appeared so similar were sharply opposed to one another, as this ceaseless dialectic of ideas continued to run its course.

The third mode of argument that played a crucial role in French political discourse was individualism. This was not initially a way of thinking about politics so much as a philosophic exploration of the delights of privacy, based on a sharp separation between public and private life. As such, however, it had from the beginning important implications for politics. It engendered a critical attitude toward authority, and encouraged the withdrawal of energy from public life. The individual made his appearance in French philosophy in the *Essays* of Montaigne. This book was the fertile source of the fascination felt by generations of Frenchmen with the psychology of the self—the passions and interests, self-exploration and self-expression of the individual. Montaigne focussed attention on the single person as a complex and intriguing microcosm rather than as defined by his role in a larger structure—the church, the family, the status order, or the state. Despite his own punctilious attention to his public duties, Montaigne expressed contempt for politics in his influential book. In doing so, he helped inaugurate a durable strain in French thought that served as a critical counterpart to the near-fanatical reverence felt by most Frenchmen for their king.

Beginning in the late sixteenth century, and continuing well into the seventeenth, at the same time that Frenchmen were deifying their monarch in a way unmatched in European thought, other Frenchmen (or even occasionally the same ones) were treating all things political as objects of contempt—petty, sordid, unworthy of sustained attention by a man with better things to do. These two extremes existed comfortably side by side because those who felt contempt for politics, like Montaigne and his successors among the *libertins*, were convinced of the importance of absolute monarchical power in providing the order that made it possible for them to live their own lives. They therefore gave scrupulous public support to the political order they mocked among themselves. The subversive potential of this approach is apparent, despite their care to avoid subversion. But as it happened, it was not the subversive but the positive aspects of this stubborn individualism that were important in French political philosophy.

In order to understand why this should have been the case, it is important to remember that France from 1560 until 1660 was rarely free from civil disorder; religious, economic, regional, dynastic upheavals marked these years. Rebellions reminded Frenchmen of the costs of civil conflict, and this bolstered their desire for security and peace. The rebellions were for the most part isolated, disconnected occurrences, and no coherent theory of opposition brought them together. The political theories of the Huguenots and the members of the Catholic League during the religious wars of the late sixteenth century are important exceptions to this rule. But during the first half of the seventeenth century, rebellion was common in France and theories of rebellion almost unknown. Even during the Fronde, in the 1650s, little that deserves the name of theory appeared to justify what was being done. Instead, the recurring disorders reinforced the tendency of those Frenchmen who wrote about politics to support the monarchy and extol the virtues of ordering power.

Montaigne's spiritual descendants were therefore quite content to cultivate their private gardens while giving firm support to royal power. During the seventeenth century, two different kinds of arguments deepened the political relevance of the individualist tradition. On the one hand, the arguments of the interest of the state developed by Richelieu and his protégés in the 1620s and 1630s to give further legitimacy to the performance of the king were taken over by such aristocratic rebels as cardinal de Retz to explain their own personal activities during the confusions of the Fronde. Interest of state was domesticated in France. The Machiavellian arguments about the strange permutations of vice and virtue in the public realm, which Montaigne had mused about, became central to political discourse. Retz and his co-conspirators fancied themselves little states, negotiating, fighting, following the rules of *raison d'état* in their dealings with the court and with one another. This provided an early model of the interested individual in politics; but it was a sterile one in several ways. These rebels could explain their own behavior according to the maxims of *raison d'état*; but they could provide no reasons for preferring one possible outcome of their struggle to any other—save that victory was better than defeat. But victory in such a situation has no substance. There was no myth, no vision of an alternative way of organizing politics, to give them energy and unity. They lacked any notion of a public or common interest that transcended the selfish individual interests of each Frondeur. Each individual was by definition isolated by his interests, divided from and suspicious of his fellows. This absence of any sense of common purpose and mutual trust was one reason this rebellion failed so dismally to make any lasting difference in the polity.

On the other hand, in the decades immediately after the Fronde, another set of arguments renewed the fascination with individual psychology and motivation that had occupied so many Frenchmen since Montaigne. Jansenist theorists associated with the monastery of Port-Royal, especially Pascal and Nicole, developed arguments that joined individualist and absolutist themes. Jansenist theory, although strictly Hobbesian in stressing complete obedience to sovereign power, used ideas formulated by earlier French individualists in such a fashion that their implications for a utilitarian social theory were made clear for the first time. The Jansenists described society as an intricate network of individual actions impelled by human passions, especially the passions of ambition and of greed. These passions had been analyzed by earlier individualists; but Jansenist authors, drawing upon insights taken especially from St. Augustine, dwelt on the rich consequences for the economy and for the entire society of behavior motivated by such passions. They showed how "virtuous" human action is normally the product of some "vicious" passion. It is behavior suggested by an enlightened self-love that happens to have beneficent consequences for others. True virtue in their eyes was *la charité*, the self-abnegating love of God and thereby of our fellow men. This is a rare quality that comes through God's grace to those blessed individuals who are participants in the community of saints.

By exploring the connections between the passions and self-interest, and by showing how men impelled by greed and ambition serve one another's interests in society, Jansenist thinkers struck a subtle blow at the foundations of absolutist theory. They undermined the crown-centered, self-sacrificing patriotism of French absolutism by preaching the stubborn prominence of self-love in the human psyche; and they ejected the monarch from his role as ordering authority for the entire society, godlike source of energy, action, and harmony within the state. They stressed the violent and utilitarian aspects of his role, rather than arcane insights and majestic governance. Since they recognized the importance of awe in instilling obedience in mortal men, the Jansenists kept the king perched high upon his pedestal. But they described him not as a god, but as the superintendent of a hospital of madmen, the source of useful fear and legal regulation. He became the overseer and referee of society rather than its keel or linchpin. And the Jansenists redirected attention from the organizing activities of the monarchy to the energetic activities of all individuals within society, as the basic constituents of social life. Thus they brought active individuals into the absolutist polity, and circumscribed more narrowly the role of the absolutist king.

The selfish greed that marks fallen man in Augustinian theology might seem unpromising material to use in constructing a portrait of a cooperative individual as a political actor. But by the end of the century, this transformation had in fact occurred. Selfish greed became more and more respectable as its social utility was disclosed, and in its new guise as enlightened self-interest, was finally accepted as a simple neutral truth about human nature.[30] A convincing and fruitful political psychology was built upon this notion. The individual motivated by enlightened self-interest, unlike the conspirators of the Fronde, sees clear reasons why he should cooperate with others and serve others' needs to get what he wants. On this basis, a theory of common interests, and finally of the public interest, could be constructed. The public interest ceased to be a vague term synonymous with the age-old *salut publique*, and incorporated within it the interests of individual Frenchmen connected with one another in diverse ways. Interests were shown to bring men together as well as divide them from one another, and the connection between the individual and the political community that had been broken for so long in French political philosophy could finally, in the eighteenth century, be repaired.

[30] Albert O. Hirschman charts the fortunes of ambition and avarice in *The Passions and the Interests: Political Arguments for Capitalism before its Triumph*. Lester K. Little, "Pride Goes before Avarice: Social Change and the Vices in Latin Christendom," *American Historical Review LXXVI* (1971), 16-49, deals with an earlier period.

PART I

The Order of the Kingdom and the Order of the Soul

CHAPTER ONE

Sixteenth-Century Constitutionalism

1. THE ANCIENT CONSTITUTION

Studies of French constitutionalism often begin by asking whether it can be said that France had a constitution during the *ancien régime*. Revolutionary leaders, convinced of the importance of a properly written and labeled document, produced a constitution in 1791; but at least one observer, Arthur Young, disapproved of their proceeding as though "a constitution was a pudding to be made by a receipt."[1] A number of their contemporaries asserted that France had always had a constitution, "for how could it be that a state which has flourished for 1,300 years was never constituted?"[2] By this they meant something more than the common-sense notion that states, like other complex entities, must have a minimum of form. As their proud reference to France's long flourishing makes clear, they assumed that their *patrie* had always had a distinctive political structure that was the basis for its health and longevity.

One indication that France had always had a constitution was that Frenchmen had constitutional disputes regularly throughout the *ancien régime*, and they tended to agree roughly on what it was that they were arguing about. The word "constitution" was rarely given political significance in France until the late seventeenth century; but questions about *la régime et gouvernement du monarchie* and *les lois fondamentales* dominated French political discourse long before that.[3] Innumerable treatises were written to stake out the precise provisions of the elusive constitution of the polity. Major steps in the argument were based on barely perceptible nuances in interpretation of familiar phrases, and impassioned disagreements founded on differences so subtle

[1] Quoted in Charles H. McIlwain, *Constitutionalism Ancient and Modern*, 3-4.
[2] André Lemaire, *Les Lois fondamentales de la monarchie française*, p. i. See also W. F. Church, "The Problem of Constitutional Thought in France," *Etudes des . . . assemblées d'état*, pp. 173-182.
[3] Roland Mousnier, "Comment les Français du XVIIe siècle voyaient la constitution," *XVIIe siècle*, no. 25-26 (1955), p. 11, follows Walther von Wartburg in arguing that Bossuet was the first to use "constitution" as a synonym for fundamental law. E. M. Beame, "Limits of Toleration in Sixteenth-Century France," *Studies in the Renaissance* XIII (1966), 255, finds a reference in a pamphlet of the late sixteenth century.

that they hardly appear to be worth bothering about. In such a complex and homogeneous intellectual universe, it is hard to draw sharp distinctions among theorists. Nonetheless, historians have commonly discovered two fairly distinct intellectual tendencies in arguments about the French polity during the *ancien régime*: absolutist and constitutionalist.[4] Most French theorists, whether constitutionalist or absolutist in temper, began with the assumption that their king possessed a *puissance absolue*. This conveyed the sense that he was not subject to the authority of any human will, inside or outside his realm. Most theorists also agreed that the king was subject to divine law, and that he should rely on the best counsellors and magistrates he could employ to help him govern beneficently and justly, rather than arbitrarily and oppressively. Beyond this, constitutionalist theorists asserted that the king was subject to the fundamental laws of the French realm, a point on which absolutists tended to equivocate, and to the ordinary positive laws that he and his predecessors had made, a point that absolutists straightforwardly denied.

Much of the frustration experienced by students of French constitutionalism arises from this apparently paradoxical assumption that power can be both absolute and limited. In order to make sense of it, it is important to remember that the *puissance absolue* ascribed by constitutionalists to the king did not include the power to extend the activities of government beyond those spheres in which it had traditionally operated; and constitutionalist theorists were quite clear that absolute power could be abused. The notion of abuse of power implies some understanding about proper uses, some notion of frameworks for monarchical activity and procedures for carrying on that activity. Constitutionalist theorists, unlike absolutists, asserted that some institutions in the state—normally the parlements—were charged with ensuring that these frameworks and procedures were respected by the monarchy. Yet such supervisory activities had to be accommodated to the notion that the parlements were also part of the monarchy itself, arms of the king for the provision of justice to the people.

French jurists and political theorists had trouble identifying firm institutional obstacles to the abuse of *la puissance absolue* because they found the notion of divided sovereign power profoundly uncongenial. Even before Bodin asserted clearly that sovereignty, by definition, cannot be divided, sixteenth-century Frenchmen took for granted that

[4] Mousnier, "Comment les Français," for example, distinguishes between those jurists who "adhered to the Constitution without reserve" and those men *du côté du Roi* who wished the same principles applied in ways more favorable to monarchy.

authority must have some specific unitary locus in the state. Most of them also took for granted that this locus must be in the king. During the religious wars, some argued that the locus ought instead to continue in the people; but arguments for popular sovereignty were very much in the minority in France. The disinclination to think in terms of a division of authority marked French theorists until the late seventeenth century, and was not seriously challenged until the *Spirit of the Laws*.

Despite this deep-seated aversion to the notion of divided power, there was an equally deep-seated attachment in French theory to fundamental law. Even if no clear-cut human sanctions for this law could be agreed upon, there was consensus on what the *lois fondamentales* were supposed to provide: a statement of conditions for accession to the throne of France, and of the legitimate extent and proper uses of power in the state. The ancient constitution of France, like that of England, supposedly determined the pattern of succession to the monarchy and regulated the relationships between the king and all his subjects, setting out rights and obligations on both sides. But while the French constitution possessed rather more precision than the English about the former subject, it did much less well at setting out clear limits on authority and obligation.

The *loi Salique*, which set out the conditions for monarchical succession, was the nucleus of the fundamental law. Its provisions were universally understood, and had sufficient sanctity that they were virtually unassailable. One royal publicist under Henry IV, Jerome Bignon, spoke of this law as "engraved on the heart of Frenchmen," not written down on paper, but "born with us, not invented by us, but drawn out of nature herself, who taught it to us as an instinct."[5] The instinct, if such it be, was given a name only in the fourteenth century, when an ancient law governing the disposition of private property was put to use to exclude Edward III of England from the throne of France; and several provisions of the Salic law still excited controversy when Henry of Navarre, a Protestant, was heir to the throne.[6] Nonetheless, the basic rules for accession to the French monarchy were almost universally acknowledged. But France had nothing comparable to Magna Carta; and it was in this vexed area of the proper uses and extent of the royal authority, on the one hand, and the privileges of subjects, on the other, that constitutional disputes were joined.

The constitutionalists were, for the most part, loyal monarchists. They were orthodox jurists, historians, and administrators, who took

[5] *De l'excellence des Roys et du Royaume de France* (1610), cited *ibid.*, p. 15.
[6] Denis Richet, *La France moderne*, pp. 46-54.

for granted the royal *puissance absolue* and depicted a close harmony among the laws and institutions of the kingdom. They must be distinguished from those polemicists who opposed absolute royal power, particularly the sixteenth-century Huguenots and members of the Catholic League, who stressed the primary authority of popular institutions and argued for strict limitations on the king. Such men were also "constitutionalists" in a different vein; but their arguments formed a tangent to the main stream of French thought. Hotman and his colleagues, including the author of the *Vindiciae contra tyrannos*, have attracted the attention of modern scholars because their doctrines of popular sovereignty and the contract of government have become central in interpretations of the development of liberal political ideas. Yet the arguments of Seyssel and Pasquier were more important in shaping French political thought in the sixteenth and seventeenth centuries, and more representative of the ideas of Frenchmen generally.

2. Philippe de Commynes and Medieval Constitutionalism

Several of the central themes and images of sixteenth-century constitutionalism were developed in medieval discussions of the polity; and while we cannot explore those roots extensively, it is well to have some notion of how things stood in the late fifteenth century. The best-known writer about politics during this era was Philippe de Commynes, who left the service of Charles the Bold of Burgundy in 1472 to become one of the most trusted advisors of King Louis XI of France. In retirement, he composed a set of vivid *mémoires* about the period, describing events, assessing characters, and offering the fruits of his experience as guidance for politicians in the future.

In Commynes's *Mémoires*, most of the themes characteristic of French constitutional argument are to be found, even though they are indicated only hastily. Unlike most French constitutionalists, Commynes was not a jurist, and had little formal education. He was a clever and devoted servant of two successive masters who were enemies, and he was rewarded for his efforts with rich lands and impressive titles. These circumstances help explain the mixture of cynical realism, ardent admiration for strong monarchy, and stubborn defense of feudal privilege that can be discerned in Commynes's book. The major differences between his ideas and those of his constitutionalist successors arise from the absence of the perspective of the legal scholar or historian. Commynes pays little attention to the *lois fondamentales*, or indeed to laws of any sort, in discussing the French monarchy. Apart from this, his arguments have a good deal in common with those of French constitutionalist writers, and provide a good introduction to three themes: the pluralistic notion of counterpoise and conflict in the state; the importance of good counsel and good training to assure that the prince's will is well-ordered and sound; and the political realism that recognizes the importance of prudence and calculation in the achievement of the common good.

Like many later French social theorists, Commynes took for granted that human beings try naturally to gain dominance over one another because of their strong passions, particularly covetousness and the love of power. "Neither our natural reason, nor our sense, nor fear of God, nor love of neighbor will restrain us at all from doing violence to one another . . . or from taking the possessions of others by all possible means," asserts Commynes. The only effective restraints come from the opposition of other human beings who attempt the same adventures against us. Fortunately, "God has created neither man nor beast in this world without establishing some counterpart to oppose him, in order to keep him in humility and fear."[7] Commynes held a general theory of counterpoise. Each of us, as individuals, as well as estates, communities, and nations, has a counterpart set over against us by divine mercy to keep our ambitions and avarice within tolerable bounds. This works fairly well within a particular society, since dissensions and divisions balance one another, and mutually opposed desires and energies neutralize wickedness; justice, the settling of disputes by superior authority, provides further constraint. But the superior authorities themselves, the princes, have no superiors on earth; and if God in His wisdom had not also given them counterparts (such as England, in the case of France), "nobody could live under their rule or even near them."[8]

Even with counterparts among other princes, the dangers of princely aggression are great, observes Commynes; and much adversity comes to the people because of it. Counterpoise works well enough among ordinary people, within a framework of justice provided by the king; but the will of the king threatens to become an unbalanced source of energy, and requires channeling to ensure that it will be used for good ends. Powerful lords can always provide pretexts to justify encroachments, and flatterers in their entourage will hasten to assure them of the rightfulness of their cause. To guard against these things, princes need to be educated carefully and provided with wise and

---

[7] *Mémoires*, ed. Calmette, v:18 (vol. II, 207-212). There is a fine translation of the first five books of *The Memoirs of Philippe de Commynes* by Isabelle Cazeaux, edited by Samuel Kinser with a useful biographical introduction.
[8] *Ibid.*, v:20 (vol. II, 237).

honest counsellors. A disordered royal will—*une volonté désordonnée*—is the evil to be avoided by these measures. The part played by the king's tutors, his ministers, his parlements, and the various assemblies of his subjects, in ordering his will and directing it to beneficent purposes was emphasized by Commynes, and was central to French constitutionalist argument from medieval times until the eighteenth century.

Commynes, like many Frenchmen before the age of Louis XIV, took for granted that no king or seigneur on earth had the right to take any part of his subjects' property without their consent. He asserted heatedly that to contravene this prohibition meant to perpetrate *tyrannie et violence* against the people. The consent to which he referred was that of the assemblies throughout France that had traditionally been consulted before new revenues were raised. The feudal roots of this idea are clear in those passages where Commynes differentiates the prince's "domain" from the properties of his subjects, and equates taxation without consent with manifest tyranny. But he does not describe these assemblies as setting limits on kingly power. In his view, those who claim that the king's authority will be diminished by calling together the estates of the realm are guilty of *lèse majesté*, since they imply that the royal will is undermined rather than strengthened by association with the wills of his subjects. Commynes asserts that the loyal subjects of the king of France have always shown themselves eager to give their sovereign what he asks, and they present petitions and grievances most humbly for his consideration. The assemblies are not described as a counterpart to the royal will. They are formally necessary to legitimate taxation, which amounts to an invasion by public authority on the private realm unless consent is given; but they facilitate royal policy instead of hampering or blocking it.[9]

In discussing the king's procedure in calling together the estates, Commynes observes that he "only summoned certain given persons whom he thought would not oppose his intentions." This is described as one of several "shrewd moves" undertaken by the king in a period of difficulty.[10] Commynes is a great admirer of royal shrewdness, a

---

[9] v:19 (vol. II, 218); Commynes goes on to say that the place where "la chose publicque est myeulx traictée et règne moins de violence sur le peuple . . . c'est Angleterre." His description of England (see also IV:1) indicates that he regarded the well-established situation of the Parliament as a great asset for the monarchy, and for the polity more generally. This opinion was an exception to the general tendency among French constitutionalists to ignore or belittle England before 1720.

[10] III:1 (vol. I, 174-175).

trait that has led some to speak of him as the "French Machiavelli."[11] But this same tone is regularly found in French social thought. Long before Richelieu institutionalized *raison d'état*, Frenchmen were comfortable with the notion that courses of action that would ordinarily appear immoral were to be sanctioned when they were undertaken for the good of the kingdom. Such policies generally fell under the heading of "prudential" actions, and prudence was consistently praised as a princely virtue in French thought. Commynes notes that such behavior might appear deceitful or untrustworthy; he says his purpose is to provide an accurate account of what happened, even if it appears questionable. But beyond that, he asserts that when the princes he describes are "compared with other princes, these two will appear great and notable," because of the benefits they brought their people. Louis XI will be even more highly regarded than the duke of Burgundy, because he "left his kingdom increased and at peace with all his enemies." Besides that, France was the final victor in their mutual conflict; and Louis's chroniclers provide the definitive account of the events in which both participated. They can therefore turn Burgundy's great projects to his "prejudice and shame; for those who win get all the honor."[12]

Such realism about politics is a hallmark of Commynes's approach. Many of his successors among French constitutionalists echoed it, without the tone of cynicism that sometimes colors Commynes's accounts. French jurists had few illusions about the efficacy of homilies and moral didacticism to keep strong kings in order. The first systematic theorist of the French constitution, Claude de Seyssel, began his major treatise by rejecting most of traditional political philosophy as useless, since no real-world polities were ordered as reasonably and virtuously as those discussed in learned treatises. Perhaps for this reason, he and most other constitutionalists paid less attention to the role of the laws of nature or divine law in ordering the royal will than one might expect. But they did rely heavily on one type of law that was comparatively unimportant in Commynes's account—the fundamental laws and ordinances of the French monarchy—as the framework within which the royal will was to be ordered and bent to good uses. In Seyssel's treatise on *La Monarchie de France*, as in French constitutionalism from medieval times until the revolution, such laws and ordinances focus discussion of the right ordering of the polity.

[11] Kenneth Dreyer, "Commynes and Machiavelli: A Study in Parallelism," *Symposium* v (1951), 38-61, discusses a number of affinities. See also more generally, Donald R. Kelley, "Murd'rous Machiavel in France: A Post Mortem," *Political Science Quarterly* LXXXV (1970), 545-559.
[12] v:9 (vol. II, 154-155).

3. Claude de Seyssel and *La Monarchie de France*

Claude de Seyssel (1450 [?]-1520) was a diplomat, jurist, and churchman active in the service of Charles VIII and Louis XII. By birth a Savoyard, by training a legal scholar, and by reason of his proven usefulness to the French king an ambassador and negotiator in several European countries, Seyssel combined a thorough acquaintance with the law with a broad experience in contemporary politics. When Louis died in 1515, Seyssel wrote a political testament called *La Monarchie de France*, and presented it to his new sovereign, Francis I. The treatise was published in 1519 under the more ambitious title *La Grant Monarchie de France* and reissued periodically thereafter.[13]

In writing about the monarchy of France, Seyssel brought to his task not only his legal training and political experience, but also an extensive familiarity with ancient history. He had translated several classic histories for Louis, including those of Xenophon, Eusebius, Thucydides, and Appian Alexandrin.[14] These were later published, and Seyssel's observations in the preface to one of them—the *Histoire d'Appien*—were as familiar to later Frenchmen as the argument of the *Monarchie de France*. In Seyssel's eyes, the major lesson to be learned from Appian's history was the effect of civil dissension and overweening ambition in the destruction of the Roman state. Machiavelli's focus upon Livy and the origins of Rome is paralleled by Seyssel's interest in Appian and its demise, as a way of showing what must be avoided if the French kingdom were to continue to flourish: the encroachment of overly ambitious people or seigneurs on other parts of the complex social organism, an encroachment that threatens the mutual interdependence of the whole.

Seyssel provides a peculiarly Renaissance rendering of the ancient theory of harmony and counterpoise. In his vision of the world, all things that come into being are necessarily impermanent. *Les corps mystiques*, political bodies, like natural bodies, must decay. The four humors that compose the human body are contrary to one another,

---

[13] For Seyssel's biography, see Jacques Poujol's introduction to his edition of *La Monarchie de France*, which includes a discussion of the various editions of the *Monarchie* and its influence. The best essays on Seyssel's political theory are J. H. Hexter, "Claude de Seyssel and Normal Politics in the Age of Machiavelli," in Charles S. Singleton, ed., *Art, Science and History in the Renaissance*, pp. 389-415; and J. Russell Major, "The Renaissance Monarchy as seen by Erasmus, More, Seyssel and Machiavelli," in Theodore Rabb and Jerrold Siegel, ed., *Action and Conviction in Early Modern Europe*, pp. 17-31. An extended version of this section on Seyssel is N. Keohane's "Claude de Seyssel and Sixteenth-Century Constitutionalism in France," in Pennock and Chapman, ed., *Constitutionalism*.

[14] Paul Chavy, "Les Traductions humanistes de Claude de Seyssel," in André Stegmann, ed., *L'Humanisme français au début de la Renaissance*, pp. 361-376.

and compete for domination; in the long run one gains excessive prominence in the body and destroys it. So the "mystical body of human society," having been "assembled by a civil and political union" must in the end, because it is "composed of multiple judgments and discordant wills repugnant to one another," decline and fall into nothingness.[15] The primary thesis is that tension is an essential feature of political society; each part will attempt to gain dominance over all the others, and unless this unhealthy monopoly can be forestalled, "ruin and total mutation" will occur. But well-governed polities can prolong their flourishing through the internal harmony and consonance of the several parts.

To support his thesis, Seyssel draws on comparative material from history and from contemporary polities, particularly Rome and Venice. His conclusion is that even the most excellent among popular and aristocratic states are more vulnerable to destruction by internal conflict than a well-ordered monarchy. Both types of regimes are marked by an increasingly particularistic pluralism. Each part of the state desires hegemony, and all have "more regard to their particular passions than to the public good." Popular and aristocratic states have no protection against these *mauvaises humeurs*; monarchy's great advantage is that it provides a single strong will above the fray to regulate conflict, forestall the process of encroachment, and ward off the day of doom.[16] This argument for the superiority of monarchy—the provision of a strong will above incessant conflict, a single authority to be revered and obeyed by all—was central to French political argument. Other reasons were also offered during Seyssel's own time and afterwards: that monarchy is rightful because the king is God's image on earth, His counterpart in the political plane of the great chain of being; that monarchy is superior to other forms of government because of its efficiency and rapidity in decision making. But two distinctive elements of Seyssel's defense recurred often in later thought: that monarchy is superior because only a single leader enjoying complete authority can control the complex forces that make up a political system, keep order among them, and prevent the fatal tendency to encroachment; and that a hereditary monarch has a clear psychological advantage over any other ruler in commanding obedience and esteem among his subjects.

Frenchmen until the eighteenth century took for granted the nu-

---

[15] *La Monarchie de France*, edited by Poujol, part I, section 3, p. 108. Cf. Paul Archambault's study of "The Analogy of the 'Body' in Renaissance Political Literature," *Bibliothèque d'Humanisme et Renaissance* XXIX (1967), 21-52.

[16] I, 2-4, pp. 104-110.

cleus of Seyssel's claim: that only a royal will obviously superior to all partial wills within the realm, unlimited by any of those wills, can prevent petty tyranny within the state. Rousseau's political philosophy, at first sight so far removed from Seyssel's Renaissance monarchy, retains this nucleus in the *volonté générale*. The notion that it is a grave disadvantage for government to be subject to the partial wills of those who are governed, that such subjection is not a source of liberty but of chaos and destruction, distinguishes French theory from the beginning of the sixteenth century, and sets it apart from Anglo-Saxon modes of thought. The second part of Seyssel's claim—the psychological advantage of hereditary monarchy, the symbolic power of kingship to elicit awe and obedience among ordinary men—was also accepted by many later theorists, including men like Montaigne and Pascal, who were more fascinated by the effect of the royal spell on other men than subject to it.

Seyssel did not write as a pure apologist for monarchy, however, and this was not the main source of his influence. The other side of his argument in the *Monarchie* must immediately be brought to bear on his defense of the superiority of kingship. For if it is true that only a single will can control the complex forces in the state, it is also true, in Seyssel's eyes, that these forces themselves provide both the restraints on the monarch's power, and also the effective basis for the exercise of his authority. Seyssel had no illusions about the excellence of kings; he knew that the personal imperfections of monarchs are the Achilles' heel of this form of government. But he was convinced that, at least in France, this weak point had been effectively secured by a constitution sufficiently pliable to make room for the active will of a talented and vigorous monarch bent upon working for his people's good, yet strong enough to restrain the disordered will of a depraved or imbecilic successor, and prevent him from destroying the kingdom while it awaited a better king.

In his preface to the translation of Appian's *History*, Seyssel asserted that "taken as a whole, the French realm participates in all three ways of political governance," that is, that there are traces of democracy and aristocracy as well as monarchy in the regime.[17] But Seyssel did not associate any particular institutions with the roles, and his contention is not reducible to the familiar assertion about mixed government. He describes a pliant interconnection of mutually limiting spheres of authority, all combining to work together harmoniously in the government of France, beginning with the king and those officers closest

[17] This "Prohème" is included in Poujol's edition of *La Monarchie de France*; p. 80.

to him, and encompassing every official, down to the merest parish clerk. Members of each estate of the realm have offices and dignities open to them appropriate to their situation.

> And in this way, the goods and honors, charges and administration of *la Chose publique* being divided and distributed among all the estates proportionately, according to their condition, and each individual in those estates maintained in his preeminence and equality, there follows a harmony and consonance which is the cause of the conservation and augmentation of this Monarchy. And the affairs of the kingdom prosper to the extent to which the kings (who are the fountain and the source from which emanate and flow all the streams of good *polices* and justice) are attentive in upholding this union and correspondence, like true and natural Princes who are concerned primarily with the common Good of the kingdom, which they identify with their own.

Seyssel speaks of the French monarch as having "all power and authority to command and do what he wishes," but holds that this "great and sovereign liberty is so well regulated and limited by good laws and ordinances, and by the multitude and great authority of officers who are near his person and in the several parts of his Kingdom," that a king can hardly manage to act violently or against the good of his subjects. The coupling of "laws and ordinances" with those officers who participate in guarding and administering the rules, is significant; it is the effective activity of the latter that gives substance to the former, in Seyssel's theory. Surrounded by counsellors, exercising his justice through a great number of officers, aided particularly by parlements, a "true Roman senate," the king finds himself hedged in on all sides by those regulations and institutions he and his predecessors have established.[18]

In his major treatise, Seyssel does not reiterate the view that the French monarchy included elements of aristocracy and democracy; he goes out of his way, in fact, to reject this notion.[19] But the notion of complex legal and institutional constraints against the exercise of a *volonté desordonnée*, and the notion of power increased rather than diminished by such constraints, recur as keynotes of the larger work. In the *Monarchie de France* they are expressed in Seyssel's most famous and fruitful contribution to French thought: the theory of the three bridles. The metaphor of the bridle was a happy choice. Unlike

---

[18] "Prohème d'Appien," pp. 81-84. From medieval times until the Revolution, this comparison between the parlements and the senate was common.
[19] *La Monarchie de France*, I, 12, p. 120.

brakes or obstacles, bridles regulate and direct energy as well as restraining it. They are flexible and sensitive, rather than mechanical and automatic. Bridles can be used to restrain the headlong energy of a runaway monarch, and then be relaxed to move in gentle harmony with a well-intentioned king, subtly informing his direction, yet setting no obstacles in the way of his productive energy. This was the sense Seyssel wished to capture in his image. And this notion of a flexible and durable constitution, responding differently to different monarchs for the long-run benefit of the polity, dominated French constitutional argument until the middle of the eighteenth century. The specific image of the bridles was sometimes used in later thought, and the corresponding verb—*refréner*—was common.

The three bridles described by Seyssel are *la religion, la justice*, and *la police*. Long indoctrination in the precepts of Christian morality helps deter kings from tyrannical behavior; but the bridle of religion does not depend on the tutelage of princes in vague guidelines that they are always exhorted to obey. The crucial thing about the first bridle is not what the prince believes, but what the people believe about his religion, based on his overt behavior. Like Machiavelli, Seyssel used the career of Numa Pompilius as an example of the benefits that accrue to leaders who have the "color and appearance of religion and of having God on their side."[20] The devout people of France obey their kings because they regard them as instruments of the divine will, and this inclination will be disturbed if the king commands something that is obviously impious. Thus even a monarch who has little use for Christian ethics cannot afford to deviate too much from their dictates if he wishes to retain the enthusiastic obedience of his people. The institutional aspect of this first bridle is also important. Any priest, however lowly, can condemn the king in his pulpit and the king will not dare to silence him, says Seyssel, because of the popular outcry that would result.

In discussing *la justice*, the second bridle on the prince, Seyssel focuses on one institution—the parlements—that ensure, in his eyes, that justice is better established in France than anywhere else in the world. Originally created by the kings to guarantee the *civilité* of the laws and institutions of the kingdom, the parlements have made themselves so respected in their authority that "kings have, so far as distributive justice is concerned, always been subject to them." Not only do they help him give justice to all his subjects; by passing judgment on his

---

[20] I, 9, p. 117; cf. Machiavelli, *Discorsi* I, 11; and Joseph Strayer, "France: the Holy Land, the Chosen People, the Most Christian King," in Rabb and Siegel, *Action and Conviction*, 3-16.

own laws and ordinances, they "effectively restrain the absolute power our kings desire to use."[21]

La police is the third of Seyssel's bridles. This is a recurrent term in French theory that is difficult to translate. Seyssel applies the notion very broadly. He uses it initially to refer to those ordinances set up by kings themselves, confirmed by time and usage, which provide the procedural patterns for the government of the realm. Here, as in the case of the parlements, institutions originally created by the king, which derive their formal authority from his will, act as restraining influences on the exercise of his power. Besides these ordinances, *la police* includes "another order and form of living in this kingdom that tends to the same end," that is, the exercise of well-tempered power.[22] This is a reference to the other part of the political *corps mystique*: the body of the nation, the three estates of the people themselves, "well-regulated and held together" in their own patterns and consonances. This is a primary source of the constitutional order that Seyssel finds in France: not only is there a single head to govern the "mystical body," but that body is itself well-ordered in several estates and conditions, so that the energies of each part of the body are controlled internally, in addition to providing a bridle upon the king who governs them. Seyssel here follows a well-established tradition in France, gradually eroded in the next few centuries—the tradition that the nation as a body possessed customary rights and privileges, distinct from those enjoyed by the monarch, and not subject to his dictates. His description of the king's power as *absolue*, like that of most of his contemporaries, refers only to a certain sphere of action appropriate to a king. Outside this sphere, in harmony with it but not completely subject to its control, was another sphere of legal right and established usage, another part of *la police* of France.[23]

In discussing each of the three bridles, Seyssel stressed the subtle connections between the bases of the monarch's power and the limits on its use. Not only do the bridles discourage abuses, they also extend the king's capacity and constitute his power. Since a large part of the king's authority comes from his status as Most Christian King, French kings ought not only to "endure and submit sweetly" to the first bridle, but also "fortify it with their power." Since the French king is traditionally revered first of all as the source and embodiment of

---

[21] I, 10, p. 117.   [22] I, 13, pp. 120-121.
[23] W. F. Church, in his magisterial study of *Constitutional Thought in Sixteenth-Century France*, pp. 77-81, refers to this "all-important doctrine" as a fundamental legacy from medieval times; see also Lemaire, *Les Lois fondamentales*, pp. 283-284.

38—Order of Kingdom and Soul

justice, he ought to "study well how he can maintain and augment it." And as for *la police*, it is by means of "laws, ordinances, and admirable customs" of the kingdom that the prince prospers; not only is he bound by his coronation oath to honor them, but if he does not, he "enfeebles his strength and thereby diminishes his glory and his own renown."[24] Thus Seyssel insists that "this moderation and bridling of the absolute power of kings is to their own great honor and profit." He uses an analogy that recurs regularly in later French constitutionalism, asserting that if the king's power "were ampler and more absolute it would be worse and more imperfect; just as the power of God is not thought to be the less because he cannot sin or do evil, but is thereby the more perfect. And in the same way, kings are to be praised and prized much more when they choose in their great authority and power to be subject to their own laws and live according to them, though they could at will make use of their absolute power."[25] It is clear that Seyssel recognizes that the effectiveness of the bridles depends finally on the voluntary submission of the king. He must be shown why he should choose to subject himself to laws. To demonstrate the great advantages of such a choice, for the king as well as for the kingdom, was Seyssel's major purpose in writing the *Monarchie*.

4. Seyssel on the Orders of the Kingdom
   and the Ordering of the Will

The central distinction in Seyssel's major treatise is between an ordered and disordered will. His theory of decision making recognizes that royal decisions are not simply formal moments of the pure disposition of *volonté*, but are shaped by advice and information, and depend heavily on the quality of the counsel given to the king. A disordered will operates hastily and erratically, on the basis of poor, unsystematic information; an ordered will works smoothly and regularly, reflecting the sober deliberation by a number of men in cooperation with the king.

Unlike some later apologists for monarchy, Seyssel recognized that it is "impossible that a single man, or even a small number, however accomplished they may be, could understand and manage all the affairs of a large kingdom."[26] Later apologists were fond of the image of the far-seeing monarch raised high above his people, enabled to encompass the whole kingdom in his vision. Seyssel referred rather to

[24] *La Monarchie de France*, II, 14-17, pp. 149-155.
[25] I, 12, p. 120; cf. II, 11, p. 143.   [26] II, 4, pp. 133-134.

the "obfuscation of understanding" that afflicts a monarch who tries to do everything himself. In his constitutional theory, the best ordering of the royal will depends on a variety of councils, ranging from a small group of trusted advisors to the Great Council of the realm, in which the notables regularly present at court are joined by representatives of the major towns and cities of the kingdom. There is no notion that the consent of such an assembly is constitutionally mandatory even for new taxes, which sets Seyssel's arguments apart from those of many other jurists. Seyssel's focus is on the utility of such councils in royal decision making. They provide information and allow the king to publicize his policies and garner support. But they are not to be depended upon for insights into the major questions of governance. The minority in such large assemblies is always wiser and more far-seeing than the mass, argues Seyssel, yet there is great pressure to adopt the majority view, *la plus grande et commune opinion*.[27] Having little use for the political opinions of ordinary folk, Seyssel provides a much more prominent place in his constitutional system for the corporate bodies of trained jurists, the parlements, than for any of the various assemblies of the people, including the Estates-General, which he does not even mention by this name.

In the polity described by Seyssel, the role of the ordinary people is primarily social and economic. Unlike the absolutist theorists, he gives the subjects of the king a vigorous and active role; but their major contributions are made through their own *métiers* and occupations. They are responsible for filling certain offices in the *corps mystique* appropriate to their rank, but have nothing to do with the functioning of the head of the body, besides providing support and obedience. Seyssel's discussion of the *police* of the mystical body is noteworthy in that the three orders he describes do not correspond to those traditional in France, but show a probable Italian influence. Seyssel distinguishes between the *peuple gras* and the *peuple menu*, the two lower orders, and gives first place to the nobility. The clergy is an estate "common to all the others," whose members are drawn from throughout society.[28]

In discussing the *peuple menu*, Seyssel warns of the dangers to be expected if these folk are given too much liberty or excited into action, because of their great number and natural envy of their betters. But then he proceeds to argue in a most untraditional vein that this same envy and energy can be a source of health in the social body when it is properly regulated, as it is in France. A member of the

[27] II, 4-8, pp. 133-141. [28] I, 13-19, pp. 120-128.

peuple gras can be ennobled for important services, and a member of the *peuple menu* can rise to the middle class by merit and industry. Such social mobility makes each individual content with his situation, since he knows he can better it if he tries; and this is, according to Seyssel, a great source of social stability as well as social vigor. The king ought actively to encourage industry and the use of talent in the state, argues Seyssel. By this same means the arts and sciences will be enriched, and Frenchmen will be spurred to emulate their brethren who are wealthy and successful. Such confidence in the political and social value of emulation became a marked characteristic of utilitarian thought in France.

In describing this incessant motion as part of *la police* of France, Seyssel uses this term, like Aristotle's *politeia*, to refer to the whole socio-political structure of the community. He includes within it the patterns of merchandise and trade, the way people make their living, the material abundance that sustains them. The term is gradually extended in his treatise, as it is in Aristotle's *Politics*, referring first to the laws and the structure of offices, and the ways of allocating power, but in the end encompassing the "way of life of a citizen-body," a constitution in the largest sense.[29] Much of the business of a king, in Seyssel's account, has to do with the maintenance of a healthy pluralistic balance in the *corps mystique*. Though individuals can move from one order to another, the comparative statuses and privileges of each order should be maintained intact. Seyssel shows, with considerable subtlety, how each of the three orders can threaten the others. Only the king is in a position to maintain equilibrium among them, while encouraging socially useful emulation and mobility, as well.

Taking his system as a whole, it is clear that Seyssel describes a complex constitutional machinery in which the prince has a central role, but much of the energy and motive power come from the people in their socio-economic activities. The exercise of power depends on the political participation of Frenchmen holding a great variety of offices. The machinery is designed to enable a vigorous and well-intentioned king to enhance his kingdom; it is also designed to function if he is weak or incapacitated, through the system of councils and advisors to the king; and finally, to frustrate a king who sets out to abuse his power.

This is true only for domestic affairs, however; and Seyssel regards the prince's responsibilities in foreign affairs as more delicate and difficult, precisely because an energetic and creative royal will makes all

---

[29] II, 17, pp. 154-155, and v, 9, pp. 216-218. Various definitions of *politeia* are given in Aristotle's *Politics* at 1278b, 1289a, and 1295a.

the difference. In the diplomatic and military arenas of the Renaissance there was no substitute for personal initiative and skill on the part of the prince himself. Accordingly, Seyssel devotes three of the five sections of his treatise to questions of war, conquest, and negotiation. His concerns in these chapters parallel those of Machiavelli closely. There is the same preoccupation with military discipline and fortification, with complex negotiation, often based on deceit and treachery, and with the conquest and governance of new states. There is also the same basic assumption about the nature of political men: "corrupt, commonly so ambitious and lustful for dominance (even Princes and others who manage great States) that one cannot trust them."[30] The wise prince will therefore always be watchful for deceit, and occasionally engage in dissimulation. But Seyssel, unlike Machiavelli and later French disciples of the Florentine, insists that though the prince must act shrewdly, he should confine himself to measures that are fundamentally honest and reasonable, "keeping always to the *ordre de la charité*."

By comparison with the constitutionalist thought with which modern readers are likely to be familiar, Seyssel's *politeia* is strikingly monarchocentric. All authority flows from the king, all institutions are organized around the throne. The patterns of activity in the *corps mystique* do not flow upwards; the only connections are from the top downward, in a pyramidal fashion. Seyssel's system, moreover, provides for neither of the two basic sets of guarantees we are accustomed to finding in constitutionalist theories: guarantees from above the political system, in the form of a higher law considered morally binding on authority; and guarantees from within the system, in the form of strong institutional expressions for popular authority. In Seyssel's theory, both respect for higher law and the use of councils are defended on utilitarian grounds, as advantageous to the king in exercising and expanding his authority.

Yet however monarchocentric it may be, Seyssel's system is not autocratic or monotonic. Nor is it, as some scholars have charged, a static or backward-looking system.[31] His theory is remarkable, in fact, for its recognition of dynamic energy in society and in the state. The institutional structure is supposed to be pliable enough to handle such flows of energy without stifling them. The central authority must regulate those flows, maintain a balance of equality amid diversity, and direct its own excess energies outward in exploits of conquest rather

[30] *La Monarchie*, IV, 3, pp. 191-192; cf. Machiavelli, *The Prince*, chs. 15-17; *Discorsi*, I, 37.
[31] For example, W. F. Church, *Constitutional Thought*, 40-42, 72-73.

than oppressing its own subjects. Seyssel describes a complex *politeia*, an intricate socio-political system in which the arbitrariness that plagues human authority is reduced not by independent control from above or from below, but by the institutional and legal instruments through which that authority itself is necessarily exercised. He shows how the exercise of this authority depends on order, regularity, and the contribution of many human wills; and how such authority is increased rather than diminished when it is in accord with the needs, beliefs, and expectations of subjects, whose enthusiastic obedience and support are thereby elicited.

In this recognition of the relationship between the foundations of political power and the limits on its use, Seyssel provided a sophisticated, durable insight for French constitutionalism. But he also left a less fortunate legacy: the tendency to overestimate both the strength of the bridles on the power of the king, and the voluntary sensitivity of monarchs to the direction of those bridles. Seyssel did not assume that princes are by nature good; but he did assume that power and energy can easily be channeled into useful patterns in a polity. And he had an excessively generous view of the abilities of well-bridled kings and their advisors to discern what must be done, and do it.

5. Etienne Pasquier and the *Recherches de la France*

In the later part of the sixteenth century, the challenges of new political theories devised by partisans in the religious wars forced a closer examination of laws and institutions that had long been taken for granted. Disputes arose about the origins of customary law—was it made by the king or by the people? And who, if anyone, had the power to make new laws? Was the king himself originally chosen by the people, and thus in some sense legitimated by their prior authority? Or was his authority superior to any popular will? What was the historical basis for the Estates-General, and how much independent power could it claim in government? Such questions were of far more than pedantic interest in the late sixteenth century in France, when the polity was torn apart by quarrels over the limits of political obligation, the rival claims of religious orthodoxy, tolerance, and civil peace.

With the vivid example of the religious wars before them, French jurists of the late sixteenth century were less generously disposed toward pluralism than their predecessors. Instead of advocating the virtues of conflict and tension, they relied on a few hallowed institutions, particularly the parlements, to temper and participate in royal governance. French thought generally moved toward a more concentrated absolutism, in an era when men longed for a strong authority to bring stability to the state; but certain constitutionalist theorists resisted this tendency. They stressed the importance of law as the constitutive structure of the polity, and the courts of law as the institutions charged with its protection. Several French jurists of this period reserved their highest admiration for the law itself, as medieval theorists had done, rather than for the person of the prince, which became common in the seventeenth century. As one of the most important of their number put it: "Just as little can a people live without law as a body without members, blood, or nerves; and there is nothing so consonant with the condition of nature as law, without which a household, a town, a nation, or all of humankind could not subsist, nor even the nature of things, the world itself. The foundation of liberty, the fount of equity and understanding, the heart, the counsel, and the wills of a state are planted and established upon law."[32]

The difficulty with such a glowing accolade, of course, is that it says nothing about how the blessings of law can be secured to a particular community, or how the ordinary laws of a human group are related to the laws constitutive of the universe. In an attempt to provide answers to such questions that would be of use in the religious wars, several French jurists undertook research into the origins of French and Roman law, and the institutions of the ancient Franks and Gauls. When one turns from Seyssel's *Monarchie* to the juristic treatises of the later sixteenth century, in fact, the first thing one notices is the different kind of evidence employed—the new reliance on historical research. The pioneer in this quest, the jurist who first turned his sustained attention to exploring the Gothic polity, was Etienne Pasquier. Pasquier foreshadowed Montesquieu in his belief that each people has a set of laws and institutions that are especially appropriate to its temper and situation, and that these laws and institutions in turn play a role in shaping the character of the people. Like Montesquieu, he spoke of *l'esprit* of these laws, and was fascinated by the variety of guises law could take in human life. Even more ardently than Montesquieu, Pasquier was determined to establish as firmly as he could the true ancient character of the institutions and customs peculiar to his own *patrie*, and in so doing, he paved the way for numerous successors among French constitutionalists.[33]

---

[32] Bernard de Girard Du Haillan, *Histoire de France* (1576), quoted by Church, *Constitutional Thought*, p. 80.
[33] The best study of Pasquier is Donald R. Kelley, *Foundations of Modern Historical Scholarship*, ch. 10.

In a letter to a contemporary who asked his opinion of a book on *La Droit de la nature*, Pasquier mused about the relevance of the law of nature to human life.[34] Gently but quite straightforwardly, he rejected the notion that human moral principles and positive laws are rooted in reason or in some higher law. Like other animals, we are subject to the law of self-preservation (including the preservation of the species); but these laws tell us little or nothing about how we should behave in any situation. In fact, Pasquier asserted that the lives of animals are better ordered by nature than our own.[35] Animals follow their simple instincts with a fair degree of success, and manage to live without laws or governments. Pasquier, like his friend Montaigne, listened to contemporary reports of encounters with the Brazilian savages. They, too, appeared to live tolerably well without political administration, or magistrates, or any form of a republic.[36] But civilized men require laws to keep their restless and covetous impulses under control. The instinct to individual self-preservation must be regulated by rules designed to make possible the preservation of the species. For the recognition of this second law of preservation, even more pressing than the first, is confined to a few "generous souls," says Pasquier, who are charged with ordering and administering human communities. Since the good of the whole people is more important than that of a single individual (here Pasquier simply rephrased a common maxim of juristic argument), when these two laws of self-preservation come into conflict, the rule must be to give preference to the public good.[37] But the ways in which such preference is to be given are left up to the wisdom of those generous souls charged with governing their fellows. Natural law has nothing to say about what the specific rules for our preservation will be.

In each locality and *patrie*, says Pasquier, laws are therefore devised over time to fit the needs and capacities, and even the environmental circumstances, of a particular people. This means that there is great relativity among our laws, an immense variety of different ways of regulating our lives in the different parts of the world. We think the Salic law is rooted in the law of nature because we live in France, Pasquier reminds his correspondent; the English believe the same of

---

[34] Etienne Pasquier, *Oeuvres*, in two volumes (1723); volume II contains the *Lettres*, published originally in 1586 and 1619. This letter to M. d'Eschacier is *livre* XIX, no. 7, pp. 551-554. D. Thickett has published a good *Bibliographie des oeuvres d'Estienne Pasquier*, as well as several volumes of selected letters.

[35] This same theme is developed at greater length in a letter to his friend Turnèbe, *livre* X, no. 1, pp. 249-257.

[36] Letter to M. de Querquifinen, seigneur d'Ardiveilliers, III, no. 3.

[37] Letter to Eschacier, XIX, 7, p. 552; cf. the letter to Eduart Molé, XIX, 1.

their own fundamental laws. But the recognition of this relativity should not lead us to undervalue our own polity and its laws. "Whatever the diversity of the law," admonishes Pasquier, "it is necessary to live according to those of one's own country, and to consider that since they are established, we ought to judge them to be good."[38] Such a sentiment, as we will see, was characteristic of French social theorists from Montaigne to Montesquieu.

Pasquier enthusiastically took his own advice. He was a most patriotic Frenchman, and his awareness that French laws were no more natural than any others did not prevent him from considering them the best he knew. He attempted to dissuade his juristic colleagues from using arguments from Roman law as though they were of superior vintage or intelligence, and pointed out the importance of the difference between Roman and French political experience. Since Roman laws and language were devised first for an *état populaire* (and then adapted to a large empire), they could have much less relevance for Frenchmen than the French language and their own customary laws, devised on the basis of the experience of a monarchy.[39] Pasquier insisted on the close interconnection between the laws, institutions, *moeurs*, and *humeurs* of a people in his appeal to his contemporaries to learn more about their own institutions and historical experiences:

> Any man of understanding, without acquaintance with the complete history of a people, can almost imagine its overall temper when he studies its ancient statutes and ordinances; and by the same token can make a sound conjecture about what its laws must have been, by looking at its manner of life. For to speak truthfully, well-ordered laws in any country form a habitude of manners and morals among those subject to them, which over the long run appears to be imprinted on them by the disposition of their nature.[40]

Among French laws and institutions, Pasquier reserved his greatest reverence for the parlements, the corporate body of jurists with which he as a magistrate was identified. He argued that the parlements had evolved steadily from the ancient councils of the earliest races of French kings, foreshadowed by the institutions of the Gauls before the Roman or the Frankish conquest. In a Machiavellian mood, he asked

---

[38] Letter to Eschacier, XIX, 7, p. 554. On the relativity of laws and the variety of human customs, see also the letter to M. Chopin, VI, 2, pp. 71-74.
[39] Letter to Turnèbe, I, no. 2, pp. 3-4; letter to M. Brisson, IX, 1.
[40] *Les Recherches de la France*, book IV, ch. 1, p. 421. The *Recherches*, Pasquier's major treatise, is included in volume 1 of the 1723 edition of the *Oeuvres*. I have relied on the 1611 edition, the last one corrected in his lifetime.

46—Order of Kingdom and Soul

whether fortune or *le conseil* had played a greater role in the preservation of the French kingdom, and decided for the latter, which he defined broadly as "*la police*, and the good conduct of our kings."[41] Within *la police* he gave pride of place to the aristocratic peers and to the parlements, which played within France a role that he thought crucial in any *République bien ordonnée*: the tempering of the authority of the sovereign magistrat, who controls the activities of the tempering body itself by his majestic presence. The harmonious balance of these interconnected authorities provides the central stability for *la police* of France.

Pasquier discovers the origins of the cooperation between prince and parlement in the era of Pepin and Charlemagne. These great monarchs, asserts Pasquier, never undertook anything of consequence for the kingdom without assembling their advisors in parlement, barons and prelates as well as jurists. It was regarded as important that the *volontez générales* of the kings (the phrase itself is worth noting) did not "obtain the force of Edicts until they had been verified and promulgated" in parlement. Pasquier observes that it is

> truly a great thing, and worthy of the majesty of a prince, that our kings, to whom God has given full and absolute power, have by ancient institution willed to submit their wills to the civility of the law. . . . And it is equally wonderful that as soon as an ordinance has been published and verified in the parlement, immediately the French people adhere to it without a murmur, as if this company were the link between the obedience of the subjects and the commands of their prince. Which is not a thing of small consequence for the grandeur of our kings.[42]

Like both Commynes and Seyssel, Pasquier insists that the grandeur and effective authority of French kings is increased, and not diminished, by the voluntary sharing of that authority with their advisors and with the parlements. Pasquier also shared Seyssel's preference for the parlements over the body that was coming to rival them as a possible claimant for a share of power in the French polity, the Estates-General. The Estates had fallen into disuse in the late fifteenth century, after an initial period in which the kings attempted to call them together with some frequency, and thus Seyssel was able to ignore them. But in the late sixteenth century they were revived to deal with financial crisis and religious conflict, and Pasquier was obliged to recognize

[41] *Recherches*, book II, ch. 1.
[42] II, 4, p. 83; the passage containing the phrase "volontez générales" is on p. 81.

them. He dealt with them harshly, asserting that members of the third estate had been added to ancient councils of prelates and nobles only to induce them to give money to the king. Flattered by the invitation to such august assemblies (Pasquier's phrase is: "puffed up with the hot air of this vain honor"), the members of the middle classes gave the king eagerly whatever new subsidies he asked. They were awed by the opportunity to present their grievances directly to his majesty, unaware that the glowing promises for the reformation of the state that they received in return were only "beautiful tapestries to be paraded before posterity."[43] Unlike the parlements, asserts Pasquier, the Estates have had no effective role in government; they should be called the "Estates-*généreux*" because of their alacrity in granting subsidies.[44] Thus he bears out Commynes's observation about the docility of delegates to such assemblies, no danger to the authority of kings.

Pasquier's biases as a jurist no doubt affected his perspective on the effectiveness of this motley group of laymen. In fact, the assemblies of the Estates at the national level held in his own era proved recalcitrant in matters of taxation. They were more trouble than they were worth to the monarchy, and this is why the kings ceased once more to convene them.[45] Yet Pasquier's assessment, however inaccurate, attests his desire to distinguish between impressive symbols in politics and hard truths, what Machiavelli called *la verità effettuale della cosa*.[46] The tone of political realism that marks this passage appears frequently in Pasquier's writings. He rejected the notion that a kingdom might be legitimately founded on wickedness, a notion that was in the air during the decades after Machiavelli's *Prince* became familiar among Frenchmen; but he took for granted that certain kinds of ruthless and unpalatable acts, such as the killing of Virginia by her father, are necessary to the establishing and maintenance of *l'estat de la chose publique*.[47] Pasquier was fond of composing dialogues, and in his most famous one, the *Pourparler du Prince*, he put forward the arguments of a conventionally Machiavellian courtier, though his own sympathies clearly lay with another figure, the *politique*.[48] In another dialogue, the *Pourparler du loy*, he put in the mouth of one of his personages, a convict, a persuasive argument for the notion that property is theft —that by nature all things belong to all men in common, and true

---

[43] II, 7, pp. 108-111.
[44] *Lettres, livre* IV, 9, in *Oeuvres*, vol. II, p. 86.
[45] J. Russell Major, *The Estates General of 1560*, chs. 6-7.
[46] *The Prince*, ch. 15.
[47] Letters to M. Chandon, IX, 7, p. 231; and IX, 8, p. 238.
[48] "Pourparler du prince," included in editions of the *Recherches* from 1560 onwards; in the 1611 edition, pp. 939-969; the Machiavellian figure is *le curial*.

thievery is perpetrated by him "who troubles the order of nature, and wishes to appropriate to his own individual usage that which is common to all."[49] The opposing interlocutor is given the last word, and insists on the importance of human and divine laws against taking what does not belong to us. But the problem of property had been posed in a most thought-provoking way.

Given his willingness to consider such ideas, as well as his articulate endorsement of the party that advocated tolerance in the religious wars —the *politiques*, to which Bodin, Montaigne, and L'Hôpital also adhered—it is not surprising that Pasquier was regarded with hostility by more conventional jurists and churchmen. In the next century he was pilloried as a *libertin* in a lengthy treatise composed by a Jesuit stung by Pasquier's hostility to Jesuits, his belief that "Loyola's error was more dangerous than Luther's."[50] Pasquier's opponents did not yet have the epithet they needed to label his position: Jansenism.

Pasquier's writing grew more somber as he lived through the devastating civil wars. His initial fascination with constitutional complexity was overshadowed by increasing anxiety about the dangers of partisan and sectarian conflict in the state. His last essay was a vociferous defense of strong royal authority, written in language that would have been welcome at Versailles. To attempt to violate something as sacred as royal authority, to lift this palladium from royalty, warns Pasquier,

> is to precipitate the state into such horrible anarchy and confusion that three kings would be less absolute than the kings of Poland or the dukes of Venice. This is a thing in which all the Orders of the kingdom have such a strong interest that there cannot be a single man of good will who would not prefer to die than to see royal authority weakened in his lifetime by the artifice of certain spirits who under the false pretext of disorders in the government serve only their own passion. . . . For their lives, their goods, their honor, even the chastity of their wives and children can be preserved only in peace and public tranquillity; and they have no light except that which they borrow from their sovereign, their only favorable star, any more than burning mirrors have any glimmer of light that they do not receive from the rays of the sun.[51]

---

[49] *Recherches*, pp. 975-976.

[50] The phrase is Donald Kelley's, *Foundations*, p. 287; the rebuttal was Garasse's *Recherches des recherches* (1622).

[51] "De l'autorité royal," 1615, in Pasquier, *Ecrits politiques*, edited by D. Thickett, pp. 287-288. The solar metaphor is used in a similar passage in the more monarchical second edition of Du Haillan's *Estat et succez des affaires de France* (1580), quoted in Church, *Constitutional Thought*, p. 122.

Pasquier wrote this in 1615, after the period of hope and progress under Henry IV was ended by assassination. In such times it is easy to see how even the most principled proponent of constitutionalism would want to lend support to stable monarchical authority.

6. FRANÇOIS HOTMAN AND *Francogallia*

Before we consider the currents of absolutism that flowed with increasing strength during these vexed decades, we should look briefly at one other important aspect of French thought. The familiar treatises of the French Huguenots are relevant to our concerns primarily by their negative impact: they closed off certain possible avenues of constitutionalist argument to orthodox jurists, because those arguments were associated with heresy and civil dissension; and they encouraged the formulation of a more extremist absolutism in response to the radicalism of the popular sovereignty they proclaimed.

The major casualty of the religious wars, from the point of view of constitutionalist argument in France, was the possibility of a theory of parliamentary government in the English sense focused upon the Estates-General. The Estates were revived between 1560 and 1588, and went through one of the most vigorous periods in their history. They initially received strong support among all the groups in the religious wars, including Huguenots and members of the Catholic League, as well as the *politiques*. When the Estates were in session, claims were put forward by some delegates that the Estates should meet regularly; that their consent should be mandatory for all new taxation; that they should supervise the monarch's councils, and that their joint resolutions should have the force of law. During these same decades the parlements, because of corporate hostility to the Estates as well as deep monarchical sentiment, obstinately blocked all attempts at reform, and hardly behaved like the "Roman Senate" to which they were so frequently compared.

It might therefore appear that the time was ripe for the development of a sustained theory justifying the legitimacy of the Estates and supporting their pretenses; yet all initiatives on behalf of the Estates were abortive, and found scant response in juristic treatises. Friction and suspicion among the Estates helped discredit these assemblies, and the general confusion of the period played its part in making it difficult for them to develop and maintain a strong position. But it is also significant that they became closely identified in many eyes with the dissidents in the religious wars, despite their initial favor among *politiques*. They were adopted eagerly as the primary focus for popular resistance in several Huguenot treatises, and occupied a similar position in Catholic extremist sentiment. This circumstance went far to discredit them in the eyes of the orthodox jurists who composed constitutionalist treatises.

The most outspoken defense of the Estates-General during this period appears in François Hotman's *Francogallia*. Hotman, an ardent Calvinist, shared many traits with more orthodox jurists. He had the same legal training, and in his younger days had extensive ties with other jurists, many of whom had themselves been initially drawn to the "so-called reformed religion." Hotman made several significant contributions to historical jurisprudence before the shock of the massacre of the Protestants on St. Bartholomew's Day in 1572 led him to devote the fruits of his researches to the defense of the liberties of French Calvinists against monarchical oppression.[52] Like Pasquier, he was Germanist rather than Romanist in his juristic sympathies; unlike Pasquier, he defended the prerogatives of the Estates. Although his book is conservative and judicious in tone, Hotman's message is radical and provocative: that the ancient constitution based in the will of the French people, whose lineaments he presents, was still in force, never having rightfully been superseded by the developing power of the monarchy. Because of his erudition, Hotman's treatise posed a more formidable challenge to orthodoxy than the many occasional pamphlets or abstract scholastic treatises produced by other Huguenots. He joined the argument on familiar ground, and with impressive equipment; and thus his treatise was influential both as a source and as a target for later generations, though he was rarely cited by name.[53]

In Hotman's account, the Frankish and Gallic peoples who formed the French nation had originally elected their own kings, and only gradually had the monarchy become hereditary. The people had never given up their residual right of election, though it had been unused for several centuries. It was therefore implied that they could rightfully depose a tyrant and install his successor, although Hotman refrained from making so explicit the contemporary corollaries of his argument. The major focus of his treatise was the authority of the Estates-General. He asserted that traditionally the kings had consulted regularly with assemblies of the people. But a series of usurping and conniving monarchs had ceased to consult, and had allowed the people to become deluded about their rights. Hotman attempted to prove, in

---

[52] Donald Kelley's fine intellectual biography of *François Hotman: A Revolutionary's Ordeal* should be consulted.

[53] On Hotman's later influence, see the rich introduction to the variorum edition of *Francogallia* by Ralph E. Giesey and J.H.M. Salmon, pp. 107-128, which also includes a good translation of the Latin text.

considerable detail and with much antiquarian gusto, that regular consultation was part of the true constitution of France, with ancient roots in the assemblies of warriors, continuing through the medieval Estates. Such a strategy, clothing a radical argument in a reactionary appeal to ancient forms, was common in French constitutionalist debate then and in the late seventeenth century.[54]

Hotman claimed the authority of Seyssel in support of his idea that the Estates-General were central to the French government, by asserting that the three estates that have so prominent a role in *La Monarchie de France* are related "not to the order of communal life, but to the public council of the nation." He thus completely inverts Seyssel's own argument about the estates, which had nothing to do with councils or assemblies, and everything to do with "the order of communal life." With an equal disregard for Seyssel's own intentions, Hotman uses him as an authority in his polemic against the corruptions and ill-founded pretentions of those "pleaders" who have "applied themselves to the practice and study of the art of verbal brawling," the *parlements*.[55] He was concerned to make as strong a case as possible; and when he found that he could take something from the most respected of French constitutionalists to illustrate his argument, he did so, even when it meant turning Seyssel's argument completely against itself.

It should be clear from even so cursory a summary of Hotman's *Francogallia* that it has a different tone from that of orthodox juristic exercises. This is true despite its adoption of the ponderous historical apparatus that characterized French constitutionalist argument from the mid-sixteenth century onward. The tone of *Francogallia* is determined by Hotman's deep commitment to his cause, and his ardent polemical purposes. Exaggeration, occasional heavy sarcasm, and a highly selective use of constitutional authorities, which sometimes amounts to obvious distortion, are characteristic of the book. One may respect his passion and credit his influence on the development of salutary doctrines, without holding a very high opinion of his achievement as a constitutional theorist, compared with the subtle analysis of Seyssel. Nonetheless, it is important to remember that Hotman's instincts about what is required to control a king effectively were sounder than Seyssel's. For the future of constitutionalism in France, it was unfortunate that the stress on the importance of the Estates-

[54] As Kelley puts it, this "conservative posture was dictated not so much by temperament as by the political conventions of this age, which demanded that all change be introduced in the form of restoration." *François Hotman*, 114.

[55] *Francogallia*, ed. Giesey and Salmon, ch. x (on the estates) and ch. ii (on the parlements); almost all references to Seyssel were added to the second edition (1576).

General became identified with heresy, and that the central thrust of the argument stemming from Seyssel and nurtured by the circumstances of the late sixteenth century was so thoroughly monarchical.

Hotman's treatise was only one among a great many books and pamphlets produced on all sides in the religious wars. At the time, it was overshadowed by several other treatises that apparently made bolder arguments and were less encumbered with historical detail. Among the most striking and popular monarchomach treatises were Theodore Beza's *Droit des magistrats*, and the *Vindiciae contra tyrannos*, whose authorship remains a point of controversy.[56] Both confirm the right of resistance against a tyrant by magistrates representing the whole community; both rely on arguments drawn from Scripture and from abstract natural right. These same arguments were repeated, with more radically democratic overtones, by publicists for the Catholic Leagues in later stages of the wars.[57]

Nonetheless, the arguments of the monarchomachs, Huguenot and Catholic alike, which have become so familiar because of their contribution to the development of liberal ideas throughout Europe, had few echoes in orthodox French constitutional argument. As the civil wars dragged on, more and more Frenchmen became convinced that the only solution lay in strong monarchical control. An occasional orthodox jurist stubbornly resisted the monarchist current, keeping the element of balance that distinguished Seyssel's *Monarchie*, maintaining the medieval focus on the community and its customs. One such theorist was Guy Coquille, voluntarily isolated in the provincial administration, resistant to the developing ideology of sovereignty. Coquille wrote several treatises between 1585 and 1595 in which he reiterated traditional limits on the power of the king and gave an important place to the Estates-General.[58] Like Hotman, he insisted that the original transfer of authority from the community to the king had not been complete; residual authority remained with the people, and should be exercised through the Estates. But such ideas were rare among ortho-

---

[56] In addition to Du Plessis Mornay and Languet, a new contender for authorship of this anonymous treatise has been advanced by Derk Visser: Johann Junius de Jonge; see Donald Kelley, *François Hotman*, p. 295n. Valuable abridged translations of Beza's *Droit des magistrats* and the *Vindiciae*, as well as *Francogallia*, can be found in Julian Franklin, *Constitutionalism and Resistance in the Sixteenth Century*. I have relied on Franklin's language in the passage about the brawling lawyers quoted above.

[57] Frederic Baumgartner, *Radical Reactionaries: The Political Thought of the French Catholic League*.

[58] Church, *Constitutional Thought*, devotes an entire chapter (v) to Coquille, concluding (p. 302) that "Coquille represented a dying cause, but his works stand as a monument to much that was best in the constitutional thought of France."

dox jurists after 1572; and by the end of the century the monarchomachs themselves were silent. They were without disciples in France until the revival of Huguenot opposition among exiles after the Revocation of the Edict of Nantes in 1685. The central current of political thought in France in the late sixteenth century proceeded in another direction altogether.

CHAPTER TWO

The Development of Absolutist Thought

1. Types of Monarchical Power

The development of the idea of absolute monarchy in the sixteenth century meant the reinterpretation of images of the king that had been familiar in earlier centuries, and the exaggeration of certain aspects of these images at the expense of others. François Olivier-Martin discusses four different bases for *la puissance absolue* invested by jurists and royal publicists in the throne of France from medieval times: the traditional view of the king as defender and embodiment of the common good against particularistic interests; the feudal *suzerain des suzerains*, peak of a hierarchy of lords and vassals; the Most Christian King, favorite son of the church and defender of the faith; and the emperor in his realm, enjoying all the powers of the Roman emperor in France.[1] In the sixteenth century, the first and last of these elements were elaborately developed by publicists of the monarchy; and the other two were recast in a way that would have been incomprehensible to medieval men.

It would be hard to exaggerate the importance of the concept of the French king as the representative of the common interest, the source and embodiment of the good of all. This image had deep roots in medieval France, and retained its power until the eighteenth century. It was understood by Frenchmen with a special directness and vividness. There was a sense of security when the monarch was personally in charge of things, a trust in the benevolence of his will, which can only be explained by the belief that he apprehended and spoke for the good of the entire society in a way no other human being could approach. In constitutionalist theories such as that of Seyssel, this notion was kept in a moderate perspective. The monarch was the central principle of energy and will within the system, defending common interests against particularism; but he was seen as a mortal who could not be expected to comprehend more than any other man, considered as an individual. His royalty depended on his agents, ministers, associates. In absolutist theories, however, the capacity of the consecrated king to see and to represent the good of all was made central

[1] *Histoire du droit français des origines à la Revolution*, pp. 303-362.

to the ideology. During the reign of Francis I, and again under Henry IV, this idea provided the inspiration for some of the most glowing tributes to the monarch as well as an important theoretical assumption about the special excellence of monarchy.

The feudal image of the king as suzerain of suzerains was also retained in the rhetoric of Renaissance royalism; but it was gradually preempted by the theory of sovereignty, which endowed the king with a type of power unlike any other in quality and scope. In the traditional conception of monarchical fealty, the king owed justice and protection to his subjects, who in return owed obedience and support in arms and monies for the defense of the state. In medieval times this set of obligations was clearly hedged about by the notion that any changes in the pattern depended on the consent of both parties. The king had no well-defined "legislative" capacity, but spoke the common wisdom of lawyers and the customs of his subjects in dispensing justice. He had no right to new taxes when he wanted them, but was supposed to request money from his subjects in emergencies. These ancient notions involved a reciprocity that took the form of comfortable ambiguity in "lawmaking" on the one hand, and on the other a sharp delineation of the king's domain from the "private" property of his subjects, unavailable to him for public purposes except on the basis of their express consent. But this ancient belief in the sanctity of private property was boldly undermined by sixteenth-century publicists such as Barthélemy de Chasseneuz, who asserted the prince's right to decide when taxes are necessary for the state, and take them virtually at will.[2] The right of the prince to prevail over persons and property throughout the kingdom, and the concomitant obligation of subjects to provide what was needed, were firmly asserted by these jurists. The other side of the old coin—the rights of subjects to what they had been entitled to, and the obligations of princes to respect certain limits on their behavior—began to be ignored.

The French king had long been described as the eldest and most favored son of the Roman church. He enjoyed certain mystical advantages denied to less-developed monarchies, such as the ability to perform miracles, especially those of the thaumaturgical variety. It was widely believed that the French monarch could heal scrofula—the king's evil—by touching the afflicted. Regular ceremonies of healing continued until the eighteenth century. As Seyssel saw so clearly, religion was for most subjects the first foundation of the throne of France. In the fifteenth and sixteenth centuries, the character of this

[2] Church, *Constitutionalist Thought*, ch. 3, has a thoughtful discussion of such transitions.

religious aura shifted from the dutiful son of the Father to the image of God Himself on earth. The king was described as a direct bearer of divine authority in earthly things, and then finally as a god himself. In the early sixteenth century the language of deification was extensively developed. Apologists for monarchy under Francis I, such as Charles de Grassaille and Pierre Rebuffi, asserted firmly "the king of France was a fleshly god in his realm, for whatever he did was not wrought by himself but by God through him; God spoke through the mouth of the king, and whatever he did was inspired by God."[3] Such rhetoric contained two rather different implications. A king inspired directly by God, a vessel of the divine word and purposes, could plausibly be expected to obey God's laws automatically, and to refrain from harassing his subjects without further need for limits on his rule. Renaissance proponents of absolute monarchy therefore ignored or rejected the idea of such limits, relying instead on the consonance of divine and royal will. As Tawney put it: "Skeptical as to the existence of unicorns and salamanders, the age of Machiavelli and Henry VIII found food for its credulity in the worship of that rare monster, the God-fearing prince."[4]

The divinization of the monarch also began to imply something quite different from automatic royal subjection to God's will—the notion that the "king is God on earth," a succinct and striking maxim that became popular in these decades. Increasingly, the ideology of monarchy placed the deified monarch himself at the center of the stage. Approximating king to God was initially associated with the notion of the "great chain of being," an enduring order in the universe in which the monarch holds the place of God, or of the sun, a conception that undoubtedly helped make this image more persuasive.[5] But the comfortable serenity of a complex and well-populated universe in which the king occupied a plane clearly less lofty than that of various natural and supernatural forces was gradually abandoned by absolutists in favor of an ideology in which the images of God and sun are used only to lend splendor to the king, not to remind him and his subjects of the greater planes of ordered universe beyond. The particular form of deification provided for Renaissance monarchs takes its character from the humanism that pervaded Renaissance thought. The king as God on earth meant not a vicar of Jehovah, but the most splendid of mortal individuals. The prince becomes the symbol of human pride in human power. It is the notion of the king as super-man, gifted with

[3] Church, *Constitutionalist Thought*, pp. 47-53.
[4] *Religion and the Rise of Capitalism*, p. 102.
[5] W. H. Greenleaf, *Order, Empiricism and Politics*.

all the attributes of an anthropomorphic God, that prevails in this ideology and sets it apart both from its medieval antecedents and from the obscurantist mystification of the oriental cult of the despot.[6]

Images of the king as God in earth, however impressive they may be as symbols to enhance the throne, do not provide a theory of monarchical power that easily supports specific extensions and aggrandizements. They have literary luster, but lack juristic strength. For that purpose the fourth element in Olivier-Martin's catalogue proved invaluable: the idea that the king, as emperor in his kingdom, inherited and exercised the sweeping powers of the Roman emperors described in the codes of Roman law. From the fourteenth until well into the eighteenth century, "Romanists" in France were closely identified with the cause of absolute royal power against any attempts to set limits on that power from within the community itself.

Some of the abstract formulae of Roman law had been familiar to medieval jurists; but as Fritz Kern shows in his classic study, these scholars had interpreted Roman dicta in ways palatable to their own society.[7] The notion that the king was *animata lex in terra*, for instance, was read to mean that the king had absorbed the law into his will. If he was deficient in his understanding of the law, this could always be asserted by others who voiced the customary legal sense of the people. Renaissance jurists read such passages in quite another light: the king was "living law" in the sense that whatever he said had the substance and rightful force of law, and there was no earthly court of appeal against his speaking of the law.[8]

Two maxims from Roman law were particularly favored by Renaissance jurists: *princeps legibus solutus est*, and *quod principi placuit legis habet vigorem*. The effect of these maxims was to put the king above the law, which then became an instrument of his will in governing. To appreciate the revolutionary implications of this development, it is important to recall the quite different sense of law in medieval times. Law was synonymous with right and with custom, the moral sense and traditional social pattern of a community. Law developed and changed imperceptibly; it was not "made" by human will to deal with novel situations. Providing justice meant ensuring to each member of the community whatever was due to him by ancient right, and defending him against encroachment. Seyssel retained this idea of justice as main-

---

[6] Jacques Ellul, *Histoire des institutions*, pp. 356-357.
[7] *Kingship and Law in the Middle Ages*, pp. 183-185.
[8] See generally Myron Gilmore, *Argument from Roman Law in Political Thought*; A. Esmein, "La Maxime *princeps legibus solutus est*," in *Essays in Legal History*, edited by Paul Vinogradoff, pp. 201-214.

tenance of customary privileges, even though he moved away from the sense of static peace that had accompanied it in medieval theory, in his idea of individual mobility and dynamic social change. In the later sixteenth century, however, this ancient notion gave way to the theory of legislative sovereignty.

Bodin was the first to state such a theory clearly, but several theorists had broached it in the preceding decades. Jurists provided long lists of *regalia*, the powers and privileges of the king, and borrowed from Roman law the notion of the *merum imperium*, which emphasized "the twin authorities of supreme jurisdiction and the promulgation of laws binding throughout the realm."[9] Men trained in the Roman codebooks were led to make comparisons between Roman laws and the traditional laws of their own community; and on the basis of this they arrived at the notion of the "positive law" of a particular society, separable from the "natural" or "divine" law that it was supposed to embody. It was then possible to conceive of the king "making law" in dispensing justice and in his ordinances regulating the kingdom, devising specific applications of universal principles. The desirability of obtaining advice and consent from various parts of the realm in the process of lawmaking was universally recognized. But the basic authority of the king himself to pronounce the law and to be personally absolved from subjection to the law he made was developed on the basis of Roman legal maxims, especially the notion of a *plenitudo potestatis* to override and change all customary law. The essential step was driving a wedge between "natural law" and "positive law" so that the prince could be held to be subject to the former but above the latter, and thus have a clear field for legislative action.

2. Guillaume Budé and Absolutist Rhetoric under Francis I

The brilliance of the person of the prince, and the adoption of categories from Roman law to define his powers, are both evident in the work of one of the most important of the early Renaissance humanists, Guillaume Budé. Budé was an extraordinarily erudite man who did more than any other Frenchman to stimulate the study of classical life and letters, language and law, in France. He was a secretary to Francis I, combining several minor administrative duties with ministering wholeheartedly to Francis' enthusiasm for art and letters. The advent of this new monarch in 1515, which led Seyssel to compose his treatise

[9] Church, *Constitutionalist Thought*, pp. 55-56; on the medieval roots of the *regalia*, Jacques Poujol, "Jean Ferrault on the King's Privileges," *Studies in the Renaissance* v (1958), 15-26.

on the realm of France for the edification of the king, produced a very different reaction in Budé. Impressed by the great potential of a strong monarch to advance the glory of France and the scholarly and artistic vigor of Frenchmen (two things fused for Budé in the same patriotic fervor), he used his pen to celebrate the individual prince and his creative powers.

For the theoretical underpinning of his idea of an all-powerful monarch who is not a tyrant, Budé relied on Aristotle's *Politics*. Aristotle's discussion of the paternalistic, superhuman ruler who has no proper place in any polity except that of full control over his fellows lends itself nicely to absolutist rhetoric. Budé provides examples of such rulers from Roman history, and also names among them "our own kings, who have everything in their own power and like Homer's Jupiter make everything function . . . by their nod alone, are human Joves . . . who nevertheless die in the manner of men."[10] Only in death do such kings reveal their mortality; and only after death may they be judged and assessed by other men. The only human bridle Budé allows, in fact, to rein in the impulse of such a king, is the anticipated judgment of posterity. The king's natural desire to impress future generations will provide the impetus for him to behave in heroic and appropriately kingly ways.[11]

Budé's most sustained discussion of monarchy is his contribution to the "mirror of princes" literature, the only book he wrote in the vernacular, his *Institution du Prince* composed for Francis I. This primer for princes relies on a Renaissance version of the Platonic image of the philosopher-monarch, requiring instruction and counsel from men of letters. Budé's contribution to the instruction of his prince is a classical portrait gallery of great rulers through which he leads the young monarch, admiring the princely qualities of each, rather than constructing a systematic argument. Budé rambles from one portrait to another, describing battles, courts of justice, encounters, and voyages, quoting Scripture and relating classical anecdotes with fine disregard for temporal boundaries.

The most important lesson of the *Institution du Prince*, reiterated in a variety of ways, is that the monarch must remain in full control of his own government, and not share too much power with his underlings. Only he has the princely capacities that make for good ruling, and all other officers in the state must be firmly subordinated to his

[10] *Annotationes in Pandectas* (1508), quoted by David O. McNeil, *Guillaume Budé and Humanism in the Reign of Francis I*, p. 22.
[11] Claude Bontems, "*L'Institution du Prince* de Guillaume Budé," in Bontems, et al., *Le Prince dans la France des XVIe et XVIIe siècles*, p. 39.

own will. Budé evoked the image of the king seated above society that dominated French thought for so many decades:

> It is written in the twentieth chapter of the *Proverbs* of Solomon: "The king sitting in his seat of justice, by his glance alone, searches out and chases from his kingdom all iniquity and disorder." So it was said of King Solomon, wise above all other men, to signify that when a king has the will, the knowledge and the grace of majesty, and full purpose to use the magnificent and venerable authority of his office, to be present and speak where he is needed, and show himself to his subjects, exhibiting the royal majesty publicly, he can do far greater and better things in peace and in war than his lieutenants or agents, because the reverence and majesty of royalty cannot be delegated by the king to those to whom he delegates his power, however much authority he grants them.[12]

Although his early treatises show support for a monarchy moderated by diverse institutions in the state—a constitutional monarchy akin to that of Seyssel—in his later writings Budé embraced an uncompromising ideal of kingly power, in which there was no room for any other source of power in the state. He firmly rejected the notion that the parlement of Paris resembled the Roman senate, and provided lengthy legal arguments to demonstrate the complete superiority of the monarch over this body, paralleling Francis' own tendency to subject the parlements more and more firmly to his own royal will. Budé's general attitude toward popular interventions or resistance to monarchy was sufficiently negative that he was willing to accept tyranny itself as preferable. Any notion that the king might be "subjected" to any other will, whether that of his ministers, his judges, or his people, was abhorrent to him.[13]

What of the relationship of the king to law? Budé defines justice as "a constant and immovable will giving to each one his due," and associates it with the light and order of reason in the universe, so that "this justice cannot be done without great knowledge and science acquired by letters." It includes the distribution of honors and profits, as well as punishments, throughout society in such a way as to advance *la chose publicque*. And it is for this reason, says Budé, that kings are "not subject to the laws and ordinances of their kingdom as others are," since they must be the ones to apply those laws for the benefit of all. "For it is to be presumed," insists Budé, "that kings are so perfect in prudence and nobility and equity that they have no need of rule or

[12] *L'Institution du Prince*, 31r.-31v., *ibid.*, p. 94.
[13] *Ibid.*, pp. 24-38.

written form to constrain them by fear and by the necessity of obedience, as others do, except for the divine law that takes its authority from God and not from men." The innate excellence that we must associate with kings, and the distributive functions of the kingly office, raise them above the laws of their own kingdoms and make them obedient only to the divine laws. However, concludes Budé, the most honorable and royal course of action is for the king to subject himself voluntarily to his own laws and advertise this subjection "in order to give authority to his *constitutions et ordonnances*." In this act he behaves in a peculiarly kingly fashion, enhancing his own laws and emphasizing that none but he can subject himself to law.[14]

And why should we expect kings to behave in this way? They will do so instinctively, asserts Budé on the authority of Solomon; for just as the several rivers of the earth are directed in their courses by the will of God, "so the heart of the king moves by instinct and by impulsion of God, who controls and attracts it according to his pleasure, to undertake enterprises that are praiseworthy and honest and useful to his people and himself, or alternatively are in line with what he and his subjects have merited."[15] In his direction of the hearts of kings, God requires human aid only from philosophers, who provide the light of reason that indicates to the monarch the way he should go, and remind him of the exacting judgment of history necessary to a hero-king.

3. MICHEL DE L'HÔPITAL ON JUSTICE AND THE ORDER OF THE STATE

The traditional notion of the prince as embodiment of and spokesman for the common good, dispensing justice throughout the polity, was central to Budé's heroic kingship, and was equally prominent in other sixteenth-century discussions of monarchy. It remained important in Bodin's work, where it was transformed into the theory of legislative sovereignty that made it the basis for a satisfactory account of the exercise of power in the modern state. In order to appreciate both the scope of Bodin's achievement and the extent of his indebtedness to earlier concepts of royal authority, it is useful to have a specific contemporary benchmark against which to measure the *Six livres de la*

---

[14] *Institution du Prince*, 7v.-8r., *ibid.*, p. 80. A. J. Carlyle, *History of Medieval Political Theory in the West*, VI, 294, cites a similar passage from the *Annotationes in Pandectas* in which the Aristotelian basis of this argument is made explicit. See also Kelley, *Foundations*, ch. 3.
[15] *Institution du Prince*, 31r.-31v., in Bontems, *Le Prince dans la France*, p. 94; cf. Linton C. Stevens, "The Contribution of French Jurists to the Humanism of the Renaissance," *Studies in the Renaissance*, I (1954), 92-105.

république. Such a benchmark is provided by the ideas of the chancellor of Catherine de' Medicis, Michel de L'Hôpital. L'Hôpital, like Bodin, exemplified the tendency toward absolutism in late sixteenth-century thought, while retaining important elements of older arguments. He extended the traditional picture of the prince as the embodiment of justice as far as possible, and drew on Augustinian motifs to show how that justice is connected with public and private interest in suggestive ways. He distinguished between adjudication and legislation, but he did not provide a description of the exercise of unitary royal will comparable to that of Bodin.

L'Hôpital was one of the most respected ministers in the history of France. He was the founder of the party favoring toleration, the *politiques*, though the solution for which he worked was accepted only after decades of bloodshed in France. Unlike many of his fellow jurists, he was a staunch opponent of the claims of the parlements to participate in lawmaking. His education predisposed him toward the humanistic absolutism of a Budé, and his experience in royal administrative service confirmed his admiration for strong monarchical power and distaste for intermediate bodies. Many of the chancellor's political ideas were expressed in speeches before the parlements and the Estates-General to which he came as spokesman for the Crown. Several political writings have also been attributed to him, including a long *Traité de la réformation de la justice* first published in 1826. This treatise is commonly accepted as L'Hôpital's, but it cannot have been written in its entirety by him, since the last five parts of the treatise contain multiple references to events that occurred decades after his death.[16] I shall refer only to the first two parts, which differ in tone and substance from the others, with the proviso that even these references are uncertain.

In the early part of the *Traité de la réformation de la justice*, there is an idealized vision of the prince as source of justice and good order in his kingdom that is consonant with L'Hôpital's humanism, his other political writings, and more generally with French political thought before Bodin's *République*. The ancient theme is given a Platonic vividness in these passages, which stress the personal role of the prince and the magistrates he chooses to help him govern, as models and exemplars of a just way of living. The good prince is "himself the law,

[16] P.J.S. Duféy, ed., *Oeuvres complètes de Michel de L'Hospital*, vols. IV-V. The manuscripts of this treatise in the Bibliothèque nationale (fonds Français nos. 18472-18474) are catalogued as "écrit par M. [Eustache] des Réfuges, et attribué à M. de L'Hôpital." They are all later copies, and do not help answer the question how much, if any, of this treatise was in fact written by the chancellor himself.

the rule and pattern for his subjects. They form their behavior on his example much more surely than on the most austere ordinances promulgated by a loose-living prince."[17] This is an unusually concrete version of the idea that the prince is living law. But the author of the *Traité* does not have a purely personalistic notion of justice; he cites Saint Augustine as his authority for the notion that justice constitutes a kingdom. The order provided by the prince in his acts and in his laws holds the people together in society, and explains why they are there. "For why else would so many thousands of men of diverse regions, languages, manners, qualities, and conditions put themselves voluntarily under the domination and the law of a single man?" Only their expectation that their voluntary subjection will bring them justice, in the old sense of protection from oppression and security in what is due to each of them, makes this behavior comprehensible. This is all ordained by God for the good of his people; this "tacit consent of peoples and of nations, this general fittingness, comes from heaven; it is the true harmony of the world, which supports human society with a firm and assured link."[18]

Thus L'Hôpital sees justice and order, power and obedience, as inextricably linked together in the divine pattern that supports society among men. In this vision, providing justice is something much more wonderful and awful than simply adjudicating disagreements; it is a profoundly constitutive act, by which the prince, reflecting divine order in his own actions and dictates, provides order in his kingdom. The chancellor draws a sharp distinction between justice and the "profit and particular interest of the prince," citing as his authority "Plato, in the fifth book of the *Laws*." But his major debt on this point is to Saint Augustine; and he foreshadows Pascal and Fénelon, who drew from the works of Augustine the same inspiration. L'Hôpital insists that

> justice is so charitable that she has no regard for her interest and her particular profit, nor for anything except that which works for the conservation and well-being of the whole.... Thus justice is properly the eye of the republic, without which all things would be indubitably in shadows and in confusion.... The eye cannot see itself, except in a mirror or reflected in the eye of another. This

[17] Duféy, IV, 23-24.
[18] Duféy, IV, 28-29; the reference in the passage quoted just above to the "voluntary submission" of thousands to the will of a single man may well be an attempt to provide an answer to the question raised by La Boétie in his *Discourse on voluntary servitude* (discussed below, ch. 3).

justice is not made for itself nor for the one who exercises it; she is wholly made for the good of the other.

> ... But injustice is so intoxicated with the love of herself that she thinks only of her own profit and particular contentment. All that is useful to her, all that will serve her avarice, her lust, her vengeance, which contributes to the augmentation of her goods, her family, her ambition, her grandeur—all these things become justice to her, licit, and honest, so that she wills to make a law of them, when in fact this would be the greatest misfortune in the world.[19]

Yet like a good Augustinian, L'Hôpital recognizes that because justice is so essential to human order—*l'anchre et soutènement de la cité*—some shadow or imitation of justice must be present even in tyrannies, even among thieves. Usurpers are compelled to set up "some form of justice," not out of love and sympathy with it, as do good princes, but "for love of themselves." Their own calculation of their selfish interest as rulers desiring to keep power leads them to imitate just actions.

The contrast between justice as charity, the pure eye that looks only outwards for the good of others, and injustice as self-love and calculated ambition that necessarily requires an imitation of justice itself, became a prominent theme in seventeenth-century French social thought. An equally prominent theme, also discussed by the chancellor, was the difficulty that faces anyone who wants to believe in abstract purity in human justice, in the face of laws and customs that differ so markedly from place to place. Like many classical thinkers, and like Montaigne and Pascal after him, L'Hôpital treats human justice as "only an image, or rather a shadow," of "true and universal justice," inevitably subject to diversity and change. But more optimistically than many of his successors, L'Hôpital insists that just as the same sun shines in Paris and in Constantinople, so divine justice is itself manifested in the laws of all peoples, American savages as well as European Christians; in his view, "as far as human laws are concerned, each people, monarch and sovereign establishes them according to the commodities and particular necessities of provinces, regions, even cities; always retaining this character, that reason must always be the soul of the law; otherwise she cannot last, any more than the human body can survive without the soul that gives it life."[20]

[19] Duféy, IV, 31 (on Plato's *Laws*), and pp. 73-74.
[20] Duféy, IV, 58-61.

Thus justice has for L'Hôpital a generous and charitable undertone of creative activity, a "vigorous and laborious life" that requires adapting universal truths to the "common utility" of each separate territory. More firmly than his traditional predecessors, L'Hôpital asserts that the prince is himself above the law he makes. In a strong speech given before the parlement of Paris in 1561, L'Hôpital defended the purity of monarchy against any pretentions to participation in power by the courts. He reproved the judges for wanting to take part in legislation, the prerogative of the king alone, and one that requires a different sort of prudence from that appropriate to judges. The courts must be sensitive to the demands of justice as equity in each particular dispute that they adjudicate. "The legislator," on the other hand, "is not bound by times or persons, and should regard that which touches everyone; this will sometimes mean that he appears to do wrong to individuals, for the conservation of the whole."[21] The idea that single-minded attention to the common good necessarily means injury to particular claims of individuals considered in themselves, a notion that had medieval roots, and later became central to the theory of the public interest, was thus voiced straightforwardly by L'Hôpital.

In his attitude toward the Estates-General, L'Hôpital echoes the language of Commynes, arguing the utility of this body to both prince and people against anyone who would hold that the prince's own power is diminished by such an assembly. For "there is no act so worthy of a king, and so appropriate to him, as to hold estates, and give a general audience to his subjects, and do justice to each." As far as the people are concerned, "there is nothing that pleases and contents a subject so much as to be recognized, and to be able to approach his prince." This conception of the assemblies is quite traditional; they provide psychological and symbolic benefits for the humble subjects and enhance the majesty of the king. There is no suggestion of active participation in policy making, nor of any constraint upon the royal will. The king's abilities to make law are enhanced when he learns "of many general complaints which concern the whole people, as well as those of private individuals."[22] The estates free the king from excessive dependence on his own ministers by revealing deficiencies that would otherwise remain hidden from even the most conscientious king, and give him new eyes and ears through which to learn about his kingdom. But there is no warrant here for

---

[21] Duféy, II, 12-13.
[22] "Harangue prononcée à l'ouverture de la session des Etats-généraux" (1560), Duféy, I, 378-382.

66—Order of Kingdom and Soul

subjects to believe that they can withhold their assent or their treasure from the king on any grounds, if he sees fit to ask for them.

Like Seyssel, however, L'Hôpital notes the subtle connection between beneficent government and healthy monarchical authority. In the *Traité* he makes this connection quite explicit, excoriating tyranny and asserting "that there is no assured power based on fear, nor any state of long duration founded on pure force. . . . And whoever conducts a state by absolute power, without restraining it with the reins of mildness and justice, is like a coachman who lets his horses gallop down a sharp descent, or whips them up to full speed, instead of moderating them and applying the brake to keep them from destroying themselves."[23] Yet, even as he uses Seyssel's famous image, L'Hôpital changes its meaning. For Seyssel had never personified the king as the coachman; his prince was in the position of the bridled horse. But L'Hôpital recalls Plato's charioteer as well as Seyssel's image, and makes the good king the firm controller of his own *puissance absolue*. For L'Hôpital, like Plato, the essential connection is between the order in the soul of the good king and the order he provides within the kingdom. The second part of the *Traité* ends with the counsel to

> seek first within ourselves this accord, this consonance, this harmony . . . which unites us with God, in which consists the sovereign good of man; and then, if we have some authority, use it in order to ensure that this same harmony is found in the body of the city, the republic, or the state, so that each one living in repose, content with his own lot, and not undertaking anything against his neighbor except to do him good, God will be served . . . the king will be more faithfully obeyed . . . the magistrates revered . . . and individuals will be maintained according to their conditions, ranks, and merit in their possessions, lives, and honors, they with their families; which is the end and purpose of justice.[24]

It would be difficult to find a better statement of the ancient idea of justice as the maintenance of order in the kingdom, combined with the Platonic and Augustinian themes of love of God and order in the soul. These parallel concepts—ordering the self and ordering society —were rarely expressed more forcefully than in the last part of the sixteenth century in France, and never more eloquently than in this passage. The same notion of justice as harmonic order was present in Bodin's social theory. But there it was combined with a host of other arguments that redirected it, arguments that derive from Bodin's distinctive notion of legislative sovereignty.

[23] Duféy, IV, 77-78.   [24] Duféy, IV, 111-112.

4. JEAN BODIN ON THE COMMONWEALTH: THE THEORY OF SOVEREIGNTY

Bodin was one of the most complex and heterodox thinkers of a complex and heterodox century. He was a jurist and humanist with wide interests in philosophy, history, and the occult.[25] He was also a political activist, an advocate of the toleration party, and an influential delegate (by his own account) for the third estate to the Estates-General of 1576. He wrote not only several different versions of one of the longest books on political philosophy ever published, but also another major work on law and history, an examination of spiritual influences in the world, and two treatises, in dialogue form, on contemporary science and religion.[26]

Yet Bodin's name is now closely associated with a single concept: sovereignty. His sharply focused idea of sovereignty was an important achievement, but in isolation it is easily misunderstood. The concept of sovereignty put forward in his *Six livres de la république* is seldom read in the context of the whole book, even less often in the context of the whole *oeuvre* of this prolific man. More than most theorists, Bodin has been approached through his supposed successors—Hobbes and Althusius—rather than on his own terms. As a result, elements of continuity between his ideas and those of earlier thinkers are overlooked, and intricate balances within his major treatise ignored. In confronting Bodin's huge book, readers have often responded (as they have to that comparably formidable *magnum opus*, the *Spirit of the Laws*) by seizing whatever straws they can, to avoid the challenge of searching out the order that undergirds the learned references and endless digressions. Yet Bodin, even more than Montesquieu, was obsessed with order. His method involved dividing his material into

---

[25] There is no satisfactory intellectual biography of Bodin; even the date of his birth and his activities during much of his life are not definitely known. Useful information is provided by Henri Baudrillart, *Bodin et son temps*, and by Julian Franklin, *Jean Bodin and the Sixteenth-Century Revolution in the Methodology of Law and History*.

[26] Details of publication of the several editions of the *République* are provided in Kenneth McRae's excellent edition of *The Six Bookes of a Commonweale*, A28-A38, and A78-A86. Bodin's other major works were the *Methodus*, which I have used in Beatrice Reynolds' translation, *Method for the Easy Comprehension of History*; the *Demonomanie*; *Theatrum naturae*; and *Heptaplomeres*, recently translated by Marion L. D. Kuntz, *Colloquium of the Seven about the Secrets of the Sublime*. Bodin also ventured into economics with his *Réponse à M. de Malestroit sur les monnaies et le rencherissement*. As Judith Shklar noted in reviewing one of the first attempts to treat Bodin's whole range of thought, the Munich colloquium on *Jean Bodin* (edited by Horst Denzer, 1973), "a full study of Bodin could help us understand the prehistory of modern social science, a prehistory which is rooted in our ancestors' mythological consciousness." *Journal of Modern History* XLVII (1975), 134-141.

broad categories, normally dichotomous, and then making further subdivisions until the field was covered.[27] The concept of order was central to Bodin's whole world view, and particularly to his view of politics. Sovereignty in the *République* cannot be understood unless the theme of ordering is associated with it; and the book itself remains inaccessible unless the order of presentation is kept in mind.[28]

Bodin begins the *République* not with a definition of sovereignty, but with a definition of the commonwealth. Like Hobbes, he was convinced of the importance of definitions in speech and reasoning; like Aristotle, he believed that a proper definition is ultimately in terms of end or purpose, an end that becomes clear only in the course of the whole treatise. In Bodin's definition, "a commonwealth is a rightful government of many families, and of that which belongs to them in common, with a puissant sovereignty."[29] Each element of this definition is carefully chosen, and the structure of the whole first book of the *République* rests upon it. Bodin discusses first what it means for a government to be "rightful"; then he takes up the role of the family in the polity; the distinction between common and private things; and finally, the concept of sovereignty that unites the whole into a commonwealth.

In each of these discussions, Bodin proceeds by separation and juxtaposition. Nothing can be understood except in contradistinction to what it is not, by setting it over against what is opposed to it. Thus a *droit gouvernement* is a regime ordered by virtue, which must be care-

[27] Kenneth McRae, "Ramist Tendencies in the Thought of Jean Bodin," *Journal of the History of Ideas* XVI (1955), 306-323, shows the affinities of Bodin's method with that of Peter Ramus, and notes that Bodin shared the common Ramist tendency to carp at Aristotle while depending heavily on his ideas.

[28] Greenleaf, *Order, Empiricism and Politics*, makes this argument, and develops it in more detail in his essay for the Munich colloquium, edited by Horst Denzer, pp. 23-39. Preston King has a useful treatment of Bodin from this perspective in *The Ideology of Order*, part III; see also Mesnard, *L'Essor de la philosophie politique du XVIe siècle*, v, 3, and Jean Moreau-Reibel, *Jean Bodin et le droit public comparée*, pp. 149-155.

[29] Bodin, *Les Six livres de la république* (Paris 1577), I, 1, 1 (my own translation). In subsequent quotations from Bodin I have used McRae's edition of the Richard Knolles translation of the *Six Bookes of a Commonweale*, indicating book, chapter, and page numbers, respectively. Knolles' translation was based on both the French and Latin versions of the work, and read in conjunction with McRae's extensive notes, is quite satisfactory. The more familiar abbreviated edition of the *Six Books of the Commonwealth* by M. J. Tooley is easier to use, but much inferior to McRae because the excessively free translation of several key terms and passages distorts the argument, and the radical abridgment mutilates the book beyond recognition. I have modernized Knolles' spelling to bring quotations from Bodin into consonance with the modern translation of Montaigne used in Chapter Three.

fully distinguished from a society dominated by vice and disorder. Bodin connects lawfulness with right action and virtue in the largest sense. Only a community constituted by such a regime, a well-ordered society, deserves the name of commonwealth.

The same kind of reasoning marks Bodin's discussion of the family. It seemed obvious to him that the commonwealth must be composed of elements that have a definite structure and sphere of action apart from that of the commonwealth, so that the public realm can be distinguished from what it is not—the private. To Bodin the family was not only the focal point for human affection and nurture, but also the locus for the possession of property and for the exercise of natural paternal authority. The family was like a little state, the state a larger family; and the order of his commonwealth required that the patterns of authority and subordination in the one be faithfully imitated in the other.[30] The citizen himself was the pivotal juncture in these two spheres of action. When he turned his face inward to domestic governance and economic pursuits, exercising his natural role as father and his economical government ("a knowledge for the getting of goods," as Bodin defined it), his activities gave structure to the private realm. When the father of the family "goes forth out of his own house where he commands, to negotiate and traffic with other heads of families about that which concerns them all in general," he ceases to be a master and becomes a "companion, equally and fellow-like with others," a citizen rather than a lord. Bodin's citizen, like Aristotle's, participated in ruling and being ruled in turn; but he ruled his family and was ruled by his sovereign in a strict hierarchical order of domination and subjection. The definition of a citizen in the *République* is "a free subject holding of the sovereignty of another man."[31]

The private world of the family, composed of paternal authority and property, was juxtaposed to the things that belong to citizens in common, the proper matter of the commonwealth. The essential thing the citizens have in common is subjection to the same sovereign. This holds them together like the keel of a ship, and makes of them a commonwealth rather than a mass of ill-connected parts, "an evil-favored hoop of wood." Beyond this, "many other things besides are of citizens to be had in common among themselves, as their markets, their churches, their walks, ways, laws, decrees, judgments, voices, customs, theaters, walls, public buildings, common pastures, lands, and treasure; and in brief, rewards, punishments, suits, and contracts." This extensive range of nonfamilial activity, comprising a good portion of civil and

[30] I, 1, 3; and I, 2, 8.   [31] I, 6, 46-47.

economic behavior as we now define it, was the common stuff that provided the opportunity, and the need, for governance. Bodin was explicitly insistent that this range of common things could not be indefinitely extended or reduced without destroying the commonwealth. There can be no commonwealth "which has in it nothing at all public or common," and Bodin asserted the equal absurdity of the attempt to have everything in common: "for nothing can be public where nothing is private."[32]

The final element in Bodin's commonwealth—the "puissant sovereignty"—can only be understood by contrast with the subject, or nonsovereign. In Bodin's succinct definition of sovereignty—"the most high, absolute, and perpetual power over the citizens and subjects in a commonwealth"—the little word "over" is among the most important. Unless there is some body for the sovereign to be sovereign over, he cannot exist. The old image of head and body still influences this conception; but Bodin's sovereignty depended on a significant shift of emphasis in the meaning of this headship over the body politic, compared with earlier notions of the king as supreme judge, possessor of a mosaic of rights and powers that comprised the *merum imperium*.[33] In Bodin's treatise, lawmaking power, instead of being one of several royal prerogatives, became central to and constitutive of sovereignty, with notable consequences.

For Bodin, the essence of lawmaking was command—the exercise of will with binding force. To him it seemed obvious that no one could be sovereign and subject at the same time, and thus that he who gives laws to others cannot give them to himself, but must be "over" the law as well as above those subjects for whom the law is made. Because of this potent concept of lawmaking, Bodin was able to present a novel picture of the sovereign as a creative, innovating force within the state rather than the traditional dispenser of justice, maintainer of an established equilibrium. Bodin shared to some degree the voluntarist view of God as pure legislative will, ordering the universe

---

[32] I, 2, 9-11; on this basis Bodin agrees with Aristotle's criticism of Plato's suggestion that the guardians should hold everything in common. On Bodin's use of Aristotle in general, see H. Weber's essay in R. R. Bolgar, ed., *Classical Influences on European Culture*, pp. 305-314.

[33] I, 8, 84. Church, *Constitutional Thought*, 51-62, 212-262, discusses the transformation of the old notion of a "mosaic of rights." Julian Franklin, *Jean Bodin and the Rise of Absolutist Theory*, argues persuasively that this definition of sovereignty in the *République* was unprecedented both by comparison with "the mainstream of French tradition" (which he regards as "tentatively constitutionalist" before 1572), and with Bodin's own earlier ideas in the *Methodus* (vii). See also Derathé's survey of "La Place de Jean Bodin dans l'histoire des théories de la souveraineté," in Denzer, ed., *Jean Bodin*, pp. 245-260.

Absolutist Thought—71

out of chaos by the exercise of divine command.[34] His sovereign prince replicated this creative power in the state, though he was limited, as God was not, by the natural laws of the universe. This concept of sovereignty as an active, ordering will, shaping and giving form to a diverse and heterogeneous mass, did not lend itself easily to multiple expression. Although Bodin recognized the existence of aristocracies and democracies, he regarded sovereignty as essentially monarchical; the single human will became the perfect paradigm of unity and control.

One of Bodin's most influential notions, derived from this concept of unitary ordering will, was the indivisibility of sovereignty. The sharing of sovereign power among several wills, in his eyes, meant the complete negation of sovereignty itself, and therefore of the commonwealth. In addition to the image of the ship's keel, he rings the changes on all the familiar analogies—the understanding in the soul, the center of the circle, God in His universe—to describe the power of the prince in the commonwealth. Bodin insists that the prince is firmly superior to the customary laws and institutions of the *corps mystique* as well as to the laws he makes himself. He dismisses any claim on the part of parlements or Estates to share in making law. In his version of the familiar assertion that convening the Estates enhances rather than diminishes the king's majesty, Bodin stresses that this is because such assemblies make very obvious the distinction between king and subjects. They come together as a body to entreat and counsel; he alone commands. And "so we see the principal point of sovereign majesty and absolute power to consist in giving laws to subjects in general, *without their consent.*"[35]

Since Bodin describes the sovereign in such clear-cut terms as a unitary focus of commanding will, his discussion of certain limitations on the sovereign appears at first glance to be inconsistent. As an early advocate of a "pure theory of sovereignty" who nonetheless accepted boundaries to the exercise of sovereign power, he is often seen as an imperfect Hobbes who did not quite see where his own ideas were leading. In fact, these limitations are essential parts of the theory itself. Bodin mentions three different kinds of limits: natural law, the fundamental laws of the realm, and the inviolability of private property. Each corresponds to part of his own definition of sovereignty—the

[34] Margherita Isnardi Parente, "Le Volontarisme de Jean Bodin," in Denzer, ed., *Jean Bodin*, pp. 23-38, and the discussion following, pp. 415-535. Bodin's discussion of the king as "above" the law is in I, 8, 91.
[35] I, 8, 98, emphasis added. For Bodin's attitude toward the parlements, see Franklin, *Jean Bodin and the Rise of Absolutist Theory*, pp. 66-69.

"rightful government" of "public" or common matters—and they cannot be dismissed as anomalies.[36]

According to Bodin, there are three different kinds of monarchy: lawful or royal monarchy, lordly or seigneurial monarchy, and tyranny. In a broad sense they are all forms of "sovereignty," but only the first involves the kind of power Bodin associated with a commonwealth, a *droit gouvernement* that respects the persons and goods of the subjects. For such a monarch, the constraints of natural law and the constitutional foundations of the state are part of the basis on which he governs.[37] Though Seyssel is not mentioned by Bodin in this connection, it makes sense to think of natural law as a "bridle" on the prince, since it provides the stuff from which he makes his laws, and prevents abuse. Not all laws embody the laws of nature in Bodin's world; some are merely useful, not honest, and the king is not bound to obey these laws. But insofar as his own laws embody precepts of natural morality, he must obey them *qua* laws of nature (though not *qua* civil law) even more strictly than ordinary mortals.

Unlike Seyssel's bridles, however, natural law takes no institutional or public form, and in Bodin's commonwealth no human sanctions can be brought to bear on a prince who abuses power. This led to a tension in Bodin's theory of lawmaking between "right," the element of virtue that is embodied in good laws, and "will," the pure voluntary act that makes a law.[38] Bodin wanted to retain the notion that action by a prince that contravenes God's law (rather than embodies or ignores it) is not, properly speaking, an act of sovereignty at all. But since he wrote his treatise partly to convince his countrymen that they must obey even a prince whose religious views were different from their own, he had no interest in discussing the vexed issue of justified resistance to abusive power. He certainly did not believe that whatever the prince commanded was *ipso facto* just; but he contented himself with concluding, as others had before him, that "if justice be the end of the law, and the law is the work of the prince, and the prince is the lively image of almighty God, it must needs follow that the law of the prince should be framed unto the model of the law of God." The prince who ignored this model was guilty of treason against God's majesty; but no way on earth was provided to call him to account.

[36] For useful discussions of this topic, see Franklin, *Jean Bodin and the Rise of Absolutist Theory*, ch. 5; and Max Shepard, "Sovereignty at the Crossroads," *Political Science Quarterly* XLV (1930), 580-603.

[37] II, 2, 199-200; II, 3, 204-205.

[38] I, 8, 92-105; III, 4, 312-313; V, 4, 585. J. U. Lewis has a good discussion of this tension in "Jean Bodin's 'Logic of Sovereignty,'" *Political Studies* XVI (1968), 206-222.

In his discussion of the fundamental laws of the French polity, and of the inability of a prince to tax his subjects without their consent, Bodin allies himself firmly with a long tradition in French juristic argument. This connection makes particularly evident the constitutionalist roots of absolutist thought. Bodin takes for granted, as most of his fellow jurists had done, that the prince is constrained by the "laws which concern the state of the realm, and the establishing thereof," since these laws constitute the monarchy itself. If any prince is so foolish as to attempt to alienate his domain or alter the conditions of accession to the throne, his successor simply annuls his action, and things are as they were before. In arguing that "it is not in the power of any prince in the world, at his pleasure to raise taxes upon the people, no more than to take another man's goods from him," Bodin echoes a commonplace assumption in French thought, voiced vigorously by Commynes a century before.[39] But in Bodin's theory this assertion finds a theoretical grounding that had earlier been absent. Having defined a commonwealth as a government of families and what they have in common, and distinguished this sharply from the private realm, inhabited by families who are themselves defined in terms of ownership of property, Bodin could not logically allow the sovereign to take property without consent of its owners except in cases of direst public need. He expects that taxation will occur; but the formal requirement of consent is needed to ensure that the structure of the family is maintained at the foundation of the commonwealth, and the public realm does not swallow up the private and extinguish itself.

The focus on "consent" indicates that Bodin expects that this third type of limitation, unlike the other two, will require regular cooperation by the subjects in the sovereign's government. His activities as a delegate to the estates at Blois support this hypothesis.[40] In the *République* itself, however, Bodin gives no indication that he expected the French Estates to take a more prominent role in consent to taxation than they had in the past, or to develop any tendency to resist a king's commands or deny his requests.

5. Bodin on the Commonwealth: Patterns of Participation in Power

The first of the six books of Bodin's *République* is devoted to defining "commonwealth" and establishing the formal necessity of uni-

[39] I, 8, 95-97.
[40] Owen Ulph, "Jean Bodin and the Estates-General of 1576," *Journal of Modern History* XIX (1947), 289-296.

tary absolute sovereignty for the existence of the polity. The limits on this sovereignty are, as we have seen, most accurately understood as conditions for its exercise. They are not lodged in specific structures or institutions that operate continually in government. This has led some scholars to see Bodin's theory as overly abstract or legalistic, and to compare it unfavorably with more realistic schemas of Machiavelli and Seyssel.[41] This judgment, however, neglects the great bulk of Bodin's treatise, since in the remaining five books he describes a complex pattern of participation in power on the part of magistrates and citizens, within the formal framework of sovereignty.

Bodin's taste for distinctions served him well in this endeavor, since it allowed him consistently to separate formal sovereignty from the actual flow of power in the governance of the commonwealth. Some of his distinctions were particularly influential for later French thought, including the distinction between command and counsel, between the "mask" and the reality of governance, between the form of state and the form of administration, and between the law itself and its enforcement. Each of these distinctions can be found in Rousseau's political theory, especially. Whether the connection with Bodin is direct, indirect, or nonexistent is of no particular importance. The parallels themselves are notable.

The distinction between command and counsel is related to Bodin's prior distinction between the willing of the law and its content (whether or not it is consonant with right principles). Only the sovereign, or those acting on his express authority, can command or promulgate the law. But Bodin remarks often on the importance of a body of wise counsellors, a small senate or cabinet of the wisest and best men who advise the king in making law. Such an assembly performs the function of "wit and reason," without which neither a human nor a political body can long sustain itself. Like Seyssel, Bodin regards large assemblies as undesirable for this purpose, since "the greater part overrules the sounder and the better." In order to be a counsellor one must be a man who can "lay down all favor toward his friends, all hatred toward his enemies, and all high conceit of himself; aiming at no other end but to the advancement of the glory of God and the welfare of the commonwealth."[42]

This concept of ideal advisors was central in French absolutist thought. For those who followed Bodin, as for Bodin himself, the purity and capacity of the counsellor depended in part on his lack of

---

[41] R.W.K. Hinton, "Jean Bodin and the Retreat into Legalism," in Denzer, ed., *Jean Bodin*, pp. 303-313.
[42] III, 1, 255-258; on the disadvantages of large assemblies, VI, 4, 710.

formal power to command. There is an implication here that power necessarily involves interest—that the ability to satisfy or frustrate desires at will means favor to friends and exclusion of enemies. Thus the most clear-sighted vision of the public good comes from those who cannot themselves issue commands, but whose superior possession of virtuous human capacities enables them to see what others need without being corrupted by power. An echo of this notion can be discovered in Rousseau's idea of the Legislator who designs the law but cannot will it. In earlier theory, from Bodin into the eighteenth century, this function was performed by a group of wise men, who described the requirements of the public good in any situation. The crystallization of their counsel into law, however, could only be done by the formal word of the sovereign.

In this theory of royal decision making, the old image of the king as the one who sees the good of the whole commonwealth was extended by the provision of the best possible counsellors. Those who perform this function inevitably share in the king's decision, and leave their impress deep on his commands. But the formal point of decision remains focused in one will; and the monarch's dependence on his counsellors is hidden by the impressive and satisfying fiction that the law is handed down by one benevolent, absolute, superhuman will rather than being the product of negotiation, compromise, or conflict. This is a theory of abstract legitimation of decision-making power that also manages to take into account the dependence on other human beings involved in its daily use.

Bodin accepted the formal possibility that the whole body of citizens could act as sovereign over themselves as subjects, but left it to Rousseau to explore the fruitful corollaries of this line of argument. It seemed obvious to Bodin that such a polity is imperfect, since the subjection of the citizens to themselves as sovereign must necessarily be as individuals, and they would lack the unity of subordination to a will over themselves that characterizes a true commonwealth. In any case, he said, "if we rip up all the popular states that ever were" to examine them more closely, we will find that except in situations of internal or external war, they have always "been governed in show by the people" but in fact by a few, "who held the place of a prince and monarch," and "the people serves but for a mask."[43] This realistic assumption that power must always be exercised by the few, whatever the form of the polity—expressed here as the distinction between the "mask" and the reality of governance—does much to liberate Bodin from the strict legalism of his opening book.

[43] VI, 4, 705. Cf. Jean-Jacques Rousseau, *Social Contract*, book III, chs. 4 & 7.

The distinction between the mask and the reality of governance corresponds to another of which Bodin was particularly proud: the distinction between "the state, and the government of the state," which he says is "a rule in policy, to my knowledge, not before touched by any man."[44] In his discussion of this distinction, Bodin follows Aristotle fairly closely, but he may well be correct in asserting that the distinction itself had not been clearly drawn before. And it is, of course, one that is central to Rousseau's politics. Bodin's distinction depends on the different principles the sovereign can follow in distributing offices and honors in the state. A state can be administered according to democratic or aristocratic principles of several different sorts—nobility, wealth, and virtue, as well as indifferent equality. This administration is quite separate from sovereignty, which may itself be held by one person, by several, or by many. This is Bodin's solution to the problem of the mixed regime, which he regarded as logically absurd. Having insisted that sovereignty is indivisible, he was able to accommodate apparent exceptions to his rule by showing that the simplicity of formal sovereignty is maintained even when citizens participate in governing in several ways. In Bodin's eyes, the commonwealth reaches its highest perfection when the state is a "royal" monarchy administered on the basis of a harmonic fusion of aristocratic and popular principles.[45] This is the most aesthetically pleasing, and most stable, of all commonwealths.

In later French thought, this distinction between the form of state and the form of administration was less often associated with the theoretical mongrel that bothered Bodin (the mixed regime) than with the concrete problem of government in an absolutist state. Theorists built upon it to show how a sovereign could reserve full unitary authority to himself, and yet ensure that a large commonwealth could be effectively administered by his agents. They often echoed the rhetoric used by Bodin in the fourth book of his treatise, which deals with the question of whether princes should dispense justice in person, and decides it in the negative. Bodin held that "nothing has ever been more dangerous, or more destructive to commonwealths, than to translate the authorities of the Senate or command of the magistrates unto the prince or the people." He even asserts that "the less the power of the sovereignty is, the true marks of majesty still reserved unto it, the more it is assured." Thus he describes a godlike sovereign showing himself to a people rarely, in order to preserve their awe, and refraining from interfering in the actual business of administration by his magistrates and officers. The sovereign human being becomes identi-

[44] II, 2, 199.   [45] II, 1, 191, and VI, 6, 755.

fied with the symbolic legislative will, and is expected to keep aloof from the daily dispensing of specific rewards and punishments, to encourage behavior that benefits the commonwealth.[46]

Bodin also assumes, as Seyssel did before him, that the best constitutional order is one that is easily adapted to the qualities of the ruler. The balance between the power of the state and the power of the administration should shift in order to reflect the vigorous capacities of an exceptionally noble prince, as well as to compensate for the lax and vicious government of an unworthy one. This conception of the constitution was common to French theorists who described the absolute sovereign in awesome terms, and yet assumed that he would normally have little to do with the business of governance. If he showed legislative talent, the constitution would make room for him; if he acted tyrannically, he could be contained. But in either case most of the governing would be done by strong administrators.

The penchant for differentiating between legal forms and the actual exercise of power that underlies all of these distinctions in Bodin's work is brought out clearly in his discussion of law and its enforcement. When we speak as though the law itself does something, we speak inaccurately, he says, since "the law in itself carries or contains nothing but commands or prohibitions, which are but mockeries and to no purpose if the magistrate and punishment were not attendant at the foot of the law, ready for him who transgresses it." Bodin's sense of political power makes room not only for the will that dictates law, but also for the ability to enforce it. The magistrate is described as "a living and breathing law," and the law without the magistrate as a hollow mockery.[47]

Some of Bodin's most striking and realistic insights about the process of governing are included in the fifth chapter of book IV, where he discusses the question of "whether the unity and concord of magistrates among themselves is good and wholesome for the commonwealth, or not?" This chapter is excluded from the abbreviated version of Bodin familiar to most English-speaking readers, but it is of particular interest, since it shows Bodin in a pluralist mood, demonstrating the importance of conflict among the powerful as a means to the protection of the weak. Bodin dismisses the simplistic assumption that all conflict is unhealthy and seditious, and argues that good men "pricked forward with an honest ambition . . . are by the emulation of their competitors incited to take in hand great matters." Thus competition and ambition, which might seem to be sources of instability in politics, can be channeled so that they serve the public good. Further,

[46] IV, 6, 517; V, 4, 584-596.   [47] III, 5, 325.

asserts Bodin, it generally makes sense to pit ambitious and energetic notables against one another, so that "the common people . . . might be safe and free from their outrages and robberies." Potential petty tyrants in high places mutually control one another through their own conflict, and the commonwealth will be "in much more safety and assurance than if they were of one accord among themselves." To conclude this argument, Bodin draws on the familiar Renaissance analogy of bodily humors that must be contrary to one another lest the body perish. The whole world "next to God," he claims, depends on "contrariety" in every part, and "even so the magistrates in a commonwealth ought in some sort to be at difference among themselves, albeit that they otherwise be right good men, for that truth, the public good, and that which is honest, best discovers itself by that which is contrary to it: and is still to be found in the middle between two extremes."[48] This notion of the public good as discovered in the conflict of opposing views had a rich future in French theory, culminating in the descriptions of the *volonté générale* in the *Contrat social*.

Always quick to find arguments for monarchy, Bodin, like Seyssel, assumes that only in a monarchy can the advantages of conflict among magistrates be fully enjoyed, since the king is the final arbiter, who provides the controlling will that keeps such conflicts from becoming destructive, and channels them in positive directions. Bodin shows how a prince can act as a "neuter" in his subjects' quarrels, maintaining the balance of power in the state by preventing unhealthy excess of factional strife. The same point is made in his discussion of "corporations and colleges" of private men and magistrates within the commonwealth. These are described as second only to the family as constituent elements of the commonwealth, since they contribute to the mutual amity among citizens that is the principal political cement. But only a monarch can deliberately encourage "the orderly conversing and combining of men" together, and prevent the "confusion and broil" that attend disorderly combining. And finally, Bodin hypothesizes that since extreme wealth and poverty excite sedition, and pure equality of goods is equally pernicious, large commonwealths will be more stable than small ones. A multitude of citizens reduces the possibility that the state will be divided into a small number of bitterly contending factions. Here he addresses directly the problem taken up later by Hume and Madison, and arrives at the same conclusion.[49]

Bodin's awareness of the dangers as well as the advantages of conflict in the state, and the necessity to control it carefully in order to turn it to advantage, is matched by his Machiavellian sense of the grave diffi-

[48] IV, 5, 494-496.   [49] IV, 7, 519-520; V, 2, 571.

culties that face anyone who sets out to alter the mass of human habit that comprises a commonwealth. Bodin assumes that natural (uncontrolled) change is always for the worse, so that the job of the legislator is reformation to a prior best state. In the best tradition of Renaissance rhetoric, he asserts that "the nature of man as of all other worldly things also, is most slippery and unconstant, running still headlong from good to evil, and from evil to worse; vices little by little still increasing, not unlike evil humors, which without sensible feeling increase man's body until it be full of them, breeds in it many most dangerous diseases, and so at length brings it to utter destruction." In dealing with such unpromising material, the skillful legislator does not attempt to do everything at once, but proceeds slowly and imperceptibly, bending rather than breaking the established practices of the people. Bodin, like Montesquieu, cautions would-be reformers that the whole intricate structure of a polity is knit together and cannot be attacked simplistically. In healing the diseased commonwealth, men must imitate not only physicians, "but even nature itself, or rather the great God of nature whom we see do all things little by little, and almost insensibly."[50] The point of the whole enterprise is the reduction of civil vice and disorder to "an apt and comely order, so that the first may be joined with the last, and they of the middle sort with both; and so all with all, in a most true knot and bond among themselves together with the commonwealth."[51]

6. JUSTICE AND THE COMMON GOOD

In discussing the qualifications that those who participate in power should possess, Bodin asserts that only those who think they have a stake in the public good can be expected to attend to it. He uses this as an argument for circulation of office-holding. Those who hold power ought to be aware of their private interest, as ordinary citizens, in what they do as public officials; and those who do not hold power should have a reasonable expectation of doing so in future. In a situation where public charges are reserved for a few, and the rest are limited to their own private business, anyone who "would take more care of the common welfare than of his own" would be "but laughed at and derided as a fool."[52] Thus the common welfare is best served by interesting all citizens in its protection, not by confiding it to a few who have permanent possession of their offices.

[50] IV, 3, 471-472.   [51] III, 8, 386.
[52] IV, 4, 479-480; cf. I, 2, 12, where Bodin argues for private property on the grounds that things held in common are "of every man smally regarded and neglected, except it be to draw some private and particular profit therefrom."

This argument connecting widespread participation and the protection of common interest against particularistic selfishness has a number of implications that later theorists explored at length. In Bodin's own discussion, however, the classical and medieval roots rather than the novel possibilities were dominant. He asserts that the most happy commonwealth is one in which "every man in his degree and according to his quality, having enjoyed appropriate preferments, and so having learned true wisdom by the managing of worldly affairs, should retire from these vain and worldly businesses, to occupy themselves in the contemplation of things natural and divine." The "managing of worldly affairs" is seen as a source of wisdom for the individual, as a transient though important part of a man's experience that prepares him for the final good of contemplation in retirement from "vain and worldly businesses." According to Bodin, the true end of the commonwealth and of the individual alike is the Platonic good of justice as contemplation and reflection of the divine order—that is, philosophy. The best man and the best citizen are one.[53] He praises the Romans above the Spartans on this score, since the Spartans sacrificed all virtue to the common good interpreted as the "increasing of their state," whereas the Romans took justice itself as their deliberate goal. He thus takes note of, and summarily rejects, nascent *raison d'état* arguments that posit the "increasing and perpetuation" of the state as an appropriate end in itself. Against such views, he asserts that justice is not only the more comprehensive virtue, but also the more desirable public goal, the true source of greatness and flourishing for the state itself.

Bodin's magisterial conception of justice stimulates some of the most powerful passages in his great treatise. He waxes eloquent about the harmonic justice provided by the king, "as of treble and base voices is made a most sweet and melodious harmony," so the king brings together good and bad, rich and poor, wise men and fools, strong and weak, "allied by them which are in the mean between both, and thus by a wonderful disagreeing concord, joins the highest with the lowest, and so all to all." The treatise concludes with a symphonic vision of a commonwealth, dissonance and variety held together in harmony and a "most sweet quiet" by the unity of the wise prince, "exalted above all his subjects, and exempt out of the rank of them, whose majesty suffers no more division than does unity itself."[54]

[53] I, 1, 4-8; cf. III, 4, 318, On this question Bodin apparently reversed himself between the publication of his treatises, since in the *Methodus*, 187, he asserts that "the best man is the worst citizen, for his whole being seeking solitude, is carried heavenward in contemplation."
[54] VI, 6, 790-794.

Throughout the book, Bodin links this notion of justice as harmonic order with a more generous sense of the content of the "common good" than that provided by later theorists of interest of state.[55] Having defined a commonwealth in terms of shared things, he gives a clear and concrete sense of what such sharing means. In his discussion of taxation, for example, he insists that the costs of public life should be borne by all alike, in proportion to their wealth, and not foisted off by the rich onto those least able to bear the burden.[56] This argument reflects the hostility of the third estate to the feudal privileges of nobility and clergy, which Bodin expressed so strongly as a delegate at Blois; it also reflects the distress at the condition of the poor that became an increasingly urgent theme in French political writing in the next century. In Bodin's view, all citizens are part of the commonwealth in a concrete sense, brought together by the creative order of sovereign power in a common search for a good public life, which is made meaningful by continual juxtaposition with important areas for private life in family and property, and by lesser common interests of corporate activity of all kinds. The most significant achievement of the *République* is precisely here: that Bodin provided a rich focus for *le bien commun*, a focus resting on classical principles of harmony and justice, while at the same time making room for a newly vigorous sense of private interests and pursuits that has characterized the modern state.

This *summa* of sixteenth-century political philosophy was sufficiently original, seminal, and magisterial to set the broad outlines of French political philosophy for centuries to come. Its most immediate influence was in the theory of sovereignty, which was seized eagerly by monarchical theorists in the reign of Henry IV, and immediately became part of the accepted canon of juristic theory. In this way Bodin's ideas were crucial for the development of absolutism in France. Many of the theorists who used Bodin's notion of sovereignty did not mention him by name, and few, indeed, attempted to come to terms with the rich possibilities of the *République* itself. Nonetheless, the elements of his arguments permeated French thought in the seventeenth and eighteenth centuries. The conception of a personal unitary will above the state, providing order by means of laws, yet acting often indirectly, almost invisibly, through the power of his administrative officers rather than intruding his own office in all areas, was central in the French tradition well into the eighteenth century. D'Argenson's

---

[55] Raymond Polin, "L'Idée de République selon Bodin," in Denzer, ed., *Jean Bodin*, pp. 343-357.
[56] VI, 2, 699.

vision of such a sovereign rests directly on Bodin's. Similarly, a good many of Montesquieu's most characteristic notions can be traced back to the *République*—not only the notorious theory of climate, but also the broader conception of the role of the legislative will incorporating natural law in civil law, and adapting universal principles to particular cases. And in insisting upon the connections between justice and *le bien commun*, and upon the fruitful tension between public and private interests for the citizen, Bodin laid down the conditions of the problem Rousseau set himself to solve.

CHAPTER THREE

Individualism and Humanism

1. Civic Humanism in the Sixteenth Century

Constitutionalism and absolutism are labels for theories of the polity, alternative conceptions of the proper ordering and use of public power. They consider human beings as political entities, and deal with them only insofar as they have a place in the public realm. Individualism, in the form it took in French psychological and ethical theory in the sixteenth and seventeenth centuries, dealt with human beings primarily as private persons, and was more a mood or temper than a theory. It found expression in a variety of ideals during those centuries. Although individualism could be associated with the solitary life of the scholar in retreat from the world, it was more often associated with a pleasurable life of like-minded men (and sometimes women) who eschewed regular public involvement to concentrate their energies in philosophy, leisured discussion, and good fellowship with one another. Individualism promoted the joys of private life, the fulfillment of each person, the *vita contemplativa* rather than the *vita activa*. It was compatible with a greater or lesser awareness of public duties that needed to be performed to make such a way of life possible for those capable of enjoying it. The primary hallmark of individualism, in all its variants, was the exploration and fulfillment of the self.[1]

Individualism dominated French ethics and psychology from the end of the sixteenth century well into the seventeenth, and proved for a time an admirably efficient ideology for the subjects of an absolutist state. It developed in reaction to quite a different temper that flourished among French jurists in the earlier part of the sixteenth century, a temper comparable to the "civic humanism" of the Renaissance in Italy. French scholars of jurisprudence, men of classical education and humanist outlook, often held minor government posts. Such men tended to be strongly monarchical in their political beliefs, and dedicated to advancing the glory of France. During the Renaissance, this conjunction of study and political involvement produced a distinctive view of knowledge as the indispensable guide to civil life, and of politi-

[1] Like most "isms," individualism is a term coined in the nineteenth century to describe an ancient and complex phenomenon. Steven Lukes has explored the diverse early fortunes of this word in *Individualism*, part 1.

cal affairs as the arena in which philosophy was tested and perfected. Adherents of this type of humanism hotly resisted the notion that philosophy was properly a pursuit of privacy, a contention regularly advanced by supporters as well as detractors of the philosophic life. They took public duties very seriously, and attempted to preach civic responsibility to those of their colleagues who preferred the privacy of their estates and libraries. In the bitter struggles of the wars of religion, however, such optimistic assessments of the quality and scope of public life sounded less convincing, and won few adherents. The delights of privacy seemed more and more compelling, and French civic humanism, along with parliamentary constitutionalism, was among the many victims of those civil wars.

Budé and the classical scholar Lefèvre d'Etaples were the guiding geniuses of French civic humanism.[2] Cicero was its patron saint, admired for his fusion of oratory and civil knowledge. Louis Le Caron (or Charondas) and Louis Le Roy (or Regius) were articulate exemplars of this unity of theory and practice. In numerous dialogues, translations, treatises, and harangues, both scholars expressed an ideal of the vigorous philosopher devoted to the advancement of useful knowledge in the *vita activa*.

Le Caron's vision of politics included a Christian humanist version of the Platonic philosopher-prince, in which divine revelation and discipleship, as well as the study of all human knowledge, become the source of civic wisdom for a king. This wisdom was described by Le Caron as *la science politique*, or *la science royale*, an admirable knowledge for knitting together men naturally needful of one another, but not naturally capable of living together in harmony.[3] Le Caron waxes eloquent in his praise of this royal science, linking civic philosophy closely with absolutist monarchy. The office of a king is "not similar to a private man, because on his good depends the public good, from his virtue shines the glory and splendor of the people, from the tranquil and tempered constitution of his person arises the enjoyment of

---

[2] André Stegmann, "Un Thème majeur du second humanisme français (1540-1570): l'orateur et le citoyen," in *French Renaissance Studies*, edited by Peter Sharratt, pp. 213-233; Eugene F. Rice, Jr., "Humanist Aristotelianism in France: Jacques Lefèvre d'Etaples and His Circle," in Anthony Levi, ed., *Humanism in France*, 132-149; more generally, Walter Ullmann, *Medieval Foundations of Renaissance Humanism*, explores the Aristotelian roots of this phenomenon.

[3] Donald R. Kelley, "Louis Le Caron *Philosophe*," in *Philosophy and Humanism*, edited by Edward P. Mahoney, pp. 30-49, has a fine discussion of this topic. Among Le Caron's own expressions of this sentiment is a harangue delivered at the Estates in 1588 (and later published as a pamphlet), "Au Roy, nostre souverain prince et seigneur."

the common repose."[4] The order of the monarch's soul is thus made directly constitutive of the order of the kingdom, and of the peace and happiness of all its members.

For Le Caron, the parallel between psychological and political order was both intimate and complex. Each body, he affirmed, has "an order and *police* among its parts," so that each individual "represents in himself some form of a true republic." Each of us is responsible for the good ordering of our souls, but this good ordering also depends on civil order and tranquillity, which flows from the right ordering of the monarch's soul. This royal order gives rise to a public and common happiness in which each individual finds his own true good and happiness. By means of the prudence of the one who exercises the royal science, asserts Le Caron, men are, as it were, "awakened from a long sleep," brought out of their isolation and made to feel love for something greater than themselves, the public good that encompasses their own good.[5] The public good is understood to include the good of every individual, because in a well-ordered kingdom each individual sees how his own happiness flows from and depends upon the public happiness, and identifies himself with the common good rather than regarding it as antithetical or opposed to his own good. This vision of a common good that institutes and encompasses the happiness of each individual, bringing him out of narrow selfhood into a larger whole, in which he discovers his personal identity and happiness, was a recurrent theme in French political philosophy from the Renaissance to the Enlightenment.

The role of the scholar in this impressively articulated order is to assist his king in understanding and applying the principles of philosophy that are the indispensable grounding of all human activity, from the conduct of the self to the government of principalities. Le Caron asserts that a philosopher true to the love of knowledge will also be a "lover of *la chose publique*, tending to no other good but common utility, not living a life contrary to that of vulgar men but a better one, and giving no occasion to trouble political order."[6] He contrasts such a life with that of the avaricious or ambitious man, the two types that became so prevalent in the social philosophy of the seventeenth century. Of the two, Le Caron regards ambition as more noble, since it imitates philosophy in its attention to public affairs, instead of remain-

[4] Loys Le Caron, *Dialogues* (1556), dialogue premier, "Le Caron & Philante," 11v.

[5] Dialogue premier, 6v-9r.

[6] Dialogue second, "Le Courtisan & Le Caron," and "Paean to the true sage," *Dialogues*, 71r-77v.

ing, as avarice must always be, caught up in the inferior world of things. But the man who desires glory for its own sake rather than loving the public good corrupts his behavior to please other men, and "nothing is virtuous or vicious to him but what pleases or displeases his master." Only *la souveraine philosophie* comprehends "the essence and truth of things" and provides a worthy motivation for excellence in human life.

Among Le Caron's contemporaries, an equally eloquent advocate of the fusion of philosophy and politics was Louis Le Roy, biographer of Budé and translator of Plato and Aristotle. In his most ambitious treatise, *De la vicissitude ou variété des choses en l'univers*, Le Roy discusses the practice of philosophy in the context of a narrative of human development rather like that offered in Rousseau's second *Discourse*. He connects the "artificial wisdom" that makes it possible for men to live together and develop complex machines, institutions, and patterns of trade with the Promethean gift of fire. Le Roy makes fun of the common notion that human morals have been decaying steadily since some past golden age, noting that if this were true, there would no longer be any faith or integrity among men. Instead of a unilinear pattern, Le Roy offers the conviction that great excellence in letters or science or virtue is rare in any age, and that successive periods of accomplishment will be swept away by Vandal visitations, to be replaced by equally impressive works at some later time.[7]

In assessing the temper of his own times, Le Roy was particularly bothered by the prevalence of public embroilment, the proliferation of sects and heresies—the harbingers of the religious wars that began in the last decade of his life. He noted that philosophy and letters languished, and ascribed this to the mistaken view that such pursuits belong to solitude and scholastic retirement. Philosophy had left the public world, no longer tested itself in action as it had among the Greeks, and therefore atrophied, unaware of its own dexterity and usefulness.[8] In what was probably his most influential work, a translation of Aristotle's *Politics* with his own extensive commentary, Le Roy expounded this same conviction. He remarked on the general revival of learning in his own times, touching even the meanest of sciences, but not extending to *la science politique*, which is "the worthiest, the most needful of all," without which men "who are naturally companionable

[7] *De la vicissitude ou variété des choses en l'univers*, edited by Blanchard Bates, books III and XI; *De la vicissitude* was a distinctive contribution to the prolonged debate about the relative excellence of the ancients and moderns that occupied so many Europeans from the Renaissance to the Enlightenment, and touches our study peripherally at several points.

[8] *De la vicissitude*, pp. 40-43.

cannot at all maintain their companying and society together." "By the forebearing of the learned to practice and the practitioners to study," the science falters, and the state declines.[9]

Le Roy's concern about the embroilments that afflicted his age was echoed by many of his contemporaries; but not all shared his view that the retreat of philosophy from public life was among the causes of these ills. The response of many of his learned countrymen, in fact, was to accelerate this withdrawal. No exercise of high-minded humanistic statesmanship, including that of such a worthy man as the chancellor de L'Hôpital, appeared to offer any solution for the evils that afflicted France. Even at the height of participatory humanism, a few men of letters (including Rabelais) and a few jurists (including La Boétie) expressed contempt for politics, and advocated some version of a life devoted to pleasant learning and good company. Both Le Caron and Le Roy perceived the need to combat this tendency and recall their philosophic brethren to the fray. But by the last third of the century, when the civil wars had exhausted France and all public life seemed deeply infected by their cruelties and treacheries, such appeals had a pitifully hollow sound. The course of action recommended most eloquently and influentially by Michel de Montaigne—the outward attention to public duties combined with private scorn for the corrupt and twisted ways of politics, cultivated in the scholar's study and at his pleasant table among friends—became the norm for most philosophic Frenchmen for decades to come. The nascent civic humanism of Budé and his disciples was supplanted by a potent and vigorous individualism. In a disordered kingdom where no order gave promise of establishing itself and *la chose publique* had become the plaything of rival extremist factions, concentration on the good order of the soul in solitude and among friends appeared to offer the best prospect for human fulfillment, and a measure of happiness.

2. THE ABBEY OF THÉLÈME: RABELAIS

The tension between the attractions of public and private life that exercised humanists in the sixteenth century pervades a letter addressed by Etienne Pasquier to a close friend who had retired from a vigorous career "to cultivate his garden," and "to nourish himself in the contem-

---

[9] Louis Le Roy, *Aristotle's Politiques or Discourses of Government* (English translation, 1598), Bi. Werner Gundersheimer, *The Life and Works of Louis Le Roy*, quotes from a letter by Gabriel Harvey to a friend in 1579: "You can not steppe into a schollars studye but (ten to one) you shall litely finde open either Bodin de Republica or Le Royes Exposition uppon Aristotles Politiques."

plation of his trees."[10] Pasquier professes himself unmoved by the attractions of such a life, which involves (in his eyes) opting for "silence as a conversation, solitude for company . . . and in brief, in place of liberty, taking the fields as prisons." The trees, who are the sole auditors of his friend's ideas, express their vegetative discontent with his intrusive presence by shedding their rich robes as he attempts to converse with them. Pastoral repose is a false ideal for man, contends Pasquier, since we are made in the image of a ceaselessly active God, and need diversion from an unhealthy preoccupation with ourselves. Virtue as well as vice are found in cities in more abundance, as well as "great traffic not only of merchandise but of ideas." He therefore begs his friend to "return not so much to us as to yourself, and collect your spirit."

For all his mockery of the delights of solitude, the arguments offered by this prominent jurist in favor of his own life style are quite as privatistic and individualist as those he rejects. The delights of the city that Pasquier holds out to his friend are not those of public participation or commitment to some community larger than the self, but the personal pleasures to be found in society—the life of the study, the excitement of a well-turned harangue in the lawcourts, the incessant activity of the marketplace as a diversion from too much attention to oneself. The sense of need for diversion, of inability to live happily with oneself, is much stronger in this letter than any notion of a common happiness. The strictures of Montaigne and Pascal about the way we tend to flee ourselves and come outside ourselves were directed at men in just such a mood as that here expressed by Pasquier. Privacy and privatism, in other words, were complicated phenomena in his era, as they are today; and the solitary life of the man in pastoral retreat was not the only pattern available to one who wanted to cultivate selfish individuality.

In one of his late writings, a "dialogue of the dead" between Alexander and Rabelais, Pasquier himself adopts a skeptical tone about the value of ambition and public life. He makes Rabelais his spokesman, questioning Alexander about what possible profit, obtained from all his grandeur, carries any value after death, or sets him apart from private men such as Rabelais himself. Alexander's brave attempt to defend the excellence of his career is punctured in the end by Rabelais's quiet conviction that he is not "at present less in grandeur or contentment" than

[10] Pasquier, *Lettres*, II, 4, to M. de Marillac, sieur de Ferrières, in *Oeuvres* (1723), vol. II, 31-40 (also included in D. Thickett, ed., *Pasquier, Lettres familières*).

the erstwhile master of the world, "since all your grand conquests evaporated to nothing, and to contemplate this now must give pain, as all the vanities of the world pale before the heavenly majesty we see before us." The vanity of incessant worldly activity, and its ultimate hollowness in the face of eternal verities, conflicts with the assessment offered in Pasquier's early letter, and indicates that over time he himself came to be less attracted by such things.[11]

Pasquier's choice of Rabelais as the interlocutor of Alexander in this dialogue is itself worthy of note—not only because Rabelais was assumed to be in a position to contemplate divine majesty after death despite his unorthodox writings, but also because he was taken as a sensible exemplar of the delights of privacy and a moderate life. One of the most striking impressions to be gleaned from Rabelais's writings is precisely this mood: the delights of good fellowship and private pleasure, a hedonistic individualism that finds fulfillment in good company. When Rabelais introduced his *First Book* with a promise of abstruse doctrine and high mysteries "concerning our religion as well as the political estate and economic life," he indulged in subtle self-mockery and a mockery of all those who mine learned texts for hidden profundities.[12] His vast humanistic education and his verbal gusto led him to poke fun at the complicated formulas of scholasticism and the pedantic multiplication of terms in Roman law. His own political ideas, such as they were, were fairly straightforward, though not simple.

Rabelais's giants, particularly his hero Pantagruel, behave in a fashion appropriate to heroic and enlightened kings when their careers involve the governance of ordinary mortals. Pantagruel's success in ordering the polity of Dipsody is based on his awareness of the durability of political loyalty imbibed with one's mother's milk.[13] This is quite consonant with the crown-centered French patriotism prevalent in the sixteenth century. In his account of Pantagruel's rule, Rabelais heatedly rejects the notion that the best way to govern a newly conquered people is by violence and vexation. A catalogue of successful conquerers is invoked to prove the superiority of the alternative course of action—coddling and carefully nurturing a new people like a newborn

---

[11] "Pourparler d'Alexandre & Rabelais," *Recherches de la France* (1611), p. 993. George Huppert, *Les Bourgeois Gentilshommes*, ch. 12, focuses on Pasquier in his solitary mood as an example of the "desire to retreat from the world" that was "becoming a noticeable state of mind among the gentry's philosophers and poets."

[12] Rabelais, *Oeuvres complètes*, edited by Jacques Boulenger and Lucien Scheler "Prologue de l'auteur," p. 5.

[13] *Third Book*, chs. 1-5.

babe. Here as elsewhere in Rabelais's books there are faint echoes of the Seysselian vision of a self-tempering monarchy controlling a healthy and vigorous populace.[14]

However, the most sustained discussion of a "good regime" in Rabelais's work is explicitly antipolitical. This is the depiction of anarchic bliss in the utopian abbey of Thélème, a monastery "unlike all others," a haven of perfect free will. The very name of the place is the Greek word for will, *thelema*. It was founded by Friar John, who rejects the opportunity to supervise an ordinary monastery with Socrates' answer: "How shall I govern others when I cannot possibly govern myself?"[15] Thélème has only one rule: "Fay ce que vouldras: Do as you like." There are no walls or laws to fence in the members, no clocks or regimens to circumscribe the day. All rise, eat, dress, study, make love, play, and work as seems good to them. Members of this community naturally evolve patterns of common action, dress, and occupation, seeking out one another's company and accommodating themselves to one another's preferences and needs.[16] Order is shown to arise spontaneously among human beings who are "free, of gentle birth, well-bred." The need for imposition of external order, and the notion of some incompatibility between the ordering of the individual soul and the ordering of the community, are decisively rejected.

Thélème attests that men and women can live together effortlessly as voluntary associates, naturally tuning their pursuits and pleasures to the enjoyment of one another's company. Freely expressed individuality finds itself in consonance with the equal individuality of friends and lovers. Men and women demonstrate instincts that bring them into perfect harmony. They are inclined to virtue and saved from vice by their own honor, by a "praiseworthy emulation" that arises among free human beings. They instinctively seek to "shake off the yoke of servitude," and make good use of common freedom.

Rabelais revels, as a good utopian should, in detailed descriptions of this society founded on principles opposed to those of poverty and chastity, as well as on the rejection of obedience. He lingers over the architecture of the handsome chateau, the extensive symbolism and ornaments of the towers, the vast libraries. The animals, the jewels, the playthings, the beautiful sounds, sights, tastes, and odors of Thélème

[14] Nicole Aronson, *Les Idées politiques de Rabelais*, part II.
[15] *Gargantua*, ch. LII; the Socratic origin of this maxim is pointed out by M. A. Screech, "Some Reflexions on the *Abbey of Thelema*," *Etudes rabelaisiennes*, VIII.
[16] *Gargantua*, LVI-LVII; as Screech points out, "this obtaining of order out of chaos by a free play of sympathy is central to the satire of obedience"; "Reflexions," III.

are all richly laid out before us.[17] The mood of utopian reverie was one that later French theorists often found appealing. None managed to convey more skillfully the tangible atmosphere of an idyllic world.

Thélème is a retreat for an elite group of men and women, not a rule for ordinary life. Physical and mental deficiencies are not allowed to spoil the perfection of the whole. Men and women who enter this community must be beautiful, learned in several languages, musical, athletic, altogether worthy companions for one another. The ideal achieved is not selfishness or solitude; but neither is it in any sense a public life. There is no authority, law, commerce, property, subjection; there are no conflicts of interest to be resolved, no hard decisions to be made and enforced. The enjoyment of the community itself, and of the varied human pursuits that it makes possible, are the only goal.

The time comes for each of the inhabitants of Thélème to leave the abbey. They marry one of their number and go out happily to confront the world. But within the abbey itself, no harsh tasks must be performed, no sacrifices made. Ample resources are magically available to provide for the needs and desires of the inhabitants. Ardent and skillful cooks and carpenters, gardeners, and seamstresses attend to all the supportive details that make such a lovely existence possible. The hedonistic, philosophic, atemporal inhabitants of Thélème symbolize one aspect of the intricate ideal of privacy, serving to demonstrate that retreat from the world need have nothing austere or solitary about it. All the hard questions, of course, have gone unanswered. But such is the acceptable license of utopia.

In the other four of the five books of *Gargantua and Pantagruel*, Rabelais also wrestled with questions about human freedom and individuality, self-love and society.[18] But there is no indication of a belief in the natural consonance of virtuous human beings. The "good regimes" of which occasional glimpses are given involve the imposition of order and hierarchy by superhuman benefactors. The last two or three of these books were written in an era of increasing intolerance and inhumanity. Rabelais, like many of his contemporaries, found it difficult to tread a middle path between fanatical Catholics and ferocious Calvinists, both bent on denying the legitimacy of any compromise. The optimistic faith in human nature, in good company and robust physical enjoyment, in humanistic education, are maintained

---

[17] *Gargantua*, LIII-LV; on the possible Renaissance models for this chateau, see Raoul Morçaye's introduction to *L'Abbaye de Thélème*; on the artistic complexity of Rabelais' description, Richard Regosin, "The Artist and the *Abbaye*."

[18] Wayne A. Rebhorn, "The Burdens and Joys of Freedom," *Etudes rabelaisiennes* IX, 71-90.

sturdily by Rabelais even in the darkened atmosphere. But in such an atmosphere, Thélème has disappeared.

3. On Voluntary Servitude: La Boétie

Rabelais's celebration of the ideal of pure liberty in good company, and his conviction that free and well-born human beings would chafe under "the yoke of servitude," were echoed in quite a different vein in a little treatise composed by one of his younger contemporaries, Etienne de La Boétie. In La Boétie's *Discourse on Voluntary Servitude*, the community of scholars devoted to the ideal of liberty is extended across time and space, rather than situated in a utopian locale. The bulk of his essay, however, is dedicated not to the celebration of liberty but to the condemnation of tyranny, and the analysis of the psychology of subjection. The fact that La Boétie was a close friend of Montaigne, and that this friendship provided the subject for one of Montaigne's most important essays, is one reason for attending to this discourse; but such attention needs no excuse. The *Discourse on Voluntary Servitude* fully repays study by its own intrinsic merits.

One of the most notorious treatises published during the French religious wars was the *Reveille-matin des français* (1574), a variegated collection drawn from several sources. Among the pieces in this collection of partisan polemical pamphlets directed against the regime was a mutilated version of a *Discourse on Voluntary Servitude* composed by a young poet and classicist who later became a magistrate in the city of Bordeaux. The discourse was composed around 1550, when La Boétie was a law student of Anne du Bourg at Orléans. Du Bourg was a notable Huguenot martyr, but La Boétie was never connected with the Huguenot cause. His discourse, for all its fiery rhetoric, was not a defense of resistance or tyrannicide, and had nothing but contempt for popular will. It was probably written under the immediate stimulus of the harsh repression of the *revolte des gabelles* in Bordeaux, which led to the execution of a number of city fathers who had failed to act with sufficient firmness against the rebels, as well as to the suppression of the parlement of Bordeaux and the humiliation of the city. Occurring before the civil wars had made Frenchmen accustomed to worse things, such an event left a strong impression on a young humanist steeped in the idealistic republicanism of the classics and of contemporary Italy.[19]

Montaigne was no doubt correct in his conviction that his friend

[19] Henri Weber, "La Boétie et la tradition humaniste d'opposition au tyran," F. Simone, ed., *Culture et politique*, pp. 355-374.

(who died in 1563) would have shared his own distress and disgust at the use made of the *Discourse* by those who "sought to disturb and change the state of our government." His assessment of La Boétie's attitude toward ideal and existing laws and governments is worth quoting, not only for the light it sheds on La Boétie's work, but also because it appears to describe Montaigne's approach as well:

> This subject was treated by him in his boyhood, only by way of an exercise, as a common theme hashed over in a thousand places in books. I have no doubt that he believed what he wrote, for he was so conscientious as not to lie even in jest. And I know further that if he had had the choice, he would rather have been born in Venice than in Sarlat, and with reason. But he had another maxim sovereignly imprinted on his soul, to obey and submit most religiously to the laws under which he was born. There never was a better citizen, or one more devoted to the tranquillity of his country, or more hostile to the commotions and innovations of his time. He would much rather have used his ability to suppress them than to give them material that would excite them further. His mind was molded in the pattern of other ages than this.[20]

This passage captures the subtle mixture of skepticism, idealism, and conservatism that characterizes Montaigne's own ideas about politics, the puzzling combination of radical private criticism with scrupulous public adherence to norms and institutions. La Boétie, unlike Montaigne, did not choose to make his private critical thoughts "public" in the sense of publication; but he did circulate his manuscript among "men of understanding." Montaigne informs us that he planned to publish the *Discourse* (which was also known by the title *Contr'un*) as part of his own *Essays* until it was taken up by the Huguenots, presumably "men without understanding." On the face of it, the *Discourse* appears bolder and more radical than all but a few passages in the *Essays*. In fact, its final message is equally conservative, and closely parallels that of Montaigne himself. The real difference between the two works is not in their attitude toward authority, but in their attitude toward common people. La Boétie shows none of the ability to identify with ordinary people that Montaigne developed with the years.[21] His most marked emotion was disdain for the vulgar

---

[20] *The Complete Essays of Montaigne*, translated by Donald Frame; 1, 28, "Of Friendship," p. 144. On the parallels between Montaigne's attitude to authority and that of his friend, see Keohane, "The Radical Humanism of Etienne de La Boétie," which is an extended version of this section.
[21] Donald Frame, *Montaigne's Discovery of Man*, discusses this "humanization of a humanist."

masses, for the credulity and lack of judgment of the mob. The *Discourse* is a strongly elitist essay, in which the only ray of hope is that a few men of superior intelligence might keep the idea of liberty alive, while the gullible masses are fed with bread and circuses, in every century.

The central purpose of the *Discourse on Voluntary Servitude* is to make us wonder how it can be that men free by nature everywhere subject themselves to a single man, who has no power except that which they give him. La Boétie skillfully stresses the amazing aspect of multitudes obeying the will of "a single little man."[22] He points out that to overturn the ruler's power no battle or conflict would be necessary, simply cessation of compliance, withdrawal of support. And he concludes that this must therefore be a peculiarly *voluntary* servitude, in which the subjects are implicated in their own subjection. Although he enjoins his hearers to throw off this yoke by becoming aware that the awesome strength of the oppressor is in fact their own strength compounded in his hands, such passages are indeed rhetorical. La Boétie clearly has no expectation that anyone will heed him. His true intention is not to spur revolt, but to analyze the phenomenon of subjection that fuses individuals together into one powerful pedestal for the colossi we call kings, and to differentiate from that mass a few special individuals who can attain a vision of brotherhood that transcends subjection.

In La Boétie's eyes, we are all by nature free and essentially equal. Nature is a kind mother who fashioned us all from the same pattern, "so that each of us might find himself reflected in the other." Some are more favored in gifts of bodily strength or of intelligence, but Nature never intended us to use these gifts to attack those who are weaker than ourselves. She has rather offered us the opportunity to show fraternal love by helping others, and lodged us all as if in the same house. She has given us, besides, the gift of speech so that we may create, "by a common and mutual declaration of our thoughts, a communion of our wills." She has generally attempted in every way possible to tighten the knot of our society and show us that she wishes us to be "not so much united, as one." None among us is destined by nature to subjection or authority; we are all free comrades. If we followed our natural inclinations we would be subject to our parents, and then only to the reason that is innate in all of us.[23]

---

[22] *De la servitude volontaire*, included in Paul Bonnefon, ed., *Oeuvres complètes de La Boétie*. Translations from this discourse are my own, though I have consulted a fairly good English translation by Harry Kurz, reissued by Murray Rothbard as *The Politics of Obedience: The Discourse of Voluntary Servitude*.

[23] *Servitude volontaire*, pp. 15-17; Rothbard, pp. 55-56.

If men are naturally free, how does it happen that they are everywhere enchained? La Boétie poses this question in terms strikingly similar to those used by Rousseau, and his answer is given in terms closely parallel to those of Montaigne. His explanation for this strange phenomenon is that men were originally constrained by force or fraud, and then became accustomed to their servitude; men are now "born and bred as serfs," and it never occurs to them that they are by nature free. Nature's power over us is less than that of custom. The seeds of nature in us are fragile, and die out unless treasured and carefully nourished. Indeed, one of the most striking things about our nature is the ease with which we adopt the form and pattern of action given us by custom. La Boétie points out that a child born in regions where there are months of darkness followed by months of continual sunlight would not long for the light if he had never seen it; we do not long for what we have never experienced. Thus he concludes that "it is true that it is man's nature to be free and to wish to be so; but his nature is also such that he naturally takes the bent [*le pli*] which nurture gives him. Let us then say that anything comes to be natural to a man if he accustoms himself to it; whereas only that to which his nature pure and simple calls him is unaffected [*naif*] in him; thus the first reason for voluntary servitude is custom."[24]

When La Boétie refers to government as tyranny, which he does consistently throughout his discourse, he does not refer to some distant Asiatic phenomenon, but to every instance where a group of men are subjected to the authority of a single man, however that authority has been acquired. He distinguished three sorts of tyrants: those raised up by election, by force of arms, and by dynastic inheritance. He finds some difference in their behavior, but nothing really to choose among them. Thus he departs from the familiar convention that a good monarch is far removed from a usurping tyrant. La Boétie holds that submission to the will of one man is heinous, however that man acquired the throne, and however well-intentioned he may be. He considers the various methods used by all rulers to "put their subjects to sleep beneath the yoke," the tricks, symbols, and disguises they employ. He is particularly harsh in his ridicule of those who pretend to be "tribunes of the people," in order to consolidate their mastery, mouthing pretty phrases about *le bien public et soulagement commun*, and those who claim to be gods so that popular imagination, working in a void, can endow them with an awful mystery. The subjects of such masters "accustom themselves to serve the more willingly for not knowing what sort of master they have, nor even in truth if they have one at all,

---

[24] *Servitude volontaire*, p. 29; Rothbard, p. 64.

and they all fear on hearsay one whom nobody has ever seen. The early kings of Egypt rarely showed themselves without a cat, a branch or a fire on their heads, masking themselves as well and generally decking themselves out like jugglers or conjurers. In behaving this way, by the very oddness of their action they inspired reverence and admiration in their subjects, whereas people not so besotted in their wits or so completely servile would simply have laughed at them."[25]

Lest anyone be so dimwitted as to suppose that only the pharaohs were given to such behavior, La Boétie mocks those who believe their king can perform miracles and cure diseases, "borrowing some splinter of divinity" to prop up their rule. He lists the major devices used by the kings of France—the fleurs-de-lis, ampoulas, and flaming standards —as examples of the "fine conceits" on which kingly power rests. This repertoire of symbols and disguises is not so important in explaining voluntary servitude, however, as another factor, the network of patron-client relationships that link the tyrant to a few intimates, and these in turn to larger groups of men who carry out their will, and so on in an ever larger series of concentric circles. By this "mainspring and secret principle of domination," half the people of the country are involved in the government and think they stand to profit from it.[26] They suffer persecution and humiliation because they are given license to treat those beneath them in the same way, in a perverse application of the golden rule.

Some readers of the *Discourse* have argued that La Boétie should have ended his treatise with a call to regicide.[27] But such an ending would be the most superfluous rhetorical touch of all. La Boétie implicates men thoroughly in their own subjection, and effectively establishes his central thesis that this is *voluntary* servitude. Thus he makes clear that if one tyrant were killed, we could only expect another in his place. The men he depicts are not chafing beneath their yoke; they are not blind to their situation; these men have come to like it. Like racehorses broken to the bit, they parade around in colorful trappings, responding to the reins in the hands of their masters. Foreshadowing Rousseau's *Discourse on Inequality*, La Boétie recounts a process of *denaturing* in which men lose even the memory of their freedom. In a mood quite like Rousseau's, he asks: "What unhappy accident can it have been that has so much denatured man, born, alone among all the animals, to live freely, and caused him to lose even the memory of his

[25] *Servitude volontaire*, pp. 35-40; Rothbard, pp. 69-72.
[26] *Servitude volontaire*, pp. 44-57; Rothbard, pp. 77-81.
[27] Bonnefon, *Montaigne et ses amis*, pp. 148-149; Wade, *Intellectual Origins*, p. 111, attributes the notion of tyrannicide to La Boétie without discussion.

original being and the desire to find it again?"[28] Men have taken a new bent under the yoke of customary subjection, and there is no hope that they would spring back upright if the yoke could somehow be removed.

Instead of calling for tyrannicide, La Boétie holds out a vision of a community of brothers, a fraternity of educated men throughout the ages that binds together the natural free spirits. These men will always keep liberty alive; they are

> a few, better born than the others, who feel the weight of the yoke and cannot abide submission to it; who never become docile in subjection, and who . . . never cease to search for their natural privileges and to remember their predecessors and their essential being. These are those who with clear understanding and far-seeing intelligence cannot be content, like the gross populace, with keeping their gaze fixed on what is at their feet. They must be looking behind and before, and think nostalgically of earlier times in order to judge those of the future and have a standard for measuring the present. . . . If liberty were completely lost, and removed from the world, they would imagine it and feel it within their spirits and still savor it. Servitude is not to their taste, no matter how it may attire itself.[29]

A reference to the "liberty of the republic of Plato" supports the conjecture that La Boétie expected such men over the ages to find their true freedom and pleasure in communing with one another. The radicalism of his treatise on servitude finds no expression in any public life. His beautiful vision of a transtemporal fraternity was an individualistic ideal quite consonant, in theory and practice, with punctilious submission to an absolutist king. If all authority is tyrannical, it matters little whether one is ruled by an Egyptian pharaoh, a senate, or a Valois king. The essential thing is to preserve space for the liberty of the mind and spirit, the only liberty possible for members of our species.

It is thus not at all surprising that La Boétie, like many others, including both Montaigne and Montesquieu, set his radical visions apart from his daily life, submitting in silence to the laws of his own land. Like Montaigne, he did the business of his king, and did it well. The

---

[28] *Servitude volontaire*, p. 19; Rothbard, p. 48. Rousseau echoes the images of the yoke of servitude and the tamed horse in the last part of his *Discourse*, without mentioning La Boétie. Rousseau was heavily influenced by Montaigne, and La Boétie's work was often read in the eighteenth century in connection with Montaigne's (according to Bonnefon, *Montaigne et ses amis*, p. 169).

[29] *Servitude volontaire*, p. 30; Rothbard, p. 65.

only other political writing ever attributed to him was a pedestrian polemic for the king's Catholic cause against the Huguenots.[30] His conviction of the continuity and liberty of men of learning throughout the ages must surely have enriched a private life lived alongside the public role of a magistrate in the city of Bordeaux. Whether La Boétie ever mused on the irony of finding himself a prominent part of the network he had once condemned so scathingly, we cannot know.

4. Montaigne's Individualism

The optimistic, public-spirited humanism of Le Roy and Le Caron rested on assumptions about ethics and politics that were called into question by several sixteenth-century thinkers, most importantly by Michel de Montaigne. Among these were the assumptions that there is a true and essential goodness available to human beings who put their minds to finding it, a virtue that is the same in all eras and situations; that the happiness of individuals is naturally in consonance with, and dependent on, the happiness of the entire community—that the individual interest and the common interest are in harmony; and that ambition, emulation, the desire to serve one's *patrie* and perform great deeds are noble motivations, virtuous and worthy of a thoughtful man. In his *Essays*, Montaigne provided reasons to doubt all these former certainties, and presented a portrait of the individual as the rightful center of his own world, determining his own values through testing and self-discovery.

The elusive and magnetic figure of this Gascon philosopher stands at the head of the tradition I have called "individualism." His book was read by almost all educated persons in the seventeenth and eighteenth centuries. Numerous references and borrowings attest its influence on the thinkers we will consider in this study.[31] Montaigne depicts a life centered in the self, a life in which all other obligations besides obligation to the self are peripheral, carefully measured, kept

---

[30] Montaigne makes a passing reference to this essay, in I, 28 (135). (All references to Montaigne are to Donald Frame's translation of the *Essays*; page numbers are in parenthesis. I have also used the edition of the *Essais* by Maurice Rat, in two volumes.) Bonnefon published a *mémoire* he took to be the one in question, as "Une Oeuvre inconnue de La Boétie: Les Mémoires sur l'édit de janvier 1562," *Revue d'histoire littéraire de la France* XXIV (1917), 1-33 and 307-319.

[31] Alan M. Boase, *The Fortunes of Montaigne in France*; Wade, *Intellectual Origins*; and Richard Popkin, *The History of Scepticism from Erasmus to Descartes*, ch. 3. Popkin stresses that in the seventeenth and eighteenth centuries, Montaigne was "seen not as a transitional figure, or a man off the main roads of thought," but as the real founder of modern philosophy.

Individualism and Humanism—99

in their places. It is not a life of retreat or isolation, but a life in which the self discovers itself by reflection upon other selves and other matter, and establishes its claims within and against the world. More than any other writer, Montaigne succeeded in making such a self-centered life attractive, in teaching men to think of this individuality as a satisfactory and appealing norm. He provided for modernity an alternative ideal, to be set over against the ancient ideal of the engaged citizen, and the medieval ideal of the self-sacrificing saint.

To get a sense of Montaigne's achievement it is useful to compare him with Machiavelli. Montaigne was generally familiar with Machiavelli's counsels for political activity, and accepted a view of the temper of public life that has much in common with his predecessor's. He incorporated into the *Essays* certain aspects of Machiavellian politics, and transmitted them to the writers of the early seventeenth century in France. Yet whereas Machiavelli assessed political activity positively and rejoiced in the vigor and glory peculiar to the exercise of political *virtù*, Montaigne denied that a life lived according to these principles was ultimately satisfying or praiseworthy for a man of judgment. Machiavelli made an influential distinction between the public and the private realms of morality and action, and gave exclusive attention to the former.[32] Montaigne made the same distinction, and the opposite choice; he recommended a course of self-absorption, with only limited and measured involvement in public life. This was the primary legacy he left for his successors.

A peculiar paradox of publicity and privacy threads its way through Montaigne's own life. He retired from public life as a magistrate in Bordeaux to the privacy of his tower library to write a book about himself. During the period when he was engaged in writing, he served two terms as mayor of Bordeaux and acted occasionally as a negotiator whose skills were prized both by the king and by Henry of Navarre. Yet these public activities are rarely mentioned in his book. He treats his public behavior as if it were too private to put on display, and publicizes in detail his most private thoughts and acts. In his note "To the Reader," Montaigne refers to his book as having a "domestic and private" goal; yet he went to great trouble to ensure for it a wide public circulation, bringing out several editions in his lifetime. He informs us that he was by nature reticent, scrupulous about his obligations, and pleasant in society, but incommunicative about himself in conversation. And yet he spent the greater part of his adult life putting his private self on public view.[33]

[32] On this aspect of Machiavelli, see Isaiah Berlin, "The Question of Machiavelli."
[33] Phillip Hallie, *The Scar of Montaigne*, ch. 8, deals with this theme; see also

The key to this paradox lies in Montaigne's conviction that men are too easily seduced outside themselves by all the attractions of the world and by the discomfort of focusing on their own "inanity and nonsense." Thus they avoid becoming familiar with themselves, and spend their lives outside themselves. Montaigne attempted to show men how to be at home in their own company, to draw us back into ourselves away from the world in which we are too much absorbed. So he publicized his private life and took his public life for granted. He discovered, though he did not name, what Pascal later called *divertissement*, our tendency to avoid looking into ourselves. One of the most powerful essays, "Of Vanity," concludes with the observation that "we are an object that fills us with discontent; we see nothing in us but misery and vanity. In order not to dishearten us, Nature has very appropriately thrown the action of our vision outwards.... Look, says everyone, at the movement of the heavens, look at the public, look at that man's quarrel, at this man's pulse, at another man's will; in short, always look high or low, or to one side, or in front, or behind you." Thus Montaigne could show that what appears to be a natural and normal exercise for men—knowing ourselves first of all —is in fact one of the most difficult things for us to do, something we must be taught to do and prodded to perform. "It was a paradoxical command that was given us of old by that god at Delphi: Look into yourself, know yourself, keep to yourself; bring back your mind and your will, which are spending themselves elsewhere, into themselves; you are running out, you are scattering yourself; concentrate yourself, resist yourself; you are being betrayed, dispersed, and stolen away from yourself."[34]

Montaigne does not preach the joys of contemplation for its own sake; he ridicules pedantry, and finds meditation in his tower library less satisfying than a good conversation over a good dinner.[35] He also recognizes the necessity of performing public duties when one is called upon to shoulder one's share of common burdens, and the continuing attractions of the public world. In all these ways, he exemplifies an attitude similar to that of the man whom he admired above all others, Socrates. In the early *Essays*, there is also a strain of Stoic virtue, over-

---

Essais III, 2 (611) and III, 9 (750), which show that Montaigne was well aware of the paradox. "For my most secret knowledge and thoughts, I send my most faithful friends to a bookseller's shop."

[34] III, 9 (766). This is among Montaigne's most constant themes; see also I, 3 (8) and III, 12 (799).

[35] I, 25 (98) and III, 8 (704); in III, 9 (750), Montaigne links solitude with old age. Michael O'Loughlin, *The Garlands of Repose*, places Montaigne within a long tradition of celebrations of "active leisure."

coming the fear of death, avoiding the vulnerability that comes from committing the self too much into the world. But of all the ethics of the past, the one that comes closest to Montaigne's, to which he regularly pays homage, is that of Epicurus.[36] He finds the counsel of regulated pleasure in good company the most satisfying precept in the world. His allegiance to the past was not to the brilliant apologists of republican virtue and martial strength, but to the alternative message of withdrawal into the self and extension into the world of nature, the focus on the individual as part of the whole wondrous universe, which characterized the Hellenistic spirit against Hellas itself. The comparison with the Hellenistic spirit is particularly cogent, since Montaigne's world, like that of the Epicureans, was breaking down. Montaigne lived in the thick of the civil wars, and described their brutal and terrible effects. Metaphors of sickness and decay are frequent in the *Essays;* like the Epicureans, Montaigne was engaged in forging new norms for use by disoriented individuals in a decaying world.[37]

Montaigne explored many different avenues in essaying his judgment, and found it easier to keep that judgment fluid and open than to come to rest. He employed all of the characteristic devices of the Renaissance, including irony and paradox.[38] Within these fluidities and paradoxes, there is a deeper dialectic, singularly appropriate to his purposes. He moved easily from positing something to positing its opposite; his thought moves by the uncovering of parts of things that reveal other parts by their very incompleteness. The matter flows with its own movement, finding its own divisions and its own seams. Socrates before him, Pascal and Hegel after, are Montaigne's intellectual companions in this serene but active fascination with unity in multiplicity. This was an individuation that depended on recognizing the place of the individual within a complex whole, and the complex whole within the individual. His book, which he described as "consubstantial with its author," records the process of Montaigne's development and self-discovery as an individual.[39] If he had written a conventional

[36] On the development of Montaigne's ideas, the central work has been done by Pierre Villey, *Les Sources et l'evolution des Essais*; the Stoic influence is discussed in vol. II, ch. 2. James H. Nichols' study of *Epicurean Political Philosophy: The De Rerum naturae of Lucretius*, brings out themes that are strikingly similar to those of Montaigne.

[37] A. J. Krailsheimer, *Studies in Self-Interest from Descartes to La Bruyère*, p. 4, gives a fine sense of the disorientation of the *moi désaxé* in the sixteenth century that prompted Montaigne to undertake this enterprise.

[38] Margaret McGowan, *Montaigne's Deceits*; Barbara C. Bowen, *The Age of Bluff*; and Rosalie Colie, *Paradoxia Epidemica*, place Montaigne with this tradition.

[39] II, 18 (504); see also II, 1 (761-762); III, 13 (824). On this aspect of Montaigne,

book of moral philosophy, presenting his findings as rounded generalizations and neat exhortations, he would have failed in doing what he wanted. The distinctive stubborn individuality of the book makes it a powerful model for individualism. Pascal paid high tribute to his success when he noted that "it is not in Montaigne but in myself that I find everything I see there."[40]

In writing about such a writer, any analytical beginning point is bound to be unsatisfactory. In Montaigne's world, as in Pascal's, it is "impossible to know the parts without knowing the whole, or to know the whole without knowing each of the parts individually."[41] But one must begin somewhere; and for the purpose of understanding Montaigne's contribution to individualism, it makes sense to begin with the theme of freedom and restraint. The tension between the free individual and the necessary restraints imposed by social order has been a central focus of individualist thought; and that same tension is apparent throughout the *Essays*.

Montaigne put a high value on freedom for the individual. There are passages in the *Essays* celebrating freedom eloquently, and others proclaiming Montaigne's distaste for any sort of mastery and domination. He gives a strong sense of his desire to face an open world, to have space and elbow-room for thought and movement, to avoid all but the most necessary constraint. In one striking passage, he gives as uncompromising a testimonial to simple freedom of movement and to open doors as one can find short of Bakunin reflecting upon Bluebeard's wife: "I am so sick for freedom, that if anyone should forbid me access to some corner of the Indies, I should live distinctly less comfortably. . . . If those that I serve threatened even the tip of my finger, I should instantly go and find others, wherever it might be. All my little prudence in these civil wars in which we are now involved is employed to keep them from interrupting my freedom of coming and going."[42]

Yet Montaigne is also exceptionally sensitive to the dangers of both thought and action if they are unrestrained. There are other equally

---

R. A. Sayce, *Essays of Montaigne*, has a good discussion; see also Olivier Naudeau, *La Pensée de Montaigne et la composition des Essais*, and Frederick Rider, *Dialectic of Selfhood in Montaigne*.

[40] *Pensées*, edited by Brunschvicg, no. 64. In III, 2 (611), Montaigne remarks: "You can tie up all moral philosophy with a common and private life just as well as with a life of richer stuff. Each man bears the entire form of man's estate."

[41] *Pensées*, edited by Brunschvicg, no. 72.

[42] III, 13 (820-821). Bakunin praises Bluebeard's wife for her inability to stay away from the one tower room that was forbidden her, in his critique of Rousseau's theory of the state; Sam Dolgoff, *Bakunin on Anarchy*, pp. 129-130.

eloquent passages where he describes the unruly raw activity of the human mind—restless, curious, presumptuous, a sharp-edged tool that cuts itself unless it is used with caution. "If it is true," he says in his most pessimistic essay, "that man alone of all the animals has this freedom of imagination and this unruliness in thought, . . . it is an advantage that is sold him very dear, and in which he has little cause to glory, for from it spring the principal source of the ills that oppress him: sin, disease, irresolution, confusion, despair."[43] The theme of the human mind in unruly motion is associated with the metaphor of the journey that dominates the *Essays*; Montaigne compares the mind to a mettlesome horse, and observes that "there is no animal that must more rightly be given blinkers to hold its gaze, in subjection and constraint, in front of its feet, and to keep it from straying here or there outside the ruts that custom and the laws trace out for it." He took for granted that some human animals can use their freedom more wisely than their fellows, and spoke of a "few souls so orderly, so strong and wellborn that they can be trusted with their own guidance" and "sail with moderation . . . in the freedom of their judgments, beyond the common opinions," using their freedom "with order and discretion."[44] But for the most part he was concerned to discover standards for behavior for the unruly human animal. Where do we find the patterns that allow us to exercise self-discipline, if we are capable of it, and impose an acceptable discipline on a whole society of restless individuals? How can we learn to enjoy freedom without destroying others and ourselves? In the course of the *Essays*, three sorts of standards for the regulation of individuals are discussed: those stemming from nature, from reason, and from custom. Each has its uses, and each its limitations.

Montaigne uses "nature" in at least three different senses: to denote the whole universe of diverse concrete particulars; to describe a primitive, instinctual pattern of behavior shared by human beings with all other animals; and to indicate an individual configuration of needs, desires, and possibilities. In all three senses, nature has positive associations for Montaigne; whatever is natural is normally desirable and good. But it is not easy to discover what is natural amidst the corrupt complexity of the modern world. Nature, for Montaigne, is both the healthiest and most original thing on earth and also the most difficult of access for "civilized" men. It is a guide for action to be preferred above all others, but one that we have covered over and muddled up, and must now teach ourselves to recognize.

[43] II, 12 (336).   [44] II, 12 (419-420).

104—Order of Kingdom and Soul

When Montaigne uses nature in his first sense, it is to remind us that everything that is, is natural, and thereby lift us from our parochial assumption that our own familiar ways of doing things are natural, whereas what is strange to us is not. One of the major purposes of the *Essays* is to help us, along with Montaigne, achieve such a larger perspective by inquiring, journeying, exercising curiosity. Montaigne chides us for being "huddled and concentrated in ourselves," so that "our vision is reduced to the length of our nose"; whereas

> whoever considers as in a painting the great picture of our mother Nature in her full majesty; whoever reads such universal and constant variety in her face; whoever finds himself there, and not merely himself, but a whole kingdom, as a dot made with a very fine brush; that man alone estimates things according to their true proportions. This great world, which some multiply further as being only a species under one genus, is the mirror in which we must look at ourselves to recognize ourselves from the proper angle.[45]

We can learn something about nature in the second, narrower sense by observing unspoiled people such as the Brazilian cannibals, whose simple morals and close communal life are described in one of the most famous of the *Essays*. This allows us to gain a precious vantage point on our complicated modern lives, and understand the disabilities that attend "civilization." Montaigne records the reaction of one cannibal who had the misfortune to be brought to Bordeaux, and who observed with surprise "that there were among us men full and gorged with all sorts of good things, and that their other halves were beggars at their doors, emaciated with hunger and poverty; and they thought it strange that these needy halves could endure such an injustice and did not take the others by the throat or set fire to their houses."[46] These passages, of course, would never be read by the beggars of Bordeaux, and were not written to incite them to revolt. Instead Montaigne hoped to lead his readers "full and gorged with all sorts of good things" to contemplate the distance they had traveled from primitive equality and natural justice, and ponder the inherent barbarism of their own lives. However useful this example might be as a benchmark for modern men, Montaigne was convinced, like Rousseau after him, that we can never return to such a condition. We have gone too far along the road. In our presumptuous efforts to find better ways to do things we have ascribed laws of our own devising to nature, and made it more

---

[45] I, 26 (116).   [46] I, 31 (159).

difficult to find her paths. We have put out our natural light by artificial light.[47]

There remains a third sense of "nature," an individual pattern of dispositions and potentialities that should be discerned and nurtured.[48] But this kind of nature, like the other two, is of little use as a restraint on our tendencies to license and unruliness. We must look elsewhere to find standards that can be relied on to accommodate the varied activities of restless individuals.

Occasionally it appears as though Montaigne believes that such standards can be discovered in the "rules of reason." He speaks of himself as "a slave only to reason," and once or twice advises relying on reason against promptings of primordial nature herself. Much more commonly, however, he argues the radical insufficiency of human reason as an instrument for obtaining certain knowledge.[49] The *Essays*, particularly II, 12, include some of the most profoundly skeptical passages in Western literature, and leave little doubt about the utility of this feeble tool. Our reason is distorted by pride, passion, prejudice; by the condition of our bodies and our environment. Conscientious reasoners regularly disagree, and objective clarity of judgment is impossible to maintain. Montaigne assumed that there are natural principles of reason in the universe, but that we as human beings can never be sure we have apprehended them. We cannot therefore hope to use them as solid common ground upon which to construct a public world, nor can we be justified in imposing our own reason upon other men. Reason is a private, not a public, guide for action.

There is a third source of standards for human behavior: custom, which on the face of it appears to be the least promising of guides—contradictory, fluid, and absurd. Some of Montaigne's most memorable passages have to do with the diversity of customs around the world, the manifold ways human beings have devised of doing things. He notes that "there falls into man's imagination no fantasy so wild that it does not match the example of some public practice and for which, consequently, our reason does not find a stay and a foundation."[50] Such passages, however, are written not to ridicule custom, but to introduce sobriety into our sanguine assumptions that there are simple ways of doing things obvious to all men. They also draw attention to the power of custom, strong enough to blot out nature and draw

[47] I, 36 (167).   [48] I, 26.
[49] III, 12 (603); III, 8 (279); and I, 31 (156). In III, 11 (786-790), Montaigne makes clear that it is the presumptuous aspect of human reason that most disturbs him, our tendency to torture and murder others to see our truths prevail.
[50] I, 23 (79).

reason in its wake. Since Montaigne regarded both reason and nature as faint voices heard by individuals in different ways, easily bent to biased uses, he was all the more impressed by the great public strength of custom. Even though men change their ways of doing things with bewildering rapidity, they adhere today with equal firmness to new customs as they shun those of yesterday. This introduces a precious element of regularity and predictability into human behavior. The brutish stubbornness of men obeying custom provides a rare fixed point in a fluid world, and makes it possible to maintain a public life. Foreshadowing Montesquieu and Burke, Montaigne described the way human societies arrange themselves over time without rational planning or direction. Our customs grow up from accidental linkages and accommodations, and thus "human society holds and is knit together." Human beings, like "ill-matched objects, put in a bag without order, find of themselves a way to unite and fall into place together, often better than they could have been arranged by art."[51]

Despite its utility and power, however, custom is not a wholly satisfactory source of standards. It is a "second nature" that has not totally obscured the first, and the two will inevitably come into conflict.[52] Proud reasoners will reject the applicability of stolid custom, and seek restlessly for novelty. Anyone who becomes aware of the incredible variety of human experience will be led to question the legitimacy of custom itself. Thus none of the three standards provides clear-cut and durable patterns for social behavior. They lead in varying directions, and even cancel one another out. As Hobbes put it later in *Leviathan*, "somewhat else" is needed to bolster and enforce the regularities of custom, to identify a common reason that can decide upon a course of action in case of conflict and confusion, and to deter individuals whose ambitious restlessness leads them to encroach on the freedom of other individuals.

5. Montaigne's Communities: Friendship and Authority

"There is nothing to which nature seems to have inclined us more than to society," asserts Montaigne, "and Aristotle says that good legislators have had more care for friendship than for justice."[53] For

---

[51] III, 9 (730).
[52] III, 10 (772); see also II, 12 (423); II, 37 (598); and III, 11 (792).
[53] I, 28 (136); Montaigne's discussion of friendship draws on that of Aristotle in the *Nicomachean Ethics*, book VIII. The singular friendship he enjoyed with La Boétie is the subject of his essay "Of Friendship." Richard Regosin, *The Matter of My Book*, part I, discusses the subtle interplay between the literary models of essays on friendship, and Montaigne's own experience.

Montaigne as for Aristotle, friendship and justice are two different modes of fitting individuals together in human society. But Montaigne describes true friendship as a relationship so rare and precious that most human beings never experience it, so all-absorbing that it can only involve two human beings at one time. A pale imitation of such a friendship may serve to cement societies together; and a derivative conception of friendship for the self may undergird the sense of public duty; but friendship as such was a most uncommon phenomenon, in Montaigne's world.

True friendship, lyrically depicted in one of the most beautiful of the *Essays*, is a perfect duplication of the self, a full communication with another human being, the most rewarding experience available to mortal men. It is not a denial but a fulfilment of individuality. It is based on equality of partners, and unfettered free choice; it is a "complete fusion of our wills," in which "our souls mingle and blend with each other so completely that they efface the seam that joined them, and cannot find it again."[54] This vision of friendship imparts the ideal of a full realization of the individual that is not singular or egocentric; it must be double, the fusing of two souls in which each human participant is reflected and enriched by the other. Later French theorists such as Pascal and Rousseau were surely influenced by the power of Montaigne's vision when they drew up their own descriptions of intimate communities in which the individual discovers his true self in something larger than himself. But Montaigne decisively rejected the idea that such a relationship could be extended to an entire community. This friendship that "possesses the soul and rules it with absolute sovereignty" cannot possibly be shared with more than one other person, since "each one gives himself so wholly to his friend that he has nothing left to be distributed elsewhere." Montaigne could never have accepted the extension of his ideal self-absorbing fraternity to a polity. He described a private relationship between two human beings, not a paradigm for public life.

In his description of the cannibals, Montaigne remarked on the close traditional bonds of their community, which was made possible by the rude simplicity of their lives. They exemplified a "naturalness so pure and simple" that their society could be maintained with "little artifice and human solder."[55] As the reaction of the cannibal who visited Bordeaux makes clear, they were bound together by a kind of

[54] I, 28 (139).
[55] I, 31 (153); Montaigne associated this condition with the poets' "golden age," whereas Hobbes uses similar language in *Leviathan* XIII to describe a condition of brutish deprivation.

fraternity that meant recognizing other men as "other halves" of themselves, by traditional filial obligations, and a direct sense of belonging to the community. In the society of the cannibals there was "no sort of traffic, no knowledge of letters, . . . no riches or poverty, no contracts, . . . no agriculture, no metal," and there was therefore also "no name for a magistrate or for political superiority" among them. They could be ruled directly by "the laws of nature" because of the simplicity and intimacy of their fellowship. In a more complex and diversified society, however, magistracy is necessary to regulate the multiple activities of strangers, and human laws replace those of nature herself. Most human associations are based not on friendship or even on the natural fraternity of the cannibals, but rather are "forged and nourished by pleasure or profits, by public or private needs," and they depart from friendship insofar as "they mix into friendship another cause and object and reward than friendship itself."[56] For such relationships another ethic than that of friendship is required, the impersonal ethic of justice, and the restraints of political authority.

Like later individualist theorists such as Hobbes and Locke, Montaigne asserted that formal structures of political authority are necessary for human beings to live comfortably in civilized society. Unlike such theorists, however, Montaigne had little confidence in the ability of human reason to devise deliberate structures for this purpose. He put great weight upon the importance of established authority, developed haphazardly over time. His comments about political authority are deeply conservative. He asserted the necessity for scrupulous obedience to the powers that be, and was profoundly pessimistic about the results to be expected from any attempt to improve on them, however corrupt they might become. Montaigne had little patience with utopian dreams, because "all those imaginary, artificial descriptions of government prove ridiculous and unfit to be put into practice." We do not find men malleable to any form we choose to impose upon them, but rather "already bound and formed to certain customs," and "we can hardly twist them out of their accustomed bent without breaking up everything." As a consequence, concludes Montaigne, "not in theory, but in truth, the best and most excellent government for each nation is the one under which it has preserved its existence. Its form and essential fitness depend upon habit."[57] He applied this doctrine

---

[56] I, 28 (136).

[57] III, 9 (730); see also I, 23 (86), and compare strikingly similar passages in Montesquieu's *pensées* 632 and 1617; *Oeuvres complètes*, edited by Roger Caillois, I, 1153 and 1460. Frieda Brown provides a rather simplistic account of Montaigne's conservatism in *Religious and Political Conservatism in the Essais of Montaigne*; a more penetrating treatment is Sayce, *Essays of Montaigne*, ch. 10.

directly in his assessment of his own polity, ravaged by civil war. Montaigne offered no hope for constructive alteration in French public life; instead, his mood was one of hanging onto the remaining shreds of order and civility, in the belief that any attempt at reform could only make things worse. He was convinced that he lived in a decaying polity, and that the road ahead was all downhill; the morals of his own age were in his eyes "extremely corrupt," yet he asserted that "because of the difficulty of improving our condition, and the danger of everything crumbling into bits, if I could put a spoke in our wheel and stop it at this point, I would do so with all my heart."[58]

This conservatism about politics is a corollary of Montaigne's assertion that "private reason has only a private jurisdiction."[59] There is no accessible public reason in the universe that can teach us how to order our societies, and no ground for supposing that the fruit of one man's private reason in such matters is superior to any other. Montaigne held no illusions that those in power were blessed with an arcane expertise that led them to see the best answers to political dilemmas. But it is essential that someone be in power to formalize the most important customs into laws, and provide sanctions so that the rest of us can get on about our private business without continually suffering from invasion and anxiety. Here once again Montaigne anticipates the arguments of Hobbes. Someone's reason must be made trump in order that society may function; someone's private reason must be raised to the status of a public reason. No one is so exceptionally clever or virtuous that he has the direct avenue to a "right" solution, but anyone can be given authority to pronounce *a* solution, and this delivers us from the chaos of conflicting opinions that tears society apart. Therefore, in politics the first virtue of the citizen is obedience.

As a result of this profound conservatism about politics, the tension between autonomy and authority—between freedom for the individual and the restraints necessary to make society possible—is particularly clear-cut in Montaigne's *Essays*. Montaigne resolves this tension for himself, at least, by setting up a double standard for behavior: a standard of private critical reflection, and public conformity, that provides a central keynote of the *Essays*. He teaches his readers to submit scrupulously to the restraints of public authority in public, but retain the freedom of private judgment in criticizing the absurd or vicious aspects of that authority in their own solitary meditations, and among close friends. The ambiguous status of the publishing of the *Essays*, as both a public and a private act, is highlighted by this advice; but the

[58] II, 17 (497). [59] I, 23 (88).

advice itself is unambiguous. We must obey the commands of princes, but not twist or submit our private reason to public use. We obey outwardly and judge inwardly; as Montaigne put it vividly, "all deference and submission is due to [kings] except that of our understanding. My reason is not trained to bend and bow, it is my knees."[60] By severing the connection between his reason and his knees, Montaigne can submit and yet remain (in Rousseau's words) "as free as before" in the only way that counts for him. Montaigne asserts that "laws remain in credit not because they are just, but because they are laws. That is the mystic foundation of their authority; they have no other." They are often made by fools or knaves, always "by men, vain and irresolute authors," and nothing is "so ordinarily faulty as the laws." Therefore, "whoever obeys them because they are just, does not obey them for just the reason he should."[61] He believes, in other words, that the most stable foundation for a state is an informed and sober obedience on the part of citizens who suffer no delusions about the supernal justice of their laws, but recognize the necessity of obedience to them simply because they are the established laws. Such men make better citizens than those who believe their laws are wholly just, since this type of obedience rests on an illusion that might be shattered at any moment.

This distinctive resolution of the tension between authority and autonomy is one of Montaigne's most characteristic counsels—but also one of the most difficult. Most individuals do not find it easy to bend their knees to something their reason cannot support. The difficulty runs both ways; men resist bending their knees to something their reason rejects; and when they have bent their knees to something long enough, it affects their reasoning. But Montaigne was firmly convinced of the necessity of this distinction. "Will and desires are a law unto themselves," he said; "actions must receive their law from public regulation."[62] Therefore

> the wise man should withdraw his soul within, out of the crowd, and keep it in freedom and power to judge things freely; but as for externals, he should wholly follow the accepted fashion and forms. Society in general can do without our thoughts; but the rest —our actions, our work, our fortunes and our very life—we must lend and abandon to its service and to the common opinions, just as the great and good Socrates refused to save his life by disobedience to the magistrate, even to a very unjust and very iniquitous magistrate.[63]

[60] III, 8 (714).   [61] III, 13 (821).   [62] III, 1 (603).
[63] I, 23 (86). J. Peter Euben, "Philosophy and Politics in Plato's *Crito*," has

The reference to Socrates is particularly telling. It helps explain how Montaigne could publish a book that probes and questions everything, and yet maintain that we must uphold established ways of doing things, and obey authority. Socrates used his private reason with devastating effect in his own world throughout his life. He taught his associates to wonder and to question everything; yet he obeyed the laws meticulously and in the end submitted to execution even by "a very unjust and very iniquitous magistrate." Montaigne admired Socrates more than any other man, and it is reasonable to suppose that in this respect he found him a particularly helpful model.

Personally, Montaigne chafed at ceremony, ritual, confinement, but he was much impressed by the power of symbols and rituals in politics. "What I myself adore in kings," he said, "is the crowd of their adorers." He noted how much men are affected by uniforms and regalia, and how difficult they find it to remember the distinction between the symbols and the office, and the ordinary man who fills it.[64] Montaigne himself was always aware of this distinction, and his own allegiance was to the office, not its human occupant. The precious stability and regularity in human action on which Montaigne depended as an individual requires subordination to custom and authority in the public realm, on the part of himself as well as others. The thoughtful man will inevitably notice the absurdities and irrationalities behind all this impressive show, but bow down reverently in public with all the rest. Montaigne's solution to the problem of how to reconcile critical individual freedom with public regularity was precisely the reverse of that of the child in the fable of the emperor's new clothes; he noticed that there was no real emperor inside the handsome uniform, but continued to act as if there were.

6. Public and Private Virtue

In one of his most provocative essays, Montaigne chides those who condemn burial salesmen because they profit from death. "This judgment seems badly taken," he observes, "inasmuch as no profit is made except at the expense of others, and by this reckoning you would have

---

a thoughtful discussion of the tensions between citizenship and philosophy revealed in this dialogue that also sheds light on Montaigne's attitudes.

[64] I, 3 (9); cf. II, 16 (477), and Pascal's *Pensées*, edited by Brunschvicg, nos. 303-334. Montaigne notices that magistrates have a hard time making this distinction when they are in power: "I see some who transform and transubstantiate themselves into as many shapes and new beings as they undertake jobs, who are prelates to their very liver and intestines, and drag their position with them even into their privy." III, 10 (773).

to condemn every sort of gain." He urges each reader to "sound himself within, and he will find that our private wishes are for the most part born and nourished at the expense of others."[65] Throughout his book, Montaigne argues that vice and virtue are not easily distinguishable, and that apparently virtuous behavior may be motivated by "vicious" passions such as ambition, lust, and greed.

> Ambition can teach men valor, and temperance, and liberality, and even justice. Greed can implant in the heart of a shop apprentice, brought up in obscurity and idleness, the confidence to cast himself far from hearth and home, in a frail boat . . . ; it also teaches discretion and wisdom. . . . In view of this, a sound intellect will refuse to judge men simply by their outward actions; we must probe the inside and discover what springs set men in motion.[66]

In these observations Montaigne inaugurates a long and fruitful tradition in French social theory, foreshadowing the *libertins* of the early seventeenth century, the Jansenists, and their English disciples such as Mandeville. Montaigne makes explicit the idea that private vices knit society together, that selfish motives lead men to serve the public good. Those who profess a passionate commitment to the public good, he observes, are normally deceiving others, and probably themselves as well. "As for that fine statement under which ambition and avarice take cover—that we are not born for our private selves, but for the public—let us boldly appeal to those who are in the midst of the dance. Let them cudgel their consciences and say whether, on the contrary, the titles, the offices, the hustle and bustle of the world are not sought out to gain private profit from the public."[67] In this context, Montaigne draws a firm distinction between the private and public realms. Although both are subject to useful vices and imperfections, the public realm is regarded by Montaigne as peculiarly infected by the "sickly qualities" with which "our being is cemented."[68] He therefore separates out the comparative purity and rigor of private morality from the tainted, twisted rules for action that must obtain in public life.

Like Machiavelli, whom he mentions disparagingly in the *Essays*, Montaigne argues that certain acts normally regarded as inherently vicious must be performed in public life in order that the state may be preserved. He provides a number of "dangerous examples, rare

---

[65] I, 22 (77); Montaigne concludes by noticing (after Lucretius) that "nature in this does not belie her general policy," for birth of any sort entails decay and alteration.

[66] II, 1 (244). The passage continues: "but since this is an arduous and hazardous undertaking, I wish fewer people would meddle with it."

[67] I, 39 (174). [68] III, 1 (599).

and sickly exceptions to our natural rules" to illustrate his point, concluding that "no private utility is worthy of our doing this violence to our conscience; the public utility yes, when it is very apparent and very important."[69] This justification is in terms of what later Frenchmen called *raison d'état*. Montaigne's language makes clear that he shared none of the admiration felt by Machiavelli, or by his own successors in the French utilitarian tradition, for men who performed such acts in the offices of state. He praises Socrates and Epaminondas, rare heroes who managed to maintain their integrity and follow the straight path of virtue in public life. But Montaigne is aware that the straight path does not always lead to public success, and speaks of a special virtue "assigned to the affairs of the world," a "virtue with many bends, angles, and elbows, so as to join and adapt itself to human weakness."[70] This hazardous, duplicitous, and opportunistic "virtue" appropriate to public action takes its peculiar character from a strong admixture of what would normally be called "vice." Montaigne points out that "in every government there are necessary offices which are not only abject but also vicious. Vices find their place in it and are employed for sewing our society together, as are poisons for the preservation of our health. If they become excusable, inasmuch as we need them and the common necessity effaces their true quality, we must still let this part be played by the more vigorous and less fearful citizens," who are ready to "sacrifice their honor and their conscience" for their country's good. "The public welfare requires that a man betray and lie and massacre; let us resign this commission to more obedient and suppler people."[71]

Twisted virtue excited distaste in Montaigne, since he was firmly committed to the straight path, the clean and constant. He noticed that too much clarity and purity of vision prove disadvantageous in public life. A man's thinking must be "thickened and obscured to suit this shadowy and earthly life."[72] The last thing Montaigne wanted was to "thicken and obscure" his own judgment. This provided, in his eyes, one of the strongest arguments against participation in public life. He had succumbed to the attractions of that life; in a late essay he confessed that he could still "listen without frowning to the seductions that are held out to me to draw me into the marketplace."[73]

[69] III, 1 (600). [70] III, 9 (758).
[71] III, 1 (600); Montaigne's complex ambivalence about the quality of public life is nicely revealed in his juxtaposition of "more vigorous and less fearful citizens" with "more obedient and suppler people," to describe the same set of men.
[72] II, 20 (511); the passages about the straight path are in II, 16 (472).
[73] III, 12 (800).

But he reached the conclusion that we should take advantage of a capacity for doubleness within ourselves, to maintain a strict demarcation between public and private selves. "The mayor and Montaigne have always been two," he tells us, "with a very clear separation." We must recognize and perform our public duties, but not allow them to dominate our lives. When people have "pushed me into the management of other men's affairs," says Montaigne, "I have promised to take them in hand, not in lungs and liver; to take them on my shoulders, not incorporate them into me. . . . We must husband the freedom of our soul and mortgage it only on the right occasions; which are in very small number, if we judge sanely."[74] In one of his most characteristic passages, he enjoins us always to reserve for ourselves an *arrière-boutique*, "a back-shop all our own, entirely free, in which to establish our real liberty and our principal retreat and solitude."[75]

The culminating argument against becoming too much involved in public life, in Montaigne's eyes, was that the public man must "live not so much according to himself as according to others." He is required to give himself away, to put himself at the disposal of others. This is to Montaigne the most threatening aspect of all, since it is such a profound constraint on individual autonomy. He insists that "I love a private life because it is by my own choice that I love it, not because of unfitness for public life, which is perhaps just as well suited to my nature. I serve my prince more gaily because I do so by the free choice of my judgment and my reason, without personal obligation. . . . I hate the morsels that necessity carves for me."[76] Thus the superiority of private over public life is defended by Montaigne on several grounds. It allows us more space and autonomy as individuals, and it relieves us from the necessity of conforming our ethical gait to the angles and elbows we face by "walking in the crowd." Moreover, Montaigne associates a well-ordered private life with "virtue" in the noblest sense. He argues that through learning to control and guide our own lives, we "render higher and more difficult service to virtue than those who are in authority." He wrests from the public realm the glory that Machiavelli took to be the special reward for political *virtù*, asserting that "greatness of soul is not so much pressing upward and forward as knowing how to set oneself in order and circumscribe oneself." Thus Montaigne neatly inverts Machiavelli's model. He attaches vigor, choice, glory, and demanding virtue to the private realm, and associates docility, suppleness, pettiness, and mediocrity with politics. Private life is the pure site of freedom; public life, the

[74] III, 10 (767, 774). [75] I, 39 (177).
[76] III, 9 (756-758).

locus of restraint. Public life must have a dull, slack, and stable tempo to avoid shocks that would disturb society. It can never be open to the fluidity that graces privacy, which is the area of creativity and true virtue. In a passage that directly contradicts Machiavelli's ethic, Montaigne asserts that "to compose our character is our duty, not to compose books, and to win, not battles and provinces, but order and tranquillity in our conduct. Our great and glorious masterpiece is to live appropriately. All other things, ruling, hoarding, building, are only little appendages and props, at most."[77]

Montaigne attempted to teach his readers to be comfortable with themselves and explore their own motivations honestly. In our search for virtue, we should not feel constrained to disguise our "selfish" purposes by reference to some larger good outside ourselves. The ethic provided in the *Essays* recognizes the primacy of the urge toward self-preservation. Montaigne quotes with approval Livy's dictum that "we feel public calamities only so far as they concern our private affairs," and counsels us to fight for the good side in any conflict, but use whatever leeway our duty allows us to look after our own interest. "In truth," he says, "I would easily carry, in case of need, one candle to Saint Michael and one to the dragon, according to the old woman's plan," on the eve of a battle. "I will follow the good side right up to the fire, but not into it, if I can help it."[78]

In Montaigne's book, public duties are defended as important for the enrichment and fulfillment of the self. The connection between the public and private aspects of our lives is a "salutary and well-regulated friendship for the self," which is the "summit of human wisdom and of our happiness." Such a friendship cannot be attained in solitude. A man who orders himself well, and correctly estimates his duties, "finds it in his part that he is to apply to himself his experience of other men and of the world, and in order to do so, contribute to public society the duties and the services within his province."[79] Montaigne approves the maxim of Seneca: "He who is a friend to himself, know that that man is a friend to all." Friendship for the self is the virtue that leads us to perform socially useful acts, and holds human communities together.

Montaigne apparently assumed that the demands of public duty would be recognized by all clear-sighted men, and that the seductions

[77] III, 13 (850-852); compare II, 16 (471) and III, 2 (613).
[78] III, 1 (601); the quotation from Livy is at III, 12 (801). Montaigne is careful to distinguish this ethic from the refusal to commit oneself to either side in a public dilemma, the "wavering and half-and-half" which he considers "neither handsome or honorable."
[79] III, 10 (769).

of ambition and interest would pull the others into the arena, so that the world's business will always be done. In discussing "friendship for the self," he pointed out that "most of the rules and precepts of the world take this course, of pushing us out of ourselves and driving us into the marketplace, for the benefit of public society." Montaigne attempted to provide a counterforce, pulling in the opposite direction, teaching his contemporaries—intolerant, feverish, overextended men—to taste the delights of privacy and understand the importance of exploration of the self. He, like his friend La Boétie, spent a good part of his life in politics, and never counseled men to withdraw from public life altogether.[80] But his disciples in the early seventeenth century ignored this aspect of Montaigne's life and teaching. They responded only to the eloquent celebration of concrete pleasures, good company, study, and a concentration on the self. These men developed an ethic of privacy that included only the most cursory attention to public duties. In withdrawing their intelligence and energy from public life, they lost sight of the ancient ideal of civic virtue that Montaigne and La Boétie had lived, but not professed. Thus these two friends, by their praise for the private enjoyments of the well-educated and leisured individual in communion with himself, with close friends, and with the sages of the past, contributed to the development of an apolitical individualism in French social theory that had far-ranging consequences in the century after the religious wars.

[80] John Parkin offers a thoughtful analysis of Montaigne's attitude towards public life in "Montaigne *Essais* 3.1: The Morality of Commitment." David L. Schaefer, "Montaigne's Intention and his Rhetoric," argues that Montaigne's conception of his public role included an awareness of his importance as a counsellor to princes through the educative influence of his essays.

PART II

Interest and Prudence: The State and the Sage

CHAPTER FOUR

Two Moralities: The Philosopher
and the *Patrie*

1. SEPARATION FROM THE STATE

France in the first half of the seventeenth century is sometimes regarded as a period when order was imposed in life and letters after the profound disorders of the late sixteenth century. To some extent this is an accurate perspective. But things are rarely that simple; and the development of the order we now call classical in France was neither serene nor unilinear. The search for order derived from recurrent radical disorder in polity and society that plagued France until 1660, and from prolonged uncertainties and questionings in morality and religion.[1] Assassinations and minority kingships followed periods of royal splendor, and the juxtaposition of the two accelerated the development of absolutist thought. Mercantilists and *étatists* produced arguments for increased state action in the economy and in society. In the great swelling up of absolutist theory that marked French political discourse from the accession of Henry IV until the beginning of the Fronde, the constitutionalist current stemming from Seyssel was incorporated, submerged, and all but lost. Individualism, on the other hand, flourished in this atmosphere, as subjects of the absolutist monarch devised new patterns of action in economy and society, and adapted old ethical arguments to justify them.

Frenchmen during these decades worked out two moralities: one for political behavior, the other for the individual. As publicists perfected absolutist doctrine, supportive codes of ethics that deviated from familiar Christian precepts were developed to condone actions by rulers and their ministers. In politics, the new moralities were those of the state and its reasons. At the same time, philosophers and theologians worked out codes for individual action, too, based on neo-Stoic and Epicurean strains, and the all-pervasive influence of Montaigne. Among

[1] Will G. Moore, *French Classical Literature*, and Anthony Levi, *French Moralists: The Theory of the Passions 1585-1659*, both make this point cogently. As Levi puts it, p. 337: "It is perhaps even possible to argue that the 'Grand Siècle' never existed until it was all over, a projection of regularity, order, and serenity in the perverse imagination of Voltaire, a myth witnessing to the insecurity of the brave new era which replaced it."

the most striking characteristics of the age was the strict separation that normally obtained between these public and private ethics, which existed in such symbiotic harmony.[2] Individualist moralists took government behavior as a given, like the laws of natural necessity. They assumed that rulers would follow policies based on their own perceptions of their interests and the interests of the state. It was also taken for granted, by philosophers and magistrates alike, that individuals would observe their strict duty of obedience to the king and refrain from any public criticism of his behavior, or any attempt to interfere in government. Within this constraint, moralists worked ingeniously to carve out a space for vigorous private action and individual achievement.

This was an era in which exaggerated personal heroism and idiosyncracy were made compatible with scrupulous obedience and outward conformity to custom. Montaigne's radical separation of public action and private life became the dominant pattern for many Frenchmen. The aristocratic and princely rebels who interpreted their own *gloire*, and that of their families, in ways not always conducive to subjection to the crown, were exceptions to this rule. So were a few moralists, such as Guillaume Du Vair, who continued to adhere to an ethic of public involvement and dedication to the common good as the standard of heroism and individual virtue. But none of these men worked out a persuasive ethic bridging that of Charron and that of Richelieu, bringing public and private moralities into a single systematic whole. The two types of morality developed and flourished side by side, occupying two different and complementary worlds.

In one sense, this was not an unexpected or a surprising situation. Active participation in politics by large numbers of persons is a fairly unusual phenomenon in any polity, and seems particularly unsuited to absolutist monarchy in early modern Europe. What is remarkable is not that most men were content to conceive of themselves as obedient subjects of the king, expecting him to worry about government while they attended to more pressing private matters, but that there was a complex and self-conscious pair of ideologies preaching the positive virtues of privatism on the one hand, and on the other hand the need for an arcane political behavior, inaccessible to ordinary men. The separation of public and private worlds is not notable; but the fact that so many Frenchmen went to such lengths to emphasize and celebrate it does appear to call for explanation.

[2] Anna Maria Battista, "Morale 'privée' et utilitarisme politique en France au XVIIe siècle," in Roman Schnur, ed., *Staatsräson*, pp. 87-119, has some valuable observations on this phenomenon.

This attitude contrasted sharply with that prevalent earlier in the sixteenth century, reflected in the treatises of Seyssel and his constitutionalist successors, the humanists under Francis I, and the active partisans in the religious wars. These authors assumed that it was both possible and desirable for men to move back and forth from public to private concerns, and never noticed any radical disjunction between the two. They regarded political participation as an important part of a satisfying human life, whether this took the form of judicial office, participation in municipal affairs, diplomatic or ministerial service, or even rebellion against a defective regime. For none of them was the stance of principled withdrawal, a conformist façade, or the strict separation between public and private personae accepted as a norm. That these norms were accepted by many Frenchmen in the seventeenth century is therefore not to be taken for granted as an obvious facet of early modern politics. The continual involvement of their counterparts across the Channel in politics during this century, and the development of civic ethics there, provide further evidence that French political culture in the age of Henry IV, Louis XIII, and Louis XIV is a phenomenon that needs explaining, not one that was somehow foreordained before Enlightenment and the Revolution drew men into action.[3]

One possible explanation that appears unsatisfactory is that this was an ideology that fit the needs of the rising bourgeoisie. Most of those who promulgated the ethic of strict separation on the side of the individual were scientists, philosophers, writers by profession, and thus bourgeois.[4] But there is no obvious way in which this stance reflects the interests of the developing bourgeoisie in France. Although the early seventeenth century was a period of economic stagnation and recession, the bourgeoisie emerged from the religious wars strengthened vis-à-vis the aristocracy, and continued to consolidate its advantages. Members of the bourgeoisie were entering the administrative and judicial hierarchies in unprecedented numbers, purchasing offices and being recruited for new posts. Such men clearly identified their own fortunes with the development of absolutist monarchy. It is therefore not difficult to see why they would have supported the monarchy enthusiastically, and accepted the necessity for obedience to the state. But in preaching the separation of public and private roles, and an

[3] Irene Coltman, *Private Men and Public Causes*, discusses the very different dilemmas faced by individuals in the English Civil War; J.G.A. Pocock, *The Machiavellian Moment*, discusses conceptions of civic virtue in that era.
[4] On the class backgrounds of these authors, see René Pintard, *La Libertinage érudit dans la première moitié du XVIIe siècle*, part II, ch. 3; and J. H. Spink, *French Free-Thought from Gassendi to Voltaire*.

ethic of privatistic withdrawal from society, writers from bourgeois backgrounds do not seem to have been voicing the interests of their class. These might just as plausibly have been expressed by an ethic of civic participation and economic activism, or by a more widespread acceptance of natural law theories such as those propounded by Grotius, who found few disciples in France.[5]

The dimensions of this ethic of noninvolvement should not be exaggerated, of course. Some of the same Frenchmen who preached this ethic sought political favor and held posts at court. Members of the aristocracy continued to engage in sporadic bitter conflict with the central government; sections of le peuple rebelled periodically to protest economic misery and the burdens of continual war. As Roland Mousnier put it, there was a "permanent state of unrest" in France in this era.[6] But what was lacking among all these groups, and also among the official and commercial bourgeoisie, was an ethic of positive commitment to the activities of the polity. There was little evidence of what might be called a "communitarian ethic" among Frenchmen who expressed themselves about ethics and politics. The ancient view, revived during the Renaissance and again in the eighteenth century, of man as a social and political animal who found his individual realization in the community, was absent. In its place was the radically individualist ethic of the "dissociated man."[7] This is one aspect of what historians have described as a "separation between civil society and the state" in seventeenth-century France; on the one hand, ordinary people going about their business, a business to which politics had only a peripheral and formal relevance, and on the other hand, the absolutist regime working to consolidate the machinery of state (primarily to make war more effectively), with little integration between state machinery and social activity. In fact, of course, the "separation" was breached in many ways—by mercantilist policies, the rationalization associated with the centralizing monarchy, and the entry of new men into office.[8]

[5] Such an ethic was voiced, as we shall see, by at least one isolated figure, Louis Turquet de Mayerne. Anna Maria Battista, "Sul rapporto tra società e stato nello Francia dell' assolutismo," summarizes and criticizes the views of Marxist historians on this question, especially Antonio Negri, who posits a "renunciation of revolutionary potential" on the part of the bourgeoisie after the Wars of Religion. See also Robert Sayre, *Solitude in Society*, pp. 44-50.

[6] Mousnier, "The Fronde," in Robert Forster and Jack P. Greene, ed., *Preconditions of Revolution in Early Modern Europe*, p. 136.

[7] Battista, "Sul rapporto tra società et stato," pp. 104-106, contrasts the ethic of the "uomo dissociato" with different varieties of communitarian ethics, and traces the appearance of the dissociated man to the writings of Montaigne and Charron. See also her essay "Appunti sulla crisi della morale communitaria nel seicento francese."

[8] Useful correctives to the tendency to overstate this separation are provided in Raymond F. Kierstad, ed., *State and Society in Seventeenth-Century France*.

But the attitudes of subjects, as well as theories of ethics and politics, were slow to reflect these facts.

Part of the explanation for the separation of public and private ethics must lie in the terrible experience of the religious wars. For those of us who have not lived through civil war, but are acquainted with other forms of political evil, the dictates of Montaigne or Hobbes about civil war as the worst thing a society can experience may seem extreme. But it is worth pondering the fact that so many men who have known civil war have held this view. A good many Frenchmen did so in the early seventeenth century, at least among those who wrote books. Noninvolvement commended itself strongly to men who had seen what passionate involvement of personal beliefs and commitments in the public realm could mean. The necessity of complete obedience to strong government, and diversion of individual energies into private pursuits to prevent renewed chaos, might well seem obvious.

A related explanation for the separation of public and private lives, which underlines the importance of the religious wars, is that the most seminal political and social theorists for men of the seventeenth century were the dominant figures of the era of civil war, especially Bodin and Montaigne. Their treatises were the source books for political and social thought for decades afterward; and both men (in quite different ways, to be sure), had drawn an explicit line between public and private in their own writings. The separation of public loyalty and private faith defended by Bodin was essential to the *politique* solution that finally ended the religious wars, a solution that won widespread support at the end of the sixteenth century. The persuasive formulas of Bodin and Montaigne, hammered out in civil war and retaining much of the force and urgency of their origins, as well as the eloquence and conviction of authors of unusual breadth and genius, provided an impressive cumulative testimony to the importance of separating public and private worlds.

Another factor that shaped seventeenth-century attitudes was that France was at war or closely involved in the wars of other countries almost continually. These were dynastic and territorial wars that excited little enthusiasm in France. The harsh burdens they imposed were resented by the people; the alliances with Protestant regimes distressed devout Catholics; and these wars must have appeared to sophisticated skeptics as excellent examples of the devious and bloody games that politicians play. This would have reinforced the general sense of dissociation from political activity for many Frenchmen.

Finally, Frenchmen during this era were still searching for new certainties to replace those destroyed in the collapse of the medieval synthesis. They were busy questioning all authorities, in science, politics, and in religion. The "general crisis" of the seventeenth century about which so much has been written lately has been described by Theodore Rabb as a "crisis of authority."[9] Philosophically inclined men were dissociated from politics, as they were dissociated from religion and other traditional beliefs; they devoted their efforts to active inquiry and contemplation, attempting to discover who they were and what the world was about. It was not an age given to commitment. Rebellion, like any other form of political participation, requires some articulated public goal; neither positive nor critical public goals, beyond the preservation of society as a shelter for individual activity, appealed to many Frenchmen during this era. The separation of public and private ethics was the central aspect of a more general distancing of the individual from the society and the world.[10]

Historians may soon provide a fuller explanation of this dichotomous temper; my purpose in this section has been to indicate a few of its roots as a background for discussing social theorists who developed ethics of both sorts. In this chapter I will first consider the absolutist theory produced by Frenchmen in the early decades of the century, and then deal with the rich growth of individualist ideas in the same period, devoting special attention to the derivative but immensely influential treatise *De la sagesse* of Pierre Charron.

2. THE ABSOLUTISM OF THE JURISTS

In the first decade of the seventeenth century, *le bon Henri* was well established on his throne, and France enjoyed a period of peace and vigorous development unprecedented in contemporary experience. Publicists vied with each other to celebrate the glories of the realm and link them closely to the person of the prince. French patriotism was, as Church has shown, "crown-centered" in a striking fashion; loyalty to *la patrie* was largely identified with loyalty to the prince.[11] At the same time, juristic discussions of the office of the monarch, the possession of sovereignty, and the new phenomenon called the "state"

---

[9] *The Struggle for Stability in Early Modern Europe*; Rabb summarizes the positions taken by historians on the use of a "general crisis" as the organizing principle for understanding seventeenth-century European history. See also Trevor Aston, ed., *Crisis in Europe 1560-1600*, and Geoffrey Parker and Lesley Smith, eds., *The General Crisis of the Seventeenth Century*.

[10] A. J. Krailsheimer, *Studies in Self-Interest*, p. 7, provides a concise statement of this thesis: "Everyone knows that *le grand siècle* revolved round *le roi soleil*; it is the contention of these pages that it only settled on that axis after an abortive attempt to fix it on *le moi soleil*."

[11] W. F. Church, "France," in Orest Ranum, ed., *National Consciousness, History, and Political Culture in Early Modern Europe*, pp. 48-51.

began to converge, so that the sovereign prince was closely identified with the state as well as with *la patrie*.

One of the most striking documents of this patriotic mood was an essay by Jean Duvergier de Hauranne, later abbé de Saint-Cyran and founder of Jansenism in France. As a young courtier, Duvergier de Hauranne took it upon himself to answer affirmatively a question posed by Henry IV: whether a subject is ever obliged to give up his own life to save his sovereign. Hauranne argued that in certain situations suicide can be a duty for a faithful subject conscious of *l'intérêt public*. In this ethic, the existence of the individual is subordinate to the exigencies of patriotic loyalty. Hauranne made much of the argument that members of a larger body are rightfully expected to sacrifice themselves for the preservation of the whole. "When a man has been made a member of a kingdom or a community," he asserts, "he has entered the most austere religion in the world, the brotherhood of the dying, where it may not be simply a question of mortifying himself, but of really dying."[12] In such a community he may be required "to give up his life for his Prince, to immerse himself in the love and memory of his fellow citizens by a generous death, in order not to engage himself in the ruin of his country." Even allowing for the conventions of court flattery, it is worth noting that this man, who later embraced one of the "most austere" religions in the world, began by assuming the validity of the political community knit together by the sovereign person of the prince, the symbol of the whole for which one must be prepared to die. In Jansenism this imagery was retained, but shifted to the plane of the community of the faithful; the relevance of such exalted sentiments to any earthly *patrie* was firmly denied.

During this same decade, jurists produced numerous treatises linking Bodin's theory of sovereignty with older notions about the divine origins of kingly power. The most accomplished of these writers was Charles Loyseau, whose magisterial treatises are still used by historians for their rich portrayal of the social and political order of the realm. Loyseau's ideas were shared by other jurists, and they allow us to follow the trend of development of absolutist thought between the time of Bodin and that of Richelieu.

Loyseau distinguished between an "office," which is a position held on suffrance from some other authority, and a *seigneurie* or lordship. He identified sovereignty firmly with the latter, and all other positions in the state with the former. He defined *la Seigneurie publique* as "an

---

[12] Jean Orcibal, *Jean Duvergier de Hauranne abbé de Saint-Cyran et son temps*, II, 160; this is an excerpt from Hauranne's *Question royale*, published anonymously in 1609.

intellectual right, and an authority over free persons and the things they possess."[13] Loyseau recognized that this right normally emerges from conquest and confusion, but insisted that over time it is legitimized by prescription. The concept of prescription was among his favorites. He used it to justify, for example, taxation by the sovereign to obtain revenue as he deemed necessary. Nonetheless, he did not wish to destroy the distinction between public and private on which Bodin insisted. Loyseau assumed that private ownership meant free disposal of one's goods whereas public ownership of power was not directly over the goods of individuals, but instead conferred rights of expropriation for the public good, and ought always to be exercised not arbitrarily, but lawfully.

Loyseau coupled *ownership* of sovereign power over a kingdom by hereditary right with the state itself, arguing that he who has the sovereignty has the state, since "sovereignty is the form that gives being to the state; the state and the sovereignty taken *in concreto* [that is, as rulership over territory] are synonymous."[14] This treats the monarch as coextensive with his monarchy, as defining the polity rather than occupying one position in a political structure. As one would expect, Loyseau was distressed by the contemporary acceleration in venality of offices in France. This practice was for him a monstrous confusion of office and *seigneurie*, since properly speaking, in his view, sovereignty is the only legitimate form of public ownership of power.[15] All other powerholders in the state are functionaries who derive their authority from the sovereign, not proprietors of their positions. Yet magistrates who had hereditary titles to their posts did enjoy a form of public *seigneurie*, and Loyseau reluctantly conferred a label on the aberration he deplored. The term he chose—*la suzeraineté*—makes clear his own recognition of this practice as a bastard form of feudalism.

Notwithstanding the practice of venality, Loyseau asserted that France was the best-governed kingdom in the world, echoing contemporary patriotic treatises like that of Duvergier du Hauranne. In his eyes, most monarchies were subject to a deficiency that reduced their excellence: divided power. Following Bodin closely, Loyseau asserted

---

[13] *Traité des seigneuries* (1608), in *Les Oeuvres de M. Charles Loyseau* (1701), p. 1. For analysis of Loyseau's ideas, see Church, *Constitutional Thought*, ch. 6; Mousnier, *Les Institutions de la France sous la monarchie absolue*, I, 14-24 and 499-524; Lemaire, *Les Lois fondamentales*, pp. 151-163.

[14] *Seigneuries*, ch. 2, p. 8.

[15] *Seigneuries*, ch. 1, p. 6; more generally, see Davis Bitton, "History and Politics: the Controversy over the Sale of Offices in Early Seventeenth-Century France," in Rabb and Siegel, ed., *Action and Conviction in Early Modern Europe*, pp. 390-403.

that sovereignty must by definition be *parfaite & entière de tout point*, a plentitude of power without external controls upon its use. He drew an elegant analogy to make his point: "as the crown cannot exist if its circle is not complete, so sovereignty does not exist where there is some deficiency." French kings suffered no such liability, but enjoyed "a perfect sovereignty," that is, one "in which the Estates have no part at all." Yet since only God himself can truly be all-powerful, Loyseau took note of three kinds of law that limit even the king of France, "without engaging the sovereignty itself": the laws of God, the rules of natural justice, and the fundamental laws of the French polity.[16] Loyseau depends directly on Bodin for the arguments by which he defended the constitutive quality of these "limits" in the possession of sovereignty.

Even Loyseau's sovereign, since he is a mortal man, cannot do everything himself; he relies on agents in all parts of his kingdom to bring him information, and execute his orders. But all these officers take their authority from the king himself, who alone possesses sovereignty. Just as theologians tell us that all virtues reside perfectly in God, and men participate in them only insofar as He wills to communicate them to us, says Loyseau, "also in *la science politique* . . . the public power of the state resides perfectly and entirely in sovereign princes." Beneath the prince, in ordered ranks, are all other offices in society, manifestations of the inequality necessary to human order and stability: "And thus by means of these multiple division and subdivisions, there is made from many orders a general order, and of several states [*états*] a well-regulated state, in which there is a beautiful harmony and consonance, a correspondence and rapport from the lowest to the highest, in such a fashion that by means of order an innumerable number converge in unity."[17]

In this paean to order, not only Bodin's *République* but the older strains of Seyssel are discernible. For many of Loyseau's successors, however, the indivisibility of sovereignty crowded out other motifs of sixteenth-century jurists. A few decades later, Cardin Le Bret provided a memorable image to crystallize this theme, an image also used by cardinal Richelieu: that "sovereignty is no more divisible than the point in geometry."[18] Le Bret contributed to deification of the king

[16] *Seigneuries*, ch. 2, pp. 8-12; the verb here translated as "engaging" is *interesser*.

[17] *Seigneuries*, ch. 3, pp. 14-16; *Traité des ordres et simples dignités* (1610), in *Oeuvres, avant-propos*, p. 1, and ch. 7, p. 40.

[18] *De la Souveraineté du Roy* (1632), quoted in Gilbert Picot, *Cardin le Bret (1558-1665) et la doctrine de la souveraineté*, p. 127; see also Church, *Richelieu and Reason of State*, pp. 268-286, and Henri Sée, *Les Idées politiques en France au XVIIe siècle*, pp. 68-78.

that marked the fruition of divine-right arguments. He insisted that God grants particular grace to the sacred persons of kings, in order to use them for conducting the lives of other men. Le Bret dwelt on the ceremony of the *sacre*—the consecration and coronation of French kings—not as a constitutional event confirming mutual duties of prince and people, but as a religious event transforming an ordinary human being into a unique royal person, a vessel of divine favor raised up to a plane above all other men.

The constitutionalist tradition of a complex and pluralistic polity gradually receded before such arguments. Echoes of that tradition can be found in speeches by delegates from the Third Estate at the meeting of the Estates-General in 1614. These men had a fairly generous view of their own prerogatives, and a program for reform doomed by disagreement with the other estates and by the policies of the crown.[19] A few jurists continued to emphasize the rightful share in sovereign power belonging to the "sovereign courts," as the parlements were sometimes called (not to set them above the prince, but to emphasize their position at the summit of the judicial pyramid). Among those jurists was La Roche-Flavin, whose treatise entitled *Treize livres des Parlements* (1617) helped keep constitutionalism alive during these decades, and provided substance and inspiration for numerous harangues and briefs.[20] La Roche-Flavin reaffirmed the essentials of the Seysselian argument, including a reference to bridles and an explicit denial that France was an absolute monarchy, in favor of the view that it was "composed and mixed of the three sorts of government together." But neither La Roche-Flavin nor any other jurist posed new challenges to absolutist dogma.

Occasional mavericks, men behind or ahead of their times, worked out political theories quite unlike those accepted as satisfactory by most of their contemporaries. Among these was a Huguenot, Louis Turquet de Mayerne, whose treatise *De la monarchie aristo-démocratique* was published in 1611. Turquet was heavily influenced by theories of natural law, and attempted to create a true science of politics to support the theory of the tempered monarchy. He also spoke directly for the interests of the new bourgeoisie. He was the son of an early capitalist, and argued for the development of a social elite of men dedicated to the public welfare, exemplifying their virtue by commercial and professional accomplishment, which would be a product of, rather than a derogation from, their nobility.[21] Unlike later defenders

---

[19] J. Michael Hayden, *France and the Estates General of 1614*.
[20] Lemaire, *Les Lois fondamentales*, pp. 164-166.
[21] Natalie Zemon Davis, "Sixteenth-Century French Arithmetics on the Business Life," pp. 46-48.

of the social utility of commerce Turquet offered a model of a successful businessman whose concern for the public interest was direct and nonselfish, rather than the indirect product of his own greed. In his attention to connections between natural and positive law, and in his defense of the nobility of the bourgeoisie, Turquet announced themes that sound more like the eighteenth century than the early seventeenth.[22] For the majority of his contemporaries, the old aristocratic ideal of personal heroism and military valor, or the contemplative ideal of the philosophic life, continued to have greater luster. A pluralistic regime such as an "aristo-democratic monarchy" had little appeal either for Frenchmen caught up in admiration for their splendid prince and robust pride in their *patrie*, or for those who wanted simply to be protected against their neighbors by efficient kingly power, and left alone to cultivate their gardens.

3. Justus Lipsius on Private Tranquillity and Public Profit

French ethical theories in the first half of the seventeenth century have received a good deal of attention from scholars, and proved difficult to categorize.[23] A number of distinct strands appeared in different combinations in different treatises, and a work of synthesis such as Charron's *Sagesse* can be shown to have influenced later thinkers whose ideas were fundamentally opposed to one another. Stoicism, Epicureanism, skepticism, the views of Seneca, Plutarch, Plato, and Augustine were all important as sources for these theories. There was a common, and profound, indebtedness to Montaigne, whose protean book provided a different inspiration to each reader, and yet also gave a characteristic flavor to all ethical speculation in this era. All these moralists were in their several ways individualists, preaching self-knowledge and the achievement of happiness and virtue for the individual, whose duties and pleasures were all subordinated to this end.

Revived Stoicism dominated a good deal of ethical thinking at the end of the sixteenth century, and survived into the seventeenth. A major source of neo-Stoicism in France was the work of a Belgian, written in Latin, Justus Lipsius' *Traité de la constance*. Lipsius' work is of special importance for the themes we are considering, since he wrote not only the treatise on constancy, but another on politics,

[22] Roland Mousnier, "L'Opposition politique bourgeoise à la fin du XVIe siècle et au début du XVIIe siècle: l'oeuvre de Louis Turquet de Mayerne," in *La Plume, la faucille, et le marteau*; Lionel Rothkrug, *Opposition to Louis XIV*, pp. 312-313.
[23] Among the best studies of these theories are Levi, *French Moralists*, and Krailsheimer, *Studies in Self-Interest*. See also works by Bénichou, Adam, and Maurens listed in the bibliography.

equally influential in France. The disparate character of the two treatises nicely exemplifies the dichotomy between public and private ethics that dominated French thought after the Wars of Religion. Both treatises were soon available in French, and were republished many times in the seventeenth century; they rivaled Montaigne's *Essais* as sourcebooks for French thinkers such as Charron and Du Vair.

Lipsius' *Traité de la constance* describes the consolations of Christianized Stoicism, a doctrine he learned after he fled from his troubled land in sorrow as a young man. His philosophic mentor, Langius, instructed Lipsius to distinguish between external goods and evils, and those within the soul, and to make the latter his primary concern. "Make your spirit firm and fortify it—this is the true way to find in yourself calm in the midst of troubles, peace in the midst of arms."[24] Langius describes devotion to our *patrie* and compassion for the ills of others as obstacles to our duty to moderate all our passions, including apparently virtuous ones such as patriotism and sympathy. These will trouble the constancy of the soul unless properly regulated. This is a strongly privatistic ethic, in which everything is understood insofar as it touches on our duties to ourselves as individuals.

Like Montaigne, Langius asserted that patriotism and compassion are normally self-centered at their core. Only because we think our own homes and lives endangered do we deplore the calamities of civil war. If we could be assured that we would escape harm to life, property, and those we love, we would watch such troubles unmoved or with a secret malice. For we instinctively take pleasure in evil that befalls others, and leaves us unscathed. This assertion is designed to shock Lipsius into realizing that the civil evils he bewails are for the most part reducible to perceived threats to his own safety and tranquillity. Public evils are simply evils that threaten a great many individuals at once, and they must be dealt with by the sage like other evils that threaten him. The first step of wisdom in this area is recognizing the common practice of dissimulation and self-deception that is involved when we cry out against public calamities.[25]

This is only the first of three thrusts, or *escarmouches*, used by Langius to disabuse Lipsius of his entangling attachment to the world. After telling him to lift the curtain, throw off the mask, and recognize the comedy of our behavior when we deplore public ills, Langius next condemns patriotism. We ought properly to feel pious devotion only

[24] Lipsius, *Traité de la constance*, French translation by Lucien du Bois, p. 135; first published as *De constantis libri duo* (1584). According to Jason L. Saunders, *Justus Lipsius*, this treatise was published in more than eighty editions by the eighteenth century.

[25] *Traité de la constance*, book 1, chs. 7-9.

to God and to our parents, not our country. We are members of the whole species, citizens of the universe, not attached specially to the land where we happen to be born.[26] He denies that there is any sense in which our "country" has nourished us—only our family, and nature itself. Any other belief is the result of the ideas and institutions established by human beings to justify the useful practice of living in society. The real root of patriotism is selfishness; men come together and begin to build public places and associate in several ways. They are devoted to these common things because of their own share in them. Things owned in common do not differ fundamentally from private possessions. We are attached to them by the same motives of avarice and pride in ownership. Our love of our country is an extension of our love of things that belong to us, bolstered by our awareness that our personal security depends on that of the community. The proof of this, says Langius, is that noble and wealthy men always care more about their country than "the plebians and the poor," since they have a larger possessive stake in the public protection.

Langius' final *escarmouche* is directed against compassion. We should feel pity—an inclination of the soul to want to help others—but not compassion—a weak and pusillanimous vulnerability to another's evil, a soft self-indulgence in another's pain. We should always retain the inviolability of the soul against infectious passion and emotion. In place of such infections we should seek tranquillity, a calmness that comes from *la sagesse*, which is a kind of wisdom that appeases troubles, implants virtue, and teaches constancy.[27]

This belief in a right reason harmonious with divine grace and providence, which brings constancy to the individual sage, was the culminating achievement of late Renaissance Stoicism. Lipsius' other major treatise, the *Politicorum, sive civilis doctrinae libri sex*, while not incompatible with the *Constancy*, viewed matters from another perspective altogether, that of the behavior appropriate to political action. In this treatise, a compilation from a variety of sources, Lipsius defined civil life as a society of men for "mutual commodity and profit, and common use of all," composed of "traffic and government," and directed by two guides: "prudence and virtue."[28] He counseled princes

---

[26] *Traité de la constance*, book I, ch. 11; Langius asserts here that the higher wisdom is to know oneself a citizen of a higher realm; "the heavens, there is your pure, your true *patrie*."
[27] *Traité de la constance*, book I, ch. 12; book II, ch. 4.
[28] *Sixe Bookes of Politickes or Civil Doctrine*, translated by William Jones (1594), I, 1; originally published in Latin, 1588. As in the case of Bodin, I have modernized the spelling of the sixteenth-century translation. On Lipsius' political thought, see Gerhard Oestreich, "Justus Lipsius als Theoretiker des neuzeitlichen Machtstaates," and Jean Jehasse, *La Renaissance de la critique*.

to exemplify piety and justice, virtues appropriate to their position at the center of human society. But his most striking observations were about prudence; they were echoed by many later writers who dealt with the thorny problems raised by the notion of reason of state. Lipsius referred to "reason" in connection with this princely prudence. But the intricate shrewdness required for political success was clearly distinguished from the pure austere virtue of right reason in the sage.

Tacitus, a popular authority in this age, was one of Lipsius' major sources. Another was Machiavelli, the Italian "who, poor soul, is laid at of all hands," but who despite his excesses had some very useful things to say. Lipsius accepts the idea that the prince's prudence must include "some dregs of deceit," to be appropriate for the "dregs of the state of Romulus" rather than a Platonic commonwealth. The dissembling fox as well as the majestic lion must be models for successful princes; otherwise a too-innocent ruler will be subverted by the "subtlety and guile" of others, and lose his kingdom. Lipsius counsels the prince to mingle the honest with the profitable and not ignore honesty altogether. But he must use deceit if "the good and public profit, which are always conjoined to the benefit and profit of the Prince, require it." Thus the conjunction of public interest and the interest of the prince was made explicit, and the dissembling prince is bolstered with the conviction that "the forsaking of the common profit is not only against reason, but also against nature."[29]

Three sorts of deceit are distinguished by Lipsius: light, middle, and great, according to how far they stray from the straight path of virtue. Only the third sort, pure treachery, a "forcible and perfect malice," is condemned. The first sort is to be cultivated assiduously, and the middling sort tolerated whenever it is "referred to the profit of the commonwealth, which easily draws and drains into itself all the venom of the vice that is therein," like poison in a potent medicine. These teachings on the prudence of deceit were Lipsius' most important legacy. A few theorists also attended to another theme (common to Machiavelli, Bodin, and Lipsius): the belief in the utility of faction, of "some small dissension" in the state. Relying on Seneca, Lipsius asserts that moderate conflict is politically healthy, since "our society is most like to the stones of a vault, which would fall, but that they hinder one another, by which means it is kept up."[30]

At the end of his *Politics*, Lipsius reverts to his Stoic voice, and counsels the honest man to sit still during civil war and not take either side in a situation in which "the leaders, under a pretext of the public

[29] *Politickes*, Book IV, ch. 13.   [30] Book IV, ch. 14; Book VI, ch. 3.

profit, do each of them strive for their private authority."[31] And yet he believes that it is contemptible not to be willing to fight to protect one's friends. The tension between his individualist ethic, and his belief in the common utility of society, is nowhere resolved. His political maxims were compiled for those who advise princes, and to teach subjects the reasons for obedience to princely government. For those who wanted to understand their own personal duties, his views in the *Treatise on Constancy* provided an attractive privatistic model in troubled times. Those counsels were antiphonal to those offered earlier by Le Caron and Budé. Lipsius insisted that the primary sphere of action and ordering for the wise man is his own soul, against the civic humanist conviction voiced by Le Caron that "the world is the true theater in which the man who wishes to be called noble and virtuous must exercise himself."[32] Le Caron had condemned solitude as brutish, and insisted that "wisdom must be sought in the world." Lipsius advocated a form of wisdom that could only be attained in solitude and self-discipline, communion with God and quiet faith in divine providence.

Lipsius' particular version of neo-Stoicism was not the only one available to early seventeenth-century moralists, however. A younger contemporary, influenced by Lipsius' treatises, provided a different form of Christian Stoicism that drew upon the activist spirit of Renaissance humanism as well as Stoic virtues of duty and self-control. His Stoicism was that of the sage in the world, and he helped create the climate in which the Corneillian hero and the generous man of Descartes could become ideals. Du Vair taught a social ethic of action and responsibility, as well as an individual ethic of tranquillity of soul. He was one of the few moralists in this era who attempted to bridge the ethic of public participation and that of the individual. As Jacques Maurens points out, Du Vair discovered "a harmony between virtue and the taste for glory," uniting "the Stoic need for security and the Christian desire for responsibility."[33] His Stoic Christian sage, unlike that of Lipsius, helped guide his country's fortunes to win the admiration of his countrymen. Du Vair offered the satisfying vision of a double reward, earthly and heavenly alike, for the elect who combined the impulse of charity, love of God, with the desire to make the world a better place.

[31] Book VI, ch. 6.
[32] Eugene F. Rice, Jr., *The Renaissance Idea of Wisdom*, p. 152.
[33] Maurens, *La Tragédie sans tragique: le néo-stoicisme dans l'oeuvre de Pierre Corneille*, p. 122; Maurens has a very useful chapter on Du Vair's humanism and his influence on Corneille.

In the last stages of the religious wars, Du Vair presented an optimistic vision of the true good for man as "the use of our right reason, that is, virtue, the firm disposition of our will."[34] He spoke of purging the passions with God's help, not for the purpose of emptying the self, but to make possible vigorous action enlightened by divine truth. He addressed himself to his countrymen who retreated to their houses or to monasteries in the face of the horrors of the civil war, exhorting them to recognize their responsibilities as "small parcels of the universe," linked and attached to others by natural law and the obligations of Christian charity alike. Renewing the strain of Roman stoicism that regarded public life as a duty for the sage, he insisted that however attractive the joys of individual tranquillity may be, we cannot rightfully achieve them at the expense of others who need our good offices in time of trouble.[35] Only when *la chose publique* is well-established can a good man retreat into sanctuary; at other times men of talent and virtue must stay at their posts, like pilots in a storm, and attempt to heal the ills and ravages around them, however hopeless this enterprise may seem. It is important to note that Du Vair provided no specific counsels for political action for the sage. His focus was on the happy consonance of charity and justice, which ensured that action taken in good faith by regulated will would bring earthly felicity and secure divine reward.

Du Vair's model of the Christian neo-Stoic sage active in the world was a major influence on the drama of Pierre Corneille. Corneille's noble heroes, driven by the need to achieve personal glory and serve lofty ideals of family or fatherland, provided a powerful vision for French ethics in the mid-seventeenth century. This ideal gave a characteristic tone to ethics and politics alike in an age that valued *panache* and thirsted for absolutes. Corneille's plays also bridged the public and the private realms, in that they dramatized the tragedies of conflicting duties and displayed the effects of powerful passions on the plane of high politics and martial conflicts. As Paul Bénichou has shown so well, the mood of "aristocratic agitation" epitomized by these heroic epics gave way, after the Fronde, before the bourgeois triumph of reason and nature.[36] But even in its heyday, the Corneillian ethic was under attack from sources that will be discussed at greater length in Chapter Six. On the one hand, theologians indebted to St. Augustine thundered against earthly glory and ambition, and taught an austere

---

[34] *La Philosophie morale des Stoiques*, in *Oeuvres de Guillaume du Vair* (1641), p. 255.
[35] *Exhortation à la vie civile*, in *Oeuvres*, pp. 306-310.
[36] Bénichou, *Morales du grand siècle*, pp. 8-9.

ethic of Christian charity against the vanities of the world. And on the other hand, more subtly but no less effectively, the *libertins* undermined neo-Stoic heroism by reaffirming the strict separation of public and private worlds, and devoting most of their energies to the more delicate pleasures of the latter. In these attacks on heroic Christianized Stoicism, Augustinians and *libertins* alike were indebted to a treatise that was itself, in several ways, a product of neo-Stoicism: Pierre Charron's *De la sagesse*.

4. Pierre Charron's *Sagesse*

Like many books that have a deep impact on the period in which they are written, Charron's treatise *De la sagesse* was a skillful popularization of themes developed by other writers, presented in accessible prose, synthesized in a superficially coherent order without too much attention to specific incongruences. Charron borrowed heavily from several ancient writers, and from Montaigne, Bodin, Lipsius, and Du Vair among the moderns. It would be wrong, nonetheless, to dismiss his book as a compilation of the ideas of other men. Charron's synthetic concept of wisdom was distinctive, and peculiarly attractive to many of his contemporaries, men of critical judgment and advanced beliefs.[37] The motifs of natural law as the light of reason, of self-knowledge and self-mastery, and the separation of moral philosophy from religious belief, lend to his work at certain points a Stoic tone of order and serenity. But there are other elements as well, and it was these that made the book so influential and so controversial. The *Sagesse* became the "breviary" of the *libertins* because of the profound skepticism, elitism, and individualism that marked the treatise. The approach to questions of faith and the treatment of the passions allowed Saint-Cyran to find inspiration there, as well, in developing his Augustinian position.

Charron retained and sharpened Montaigne's division between the internal and external lives of the wise man, between critical inquiry and public performance. He dwelt on this theme at considerable length, often repeating Montaigne's counsel word for word, but offering his own distinctive version of it. Charron entirely lacked Montaigne's humor, sensitivity, and lively curiosity about the ordinary world; this gives his book a coldness that is quite absent from the

---

[37] Renée Kogel, *Pierre Charron*, ch. 6; Wade, *Intellectual Origins*, pp. 170-179; Anna Maria Battista, *Alle origine del pensiero politico libertino*. Levi, *French Moralists*, pp. 95-97, observes acidly that Charron's influence, "ambivalent to the point of contradiction," was rooted in "unsteadiness of judgment."

Essays. On the other hand, Charron was more explicit than Montaigne about the civic duties of the wise man. But he was quite clear that these are secondary to the duty to oneself. His discussions of the role of the sage in the world include a few arguments used earlier by Du Vair; in his treatise they take on a very different tone.[38]

Charron distinguished three lives men live—the "interior or private," the domestic, and the public. Each has its duties, vices, and temptations. The most admirable man achieves wisdom (and therefore virtue) in all three spheres, making his life a beautiful composition of behavior appropriate to each. Charron disapproved of men who live only in themselves and flee the world for solitude. They choose the easy way, and have no occasion to develop true *sagesse*, which can only be done by men living in the world, coming to terms with its necessities. They also fail in part of their duty. "To flee the world and hide oneself," admonishes Charron, "for whatever private or individual motive, while we have the means to profit another person and aid the public, is to become a deserter, to bury one's talent, hide one's light."[39] This is a "fault that deserves to be rigorously condemned." But Charron was far more rigorous in his condemnation of those who err in the other direction. The man who flees himself to lodge only in the world forgets his primary duty, "the principal and most legitimate charge we have, which is our own conduct. This is why we are here; we should maintain ourselves in tranquillity and liberty." We should be charitable to others, and contribute to public society the offices and duties that are its due, but with great moderation and discretion, lending ourselves but never giving ourselves to others. And we must always know how to

> distinguish and separate ourselves from our public charges. Each one of us plays two roles and has two personae, the one alien and in appearance only, the other our own and essential to us. It is important to know the difference between the skin and the costume. The skillful man will perform his office well but never forget to judge clearly the folly, the vice, the knavishness he finds there. He will exercise his charge because this is the practice in his country; it is useful to the public and can be also to himself; this is the way the world runs,

---

[38] This assessment is shared by Hans Baron, "Secularization of Wisdom and Political Humanism in the Renaissance," pp. 148-150, in reviewing Eugene Rice's generally excellent study of *The Renaissance Idea of Wisdom*, which presents Charron as an advocate of civic humanism.

[39] *De la sagesse*, edited by Amaury Duval in three volumes (originally published 1600); Book I, chs. lv-lvi (I, 403-410). It is worth noting that Charron equates the "interior" life of the individual mind with the "private," and separates it from family or domestic life, as well as from public life in the larger society; this distinction had not been made so clearly by Montaigne, for instance.

and he should do nothing to damage it. One must make use and avail oneself of the world as one finds it, but nevertheless consider it as a thing alien to oneself, know how to enjoy oneself apart from it, commune confidently with one's own good, and at the worst, walk by oneself.[40]

The concept of "wisdom" set out in Charron's treatise is designed to make possible excellence in all three spheres of human life. It is associated with reason, nature, and practical prudence alike, and gains much of its appeal from Charron's refusal to be quite clear about how all these good things differ from one another. However, *scientia*—that is, pedantry, too much bookish knowledge for its own sake—is firmly excluded from this *sapientia* that befits a man of prudence and good character. The allegorical device Charron created for the title page of his treatise makes this point clearly.[41] It shows wisdom as a strong and clear-faced naked woman, standing solidly on the cube of justice, gazing eternally at her own face in a mirror, to symbolize the central purpose of self-knowledge. She is surrounded by a good deal of open space, to indicate the freedom that belongs only to the wise. Floating in the space are her two mottoes, *Paix et peu* and *Je ne sçay*, a reworking of Montaigne's motto *Que sçay-je?* which has quite a different tone. Underneath her pedestal, enchained to it, are four other female figures, representing Passion, Opinion, Superstition, and Science, the four "authorities" from which the sage must free himself. They make up an interesting quadrumvirate. Passion is luxuriously dressed, but contorted and obviously uncomfortable; Opinion is supported rather unsteadily by the uplifted hands of a small crowd of People; Superstition cringes fearfully; and Science, who might seem an unexpected companion for the others, is absorbed in reading a heavy book on whose pages appear only two words: *oui* and *non*.

These four sources of danger to the sage are all to be dealt with in the same way, by the attainment of wisdom, which begins with knowledge of the self. Charron incorporates into his treatise long passages from the *Essays* of Montaigne on this topic, and echoes all he says about the importance of self-exploration, retreat into the self. He also echoes Montaigne's view of nature, revealed by this process of self-exploration through a continual attitude of inquiry.[42] But in his under-

---

[40] *De la sagesse*, Book II, ch. ii (II, 70-72); I have translated *estranger* as "alien," and *personnages* as "personae."
[41] This device is reproduced in Rice, *Renaissance Idea of Wisdom*, between pp. 128 and 129.
[42] Preface to *De la sagesse* (I, lvii). Book I, ch. I is devoted to the theme of self-knowledge. The most sustained discussion of the Stoic theme of the

standing of the connections between nature and self-knowledge, Charron moved beyond Montaigne in the direction later taken by Pascal. For Charron asserted that man is not only a wondrous and infinitely complex being, but also a being who engages in self-deception. This radically compounds the difficulties of self-exploration. In order to penetrate the mask we wear even before ourselves, as well as the manifold roles in the human comedy that are played by other men, we must seek knowledge of the full range and variety of *la condition humaine*. This allows us eventually to come to a fuller understanding of our individual selves, beneath our complex disguises.[43]

The goal of self-exploration in Charron's ethic is self-control, the regulation of the passions by reason and will. Charron describes the passions as forms of love, and distinguishes three principal passionate and vicious loves: ambition, the love of grandeur and honor; avarice, the love of goods; and lust, voluptuous love. There is also a virtuous form of love, the inclination toward God called charity. But Charron pays little attention to charity, the virtue that arises from the irrational gift of divine grace. In his ethical system, virtue is achieved by human reason and judgment taking charge of the will, and thereby controlling the vicious passions. Of the three passions that must be controlled, ambition is the most easily bent to good purposes, since the human desire for reputation can be channeled by politics and education into socially useful behavior, and spur men to heroic acts. Charron does not mention the social utility of avarice, though Montaigne had suggested it and some of his contemporaries were exploring this idea.[44]

One of Charron's constant motifs is liberty, the pure free space that surrounds the sage. It is crucial to his freedom that he does not commit himself. This does not mean inability to take action, for the sage proceeds according to his best understanding of the prudence that guides

---

law of nature in Charron's work is in the *Petit traicté de sagesse*, a concise version of his major treatise that Charron was working on when he died (see Duval's edition, III, 289-90). Maryanne Cline Horowitz, "Natural Law as the Foundation for an Autonomous Ethic: Pierre Charron's *De la Sagesse*," argues that Charron's wisdom should be understood primarily within this tradition.

[43] "For each man is extremely painted over and disguised, not only to other men, but each one to himself; each one of us takes pleasure in deceiving himself, hiding himself and escaping from himself, betraying himself"; *Petit traicté* (III, 271).

[44] *De la Sagesse*, Book I, ch. xxi (I, 155-157); Charron repeats Montaigne's challenge to "those who are in the midst of the dance" to examine their motives; but he specifically exempts the sage from the attractions of reputation, or the need to be spurred toward virtue by such glittering prizes. Compare his condemnation of avarice as *une passion vilaine et lasche des sots populaires* with Montaigne on greed, *Essay* II, 1, p. 244.

his relations with the world. But it does mean the avoidance of any pledging of the self, any fixing of the judgment on doctrine or authority; and it entails the primacy of duty to the self over duty to any other person or to society. Outwardly always conforming, inwardly always critical, making use of the world for his own purposes, "always holding [himself] ready to receive something better if it comes along," Charron's sage is committed only to himself.[45]

5. Charron's Politics

The sage described in Charron's treatise occupies the highest of three planes of spiritual existence, introduced by Charron to differentiate among three sorts of men: *les esprits faibles*, *les esprits médiocres*, and *les esprits supérieurs*.[46] The weaker, lowest spirits are dismissed contemptuously as men born to obey; they do not trouble the world because they lack the strength of spirit to do so. The middling sort make the greatest noise in the world; they are the presumptuous agitators who stir up disputes and upset routines. Yet these mediocre folk are also the ones most attached to the world as it is, lacking the vision needed to attain true wisdom. They submit to the opinions and the laws of their society, not with unthinking stupidity, like the lower sort, but with impassioned zeal, believing their way of doing things the only right way in the world. They are the world's Aristotelians, says Charron: "affirmative, positive, dogmatic." They govern the world as well as trouble it, since the most skilled among them are usually in charge of things. Among the third and higher sort, we find a few rare men of a clear and lively spirit, firm and open judgment, who look critically at everything and search for a more universal truth than that in which they happened to be born. They examine everything and sound it to the root; but they possess too much self-sufficiency and firmness to bother about troubling the world. They are content to go along with local laws and customs, not from impassioned commitment, like the mediocre sort, or from brute habit, like the lower sort, but from a reasoned view that all laws and customs are equally deserving of obedience. The cultivation of a rich internal life of judgment was the true meaning of the freedom of the sage, and Charron insisted that this freedom was harmless to the received opinions of the world, and to authority.[47]

[45] *De la sagesse*, Book II, ch. ii (II, 33); preface (I, xliii).
[46] *De la sagesse*, Book I, ch. xlv (I, 333-337); cf. Pascal's analogous distinction of the three orders discussed in Chapter Nine below.
[47] "All my liberty and daring," he asserted, "have to do only with my

140—Interest and Prudence

Prudence, along with liberty, was among the concepts central to Charron's *Sagesse*, and one might suppose that such statements were made prudentially, to avoid attracting official censure for unorthodox ideas. If so, the gambit failed, since Charron's implicit message—that a man can achieve virtue in the world unaided by religion and, for all practical purposes, has no need of grace—attracted immediate ecclesiastical disapproval.[48] It is, I think, more likely that Charron was sincere in his contention that the *esprits supérieurs* have no need to trouble the waters of this world. His attitude toward politics was straightforwardly utilitarian: a good ordering of the affairs of men makes it possible for the sage to pursue his goals without worrying about continual encroachments on his private space. Some measure of participation in that ordering may occasionally be required of the sage, and his wisdom is gained partly by worldly experience; but there is no reason to expect any positive outcome from an attempt to make major changes in the way the world is run.

In his comments on politics, Charron develops the prudential themes put forward by Lipsius and Montaigne, the discussion of the special political skills necessary for the government of this world. He showed little of Montaigne's revulsion and disdain for this "twisted virtue," perhaps because he had never been involved and then disillusioned, as Montaigne had been. By the time Charron wrote his treatise, Frenchmen had begun to take for granted that politics has an ethic of its own; and he contributed several elements to the developing canon of *raison d'état*.

In Charron's view, prudence is the first virtue, in public and private life alike. Justice explicitly takes second rank, and in the end the world's justice and the counsels of prudence become indistinguishable. The major element in political prudence, as in all other kinds, is knowledge —the knowledge of the matter with which one is concerned. In the case of governance this means knowledge of men, of sovereignty itself, of one's state and its resources. It also means familiarity with the special qualities appropriate to ruling, for we should be aware, cautions Charron,

> that the justice, virtue, and probity of the sovereign have a slightly

---

thoughts, judgments, and opinions, in which no one has any share or concern except those individuals who have them each in his own right." Preface to *De la sagesse* (I, lix).

[48] *De la sagesse* was placed on the Index long before Montaigne's *Essays*. On the intellectual backgrounds and fortunes of his book, see Albert Soman, "Pierre Charron: A Revaluation," which casts doubt on the widely accepted story that Charron was a close friend of Montaigne.

different course from those of private men; it has its own ways of marching, larger and freer because of the great, heavy, and dangerous burden it carries and leads forward. Therefore it suits the justice of the prince to march with a step which would seem, in other situations, to be disordered and unregulated, but which is necessary, loyal, and legitimate in its own terms.[49]

The peculiar princely gait is a sideways movement; the prince must know how to dodge and evade, to play the fox and the lion, the serpent and the dove. He must be willing to bend the strict rules of justice to accommodate prudence for "the utility of the public, which is to say, of the state and of the prince, which are all conjoined." The prince should mix the useful with the honest, as Lipsius had said, never actually turning his back on honesty, but approaching it obliquely, employing artifice and ruse, like mothers or doctors deceiving children or patients for their own good.

When Charron deals with justice directly, as the second virtue, he defines it as "rendering to each one that which belongs to him, *first of all to oneself and then to others*."[50] It is in this context that Charron discusses charity. He seizes eagerly on the admonition to "love thy neighbor as thyself" as evidence that even in Scripture we are taught to love ourselves first of all, and model all our other loves on this. Thus, though he does not speak explicitly of the *amour-propre* that was shortly to become so central in French moral discourse, Charron offers what must have seemed to some of his contemporaries a blasphemous reading of *la charité*. It is rooted first of all in love of self, and proceeds thence outward to love of others; the love of God, which was for Augustinians identical with charity, is hardly mentioned. Justice is equated with this love, and also with the sovereignty of reason over the passions in the soul. Montaigne's distinction between two kinds of justice, the one "natural and universal," the other "a special national justice constrained to the need of our governments," is taken up by Charron, who is concerned primarily with the second sort.[51] He shows how this justice, in order to be effective, must necessarily be mixed with injustice and deceit.

In an age when absolutists were fusing Bodin's logic of sovereignty with older, more mystical notions of the king as touched with divinity,

---

[49] *De la sagesse*, Book III, ch. ii (II, 302-303). Compare his description of prudence as "a universal virtue, because it extends generally to all human things, not only in gross but in detail to everything; thus it is as infinite as individuals themselves." Book III, i (II, 283).
[50] *De la sagesse*, Book III, ch. v (II, 431-433); emphasis added.
[51] *Essays*, III, 1 "Of the Useful and the Honorable," p. 604.

Charron kept these strands deliberately separate in his own treatise. He repeated Bodin's discussion of sovereignty virtually without alteration, as the explanation for the central role of monarchical authority in human life, and as the justification for the obedience of the sage.[52] He also used the language of divine right, but for two quite different purposes. Such language was not for the edification of the sage himself, far too intelligent and critical to believe in such illusion, but for the people and the king. Charron wanted the sovereign to think of himself as the living image of God on earth, so that he might remember his duty to be virtuous and provide an excellent model for his people in his elevated role. Such beliefs are also central in the political psychology of obedience for ordinary people. Charron, like La Boétie, stressed the role of symbols and artifice in evoking the awed obedience of the vulgar, and in this context discusses the belief that kings possess a godlike authority. He presents men as difficult to tame and dominate, like savage beasts. If they are to live together peaceably, force and artifice must be effectively conjoined. They must be awed and frightened before they can be taught their duties. "And the appropriate means for doing this is a great authority, a brilliant and striking power, which blinds them with its splendor and gravity. . . . There is nothing grander in this world than authority, which is an image of God, a messenger from on high; it is sustained by two things, admiration and fear mixed together. . . . By this means the foolish are reduced, constrained, and guided; here is the weight, the necessity, and utility of authority and law in this world."[53]

Thus Charron brings off an adroit and impressive alliance of Bodin, Montaigne, and Lipsius in a political philosophy for the initiated. He is quite explicit about his audience: "This book is not for the common run of folk or the ordinary man, and if it were to be popularly received and accepted, it would have completely failed in its intentions."[54] Much of the power of the book must have come from the sense that it was written only for a few superior men, so that anyone who read it and accepted its view of the world could feel comfortably sure that he could count himself among them. It was, no doubt, peculiarly satisfying for Charron's readers to think of themselves as among the *esprits supérieurs* who could see beneath the masks worn by governors and kings; and peculiarly difficult to look critically at Charron's own

[52] *De la sagesse*, Book I, ch. li (I, 375-378).
[53] *De la sagesse*, Book II, ch. VIII (II, 191-194). Cf. Priézac's invocation of the stunning effect of majesty, discussed in Chapter Eight.
[54] From the Preface to the *Petit traicté*, where Charron defends his major treatise against charges that he offended common beliefs and undermined authority.

critical approach, since to do so might indicate that one was, after all, only a mediocre or a brutish man. It was a book for insiders who could think themselves elevated not only above the masses, but above the powerful men who run the world, by virtue of their own superior *sagesse*. Within this seductive framework Charron put forward a powerful justification for obedience that set the tone for French political philosophy for decades afterwards.

In Charron's politics, as in Bodin's, sovereignty—the unquestioned power to command in giving law—is the cement that holds society together. The other side of this is necessarily the obedience of all members of society subject to this power. Judged by the lofty standards of the sage, ordinary laws promulgated by human sovereigns are sadly deficient; but he can nonetheless obey serenely, because he recognizes that the laws and customs of his community retain ther credibility and perform their functions precisely because they are established and obeyed. The world has proceeded fairly smoothly for a long time, Charron reminds his readers, on the basis of unjust and deficient laws. Whoever wishes to make radical changes in these laws not only shows his own imperfect understanding of the world, but also becomes "an enemy of the public." Human nature "accommodates itself to everything in time, and having once taken its own bent, it is an act of hostility to try to redirect it."[55] Therefore the sage can acquiesce serenely, performing his formal duties to society, relieved of any nagging sense that something better could be done and that he might have some obligation to attempt to do it. This is one of the most potent and satisfying conservative philosophies ever put forward. It left its mark on French political theory into the eighteenth century and after, since critics of the Revolution argued, in effect, that its validity was vindicated in the very act of trying to disprove it.

The vision of the schizophrenic sage who finds the appropriate composition of his character in a strict separation of his internal and external life, who walks through the world with equanimity but as an alien, was a very attractive model for Charron's contemporaries. As we shall see, it was taken up eagerly by the *libertins*; and it has certain parallels in the Augustinian conception of the saint who lives in the world but is not truly of it. The withdrawal of creative energy from the world, the absorption in community with oneself, and the sense of ordinary life as alien folly, provided a refuge and a source of tranquillity for many Frenchmen in the seventeenth century, and delayed for several decades any renewed sense of robust civic involvement in in the world. Charron's sage was an excellent subject for an absolute

[55] *De la sagesse*, Book II, ch. viii (II, 207-213); see also Book I, xlvii.

monarch. He obeyed scrupulously and performed his civic duties punctiliously, but had no desire to try to make the world a better place, or to comment critically on the king's governance. He took for granted, with a patronizing approval of necessary mediocrity, that the prince would engage in devious practices and hoodwink his subjects. *Raison d'état* was perfectly acceptable to this sage, for it strengthened the protective shelter within which he bent his energies to cultivating his own reason, and exploring his own self.

6. The Erudite Libertines and the Double Arcana

The separation of public and private lives counseled by Montaigne and Charron came to fruition in the habits and teachings of a set of philosophers prominent in French life and letters in the first four decades of the seventeenth century, generally known as *libertins*. *Libertinage* was an all-purpose term in this era, used primarily by those who disapproved of heterodox opinions and styles of life. In a dictionary published in 1611, the term was linked with "epicureanism, sensuality, licentiousness, and dissoluteness."[56] In a world where orthodoxy was both rigid and detailed, there were many ways to be unorthodox. *Libertinage* was associated in the eyes of its opponents with atheism and deism, Machiavellism and the *politiques*, free thought and loose living. Some of those to whom the term was applied, particularly among noble Parisian youth around 1620, professed a dissoluteness of life, an obtrusive irreligion, and a radical cynicism that came to be associated for many contemporaries with being *libertin*. Thereafter, the reputation for debauchery surrounded even those free-thinkers who were austere in their morals. The *libertins* included "radical naturalists" such as Cyrano de Bergerac and Théophile de Viau, visionary, utopian, "restless, proud, and unsubmissive of spirit," who shared something of the Corneillian taste for *la gloire* and the aristocratic impatience at moderation.[57] These were the intellectual ancestors of men like Denis Veiras and Jean Meslier. At the other extreme, there were among the *libertins* men like Mersenne, circumspect Christians of regular habits and orthodox faith, who were free only in their approach to science and their belief that untrammeled questioning of the universe and experimentation would support, rather than call into question, the doctrines of Catholicism. In between were the *libertins*

[56] Cited by Renée Kogel, *Pierre Charron*, 143.
[57] J. S. Spink, *French Free-Thought*, has a good discussion of the various types of *libertinage*, and proposes the category "radical naturalists" (ch. 2). F. T. Perrens, *Les Libertins*, emphasizes the atheistic and socially nonconformist aspect of *libertinage*.

érudits, men such as Naudé, Gassendi, and La Mothe le Vayer, the intellectual ancestors of Bayle and Fontenelle.[58]

The erudite libertines were followers of Montaigne in many things: in their empiricism, their curiosity, their Epicurean ethics. They evinced a skeptical spirit similar to Montaigne's, although the *libertins* tended toward a more corrosive cynicism, a more self-conscious posture of Pyrrhonian doubt. They thought of themselves, along the lines suggested by Charron, as *esprits forts*—strong spirits, able to face the uncertainties and complexities of nature and the universe without taking refuge in the superstitions that comforted lesser men, the *esprits faibles*. They shared with their contemporary Descartes the notion that the individual reason can be radically purified of all accumulated knowledge based on custom and authority, then sharpened as an instrument to use in and against the world. But they were less certain than Descartes that such an instrument would prove reliable in discovering truth.

In his *Syntagma de studio liberali*, composed at the same time as Descartes's *Discours sur la méthode*, Gabriel Naudé outlines an attitude toward knowledge shared by the whole group of erudite libertines.[59] His first principle was "to persuade oneself that truth lies hidden at the bottom of a well, that it has never yet appeared to human eyes, and that those who vaunt themselves on possessing it are imposters." The second was "to understand that nothing in this world is stable," that all the arts, sciences, and kingdoms of the earth "dance in a perpetual round," so that the wise man admits nothing as definitive, but continually adjusts his own beliefs "with that supple imperturbability of spirit that knows itself to be the only stable point in the midst of development." Third, to know that all accounts or origins and traditions are infected with legends and lies; fourth, to recognize that all things tend to produce monstrosities, overstepping their natural limits, so that science is marred by "purulent excesses"; and finally, "to maintain an independent spirit," exempt from the constraints of passion and authority, borrowing from all masters and subjecting oneself to none.

This radical sense of individual independence in the world, and of thorough-going skepticism about all authority and science, coupled with a fascination for knowledge, was typical of Naudé's colleagues.

---

[58] The basic work is René Pintard, *La Libertinage érudit*; for a different view that must be considered, see Richard H. Popkin, *The History of Scepticism*, ch. 5. Antoine Adam, ed., *Les Libertins*, includes excerpts from the work of several of these men.

[59] Summarized by Pintard, *Libertinage érudit*, pp. 454-455. Naudé's method, more clearly than that of Descartes, shows the influence of Montaigne's "Apologie de Raimond Sebond," *Essays* II, 12.

Montaigne would no doubt have poked fun at their arrogant conviction that they were superior to ordinary folk in their style of life and understanding of the world. But he would have understood their desire to keep their beliefs and inquiries separate from their public roles. They regarded custom and political authority as necessary for the stability of society, and conformed outwardly to what they questioned in secret. They took their motto from Cremonini, and it could have served as well for Montaigne, La Boétie, or Charron: *intus ut libet, foris ut moris est*.[60] These prudent men had no desire for martyrdom; and whatever they may have thought about their own moral character, they were convinced that ordinary men were dangerous unless strictly controlled. They were sensible enough to recognize the need for their own obedience in order to *encourager les autres*. Against the Stoic belief in rationality, they stressed the strength of passions and the tendencies to brutality among men. In this they joined hands with the Augustinians in a curious alliance that was to have important ramifications later in the century.

Most of the *libertins* took seriously the Epicurean counsel to avoid the business of the world. They conformed to its demands as far as necessary, and found their true pleasures in the company of friends. Within this limited framework, they were inveterately social. Like the Jansenists, and many of their own successors in the late seventeenth and early eighteenth centuries, the erudite *libertins* formed alternative communities—academies, discussion groups, research societies in which they found the satisfactions of fraternal support and like-mindedness that made it easy for them to remain emotionally detached from the rest of the world.

A few of the *esprits forts*, particularly Naudé and La Mothe le Vayer, were also active politically, the one as polemicist and librarian for Richelieu and Mazarin, the other as publicist and tutor to princes. We will encounter these two again in their public roles, for each of them made important contributions to the developing theories of the public interest and *raison d'état* in France. There were obvious parallels between the reasoning associated with *raison d'état* and the approach to truth adopted by the *libertins*. The special morality of princes and their ministers, different from that of the sage, but equally inaccessible to ordinary minds, following its own special rules, had much in common with the morality of the sage derived from Charron's *Sagesse*. It is not, therefore, surprising that some of the *libertins* contributed to the literature of reason of state, not simply because it

---

[60] "Inwardly as though free, outwardly as though bound by custom." On this motto and the spirit behind it, consult Spink, *French Free-Thought*, ch. 1.

fit their own interests to strengthen the mystery of the monarch in the eyes of ordinary men (and therefore bolster obedience), but also because they were fascinated by, and peculiarly well placed to understand, the intricate reasoning about morality associated with reason of state.

François de La Mothe le Vayer was one of the most prominent of the erudite libertines. He was a member of the *académie putéane*, the gathering of book lovers in the library of De Thou that was a central focus for libertinage, and of the intimate *tétrade* that also included Gassendi, Diodati, and Naudé.[61] He was a prolific author, admired for his erudition, and courted by Richelieu as a publicist. Although he occasionally lent his pen to Richelieu's service, his better-known works defend the fruits of the philosophic life. Two of his *Dialogues faits à l'imitation des Anciens* deal with the theme of public versus private pursuits, and the comparative merits of each.[62] They offer a particularly explicit formulation of the dichotomy we have already encountered in Montaigne and Charron. The dialogues were composed with humor, skill, and polish, and include character development and a real exchange of views; they were popular and widely read. But the conclusion is obvious in each case from the beginning of the dialogue. These are exhortatory rather than exploratory pieces, written to persuade readers of the superiority of private life.

The "Dialogue sur le sujet de la vie privée" is a conversation between two friends, Philoponus—whose name bespeaks his commitments to the burdens of the world—and Hesychius, who speaks for the author, and wins the debate. Philoponus berates his friend for his retiring habits, asking why "neither honor, nor the consideration of utility," nor any other of the goods discovered "in the offices and diverse employments of civil life," can dislodge his friend from his "reclusive sloth." To Philoponus such "a particularistic manner of living" hardly counts as living at all. "Your house serves you as a tomb," he says, "and I can hardly pass it without wanting to put up a marker inscribed 'Here lies poor Hesychius.' "[63] Hesychius, however, asserts that true virtue and happiness can only be found in the contemplative life, and that "those puissant demons of human life" called

---

[61] All discussions of the *libertins* devote a good deal of attention to Le Vayer; see particularly Pintard, *Libertinage érudit*, pp. 127-147, 296-303, 505-541; and Wade, *Intellectual Origins*, pp. 179-187.

[62] These nine dialogues were published in two installments in 1630-1631, under the pseudonym Oratius Tubero. I have used the 1716 edition in two volumes. The *Dialogues* originally appeared with a false place and date (1606) of publication. According to Popkin, *History of Scepticism*, p. 92, this was done "for peculiar reasons of pedantic perverseness."

[63] *Dialogues*, I, 175-182.

forth by Philoponus—"honesty, utility, and pleasure"—are really on his side. Philoponus assumes that virtue can only be displayed in action; Hesychius points out that since our rational faculties are what is most distinctive about our species, it follows that our highest pleasures and accomplishments must be associated with these. Growing bolder, he claims that the man who practices philosophy is like a god, invulnerable to fortune, self-sufficient, entirely contained within himself. "Here, Philoponus," he says, "you have a summary of the good and the utility that spring from a covered and individual life such as our own."[64]

The notion of a "covered and individual life" is central to this conception of philosophy and human good. Philoponus charges his friend with behaving inhumanly because he retires from society into his cave, like a sullen toad. Hesychius replies that he had felt and even tasted the attractions of the worldly life, but came to see the greater joys of solitude; in his view, those men who succumb to ambition demonstrate their own radical insufficiency, their inability to be at home with themselves. Because those who lack the self-sufficiency of the philosopher cannot understand it, they assume that philosophers are subverting or criticizing the world; to avoid such animosity, says Hesychius, great men "cover and hide themselves as much as possible," like animals who blot out their tracks to escape attention. Philosophers claim they are incapable of action, and then the worldly types are content to leave them to their second-rate pursuits, as silly dreamers unfit for the real world. In fact, claims Hesychius, philosophers are men of the highest gifts who could do the public business brilliantly, but have learned that it is not worth doing. Such superior beings are ill-fitted for citizenship of an ordinary republic, as Aristotle had said. They are citizens of the universe, finding perfect solitude even in great cities, taking marvelous journeys of the intellect in company with bookish companions alive or dead. Only they enjoy true freedom. Philoponus, a bit bemused by all these revelations, is forced in the end to admit that Aristotle was right to call the solitary man a beast or a god, since Hesychius' bestial metaphors and godlike visions are alien to his world.[65]

A second dialogue, "Traictant de la politique sceptiquement," opens as its counterpart had closed, on an Aristotelian note. Whereas the earlier dialogue was about action and contemplation, this one is about the relations between knowledge and politics. Telamon, who is gen-

[64] *Dialogues*, I, 208-209; note that Hesychius speaks of a life such as "*our* own," not "*my* own," which underscores the intimate social nature of the philosophic life.
[65] *Dialogues*, I, 215-216, 238-239.

erally recognized as Le Vayer's friend Naudé, gives an enthusiastic paean to politics, and more particularly to political philosophy. Since man is the most political of animals, we can infer that his highest and most distinctive knowledge is about politics, so that the science of politics becomes the crowning science. Naudé himself admired political philosophy; he composed a compendium of the teachings of the major writers on politics from Plato to his own time, and made his own contribution to the craft with his *Considérations politiques sur les coups d'estat*.[66] But in this skeptical dialogue, Le Vayer undertakes to demonstrate that the entire science of politics is a mass of confusions and contradictions. "All these interests of state and these political ditties are vain things to anyone who knows more solid things," claims his mouthpiece, Orontes. Anyone who sees clearly "of what type, and how weak, are the springs that move the great machines of states" will "doubtless be touched with pity rather than envy for those whom he sees engaged in such a miserable business, unless the splendor and pomp that accompanies them obscures his judgment."[67] Those great men who have written about politics, like Plato, have done so in a playful mood, and quite as many worthy men have spurned the "base and frivolous occupations of government," says Orontes, as have become involved in it. He cites as his examples Ulysses, "the first of all the Statists," who chose to be reborn as a private man, and Socrates, whose demon continually warned him against political participation.

The conception of politics as a miserable pursuit, and of political philosophy as at best the utopian pastime of great minds, was common to a number of French theorists. Le Vayer's inventive debunking of the celebrated *arcana imperii* of government, in which he demonstrates that every political maxim has its countermaxim, that every supposed truth in political science is contradicted by another put forward with equal certainty by another advocate, was also echoed by such theorists, and especially by Rousseau in his condemnation of this "vast and useless science." Le Vayer also broached a theme dear to Rousseau when he attributed most evils suffered by our species, including "wars, tyrannies, plagues, and famines," to our much-vaunted political inven-

[66] Naudé's compendium, one of the first textbooks in the study of political science, was entitled *La Bibliographie politique contenant les livres & la méthode necessaires à estudier la politique*. It was composed in Latin, and published in a French translation in 1642. His better-known *Considérations politiques* was published in 1639. Naudé's political ideas will be discussed in connection with *raison d'état*, in Chapter Five.

[67] *Dialogues*, II, 243-246; the metaphor of the springs that move the machine of state was used to very different effect in Le Vayer's own treatise composed for the instruction of the dauphin, discussed in Chapter Five.

tiveness. All our diverse polities have simply provided so many different ways "to enchain our beautiful natural liberty, whose loss cannot be recompensed in any way."[68]

At the conclusion of the dialogue, Telamon/Naudé is won over completely by his friend. The two join in celebrating the joys of the contemplative life, pledging to "try to be among that small number of the elect," keeping their happiness hidden, imitating those animals who seek food and tranquillity *à couvert*, out of sight.[69] This was the course of action followed by many of the erudite libertines as the world swirled on about them. But neither Naudé nor Le Vayer held to it. As Pintard puts it: "The time was coming, was at hand, when Le Vayer would betray Orontes; he was to accept those obligations from which his double had recoiled; he was to alienate the precious repose of which he had boasted in the *Dialogues*." Betrayal is one way to look at it; one might also suppose that Le Vayer was not immune to the patriotic sentiments expressed by some of his contemporaries.[70] In any case, it is clear that in the world of Richelieu even an Orontes could be seduced into action, for all his harsh mockery of *la science politique*. High politics and reason of state exerted a special fascination in this regime. The arcane hidden rituals of the philosophic life were based in part on a disdain for the parallel *arcana* of the politician. But a devotion to the one sometimes led, as in Le Vayer's case, to a desire to explore the other also. The two *arcana* complemented one another nicely, just as the stability promised by the absolutist monarchy fit well with the privatistic independence cherished by the sage.

[68] *Dialogues*, II, 257-259. [69] *Dialogues*, II, 359-360.
[70] Pintard, *Libertinage érudit*, 541; Popkin, *History of Scepticism*, ch. 5, takes issue with Pintard's stress on the reclusive nature of the *libertins*, and draws attention to the links that bound several of them to the court of Louis XIII.

CHAPTER FIVE

Public Utility Preferred to Private: Mercantilism and *Raison d'Etat*

1. THE PASSIONS AND THE INTERESTS

In moral philosophy, the management of the passions has often been a primary concern. It is also common to distinguish, as Charron does in his *Sagesse*, between two kinds of management of passion, one appropriate to superior men capable of philosophy, the other to more mediocre folk. Charron's first model, designed for sages, perpetuates an ideal familiar since antiquity: the disciplining of the passions by reason. This discipline is identified with true virtue, achieved through wisdom, exemplified in the good ordering of the soul. The benefits of such discipline are felt directly by the virtuous individual: good order provides internal harmony and outward tranquillity, the goods deemed worth striving for in this philosophy. This vision of the ordered individual soul appealed to philosophers, or would-be philosophers, who read Charron's treatise and others in this same tradition in the early seventeenth century. The alternative model, intended for the management of the passions of ordinary men, had also been familiar since antiquity; but in developing this model, moral philosophers of Charron's era and of the later seventeenth century suggested themes that became increasingly important for modern morality, as the image of the self-disciplined sage appeared less and less pertinent. Like the philosophers of classical virtue, Charron took for granted that ordinary men, whether marked by brutish unconcern or driven by violent passions, are incapable of self-control. They possess inherently disordered souls that must be controlled by order imposed from outside themselves. From the lofty perspective of the sage, Charron disdained men motivated to act nobly, not out of love of virtue, but from a desire to be praised and thought well of by others. Yet despite his disdain, he recognized the useful part such motivations played in channeling the potentially dangerous passions of ordinary human beings into beneficent activity.

The notion that pride and ambition could be channeled into noble and heroic deeds was hardly novel. What was novel in seventeenth-century moral theory was the general fascination with the idea that diametrically different motivations, "vicious" as well as "virtuous," could lead men to engage in socially useful behavior, and the awareness of the rich possibilities for social policy and political control that followed from this. Such ideas had been suggested by Renaissance philosophers, and antecedents can be found long before that; but in the seventeenth century they were moved from the periphery to the heart of ethical discourse. The recognition that selfish passion provides a pure motive energy that can be turned to good as well as to evil purposes, that not only ambition (always a vice easy to excuse and justify), but lowly avarice could be put to good use, inspired several significant developments in moral argument. In *The Passions and the Interests*, Albert Hirschman discusses these developments in terms of the "harnessing" of the passions. Hirschman argues that the notion of harnessing replaced an earlier view that called simply for repressing passions, damping them down and preventing them from finding outlets, and preceded a later notion of countervailing passions, in which avarice was used to counteract ambition.[1]

The image of "harnessing" unruly passions had been familiar since Plato's description of the soul composed of a charioteer and two horses in the *Phaedrus*. Disordered souls of the seventeenth century were not expected to harness themselves, however. Their passions were channeled by their situation, by some outside intelligence manipulating their choices, or by the attractiveness or repulsiveness of objects of desire. Rather than striving consciously and autonomously for virtue, as does the sage, the ordinary man in moral philosophy of the seventeenth century is led to act well despite himself. All he provides is the motive energy of passion. The benefits of the channeling of his energy do not accrue directly to him, as does the virtue of the sage; instead, the channeling leads to benefits for the whole society, as disruptive passions are harnessed for the advantage of the community.

The central question in all this, of course, is precisely how the useful channeling occurs. How much deliberate structuring must occur by political manipulation, and how much is it possible to count on other factors to direct selfish choices to generally advantageous goals? The need for artificial provision of political structure—laws, rewards, and punishments—to direct choices that ensure the consonance of selfish

---

[1] Hirschman, *The Passions and the Interests*, pp. 14-20. The term "harnessing" was not commonly used with reference to the passions in seventeenth-century French moral discourse, but Hirschman's term nicely conveys the general sense of passionate energy channeled toward useful ends that is central to this discourse. The notion of "countervailing" passions and powers is mentioned, as we have seen, in the more pluralistic passages of Commynes' *Mémoires* and in the fifth chapter of Bodin's fourth *Livre de la République*.

action with the good of society was emphasized by some theorists, in arguments akin to that of Hobbes. Other theorists stressed the natural consonance of selfish purposes and social good, a consonance that can be counted on because things have been providentially arranged so that the successful pursuit of my own happiness requires me to satisfy the needs of others in human commerce. The two positions were not very far apart on the larger spectrum of political philosophy. No one denied the need for some artificial framework of coercion and reward to help out the divine intelligence; the position of pure anarchism, in other words, was not defended. On the other hand, what set these arguments apart from repressive authoritarianism was the delighted recognition that human beings working within some political framework could cooperate in building a more commodious life for themselves, instead of having continually to be supervised in every detail of their lives by an all-seeing earthly father.

One of the durable tensions in this discussion sprang from the recognition that princes and governors charged with imposing political structure on other men, and thereby harnessing passions and channeling choices, are themselves only mortals who possess passions of their own. What is to guarantee that *their* passions will be channeled in socially useful directions—that is, that they will use their power to benefit instead of harm society? The vocabulary of interest was developed in connection with this particular concern, and proved an appropriate vehicle for discussions of social utility and selfish desire. The whole set of developments in moral and political philosophy that had to do with channeling human energy in socially advantageous ways rested on successive refinements in this concept, as seventeenth-century moral argument moved from the undifferentiated notion of "passion" to the more focused notion of human "interest."

The concept of interest, as Hirschman has shown, occupies a middle position between reason and passion, indicating a particular attitude toward the pursuit of selfish goals.[2] Differing from the absurd blindness of pure passion on the one hand, and the clear calmness of pure reason on the other, the interested pursuit of personal happiness involves predictability and calculation, discipline and prudence, as well as aspiration and desire. Interest refers to concrete objectives as well as to the sentiment of selfish identification with those objectives; it nicely bridges the impersonal and the private spheres. It is possible by argument to convince someone where his "true interests" lie, whereas it is more difficult to provide someone with information about his "true

---

[2] Hirschman's discussion of this topic, pp. 31-54, is particularly illuminating.

passions," since the possessor of the passions has privileged access to them (or was assumed to have such access before the development of psychotherapy). Yet the appeal to interest, unlike the appeal to "abstract reason," includes attention to selfish profit, that is, to satisfaction of desire and passion. Interest is thus more accessible to argument and direction than passion itself, and yet does not depend on the ability to consider matters "objectively," without reference to one's own stake in them. Because of this uniquely "middling" quality, the advent of interest was greeted with optimism. It offered hope for the moderation of selfishness and the resolution of conflict, while not requiring ordinary men to become angels, or even philosophers.

At the outset, however, the notion of interest had little or nothing to do with ordinary men. It was a term initially confined to discourse about states.[3] The concept had been developed in the sixteenth century under Machiavelli's influence to denominate a cluster of purposes of princes and their ministers. It was a deliberately "realistic" concept, designed to draw attention to actual objectives and motives rather than to the goals prescribed to princes by moral philosophers. In political terms, this concept was distinct from royal caprice or tyrannical whimsy on the one hand, and abstract self-abnegating concern for the public welfare on the other. The most common formulations were "the interests of the prince" and the "interests of the state," taken as synonymous, and used to denote national power and glory. These were understood as fairly tangible objectives: territorial defense and aggrandizement, military vigor, social stability, royal splendor, dynastic health, and general prosperity.

From the late sixteenth century onwards, *les intérêts publiques* was used as a synonym for princely and state interests, alongside older terms such as *le salut public* and other phrases for the ancient *bonum publicum*. In some contexts, "public interests" were interchangeable with "public welfare"; but for many publicists, the new term was more concrete and meaningful in its referents than the older ones. Appeals to a vague "public good" were held to be threadbare and worthless. Montaigne's notion that such appeals always cloak selfish purposes was widely accepted. "The notion of *le bien public*," remarked Jean Sirmond, a member of Richelieu's entourage, "is a mask so old and so frequently employed that it is wonderful that anyone is able to use it any longer."[4] To such men, the idea of "public interests" appeared

---

[3] J.A.W. Gunn, *Politics and the Public Interest in the Seventeenth Century*, provides much useful information about the development of this term in English politics; there is nothing comparable for France.

[4] *Advis du François fidelle aux Malcontens*, quoted by Sutcliffe, *Guez de Balzac et son temps*, p. 165.

Public Utility and Private—155

solider and more reliable. Since these interests were held to be identical with the interests of the prince himself and of his state, it was reasonable to expect that the prince would pursue them automatically without straining for virtue or disguising his true purposes.

The classic early formulation of the concept of "interest of state" in French was in the duc de Rohan's famous and influential treatise *De l'interest des princes et des Estats de la Chrestienté* (1638). Rohan asserted that

> princes rule people, and interest rules princes. An understanding of this interest is as influential over princes' actions as the latter are over the people. The prince may be deceived and his council may be corrupt, but interest alone is forever sure. According to [whether] it is well or badly understood, it preserves or ruins states. And since it always has gain or at least preservation as its objective, it must change with the times in order to be successful.[5]

The sense of *necessity* that interest will prevail conveyed by this passage is one key to understanding why the concept proved so attractive. It can be taken for granted that princes will be moved by what they think will conduce to their "gain or at least preservation," that they will be ruled by their perceptions of where their interests lie. It is possible for them to misunderstand their interests, to be deceived about their situations; in such cases, they will still act on what they understand their interests to be; and yet their "true" interests will retain some objective status apart from the princes' understanding of them.

However, the connection between these "interests" of princes, defined as a set of realistic goals for state policy consonant with the narrow selfish interests of the prince, and the lowly pursuit of happiness by ordinary subjects, was not at all self-evident. The old threadbare notions of the "public good" carried connotations of justice and benevolence in governance that were absent from the concept of *les intérêts publiques*. It was easy to say, and often said, that in the long run prince and people alike profited from general prosperity; that a prince had no interest in ruling over a population of miserable slaves; that national glory and military vigor depended on a flourishing popu-

---

[5] This translation is that of W. F. Church, *Richelieu and Reason of State*, p. 352; a more familiar rendering of the maxim coined by Rohan here is "Interest never lies." On the widespread influence of Rohan's work, see J.A.W. Gunn, "'Interest will not lie': A Seventeenth-Century Political Maxim"; Friedrich Meinecke's classic study of *Machiavellism: the Doctrine of Raison d'Etat and its Place in Modern History*, ch. 6; and J.H.M. Salmon, "Rohan and Interest of State," in *Staatsräson*, edited by Schnur, pp. 121-140.

lation; that taxes were easier to collect, and allegiance more likely to be forthcoming with alacrity, from a fat and happy people than from grumbling paupers. But exactly when and how the pursuit of individual goals by millions of subjects was in consonance with the pursuit of *les intérêts publiques*, and when and how the two conflicted, was open to dispute. This was, in fact, an aspect of that same basic dispute in seventeenth and eighteenth-century French social and political philosophy that we have already come upon from a different direction. How much manipulation, and what kinds, were necessary to ensure the dovetailing of public and private utility?

It was uncommon to speak of private or individual *interest*, as such, in France before 1640 or so, when it occurred first in connection with political polemics and theological disputes. But the concepts of public and private utility have been familiar since medieval times, and thus the vocabulary for carrying on the dispute was readily available. The maxim *utilitas publica prefertur utilitati privatae*—that public utility should be preferred to private—had been voiced by innumerable writers from Tacitus to Saint Thomas.[6] Sometimes the phrase was a vague admonition to look out for the general welfare; in other instances it came close to a full-blown formulation of what was later known as *raison d'état*.[7] In any case, it was generally accepted long before the seventeenth century that public utility—whether as the utility of the largest number of individuals, or as the good of some entity larger than the sum of individuals—took precedence over private utility when the two were in direct conflict. The seventeenth century uncovered a number of new complexities within such issues. When were direct conflicts between public and private utility likely to occur, and how, if at all, could they be avoided? What understanding of public and private utility increases the chances that the two will work together harmoniously? How can those responsible for public utility be led to interpret it so that private utility is not forgotten? And how might ordinary selfish subjects be made to accept the necessity of submitting to public utility in some instances of conflict, and in general to find their own private utility engaged by, and involved in, the interests of the society larger than themselves?

Such questions will occupy us throughout this study. In this chapter, we will explore the answers provided by two early seventeenth-century systems of thought: mercantilism and reason of state. Political writers identified with the origins of mercantilist thought, such as Antoine de Montchrétien, stressed the consonance of public and pri-

---

[6] Walter Ullmann, *The Individual and the Society in the Middle Ages*, p. 36.
[7] Gaines Post, *Studies in Medieval Legal Thought*, chs. 1 and 5.

vate utility, as well as the necessity for political intervention to ensure that this consonance would be realized. Reason of state theorists, on the other hand, tended to emphasize the necessary sacrifice of individual utility to the demands of the public interests.

Mercantilist treatises were composed for policy makers, to convince them of the advantage to be expected from certain kinds of policies. They were not intended primarily for general consumption by educated readers. However, mercantilism, unlike reason of state, needed more from ordinary Frenchmen than simple obedience and punctual performance of a few minimal duties. Mercantilism required the stimulation and harnessing of the economic energies of subjects, and their patriotic identification with the power and glory of their country. This meant that Frenchmen were encouraged by mercantilist argument (how effectively we do not really know) to think of themselves as part of a nation, and consider the profit or glory won by any section of the French state as a cause of rejoicing, and ultimately as a contribution to their own well-being.

Those tracts and treatises in which the ideas associated with *raison d'état* are set forth fall into two groups: those written primarily for the initiated, for policy makers themselves, such as Richelieu's *Testament* and Gabriel Naudé's *Considerations politiques sur les coups d'Estat*; and those intended as propaganda for the monarchy, such as Daniel de Priézac's adulatory essay "De la majesté." Both types of treatises emphasize the arcane aspects of governance, the need for a special type of "reason" and skill for rulership. Books composed for insiders develop the concept of prudence appropriate to political action, and work out its implications in a variety of situations. Propaganda pieces invoke the mystery and impenetrability of governance, to maximize awe-struck obedience to the king. In both types, what initially appears unjustifiable is boldly justified by associating it with necessity, with divinity, and with the interests of the state.

Both mercantilist and reason-of-state arguments were part of the concurrent development of individualism and absolutist thought during this period. They said little about constitutionalist aspects of politics, and almost nothing about any limitations on the power of the prince. Both arguments were premised on "absolute" power held by the monarchy, and had to do with the way that power was used, the ends to which it would be directed, and the importance of the concurrence of ordinary subjects in absolutist rule. Both had also to do with the motivations of individuals concerned to maximize their own utility and better their own situations, whether they were private persons, ministers, or princes.

2. Mercantilism and the Socialization of Avarice

The concept of mercantilism, more than most "isms," is closely connected with a few names, especially those of Eli Heckscher, author of the magisterial treatise that is the core reference in any discussion of the term, and Jean-Baptiste Colbert, preeminent practitioner of mercantilist policy. Some scholars question whether mercantilism ever existed as a coherent system of ideas except in Heckscher's fertile brain. A. V. Judges contends that the whole concept was "an affair of archaeological reconstruction" foisted on seventeenth-century statesmen by eighteenth-century economists, and endowed with artificial structure by nineteenth-century historians.[8] Nonetheless, it seems plausible to continue to use the term, as Heckscher himself used it, to denote a cluster of ideas and practices that characterized political economy in the seventeenth century, particularly in France, and gradually gave birth to its apparent opposite, the ideals of laissez-faire. As in most such instances, the "opposite" doctrine turns out to have more in common with the parent system than first meets the eye.

Mercantilism was associated with, and may even be understood to include, those concepts of rationalization and consolidation that we have identified as parts of the program of the absolutist regime in France. The breaking down of residual diversities of feudalism—the plethora of tolls, taxes, and jurisdictions that hampered the development of trade and industry—was dictated by the mercantilist desire to increase the national wealth. "State building," that is, the strengthening and centralizing of the administrative structure, was necessary not only for effective political control, but also for the encouragement and integration of economic activity throughout the realm. The glory of France, the wealth of her people, and the strength of the state were all understood as bound up with one another in this political economy.[9] For our purposes, the question of how the prosperity and power of the nation were thought to be connected with efforts by individual subjects to maximize their private happiness is the crucial one.

Mercantilist theorists assumed an "identity of interests between the monarch and his subjects," an essential congruence of economic pur-

---

[8] A. V. Judges, "The Idea of a Mercantile State," in D. C. Coleman, ed., *Revisions in Mercantilism*, p. 35; see also Coleman's own essay on "Eli Heckscher and the Idea of Mercantilism" reprinted in the same volume.

[9] According to Coleman, "Eli Heckscher . . . ," p. 95, the concept of mercantilism as state building is associated primarily with Gustav Schmoller. Jacob Viner discusses the congruence of the several goals of mercantilists in "Power *versus* Plenty as Objectives of Foreign Policy . . ." in Coleman, *Revisions in Mercantilism*, pp. 61-91.

poses.[10] The prosperity of subjects was the basis for the wealth of kings, understood in the narrow sense of money available from taxation of all sorts; more generally, the wealth of the society contributed to the power and prestige of the monarchy. In this insight, mercantilists and their successors who advocated laissez-faire agreed. The economic interests of prince and people were basically the same, not at odds with one another. Both kinds of theorists also asserted the desirability of rationalizing the taxation system, to make it more efficient, more productive, and less burdensome for the people. Aware that the wealth of the prince depended on vigorous activity by the people in all branches of the economy, mercantilist writers were led to investigate the motives that draw people out of sloth and custom, and encourage inventiveness and productivity. They stressed the social utility of ambition, and explored the uncharted territory of avarice as a source of social good. In their musings on this subject, mercantilists offered counsels strikingly similar to those given later in the century by the pioneers of laissez-faire in France. Both types of theorists advocated liberty, rationality, and the stimulation of economic energies.[11] Both believed in a natural economic order underlying the economic order of all states.

The major difference between mercantilists and their successors was that mercantilists believed that vigilant direction by political authority was needed to ensure that the natural economic order would be exploited for the benefit of the state, whereas laissez-faire theorists rejected this idea.[12] Mercantilists assumed that unhampered pursuit of private utility would not automatically lead to economic benefits for the whole society. Governments were needed to shelter and protect industry, and to encourage internal trade. Theorists who advocated laissez-faire at the end of the seventeenth century decided that government direction and intervention hampered rather than facilitated economic activity. Such tutelage, they argued, interfered with the smooth workings of the natural economic order established by divine providence. Mercantilists were enthusiastic advocates of absolutist monarchy, since they saw the necessity for strong government if the kind

[10] Martin Wolfe, "French Views on Wealth and Taxes from the Middle Ages to the Old Régime," in Coleman, *Revisions in Mercantilism*, p. 196.

[11] Eli Heckscher, *Mercantilism*, volume II, part v, ch. 1, argues persuasively that the world views of mercantilists and laissez-faire theorists were very much the same on these dimensions. In his shorter study of "Mercantilism," reprinted in Coleman, *Revisions of Mercantilism*, p. 32, he asserts that "mercantilist authors and statesmen" including Colbert "actually harped upon 'freedom,' especially 'freedom of trade.'"

[12] This comparison is pursued in greater detail in Chapter Thirteen; Wolfe, "French Views on Wealth and Taxes," pp. 204-209, has a succinct discussion.

of direction they envisioned was to be provided in the economy. The early French theorists of laissez-faire were too circumspect to attack absolutism head-on; but their ideas arose amidst a general climate of dissatisfaction with absolutist politics; and the view that governmental power should be used sparingly in the economic realm amounted to criticism of absolutism itself.

A second important difference between mercantilism and laissez-faire was that the former system of ideas entailed a narrow and sometimes xenophobic identification with the national state. The focus of mercantilist efforts was the aggrandizement of *national* power and prosperity, understood as necessarily opposed to the power and prosperity of other nations. For French mercantilists, trade among nations was a zero-sum activity. Internal trade was thought advantageous to all parties; but trade with other countries meant loss of sustenance and strength for the nation itself, unless France's stock of specie was enriched by such transactions. The intense crown-centered patriotism of the early seventeenth century, which we have already noticed in other contexts, expressed itself in economic thought, as well. Not until the eighteenth century was the cosmopolitan spirit of world order revived, in connection with a different system of ideas. For laissez-faire theorists, the whole world economy was interconnected, and prosperity for every land would be increased by the unhampered flow of commercial enterprise across all kinds of boundaries.

The roots of mercantilist theory in France go back into the fifteenth century, at least; but only at the end of the sixteenth century were systematic ideas about political economy formulated. Jean Bodin was among those who reflected on this subject; he exemplifies the tension between the old medieval sense of the natural unity of Christendom, and the more novel desire to strengthen the realm of France itself. In his *Réponse au paradoxe de monsieur de Malestroit*, Bodin reproved those who thought France should attempt to achieve economic autarchy, men who thought the country so well-endowed that it had no need of foreigners. Bodin pointed out that France gained greatly by international trade in a variety of commodities, and asserted that the duties of friendship required men to "traffic, sell, . . . exchange" with others.[13] "God in His admirable prudence has ordered these things

[13] *La Réponse de Jean Bodin à M. de Malestroit*, edited by Henri Hauser, p. 34. The political importance of cultivating the economy, and of foreign trade, is also insisted on in Guillaume de La Perrière's *Miroir politique*, pp. 114-124. Wealth, agriculture, mechanical arts are essential to the polity, says La Perrière; and "communication with pilgrims, aliens, and strangers is often quite useful to the republic because of the merchandise they bring." Since "nature has not wanted to convey all her goods in a single place, but rather parcels them out in

well," contends Bodin. "For He has distributed His bounty in such a fashion that there is no country in the world so plentiful that it does not lack many things." In Bodin's eyes, God chose to do this to bind all peoples "together in His republic of friendship" and mitigate hostilities, "by ensuring that they have business with one another." These same sentiments can be found in other writings of this same period, and a few decades later in Sully's *Economies royales*.[14] They are strikingly similar to the assumptions expressed in the treatises written by early laissez-faire theorists a century later.

For Bodin or Sully, such internationalist sentiment coexisted with advocacy of measures to ensure French economic health, with no sense of incompatibility between these views. Both proposed strict taxes on exports of raw materials and on imports of finished goods, to encourage local manufacture and bring revenue to the crown. In his *Six livres de la république*, Bodin connects such ideas with the theory of sovereignty, and voices his disapproval of luxury because it drains off national resources to exotic lands.[15] In the more systematic mercantilist writings of one of Sully's contemporaries, Barthélemy de Laffemas, controller-general of commerce for Henry IV, there is explicit recognition that putting the French economy first means that the interests of foreigners cannot be equally regarded. Internationalist sentiment is absent from Laffemas' writings, and the focus is on measures that will strengthen the economy of France at the expense of other economies. Laffemas touched on most of the points important to mercantilism: the undesirability of allowing gold and silver to flow out of the country, the disapproval of imported luxuries, the emphasis on keeping raw materials at home for French manufacturers, the suggestions for putting the poor to work and reducing vagrancy and laziness, the importance of controlling and encouraging internal trade, and the general necessity of ensuring that foreigners could no longer "ravage France of her treasures."[16]

In Antoine de Montchrétien's *Traicté de l'oeconomie politique*, the classic mercantilist tract, these same ideas are expressed more systematically, and the dislike of foreigners who profit from French pros-

---

different climes," even old enemies, such as France and England, find profit in exchanging wine and cloth.

[14] Rothkrug, *Opposition to Louis XIV*, ch. 2; on the *Economies royales*, see David Buisseret, *Sully and the Growth of Centralized Government in France*, ch. 9.

[15] See particularly Book VI, ch. 2.

[16] Charles Woolsey Cole has a good discussion of Laffemas' system in *French Mercantilist Doctrines before Colbert*, ch. 2; see also G.R.R. Treasure, *Cardinal Richelieu and the Development of Absolutism*, ch. 15.

perity approaches xenophobia. Montchrétien also included an element in his system that had not been prominent in earlier mercantilist writings: an explicit recognition of the social utility of avarice. We have seen how the value of ambition and emulation as spurs to socially useful behavior was recognized by several moralists in France; the notion that avarice might also have some benefit was novel. It was suggested in the concluding lines of Montaigne's essay, "Of the inconsistency of our actions" (II, 1), and developed more fully in an essay published by Antoine Hotman, the brother of François Hotman of the *Francogallia*, in 1598. The title of the essay—"Deux paradoxes de l'amitié et d'avarice"—indicates Hotman's awareness that the views put forward were paradoxical.[17] No doubt he deliberately set out to shock his readers by arguing an apparently perverse position. But before long similar ideas were expressed in a straightforward fashion by serious moralists.

Hotman asserts that insofar as friendship is a passionate attachment, it is incompatible with virtue, which requires the control and restraint of passion; insofar as it is an exclusive attachment that can be shared only with a few intimates, it interferes with civic duties and constitutes a kind of treason. He argues from a Stoic perspective that we should be aware of our brotherhood with all men, and not display special affection for a few; and that we should not confuse the love of others with the duty to love God, since love of God stems from acknowledgment of His perfect goodness, which cannot be possessed by human beings. This paradox was novel enough, given the assumptions generally made in ethical literature at this time. But it pales before the paradox of avarice.

If anything had been taken for granted in the moral code of Christian Europe (as opposed to its habits and conventions), it was that wealth was a heavy and ambiguous blessing, an obstacle to all virtue except generosity. The desire for wealth in its own right was assumed to be the very root of evil. But Hotman argued boldly, like a Machiavelli in economics, that "it is best to be as rich as one can," and that "whoever rejects the riches that bring with them the commodious things of life is unnatural [*desnaturé*] and does not know what it is to live." Although formal ethics condemn the pursuit of wealth, said Hotman, "the laws themselves invite men to do good by proposing riches as a reward and recompense, and deter them from evil by the threat of loss of their wealth." Hotman asserts that amassing riches is a socially desirable act; the wealthy provide employment for many other men, and establish useful institutions.[18]

[17] This essay is included in the *Opuscules françoises des Hotmans* (1616), pp. 113-183.
[18] *Opuscules françoises*, pp. 158-169. Hotman notes that men blame avarice

These two paradoxes in Hotman's essay are connected by the observation that since men have no duty to love one another as friends, and are not warranted in devoting themselves to a few neighbors at the expense of all the rest of the species, virtue must be defined in terms of actions that benefit society as a whole. This justifies acquiring substantial wealth and using it for the diffuse enrichment of society without reference to personal relationships. Since his essay attracted little notice, at the time it was published or afterwards, we must be cautious about taking these arguments as the dawning of a new era.[19] But the argument itself, even if intended as a set-piece of Renaissance rhetoric to amuse and shock, is unusual, to say the least. And in the next few decades an increasing number of Frenchmen began to take utility seriously as a major component in social ethics, and defend the uses of avarice.

3. MONTCHRÉTIEN'S POLITICAL ECONOMY

Antoine de Montchrétien, a well-known dramatist of the early seventeenth century who occasionally ventured into economics, was one of this number. In his influential *Traicté de l'economie politique*, the hope for gain is presented as a fundamental aspect of human psychology, with great social utility. Montchrétien, like Charron, draws a distinction between nobler and commoner sorts of men, and counsels different strategies for inducing good behavior in each sort. But the lofty sage is not one of his concerns. Using the example of competing troupes of comedians in a small town, Montchrétien describes ambition as "a powerful spur to doing well," and generalizes from this to note the utility of the desire for honor and glory as a way to draw talented individuals out of the masses and encourage them to develop and display productive skills.[20] For ordinary individuals, the hope for gain and private profit, asserts Montchrétien, can have the same effect. The passage in which he first broaches this observation begins with a para-

---

in general, but honor and envy specific instances of successful avarice. "Nature herself invites us to seek riches," he asserts; "for she gives us so many and such powerful emotions to acquire wealth." Such arguments were unusual, but not unprecedented. Quentin Skinner, *Foundations*, I, 42-74, notes several defenses of the public utility of wealth in the Italian republican tradition.

[19] Cf. Rothkrug, *Opposition to Louis XIV*, p. 308.
[20] Montchrétien, *Traicté de l'oeconomie politique* (1615), edited by Theodore Funck-Brentano, pp. 34-37. On the later fortunes of this powerful idea (which Montchrétien did not, of course, originate), Arthur O. Lovejoy's *Reflections on Human Nature* remains the classic study. On Montchrétien's life and his career as a dramatist, see Richard Griffiths, *The Dramatic Technique of Antoine de Montchrestien*, ch. 1.

164—Interest and Prudence

phrase of Machiavelli's famous argument about the *verità effettuale della cosa* in chapter xv of *The Prince*:

> Since we are not perfect and do not live among perfect men, let us speak to this point according to the way the world actually operates. It is a world in which each individual sets his sights on profit, and his eyes are caught by the glittering of each little spark of utility, to which a man is drawn, whether by nature or by the education and custom which we speak of as second nature.

The reference to "custom as second nature" is reminiscent of Montaigne. It is followed by another phrase of the same vintage, after which Montchrétien gradually sharpens the *economic* thrust of his moral contentions. The passage continues as follows:

> Therefore the most skillful, who have studied most carefully the book of common experience, have held that the diverse necessities which each individual senses strongly as pertaining to himself have been the first cause of general communities. For the most ordinary liaison between men, and their most frequent assembling together, depends on the help they provide for one another and the mutual offices they render to each other, in such a fashion that each is primarily motivated by his individual profit, as he perceives it, rather than by nature, the real prime mover here, of which he is unaware. So many efforts, so much labor of so many men has no other goal but gain. The circle of affairs reduces itself to a single point; the necessity of movement depends on this.[21]

Thus one of the major theorists of mercantilism sets forth clearly what later became the foundation stone of laissez-faire economics, and the ethic of utility with which it was associated. Men are motivated primarily by the desire for private gain; their activities in society all have selfish profit as the central goal; wise nature, working through custom, brings all these scattered efforts together for the good of the whole.

Unlike the theorists of laissez-faire, however, Montchrétien believed that "wise nature" requires the aid of human authority to turn the pursuit of profit to public advantage. He argues that such aid should come from a powerful government operating according to the same principles as nature herself: that is, recognizing the centrality of the "bait of honor and the lure of profit" in human life, and making sure that these motives are encouraged, given free scope, and properly rewarded.[22] Montchrétien describes the human understanding as *une table raze* on which can be imprinted socially useful motives and goals

[21] *Traicté*, pp. 38-39.   [22] *Traicté*, pp. 101-103.

as easily as slothful ones. Like his successors who developed a systematic utilitarian philosophy, Montchrétien regarded "the useful and the pleasant" as "the two great points on which all human action depends."[23] A government that uses these insights skillfully will find that even small efforts are richly rewarded.

Quite often in his *Traicté*, Montchrétien asserts the interconnectedness of public and private good, and in the same breath the necessity for wise policy to nourish this natural liaison. He speaks of political communities, like physical bodies, deriving energy from the close interaction of the participating parts; and then asserts that "it follows from this, that the grandest policy one can practice in a state is to make sure that no part remains unproductive." Montchrétien saw no incompatibility in believing in natural harmony and in the importance of human artifice to ensure that harmony. He described it in terms of "polishing with industry and judgment the natural faculties" of subjects, "making them harmonious and profitable to the support and conservation of the universal body of which they are animated members."[24] Unlike many of his successors in this tradition of moral argument, Montchrétien had no clear conception of enlightened self-interest or self-love; he did not believe that ordinary human beings can be counted on to direct their own pursuit of profit in a sophisticated fashion. Instead, he put his faith in enlightened absolutist politics. His major purpose in writing the *Traicté* was to demonstrate to the king and his ministers that public and private utility are so closely intertwined that if they wish to achieve the former they must consider carefully the sources of the latter.

"Private activities make up the public," Montchrétien says several times. Work in the household and the marketplace is the source of public prosperity, and the great river of state is composed of all the little streams of private affairs. Bodin's argument about the family as the foundation of the state is taken over by Montchrétien to make this argument, as well as to remind kings that the management of the family is a good model for management of the polity. Hence the inspiration for the title of his treatise, in which he coined the term "political economy." Montchrétien wrote to convince the king to become an economist, to recognize that the central aspect of good government is good management of the economy, on which the strength and glory of his state depend. He was particularly anxious to direct the king's attention to the neglected members of the third estate, "apparently the

[23] *Traicté*, pp. 20-21, 337-338.
[24] *Traicté*, pp. 22-23. The Renaissance flavor of Montchrétien's conception of unity among animated members of a whole is brought out in several references to the "humors" in the body of the state, as on pp. 12 and 43.

most negligible of all, but in fact extremely important" to the prosperity of the whole. He speaks of laborers, artisans, merchants not as the belly of the state (the function traditionally assigned them in the body politic), but as skillful fingers that should be controlled by the ruling intelligence to increase the well-being of the whole.[25]

The major preoccupation of government, on this account, should be ensuring that each subject does what he is best equipped to do, is given the liberty to do it creatively, and then properly rewarded. Montchrétien thinks of men as complex instruments of policy to be manipulated by a general framework of laws and good policies provided by well-informed government. He wants to free Frenchmen, not constrain them—to draw them out of sloth and stimulate them to healthy activity. He does not propose a detailed scrutiny of all individuals in the economy, but a few simple policies to encourage productivity: the strict regulation of external trade, the requirement that all able-bodied men must work, the rewarding of good efforts, the removal of obstacles to internal commerce. When these things are taken care of, ambition and avarice will do the rest. Montchrétien bids his sovereign to look at England and the Netherlands, France's major commercial rivals, for examples of what can be done by a government bent on encouraging productivity. His own interest in economics had been awakened by an extended stay in both these countries, and he was only the first of many Frenchmen to advise his government to learn lessons of this sort from neighbors to the north and west.[26]

Montchrétien's glowing description of the enterprise of government in the polity he advocated for France was full of images particularly dear to absolutists. He spoke of linking the arts and sciences of the whole realm in a single well-ordered chain held by the hands of the *souverain maistre de police*, like the golden chain of earth and sky held in the hands of Jupiter. He entreated the king to model his actions on the deity, "who gives being and conservation to the smallest things as to the grandest." In such a model, "virtue, honor, and utility are fused together" with true Christian charity. Besides imitating God and wise nature, the king is exhorted to imitate the sun, in the most glorious and honorable of earthly work, doing something "in whose utility everyone can participate"—providing, as we should say nowadays, the ultimate collective good: sunlight.[27] In these passages, Montchrétien an-

[25] *Traicté*, p. 12; Vauban echoes the same concern, in almost the same words, more urgently and sorrowfully in his *Dixme royale* addressed to Louis XIV a century later.

[26] *Traicté*, pp. 101-103; Montchrétien also anticipates Adam Smith's celebration of the division of labor, citing the Flemish and the Germans as models to be imitated, on pp. 37-38.

[27] *Traicté*, pp. 17-18, 112-127.

ticipates the assertions of Louis XIV himself, who had a special fondness for solar imagery, and urged on his heir the unequaled pleasure of doing something gloriously useful for the whole world at once.

In his descriptions of the motives that lead ordinary individuals to engage in productive activity, Montchrétien uses quite different language. He stresses the importance of the selfish sense of having a stake in something, standing to gain directly from the outcome of one's labors. The cause of the poverty and wretchedness of the French peasantry, he asserts, lies not in their nature or the climate, but in the fact that they do not share in the profits of their own labors, which are all drained away by dues and taxes. Few own their own land, "and since their work is always done for someone else, is it surprising that they have no care or desire to do it well?"[28] In discussing merchants, Montchrétien asserts that their willingness to take risks and expose themselves to all kinds of inconveniences, on which so much of the prosperity of the realm depends, flows directly from their "lust for having things and desire for gain," which ought therefore to be encouraged by the government instead of treated as vicious or ignoble. Montchrétien warns that those who "measure the felicity of a state solely by virtue simply considered" make a grave mistake, since men are no longer content to subsist on acorns, and to give them what they desire requires an industry and commerce that spring from motives quite contrary to those of pure and simple virtue. Of course, he says, merchants act not out of "affection for the public," but rather from "their own lust for gain," and "the splendor of gold" regularly "blinds them and leads them away from equity. But to speak politically, we should not for that reason cast them out of the republic and make them a species of helots rather than citizens. One draws a good antidote from this viper itself; it is a cantharide with good feet and wings."[29]

This suggestion for drawing remedy out of poison indicates that Montchrétien, like Montaigne in his own use of such imagery, was not entirely happy with the moral condition of the world he described. Although he saw that vicious motives as well as virtuous ones could lead to social benefit, he retained a sharp sense of the difference between the two. He regarded men of his own era as petty and sordid, caught up in vanity and luxury. "Avarice and ambition possess all

[28] *Traicté*, pp. 42-43. On p. 52 Montchrétien appeals to the king and queen mother in language that amounts to an odd inversion of terms later used in laissez-faire arguments: "Make us then the possessors of the fruit of our industry; that is to say, restore us to ourselves [*rendez nous à nous mêmes*]."
[29] *Traicté*, pp. 137-138; the reference to the cantharide, or Spanish fly providing its own antidote, is lifted directly from Montaigne's essay "Of conscience," II, 5.

the rewards of virtue," and this makes it impossible to tell the good men from the knaves. Montchrétien nostalgically assumed that human beings in the past must have been nobler, and regretted the absence of direct affection for the public good, or love of virtue, among his contemporaries. His own first love was not political economy, but drama; and in his tragedies he dwelt on nobler themes. But in the imperfect world described in his political economy, each man "looks to his individual profit without ever thinking of the public utility. He remains in his house to give himself over to his pleasure; if he is called to office, he uses it to fill his purse like everyone else."[30] In such passages Montchrétien vividly captures the privatistic spirit he found characteristic of men in his own time. But the remedy he suggests is not to exhort them to public spiritedness, or to try to revive lost civic virtue. Instead he proposes to take men as they are, motivated by ambition and avarice, and by skillful political economy ensure that they contribute to the public good despite themselves. Such management requires flexibility and suppleness, rather than rigid adherence to strict codes of virtue, on the part of rulers. New remedies must be sought for new evils in a changing world, laws quietly adapted when they cease to be effective. The language of medicine lingers in this notion of governance. Special and esoteric skills are needed to cure human ills, as Montchrétien sees it; and "the reason of state is not always the same, any more than that of medicine."[31]

4. THE POLITICS OF REASON OF STATE

In the development of the modern state, *ragion di stato* was the term adapted in all European languages to connote the particular mode of action and justification concerning the interests of this novel entity. It was a form of reasoning confined to politics, more specifically identified with the politics of absolutist monarchy. In France, the term evokes the name of Cardinal Richelieu. This is not because the cardinal put forward a clear-cut theory of *raison d'état*. Indeed, it may be doubted that such a theory could be constructed, since reason of state is "more a mentality, an attitude, a climate of opinion," than a concept that lends itself to systematic analysis.[32] But as a climate of opinion, reason of state surrounded Richelieu's regime; and the most thorough discussion of what it means to govern according to its precepts was undertaken by publicists who wrote to defend his policies.

[30] *Traicté*, pp. 243-244.   [31] *Traicté*, p. 120; see also p. 36.
[32] J.H.M. Salmon, in contributing to discussion in an International Colloquium on the Historical Role of the Concept of Reason of State, held in Tübingen, 1974; proceedings edited by Roman Schnur, *Staatsräson*, p. 230.

There was no necessary connection between absolutist theory and reason of state; as we have seen, the theory of absolutism was well developed in France before the age of Richelieu. But there was a close consonance between the two that led Charles McIlwain to observe perceptively that "the end product of divine right sovereignty was reason of state."[33] Citizens of republics were suspicious of the term because of its paradoxical connotations of irrationality and mystery, of justification beyond the rules of ordinary justice.[34] These very aspects made reason of state attractive to absolutist publicists, who took advantage of its ambiguity in their support of specific royal policies. Reason of state was sometimes identified with a superior law, embodied in the person of the prince, yet it could also denote a form of action that was characteristically alegal, irregular, extraordinary. Most basic, perhaps, was the tension between the justificatory intent and the undertones of immorality or amorality connoted by the term.

The Machiavellian roots of this concept were generally recognized, although the notion of princely prudence and the preference for public over private utility were familiar long before the sixteenth century.[35] During the religious wars in France, adherents of all factions accused one another of unsavory and irreligious behavior in politics, and pointed an accusing finger at Machiavelli for having invented such activities. But Richelieu was responsible for making the notion of *raison d'état* acceptable as an approach to governance. He authorized writers to expound the concept, and sought to legitimize its precepts. Fully conscious of the power of words to shape men's minds, and of the central role of opinion in governing states, Richelieu undertook the deliberate direction of an impressive panoply of propaganda.

Frenchmen during the age of Richelieu saw close connections between the power of language and the power of the prince. Guez de Balzac wrote a pretty letter to chancellor Séguier in 1636 noting that not all those who serve the king kill men or make machines; some pray, others write dispatches, and others work in their studies to honor the prince and edify his subjects by their art. Racine, some decades later, testified to the solidity of this alliance in a paean to the Académie française: "All the words of our language, all its syllables appear precious to us because we regard them as so many instruments to serve the

---

[33] W. F. Church notes in the preface to *Richelieu and Reason of State* that this observation by McIlwain, his former teacher, inspired that study. Cf. a similar remark by J. Declareuil quoted by Thuau, *Raison d'état et pensée politique*, p. 11.

[34] E. H. Kossman, in Schnur, ed., *Staatsräson*, pp. 233-234.

[35] In addition to the medieval references provided in the works by Post and Ullmann cited above, discussions of public vs. private utility by Pasquier, Montaigne, and L'Hôpital have been noted in earlier chapters of this study.

glory of our august Protector, Louis XIV."[36] Several scholars have noted the consonance between the development of French classicism and the development of absolutist monarchy under Richelieu and Louis XIV. Beyond an awareness on the part of some authors of their contributions to shaping public opinion in favor of the monarchy, this involved a more general parallel between the focus on order and rationality in the program of the centralizing monarchy, and the stress upon regularity and discipline in the genres of classical literature, philosophy, and art. There may even have been a connection between the idea, central to classicism, that each genre—poetry, tragedy, the epic—has its own particular rules of order, and the idea that the state had its own rules of action distinct from those governing social morality, the economy, or the church.[37] This latter idea, in any case, was fundamental in the discussion that surrounded reason of state.

At the core of this discussion was the matter of justice and justification. Must actions undertaken for the advantage of the state ultimately conform to justice to be justifiable? Is there a special sort of political justice, like that mentioned by Montaigne, Lipsius, and Charron, which can serve as a standard for such justification or are princes held to the ordinary forms of justification in Christian ethics? Does effective governance sometimes require unjust action in the defense of the basic interest of the state? Or is the interest of the state the final measure of justice itself? All these positions were defended by publicists writing under Richelieu. Guez de Balzac expressed a representative view when he condemned "that punctual and scrupulous Justice" that invites the ruin of the state because of its overly fine respect for the specific forms of justice, "which means that by observing the terms of a particular law one lets all laws perish." Balzac defined this rigid standard as a "sovereign injustice," and asserted that "prudence must come to the aid of justice in many things," if the precarious order on which imperfect human society rests is to be preserved.[38]

In a slightly different vein, other writers dealt with this same problem by identifying the king's will with justice itself. The problem was

[36] Thuau, *Raison d'état et pensée politique*, p. 172, quotes Balzac; Mousnier, *XVIe et XVIIe siècles*, p. 258, Racine. More generally, see G.R.R. Treasure, *Cardinal Richelieu*, and F. E. Sutcliffe, *Politique et culture*; here as elsewhere, Hobbes provides the most striking formulation of this connection of language and power in *Leviathan*, chs. IV-V.

[37] This is suggested by Julien Freund, Schnur, ed., *Staatsräson*, pp. 231-232.

[38] Guez de Balzac, *Le Prince* (1631), included in *Oeuvres de J.-L. de Guez, sieur de Balzac*, edited by L. Moreau, I, 98, from ch. XVII; cf. Jean de Silhon, *Le Ministre d'Estat* (1632), discours XI, for a similar formulation in one of the best-known works in the development of *raison d'état*.

solved by defining it away. The king himself was depicted as the embodiment of divine justice, gifted with special grace so that he could rule the kingdom as a living law. This argument invoked lofty assumptions, and was expressed by devout Catholic jurists such as Charles de Noailles.[39] In practice, it was indistinguishable from a purely positivist assertion that whatever the king did was just. The bishop of Chartres in 1625 asserted that the king had gone to war "because to do this was just and reasonable; or rather such a way is just because the king has undertaken it."[40] The bishop was probably assuming a framework of divine-right absolutism in which the justice of the king was a gift of divine charisma; but what he said was very close to the view expressed by Gabriel Naudé, the bold and cynical erudite libertine, who surely did not make this assumption. In both cases there was an explicit denial of any higher reference point that could be used to evaluate and criticize the actions of the ruler.

During the Fronde, Naudé observed that in the preventive arrest of a suspected traitor, "the king acts perfectly justly, because he has the power to act this way, and because he has on his side reason of state, before which all other considerations must give way."[41] This assertion is consonant with, though less subtle than, the views put forward by Naudé in his best-known work, the *Considérations politiques sur les coups d'Estat* (1639), which comes close to being a manual of *raison d'état*. Many treatises in this genre were written to convince subjects of the necessity for acceptance of royal policies, even those that deviated from the ordinary expectations about morality, when the king was obliged to meet fox-like enemies and potential rebels on their own terms in order to protect the state. Such apologetic tones were absent from Naudé's treatise. He did not write at the instruction of the cardinal prime minister, nor did he write for general consumption.[42] Naudé wrote to show what must be done by a prince determined to rule his kingdom firmly and act according to the interests of his state.

---

[39] *L'Empire du juste, selon l'institution de la vraye vertu* (1632), cited in Church, *Richelieu*, pp. 277-279.

[40] Quoted by Mousnier, *Peasant Uprisings*, p. 33; this opinion was quickly repudiated by the assembly of the clergy before whom the bishop had expressed it.

[41] *Mascurat*, quoted by Thuau, *Raison d'état*, p. 332.

[42] In Introducing his *Considérations*, Naudé remarks that kings are required to "manipulate the people and persuade them by pretty words, seduce them and deceive them by appearances," by employing preachers and spokesmen "or by means of skilful pens . . . to lead the people by the nose, and make them approve or condemn, on the basis of outward appearances, the substance of what he does." Meinecke devotes an entire chapter (VII) of *Machiavellism* to Naudé.

172—Interest and Prudence

Naudé follows Montaigne and Lipsius in distinguishing two kinds of justice and three kinds of prudence. He asserts that the universal and noble justice admired by philosophers is "often useless and inconvenient in the affairs of the world," compared with the special artificial justice appropriate to "the needs and necessities of police and of states." Like Charron, Naudé sees the necessity of twisting justice in small matters to serve it in greater ones, and he fuses knowledge and practice under the more general heading of prudence. This is defined as "a moral and political virtue that has no other goal but the seeking out of diverse expedients . . . for dealing with and succeeding in the affairs a man proposes to himself."[43] This prudence dictates three different approaches for governments appropriate in different kinds of situations. First there is "the general science" of politics propounded in the great tradition from Plato to Bodin, containing principles of duty, love, and obligation. This lofty science is not Naudé's primary concern in the *Considérations*, although his *Bibliographie politique* revealed his extensive familiarity with most of the great works on this subject.[44] In the *Considérations*, Naudé moves on to the second type of political knowledge, of greater moment for his argument: the maxims of state or *ragion di stato*, rules for the preservation of kingdoms that include some things accepted in ordinary morality, and others that cannot be justified by natural or civil law but must be practiced occasionally to preserve the state. Beyond these, Naudé identifies a third category of political science and practice he calls *coups d'Estat*, bold and desperate actions in times of crisis that are completely outside the order of justice and cannot be reduced to maxims.[45] According to Naudé, such *coups d'Estat* undertaken with an eye to public utility

[43] In the *Considérations politiques* (1679 edition), the reference to Montaigne's distinction is on pp. 339-340, and the discussion of Charron (whom Naudé greatly admired) is on pp. 19 and 56-58.

[44] The *Bibliographie politique* ends with a list of authors mentioned in the text; the names of most Greek and Roman moralists and historians are included, as well as many of the moderns. Tacitus, Commynes, Saint Thomas, and Machiavelli are there, but not Thucydides, Marsilius, Saint Augustine, or Seyssel. Several Frenchmen of the sixteenth century are on the list, as are Erasmus and Campanella; but there are no English names, not even that of Thomas More. Montaigne and Charron are praised for their moral insights, but the highest accolade is reserved for Jean Bodin, the first after Plato and Aristotle to have arrived near perfection in politics; "a vast spirit," who brought order to the entire subject; a man alien to repose, who at the end, "like another Phoenix of our century, consumed himself in the contemplation of this sovereign wisdom" (pp. 40-43).

[45] *Considérations*, pp. 98, 110-111. Naudé's prime example of such politics was the massacre of Saint Bartholomew. On the defense of that slaughter of the Huguenots, and Naudé's treatise generally, see Julien Freund, "La Situation exceptionnelle," in Schnur, ed., *Staatsräson*, pp. 141-164.

are clearly distinct from tyranny, which is defined as the tendency to resort to such measures regularly for the narrow interests of the ruler. Such potent medicine is not for daily use; it must be administered carefully for the good of the state, like a father performing radical surgery to save his child. Among situations in which such action is likely to be necessary, Naudé names the founding of a kingdom, the restoration of a corrupt state, and instances in which privileges enjoyed by certain subjects threaten the prince's authority. In more "normal" times, the rule for princes and their ministers should be to "unite and bring together insofar as possible utility and honesty."[46]

The focus on prudence in the *Considérations* is typical of treatises discussing reason of state, though Naudé's is bolder than most of them. Publicists writing about reason of state tended to identify a special kind of reasoning as the central quality of a capable ruler. Such reason was equated with prudence, the shrewd pragmatic calculation about utility and necessity in specific situations, and concerned interests—the interest of the public, of the state, of princes and their dynasties. Thus the most important long-run effect of *raison d'état*, in France at least, was to provide political argument with a new central focus: interest. Phillippe de Béthune formulated the connection concisely when he asserted that "reason of state is nothing other than reason of interest."[47]

The effects of this preoccupation with interest are clear in innumerable treatises composed in this period and afterwards. One of the most striking illustrations is the material prepared for the instruction of the dauphin by another erudite libertine, La Mothe le Vayer, when he was a candidate for the post of tutor to the future Louis XIV. In his section on "La Politique du prince," Le Vayer incorporated a good deal of commonplace material from the "mirrors of princes," but struck some novel notes in the key of interest. "The interest of state," he asserted, "is the point on which all sorts of government turn; utility is their sphere of action, outside of which they do not act at all; and the jealousy of power makes instant enemies of those who a moment before appeared to be united most closely." Le Vayer attributes preoccupation with selfish interests to the rulers of aristocratic regimes as well as monarchies, and asserts even in "the most perfect democracies, where the passion for the common good is esteemed to be

[46] *Considérations*, p. 341; this formula reflects an enduring preoccupation in French thought. On Naudé's scholarship and influence, consult Kristeller, "Between the Italian Renaissance and the French Enlightenment."

[47] Quoted by Thuau, *Raison d'état*, p. 400; the same connection was made by Giovanni Botero in the *Aggiunte* to his famous treatise on *Ragion de Stato* (1598), according to Church, *Richelieu*, p. 64.

most violent, this interest does not cease to prevail in the most perfect spirits."[48] The lesson for a budding monarch is that the passion of self-interest dominates not only his rivals on the thrones of other states, but each of his subjects, as well, so that he must be always vigilant. There is also a positive aspect to the universality of interest; the prince who can use it to manipulate the actions of other men, so that "like the greatest artisans who move the largest machines by the tiniest engines, skillful princes can often succeed in the most important affairs by seemingly insignificant measures."[49]

5. Richelieu on the Interests of the Monarch and the Interests of the State

The concept of the "interests of the state" that paved the way for such sophisticated discussions of the centrality of interest was first formulated to advance understanding of the motives and objectives of different actors in international diplomacy and war. From early in the seventeenth century until the middle of the eighteenth, numerous treatises were devoted to the "interests" of the several states of Europe. By the time Rohan published his influential work *De l'interest des princes et des Estats* in 1638, it was a well-established maxim that princes and republics are moved by interest. Rohan claimed to be able to chart out the "true interests" of each of the great powers, even though these interests were not always understood by the rulers of those states. For Rohan, as for Richelieu and other Frenchmen of this era, interests of state are objective facts that can be discerned or misunderstood; they are not reducible to those attitudes or beliefs that interested parties themselves hold or express. They are analogous to the positions of players in a complicated game, whose strengths and weaknesses can be analyzed by a knowledgeable observer, but may or may not be correctly perceived by the players themselves.

For Rohan and his contemporaries, success in the game of politics depended on the accurate perception of one's own interests and those of the rulers of other states; and these were understood to be fundamentally opposed. Interest in such a context is defined by opposition to other interests. It was not surprising, therefore, that as the concept of "the interests of the state" began to be used in discussing domestic

---

[48] La Mothe le Vayer, *Oeuvres*, vol. I: *De l'instruction de Monseigneur le Dauphin*, part II, sec. v, p. 315. This treatise did not win for Le Vayer the post he coveted; but he was appointed preceptor to the duc d'Anjou seven years after the *Instruction* was published in 1640.

[49] *Instruction*, p. 325. This notion of the "great machines of state" moved by tiny springs fascinated later theorists, including Saint-Pierre and Montesquieu.

politics, it was defined as an objective position advantageous to the ruler, his government, and the nation as a whole, that was distinct from and even sometimes opposed to the specific interests of the individual subjects. The "true interests" of one special individual—the prince— were assumed to be identical with the interests of the public and of the state. Little attention was paid to potential dissonance between the prince's personal desires and the good of the whole polity. But the interests of all other individuals were regarded as potential threats or obstacles to the realization of the public interests. These public interests were not composed of the collected interests of all individuals in the community, but were instead of an entirely different nature from those of private individuals.

This conception of *les intérêts publiques* is particularly clear in Richelieu's *Testament politique*.[50] The approach to politics in this treatise is Machiavellian in its single-minded focus on the interests of the prince and the state, regarded as synonymous and quite separate from those of private individuals. Richelieu much more often sounds like Machiavelli than he does, for instance, like Bodin. He takes sovereignty for granted, and includes few juristic arguments. He focuses on those things a prince must do to maintain his authority and strengthen his state, measures he must take to ensure that he can govern effectively and make his will prevail. The cardinal makes frequent use of the notion of "interest" in this enterprise, to show the monarch how he can be better obeyed by engaging the private interests of his subjects to advance the public interest. These two types of interest, in other words, are not regarded as irretrievably in conflict, although separate and potentially opposed. The good monarch is the one who shows his subjects their own interests in actions that promote the interests of the state. Richelieu assumes that all men are moved by their perception of where their interest lies, and that a skillful ruler is aware of this fact and takes perpetual advantage of it. Only the monarch and his advisors can perceive the public interest; and it is the business of the king to be sure that this prevails over others at all times. This does not mean summing private interests to arrive at a majority solution, nor even weighing broader interests against narrower ones, but instead caring for a specific entity, the public interest, which has an objective

[50] The authenticity of Richelieu's *Testament* has been debated for centuries. Scholars now accept it as an accurate statement of the cardinal's own views and principles, probably compiled by his secretaries and incorporating certain passages he had composed himself. This conclusion is reached by Church, *Richelieu*, pp. 480-485. See also Dietrich Gerhard, "Richelieu," in Leonard Krieger and Fritz Stern, ed., *The Responsibility of Power*; and Edmond Esmonin, "Sur l'authenticité du *Testament politique* de Richelieu," in his collection of *Etudes sur la France*.

reality of its own, visible to those charged by God with responsibility for the state.

On one issue much debated in this era—the relation between politics and religion—Richelieu argues that the prince is charged with looking after the health and power of the state, while the pope and other officials of the church are charged with matters of religion. The prince must respect the papal tiara in all that concerns the spirit, but he must also preserve the power of his crown. And the purposes of the state itself are not defined with reference to specifically religious objectives.[51] The focus of the *Testament* is not on how to build a Christian commonwealth that will work for the salvation of its subjects, but on how to build a strong and well-ordered state able to act effectively in pursuit of its military, commercial, and administrative objectives. In pursuit of such objectives, certain harsh measures are condoned by the cardinal that would be reprehensible were they not required by the interests of the state, such as rigorous exemplary punishments imposed on a few subjects. The notion of prudence is at the heart of this *Testament*. Richelieu advises his prince to calculate carefully, choose advisors well, and exercise skill in negotiation. He asserts that different kinds of probity are required for honor in God's sight and for success in the world's affairs.[52] He does not touch directly on lying and deceit, either to counsel or condemn it. But in a *mémoire* he drew up for his own use just before he began to build his career at court, Richelieu analyzed the complicated strategies of the successful courtier, including "a very difficult science: dissimulation."[53] It is reasonable to suppose that this was equally central in his counsels to his prince when he became prime minister, although he was prudent enough not to explore the subject in a *Testament*.

This private *mémoire* containing the principles Richelieu followed on his own path to power connects dissimulation and craftiness with "reason." In the *Testament* composed several decades later, the notion of "reason" is central to Richelieu's discussion. For Richelieu, reason is the prerogative and ought to be the guide for all human beings; but it should be specially evident in the conduct of a prince. Not only is it appropriate for a king raised above all other humans to provide a model of sovereign reason; rationality is also an effective method of

---

[51] *Testament politique*, edited by Louis André, part I, ch. 2, sec. 9 (pp. 202-203).
[52] *Testament politique*, I, 8, sec. 3 (p. 291); see also II, 9 sec. 7 (p. 444), and Richelieu's instructions to Schomberg: "Autres sont les intérêts d'Etat qui lient les Princes et autres les intérêts du salut de nos âmes," quoted by Thuau, *Raison d'état*, p. 205.
[53] "Mémoire . . . écrit de sa main," written in 1607 or 1610, edited by Armand Baschet, pp. 21-23.

Public Utility and Private—177

governing, compared to the attempt to evoke brute fear. The cardinal asserts that "authority constrains men to obedience, but reason persuades them to it. It is much more fitting to conduct men by measures that insensibly win over their wills, than by means that usually make them act only when they are forced to do so."[54] Nonetheless Richelieu, like Machiavelli, recognizes that the foundation of obedience is fear; and he emphasizes throughout his book that the prince must maintain the strength of his own position as a monarch so that he may be feared by his subjects and by other rulers. "Among all the principles capable of moving a state, fear, which is founded on esteem and reverence, is the strongest," according to the cardinal; "for it is this which engages most directly the interests of all those with whom the prince must deal."[55]

In discussing the several orders of the state—the clergy, nobility, and third estate, Richelieu's primary interest is in their contributions to the health and strength of the polity. He refers to the king's duty to protect all his subjects, and assumes the legitimacy of the traditional pattern of the orders in society. But his major concern, here as elsewhere, is with the ways in which the order or disorder of these several sections of the state affects the interests of the whole. He excoriates the first estate, his fellow clergy, for teaching rude folk the elements of a learning that is useless to them. This "tincture of learning" has seeped down to the lowest orders, so that men are readier to doubt than to believe, and pride and presumption have replaced docility and obedience. Like a body with eyes in all its parts, a state whose subjects are all savants is a monstrosity. According to Richelieu, "the commerce of letters absolutely banishes that of merchandise, which brings wealth to states; it ruins agriculture, the true nursing mother of the people, and sooner or later it will completely empty the nursery of soldiers, who spring up faster in the rudeness of ignorance than in the *politesse* of the sciences."[56] Men desert the mechanical arts for the liberal arts, and France is deprived of productive subjects and overrun with parasitic *chicaneurs* who disturb the public repose. The consequences of the widespread privatistic spirit of his times, the burgeoning of new offices, and the spirit of *libertinage*, are very clear in the cardinal's assessment. To halt such dangerous tendencies, the king should ensure that men of the lower orders are taught mechanically useful skills and

[54] *Testament politique*, II, 2 (p. 325).
[55] *Ibid.*, 9, sec. 1 (p. 372); the rather elliptical wording in the last part of this passage is: "puisque c'est celui qui intéresse davantage chacun de ceux dont il est intéressé."
[56] *Ibid.*, I, 2, sec. 10 (p. 204).

the rudiments of literacy. Only the most gifted will be singled out for higher education in a small number of institutions where the flame of learning can be maintained in purity.

The cardinal deplores the internecine squabbles and violent habits of the nobility. He also regrets the influx of newly ennobled officers from the bourgeoisie who crowd into their midst. Richelieu's own aristocratic biases and conservative sense of order are clear when he remarks on this monstrous reversal of the proper order of things. The strength of the aristocracy must be renewed by purifying their ranks, providing them with posts, and suppressing the luxury that drains away their livelihood. This renewed strength must be properly channeled, in defense of the state and their own class interests, rather than in duels and against the common people. Since they have shown that honor is dearer to them than life, this channeling should be accomplished by threats of loss of honor and derogation to common status —much more likely to prove effective than the threat of death itself.[57] Thus the cardinal echoes the contemporary assumption that passions can be properly channeled for good purposes.

In discussing the third estate, Richelieu broaches the possibility of tax reform and the abolition of venality of offices; but he rejects these measures as inappropriate in an ancient monarchy. He distinguishes sharply between policies that would make sense if one were starting out afresh, and those that can be put into effect in an established state. Like Montaigne, Descartes, and Montesquieu, he argues that corrupt and irrational practices have rough utility as integral parts of a developed system. To wrench them out would mean the destruction of the whole edifice.[58] Richelieu was aware of the misery caused by excessive taxation. In his *Testament* he condemns heavy burdens as unjust even if they are useful to the public, and urges the king to tax his richer subjects first. This is the only place in the treatise where he argues that justice should be honored when public utility suggests another course of action.[59] However, such a concern for the condition of the poor

[57] *Ibid.*, 3 (pp. 218-229). The isolation of honor as the spring of noble action was also central in Montesquieu's analysis of monarchy. Richelieu implies that it would be useful for the state and envigorating for the nobility as a class if they could engage in commerce, but that this policy would be impossible to put into effect, because of the strength of *honneur*.

[58] *Ibid.*, 4, sec. 1 (p. 236). According to the cardinal, "un architecte, qui, par l'excellence de son art, corrige les défauts d'un ancien bâtiment et qui, sans l'abattre, le réduit à quelque symétrie supportable, mérite bien plus de louange que celui qui ruine tout à fait et construit un nouvel édifice parfait et accompli."

[59] *Ibid.*, secs. 1-4 (pp. 230-253). Richelieu returns to this same theme at the end of the treatise; in II, 9, sec. 7, he proposes a fairly extensive reformation of the tax collection system—but only when peace is attained.

is not much in evidence in the bulk of the *Testament*, which assesses the status of the common people solely from the point of view of their contribution to the power of the regime.

One of the most notorious passages of the *Testament* is that devoted to *le peuple*. The cardinal asserts that *tous les politiques* agree that "if the people were too comfortable, it would be impossible to contain them within the regulations of their duties." Having argued earlier that it is not in the interest of the state that they be educated beyond their station, he now asserts that "since these people have less knowledge and are less cultivated and instructed than other orders in the state, they can be kept within their proper duties only by the imposition of some necessity." One thing emerges clearly from this peculiarly circular reasoning: the people exist to perform their functions as farmers, soldiers, merchants, so that governing them requires treating them primarily as working parts of the whole state. This means ensuring that they are not so well off that they have no incentive to work, and not so crushed by harsh demands that they can no longer work productively. It is precisely the same reasoning that underlies the discussion of the nobility and clergy; all are viewed as having a particular function to perform as parts of the whole body. In the context of a discussion of the third estate this reasoning has especially harsh connotations, as in this famous passage:

> Reason does not permit that the people be exempted from all taxes, because in that case they would lose the mark of their subjection and with it the memory of their condition. Free of tribute, they would assume they were also released from obedience. They should be compared to mules who, being accustomed to bearing burdens, are more damaged by long rest than by work.[60]

In dedicating *The Prince* to Lorenzo de' Medici, Machiavelli wrote that just as "landscape painters station themselves in the valleys in order to draw mountains or high ground, and ascend an eminence in order to get a good view of the plains," so one must be a prince to understand the nature of the people, and one of the people to achieve perspective on a prince.[61] Absolutist publicists were usually men of letters or minor courtiers who looked up from among the people and drew the lineaments of the prince in awesome and magnificent design.

[60] *Ibid.*, 1, 4, sec. 5 (pp. 253-254); it is the next sentence, however, which advocates moderating the burden out of concern for justice rather than utility. W. F. Church, "Cardinal Richelieu and the Social Estates of the Realm," *Album Helen Maud Cam*, II, 262-270, provides a good overview of this topic.
[61] *The Prince and the Discourses*, edited by Lerner, p. 4.

180—Interest and Prudence

Cardinal Richelieu, France's first "prime minister," achieved the height of power and then looked down from that eminence to describe the nature of subjects and the best way of ruling them. In his *Testament politique* he wrote from a perspective very close to that of the prince himself. That *Testament* stands as the consummation of the tendency for French constitutionalist thought in the seventeenth century to dissolve itself in absolutism. The orders that in Seyssel's *Monarchie* had helped bridle princely power were viewed by Richelieu solely as objects of government, as the stuff the monarch must organize in his pursuit of the objectives of the state. Richelieu's state was neither uniform nor undifferentiated. But it was firmly united by the prince embodying and working for the interests of the whole, which was subordinated to his ordering will.

Richelieu's is one of the most clear-cut statements of the theory of concentrated power in the history of politics. It is hostile to any pluralism that cannot be effectively controlled and managed by the state. It depends upon an explicit rejection of any conflict among powers, any balancing of authorities, and upon a firm conviction that effective political authority must derive from a single source, and be ordered by a single omniscient intelligence that directs the whole. In discussing the actual organization of the government, the cardinal recognizes that the prince needs ministers and counsellors; even God relies on "the ministry of secondary causes" to do His work in the world. But all lines of authority must radiate out from one center, in imitation of the sovereign Deity Himself. Assemblies of subjects are worthless, since "there is no community where one does not find many more bad subjects than good ones . . . and the greater number corrupt the better ones."[62] Conflict among counsellors is abhorrent because the good ideas of each will be frustrated by the programs of the others, and each leader will deploy his own supporters, thus dividing the forces of the state. Turning one of the favorite images of the Renaissance to his own purposes, Richelieu asserts that "just as the maladies and death of men come only from the ill accord of the elements of which they are composed, so it is certain that the contrariety and absence of union that is always to be found among equal powers will alter the stability of States to whom they are entrusted and produce divers accidents that can finally lead to ruin." To avoid such a disaster, a single pilot must control the ship. If the king cannot do the job himself he should entrust another person with superior authority, who will be "like the prime mover, who causes all others to move

[62] *Testament politique*, I, 8, sec. 1 (p. 289); and II, 9, sec. 4 (p. 392).

without himself being moved save by his own intelligence."[63] The prime minister as prime mover provides the prince with a surrogate through whom he can imitate the ordered government of God over the world, and prove the surpassing excellence of a monarchical regime.

The goal of this impressively coordinated regime, with all parts of society marshaled and protected in humble and productive obedience in their several ranks and orders beneath the throne, is the advancement of the interests of the whole. This central concept is stubbornly elusive, although the term *intérêts* appears on almost every page of the *Testament*. The cardinal asserts that "the public interests ought to be the sole end of the prince and his councillors, or at least they are obliged to treat them as singularly important and prefer them to all particular interests." This indicates that such interests are there to be discovered in the business of governing, and that particular interests will often have to suffer in order that they may prevail. In practice, the cardinal and his sovereign interpreted these interests to mean the strengthening of the monarchy and the aggrandizement of the French state at the expense of other states. The interests of ordinary individuals and groups were regarded not simply as less important, but as incommensurate with the interests of the whole, a completely different order of interest that must not be allowed to weigh against the concerns of the state.

> If someone says that the public interests should be preferred to those of individuals, while accepting his contention, I beg him to consider that in discussions of this kind, these different types of interest should not be weighed off against each other, but those of the public should be weighed only against others of the same species, those of the future against those of the present, which pass in an instant.[64]

Yet Richelieu also proposed to tap those individual interests to bring all subjects into ordered conformity with the sovereign will. Such interests were instruments for the consolidation of obedience, rather than legitimate claims by subjects on the attention and benefaction of the prince. They existed to be manipulated, not to be harmonized or legislated for.

Thus the utility and universality of selfish interest, as well as the objective reality of the public interests to be achieved, if necessary, at the expense of private goods, were central to the political corpus

[63] *Ibid.*, I, 8, sec. 6 (pp. 305-306).   [64] *Ibid.*, II, 9, sec. 7 (p. 444).

associated with the age of Richelieu. This set political philosophers a formidable task: to reinterpret the public interests in such a way that the interests of individuals within the state are encompassed by them, realized through them, rather than being quite separate entities, opposed to the interests of the whole. The older, vaguer notion of the *bonum publicum*, with its more generous and humane overtones, had been discredited in Richelieu's milieu as a transparent and useless cloak for private political ambition. It had somehow to be rescued from these connotations, and joined to the newly powerful concept of an objective interest identified with the fortunes of the state. To do this required rethinking the concept of interest, and the concept of self-love with which it was closely connected; and this was begun during this same era by philosophers and theologians who explored the fascinating intricacies of *l'amour-propre* and *la charité*.

CHAPTER SIX

A Variety of Loves and the Sovereignty of Will

1. AUGUSTINE AND FRENCH THOUGHT

While Richelieu and his publicists met the challenges of war and domestic intrigue by refining the concept of "interests of state," several of their contemporaries working in a different context developed the notion of individual interests. These were theologians, wrestling with the challenges of vice and virtue, felicity and damnation. They composed treatises that had important consequences for political philosophy, and occasional reverberations in contemporary politics, as well. One of the central motifs in these treatises was love: the first of all the passions, the mainspring of desire. The classical notion that virtue is knowledge, and the Stoic ideal of reason controlling the passions, were rejected by these authors in favor of an Augustinian conception of human life as controlled by two different kinds of love. It was on the basis of such conceptions that theories of individual interests were first carefully worked out.

Saint Augustine was a dominant figure in seventeenth-century French thought. His influence was felt from at least three sources: by way of Montaigne and several other sixteenth-century writers who admired him; through the austere Augustinianism associated with Cornelius Jansenius, a Dutch theologian whose work spurred the formation of a movement in France bearing his name; and most important, through the direct familiarity of many Frenchmen with the *Confessions* and the *City of God*. As Nigel Abercrombie has shown, the multipurpose term "Jansenism" obscures the direct importance of Augustine's thought for Saint-Cyran, Nicole, Pascal, and Arnauld, the major French Jansenists.[1] The fortunes of Jansenism in France will occupy a good deal of our attention later in this study. But many of the concepts associated with that movement were in common use among theologians and moral philosophers earlier in the century.

Saint Augustine's primary importance for political philosophy, in

[1] Nigel Abercrombie, *Saint Augustine and French Classical Thought*, pp. 6-13; on Montaigne's use of Augustine, see Abercrombie, pp. 40-56, and Elaine Limbrick, "Montaigne et Saint Augustin."

France as elsewhere, lay in the vivid political imagery of the *City of God*. This book held a special fascination for Pascal and several other Jansenists. The community of the faithful, sojourning according to the Founder's plan toward its glorious establishment "in the fixed stability of its eternal seat," provided the paradigm of a true community for these men.[2] The power of their vision shaped secular conceptions of what a good human community must be like. Augustine's conviction that "the blessedness of a community and of an individual flow from the same source; for a community is nothing else than a harmonious collection of individuals" proved a durable motif in efforts to join individualist sentiments with allegiance to something wider than the self.[3] The descriptions of the politics of the earthly city that place Augustine in the company of Hobbes were also important to Pascal and Nicole. But for the theologians in the early decades of the century, the *City of God* was relevant above all for the conception of the two types of love that mark the citizens of the two cities.

Citizens of the earthly city are described by Augustine as "those who wish to live after the flesh," as opposed to "those who wish to live after the spirit," who inhabit the heavenly city.[4] This puts the emphasis on an inclination in the soul toward two types of objects, things of the earth that weigh the soul down, and higher things that attract it upward. These two inclinations are discussed by Augustine as two different loves: the love of self, even to the contempt of God, and the love of God, even to the contempt of self. Both love and will are present here. They are brought together in a passage that initially suggests the priority of will, but then gives love the power to give character to will: "He who resolves to love God, and to love his neighbor as himself, not according to man but according to God, is on account of this love said to be of a good will. . . . The right will is, therefore, well-directed love, and the wrong will is ill-directed love."[5] Some readers of Saint Augustine followed out the notion of a willing choice among different types of love. For most French theologians of this era, however, the necessity of irrational grace bestowed upon the human individual who loves God is given prominence, and the quality of love is regarded as determining the quality of the will.

Love of self (Augustine's *amor sui*) can be translated either as *amour de soi* or as *amour-propre*, a term of great importance in French moral argument. From the early seventeenth century onward, *amour-*

---

[2] *The City of God*, translated by Marcus Dods, preface, p. 3.
[3] *City of God*, book I, sec. 15, p. 20.
[4] *City of God*, book XIV, sec. 1, p. 441.
[5] *City of God*, book XIV, sec. 7, p. 449; sec. 28, p. 477.

propre almost invariably had a pejorative connotation, whereas *amour de soi* could be used neutrally, or even have benign connotations. Self-love was connected with flesh and earthiness in Augustine's treatise, and *concupiscence* (the desire for fleshly things, lust, or covetousness) was a term used interchangeably with love of self. Both were opposed to *la charité*, the love of God and thence of one's neighbor according to the command of God. This love was sometimes described as *pur amour*.

This conception of two fundamentally dissimilar loves dominated ethical treatises composed by theologians during this period; but a variant conception indebted to Italian neo-Platonism had adherents also.[6] Augustine's own conception of love as an inclination toward an object taken to be good, with physical overtones of weightiness and soaring, was influenced by Platonism. Platonic *eros* was even stronger in the notion of human desire for felicity as a single rather than a double motivation, found in several of these treatises. On this view, human love originates in the lowly desires of the flesh and preoccupation with the self, and has within it the potential to move upward and outward into love for other persons, for higher things, for God Himself. This soaring movement can, however, be deflected or arrested; and when a person remains fixed upon himself, we may speak of self-love as corrupt and deficient. But since love of self is the root of all loves, even the love of God begins as a form of self-love; we are first drawn to Him as a source of good for ourselves, the fount of sovereign felicity. Adherents of strict Augustinianism vigorously denied that love of God predicated on hope of reward for the self is the same as true *charité*. They asserted instead the absolute irreconcilability of the two forms of love, springing from different sources, eternally fixed on different objects.

These various types of love of self were discussed in several treatises in terms of different types of interest. Corrupt and fixated self-love was identified as a vicious or false interest, and praiseworthy love of self, embracing the awareness of divine things as the source of true happiness for the individual, was described as a true and acceptable interest. Although the notion of "interest" was a tangential concern in these theological treatises, the sorting out of different interests, and their various connections with the love of higher things, proved seminal for secular social theory. In the moral philosophy of Descartes especially, these different types of self-love are associated with the capacity (or lack of capacity) to love something higher than the self, in the sense

[6] Levi, *French Moralists*, chs. 2-3.

of identification with an earthly, as well as a heavenly, community. A patriotism predicated on enlightened love of self, in other words, was distinguished from a narrow reading of self-interest that opposed the individual to the community. This line of argument proved a particularly promising way to integrate the self-interested individual into the larger whole. Yet, at the same time, there were the germs of quite a different argument, also parallel to theological dispute, in which pure self-abnegating patriotism was regarded as superior to any devotion to public interest that takes selfish interests into account.

Another major theme in seventeenth-century moral discourse was the dominance of will. Political images were common in such discourse to convey the sense of the sovereignty, or absolute decision-making power, of will within the soul. The possession of free will was made one of the distinctive characteristics of our species, marking us off from animals who live by instinct alone, making it possible for us to choose good or evil, God or self, life or death.[7] Here again, there are parallels between religious and secular ethics. The connection between sovereignty and liberty was used to show that just as the king is not bound by law, so the human will is free of submission even to the moral laws of nature, unless this submission is freely chosen. In theological treatises on the sovereignty of the will, there is a note of celebration and optimism like that found in aristocratic conceptions of personal *gloire* and self-fulfillment. The exercise of will was central in the ethic of Corneille, Balzac, and Descartes—the ethic of *la gloire*—which provided the ideal of the noble hero, the self-realizing individual, as an alternative to the retiring and skeptical sage who was the *libertins*'s ideal. Such ideals were condemned by the more austere Augustinians, since they were infected with, indeed predicated on, the primacy of self. *Amour-propre* was identified by these writers both with the notion of heroic *gloire* and with the self-centered isolation of the philosopher. Sage and hero alike were rejected as moral models, in favor of the saint.[8]

The blessedness of citizenship in the heavenly city, the pleasurable intellectual fellowship of the *libertins*, and the noble *gloire* of the aristocratic hero thus provided sharply opposed ethical ideals during this era. Yet there were similarities within these teachings that make it

[7] This notion, which has a number of classical antecedents, was central in the theory of *la volonté* developed by Raimond Sebond in his *Théologie naturelle*, translated by Montaigne; see the discussion in chs. 82-83, pp. 142-144 in the 1603 edition.

[8] On these diverse ideals, part III of Orest Ranum's essay on *Paris in the Age of Absolutism* is particularly useful.

unwise to treat them as wholly distinct. The attitude of the Augustinians toward the ambitious heroes of the earthly city was not far removed from that of the skeptical *libertins*. Augustine himself in his younger days had professed a Stoic ethic that regarded earthly bliss as available only to the fortunate sage, and saw virtue in the world as the fruit of wisdom. Perhaps the residues of this aristocratic intellectual elitism continued to color his attitudes toward the brutish pursuits of worldly men. In any case, there were several consonances between the *libertins* and the Augustinians, who seem at first glance so fundamentally unlike.

Both parties rejected the bold aristocratic faith in free choice and untrammeled will, as well as the Stoic belief in a scrutable providence operating according to principles of natural law that men could understand. They preached a hidden God, inaccessible to human reason. The *libertins* were professed fideists; some may have been deists, if not atheists, at heart. The Augustinians stressed the awful inscrutability of God to human understanding for quite different reasons, to highlight the necessity of mysterious grace. But the effects were oddly similar. The more flippant of the worldly *libertins* welcomed Jansenist pronouncements on the inefficacy of good works and the irrationality of grace. "If we have grace we are saved, and if we don't we are lost anyway," they said.[9] Both Jansenists and *libertins* rejected worldly values to concentrate on charity or inquiry, and the specialized intimate communities built on shared devotion to these things. Most of the Jansenists were, for some part of their lives, committed to solitude. They were known as *les solitaires*, and like their philosophical counterparts, they interpreted solitude to mean not complete isolation from all other men, but retreat from the world in small companies of like-minded men and women, in this case for prayer and study, introspection and wrestling with sin. In neither case, libertine or Jansenist, was there any strong motive for intervention in the world. Saint Augustine, long before Charron, taught the necessity of obedience to the powers that be, to maintain the framework of earthly justice. The subversive potential of Augustinian ideals, including severe disapproval of luxury and aggrandizement, allegiance to alternative communities, and subordination of worldly politics to higher things, was recognized early on by Richelieu, among others, and caused recurrent tension between the Jansenists and the government for a century. But the profoundly critical implications of these ideals did not become the basis for sustained

[9] As reported by Mme. de Choisy later in the century, quoted in Mousnier, *Les XVIe et XVIIe siècles*, p. 188.

reformist ideologies or alternatives to absolutist doctrine. This does much to explain the apparently consensual and serene face of political theory in seventeenth-century France.

The ethic of *la gloire* was a more immediate source of subversion, in the hands of the noble participants in the Fronde. Loyalty to *la patrie* could be interpreted in such a way that it became difficult to distinguish it from the requisites of personal or family glory. Yet a genuine commitment to society and public service was also central to certain versions of this ethic, including those put forward by Balzac and Descartes. Obedience to sovereign power, and identification with the *patrie*, were regarded by these men not as burdensome necessities, but as voluntary acceptance of the rightful authority of the monarch over the individual will, the interests of the larger whole of which the individual forms a part. In this ethic, expanding the concept of individual interest to embrace something wider than the self was first suggested. It proved to have a great many fruitful corollaries for later work.

2. SELF-LOVE FROM SEBOND TO SÉNAULT

After Augustine, one of the most important source-books for French theologians of the early seventeenth century was *La Théologie naturelle* of Raimond Sebond, a fifteenth-century Spaniard. Sebond had been "divested of his barbarous [Espano-Latin] costume and put into good French dress" by none other than Michel de Montaigne. Montaigne translated Sebond at the urging of his father, who admired the work and wished his son to have some occupation worthy of his classical learning and his literary style. The translation is fairly faithful, apart from the preface, which was considerably altered; but throughout the work, Montaigne promised his "delicate and curious" readers that they could expect to discover "some trait and bent of the Gascogne."[10] The impact of Sebond's ideas on Montaigne's developing skepticism and fideism is clear in the reactions that form the basis of his best-known essay, the "Apologie de Raimond Sebond." Sebond purports to offer evidence for Christian doctrine so clear and indisputable that each reader will find himself convinced; nothing is so certain, he says, as the witness of our own acceptance; nothing so close to us as ourselves. This view of an ordered cosmos in which all ranks

[10] This message is in the dedicatory address to Montaigne's father. On the translation itself, and its importance to Montaigne as author of the *Essais*, consult Joseph Coppin, *Montaigne traducteur de Raymond Sebond*. On the circumstances of the translation, Donald Frame, *Montaigne*, ch. 7.

are held together by "the general police of this universe," and each part works to the profit of things above and below, had too much about it of natural-law certainty for Montaigne's taste. Sebond's notion of a diverse nature infinitely present in each individual, and each individual a part of an infinite whole, is closer to his heart.[11] For our purposes, however, Sebond's ethics are more relevant, both in understanding the development of Montaigne's ethics and in seeing what happened to the notion of self-love in the seventeenth century.

The Spanish theologian's ideas about ethics are an amalgam of Augustine and the Stoics, in which will and love are conflated cavalierly. On one issue that later became crucial for debate—whether we must love God unselfishly, for His own sake, or whether we may love Him as the source of our own happiness—Sebond tried to have it both ways. He said that since we are obliged to our creator for all things, we owe Him a debt that can only be paid by unfeigned love, the first gift of the will; he also said that since our sovereign good is to be joined with God, the service we do to Him redounds entirely to our own profit and utility.[12] Sebond insisted that Augustine's two types of love—of self and of God—are fundamentally dissimilar; that the love of self is a disordered and unnatural love, the first of all the vices, in which a man makes of himself a god. But he also said that since God Himself needs nothing, and all things are created with a purpose and utility, the love we bear for God must be understood in terms of the good it brings to us.

The most interesting part of Sebond's argument has to do with the connections between self-love, godly love, and the larger society of which we are members. He argues, in a Stoic vein, that our obligation to love our neighbors commits us to love all men alike and not show favoritism to friends; this mutual love binds all men together in perfect peace. The love of neighbor is derived from love of God, for divine love makes our will "common, universal, and communicable"; it dilates and enlarges our will.[13] Since God Himself is common to all creatures, when we love Him we open ourselves to His uniting and transforming power. Godly love gives the will self-mastery, and sets it free. Narrow love of self, on the other hand, has all the opposite effects. It imprisons us, chains us down, and isolates us from others. The isolating quality of this love is one of Sebond's major themes: the love of self makes us singular, private, shut up in ourselves, and incommunicative to other men. Although Montaigne did not use the term *amour-propre* in translating Sebond, his discussion must have suggested such a term to later

[11] *Théologie*, chs. 1 and 5.   [12] *Théologie*, chs. 108-123.
[13] *Théologie*, chs. 139-145.

readers; Montaigne speaks of *amour de nous-mesmes* and *amour particulier*, and the term *propre* occurs in close connection with these phrases several times. Sebond's whole discussion stresses the proprietary, singular, and covetous aspects of such love, contrasted with the enlarging and unifying love of God. "Who loves himself alone," says Sebond in the language of Montaigne, "loves himself not as man, but as this or that individual . . . concentrating on what is singular and particular about himself rather than what is common, and that about him which is generally human."[14] The eccentric love of what is singular about the self cannot be expanded and extended to love of other men by virtue of what we share with them as human beings.

This striking notion of self-love, rarely improved upon, deserves close consideration. Love-of-self because of what is unique and different about me as a particular individual, as Peter or as Mary, rather than as a human being, alienates me from other human beings; it blocks my ability to extend my love and understanding beyond myself to others because they are also human beings. Men caught up in such a love can think only of what profits and enhances the particularity of the self, instead of thinking about what would be for the benefit and profit of all the men with whom they share society. The notion of narrow interests of the self understood in opposition to the interests of all other individuals is sketched out here, and contrasted with the notion of shared good and profit enjoyed in communion with other human beings, recognized as similar to ourselves and loved by virtue of common humanness.

In the first half of the seventeenth century, a number of theologians used Sebond's treatise either as a source of images and ideas, or as a target for dispute. One of the most eminent was Saint François de Sales, whose influential *Traité de l'amour de Dieu* reiterated the notion that since love tends toward union with the loved object, the love of God and our neighbor brings us outside ourselves, while love of self deflects us back into absorption with our narrow self. Saint Francis elaborates the image of the natural monarchy of the will within the soul; yet he also echoes Sebond's notion that the will is drawn and fixed by the primary object of love. One of Sebond's own images is used to make this point: just as a wife takes her status from her husband, submits to him, and follows him in marriage, so the will is ennobled or degraded by the quality of the object of love.[15]

---

[14] *Théologie*, ch. 145, pp. 271-272. According to etymological dictionaries such as the *Trésor de la langue française*, the term *amour-propre* first appeared around 1613.

[15] *Traité de l'amour de Dieu* (1616); I have used the 1630 edition. Saint Francis'

The will as "natural monarch" in the "internal polity" or "private empire" of the little *pays* that is the soul was a favorite theme for Pierre Le Moyne, who composed his *Peintures morales* a decade or so later. Le Moyne's neo-Platonism led him to stress the neutral quality of love, as a natural inclination toward the sovereign good that could be fixed on lower things or could soar into the light. Against Sebond, he argues explicitly that *amour-propre* cannot be an original motivation to action parallel to love of God. It is rather a deficiency or disease in the soul, like a malady arising from *mauvaises humeurs*; Le Moyne denies the very name of love to this "avaricious, sedentary, excommunicated affection" that cannot bear company.[16] For him, as for Sebond, love is a sociable and unitary passion that links hearts together; self-love is a deformation, a mutilation of such affection. Le Moyne depicts the passions as eager officers in the individual *république*, ready to take their character from the object fixed upon by love, submissive to the dictates of reason. They are directed by *la volonté*, the sovereign mistress of the soul, who enjoys the full liberty appropriate to sovereignty in governing her little realm. Each part is guided by different means, a different combination of force and reason, like the three estates of the realm of France.[17]

In the space of a few years around 1640, a number of treatises were published that intensified the discussion of self-love, the love of God, and the connections of love and will. This was the same period that produced the most important works in the arsenal of *raison d'état*; and there were close connections between these two endeavors. Richelieu was under attack by a group of critics known as *les dévots*, who disapproved of what they saw as the cardinal's willingness to subordinate the interests of the Catholic faith to those of the kingdom of France. The *dévot* party was unhappy about the anti-Hapsburg enterprises that allied France with Protestant regimes, and also about the domestic consequences of war for the king's poorer subjects.[18] It was

---

ideas on love and will are presented in Book I, chs. 1-10; the image of husband and wife is in ch. 2, p. 5. Sebond's characteristically more voluminous discussion of these same topics is in the *Théologie*, chs. 130-135, with the marital analogy on pp. 250-251.

[16] *Peintures morales* (1640 edition), Book III, ch. 6 (pp. 350-353).

[17] *Peintures morales*, IV, 1-2 (pp. 358-403). Le Moyne attacks the *esprits forts* in this section, for their heinous doctrine that will and reason are the aid and companion of the passions in their search for pleasure, rather than their stern mistress and opponent.

[18] This conflict is described by Church, *Richelieu*, pp. 201-207, and by Alexander Sedgwick, *Jansenism in Seventeenth-Century France*, pp. 25-46. Sedgwick brings out the sharp conflict of views by juxtaposing two quotations, from Richelieu

largely in response to such attacks that Richelieu commissioned publicists to defend his policies. The prudential politics of *raison d'état* were linked to a theology and a private ethic (propounded by Richelieu himself, among others) at odds with the austere ethic of the Augustinians, who were the most prominent of the *dévots*. Thus theology and politics were intricately linked on several different levels, as was so often true in the *ancien régime*.

One of the most prominent of the *dévots* was the abbé de Saint-Cyran, who as a young scholar-courtier had voiced the self-abnegating patriotism of the epoch of Henry IV. In the 1630s he turned more and more against the government's policies, as his conversion to austere Augustinian theology drew him away from earthly entanglements into the care of souls as spiritual director of the convent community of Port-Royal. Saint-Cyran still preached abnegation of the self, but in favor of God, and not the prince. He became a symbol for nascent opposition not only to the policies of *raison d'état*, but also to the whole ethic of aristocratic *gloire* that characterized the court of Louis XIII. In 1638, Richelieu had his former friend arrested and confined. Although the charges of heresy against Saint-Cyran could not be supported in his writings, the abbé remained in prison until after Richelieu's death in 1642. His letters from prison to men and women dependent on his spiritual guidance became cornerstones of Jansenist theology.

The ideas of Saint-Cyran were very close to those expressed by his friend Cornelius Jansenius. The abbé argued in his prison writings that there was a great gulf between the condition of Adam before the fall and all human beings afterwards. Greater than any mortal ruler, Adam was "endowed with such absolute power that no creature was able to oppose him, and all the movements of his body and soul depended upon his will to the extent that he could not feel any joy or sorrow or have any thought that he had not willed."[19] The perfect sovereignty of Adam's will, over himself and over all other creatures, entailed perfect liberty to do good or ill; but in choosing ill, Adam condemned his children to corruption of the will, so that they no longer had power to will the good on their own responsibility, but

---

and from Saint-Cyran; the cardinal is willing to assert that "the aversion of the lower classes towards war does not deserve consideration as a reason for making . . . peace," while the abbé contends that God "makes peace because of the poor, who are the most afflicted by war and who feel its effects worse than anyone else in their persons and in their possessions."

[19] Saint-Cyran, *Oeuvres chrestiennes et spirituelles*, quoted by Sedgwick, *Jansenism*, pp. 31-32.

could only choose between different types of evil. Only the gift of God's grace lifted a few men out of infection and made it possible for them to seek the good. In his huge treatise on theology written in the mid-1630s, entitled the *Augustinus*, Jansen expressed similar ideas about will, love, and grace, before and after Adam's fall. Jansen's treatise, together with Saint-Cyran's devotional writings, were embraced and defended by members of the Port-Royal community, and became the basis for the movement called by Jansen's name.[20]

Both Jansen's works and those of Saint-Cyran were anathema to Richelieu. The cardinal minister himself wrote treatises about the Christian life, and his views were sharply opposed to those of Port-Royal. Richelieu asserted that although most men are incapable of sincere self-emptying penitence, a desire to sin no more that is based on the highly pragmatic fear of damnation is sufficient to merit forgiveness. "And even if the principal motive of a man in these circumstances is self-interest," insisted Richelieu, "yet he is also inspired in part by love of God." The desire for heaven as the ultimate source of personal felicity, is by God's mystical power reconciled with love of God himself, in this theology. Richelieu viewed with marked disapproval the tendency to solitude and retreat evinced by the Augustinians; he argued "that one cannot do better than to labor in the vineyard, where much needs to be done." Against those who believe that godly thoughts are promoted by repose and leisure, Richelieu asserted that "the less leisure one has, the better off one is, because leisure degenerates into idleness." The preoccupation with the condition of their own souls that marked the inhabitants of Port-Royal seemed to Richelieu to be self-defeating, more likely to nurture self-love than its opposite. For the cardinal minister, "action is more meritorious than contemplation. It is better to love God than to spend one's time wondering whether one loves God or not."[21]

Richelieu's deep hostility to the theology of Port-Royal was inevitably colored by his perception that devotion to alternative communities and flirtations with unorthodox ideas threatened the stability of state and church. Above all, he was angered by *dévot* criticism of his foreign policies, which he identified with Port-Royal, particularly after Saint-Cyran was implicated in the attempt to oust Richelieu that culminated in the cardinal's victory on the Day of Dupes in 1630. The

[20] On Jansen's ideas and their impact in France, see A. Adam, *Du mysticisme à la révolte*; Jean Orcibal, *Jean Duvergier de Hauranne*; Levi, *French Moralists*, pp. 199-228; and Sedgwick, *Jansenism*, pp. 47-51.

[21] These quotations from Richelieu's devotional works (particularly the *Traitté de la perfection du chrestien*) are all taken from Sedgwick, *Jansenism*, pp. 29 and 39.

most outspoken attack on Richelieu's politics, entitled *Mars Gallicus*, was published by Jansen in the Spanish Netherlands.[22] It circulated in French translation after 1637, which predisposed Richelieu to look with disfavor on Jansen's *Augustinus* when it appeared in 1640. Richelieu supported the Jesuit opponents of Jansenist ideas in their attempts to set out a less severe ethic consonant with his own theology and with the politics of prudence. His hostility to the Augustinians extended to disapproval of ideas put forward by theologians unconnected with Jansenism and Port-Royal who were too harsh in their condemnation of self-love, and too rigorous in their requirements for virtue.

Such views were held by the bishop of Belley, Jean-Pierre Camus, a disciple of Saint Francis of Sales and a prolific author. The titles of two of Camus's treatises on this subject are an accurate indication of his position: *La Caritée*, and *La Défense du pur amour contre les attaques de l'amour propre*. Camus was recognized as an ally by Fénelon many decades later, in the quarrel over quietism and *pur amour*, when Fénelon's ideas were attacked by Bossuet and suspect at court. In both cases the government decided against *pur amour*. Camus was in some danger of arrest, and Richelieu himself commissioned Antoine Sirmond to compose a refutation of Camus's *Défense*, entitled *La Défense de la vertu*.[23] The most striking contribution made by Camus was the distinction between two types of self-love, in which each type is linked with a parallel type of interest. This distinction proved durable and influential for many later writers, including Jean-Jacques Rousseau.

According to Camus, the primary characteristic of *pur amour* (or *la charité*), that in which its purity consists, is that it has no thought of its own interest, but is instead directed wholly toward the glory of God. Charity is not the same as hope, which is a lesser virtue that involves love of God as the source of our own sovereign good. Hope can lead us outside ourselves as well as returning us back into ourselves; but it will not give eternal life. Only the pure love of God, which means abandoning all thought of our own profit, is sufficient for salvation. For Camus, covetousness, concern with one's own individuality and narrow interests, is the root of all sin; the viciousness of such a motivation lies precisely in its concentration on *proprieté*, on the selfish as opposed to common and the universal. He distinguishes between

---

[22] Church, *Richelieu*, pp. 385-390, discusses the controversy surrounding this treatise.
[23] Henri Brémond, *La Querelle du pur amour au temps de Louis XIII*, pp. 3-5. On Camus, see also Levi, *French Moralists*.

amour-propre—the defective self-love based upon such grasping and proprietary attitudes—and the neutral *amour de nous-mesmes*, which does not necessarily conduce to charity, but at least presents no obstacles to it.[24] Neutral self-love is sanctioned by God Himself, points out Camus, when He commands us to love our neighbors as ourselves; this is the beginning of the route that leads us to *la charité*. Neutral self-love is compatible with the *amour de l'amitié* for other men, with a genuine desire for their own good and happiness; *amour-propre*, however, is connected with *amour de convoitise*, in which we look to other men only for what they can do for our selfish satisfaction.

Amour-propre corresponds to a particular type of interest, an *intérêt propre*, or narrow concern for our own selfish profit, that is fundamentally opposed to our true interest, which Camus calls *intérêt nôtre*.[25] This embraces all things that really matter to us as human beings, and leads to our salvation; it is our true interest to seek the kingdom of God, and all else will be added unto us. Camus is quite clear that proprietary interest and self-love cannot themselves motivate us to act virtuously. They provide a starting point to gain the attention of a soul lost in mortal sin; for such men, it is permissible to begin by appealing to the crass fear of damnation. But unless this servile motivation is then replaced by a less selfish love, we cannot speak of virtue. One difficulty we encounter in the cure of souls, says Camus, is that *amour-propre* is clever enough to hide itself "under the sheepskin of *amour de nous-mesmes*," feigning disinterestedness to escape recognition and attain its ends. This makes it hard to be sure about virtue among mortal men. Beneath the cover of our just and reasonable *intérêt nôtre* glides the serpent of *intérêt propre*, disguising itself for its own ends. Only the pure love of God provides the light that allows us to distinguish with certainty between the two, even within our own souls.[26]

By marking off *amour-propre* from *amour de nous-mesmes*, connecting the former irretrievably with vice, and the latter with the possibility of charity, and pointing out how hard it is to tell the difference between the two, Camus provided key terms for subsequent French social and moral philosophy. Of course, he was only suggesting a slightly new structure for old themes, since the complexity of vice and virtue and the diffuse connotations of love of self had been central

---

[24] Jean-Pierre Camus, *La Défense du pur Amour* (1640), pp. 12-20.
[25] *Défense*, pp. 33-34.
[26] *La Caritée*, quoted by Brémond, *La Querelle du pur amour*, pp. 36-39; Camus here compares the two sorts of self-love to parsley and hemlock, so similar in appearance yet so different in character. The image of the wolf hiding under the sheepskin is used to make the same point in *La Défense*, pp. 24-26.

to French ethical discourse since Montaigne translated Sebond and wrote his own *Essays*. But for whatever reasons, Camus's way of stating the problem proved useful for his successors.

A similar treatise composed at roughly the same time, Sénault's *De l'usage des passions*, also helped convey Augustinian ideas to secular moralists such as La Rochefoucauld a few decades later.[27] Sénault, like Camus, was not a Jansenist, and he took pains to make his work acceptable to the government by an effulgent dedication to Richelieu himself. But the tenor of his argument is much the same as Camus's *Défense du pur Amour*. Sénault asserts that before the Fall, *amour-propre* was identical with charity; Adam's self-love was in full harmony with love of God and good will toward all creatures. But since the Fall, our initially undifferentiated *amour naturel*, a restless striving of the soul toward felicity, has taken two opposed routes in different individuals: that of *amour-propre* and that of *la charité*. Sénault connects *amour-propre* with preoccupation with selfish profit, and describes how men since the Fall are blinded by the sinful illusion that advantage to the self is something quite separate from (and even opposed to) the good of all other men. This poisonous tendency to self-aggrandizement, according to Sénault, has infected the depths of human nature; it is not a mere defect of the individual will. Only God's grace can heal it by the infusion of charity. Men touched by charity are able to experience *l'amour de l'amitié*, the true selfless love of friendship in which souls are mingled (just as Montaigne had said) in perfect community, in which all divisions of mine and thine are banished. Such love is contrasted with the narrow *amour d'intérêt*, Sénault's term for the more common human motive, the search for particular utility and pleasure.[28]

Sénault's treatise is set off from those of Camus and Saint Francis by its strongly political coloration. In his dedication, the government of France by the cardinal prime minister is compared to the sovereignty of a good will in a well-ordered soul. An elaborate figure is sustained at great length to work out this comparison; Richelieu is described as "the intelligence that makes the entire state move," and the love he bears for his country "has extended so thoroughly in every part that nothing happens" without his feeling it.[29] The potentially rebellious passions in the soul are ruled by reason informed by charity, just as

---

[27] Levi, *French Moralists*, pp. 225-233, asserts the probability of this influence. Voukossava Miloyevitch, *La Théorie des passions de P. Sénault*, shows how Senault's ideas were based on those of St. Francis de Sales.

[28] François Sénault, *De l'usage des passions* (1641), pp. 219-235.

[29] From the opening paragraphs of the dedication to Richelieu, *Traité de l'usage des passions*.

Richelieu himself, acting as the instrument of sovereign majesty, repressed the Huguenots at La Rochelle. He skillfully deploys rewards and punishments to move subjects to behave properly, studying human inclinations and desires to control men's passions, just as sovereign reason acts within the soul. Like divine Providence, Richelieu holds human passions by many chains of direction and control; all his designs serve his own glory and the profit of the people, who carry out his larger purposes without any awareness that they are doing so.

The political utility of the desire for personal happiness and aversion to pain is one of the most memorable themes of this book. Sénault's treatise developed ideas suggested by other men about the way in which government can take advantage of such motives to serve political goals. But Sénault also retained the notion of the well-ordered individual soul as one in which such passions are firmly subordinated to charity, which he regarded as essential both to the good man and the good citizen. Although selfish passions provide apt material for governance, no state can be happy unless its citizens prefer the public good to their own selfish good, asserts Sénault. When he suggests that "*amour propre* must be sacrificed to *l'amour universel*," the theological consistency of his work suffers, but the message is clear. Unless men regard themselves not just as narrow individuals, but as parts of a number of larger wholes—the state, the universe, the body of Christ—they can never find true happiness.[30] The political relevance of *la charité*, which binds us by ties of friendship to our fellow men and to God Himself, is confirmed in this theology against the alternative Augustinian doctrine that the politics of the earthly city have nothing in common with the community of saints.

3. BALZAC AND THE GLORY OF THE INDIVIDUAL

La gloire is a pervasive term in French political discourse. It is associated with authoritative figures such as Louis XIV or Richelieu, who identified their own activities with the glory of the French state. But in the first part of the seventeenth century, a good many French aristocrats were assiduous in pursuit of their own individual *gloire* and that of their family and their order. The sense of destiny that attends Corneille's magnificent heroes found diverse echoes in the society that admired these heroes. In at least one formulation, that of Guez de Balzac, the expression of heroic *gloire* was identified with subordination to the monarchy and service to society. His political ideal was an equilibrium of wills, in which strong individuals voluntarily accept

---

[30] *Usage des passions*, p. 245.

the king's authority as a brilliant incarnation of reason in the state, and source of comely order. Balzac's political theory has a good deal of the baroque about it. It relies on an harmonious tension of seemingly dissonant elements, and its appeal depends more on the grandeur of this very tension than any concern for logic or realism.

Balzac's life and work exemplify the accommodations of self-conscious individualism with absolutist monarchy in ways rather different from any we have yet encountered.[31] The motivation for his brilliant absolutist portrait of *Le Prince* was undoubtedly the desire to win a high post for himself in church or state. When he consistently failed in this endeavor, this assiduous courtier turned against Richelieu, and expressed considerable hatred for him after the cardinal's death. He directed his attentions toward Mazarin instead, with no greater success; and he was then suspected of sympathy for the Frondeurs. Balzac's absolutism, in other words, however persuasive as a literary exercise, was based on calculations of where his political fortunes lay. He was famous for his ambitious pride, and his writings as a publicist must be understood in this light; as one assessment has it, "he never ceased, throughout his life, to think like a possible first minister."[32] In Balzac's case, therefore, the problem of the "sincerity" of absolutist rhetoric is particularly vexed. Perhaps he wrote most straightforwardly when he expressed admiration for the citizens of the Netherlands, and criticized the warlike policies of his own regime. Or perhaps these positions were also calculated for some purpose we cannot so easily retrieve. In any case, Balzac presents some baffling complexities that can serve to illustrate those of other aristocrats of his time.

As a young man, Balzac was influenced by an idealized Roman past, both the republican and the classical aspects of this vision. He was an associate of several libertines and suspected of libertine tendencies himself, although he vociferously denied this, and was active in the attack on the prominent libertine Théophile de Viau, even though (or because) he had been a friend of the accused. He paid tribute to Saint-Cyran, whose teaching had helped form his own faith, but he was not himself a Jansenist. Balzac thus stands at the intersection of several movements of thought and policy during the first half of the seventeenth century, but stands alone. He cannot be encompassed by any one of them. There is no reason to doubt his sincere admiration for his king, his pride in his noble blood and attachment to his own *gloire*;

---

[31] The most comprehensive account of Balzac's life and *oeuvre* is Sutcliffe, *Guez de Balzac et son temps*, particularly ch. 1.

[32] Antoine Adam, quoted by Etienne Thuau, *Raison d'etat*, p. 252.

beyond this, one must pick one's way carefully amidst the complex strands of his personality.

Balzac made a trip to Holland when he was a youth, and was inspired by the spectacle of that people's struggle for freedom from Spain. "A people is free once it will no longer serve," he wrote enthusiastically. The example of Holland could be held up to "give warning to all rulers of what duties they owe their peoples, and provide all peoples with a memorable example of what they can do against their rulers." The Dutch "deserve to have God alone for king, since they could not endure a king for God." Their former master having become their enemy, treating his subjects like animals, "has lost his right over them" and "compelled them to return to natural right by acquisition of their liberty."[33] Such language is unusual in French political writing during this period; it seldom recurs in Balzac's own later work. But two themes expressed here did color his political attitudes: the vigorous stress on liberty, and sympathy for the mass of the people unusual in such an aristocratic man.

When he later discussed the place of liberty in an absolutist polity, Balzac touched on themes advanced by other aristocrats of his time, including Saint-Cyran in his own heroic phase. The future dissident abbé had argued that dignity and nobility make possible extraordinary actions. To be free is to have "the possibility of exteriorizing, in one's acts, the virtues that one possesses and which need only the opportunity to manifest themselves."[34] On this account, the king is the only human being who can be said to be entirely free, but those who approach him in status are hardly less so. The grander scale for virtuous actions open to aristocrats (as compared with common folk) makes possible the fuller realization of individual potential, of one's self. For Balzac, such grandiose realization of the self was identified with service to the polity by brilliant acts that display exceptional virtue; and deliberate submission to royal authority was interpreted not as a constraint upon liberty, but as a pure exercise of enlightened free will. He attacked the libertines' rejection of public life, insisting that such a life was the highest expression of the virtue and the essential freedom of the noble individual. Extraordinary men come into the world, asserted Balzac, either to be kings or to counsel kings; in either case they should use their talents for the benefit of the whole society. Balzac's failure to

[33] *Discours sur l'estat politique des Provinces Unies*, quoted by Pierre Watter, "Jean Louis Guez Balzac's *Le Prince*: A Revaluation," p. 216.
[34] Orcibal, *Origines du Jansenisme*, cited by Sutcliffe, *Guez de Balzac*, pp. 131-132.

secure office meant that the only outlet for his personal virtue was in his writing, but within that constraint he did the best he could, putting his pen to enthusiastic service of royal policies, embellishing the portrait of the absolutist prince.[35]

One of the services Balzac thought he could perform for the regime was to persuade ambitious nobles, whose motives he understood clearly, of the glory that lay in reasoned submission to the king, as the embodiment of reason in the polity. He sought to give substance to the ideals of greatness dismissed by many of his contemporaries as *des biens de théatre*, in order to ennoble the corrupt disordered era in which he lived. But his sympathy for ambitious compatriots did not extend to avaricious ones, who preferred profit to glory and loved dead metal; his harshest strictures were directed at those who "work uselessly night and day to fill an abyss, to satisfy the infinite."[36] He noted sorrowfully how his beloved nation had succumbed to this contemptible vice, "this unhappy interest," which had become a god at court; this may be taken as evidence of Balzac's distaste for the mercantilist policies favored by the regime.

However, Balzac shared with mercantilists such as Montchrétien the view that the whole French nation was bound up together in intricate mutual dependence. He arrived at this view from an Aristotelian conception of society as necessary to human perfection, and solitude as unnatural to our species. According to Balzac, "only God can be fully content in Himself." Like the Augustinians, although in a thoroughly secular mood, Balzac insisted that the healthy condition for human beings is not narrow isolation in self-love, but participation in a community. "Each individual is not enough even to be one unless he tries to multiply himself in certain ways with the help of many; and to consider us in general, it seems that we are not so much whole bodies as disconnected parts that are reunited in society."[37]

This awareness of the necessity for society expressed itself in several ways in the last years of Balzac's life. He withdrew from court activity in disappointment at his failure to be given what he took to be his due, and lived in self-imposed exile. But like Machiavelli, Balzac found such a condition little to his taste. He wrote wistfully to a friend that he was

> reduced to nourishing himself with his own juices. I can communicate only with our friends from antiquity. It is true that they make

---

[35] *Discours de la gloire*, dedicated to the marquise de Rambouillet, in Balzac, *Oeuvres*, edited by L. Moreau, I, 267. Balzac's major work in this genre, *Le Prince*, was mentioned in Chapter Five in connection with *raison d'état*.
[36] *Discours de la gloire*, in *Oeuvres*, I, 268-269.
[37] Balzac, *Aristippe*, discours première, in *Oeuvres*, II, 166.

very good company, but they are always the same, and do not say this year anything they did not say last year. To animate my thoughts I need a library that is more animated, and I need conversation here as much as I needed leisure elsewhere. . . . Solitude is certainly a lovely thing; but there is pleasure in seeing someone occasionally who can talk back, to whom one can remark from time to time on how nice a thing is solitude.[38]

Balzac's awareness of the other parts of the body of the nation of France, and the terrible sufferings inflicted on them by war, also increased in the last years of his life. In the 1630s, he had been a prominent defender of *raison d'état*. But his acceptance of prudential policies and diplomatic intricacy declined with the years, and in the last parts of his life-long project, the *Aristippe*, Balzac's defense of reason of state takes on another tone. He echoes Montaigne in his sad sense that the world has lost its innocence; "we live in the corruption of centuries," he says, and "all is diseased in assemblies of men." Successful government for such men depends on ridding oneself of "that importunate virtue of which your age is incapable." Ages such as his own require poisonous remedies appropriate to their diseases, "maxims unjust by their nature, but which their use justifies."[39] The robust sense of the glories of the absolutist king and his great minister found in Balzac's *Prince* is quite absent in this passage. After the cardinal's death, Balzac gave vent to his hostility and bitterness in an excoriation of Richelieu's warlike tendencies, and called upon the cardinal's successors to go and do otherwise. In his *Discours à la Reine* Balzac sounds like a *dévot* rather than a courtier. He voiced sentiments heard again with greater urgency at the end of the long reign of the five-year-old king who ascended the throne in 1643. They were never voiced more eloquently than in Balzac's prose:

> The people, Madam, are made up of wretches and constantly present to your sight or imagination only infirmities and wounds, groans, and pain. They are not nourished by the momentous news that comes from your armies nor the great reputation of your generals. Their desires are more rude and their thoughts more tied to the earth. Glory is a passion that they do not know, that is too subtle and spiritual for them. They desire more wheat and fewer laurels.

---

[38] "Preface de l'histoire du mois prochain," addressed to Dom André de Sainct-Denis, included in Balzac's *Entretiens*, in *Oeuvres*, II, 280; this passage recalls Machiavelli's own description of his conversations with the great men of antiquity in his retirement, in the letter to Vettori. Another of Balzac's letters, in praise of solitude, is quoted by Sayre, *Solitude in Society*, p. 41.

[39] *Aristippe*, sixième discours, as translated by Church, *Richelieu*, p. 439.

They often mourn the victories of their rulers and are chilled beside their bonfires because the benefits of war are never perfect nor victories complete, because mourning, losses, and poverty often accompany triumphs. . . . And the condition in which we are is not a true prosperity; it is a misery that is praised and in good repute.[40]

4. Descartes' Provisional Morality

At least one famous Frenchman of this era harbored intellectual and personal complexities even more tantalizing than those of Balzac himself: René Descartes. In a set of private notes jotted down as he began to publish, Descartes wrote: "In the year 1620, I began to understand the foundations of a wonderful discovery."[41] In those same notes he also said that "just as comedians are counseled not to let shame appear on their foreheads, and so put on a mask, so likewise, now that I am to mount the stage of the world, where I have so far been a spectator, I come forward in a mask." The use of a mask did not mean that Descartes simply obscured himself or falsified his ideas in the act of publishing; it would be more accurate to say that he was aware of the formal and ritual aspects of publication, as well as its dangers, and took great care in presenting his ideas. It is often said that Descartes began where Montaigne ended, questioning all knowledge, establishing the priority of introspection and judgment, and then worked from there to the certainty that Montaigne never found. Montaigne had left the status of the publication of his private thoughts ambiguous. Descartes was quite clear that it was a public act, and that this entailed certain responsibilities about what he should and should not reveal about his "wonderful discovery." The paradox of Cartesian thought is that of a prudent man who made a revolution in philosophy.

Descartes valued tranquillity very highly. He knew from his own experience and that of contemporaries such as Galileo that the guardians of orthodoxy sniffed heresy in the most harmless-looking arguments, and he had no wish to give anyone an occasion to sin against philosophy by persecuting him. Yet he also enjoyed publicizing his ideas, and was flattered by admiration, particularly the admiration of learned princesses. Thus he always professed ambivalence in the very act of publishing.[42] He shared the great fear of disorder expressed by

---

[40] *Discours à la Reine, sur sa Regence*, as translated by Church, *Richelieu*, p. 442.

[41] Descartes, *Philosophical Writings*, edited by Anscombe and Geach, p. 3.

[42] In a letter to his friend Chanut written towards the end of his life, Descartes offers a wry insight into his own behavior: "They say the savages imagine the apes could speak if they wished, but abstain from doing so lest they be put to

most of his contemporaries, and wanted to be sure that his ideas would help mankind, not lead to the embroilment of society. So he generally skirted theological issues, avoided publishing his views on ethics, and rarely touched on politics even in his private letters.[43] He accepted as his own device that of Ovid: "to live happily, live hidden."[44] He also professed the philosopher's inability to act effectively in politics, just as Hesychius had described it in La Mothe le Vayer's dialogue. Descartes humbly noted that politics is the business of sovereigns, not private individuals; his sense of priorities for philosophy relegated politics to a derivative status, in any case. Yet his ethics and his epistemology suggest the possibility of a wonderful new community for humankind, made up of rational individuals devoting their energies to useful activities for the progress of the species, united willingly in love and service to one another. It is impossible to be sure how much Descartes himself was aware of these possibilities. His own scattered statements on politics are consistently conservative, and he wanted to protect society against confusion or disorder from the premature or ill-conceived application of his radically new methods. But his books suggested bold ideas to other political philosophers.

Descartes placed ethics among the topmost branches of the tree of knowledge, "the last degree of wisdom" that would flow from an understanding of all other parts of science.[45] Yet since men cannot simply stop living in the world as they make their way up the tree, he offered a conditional morality to guide men before they discover how they really ought to live. This provisional code, set out in his *Discourse on Method*, contains four maxims. The first enjoins us to accept the laws, customs, and religious practices of our associates, imitating "the most moderate and least extravagant" behaviors of "the

---

work. Since I lacked an equal prudence, I do not have as much leisure or repose as I would have had, had I the wit to hold my peace." *Correspondence*, edited by Adam and Milhaud, VII, no. 558, p. 199.

[43] In another letter to Chanut, Descrates admits that "it is true that I customarily refuse to write down my thoughts on ethics, for two reasons: one is that there is no other matter from which ill-intentioned men can so easily draw pretexts for calumny; the other, that I believe it is the business only of Sovereigns, or persons whom they authorize, to become involved in regulating the morals of others." This letter (from Egmont, 20 November 1647) is included in André Bridoux' edition of Descartes' *Oeuvres et lettres*, p. 1285, as well as in the *Correspondence*, VII, no. 609, p. 366. Descartes expressed the same view in his "Entretien avec Burman," in the *Oeuvres et lettres*, pp. 1398-1400.

[44] Letter to Mersenne, April 1634, cited by Geneviève Rodis-Lewis, *La Morale de Descartes*, p. 6.

[45] Author's letter to the translator of the *Principles of Philosophy*, in *The Philosophical Works of Descartes*, edited by Haldane and Ross, I, 301-302.

most judicious men" among those with whom we live.[46] But this same maxim counsels us to avoid "all promises by which one renounces some of one's freedom," including the freedom to embrace other principles in the future. Here Descartes's provisional morality comes very close to the attitudes of the *libertins*. The other maxims have a strongly Stoic flavor, enjoining resoluteness of action even on confused principles, once one has decided what to do, and the conquest of the self rather than fortune. Only the first maxim is truly provisional and could not stand unrevised in a more systematic moral science. When the moral rules were restated ten years later in a letter to Princess Elizabeth, Descartes altered the first to counsel the individual to obtain the best moral wisdom he can find, among his contemporaries and elsewhere, and then use his own reason to decide what to accept and what to reject in the guidance of his own life.[47]

This letter to Elizabeth of Bohemia was part of a set of reflections on Seneca's essay *De vita beata* that Descartes composed during the same period when he was working on his treatise on *The Passions of the Soul*, in 1645-1646. Taken together, the letters and the treatise offer his most extended reflections on ethics. Love, desire, and will are central to those reflections, just as they were in so many moral treatises of this era. In Descartes's philosophy, as in that of Hobbes, definitions are important as the building blocks of the whole argument. Descartes defines love as "an emotion of the soul caused by a movement of the spirits that incites it to join itself willingly to objects that appear to it to be agreeable," and ranks it among the passions, along with desire, which is a passion specifically directed toward the future. Passions, in Cartesian philosophy, are perceptions in the soul directly related to some "commotion" in the body; all passions are to be distinguished from deliberate judgments, "which induce the soul by its free will to unite itself with those things that it esteems to be good, and to separate itself from those it holds to be evil." Will, a central concern in Descartes's morality, is a pure free attribute of the soul itself, defined as "the consent by which we consider ourselves from this time forward united with what we love, so that we imagine a whole of which we conceive ourselves as only constituting one part, while the thing loved constitutes another part."[48]

In analyzing different kinds of love, Descartes drew a distinction between the love that takes the form of desire for possession of the

[46] *Discourse on Method*, in *Writings*, p. 24.
[47] *Correspondence*, VI, no. 494, 4 August 1645, p. 280; Pierre Mesnard, *Essai sur la morale de Descartes*, pp. 48-64, has a useful comparison of Descartes' provisional and mature moralities.
[48] *Passions of the Soul*, article LXXIX, in *Works*, p. 366.

other as an object, and the purer love that is not distorted through the possessive mode, but instead wills unity with the loved person, without desiring anything from that person except participation in unity. Among the former loves are the miser's passion for money, the ambitious man's for *gloire*, and the brutal man's desire for a woman he wants to violate. The love of a parent or a friend is ideally of the latter sort, which entails seeking the good of the loved one as ardently as one's own, or even more ardently, since the lover has a vision of himself together with the loved one as a "whole of which he is not the best part," and therefore "often prefers their interests to his, and does not fear losing himself in order to save them."[49] Thus Descartes puts into two compartments those same loves that his theologically minded contemporaries described as the narrow *amour de convoitise* and the generous *pur amour*. Descartes asserts that it is appropriate to feel such a love for other parts of those larger wholes in which we place ourselves, in proportion to the esteem we bear for them; devotion is owed to God above all, but we may also have devotion for our prince, country, town, "and even a particular friend whom we esteem highly." The Cartesian individual is isolated only in the initiating moment of his singular experience of the complete rejection of everything except the thinking self, the *cogito, ergo sum*. For the rest of his life, before and after, he is expected to be aware of his existence as part of a concentric circle of larger communities, including ultimately the entire universe.

In the last part of his *Treatise on the Passions*, Descartes offers a portrait of the "generous man," the noble embodiment of virtue. A man who esteems himself "as highly as he legitimately can," and resolves firmly to exercise his free will to act rightly in every situation, easily conceives of other men feeling the same way, and thus assumes good will in others instead of despising them. Such men are led "to do great things . . . and because they do not hold anything more important than to do good to other men and to disdain their individual interests, they are for this reason always . . . obliging toward everyone." Against the rigorous morality of the Augustinians, Descartes allows for the psychological power of *la gloire*, the desire to be esteemed, as an acceptable road to virtue. Even though "common people judge very ill" at times, we cannot live without other people, and thus it is important to have their esteem; this frequently entails, in Descartes's ethic, following "their opinions rather than ours respecting the external aspect of our actions."[50]

[49] *Passions of the Soul*, arts. LXXX-LXXXIII, pp. 366-368.
[50] *Passions of the Soul*, arts. CLII-CLVIIII, and CCIV-CCVI, in *Works*, pp. 201-204.

The ethic of *le généreux*, like all Cartesian morality, depends on the recognition by the virtuous man that he is part of a set of larger wholes, like those described by Sénault in his own *Treatise on the Passions*. This stipulation is made not only in Descartes's *Treatise*, but also in his letters to Elizabeth, particularly when he says

> that while each of us is a person separate from others, whose interests therefore are in some way distinct from those of the rest of the world, one should always be aware that no one could subsist all alone and that each of us is, in fact, one of the parts of the universe, and more particularly one of the parts of the earth, the state, society, and family to which one is joined by residence, obligation [*serment*] and birth. And that each of us ought always to prefer the interests of the whole, of which one is a part, to those of his person in particular.[51]

This theory of obligation based on our membership in a larger whole requires us, says Descartes, to accept the authority of the sovereigns who rule the polities of which we form a part. But apart from that, this counsel should be used "with measure and discretion," since it would be foolish to risk great danger to oneself to bring about a tiny advantage to one's country, and "if one individual is worth more in himself than the rest of his city together," he should not waste himself to save it. This hierarchy of degrees of worth means that some individuals benefit society a great deal more than others; if the good of the whole will not be advanced by their sacrifice of self, this moral calculus allows them to save themselves at the expense of others. The Cartesian sense of the interconnectedness of all men does not entail their equality.

Cartesian morality has none of the sense of anguish and struggle that sometimes accompanies ethical discussions. Descartes assumes that noble souls are naturally inclined to love virtue, and the rest of us will be brought to do good in spite of our inclinations, by the divinely established order of things. This is arranged so skillfully "that even if each individual thought only of himself, and had no charity for others, he could not fail to exert himself on their behalf as much as possible if he uses his prudence."[52] This dichotomous assumption of

---

and 423-424. On the ethic of *le généreux*, see Geneviève Rodis-Lewis, *La Morale de Descartes*, pp. 82-101.

[51] *Correspondence*, VI, no. 500, pp. 301-302.

[52] *Correspondence*, VI, no. 504, 6 October 1645, p. 320; Descartes qualifies the passage quoted here by noting that it holds at least for "an age when *les moeurs* have not become corrupt."

moral motivation—noble souls will choose virtue for its own sake, the others will be unwittingly channeled into beneficent activity by the dictates of their own self-interested prudence—was parallel to assumptions made by Jansenist moralists such as Nicole a few decades later, and recalls Montchrétien's mercantilism, as well. Throughout the seventeenth century, in fact, the assumption that selfish men who act with a minimal degree of prudence will be led to benefit others to achieve their own happiness was reiterated in several different ways. Descartes's own view of the matter was as follows:

> the reason I think that those who look only to their individual utility must work for that of others and try to bring pleasure is that one normally observes that those who are known to be obliging and prompt to please others receive a great number of good offices even from persons they have not yet helped; . . . the effort it costs them to bring pleasure to others is outweighed by the commodities they gain because of their reputation for good will.[53]

The moral system in these letters to Elizabeth fuses duty and satisfaction, public and private benefit. The individual who relates everything to himself and harms others for some small advantage fails in his duty, and is also deprived of the greatest satisfactions in life; he never experiences true friendship or fidelity, nor can he perform heroic acts that bring the highest pleasure. At the other extreme, the truly generous individual, who acts in full consciousness of his duty, "abandoning everything to the divine will, divesting himself of his own interests," finds therein his own highest pleasure, and the satisfaction that attends such acts does not detract from their goodness, but enhances it. Descartes asserts that the goods available to isolated individuals are but a small part of life's pleasures; the generous man can enjoy these along with the greater goods common to the larger whole in which he consciously participates.[54] This awareness that there is a set of goods that can only be enjoyed by men in common was a major antidote to radical individualism in French ethics; it became central in the writings of Pascal. Descartes depicts a community of individuals, each of whom esteems himself and all his fellows highly, all of whom are aware of their existence as part of a larger whole, drawn to that

---

[53] *Correspondence*, VII, no. 516, January 1646, p. 5.
[54] *Correspondence*, VI, no. 500, p. 302, and no. 504, p. 314, where Descartes observes that "if we think only of ourselves alone, we can enjoy only those goods particular to ourselves; whereas, if we consider ourselves as parts of some other body, we can also participate in the goods which are common to that body, without being deprived thereby of any of those proper to ourselves."

whole by their recognition of its excellence as well as its advantages for them. Instead of a social contract among coldly calculating Hobbesian units, Descartes suggests a community based on mutual love and esteem, formed by the passionate consent of all individuals willing their own unity. All these things were developed much more fully by his successors, particularly Rousseau. In Cartesian thought they remain only potentialities sketched out in passing.

5. THE PHILOSOPHER AND THE CITY

Descartes's voluminous correspondence contains few references to contemporary events, and these only when such events impinged on his own private world. He visited his native France briefly at the outbreak of the Fronde and hurried back to Holland, professing himself satisfied with living as he did, "one foot in one country, the other in another," since this assured him the freedom he so highly prized.[55] He devoted his sustained attention to politics on only one occasion, when Princess Elizabeth commanded him to give her his opinion of Machiavelli's *Prince*. In his long letter on this subject, Descartes approves some of Machiavelli's dictates, but takes issue with others that strike him as *très tyranniques*. The most interesting aspect of his discussion is that while Descartes, like most of his contemporaries, accepted the necessity of a special sort of prudence in government (asserting that "justice among sovereigns has other limits than that among individuals, and it seems that in these encounters God gives the right to those to whom He has given force"), Descartes goes on to add that "the most just actions become unjust, when those who do them believe them to be so."[56] This novel twist in an old argument indicates that in Descartes's eyes, the important thing is that the prince should *believe* he acts justly, lest he fall into the dangerous habit of doing injustice consciously, which leads easily to tyranny. Since the precise requirements of justice are hard to determine in complex political situations, Descartes concentrates on stating the conditions under which a prince, who has the power to do almost anything he likes, will be most likely to revere the name of justice and avoid egregious injustices. He warns against teaching princes that there is no difference between the

[55] Letter to Elizabeth, June/July 1648, *Correspondence*, VIII, no. 636, p. 55. Cf. his letter to the princess after the execution of Charles I, in February 1649 (no. 656, pp. 142-143); his reaction to the "disastrous conclusion to the Tragedies of England" is primarily governed by his desire to comfort his royal friend, Charles' niece, on her bereavement.

[56] *Correspondence* VII, no. 548 (September 1646), p. 164.

two, and that they can act as they please, so long as they are successful and preserve their state.

The same subtlety is apparent in a note on Thomas Hobbes; Descartes reproves Hobbes for his principles, "which are very bad and very dangerous, in that he supposed all men to be knaves, or *that he gives them cause to be so.*"[57] This recognition of the role of belief about the moral quality of one's own behavior in politics provides a fleeting but fascinating insight into Descartes's political ideas. He regarded politics as a complex, arcane, and rather messy business, in which sovereign and subjects alike are moved by what they believe about themselves and about their world. He therefore disapproved of those, like Machiavelli and Hobbes, who teach men to think of the world as fundamentally fluid and amoral; and he insisted on the importance of certain basic ethical distinctions even in the political realm. In his letter on Machiavelli's *Prince*, he differentiates carefully between behavior that is appropriate in dealing with one's enemies—in which case virtually anything is permissible "so long as one derives from it some advantage for oneself or for one's subjects"—and in dealing with one's friends. No one should ever pretend to be friendly in order to take advantage of someone else. This is in a most profound sense disadvantageous to society, since it is friendship that holds society together. Beyond this, Descartes refuses to offer his opinion. He elegantly protests the inappropriateness of his advising a princess about politics, and never attempted elsewhere to meddle with the business of sovereigns.

Yet although Descartes asserted that the philosopher has no direct competence in politics, he may well have recognized that philosophers shape moral and political attitudes in their own way. This emerges most strongly from the *Discourse on Method*, that "history, or if you like, a fable," in which Descartes describes his discoveries in philosophy. The analogy that dominates the *Discourse*—tearing down an old building to construct another according to the best principles of architectural design—is offered in the context of several explicit references to politics. To bolster his observation that human reasoning is imperfect because it has grown up haphazardly in each individual by custom and ill-regulated education, Descartes points out that the best polities (such as Sparta) proceed from the creative legislative intelligence of a single man. In his *Discourse*, each individual is invited to become the

[57] *Correspondence*, VI, no. 419, p. 88, emphasis added; Descartes does allow that he finds the author of *De Cive* "more skillful in Morals than in Metaphysics or Physics."

legislator-architect of his own intelligence, throwing off all accumulated "knowledge" and scrutinizing everything to make it "square with the norm of reason" before accepting anything new or old as part of his mental furnishings. However, Descartes specifically denied that any private individual (*un particular*) had any business attempting such a reformation in society as a whole. He castigates those "turbulent and restless characters who, although not summoned by birth or fortune to the control of public affairs, are yet constantly effecting some new reform—in their own heads."[58]

Descartes's distaste for reformation in politics (except when undertaken by a sovereign legislator by virtue of his office and his genius) rests on his assumption that changing society is much more complex and difficult an enterprise than scrutinizing individual knowledge. With reference to states, Descartes says specifically that "such large bodies are very hard to raise up when once they fall, or even to keep up when once they are shaken." No doubt many polities are imperfect, since there are so many variants under the sun; but these imperfections, insists Descartes, have been softened by custom, and "custom has even avoided or imperceptibly corrected many faults that prudence could not so well provide against." This conservative awareness of the beneficent effects of custom can be found in a number of French theorists from Montaigne to Montesquieu. Like Montesquieu, Descartes believed that his new philosophy would "provide every man with new reasons for loving his duties, his prince, his country, his laws."[59]

The Cartesian reformulation of old truths of metaphysics and religion after they have passed before the scrutiny of reason is often quite conservative. Yet the vision of the citizens of the city of the mind adopting Descartes's method, tearing down their houses and rebuilding them according to a more rational design, and in the very act of doing so, creating a new and better-ordered city for themselves, is suggestive of a very different mood. Descartes must have been aware that a renewal of ideas and beliefs by individuals would eventually change the shape of the whole city; and although he wrote for a small number, he was a firm believer in the importance of intellectual guidance for more ordinary minds. His conviction of the necessary patterns

---

[58] The references to the *Discourse on Method* in this section are all to the second part of the treatise, in *Writings*, pp. 15-19; the description of the books as "a history or fable" is on page 9.

[59] Preface to the *Esprit des lois*; cf. the second part of Descartes' comment on Hobbes in the letter cited above: "His whole aim is to write in favor of Monarchy; but this could be done much more advantageously and soundly than he has done, if one chose more virtuous and solid maxims."

of connection among clear and distinct ideas implies that these new mental houses will be similar in basic form and pleasingly consonant with one another, though not identical.[60] Here, despite his oft-expressed incompetence in politics, the philosopher appears, for a brief moment, in the guise of the "great-souled legislator." It is only for a moment, and one must not push such a fancy very far; but it is clear that in Descartes's eyes the development of philosophy was expected to have manifold benefits for mankind, not only in science and technology, but in ethical understanding and political cohesiveness. This is the mood in which we should read his summary reflection on the utility of philosophy in society: "Since it extends over the whole range of human knowledge, we are entitled to hold that it alone is what distinguishes us from savages and barbarians, and that the civilization and refinement of each nation is proportionate to the superiority of its philosophy. In this way a state can have no greater good than the possession of true philosophy."[61]

Descartes's new method, which at first glance appears to have such a subversive potential in social thought (and was used to such ends by several Cartesians with radical propensities), was seen by Descartes himself as bolstering rather than undermining established authority.[62] In his moral system sovereigns are not overturned but strengthened; they are provided with more devoted, as well as more enlightened, subjects. This optimistic faith in the consonance between "true philosophy" and a strong and stable polity was reflected in the ideas of several Cartesians at the beginning of the Enlightenment, including the abbé de Saint-Pierre, who was firmly convinced that the radical utilitarian potential of philosophy would benefit mankind as well as absolutist monarchy.[63] But along with Cartesian optimism, the abbé also re-

[60] Descartes' belief in such connections is demonstrated on p. 21 of the *Discourse*, and also in his "Search after Truth," *Works*, p. 306.

[61] Author's introductory letter to the *Principles of Philosophy*, *Works*, p. 204; cf., in this same vein, the "Search after Truth," and the first of the *Rules for the Direction of the Mind*, in *Works*, p. 2.

[62] One example of a radical Cartesian approach to society was that of François Poulain de la Barre, whose bold essay *De l'égalité des deux sexes* (1673) applied Descartes' own method of doubt and radical scrutiny to social institutions. Poulain de la Barre did not shrink from the anarchical implications of his own discoveries about equality, according to Carolyn C. Lougee, *Le Paradis des Femmes*, pp. 18-19. Other perspectives on Cartesian politics are offered by Augusto del Noce, *Riforma cattolica e filosofia moderna*, vol. I, *Cartesio*; Roger Lefèvre, *L'Humanisme de Descartes*, part II, and Henri Lefebvre, *Descartes*, pp. 37-42.

[63] On Saint-Pierre, see Chapter Thirteen below. In his theory of an enlightened absolutist monarchy rationalizing the state, the abbé developed a line of argument that Descartes himself had hinted at, when he observed that although private individuals should not attempt to reform society, "those whom God has

tained some of the tensions in Descartes's thought. By bringing individuals into their communities as energetic, passionate participants in a larger whole, and offering bold new philosophy a prominent position in society, while at the same time requiring subordination to monarchical authority in the polity and insisting on the absence of any involvement of ordinary individuals, or philosophers, in government, Descartes sharpened some of the contradictions in the world view of absolutist monarchy.

---

favored more highly will very likely have loftier designs." *Discourse on Method, Writings*, pp. 17-18.

CHAPTER SEVEN

The Politics of Interest
in the Fronde

1. REBELLION IN FRANCE AND EUROPE

During the same period in which the English beheaded a king and established the power of Commons and of Cromwell, a number of other European peoples were also engaged in civil war. Of these contemporaneous rebellions, that which occurred in France was "both geographically and socially . . . the most widespread."[1] Since 1620, peasant uprising and urban protests had been a serious problem in France almost every year; but the conflicts had been localized and sporadic.[2] Between 1648 and 1653, such events occurred in many parts of France at the same time, and were matched by rebellious activities among the high nobility (including the princes of the blood), and within the most important courts in Paris and the provinces. Although much of France was reduced virtually to anarchy for a time, when the revolts were suppressed it was apparent that this *révolution manquée* had made little difference in government.[3] The name attached to the collection of rebellions—the Fronde—was that of a children's game played in the streets of Paris. This nicely captures the occasional frivolousness, and ultimate ineffectiveness, of the revolts. Several of the reforms won by the Frondeurs remained on the books but were circumvented or ignored by the government. The Fronde strengthened the king's determination to consolidate his position, and increased his distrust of other power-holders. Thus a rebellion fought to undo what

[1] A. Lloyd Moote, *The Revolt of the Judges*, p. 368; Theodore Rabb, *Struggle for Stability*, and Robert Forster and Jack P. Greene, ed., *Preconditions of Revolution in Early Modern Europe*, present comparative evidence about other rebellions.
[2] Boris Porchnev, *Les Soulèvements populaires en France de 1623 à 1648*, is the pioneering study of these revolts; see also the essays in P. J. Coveney, ed., *France in Crisis, 1620-1675*, and William Beik, "Magistrates and Popular Uprisings in France before the Fronde: Toulouse." There were uprisings in the decades after 1654, but they differed in intensity and character from those of the earlier period, and were less threatening to the regime, according to E. Le Roy Ladurie, "Révoltes et contestations rurales," and Leon Bernard, "French Society and Popular Uprisings under Louis XIV."
[3] Louis Madelin coined this term in his study of the Fronde, *Une Révolution manquée*.

Richelieu and Mazarin had done, to return to the constitutionalist and tempered monarchy of the past (as it appeared to nostalgic constitutionalists in 1650) had the ironic effect of spurring the development of absolutism in France.

There are a number of reasons for the failure of the Fronde. Although men of different social orders were involved in the revolts, they never united to make their combined power felt. There were, in fact, several Frondes—parlementary, princely, and popular. The revolutions proceeded separately, and participants in each were as hostile to one another as they were to the king's ministers.[4] This made Mazarin's policy of "divide and rule" an effective strategy. The Fronde began when members of two privileged groups (the judicial magistrates and the old aristocracy) took advantage of the minority of Louis XIV to attempt to win back power they had lost. But the two groups had little in common beyond their antipathy to the "reign of the cardinals," and to the new officers of the royal administration, especially the intendants. Throughout much of the century they contributed to the growth of the monarchy by making it the arbiter of disputes between themselves, and they failed to find a basis for sustained cooperation in the Fronde. Uprisings by artisans and peasants were never meshed with either the princely or the parlementary Fronde. The people rebelled out of despair at economic misery, and above all to protest oppressive taxation. The judges included relief of the tax burden among their proposed reforms, but this was less central to their concerns than the institutional interests of their corporations and their judicial order. Neither the princes nor the judges provided leadership for the popular rebellions. A few noble leaders fired the people's imagination, but this asset was used cynically or not at all. In many instances the people rebelled as much against the local oligarchies as against the crown; and when the people began to take matters into their own hands, the members of the upper classes reacted with distaste and fear.

Despite the coincidence in timing, the French rebellions had little in common with events across the Channel. The example of England was generally taken as a cautionary tale rather than a model to be followed, and outright republicanism was rare. Only in a few areas such as Bordeaux, where English agents made a concerted effort to

---

[4] On the parlementary Fronde, see Moote, *Revolt of the Judges*; Sharon Kettering, *Judicial Politics and Urban Revolt*; and Paul Rice Doolin, *The Fronde*; on the role of the peasants, Roland Mousnier, *Peasant Uprisings in the Seventeenth Century*; on the princely Fronde, Mousnier's article, "Monarchie contre aristocratie dans la France du XVIIe siècle," and Pierre Deyon's essay from the *Revue historique*, translated in Coveney, *France in Crisis*.

propagandize Frenchmen, was any sympathy displayed.[5] The Fronde lacked specifically those elements that were crucial to the outcome of the English civil war: the participation of large numbers of ordinary bourgeois citizens; the presence of a generally accepted institutional machinery for expressing opposition to the monarch; and control of an army. In most cities the members of the bourgeoisie, apart from the judges, were conspicuous for their "profound neutrality."[6] The Estates-General had demonstrated in 1614-1615 their incapacity to take any action requiring cooperation among the three orders, and had scant appeal for most Frenchmen. The Estates had never won the right to assemble regularly, and held little promise as a focus for opposition in a crisis. There was a half-hearted attempt to convene them during the Fronde, but the governors of provinces and other notables managed the elections so that only candidates faithful to the king were chosen, and in the general confusion the body never met.

According to their own theory of the constitution, the sovereign courts (especially the parlement of Paris) were the successors to the moribund Estates-General as the representatives of the French people in negotiations with the Crown. The courts set aside ancient rivalries to draft a unified program of reforms in the Chambre Saint Louis during the summer of 1648.[7] There was a fairly successful attempt to win support for these twenty-seven articles among sister courts throughout France. But the effectiveness of the proposed reforms was blunted by the unwillingness of the judges to attack the privileged financial status of various persons and provinces (including themselves), and their desire to retain control over their offices as their own property. The judges also failed to deal with the constitutional questions raised by their own activities, and describe exactly what sort of tempered monarchy they wished for France. Sheltering under protestations of complete loyalty to the king, they avoided bringing such matters to the forefront, so as to proceed with as much support and as little upset as possible. But this rendered their reforms technical and negative, rather than providing any unitary vision of a constitution for the polity within which the reforms would take their place.

For all these reasons, it is not surprising that the Fronde failed to issue in a constitutionally limited monarchy in France. It is rather more surprising that it prompted little sustained discussion of what such a monarchy might look like. Princes and judges alike claimed to be

[5] Philip A. Knachel, *England and the Fronde*.
[6] This term is used by Ernst Kossmann in *La Fronde*, p. 63; Kossmann's is the best single study of all facets of these events. In English, the most helpful succinct discussion is ch. 10 of Ranum's *Paris in the Age of Absolutism*.
[7] Moote, *The Revolt of the Judges*, ch. 5.

defending the ancient constitution against the vandalizing enterprises of Richelieu and Mazarin; and they regularly raised constitutional questions in asserting their traditional privileges to participate in government. But their views were couched in vague language recalling a better order in the past, and were rarely given concrete or systematic form. There was a great outpouring of pamphlet literature, which has not yet been studied as carefully as it should be; but most of the pamphlets were directed toward specific issues and personalities of the day.[8] They were known as *mazarinades*, after the cardinal minister who was their chief target. General questions about how France should be governed were raised by the pamphleteers, but few answers of any force and originality were given. Some thoughtful speeches were made by judges; serious treatises devoted to constitutional issues were rare. The one treatise normally identified with the parlementary Fronde, Claude Joly's *Recueil de maximes véritables*, was a collection of quotations from earlier authorities.

In the past, clear-cut constitutional alternatives had been raised primarily by the dissidents in the religious wars, first the Huguenots and then the Catholic Leaguers. Protestantism was not an issue in the Fronde, and most Huguenots were anxiously silent for fear of losing those precarious rights they had fought so hard to win. However, one aspect of the rebellion (sometimes known as the "ecclesiastical Fronde") involved the staunch Gallicanism of the judges, and touched on Jansenism, as well.[9] There was a good deal of circumstantial evidence linking the Jansenists with the Frondeurs. They had close family and class ties with the rebellious judges, and several prominent participants in the noble Fronde were patrons of Port-Royal. Several Jansenists, including Saint-Cyran, had been implicated in conspiracies against Richelieu, and Jansenist disapproval of the regime's aggrandizing policies was known to all. One of the best known of the *mazarinades*, *La Vérité tout nue*, may have been composed by a prominent Jansenist, Arnauld d'Andilly.[10] The leader of the Fronde in Paris, Cardinal Retz, carefully cultivated Jansenist sympathies among the lesser clergy for his own political purposes. One reason the regime was suspicious of Jansenism from the outset was the aura of alternative com-

---

[8] Porchnev, *Soulèvements populaires*, pp. 515-520, points out how little we know about the popular ideology of the Fronde, and argues the strength of radical views on the basis of comments in contemporary *mémoires*.

[9] Sedgwick, *Jansenism in Seventeenth-Century France*, ch. III.

[10] This attribution was first made by Tom T. Edwards, "Jansenism in Church and State," Ph.D. dissertation, Harvard, 1960; it is supported by research presented in Hubert Carrier, "Port-Royal et la Fronde," and accepted by Sedgwick, *Jansenism in Seventeenth-Century France*, p. 215.

munity, a republic of the saints, that was associated with the houses of *les solitaires*. But none of the brotherhood, during the Fronde or any other time, showed any inclination to extend those principles to secular republicanism. Noninvolvement in the world's affairs was a principle to which they generally adhered unless the world insisted on becoming involved in their affairs, which happened with considerable regularity. Nonetheless, the Jansenists professed complete loyalty to the king, and none of them declared openly for the Fronde.

2. THE ORMÉE IN BORDEAUX: THE PEOPLE'S FRONDE

Although the Jansenists were not republicans, some other Frenchmen of this era were. Republicanism was not a prominent motif in the *mazarinades*, partly because of the widespread loyalty to the king himself, perhaps also because of the effects of government censorship on men's habits of thought and writing, even during a civil war. However, in a few cities, including Aix-en-Provence, Angers, Carcassonne, and Rouen, artisans and minor bourgeois showed republican sympathies as they threatened to take control of municipal government, and in a few instances managed to do so for several days or weeks.[11] Our knowledge of these incidents is hampered by lack of evidence; in 1668, Louis XIV ordered all public documents concerning this era (particularly those in Paris) to be destroyed or altered to delete references to Frondeur activities.[12] But enough remains from the most sustained of these communard incidents (that which occurred in Bordeaux) to show how ordinary Frenchmen, at first reacting to specific grievances of an economic sort, were finally led to consider declaring their city an independent republic and appealing for English aid.

Bordeaux was governed for several months during 1652 by a group of artisans, lesser bourgeois, and proletarians who called themselves the Ormée, after the elm-shaded platform on which they met.[13] These men rebelled against the privileged status and economic oppressiveness of local tax officers, and the distorted justice provided by the local courts. They were, at the outset, completely loyal to the king. In time-honored fashion, they assumed that if he only knew about their plight he would surely aid them. The Ormists were disabused of this idea when the king sided with their oppressors and refused the alliance of *le roi et le peuple* that they offered him, and they gradually moved

[11] Sal Alexander Westrich, *The Ormée of Bordeaux*, pp. 134-136.
[12] Porchnev, *Soulèvements populaires*, pp. 505-506.
[13] The following paragraphs draw heavily on Sal Westrich's study of this movement, *The Ormée of Bordeaux*, especially chapter III.

to profess open republicanism. Their tracts were influenced by Leveleer ideology, particularly Lilburne's *Agreement of the People*, brought to Bordeaux by Edward Sexby in 1651. But their ideas were also derived from their own experiences as members of self-governing guilds and corporations, and from traditions of municipal government that still survived in France. If they became critical of the king only when they were on the verge of defeat, they were republicans in another sense much earlier—in the ancient sense of citizens of a proud city, in which Guillaume de la Perrière spoke of himself as a citizen of Toulouse.

The tracts composed by the Ormists at the height of their revolt have a strongly egalitarian tone.[14] "It is equality that makes for perfection among individuals," proclaims the *Apologie pour l'Ormée*, because "it unifies all parts of the republic, fosters peace, and produces concord among the citizenry. The actual cause of sedition and political strife is the excessive wealth of the few." The linkage of economic and political oppression was also made in the *Manifeste des bordelois*, which asserted that "princes and magistrates are the accomplices of tyranny. If the people expect deliverance from leaders who do not come from their midst, they will only prolong and worsen their miseries." The egalitarianism of the Ormée, however, was that of the lower-middle class, focused on resentment of the privileges of the wealthy few, with no notion of equalizing the status of those beneath themselves such as journeymen, apprentices, landless peasants. Their ideology was dominated by overtones of the guild experience; they spoke of their movement as "the Company," and their tracts detail the ways in which the members of the Company would be protected against oppression and provided with welfare and security.

In their plan for reorganizing the government of the city in the hands of members of the Company (as in their perception of the connections between economic imbalance and civil strife), the Ormists demonstrated the Aristotelian influence that had dominated French civic humanism so strongly since the sixteenth century. They placed sovereignty in the assembly of the people, asserting that "assemblies are founded on man's desire for society, which is one of the strongest impulses that nature has implanted in us. . . . It is upon this foundation that cities and republics have been built so that men may find in them all the goods they need, whether for survival or pleasure, and for which they have such strong appetite." The Ormists associated assembly with the practices of the ancient Gauls, and were proud of their own habit of convening beneath the trees, as their ancestors had done,

---

[14] Quotations from these tracts are all taken from Westrich, *The Ormée of Bordeaux*, pp. 48-59.

"in the very manner of our Ormée." They considered themselves democrats, at least the more radical among them, and juxtaposed their own democracy to the "aristocratic estate" which was naturally hostile to their own. They were aware that instituting a democratic sovereignty was a bold and novel act, and their language resonates with phrases dear to revolutionaries in all eras: "When it becomes necessary for individuals to constitute themselves into assemblies, it is the height of temerity to attempt to dissolve them; for a society that is bound by the common good [*le bien commun*] is indissoluble. The sovereign law being the common weal [*le salut du publique*], it is the latter that will decide the fate of all states, lowering and even destroying them in order to assert itself."[15]

The use of these ancient phrases—*le bien commun, le salut du publique*—in this context indicates that the Ormists were aware that they were rejecting the politics of *raison d'etat* for a very different vision, the vision of an assembled community of men pursuing the common good together. They had grandiose thoughts of extending their vision to other parts of France, liberating other Frenchmen as they themselves were freed from tyranny and oppression. The *Manifeste des bordelois* asserted that "the Bordelais have shown themselves ahead of all Frenchmen in their zeal for the public good. They have struggled mightily to break their chains and restore to the entire kingdom the liberties lost in the course of all those centuries." Balzac's trenchant observation that Frenchmen wanted "more wheat and fewer laurels" was doubtless true when the laurels were those of the king and his noble soldiers; but his contemporaries in Bordeaux attested the importance of another kind of laurels when they proclaimed: "Bordeaux's actions will soon be approved by all France, for its cause is so just, that its laurels must spread throughout the kingdom."[16]

Although the hopes of the Bordeaux revolutionaries were dashed almost as soon as they were formulated, they provide an interesting exception to the general absence of genuine republican ideology in French thought before the eighteenth century. They also offer a marked contrast to the cautious and colorless ideology of the more prominent Frondeurs, the members of the Parlements and other courts, who consistently asserted their allegiance to the monarchy, and pictured themselves as fighting for the best interests of the king himself. These men accepted the ancient formula describing the king's power as *absolue*, and wished only to revise the way that power was dele-

[15] *Généreuse résolution des gascons* (1652), quoted by Westrich, p. 51.
[16] *Manifeste des bordelois* (1652), quoted by Westrich, p. 57; the phrase from Balzac's letter to the queen-regent is discussed in Chapter Six above.

gated and deployed. Several students of the Fronde have noted that the Frondeur judges benefited from the amorphous nature of absolutist ideology in France.[17] They could make their reformist claims without treading on subversive territory. To remain well within the bounds of orthodoxy was no doubt comfortable and convenient for such conservative revolutionaries; but they were the prisoners as well as the beneficiaries of the rhetoric they used. They found it hard to locate a firm basis for expressing opposition and suggesting broad alternatives to the status quo; yet when they voiced their rather timid and traditional conception of the monarchy, they were castigated by the Crown as political heretics. This is a thought-provoking indication of the extent of absolutism's victory over the principles of early sixteenth-century constitutionalism.

3. Claude Joly on the Ancient Constitution: The Parlementary Fronde

The first Frondeurs were neither artisans nor peasants but judges, members of the king's own administration who saw their rights to participate in government circumvented in novel ways by Richelieu and his successor, and who also feared that the value of their own offices and that of other magistrates would be diluted by the flooding of the market to raise revenue for the Crown. At the height of their rebellion, the judges made claims about their legitimate place in the state that would have given them a more powerful part than they had ever played before. They also drafted reforms that limited the proliferation of offices, dismantled the administration of the provinces by the intendants, and reduced the tax burden for ordinary Frenchmen. But their reforms had virtually no effect in the long run, and their role in government for the next half-century was more circumscribed than before.

Despite the meager results of their rebellion, the judges broached some crucial constitutional contentions.[18] That they failed to develop them is probably due to the ambiguities surrounding their role, the greater visibility of immediate practical issues, and the lack of a spokesman able to give systematic form to their position. They did possess an eloquent orator in Omer Talon, the *avocat-général* of the Parlement

---

[17] This point is made by both Kossmann and Moote, as well as by Denis Richet, *La France moderne*, pp. 135-138.

[18] In his chapter on the Fronde in Forster and Green, *Preconditions of Revolution*, Roland Mousnier stresses the revolutionary potential of the judges' claims, had they been developed and sustained.

of Paris. In his excellent history of the Fronde, E. H. Kossmann chooses Talon as the best exponent of the baroque Frondeur conception of the state. In the eyes of such men, the polity still depended on pluralistic tensions arising from the participation by the several orders and institutions in the state. As Kossmann puts it: "The State, for them, was like a baroque church where a great number of different concepts meet, collide, and finally absorb themselves in a magnificent system." To illustrate his generalization, Kossmann quotes from some of Talon's speeches, especially that of July 31, 1648, the high-water mark of the parlementary Fronde. Talon referred to the several powers in the state as dynamic and mobile forces, and described the "respectful resistance" of the judges not as disobedience, but as a function of their office, in the same way that "the general economy of nature consists not only in the difference but even in the contradiction of those principles which, working incessantly to destroy her, subsist in that domestic struggle in such a way that the total desolation of the universe and the destruction of our own bodies cannot arise until one of these elements or qualities has defeated and surmounted all the others."[19] Talon tried to convince the king that even so central and splendid a natural element as the sun could not gain hegemony over the others without destroying the universe. But this elegant reminder of the virtues of pluralism apparently made little impression on the prince, and neither Talon nor any other Frondeur developed a systematic theory of the baroque state.

The most prominent treatise associated with the parlementary Fronde was Claude Joly's *Recueil de maximes véritables*. As the name implies, this treatise was a collection of maxims from constitutionalist writers of earlier periods. This tactic of resurrecting the past to bolster present arguments was well designed to enhance the legitimacy of the judges' revolt, ostensibly on behalf of the traditional constitution. But it hindered the emergence of arguments for a liberal regime better adapted to the mid-seventeenth century. Joly's treatise is a "mirror of princes," spiced with indictments of the alien ideas introduced by the two cardinals: that the king is master of the persons and goods of all Frenchmen, and that the requirements of successful policy include a shady morality incompatible with true Christian virtue.[20] The most interesting thing about Joly's treatise is not the text itself, but an appended commentary on its reception by contemporary Frenchmen.[21]

[19] Kossmann, *La Fronde*, pp. 24-27.
[20] Claude Joly, *Recueil des maximes véritables et importantes pour l'institution du roy* (1653), "Avertissement au lecteur."
[21] "Lettre apologétique pour le *Recueil des maximes véritables*, etc." appended

The list of principles set out in that appendix sounds innocuous enough; most of them were common wisdom at the time of Seyssel. Joly points out that they are drawn from sacrosanct juristic sources —Seyssel, Bodin, and Hôpital, as well as Commynes, Pasquier, Budé, Loyseau. They describe the ancient fundamental laws of the French monarchy. These maxims remind the king that he possesses only a finite power, limited by divine law, as befits a human being who is not God Himself; that the French kingship is a *monarchie royale* rather than a *monarchie despotique & seigneuriale*, which means that Frenchmen possess just claims to their lives and properties, and are not the slaves of a tyrant; that the "royal monarchy" of France, although a true monarchy, is tempered by elements of aristocracy and democracy introduced by the participation of the parlements and the Estates; that the king derives his authority originally from God, and more directly from the people of France, who act as secondary causes to do God's purposes in the world; that the king cannot rightfully tax his subjects without the consent of the assembled Estates; and that the judges are officers of the people as well as of the king. These are the principles for which Joly was reviled as a rebel and a traitor. They have been swept away, he mourns, by new principles that hold the king to be above all law, wielding an unlimited authority over his subjects. In Joly's eyes this is a "pure usurpation," a political monster bred in the dens of Machiavel and Pope Alexander VI.[22]

Thus Joly's *Recueil des maximes*, however derivative and unimaginative, illumines an important facet of seventeenth-century political theory in France. The broad general statements of sixteenth-century constitutionalists, in which assertions about absolute monarchical power and statements about bridles and moderation were combined in apparent harmony, could no longer be accepted by both sides in this dispute. The absolutists had developed a conception of the monarchy in which statements about tempering were unacceptable; and their own conception of the kingship had become something the defenders of traditional constitutionalism could no longer recognize. From this

---

to the collection itself in most editions. The letter is addressed to Joly by an anonymous defender, but it is reasonable to suppose he wrote it himself.

[22] "Lettre apologétique," p. 41; in this attribution Joly echoed a common theme among Frondeurs, who incessantly identified Machiavelli as the source of the evil principles of Mazarin. See Albert Cherel, "La Pensée de Machiavel en France au temps de la Fronde." Joly himself, however, also cited Machiavelli several times with approbation in his *Recueil* (pp. 169 and 381), taking care to distinguish between his useful and his evil maxims. The non-French theorist upon whom Joly relied most heavily was, as we would expect, Aristotle, by far the most prominent political philosopher for sixteenth-century jurists and humanists.

time onward, the division between them was more sharply drawn; and when constitutional theory was revived a few decades later Fénelon and Boulainvilliers placed much more emphasis on institutions designed specifically to set limits on the king.[23] In place of a vague but generally acceptable set of formulas that acted in the sixteenth century as a hospitable framework for varying positions about power in the state, discussion about the French constitution in the early eighteenth century took the form of the rigidly opposed positions of the *thèse nobiliaire* and the *thèse royale*. Reading Joly's collection and reflecting on the royalist response to it makes clearer how this change came about in the mid-seventeenth century.

4. Retz in Paris: The Noble Fronde

The aristocrats who participated in the noble Fronde were among the first Frenchmen to adapt the pattern of thought associated with "reason of state" to domestic politics. In carrying on their civil war, they reasoned about the "interests" of a noble house or an individual as they had become accustomed, under Richelieu, to reasoning about the diplomatic interests of the state in the international arena. "But whereas the notion of interest introduced an element of stability into foreign politics," as Kossmann puts it, "it wrought havoc with domestic politics and made it more complicated than ever."[24] Plagued by a "romanticism of interest," the Frondeurs became absorbed in staking out positions; in the delights of intrigue for its own sake, they failed to set more general or lasting goals.

Kossmann's account of the Fronde is borne out in the writings of one of the most prominent participants, the coadjutor archbishop of the diocese of Paris, and later cardinal, de Retz. In his *Mémoires* of the period and the pamphlets he wrote during the Fronde, one of Retz's most distinctive themes is the conflict and congruence of interest among the diverse parties. He retains the heroic aspiration after *gloire* of the aristocrat in Corneillian drama, but distinguishes between true and false *gloire*, on the grounds that the former involves the pursuit of "grand and solid" interests, whereas the latter means a preoccupation with petty and trivial concerns. Thus he brings together the

---

[23] Since no attempt has been made by scholars to place Joly in the development of French constitutionalism, and seventeenth-century jurists were not in the habit of citing sources, it is hard to tell exactly who read his book and used it later in the century. One of the few studies of Joly himself is Jean Brissaud's superficial essay, *Un Libéral au XVIIe siècle*.

[24] Kossmann, *La Fronde*, pp. 151-154; in this connection, Kossmann refers to *une épidémie d'égoisme*.

morality of *la gloire* with the analysis of different types of interest and self-love pursued by contemporary theologians, to bridge the era of Corneille and that of La Rochefoucauld.[25] He also retains the focus on the *moi* associated with the *libertins*, although his own reputation as a libertine rested more on his morals than on his ideas.[26] In Retz's writings all these elements are combined with a cavalier unconcern for their incompatibility. He is to be read not as a systematic social theorist, but for insights into the psychology of an individualistic aristocrat in rebellion against absolutism in seventeenth-century France.

As a student at the Sorbonne, Retz gave notice of his propensities as a rebel by insulting the cardinal prime minister. Shipped off to Italy to be withdrawn from Richelieu's attention, Retz rewrote the story of a famous conspiracy against Andrea Doria, depicting the rebellious Fieschi as the glorious heroes of the piece, and Doria as a tyrant. This "catechism of a revolutionary" circulated in manuscript for several years, and its strong Corneillian flavor enhanced Retz's reputation among his aristocratic countrymen.[27] He was subsequently involved (along with other members of his family) in plots to destroy Richelieu himself. Yet Retz admired his antagonist greatly, for his political creativity and singlemindedness; and Retz's own tactics as a conspirator during the Fronde have the flavor of *raison d'état* about them. "What is vice in an archbishop," said Retz, "can perhaps, in a great many situations, be the virtues of a party chief."[28] He had learned Machiavelli's lessons about engineering popular imagination, and drew on this resource often, capitalizing on his reputation as respected and popular priest, while taking care to keep his pursuits as conspirator and accomplished libertine away from public view.[29] Like Richelieu, Retz had a good deal of contempt for ordinary people. He had a shrewd sense of the power of irrational human emotion, and managed mobs quite skill-

[25] In his chapter on the cardinal in *Studies in Self-Interest*, Krailsheimer draws explicit connections between Corneille and Retz.

[26] J. T. Letts, *Le Cardinal de Retz, historien et moraliste du possible*, pp. 167-183, has a good discussion of this aspect of Retz' personality; he quotes Retz' statement that *rien ne me touche que ce qui est dans moi*.

[27] J.H.M. Salmon, *Cardinal de Retz: The Anatomy of a Conspirator*, ch. 2, provides an engrossing account of Retz' experiences as a youthful rebel.

[28] *Mémoires* of Cardinal de Retz, edited by Maurice Allem, pp. 95-96. Retz described himself as a *chef de parti*, in the style of a Plutarchian hero.

[29] The *Mémoires* provide ample evidence of Retz' sensitivity to the importance of manipulating popular opinion by the adroit use of symbols, as in his discussion of the way he and his colleagues took advantage of a derogatory nickname to focus popular sentiment in "la Fronde" (p. 286). An even more striking instance from the early stages of the conflict (pp. 24-25) relates how Retz distributed a gift of money from an aspiring noble rebel to gain support in Paris, taking advantage of the sponsorship of an aunt famous for her piety.

fully. But he saw the people only as material to be used for his own purposes. He mentioned the incidence of republicanism in Paris on one occasion as a tactic to strengthen his negotiating position with Le Tellier, and this story was conveyed to Mazarin to paint Retz as a republican.[30] His political attitudes were in fact quite conservative. He stressed the importance of maintaining awe in politics, in the language dear to proponents of *raison d'état*. In one powerful speech he invoked the useful mystery of majesty and chastised the Parlement of Paris for recklessly threatening to rip away the veil enshrouding *le mystère d'état*. To let ordinary people peer behind this veil or value it too lightly, said the cardinal, would destroy the essential sacredness of the French monarchy.[31]

Devotion to the sacredness of the monarchy did not prevent Retz from playing a central role in the noble Fronde. Like most Frondeurs he directed his activities not against the monarchy itself, but against the distortions introduced by the two prime ministers. In Retz's version of French history, French kings had never before been as absolute as they had become in his own time. In the traditional constitution, as he described it in his *Mémoires*, the power of the prince was "tempered by customs" received and "kept in trust" first by the Estates-General and later by the courts. Provisions for registering edicts in the parlements were "like images, now almost effaced, of that *sage milieu* that our ancestors discovered between the license of kings and the libertinage of peoples." This middle point was "always taken, by the best and wisest princes, as a seasoning to make their power palatable and attractive to their subjects," whereas "maladroit and ill-intentioned" monarchs regarded it as an obstacle to their will. In Retz's view, Richelieu collected all the practices devised by ill-intentioned monarchs and made a "capital fund" of them, dressed out as "useful and necessary maxims for the establishment of the royal power." Thus the cardinal minister "created, within the most legitimate of monarchies, the most scandalous and dangerous tyranny that any state, perhaps, has ever submitted to. Habit, which has been powerful enough in certain countries to make men accustomed to enduring fire, has hardened us to things which our fathers feared more than fire itself. We no longer even feel the servitude which they so much abhorred."[32]

---

[30] Moote, *The Revolt of the Judges*, p. 280.
[31] *Mémoires*, pp. 124-125.
[32] *Mémoires*, p. 64; Retz concludes this passage by challenging the absolutist identification of kings with gods in language that recalls Machiavelli: "Only God can stand all by Himself. The most stable kingdoms and the best-supported kings can sustain themselves only by the combination of arms and law, neither of

According to Retz, Richelieu was clever enough to know that these maxims were not in the true interests of the people or the prince himself, but was willing to sacrifice those to his own interest as a prime minister. He was a politician of great skill, motivated by pure interest, doing good or evil as the case required. Mazarin, however, was a different story; he tried to ape his master and failed miserably. He assumed that the subversion of France's ancient regime undertaken by Richelieu was the way things had always been, and he pursued the same course without noticing that it was hedged about with precipices. Retz reserves his greatest scorn for Mazarin precisely because he thought he was being Machiavellian, and made such a mess of it. As a result, the politics of the age had become not only totally corrupt, but also stupid.[33]

Several times throughout his writings, the rebel cardinal asserts that "the truest maxim for judging sanely the intentions of men is to examine their interests, which are the most ordinary rule of all their actions."[34] Occasionally he qualifies this generalization by noting that one must also take into account their inclinations (that is, their passions), which "affect unconsciously" the motives that propel men to act, and divert them from the rational path that they would take if interest were their only guide.[35] In an essay on "Les Intérêts du temps," he put all this quite succinctly, in a harsh indictment of his own times: "In a time when virtue reigns, one can judge men by their duty; in corrupt ages where there are nonetheless skillful and clever people, one should judge them by their interests; in ages in which one encounters much depravity and little ability, such as that in which we live, it is necessary to join men's inclinations to their interests, and to make of this mélange the rule for judgment."[36] In his own activities as a Frondeur, and his later descriptions of those events, Retz demonstrated his faith in his own maxims, as well as his conviction that men (including monarchs) are open to persuasion about where their own

---

which can stand without the other. Disarmed laws fall into contempt; arms that are not moderated by laws soon fall into anarchy."

[33] Retz returns to this charge often in his *Mémoires*; see, for instance, pp. 63-70, 152-157, and 345, as well as the last of his *mazarinades*, the "Remontrances au roi . . . ," reprinted in the *Oeuvres du cardinal de Retz*, v, 317.

[34] "Remontrances au roi," in *Oeuvres*, v, 307; see also "Le Vrai et le faux . . . ," *Oeuvres*, v, 229, another statement of the same view.

[35] Albert Hirschman notes this insight as evidence of Retz' "fine psychological acumen," in *The Passions and the Interests*, p. 45, arguing that in emphasizing interest, Retz was repeating a commonplace, whereas in delving beneath interest to unconscious inclinations, he was saying something more original.

[36] "Les Intérêts du temps," *Oeuvres*, v, 251.

"true interests" lie.[37] He saw that men could be moved by imaginary interests as well as those of a more solid kind, and that this flexibility makes them malleable to the interests of the *chef de parti*.

Retz adroitly adapted his language to his audience. In addressing his coconspirators, he used the terms of interest politics straightforwardly. He asserted, for example, that he could be counted on to work for the survival of the city of Paris, since the city provided his base of political operation, as coadjutor archbishop.[38] In his pamphlets for popular consumption he uses quite a different tone. His first *mazarinade* opens with the assertion that "the reputation of Monsieur le Coadjuteur is as far above calumny and imposture as his heart is above fear and his spirit above interest."[39] His second pamphlet, which appeared a few months later, begins: "I break my silence, I come out of my solitude, I quit my retreat from which, like a high rock, I have regarded for some time this violent agitation of so many different spirits; and, free from all the prejudices so common in this unfortunate century, I come to bring to the people the sentiments inspired in me by the purest truth."[40] In his *Mémoires* addressed to posterity, the cardinal employs both kinds of language to describe his role. His motives were no doubt complex. He wanted to leave an admirable portrait of himself, establishing his own nobility; but he was not simply being hypocritical. Retz apparently needed to believe in his own high-mindedness, even as he recognized the centrality of interest in his own behavior, as well as that of his contemporaries.[41] He appears to have been genuinely convinced that his efforts in the Fronde were directed toward reestablishing the public order and tranquillity that he associated with the "public interest," despite his personal predilections to conspiracy and intrigue.

[37] On his own account, Retz used this form of argument in speaking with the king himself, attempting to recall him to his ancient duties; see his *Mémoires*, pp. 65-66, and his powerful speech when he received his cardinal's hat, pp. 714-718; on that occasion, Retz' eloquence in describing the misery of the French people sounds very much like that of Fénelon at the end of the century, in a letter that that archbishop prudently decided not to send to that same king, discussed in Chapter Twelve.

[38] *Mémoires*, pp. 126-129.

[39] "Défense de l'ancienne et légitime Fronde," *Oeuvres*, v, 176.

[40] "Le Solitaire aux deux désintéressés," (1651), *Oeuvres*, v, 184; the image of the *solitaire* was closely connected with the Jansenist community during this era, and this connotation may have been intentional; Retz was not himself a Jansenist, but was intimately associated with the group in a variety of ways.

[41] Among many instances that could be cited, see *Mémoires*, pp. 241-243, 347-349, 432-448, and 701-702; Salmon's biography of *Cardinal de Retz* includes a thoughtful analysis of his "quest for identity" in the *Mémoires*.

In Retz's writings, the public interest is not described as an harmonious sum of individual interests. He assumed that the interests of members of his own class were often in conflict with the public interest, since they required the demonstration of military valor in pursuit of noble *gloire*. Yet there was a sense, insisted Retz, in which they too, as members of the "public," shared the general interest in peace.[42] Occasionally this *chef de parti* appealed to public interest as a reason for taking action, but he did not rely on it to move his noble colleagues. He saw this appeal as having some persuasive force, but not enough to bring a man to act against his direct personal interest as he saw it. Retz's appeal therefore takes this form: "Do X because it serves your own interest and has the additional fortunate advantage of furthering the public interest, too." This emerges clearly in his speech before a small strategy council of his aristocratic allies, as he describes it in his *Mémoires*:

> We have in our party two great and very rare advantages. The first is that the two interests that we have, the public and the particular, are here closely in harmony, which does not often happen. The second is that the ways for achieving the one and the other interest are united and are soon to become the same, which is even rarer. The true and solid interest of the public is general peace; the interest of the people is alleviation, relief; the interest of the companies is the reestablishment of order; your interest, Monsieur, and that of myself and the others here, is to contribute to this peace in such a fashion that we are, and that we seem to be, the authors of it. All other advantages are connected with that one.[43]

It is worth noticing that Retz refers to both public and private interests as "interests *that we have*"; public interests, in other words, are not wholly separate from the interests of individuals, but are one type of interest they have among others. He also assumes that the two types of interest will not normally be in harmony; when they are, a rare opportunity for civic action presents itself.

Yet Retz's listeners rejected his strategy because it was not in their interests as heads of noble houses. This response is symptomatic of the Fronde. It supports Kossmann's contention that the absence of any general interest pursued by all participants was a major reason for its failure. Frenchmen lacked a coherent theory of the connections between the various selfish interests of individuals or parts of the state,

---

[42] "Les Intérêts du temps," p. 258, and "Remontrances au roi," p. 317-318, in *Oeuvres*, v.

[43] *Mémoires*, pp. 214-215.

and some overarching common interest. The preoccupation with cynically construed self-interests that was a hallmark of the Fronde was an important stage in the development of such a theory. But the failure of the Frondeurs to fashion vigorous philosophies of opposition, and to unite in durable coalitions, made clear the poverty of such arguments isolated from any conception of *le bien de l'état*. Frenchmen during the Fronde began to speak politically of their own interests as individuals. Like Richelieu, they associated "public interests" either with the interests of the state (counterposed to those of individuals) or with the old vague notion of public welfare. In attempting to show their countrymen how the public welfare necessarily involved their own, the descendants of the Frondeurs had their work cut out for them.

5. Saint-Evremond and Cyrano: The Libertines and the Fronde

The contempt for politics characteristic of the early seventeenth century appeared more appropriate than ever in the confusions of the Fronde. As one disgusted *libertin* put it: "Never have there been so many exchanges of generosity without honor; never so many beautiful discourses and so little good sense; never so many designs without pursuit; so many enterprises without effect."[44] Several of the *libertins* sought better societies elsewhere. Cyrano de Bergerac found his in the utopias of the sun and the moon; Charles de Saint-Denis, seigneur de Saint-Evremond, in republican polities past and present. Both men displayed fluid loyalties during the Fronde itself. Saint-Evremond fought on the side of the government and composed at least one royalist version of the *mazarinade*; but his association with men who fought as rebels, and his penchant for insouciance, made his loyalism suspect.[45] He spent two brief stints in the Bastille for displeasing Mazarin, and was eventually exiled for writing a letter containing passages critical of the cardinal minister. Cyrano, another well-known *libertin* of the era, apparently composed pamphlets for both sides, on commission, disguising his own political ideas beneath the Swiftian mockery of his imaginary voyages.[46] The skeptical essays produced by both men dur-

[44] Saint-Evremond, "Retraite de M. le duc de Longueville," in René Ternois, ed., *Oeuvres en prose*, I, 57 (1649).
[45] "Apologie de M. de Beaufort," written at the behest of one of Saint-Evremond's noble patrons during the Fronde, included in *Oeuvres*, I, 77-96 (1650).
[46] Erica Harth, *Cyrano de Bergerac and the Polemics of Modernity*, pp. 198-209, discusses Cyrano's activities during the Fronde, based on the researches of Frédéric Lachèvre, who published Cyrano's *mazarinades* in his edition of *Les Oeuvres libertines de Cyrano de Bergerac*, II, 235-289.

ing the Fronde influenced philosophers later in the century, and form a link between free-thought in the time of Richelieu and the skepticism of the early Enlightenment in France.

Saint-Evremond lived from 1615 until 1703, and was a contemporary of Bayle as well as Gassendi. He was thus a personal, as well as a spiritual, link between the generations before and after the Fronde.[47] His brilliant reputation was acquired late in life, when his works were published in the 1680s. Thus Saint-Evremond is often treated as an immediate precursor of the Enlightenment. But most of his writing was done before 1670, and his ideas were strongly influenced by the experiences of the Fronde, recalled in exile. In Saint-Evremond's philosophy the skeptical individualism of the *libertins* begins to turn upon itself, and prepares the way for quite a different temper. Knowledge of all kinds, including especially knowledge of the self, is regarded as problematical, and Montaigne's most hallowed legacy—the emphasis on living well within the self—is questioned. Saint-Evremond urges us to come outside ourselves to find distraction in society, and blames individualism for the corruption of the robust civic life of ancient Rome. The pendulum of withdrawal from public life into pleasures of privacy begins to swing in the opposite direction, in a philosophy where the ultimate sterility of individualism and cynical self-interest is demonstrated on the principles of the individualist tradition.

Perhaps Saint-Evremond was reacting to the somber Jansenist brooding about the self when he urged men to avoid preoccupation with themselves, and seek diversion from their deficiencies in society. His Epicurean ethic gives pride of place to the delicate pleasures of measured hedonism shared with others, rather than the delights of introspection and communing with the self. "To live happily," he says, "it is necessary to reflect seldom about life, and instead go often outside oneself; and among the pleasures afforded us by things alien to ourselves, to divest ourselves of the consciousness of our own evils." Such a desire for *divertissement*, the deliberate attempt to avoid oneself, was seized upon by Pascal as the paradigm of bad faith and delusion. Saint-Evremond insisted, however, that "it belongs to God alone to meditate upon Himself, to find within Himself felicity and repose. As for us humans, we can scarcely cast our eyes upon ourselves without encountering a thousand flaws, which oblige us to seek outside ourselves for what we lack."[48] The deficiency of the isolated *moi*, which Pascal

[47] Enzo Caramaschi, "Un Honnête homme libertin: Saint-Evremond," discusses his connections and influence; see also Quentin Hope, *Saint-Evremond: The Honnête Homme as Critic*, and H. T. Barnwell, *Les Idées morales et critiques de Saint-Evremond*.

[48] "Sur les plaisirs," *Oeuvres* IV, 12-22. Joachim Merlant, *De Montaigne à*

wanted us to experience with anguish in order to seek wholeness in God, was regarded by Saint-Evremond as unpleasant and irreparable, and therefore to be escaped in the diversions of society. Carrying *libertin* skepticism to its ultimate conclusion, Saint-Evremond insisted that we can never know the truth about ourselves as human beings; God "animates the springs of our soul but hides from us the wonderful secret of what moves them," and in this sphere closest to ourselves, our "excessive curiosity to know everything" is doomed to remain forever unsatisfied.[49]

Saint-Evremond also attacked the unprincipled prudence of *raison d'état* politics that the *libertins* had found so fascinating. For Saint-Evremond, the ultimate emptiness of political cynicism was confirmed by the sterile machinations of the Fronde. In an essay composed in the midst of the conflict, he scorned those Frondeurs who fled from Frenchmen who were truly in misery, lest they be contaminated by misfortune, and concentrated on playing their own strategic games. As his own moral ideal Saint-Evremond chose the *honnête homme*, a figure who became prominent in France in the decades following the Fronde. He defines the *honnête homme* as a man who cultivates a "true honor that regulates the conduct of reasonable persons." His behavior is contrasted, on the one hand, with that of narrowly self-interested men, "occupied with their own affairs," immune to pity, without moral scruple; and on the other hand, men moved by passion and the search for pleasure, open to appeals of human feeling, but mutable and ineffective in their conduct. The *honnête homme* may have "his ambition and his interest," but pursues them only along honorable paths; he has "skill without finesse, dexterity without deceit, complacence without flattery."[50] The *honnête homme*, like Descartes's *homme généreux*, appeared in reaction to the practices of an age when *raison d'état* had overreached itself in absurd self-caricature. A few years later, in exile, Saint-Evremond reaffirmed this counsel of moderation, in a dialogue dominated by an "honest and skillful courtier," who attacks bald self-interest as well as overly rigid moralism.[51] To reach the corrupt man of our own times, says the *honnête homme*, we cannot simply preach virtue to him; but we should not allow him to think that narrow self-interest is the most effective policy for life. We must

---

Vauvenargues, treats Saint-Evremond as the antithesis of Pascal on these grounds; cf. similar sentiments expressed by Etienne Pasquier, discussed in Chapter Three, above.

[49] "L'Homme, qui veut conoistre toutes choses . . . ," *Oeuvres*, II, 18 (1647).
[50] "Observations sur la maxime . . . ," *Oeuvres*, II, 149-153 (1651).
[51] *Oeuvres*, III, 6-20.

show him the advantages of virtue, and thus purify his notion of his interest. Both rigid virtue and corrupt interest make society impossible, since both are narrowly focussed on the self, whether the purity of one's soul or the security of one's possessions. What later came to be called "enlightened self-interest" is the course recommended here.

Saint-Evremond regarded his era as a time of corruption and narrow self-interest, when men of rigid virtue reacted by rushing to the opposite extreme, and coming full circle in their preoccupation with the self. He sought the society of other moderate, honest, polished men and women, in salons and in his extensive correspondence. He also found much to admire in two republican societies where men shared a true social life: contemporary Holland and ancient Rome. Saint-Evremond spent most of his life as an exile in England, but fled to Holland when the plague ravaged London. In a "Lettre écrite de la Haye," he noted his reactions to the republican politics of the Netherlands. The first thing he remarked upon was liberty—republican liberty, described in terms that show his appreciation for the extent of individual security and prosperity in a popular state. His awareness of the misery suffered by his poorer countrymen, overlooked by the self-interested Frondeurs, must have disposed him to be particularly sensitive to the blessings of liberty for ordinary citizens of the Netherlands. His experiences with capricious authority must have prepared him to see that "it is sweet to live in a country where the laws protect us from the wills of men," and where magistrates are indistinguishable from everybody else. "One does not see here," notes Saint-Evremond, "those odious differences based on privilege that wound equality." Although the maintenance of liberty and popular authority requires large sacrifices from the people, these are given cheerfully because they are recognized as necessary to protect the public good, and thus each contributor has "the consolation of contributing for himself. Therefore, one should not be astonished to find there a great Love for the Patrie, since it is, in fact a true self-love [amour-propre]."[52]

In a mood very like that of another French aristocrat visiting a robust young republic almost two centuries afterwards, Saint-Evremond notices the connections between love of country and enlightened love of self, as well as the consonance between ordered liberty and equality. Like Tocqueville, he also notices that these advantages have their corresponding defects. The Dutch are distinguished more for their honesty than for cleverness, and have good sense rather than brilliance or

[52] "Lettre écrite de la Haye," in Oeuvres, II, 24-25; a slightly different version of these same lines is included in the "Lettre à M. le marquis de Créqui," p. 34 of that same volume.

delicacy. In later years, Saint-Evremond noticed other defects as well, including the avaricious narrowness of the Dutch. After spending several years reflecting on the history of Rome, he identified republican patriotism with pure love of liberty, and asserted that although the Dutch appear to love liberty, in fact they simply hate oppression. Their republic is held together by the external threat of French and Spanish armies rather than by true patriotism; they love their country "for the interest of their commerce, more than for the satisfaction that they derive from being free."[53]

In a set of reflections on the "diverse characteristics" of the Roman people, Saint-Evremond, like Machiavelli and Montesquieu, stressed the psychological changes that accompanied the stages of Roman political development. Before the founding of the republic, the Roman people took their character from the priorities of each king in turn, and there was no sense of steady purpose in the polity. But during the republic there was a steadfast focus on a common goal; for the people became "enraged with liberty, if one can speak so, and with the public good; the love of the *patrie* left nothing to the movements of nature. The zeal of the citizen hid the man from himself."[54] This patriotic zeal, in which the individual was submerged in the citizen, is described by Saint-Evremond as a wild rustic virtue, not the moral excellence that arises from a struggle between tempting alternatives. The much-vaunted frugality of the Romans, says Saint-Evremond, was not a principled rejection of luxury, but rather a "gross usage of what they had ready to hand. One does not desire riches that one does not know." The citizens of ancient Rome were a savage people, fearsome in their devotion to the common good, ferocious in their justice. Finding in their polity "not only commodity and protection, but glory and power too, can they do better than give themselves wholly to the public, from which they draw such great advantage?" Although several Roman heroes strike Saint-Evremond as "true fanatics," he points out that "such men appear quite sensible in the passion that they have for a grateful republic, which had at least as much concern for them as they did for it." Rome in those days, he continues, was "like a true Community, in which each individual dispossesses himself in order to find another good in that of the order. But this spirit cannot long subsist except in little States."[55]

[53] "Sur les historiens français," *Oeuvres*, III, 89-90; letter from the Hague, *Oeuvres*, II, 27-28.
[54] "Réflexions sur les diverse génies du peuple romain . . . ," *Oeuvres*, II, 224-233. This same view is expressed in the "Jugement sur les sciences," *Oeuvres*, II, 12-13.
[55] "Réflexions," *Oeuvres*, II, 255-256; cf. Montesquieu's *Spirit of the Laws*, book

For Saint-Evremond, Rome at the time of the second Punic War was at the height of her development, her virtue less savage and austere than formerly, her people not yet corrupted from their devotion to the common good. But after the war was over, the Roman people ceased to discover their interests in the interests of the whole. "A certain individualistic spirit hitherto unknown in the Republic" began to appear, and men regarded one another "less in common than as individuals; the social links that had been found so sweet began to seem like burdensome chains, and each individual developed a distaste for the Laws, and wished to enter again into his original right to dispose of himself."[56] Corruption of savage liberty is thus identified with the individualistic withdrawal from community; political conflicts are no longer between diverse conceptions of the public good, but center around the taste for privacy and avoidance of public office. Laws are no longer perceived as the "ligaments of the community," but as "the pure will of the magistrates"; the people in such a mood "returned from the Republic to themselves" and worshiped heroes such as Scipio instead of rejecting leadership. The new stress on glory and ambition increased Roman strength and brilliance, but it was fatal for liberty and community. Gradually this taste for honor gave way to a purely selfish interest, pursuit of narrow individual advantage and possessions. Whether as noble ambition for glory or avarice for gold, however, personal advancement rather than the good of *la patrie* dominated Roman minds.[57]

Saint-Evremond's account of Roman history parallels that of several other historians, as well as Plato's description of the decline of an ideal republic. He must also have been thinking of his own times, which he, like many of his contemporaries, saw as dominated by ambition and avarice, compared with a nobler and more virtuous past. The admirable aspects of republican liberty, the joys of true community in which the individual is subordinated to something more important than himself, are set forth in Saint-Evremond's essays along with the disadvantages of such regimes. From the perspective of the individualist tradition, the most important point is that preoccupation with the self is associated with corruption and sterility, compared with the virtues of men in society and in true public life. Ferocious republican liberty is not suited to contemporary France; but lessons can be learned from the Augustan

---

v, ch. 2, for a very similar estimate of ancient republican virtue as akin to that of a monastic order.

[56] "Réflexions," *Oeuvres*, II, 307-308; the assessment of Roman excellence during the war is on pp. 269-271.

[57] "Réflexions," *Oeuvres*, II, 318-319.

polity, which Saint-Evremond particularly admires. Such a regime is well suited to men not distinguished by exceptional patriotism, but capable of being guided away from corrupt self-interest into some sense of identification with a glorious *patrie*. In offering the tempered monarchy of Augustus as a model for his times, Saint-Evremond praises the emperor for including the Senate and people in the constitution of his government, and ensuring that the citizens saw their own interest in obeying his commands. Augustus wanted not slaves but free people for his subjects, and was thus content with moderate power; the Romans in turn submitted happily to a "sweet and agreeable domination." The key to Augustus' success, concludes Saint-Evremond, was that he "understood by the good of the State, the true interest of all of those who composed it, his own first and then that of others, which he did not think could ever be separated from one another."[58]

Thus Saint-Evremond broaches a conception of the public good compounded of the interests of all individuals, beginning with the prince, as a modern alternative to the fanatical devotion to the community that marked the classical republic. His conception of the quality of ancient virtue, and his juxtaposition of republican and monarchical regimes, introduce a number of themes that characterized Montesquieu's political thought. The work of that other *libertin* Frondeur, Cyrano de Bergerac, may well have influenced Montesquieu in another way altogether, in the humorous relativism that marks the *Persian Letters*.[59] Cyrano's satire depends on the inversion of the comfortable and the adoption of an alien perspective on the familiar, in this case the perspectives of the lunarians, and the avian citizens of the *Estats du soleil*. In a mood much like that of Montaigne, Cyrano attacks human parochialism, particularly our anthropocentrism, to defend the essential equality of all beings in the republic founded by mother Nature, and attack the human propensity to treat other creatures as though they were made to be exploited by man.[60]

Cyrano also criticizes the human propensity to allow ourselves "to be commanded by the biggest, strongest, and cruelest" among us, counterposing this to the practices of the residents of the sun. These bird-citizens make fun of their human visitor for assuming that the

[58] "Réflexions," *Oeuvres*, II, 327-351.
[59] Erica Harth's excellent study of *Cyrano de Bergerac* uses the phrase "satirical relativism" to describe Cyrano's work, and remarks upon the close kinship between certain passages in Cyrano's writings and the *Persian Letters* (p. 250).
[60] Cyrano de Bergerac, *Other Worlds*, translated by Geoffrey Strachan; this is from *The States and Empires of the Sun*, pp. 179-180; in Frédéric Lachèvre's edition of *Les Oeuvres libertines de Cyrano de Bergerac*, pp. 158-159.

236—Interest and Prudence

lofty eagle must be their king. "Our policy is quite different, for we choose none but the weakest, the most gentle, and the most pacific to be our king, and in addition, we change him once every six months. We choose him weak so that the least one of us who might be wronged by him could take his revenge," and furthermore "desire him to be of a peaceful disposition, in order to avoid war, the source of all injustice." The reigning sovereign during Cyrano's visit was a dove, and the practices of the monarchy included holding a weekly Estates-General, "where everyone with a complaint" against the king has an opportunity to express his grievance. "If but three birds are found dissatisfied with his rule, he is dispossessed and a fresh election is held." The king spends the day of the Estates-General bound to a yew tree, and if any citizen knows him to be guilty of a capital crime, he is thrown into the lake.[61]

Unfortunately, Cyrano showed no interest in developing such vivid fleeting comments into a sustained discussion of the politics of the lunar and solar worlds he visited. His influence on social theory lay not in his political ideas, but in helping to excite the general taste for extraordinary voyages that overwhelmed his countrymen a few decades later, and lay behind the enthusiastic reception of the *Lettres persanes*. However, his apolitical, cynical, opportunistic, witty writings, marked by a stubborn individualism and a fierce but amorphous devotion to liberty, are perhaps a better symbol of the spirit of the Fronde than the learned treatise of Joly, the nostalgic guild republicanism of the Ormée, or the retrospective reminiscences of Retz.[62] The Fronde was a field day for individualism and opportunism, for liberty and wit, until men gradually exhausted by it all returned to the fold of absolutist monarchy with more fervor than before.

For all its diffuseness and ideological sterility, the Fronde was a watershed of sorts in French history.[63] It marked an end to the unrest and discontentedness of various different groups that had made France such an unsettled polity since the death of Henry IV. By revealing the impotence of the Estates, the narrow corporate selfishness of the judges, and the equally narrow personal and family selfishness of the

[61] *Other Worlds*, pp. 175-177; *Les Estats du Soleil*, in Lachèvre, *Oeuvres libertines*, pp. 155-156.

[62] Madeleine Alcover, *La Pensée philosophique et scientifique de Cyrano de Bergerac*, ch. IV, emphasizes the individualistic ethic of Cyrano; Howard G. Harvey, "Cyrano de Bergerac and the Question of Human Liberties," stresses his taste for freedom.

[63] Theodore Rabb, *Struggle for Stability*, pp. 64-65; but cf. Mousnier's contribution to the symposium on Trevor-Roper's "general crisis" theory in Trevor Aston, ed., *Crisis in Europe 1560-1660*, pp. 102-103.

nobles, the Fronde also paved the way for the ascendancy of Louis XIV. Frenchmen, worn out by the latest round of civil war, were convinced that there was no satisfactory alternative to absolute monarchical rule in France. They therefore welcomed Louis's efforts to consolidate his position by weakening the nobles and judges. Perhaps the most important element in the Fronde's "ambiguous legacy" was that Louis XIV was able to bring absolutist monarchy to its zenith in an atmosphere of virtually unanimous support among his subjects.[64] The king himself was left with somber memories of fleeing Paris as a child, and a deeply suspicious scorn of those countrymen who might have tempered his power. He was also left with a strong determination that such a thing should never happen to the monarchy again.

If we assess the importance of the Fronde for our three traditions of argument, it appears that constitutionalism suffered a temporary defeat, absolutism was strengthened, and individualism was transformed. The repetitive maxims of Joly and the cautious formulas of the Frondeur judges failed to challenge absolutist dogma, or to advance constitutionalist arguments in any significant direction. The preoccupation with the needs and interests of the self that marked individualism in the early seventeenth century, on the other hand, was called into question by the conflicts of fruitless self-interest in the Fronde. Societies in which liberty was realized not against but within community, and in which honor as well as patriotic vigor played a part, began to appear more attractive. The motifs of individualist argument were joined with a sense of the integration of the individual in a larger whole, common to heirs of the *libertins* as disparate as Descartes and Saint-Evremond. On such a basis, the relevance of individualism for politics could be established later in the century. Immediately following the Fronde, however, it was absolutist rhetoric that dominated French political discourse, focussed on the brilliant person of the prince, Louis XIV.

[64] A. Lloyd Moote, *The Revolt of the Judges*, p. 355, refers to "the ambiguousness of the legacy of the Fronde."

PART III

The Zenith and Decline of Absolute Monarchy

CHAPTER EIGHT

Orthodox Absolutist Theory and the *Métier du Roi*

1. Absolutist Rhetoric in the Wake of the Fronde

Our perspective on the Fronde is affected by our knowledge that it was followed by the long and sometimes splendid reign of Louis XIV. Therefore, it is easy to underestimate the anxiety supporters of the monarchy felt during those years. It was possible to believe that the monarchical regime, and even the king himself, were in grave danger from nascent republicans, English spies, and restless princes. As the Fronde drew towards a close, ardent defenders of the monarch produced propaganda in which absolutist rhetoric reached new levels of adulation and intensity. In the time of Richelieu, one of the favorite conceits of monarchical publicists had been to refer to the words of the language as so many tokens in praise of the prince. In the years immediately after the Fronde, mere words were insufficient. Frenchmen were bidden to worship their king in awe-struck silence. Francis I had been idolized, and so had Henry IV; but the divinization of the monarch reached its height in the early years of the Sun King's majority. Daniel de Priézac compared monarchical sovereignty to a "great light that never sets," asserting that "the source of the majesty of kings is so high, its essence so hidden and its force so divine that it should not seem strange that it should make men reverent without their being permitted to understand it, just as is true with celestial things. The grandeur of majesty stuns them, its brilliance blinds them, its pomp, which bears the image of a perpetual triumph, suspends all the powers of their soul, and it seems that the same band which so gloriously encircles the monarch's head ties our tongues to prevent us from speaking of it."[1]

In such florid passages, the kingly office was described as a sacred mystery beyond the ken of ordinary men. The rather shady, all-too-human prudence associated with *raison d'état* under Richelieu gives way to an affirmation that the divine reason associated with govern-

---

[1] Daniel de Priézac, *Discours politiques* (1652), "De la souveraineté," p. 111 in the second edition (1666); the reference to *une grande lumière sans couchant* is on p. 77.

ance is the highest knowledge. Priézac insisted that kings are like true philosophers, who "use the mysteries of their science to enhance its dignity and the admiration of those who do not understand it."[2] In that same passage, we might note, he felt obliged to reject indignantly the notion (suggested long ago in La Boétie's mordant prose) that kings are like magicians relying on illusion and fraud to hoodwink subjects.

At the opposite pole from Priézac, several Frenchmen known for their skepticism and libertine tendencies reacted to this same period by producing defenses of monarchy in which adulatory imagery and mystery are completely absent, and the necessity for strict obedience is argued on the grounds of the incapacity of people to govern themselves, and the corruption of contemporary society. The most prominent of these men was Samuel Sorbière, the translator of Hobbes's *De Cive* into French. Sorbière had been a prominent *libertin* before the Fronde, an associate and disciple of Gassendi and Mersenne, as well as an admirer of Hobbes.[3] He lived in Holland from 1642 until 1650, and later published a collection of letters and discourses that include two essays on the economy and government of the Netherlands. Like Balzac before him and Saint-Evremond after, Sorbière admired the Dutch for their liberty and energy. He connected Holland's prosperity directly with the participation of all citizens in the economy and polity, and with the general love of *la patrie*. The equality of the Dutch also impressed him, as it had Saint-Evremond. Sorbière commented on the fact that magistrates were indistinguishable from ordinary people, and that anyone of merit could hope to rise to high office.[4] Such praise for republican Holland, linking prosperity with liberty and equality, with an implicit or explicit critical comparison to French politics and society, was a recurrent theme in French political thought from that time onward.

When he turned to the analysis of politics at home, in a set of three "Skeptical Discourses" composed after the Fronde, Sorbière wrote in a very different vein. He combined a Hobbist argument with the sar-

---

[2] "Des secrets de la domination, ou de la raison d'état," quoted by Church, *Richelieu*, 456.

[3] Pintard devotes a good deal of attention to Sorbière in his *Libertinage érudit*, as does Ira Wade in *Intellectual Origins*, pp. 195-204.

[4] *Relations, Lettres et Discours sur diverses matières curieuses* (1660), letters II and III, pp. 32-55. For a general overview of the place of republics in the seventeenth century, see Yves Durand, *Les Républiques au temps des monarchies*. Sorbière was also responsible for informing his countrymen about England; he traveled for three months in that country and then produced a *Relation d'un voyage en Angleterre* (1663), which discussed science, religion, and politics as well as the *génie* of the English people.

donic skepticism of the libertines, to contrast French society with virtuous republics past and present. Using the tactics of inversion employed so successfully by Montaigne and Cyrano, Sorbière set out to shock complacent readers proud of their civilized community by calling contemporary Paris "savage" and "barbaric." The city is unhealthy, morals are corrupt, and Parisians have no care for the public good. "The poorest villager in Holland has a better house than our rich townsmen," proclaims Sorbière, asserting that his countrymen are so indolent that they cannot even keep up their own property. Far less do they show concern for anything common to them all. Public buildings are vandalized, bridges are in chronic disrepair, and any man who considered doing anything individually to add to the beauty or security of the city would be thought a hopeless visionary, a "citizen of the Republic of Plato."[5] Sorbière discusses the prudential deceits and trickeries unavoidable in the politics of his own society, and accepts the necessity for the virtuous man to adopt the weapons of the vicious to avoid defeat. This is familiar enough; but there is a new tone here, a new bitterness about the bestiality of modern men preying on the body politic. Since they lack all sense of a common good, individuals make sure they get back more than they contribute; they think of *la chose publique* as "a great body that cannot easily be weakened; and each individual takes thought only for the piece that he tears off."[6]

The logical conclusion to this harangue is advocacy of republican government, since Sorbière consistently praises the Dutch for possessing those public virtues the French lack so completely. Instead, however, Sorbière praises the good order brought to France by the conscientious young king, and asserts that the national character of his countrymen is sufficiently malformed that they would behave this way no matter how they were governed. His suggested remedy, in fact, is that they should move further in the direction of oriental tyranny. He argues that European tempered monarchy is the worst form of government for human beings. The influence of Hobbes is strong in those passages where Sorbière describes his countrymen as torn between subjection and liberty, lacking the full advantages of absolute submission on the one hand and untrammelled liberty on the other, thus becoming both restless and corrupt. Unlike Hobbes, Sorbière depicts the state of nature as a pastoral golden age where men of simple

---

[5] Sorbière's "Trois discours sceptiques" are included in the *Mémoires de Michel de Marolles*, to whom they were originally addressed (1664). I have used the edition published at Amsterdam in 1755. These references are from the first discourse, in II, 349-350.
[6] Third discourse, *Mémoires*, III, 46.

vigor lived together in instinctual moderation like that of beasts. At the other extreme, as the subjects of an absolute despot, they would live much the same way, he argues, in serene simplicity, totally dependent on the sovereign for their lives and fortunes, protected against the encroachments of their fellows, happy in their slavery. Subjects of European monarchies have the worst of both worlds—no longer acting by instinct, but unable to depend on a master to provide for them; not so far removed from liberty that they no longer wish for it, but no longer capable of living in liberty. Their states are full of conflict, people attacking sovereigns, sovereigns despoiling subjects. These are the defects we as a species have contracted by entering civil society without going all the way to despotism, argues Sorbière; and as proof he points to "that which you have seen in this very city in the fury of its disorders, in which it was solidly demonstrated that the liberty to which the people aspire is a thousand times worse than the *ministériat*, and with which the present order of the monarchy contrasts so favorably."[7]

2. Louis XIV and the Business of a King

The young man responsible for bringing this order, and for evoking an outpouring of support from subjects worshipful and cynical alike, was a monarch very conscious of his role. Louis XIV was sensitive to the importance of projecting a kingly image to his people, from the beginning of his reign.[8] He also attempted to *live* the awesome role assigned him by the formal ideology, as the focal point of will and reason in the state. The intricate ritual of kingship absorbed all his waking moments, and the separation of private man who wore the crown and public figure embodying the state was all but overcome in the person of this king.[9] He was sufficiently sensible, however, not to be overwhelmed by his own majesty; his conception of the kingship was that of a solemn business, a distinctive craft at which he determined to excel. In the *Mémoires* written for his son, Louis coined the

---

[7] Second discourse, *Mémoires*, II, 391.

[8] Joseph Klaits, *Printed Propaganda under Louis XIV*, describes the care with which Louis and his advisors controlled public opinion in their "deep concern for the psychological components of kingship" (p. 12).

[9] For a vivid description of the detailed ceremonies that made up Louis's life, see the duc de la Force's essay on "The Daily Life of the Great King," in *Louis XIV: A Profile*, edited by John B. Wolf. W. F. Church, "Louis XIV and Reason of State," in John C. Rule, ed., *Louis XIV and the Craft of Kingship*, p. 370, asserts that "his public capacity was the essence of his being."

term *le métier du roi* to draw attention to the daily routine occupations of the king.[10]

It was part of Louis's conception of his *métier* that he should do as much of this business himself as possible, and should be quite familiar with those parts of it that were being done by other people, so that he could evaluate their work. He intervened in details sufficiently often that men in every office were aware of the close supervision of the king. When Louis used the image of the king as God, he did not propose a mystic serene symbol of unity, but a worker and creator, whose hand and mind are active in all parts of his world, though this may not always be visible to ordinary mortals. In a sense, Louis violated the stratification of the old vision of the great chain of being, wishing not only to be king, but also God, sun, father, tax-collector, general, judge, priest, and schoolmaster. The French regime had long been one in which everything depended formally on the will of a single man; Louis attempted to make this formal truth a practical reality in a polity where everything derived its vitality from the willing of the king.[11]

The *Mémoires for the instruction of the dauphin* have a trace of the tutorial tones of the traditional "mirror of princes." But this is a mirror with a difference, a mirror held up by one of the most powerful of princes to himself. We see him striking the poses he was accustomed to strike and divulging secrets he usually kept hidden, in an extraordinary description of the uses of self-conscious power. It is clear from these *Mémoires* that Louis enjoyed being king, and that his pleasure came from the sense that he was doing something very useful. Being king, he confided to his son, is not like mastering a discipline in the "thorny and obscure recesses of the sciences," where the mind struggles painfully. Instead, "the function of kings consists primarily of using good sense, which always comes naturally and easily. Our work is sometimes less difficult than our amusements. Utility always follows a king. . . . Success, which gratifies even in the smallest things of this

---

[10] The *Mémoires for the Instruction of the Dauphin* are available in a good modern edition by Paul Sonnino; Louis reveals (p. 22) that he has two purposes in writing these *mémoires*: to teach his son how to be king, and to give a "public accounting of his actions . . . to the entire world and to all time."

[11] Jean-Louis Thireau, *Les Idées politiques de Louis XIV*; Emile Lousse, "Absolutisme, droit divin, despotisme éclairé"; and Herbert H. Rowen, "Louis XIV and Absolutism," in Rule, ed., *Louis XIV*, are useful studies of the convergence of formal doctrine and practical effort in Louis' monarchy. As Rowen points out (pp. 302-303), "absolutism was historically defined to fit the case of Louis XIV," which means that "defining the policies and activities of the Sun King in terms of absolutism is pure circular reasoning."

world, charms in this the greatest of all, and no satisfaction can equal that of following each day the progress of glorious and lofty undertakings and of the happiness of the people, when one has planned it all himself." An important source of Louis's delight is this sense that he has "planned it all himself," coupled with the special perspective on the activities of all his subjects that comes with being king. The pleasure of being king, "consists, in short, my son, of keeping an eye on the whole earth," learning the secrets of every court, "being informed of an infinite number of things that we are presumed to ignore, . . . discovering the more remote ideas and the most hidden interests of our courtiers coming to us through conflicting interests." This king, who had at his command all sorts of human pleasures, confessed to his son that this continual satisfaction of curiosity was the most pleasant of them all.[12]

Critics of monarchy often list among the defects of this type of regime the blockage of information somewhere along the hierarchy from the grass roots to the throne. Kings are notoriously susceptible to flattery and unhappy at bad news, and are often the last to know when something goes wrong. Louis himself was aware of this danger; the main reason he was so assiduous about attending to the details of the *métier du roi* was to be well informed about every aspect of his kingdom. In the passages I have just quoted, Louis describes the king's vantage point on the conflicting interests of his courtiers as an important source of information. He alone sees all the pieces of the puzzle, and can fit it all together. James King has compared this monarch's conception of kingly reason with that of Descartes: "the ability to select from a body of evidence a right opinion." On this view Louis regarded his own role as that of exercising kingly judgment, which meant "the proper selection of policy from a mass of presented issues."[13] The primary purpose of his intricate governmental machinery was not to relieve himself of work, or delegate power more efficiently, but to provide him with all the information from which he, as king, would discover the right answer to any problem. Such a conception was not peculiar to Louis XIV. From Bodin to Rousseau, French political theory depicted the absolute sovereign will as deciding on the proper course of action on the basis of a variety of conflicting perspectives collected into the single right answer to the problem.

[12] *Mémoires*, p. 30.
[13] James King, *Science and Rationalism in the Government of Louis XIV*, pp. 116 and 310-311. Several aspects of King's thesis have been discredited by other scholars; on this particular point, however, his reading is supported by several passages in the *Mémoires* themselves; see, for example, pp. 215-216.

Looking at the record of Louis XIV's reign, one cannot say that he always lived up to his ideal of being as well-informed as possible. This was not, at least at first, for lack of trying. One of his first provisions, on taking charge of his kingdom, was to insist that "all requests for graces of any type had to be made directly to me," granting "to all my subjects without distinction the privilege of appealing to me at any time."[14] Although the petitions were "initially very numerous," Louis persisted in this practice. He took a special pride in direct contacts between king and people, and disliked intermediaries. This personal style of authority was an important characteristic of Louis's reign; he regarded such contacts not only as a source of information but as an affirmation of the close bond of affection and trust between king and people. "It is a community of justice between them that holds monarch and subject," said the king, "in a mild and courteous association, notwithstanding their almost infinite difference in birth, rank, and power."[15]

As the reference to "infinite difference" makes clear, Louis was no populist, for all his stress on accessibility. He was unwilling to entertain the notion that more systematic popular advice and information might be useful, and distrusted assemblies of all sorts.[16] Nor was he any sort of leveler. Although he deliberately weakened the power of the old noble families who had threatened the crown, by domesticating them at Versailles, and humbled the sovereign courts to make them malleable instruments of his own policy, Louis insisted on the importance of ranks and hierarchies that give order and stability to the state so long as they are firmly subordinated to the king.[17] We find occasionally in his writings the old-fashioned notion of justice as the maintenance of harmonious proportion among the several parts of the society, merging with a more novel notion of the functional contributions by each part to the bustling productivity of the whole. He reminds his son of the useful services performed by the merchant, who "by his cares assembles from a thousand different places all the useful and pleasant products of the world in order to furnish them to each

---

[14] *Mémoires*, p. 31.

[15] *Mémoires*, p. 101; this aspect of Louis's monarchy resembled the political style of a later French monarch equally preoccupied with *la gloire de la France*, Charles de Gaulle.

[16] *Mémoires*, p. 130.

[17] Louis's continuing (and largely successful) efforts to transform the nobles into docile courtiers and render the parlements meekly submissive to his will are described in Robert Mandrou, *Louis XIV et son temps*, ch. iv, entitled "La Soumission de la société Française." Pierre Goubert's *Louis XIV and Twenty Million Frenchmen* is also useful.

individual whenever he needs them." The merchant is assigned a place in Louis's ordering of socially useful tasks midway between the peasant and the artisan, on the one hand, and the financier, the judges, and the clergy on the other. "Each profession contributes in its own way to sustaining monarchy. . . . This is why, far from scorning any of these conditions or raising one at the expense of the others, we must take care to make them all, if possible, exactly what they should be."[18] Such passages make clear that Louis was influenced by the new notions in economics that stressed the importance of cultivating commercial enterprise; but this was conjoined in his mind with a feudal-proprietary attitude of the monarch toward his realm. He tells his son to "rest assured that kings are absolute lords and naturally have free and full disposition of all the goods possessed by clergymen as well as laymen, in order to use them at any time as wise administrators, that is, according to the general need of their state."[19]

There is good evidence, from the *Mémoires* and from other sources, that Louis was familiar not only with the economic arguments that characterized his era, but also with the heated debates in ethics, theology, and politics.[20] A notably pessimistic conception of human nature, with overtones of Hobbes and Machiavelli, characterizes his world view. Louis notes that the advantages of firm government are seldom appreciated; "man, naturally ambitious and proud, can never understand why another should command him until he feels the need for it." Only "extraordinary incidents" remind an individual that "without authority, he would himself fall prey to the strongest, finding in the world neither justice, nor reason, nor security for his possessions."[21] Even the king's ministers can seldom be trusted to do good without supervision, says Louis; for "it can be established as a general principle of human conduct that there is hardly anyone who does not have some natural and secret inclination toward his personal advantage." "The virtue of the most upstanding people" will fail to protect them "against

[18] *Mémoires*, p. 155; on p. 63, Louis applies this functional conception to his own role, asserting that "all these different conditions that compose the world are united to each other only by an exchange of reciprocal obligations. The deferences and the respects that we receive from our subjects are not a free gift from them but payment for the justice and the protection that they expect to receive from us."

[19] *Mémoires*, p. 165; see also pp. 154-155, and Herbert Rowen, "L'Etat c'est à moi: Louis XIV and the State," on Louis's proprietary attitudes towards his realm.

[20] G. Lacour-Gayet, *L'Education politique de Louis XIV*, is an excellent account of Louis' intellectual training, as is John B. Wolf, "The Formation of a King," in his *Louis XIV: A Profile*.

[21] *Mémoires*, pp. 84-85.

Orthodox Theory—249

their own interests if it is not occasionally sustained by fear or by hope." Thus the wise king must "play on these great springs" of fear and desire to accomplish his own purposes.[22] He should not place all his trust in one minister, but have an array of experts advise him on every question, and deliberately pit them against one another in debate to correct for the distortions of personal advantage. Using the language of countervailing interests and passions, Louis advised his son that "the jealousy of one often serves as a brake to the ambition of the others," and the ensuing conflict of views among self-interested ministers can work for the advantage of the crown.[23]

But what about the king himself? What exempts a monarch from these traits of human nature, which entail that no one can be trusted with sole power to do good? Upon occasion, Louis did remember that he and his royal brethren were only human, and prone to the ills that flesh is heir to. There are times, he confesses to his son, when even sovereigns "become as biased as, if not more than, the lowliest private individual," because "the fire of the most noble passions, as well as that of the most common, always produces enough smoke to obscure our reason."[24] But such references to royal fallibility are rare. Louis believed that a king has special advantages over ordinary mortals that make it unnecessary and dangerous to think of limiting his power. By birth, by training, and by his special position in the state, a king is uniquely qualified to avoid temptation and act in the best interests of the whole.

The Sun King took literally the notion that kings are "above" everybody else. Placed high above all other individuals, the king can look down on the entire society and see the best solution to its problems, a pattern invisible to those in the midst of that society. He is therefore much more likely to make decisions in the interest of the whole, and less likely to have a petty interest in oppressing anyone. For Louis, as for most of his countrymen, the alternative to monarchical absolutism was oppression by "thousands of tyrants," petty harassers and exploiters of the people.[25] However, it was not merely because the king

[22] *Mémoires*, p. 162; Andrew Lossky, "Some Problems in Tracing the Intellectual Development of Louis XIV from 1661-1715," in Rule, ed., *Louis XIV* (reprinted in Hatton, *Louis XIV and Absolutism*), discusses Louis's concept of human nature.

[23] *Mémoires*, pp. 238-239.   [24] *Mémoires*, p. 228; see also p. 26.

[25] Louis tells his son that "a sovereign may be sure of this about himself: that since his rank is above other men, he can also see things more clearly than they, and he must rely on his own insights more than on reports from the outside. . . . In our higher sphere we are further removed from the petty interests that might lead us to be unjust," *Mémoires*, p. 227; see also p. 45, where Louis describes

was lifted above other men that he could see things more clearly; Louis asserted a virtual identity between the personal interests of a king and those of his state. This led kings, motivated by the same interests and passions that moved ordinary men, to work more enthusiastically and successfully for the public interest than other men could ever hope to do, since kings identified this interest with their own. The glory of the kingdom was the glory of the king himself—his armies, his palaces, his diplomats, his dynasty. This was the same argument Richelieu had made, in which the public interest was equated with the interest of the state and of the prince. Balzac's message that such glory did not warm a worker's cottage or fill a peasant's plate was not part of the information that this king accepted.

On the basis of his convictions, Louis XIV rejected the idea that anyone else could claim to speak for the interests of the people against the prince. For "these two interests are but one," he said. "The tranquillity of subjects lies only in obedience," and "there is always a greater evil in popular control than in enduring even the bad rule of kings." Sometimes a king's behavior may seem reproachable to his subjects, but this is because of their limited understanding of "reason of state, which is the first of all laws by common consent yet the most unknown and the most obscure to all those who do not rule."[26] Unlike some others who have written in this vein, however, Louis seems to have believed sincerely that he would have God Himself as judge of the way he had used his "reason of state." Louis took for granted, but never took lightly, the notion that he was ordained by God to perform God's work on earth, and in so doing should copy divine methods as closely as he could.

The Sun King had a strong sense of the movement of Providence in the world, which apparently grew stronger with the years.[27] During the early optimistic period, when he directed the composition of his *Mémoires* for his son, he assumed confidently that Providence is not inscrutable, that God works through regular and ordered processes that can be used as a basis for calculation in human action. It was inconceivable to Louis that God might not behave as carefully

---

what happens when a "king relents on his commands," and all those "down the line" in positions of power seize the opportunity to oppress those beneath them.

[26] *Mémoires*, pp. 43-44; with such passages in mind, one is better placed to appreciate Saint-Évremond's conclusion that "reason of state is a mysterious reason invented by politicians to authorize everything they do without having a reason" (quoted by Thuau, *Raison d'état*, p. 401). Other passages in the *Mémoires* where Louis employs the concept of "raison d'état" include pp. 57, 99, and 208.

[27] Lossky, "The Intellectual Development of Louis XIV," pp. 324, 344.

and rationally in His *métier* as the king did in his own. The notion that "the world is governed by certain fortuitous and natural changes that were impossible to predict or avoid" is rejected as an excuse for laziness.[28] God depends on good and powerful men acting as the instruments for His blessed Providence, and this made Louis confident of the efficacy of good works. It was a source of consolation to this king in difficult or painful situations that if a decision is made in good faith, "we can be sure that it is He Himself who makes it for us." The Jansenist notion of a hidden God acting in ways inaccessible to human reason was wholly alien to Louis's faith. His ability to perform his role depended on his certainty that in "taking, so to speak, the place of God, we seem to participate in His knowledge as well as in His authority."[29]

Comparing oneself so frequently with God might be a source of psychological difficulties for a lesser man. Louis XIV's faith in himself was sufficiently strong that his faith in the consonance between the Deity's ways of acting and his own was rarely shaken. Mme. de Sévigné's familiar *mot* about the tactics used by certain flatterers of the king can be adapted to describe the king's perception of himself: he is not content to compare himself to God; he compares in such a manner that it is clear that it is God who is the copy.[30] This certainly holds true, in any case, of Louis's conception of the sun, which he took as his special device. Louis's sun, like his Deity, was comprehended as another version of the king himself; he described it as

> the noblest of all, . . . which, by virtue of its uniqueness, by the brilliance that surrounds it, by the light it imparts to the other heavenly bodies that seem to pay it court, by its equal and just distribution of this same light to all the various parts of the world, by the good that it does everywhere, constantly producing life, joy, and activity everywhere, by its perpetual yet always imperceptible movement, by never departing or deviating from its steady and invariable course, assuredly makes a most vivid and a most beautiful image for a great monarch.[31]

3. Bossuet: The Apogee of Absolutist Thought

Louis XIV's description of the business of a king is interesting above all because it was formulated by the monarch himself. It is, for that

[28] *Mémoires*, pp. 99-100.   [29] *Mémoires*, pp. 106-112, 127.
[30] Mme. de Sévigné's witticism is from a letter to the chevalier de Grignan, 13 June 1685; in *Correspondence*, ed. Roger Duchêne, III, 202.
[31] *Mémoires*, pp. 103-104.

reason, not very representative of absolutist theory in France. Nor is Sorbière's cynical authoritarianism. Priézac's refulgent prose comes closer to being typical of the genre. But perhaps the best example of what we might call "orthodox" absolutist thought is the work of Louis's court theologian and preacher, Jacques-Bénigne Bossuet, bishop of Meaux. To see absolutist theory at the height of its development, we must step back from the great king and see the kingship through the eyes of one of his most faithful and articulate servants. In the late 1670s, Bossuet drew together scriptural, juridical, and metaphorical arguments that had been common in France for centuries, and combined them with more novel Hobbesian arguments characteristic of his own day.

In one of the most powerful passages in the canon of absolutism, Bossuet asserted that "Majesty is the image of the grandeur of God in the prince. God is infinite, God is all. The prince, as prince, is not to be considered as an individual man: he is the public person, the whole state is included in him, the will of all the people is enclosed within his own. Just as all perfection and all virtue are united in God, so all the power of the individuals is brought together in the person of the prince. What grandeur, that a single man can contain so much!"[32] Here Bossuet combines the ancient idea that the king in the kingdom occupies the same position as God in the universe with language that directly parallels a passage in Sorbière's translation of *De Cive*, where Hobbes asserts that *tout l'Etat est compris dans la personne du roi*.[33] Hobbesian overtones are even stronger in the passage where Bossuet asserts that "All the powers of the nation flow into one, and the sovereign magistrate has the right to pull them together.... Thus the sovereign magistrate has in his hands the entire strength of the nation which has submitted to obey him.... Each person gains by this exchange, for each discovers in the person of this supreme magistrate more force than he has given up in order to authorize it, for each finds here the force of the united nation for his support."[34] These passages from Bossuet's *Politique tirée des propres paroles de l'Ecriture sainte* (*Politics Drawn from the Actual Words of Holy Scripture*), indicate clearly how useful the ideas of the sage of Malmesbury were to the defense of absolute monarchy across the Channel. Excoriated

---

[32] *Politique tirée des propres paroles de l'Ecriture sainte*, book IV, ch. 1; I have used the modern edition by Jacques Le Brun, in which this passage appears on pp. 177-178.

[33] In ch. VI, sec. 13, of Sorbière's translation of Hobbes' *Elémens philosophiques du citoyen*; in the 1787 edition of Hobbes' *Oeuvres philosophiques et politiques*, this is on p. 115.

[34] *Politique*, I, 3, 5.

by bishops in his own land as the embodiment of anti-Christ, Hobbes was made to dwell comfortably with the prophets and the evangelists in Bossuet's magisterial treatise.

Locke, on the other hand (particularly Locke as used by Huguenots in exile after 1685) was firmly rejected by Bossuet. The Lockean conception of a group of people coming together in society and acting in concert to choose their form of government appeared absurd to him. Before there was sovereignty, there can have been no people; at best, there was a confused troop of families; at worst, a wild and savage anarchy of isolated individuals. "But there could not have been a people, because a people already supposes something that unites it, some regulated conduct, some established right," insists Bossuet.[35] The social order was imposed by sovereign authority, and the will and power of the king hold the individuals together in a nation, just as the will and power of God controls the universe. In his *Discourse on Universal History*, Bossuet relates how God had worked through a "long concatenation of particular causes" to make and unmake empires from Adam to Charlemagne. "From the highest heavens God holds the reins of every kingdom and holds every heart in His hands," asserts the bishop. "At times He bridles men's passions, at others He gives them free rein; and that is how He moves all of mankind . . . and it is only because we fail to understand the whole design that we see coincidence of strangeness in particular events."[36] In his *Politics Drawn from Holy Scripture*, Bossuet applies this same conception to the king: "The power of God makes itself instantly felt from one end of the world to the other; the royal power acts at the same time throughout the kingdom. The royal power constitutes the kingdom, holds it all in its condition [*tient tout le royaume en état*] as God holds the world together. If God were to withdraw His hand, the world would fall into nothingness: if authority were to cease within the kingdom, all would be in confusion."[37]

This celebration of the directive and constitutive power of the monarchy must not be dismissed as overripe rhetoric if we are to understand the absolutist concept of the state. In this theory, the king was

---

[35] *Cinquième avertissement aux Protestans* (1690), in the 1740 edition of Bosseut's *Avertissements aux Protestans*, III, 321-322.

[36] *Discourse on Universal History*, edited by Orest Ranum, part III, 8, 373-374; note the image of "bridling" the passions here.

[37] *Politique*, IV, 1, 178; cf. also the well-known passage in Bossuet's *Sermon sur les devoirs des rois* (1662), where Bossuet quotes the Psalmist: *Vous êtes des dieux*; Jacques Truchet, *Politique de Bossuet*, p. 83. Compare a strikingly similar passage in a funeral sermon for Henry IV preached by André Valladier, in Jacques Hennequin, *Henri IV dans ses oraisons funèbres* (Paris, 1977), p. 117.

indeed envisioned as the moving intelligence and ordering force of the whole society. "Consider the prince in his cabinet," continues Bossuet. "From thence go out the orders that make magistrates and captains, citizens and soldiers, provinces and armies on land and sea, all move in concert. He is the image of God, who, sitting on his throne above the skies makes all nature move." In this ideology, a multiplicity of wills within the state was as unthinkable as a plethora of deities, or a variety of brains within the body.

In his diatribe against the Protestant preacher of popular sovereignty, Pierre Jurieu, Bossuet gives in the *Cinquième avertissement aux protestans* the absolutist argument against the constitutional theory of limitations on the prince. He asserts that those who have experienced the evils of anarchy will give anything to avoid them; and that since it is impossible to give to another man power that cannot be abused, a people will prefer to risk occasional abuse by the sovereign himself rather than opening itself to the much more awful danger of its own furors if it reserves to itself some power. This does not mean that there will be no limits on the exercise of sovereignty; but they will be inherent in the sovereignty rather than imposed from outside. Should a particular king not feel bound by "the limits of reason and equity," there are also the "limits of his own interest," much more visible and pressing, and therefore more to be relied upon than exhortations about justice. It follows, says the bishop, that the people will be governed best when the prince feels the strongest interest in governing them well. This is true when he regards the state as his possession, to be cultivated and passed on to his descendants. To believe that the only effective limits on power are rights against its exercise, argues Bossuet against Jurieu, is a fundamental error in judgment. For "that which you wish to weaken in its ability to harm you . . . becomes in the same degree weak in its ability to do you good."[38] Here Bossuet reiterates a theme in French theory common since the days of Seyssel: it is irrational to set rigid limits on the use of power to prevent abuse by a bad monarch, since this also hampers the ability of a good king to use his power for your benefit. Seyssel's ideal was a set of flexible bridles; Bossuet relies on interest, that all-powerful human stimulus. "Instead of limiting the power by the force you can reserve against it, the most natural means to prevent it from oppressing you is to interest it in your salvation."

[38] *Cinquième avertissement*, 333-334; cf. the *Politique*, IV, 1, 92-93, where Bossuet asserts that "without that absolute authority" the king "cannot do good nor repress evil: it is necessary that his power be such that no one can hope to escape it, so that in the end the only defense of individuals against the public power ought to be their innocence."

Like most of his contemporaries, Bossuet takes for granted that men are primarily moved by their perceptions of their interest. Kings who see their true interests clearly will govern well. It is the business of their teachers, and of their ministers and subjects, to ensure that kings understand their interests in the conservation of their people. *La puissance outrée*, observes the bishop, always destroys itself in the end; a sovereign who provides good government for his people can look forward to a long and glorious reign. Bossuet attributes to Marcus Aurelius the idea of establishing "in the most absolute monarchy the most perfect liberty of the subject people." By this "perfect liberty," he means not participation in governance, but scrupulous protection of all citizens against oppression and exploitation of any kind. Such a policy, says Bossuet, ensured that the people were enthusiastic supporters of Aurelius and maximized his power. Building a strong kingdom by combining absolute power for the prince with perfect liberty and security for the people, the idea which intrigued French theorists so deeply in the next century, is here suggested by Bossuet himself. Government organized along such lines, he contends, "proceeds and supports itself, so to speak, by its own weight."[39]

The bishop also relies on interest to explain the origins of society. In this part of his argument, Bossuet distinguishes two kinds of interest: those that draw us together, based on our common needs and diverse gifts, and those that lead us into conflict with one another, derived from our passions and our humors. The first sort attaches men together in society, knitting together diverse talents in the production of a common life; the second sort divides us so profoundly that we can hope to find unity only in common submission to a higher power.[40] Despite such suggestive uses of this concept, however, Bossuet obviously regards *l'intérêt* with ambivalence. In his thundering *Traité de la concupiscence*, he refers to *amour-propre* as "the radical vice from which all other vices swarm," the "privation" of *la charité*.[41] Since the notion of interest was intricately connected with self-love, Bossuet found it hard to rest his case upon it. The proper focus for a human soul is love of God, and he who loves himself is an unjust, tyrannical, rebellious child. Self-love as the fundamental motive energy of human society, accepted by his Jansenist contemporaries such as Nicole, was firmly rejected by Bossuet.

---

[39] *Cinquième avertissement*, pp. 334-336.
[40] *Politique*, I, I, v-vi; 2, 1-2, pp. 9-14.
[41] *Traité de la concupiscence*, in *Oeuvres choisies de Bossuet*, IV, 92-93. See also the *Maximes et réflexions sur la comédie* (1694), where he condemns *concupiscence* as an "envenomed root that branches out through all the senses," to warn against the seductions of the theater.

Thus, although Bossuet insists that prince and people must understand their true interests, he also attempts to place the king in a pure exalted sphere above all interests, whence he can discern the pattern of *le bien général*. The king should strive to govern as God governs, exhorts the bishop: "in a fashion that is noble, *disinterested*, beneficent, in a word, divine."[42] Kings are capable of becoming disinterested because "God has raised them to a condition where they no longer have anything to desire for themselves."[43] At first glance this may appear absurd, in light of the well-established moral truth that no man is so haunted by unsatisfied desire as he who can have everything. Bossuet, however, was convinced that the absolute monarch, who possesses everything a human being could desire, no longer has any reason to be ambitious. There is no higher goal he can set for himself, no greater prestige. Therefore, the king can turn his thoughts and energies single-mindedly to working for his state (whose glory is identical with his own), and remain free from lesser entanglements and wants. He is so far above particular interests that no partial purpose in the state can attract or threaten him. Whatever the merits of this argument, it offers insight into the seventeenth-century conception of ambition, and the psychological structure of the theory of absolutism. It was repeated by several of Bossuet's successors, including the marquis d'Argenson.

In Bossuet's mind, there was apparently no dissonance between the interests of the state, the interests of the prince, and the general good. He asserts that "no one can doubt . . . that the whole state is in the person of the prince. . . . In him is the will of the whole people. It pertains to him alone to make everything together [*conspirer*] for the public good. . . . For we have seen that in him resides the reason which conducts the state."[44] However, Bossuet did attempt to make his monarch think of the public and its welfare not as an impersonal abstraction, but as a great number of individuals with needs and wants dependent on the king for protection and sustenance. "Love for the public good," he contended "means having every possible and necessary regard for each individual, because it is of individuals that the public is composed."[45] This concept of *le bien général* is far removed from that of Richelieu. It resembles the generous and humanitarian conception of "the public" that was held later by a number of critics of Louis XIV. Bossuet also showed a good deal of concern for the

[42] *Politique*, III, 2, 4, p. 71, emphasis added.
[43] *Politique*, III, 3, 1, p. 72; Bossuet often employs the image of the king placed "above" society, as in *Politique*, IV, 1, 3, p. 96, and V, 1, 17, p. 141.
[44] *Politique*, VI, 1, 1-2, pp. 185-186.
[45] *Instruction à Louis XIV* (1675), included in Truchet, ed., *Politique de Bossuet*, p. 295.

misery the French people suffered on account of Louis's wars.[46] But this had no discernible effect on government policy, any more than did the bishop's eloquent sermons against the amassing of worldly goods by the rich at the expense of the subsistence of the poor. Bossuet asserted that the division of goods among men by private property and along national boundaries by reason of custom and convenience should not obscure the more fundamental *société général du genre humaine*. Instead of simply protecting the rich in their possessions and denying the poor all recourse against them, the law ought rather to encourage "that spirit of mutual aid" that distinguishes a true community, in which each cares for the goods of others as though they were his own, and gives whatever anyone needs from his own stock.[47]

In his survey of universal history, Bossuet notes how citizens of Greek polities "were all the more attached to their country since they all had a share in its government and since every individual could aspire to the highest office." This awareness that attachment to the common good often comes from sharing in its creation and protection never led him, however, to show any faith in the human capacity for self-government. He notes that the Greeks "preferred the hazards of liberty to those of lawful submission, though in truth the hazards of the latter are not nearly so great," and that "the liberty enjoyed by Rome even under its kings is not suitable to a monarchy as we know it."[48] Throughout his *Discourse*, particularly in his discussions of the admirable regimes of Egypt, Greece, and Rome, Bossuet is unswerving in his conviction that the keystone of good government is well-established law, as opposed to popular license, restless innovation, or brutal caprice. Even in the idealized pure monarchy of the *Politique*, the orderly expression of views by ordinary citizens aids the monarch in making law. "In solemn actions that concern some great good for the state," he informs his readers, "good kings, like Josias, bring together senators" to discover "from their *concours*, what ought to be done for the common good, both for the state in general and cities in particular."[49]

Bossuet rejects a favorite image of prudential politics, to insist on the close relationship between justice and equality. "A rule is no longer a rule," he says, "when it marches with an uneven step." He asserts

---

[46] For instance, in the *Lettre à Louis XIV* written in 1675, in Truchet, ed., *Politique de Bossuet*, pp. 250-251.

[47] *Politique*, I, 5, 29-30; see also the *Esquissee d'un sermon de charité* (1663), the *Sermon du mauvais riche*, and the *Sermon contre le luxe*, in Truchet, ed., *Politique de Bossuet*, pp. 210-223.

[48] *Discourse on Universal History*, part III, 5 and 6, pp. 332-340.

[49] *Politique*, VIII, 3, 6, p. 302.

258—Absolute Monarchy

that what makes it meaningful to speak of sovereigns as gods is "the independence with which they should judge, without distinction of persons, and without fearing the great any more than the small."[50] Great and small are to be equally protected by the public power against oppression by private power of any sort. This maintains the traditional advantage of the great, who have more to protect. But it also draws attention to the duty of the king to protect the little people against the powerful; and by reminding princes that they have responsibilities as well as prerogatives, it carries within it a rebuke to sovereigns who attend only to their own *gloire*.

4. Apollo at Noonday

These passages on popular consultation and equality in justice are taken from the eighth book of Bossuet's magisterial treatise; the other citations are all from the first six books. The difference in temper and argument between the first six books and the last four, written about a quarter of a century later, indicates the change in the mood of Frenchmen contemplating absolute monarchy from the first part of Louis's personal reign to its end. The first six books were written when Louis's power and prestige were at their height; the last four, around 1700, when the old king had reigned for longer than most of his subjects could remember, and his power and prestige were enfeebled and tarnished by war, religious conflict, and economic adversity. Even his staunch supporters, with Bossuet among the staunchest of them all, were more inclined to think of duties of sovereigns toward their subjects in contexts where, a few decades before, they had referred only to the duties of subjects to obey their majestic monarch.

But in those glorious years between 1661 and the early 1680s, such mild reminders of the duties of sovereigns and the possible advantages of popular consultation as those advanced by Bossuet in book VIII of his *Politique* were absent from absolutist rhetoric. Discussions of monarchy such as those of Priézac or Sorbière, or Louis XIV himself, tended toward a perfect polarization of capacity and activity in the state. On the one hand, there was an all-knowing, all-willing sovereign embodying all political energy, and on the other hand a passive people whose only role in politics was to act as spectators for the performance of the king and material for his governance. The zenith of absolutism in France was the nadir of general participation in government, in fact as well as rhetoric. Citizens of towns and villages, judges, magistrates,

[50] *Politique*, VIII, 4, 3 and 1, 1, pp. 305, 287.

holders of ancient officers throughout the realm found their powers more curtailed and circumscribed than they ever were before or afterwards.

At Mazarin's death in 1661, Louis amazed his subjects by announcing that he would be his own prime minister, and he kept his word.[51] Within the first twelve years of his personal reign, he succeeded in withdrawing from the parlements their ancient right to delay registration of his laws by remonstrating with the king. They were confined to their strictly judicial duties, and to the simple recording of his edicts until his death in 1715. Throughout his reign, therefore, the most regular source of traditional constitutionalist assertions, the parlementary remonstrance, was muted or silenced altogether. Municipal governments, already weakened when Louis took power, were deprived of many of their remaining privileges and duties in favor of officers chosen or created by the crown. There was no serious effort to convene the Estates-General during his reign, and the provincial estates and parlements were rarely troublesome. The noble governors of provinces lost their remaining powers in favor of Louis's own commissioned men, the intendants and their subdelegates, despite the reform forced on the Regent in 1648 by Frondeur magistrates, which forbade the creation of intendancies. Even powerful religious companies, including Port-Royal, were weakened or dispersed.

The nadir of participation did not bring dissatisfaction with the regime on the part of those of Louis's subjects who expressed themselves on such matters in print. They were enthusiastically supportive and proud of his glorious achievements. The air of theatrical display and ritual that had marked the French monarchy since the Renaissance was used particularly effectively by Louis XIV. In his young adulthood he was an avid participant in the elaborate charades that entertained courtiers at Versailles. This mood of charade and enchantment pervaded his poses for his admiring subjects. The image of the "great light that never sets" was associated with the figure of Apollo, who combined Roman strength with solar splendor. This was Louis's favorite image of himself. Another favorite was Augustus Caesar, with none of the overtones of tempered monarchy included in the Augustan polity as it was described by Saint-Evremond. It was the imperial Augustus that Louis imitated.

The sense of the "infinite distance" between the lofty monarch in his Apollonian splendor and his earthbound subjects of all sorts, which

[51] On the course and impact of these events, one of the best accounts is Pierre Goubert, *Louis XIV and Twenty Million Frenchmen*, part 2.

is so strong in Louis's *mémoires*, was more than a rhetorical image for this king. He treated his most venerable officials as naughty children when they failed to carry out his will, and his more ordinary subjects do not appear (despite Bossuet's admonitions) to have struck him as human individuals, but rather as abstract objects of his pity, beneficence, or use. They existed to admire his glory, to pay their taxes, and to fight his wars. When they grumbled or got out of hand it was assumed that their superiors had failed to keep them well in line. One reason the upper classes feared disruptions, beyond the threat to their own lives and properties, is that they were held accountable and punished by the regime for such events. Either they were accused of instigating the riots for their own purposes, goading the masses to rebel against the crown, or of being lax in their duties of supervision. As Orest Ranum puts it, "an inferior was like a dog on a leash; if the dog bit someone, the person holding the leash, rather than the dog, would be considered responsible for the animal's conduct."[52] It was inconceivable to the king and his ministers that ordinary artisans and peasants could act as political beings, cooperating to take deliberate action on their own behalf without elite direction. The mood of men such as those who composed the Ormée in Bordeaux was completely alien to absolutist thought.

The image of the sun appealed to Louis XIV as the source of all light, heat, energy, of life itself, for mortal beings. Another variation of the theme of light was suggested by at least one courtier, that same Sénault who dedicated his *Traité de l'usage des passions* to Richelieu. In the years immediately before Mazarin's death, Sénault composed another treatise, entitled *Le Monarque, ou les devoirs du souverain*. This is an orthodox and unimaginative piece of work, which pulls together a number of commonplace themes. Among Sénault's points is that princes themselves need *lumières* as well as force. The good ruler should be "as enlightened as he is absolute."[53] But enlightenment in this sense, which was also the sense intended by those who described the eighteenth century as the age of light, was not part of Louis's conception of his own role. He was not king to be enlightened from some other mortal source; he was there to provide light for others. And while his sun was at its zenith, his admiring courtiers were content to bask in his reflected splendor. It was during those years that Bossuet composed the first books of his *Politique*, an optimistic and serene conception of unlimited sovereign power without equal in French

---

[52] *Paris in the Age of Absolutism*, p. 200; Ranum also shows how town fathers were treated like "children who had broken the rules" on p. 204.

[53] Sénault, *Le Monarque* (1661), v, 2, p. 256.

literature. After his magisterial treatise was completed, no other Frenchman attempted such a thorough and confident account of absolute royal power. After Bossuet, political theory in France took a different route, and left his treatise as the summation of an entire tradition, a monolithic impressive bulk upon the landscape.

CHAPTER NINE

Authority and Community in the Two Cities

1. JANSENISM AND OPPOSITION

Between 1660 and 1685, most Frenchmen regarded monarchical absolutism as the best form of government for France. There were, however, a number of forms of absolutist doctrine. One of the most interesting alternatives to the orthodox theory of Bossuet was put forward by Blaise Pascal. His Augustinian conception of the importance of order among fallen men reduced the office of the king to something less than sacred, while nonetheless stressing his absolute power. Other Jansenists, especially Pierre Nicole and Jean Domat, combined such ideas with elements of more orthodox French monarchist doctrine to fashion distinctive theories of their own. Our major interest will be in these Jansenist political philosophies; but we must also notice the complex role played by Jansenism as a movement in French politics from the mid-seventeenth to the mid-eighteenth centuries, for it touches upon our study in several ways.[1]

Jansenism in one form or another was a lightning rod for opposition to the monarchy in France. On the face of it, the Jansenists appear unlikely candidates for this role. Not only were they staunchly absolutist, convinced of the crucial part played by monarchical authority here on earth; they were also distinguished by their asceticism and otherworldliness. The doctrines most closely associated with Jansenism were purely theological, intricate variations on themes of divine grace and human sin, having nothing directly to do with politics. Nonetheless, the Jansenists often provided a focal point for criticism of royal policies between 1660 and 1760 in France. For the doctrines, values, and aspirations of the Jansenists were in conflict with the dominant doctrines, values, and policies of the regime.

Certain traits associated with Jansenism were regarded by the government as dangerous from the start. A *mémoire* published by a coun-

[1] René Taveneaux, *Jansénisme et politique*, provides a lucid summary and a good bibliography; see also Adam, *Du mysticisme à la révolte*; Sedgwick, *Jansenism*, chs. 7 and 8; and Van Kley, *The Jansenists and the Expulsion of the Jesuits from France*, ch. 1.

sellor of the king in 1654 names three of them.[2] First, religious novelty of any sort creates a division in the nation. Second, the Jansenists were, according to this *mémoire*, more a *secte d'Estat* than a religious sect, since their Gallicanism and frequent assemblies made them too much like the Calvinists for comfort. Finally, the Jansenists regarded all worldly virtues as infected, and taught men to avoid reasonable acts of social utility in the pursuit of charity. Such charges had been heard from the time of Richelieu. But in the general calm that descended in the 1660s, the Jansenists became a more visible source of royal displeasure. Their major spokesmen became aggressively dogmatic in response to attacks from the church establishment, particularly in clashes with the Jesuits. This clear source of division in the state was compounded by the diffusion of Jansenist ideas on ethics and psychology from the small ascetic communities of Port-Royal outward into the world. Jansenist contempt for worldly accomplishment and worldly virtues penetrated the salons and the theater, and lent their distinctive flavor to the moral attitudes of the age, a flavor that was distasteful at Versailles.[3]

One of the most worrisome things about the Jansenists was their self-sufficiency as little communities within the state. It was partly for this reason that they were seen as *républicain*, professing ideas about social organization that went deeply against the grain of Louis's monarchy.[4] The Jansenists never professed republican principles in politics; that is, they never questioned the importance of a strong monarchy at the head of the state. But the organization of their communities, their dislike for papal absolutism, their growing emphasis upon the role not only of bishops but even of parish priests in the governance of the church, and upon the participation of the ordinary believers in the mass and in the reading of the Scripture, appeared to contemporaries as subversive of established authority and tradition.

There is much here that was shared by Jansenists with Calvinists. In addition to their distrust of Rome, Augustinian doctrines on the subject of grace, and congregationalist ideas, both movements appealed primarily to members of the bourgeoisie.[5] Marxist historians have dwelt upon this, regarding both as ideologies of the rising bourgeoisie. According to these historians, Jansenism was a continuation of the

[2] *Inconvéniens d'Estat procédans du Jansénisme*, by the sieur de Marandé, cited in Taveneaux, *Jansénisme et politique*, p. 16.
[3] Paul Bénichou, *Morales du grand siècle*, pp. 76-130.
[4] On this point see Henri Lefebvre, *Pascal*, I, 56-66; II, 20-26; and Taveneaux, *Jansénisme et politique*, pp. 17-22.
[5] Bénichou, *Morales du grand siècle*, pp. 127-129; Lefebvre, *Pascal*, II, 35-41.

abortive bourgeois revolution that was one aspect of the Fronde. Frustrated in their attempt to challenge the regime openly, members of the upper bourgeoisie who had become part of the *robe* nobility turned to theological opposition and rejection of the world. Jansenism, in this view, was the oblique reflection of discontent with limited opportunities available to the *robe* nobility, and with the continuing power of the old aristocracy. Not yet conscious of their true interests as a class, the upper bourgeoisie expressed dissatisfaction through theological heterodoxy; their opposition to the monarchy on which they still depended was deflected into religious dissent.[6]

Non-Marxist historians have rejected the argument that members of the *robe* felt frustrated by the decline in opportunities during these years, presenting data to show that this was a high point for *robe* ambition and accomplishment.[7] They have demonstrated that Jansenism and Calvinism appealed to different sections of the bourgeoisie, and denied that Jansenism can be explained as the sublimated expression of economic and political discontent. However, it is important to remember that the movement was regarded by the regime itself as an expression of nascent opposition in the state. Louis XIV did all he could to suppress the movement. Partly as a result of the sustained persecution meted out to members of the sect in the last decades of his reign, Jansenists won a good deal of popular sympathy and quite a few adherents.

In the eighteenth century, Jansenism was no longer narrowly identified with doctrines of grace and personal salvation, or limited to members of a few legal families with a taste for solitude. The term came to denote a mood of growing opposition by the parlements and their supporters to religious and fiscal policies of the regime. In 1713, the pope promulgated the bull *Unigenitus* declaring Jansenism heretical, largely to satisfy Louis's persistent demands. In the wake of the persecution that followed, in an era when parlementary energies were revived in the new atmosphere of the Regency, Jansenism became identified with religious liberty and the principles of Gallican ecclesiastical politics. The *robe* nobility moved from religious liberty and Gallicanism to more general opposition to the government's policies, and attracted widespread support. In the 1730s and again more vigorously in the 1750s, they attacked the financial as well as the ecclesias-

[6] The Marxist view is put forward by Lefebvre and by Lucien Goldmann, *Le Dieu caché*, translated by Philip Thody as *The Hidden God*.

[7] See, for instance, the preface to Adam, *Du mysticisme à la révolte*, and Taveneaux, *Jansénisme et politique*, pp. 20-21; Goldmann, *The Hidden God*, ch. VI, summarizes the arguments against his position advanced in several places by Roland Mousnier, and his own reply.

tical policies of the crown, and defended the traditional interests of the *officier* class.[8] This was a time when discontent with the monarchy was growing. In the absence of any other institutional focus for opposition to the crown, the judges found themselves once again in the unlikely role they had played during the Fronde, of popular champions. This time they took advantage of popular support to strengthen their situation as a "national senate." Thus Jansenism played a key part in French politics for more than a century. At the same time, Jansenist ideas about ethics, psychology, and politics diffused outward from austere theological treatises to shape the attitudes of the age itself.

The most famous of the Jansenists was Blaise Pascal, author of the satirical *Provincial Letters* and the sketches published after his death as the *Pensées*. Pascal's writings express ideas that are inherently fascinating, and were influential in the subsequent development of French thought. However, like the essays of his intellectual ancestor Montaigne, Pascal's complex and subtle judgments do not lend themselves easily to critical analysis. He asserted that things are so closely interconnected that we cannot expect to understand a part without understanding the whole, and that any part provides as good a place to begin as any other part.[9] To pull out part of Pascal's philosophy and treat it as self-sufficient is to do violence to his whole approach.

Another difficulty that faces us when we try to assess Pascal's place in the history of ideas is that the *Pensées* we read today is not the book that went by that name in the eighteenth century.[10] At Pascal's death, the fragments he had written for a major apology for Christianity were edited by a committee of his colleagues at Port-Royal and published as his *Pensées*. Pascal's editors reversed the order that Pascal had himself envisioned for the book, thus reducing its originality.[11] They put the traditional Christian material first, and broke up the psychological considerations on the human condition, intended by Pascal to appeal to fallen man and excite his interest in religion, in scattered chapters later in the book. More important, they left out

[8] See Roger Bickart, *Les Parlements et la notion de souverain eté nationale au XVIIIe siècle*, and Jules Flammermont, ed., *Remontrances du Parlement de Paris au XVIIIe siècle*.

[9] *Pensées*, edited by Brunschvicg, fragment 72. I have used the Brunschvicg edition throughout, and abbreviated references to the *pensées* by the number in the Br. edition. I have consulted the translation by W. F. Trotter for Everyman when there appeared to be some question about interpretation.

[10] Mara Vamos' careful analysis of the differences between the Port-Royal edition of the *Pensées* and those with which we are familiar is indispensable in dealing with this problem: *Pascal's Pensées and the Enlightenment: The Roots of a Misunderstanding*.

[11] *Ibid.*, ch. 3; see also Sainte-Beuve, *Port-Royal*, II, book III, ch. 19.

many fragments, among them a number of those having to do with politics and society. Several of the most striking *pensées* dealing with these matters were suppressed; others were broken up, rewritten, or truncated. Thus we must be especially careful about assuming that anyone in the eighteenth century was influenced by Pascal on these matters. Fortunately, enough of the material was included so that we can see some possible connections; and several of the most distinctively Jansenist notions about society and politics found more systematic expression in a book that was widely read, the *Essais* of Pierre Nicole. In the later eighteenth century, Pascal's own fragments were rediscovered, pasted together haphazardly in a large notebook by a later compiler. Each subsequent editor has made his own decision about how to present the fragments.[12] Each edition therefore presents a different book; and because of their unfinished and fragmentary status, the *Pensées* require the active participation of the reader in connecting these provocative and disparate ideas in a coherent argument. This is peculiarly appropriate to Pascal's intentions for the book and to his own way of thinking. But it makes it hard to determine his influence on any other reader.

2. PASCAL ON AUTHORITY, CUSTOM, JUSTICE

The most distinctive and pervasive aspect of Pascal's philosophy is the notion of the three orders of human life and discourse: the *ordre de la chair*, the *ordre de l'esprit*, and the *ordre de la charité*, or *la volonté*.[13] The *ordre de la chair* comprises the realm of flesh and worldly pleasures; the *ordre de l'esprit* is the realm of intellect, reason, science; the *ordre de la charité* is the realm where God touches men and men reach for God by means of a pure good will, and a comprehension greater than that of human reason. Pascal's ideas about politics and ethics are for the most part written about *le chair* in the language of *l'esprit*; but the higher *charité*, his effort to illuminate and convert the worldly, is always part of his intent. This notion of the triple orders must be kept in mind in analyzing Pascal's ideas, to see the place and purpose of his different concepts. By putting politics firmly in the

[12] Fortunat Strowski, *Les Pensées de Pascal*, ch. 2 has a useful analysis of the procedures of the several editors of Pascal; Lefebvre, *Pascal*, II, 89-95, advances the provocative idea that Pascal would not have reduced the fragments to a systematic order even had he lived to publish them, since such an attempt at linear rigidity would have lessened the rich attraction of the argument.

[13] Pascal's most sustained discussion of the three orders is in Br. 458 and 460. A.W.S. Baird, *Studies in Pascal's Ethics*, is the best commentary on the ethical dimensions of this topic.

world of *concupiscence* he follows Augustine, demonstrating both its necessity and its lowliness; by suggesting that salvation lies in charity, and using social metaphors to make his point, he opens up, as Augustine did, the vision of a fuller community, as an alternative to worldly politics.[14] He has, like Augustine, two different social theories —the overt analysis of power among worldly men, the psychology of authority, on the one hand; and on the other, the appealing conception of the participation of the saved in a *corps pensant*, a body of organically connected thinking members.

To each realm Pascal assigns a distinctive grandeur, mode of life, and set of heroes. To those who demonstrate extraordinary accomplishment or hold high office in any realm, honor is due according to the character of the realm; but we do not owe to the great in the world of flesh anything appropriate only to intellect or to charity. In the world of flesh or concupiscence, the great are kings, captains, wealthy men. We owe them respect, deference, honor for their offices, but not esteem.[15] In the order of the intellect or *esprit* we find scientific geniuses, whom we should esteem for their brilliance, an esteem that kings and wealthy men can never properly command of us unless they have demonstrated the same accomplishments. Only to saints and to Christ himself do we owe the highest veneration of *la charité*. Pascal insists firmly that the three realms are infinitely removed from one another. Just as the world of intellect is of a different quality from that of flesh, so is the realm of charity from that of intellect. Human beings are appropriately suspended in the middle. They are made up of flesh and capable of charity through grace and perseverance. They are also, distinctively, *esprit*; and their peculiarity is that they are wretched and yet by *knowing* they are wretched, by being conscious of their misery, they transcend it and reach a kind of grandeur.

By placing human authority, and specifically the authority of kings, firmly in the lowest realm of human consciousness and action, and by indicating that the honor owed to kings is well below the esteem we ought to show for scientific genius and the veneration due to saints, Pascal struck subtly at the very heart of absolutist doctrine. Instead of the god-like monarch, lieutenant and copy of God on earth, Pascal's kings are part of the lowest order of human accomplishment, ruling over that which is most bestial within us. Rather than being asked to

[14] On Pascal's debt to Augustine, see Gilbert Chinard, *En lisant Pascal*, and Nigel Abercrombie, *Saint Augustine and French Classical Thought*, ch. 4.

[15] Br. 461 and 793; see also the "Lettre à la sérenissime reine de Suède" (1652), in which Pascal honors the queen for combining sovereign authority and intellectual accomplishment, included in Jacques Chevalier's edition of Pascal's *Oeuvres complètes*, 502-504.

venerate them or to regard their majesty with awe, we are counseled to pay them scrupulous honor and obedience, but never to grant them the esteem inappropriate to their world. In this, as in much else, Pascal was the disciple of Montaigne.[16] Montaigne also drew a distinction between the honor owed to kings and the esteem that ought to be reserved for men who truly deserve it.

Pascal was much more conscious than Montaigne (or most other philosophers, for that matter) of the important role played by brute force, command of armed strength, in the relationships between monarchs and their subjects. Pascal identified *la concupiscence* and *la force* as the sources of all our actions—the one of voluntary acts, the other of involuntary (Br. 334). He was particularly acute in his perception of the way force combines with other things to determine domination among men. Here, for example, is his characteristically oblique and intricate discussion of the interplay of force and opinion, in which one can see the dialectic fluctuate before one's eyes:

> Force is the queen of the world, and not opinion. —But opinion is that which makes use of force. —It is force that makes opinion. Softness is attractive, according to our opinion. Why? Because he who would be a rope-dancer dances alone; and I can make a stronger cabal of men who will say that such dancing is unseemly (Br. 303).

The next *pensée* in Brunschvicg's edition takes up the theme of ropes and shifts to another aspect of political life:

> The ropes that bind the respect of some among us to others are in general cords of necessity; because it is necessary that there be different degrees among us, all men desiring to dominate and not all able to do so, but some can do so.

This moves Pascal to consider, in the next paragraph of that same *pensée*, the more general question of the origins of political communities, which brings him back to force and opinion:

> Let us imagine how it happens that the powerful form themselves. There is no doubt that they struggle until the stronger party conquers the weaker and a dominant party is established. But when

---

[16] Bernard Croquette, *Pascal et Montaigne*, provides a detailed listing of Pascal's borrowings from the *Essays*, which span eighty pages of small print. See also J. H. Broome, *Pascal*, ch. 4, and Léon Brunscvicg, *Descartes et Pascal lecteurs de Montaigne*. Of Pascal's several references to Montaigne in the *Pensées*, perhaps the most notable is Br. 64: "Ce n'est pas dans Montaigne, mais dans moi, que je trouve tout ce que j'y vois." His own critical appreciation of the *Essays* is given in the *Entretien de M. Pascal et de M. de Sacy sur la lecture d'Epictète et Montaigne*.

this is once determined, then the masters who do not want war to continue, order things so that the force that is in their hands will be handed down as they please; some give it over to popular election, others to heredity, etc. And it is here that imagination begins to play its role. Until then, power forced reality: now it is the force that is contained in the imagination of a certain group, in France the gentlemen, in Switzerland the commoners, etc.

And the next sentence, the last one in this *pensée*, picks up the notion of ropes once more:

These ropes that attach respect to such and such a person in particular, are thus imaginary cords, cords of the imagination (Br. 304).

A few paragraphs further on is another *pensée* that I suspect originally preceded the one with which we just began, or it could have followed directly on the one just finished:

Domination founded on opinion and imagination rules sometimes, and this empire is sweet and voluntary; that of force reigns continually, always. Thus opinion is like the queen of the world, but force is its tyrant (Br. 311).

In Pascal's philosophy, human authority depends on the subtle interplay of brute strength, the force of numbers of men in groups, and the control of the imagination and of opinion by means of symbols. The more powerful a man is, the less need he has of the symbols that provide an alternative avenue to domination by the power of the imagination. Kings and soldiers use uniforms, but do not really need them to command respect, whereas a judge or magistrate depends on his regalia. Pascal muses about the probable outcome of a direct encounter of *la force* with *la grimace*, his word for the symbols that shape our imagination: "an ordinary soldier grabs the mortarboard of a first magistrate and sends it flying out the window . . ." (Br. 310).

All kinds of human authority, both the authority of the soldier, which rests directly on force, and that of the judge, which depends upon the power of *la grimace*, are rooted in fundamental human needs and motivations. All men desire rank and dominance; not all can have equal dominance at once. Pascal, who was an exceptional mathematician, might have accepted the language of game theory to express his meaning here: power is a zero-sum game.[17] For some to dominate, others must be dominated. What, then, decides which of us is to be

---

[17] Ian Hacking, "The Logic of Pascal's Wager," speaks of Pascal as the inventor of decision theory on the basis of the argument of the *pari*.

where? The preponderance of force provides an excellent shorthand way of solving the dilemma. To put it at the simplest level, says Pascal, it is obviously reasonable that I cede precedence to someone who commands four lackeys when I command but one. We have only to count them up; the outcome is clear (Br. 319). In the same way, we avoid eternal strife by determining a simple way for transferring power in the state.

Pascal takes deliberate advantage of the absurdity inherent in the idea of hereditary monarchy, to argue that this very irrationality makes it a reasonable way to hand on power, in the context of the fundamental irrationality of human affairs. In politics it is madness to look for sense—the brute established ways of doing things have to recommend them at least that they are simple and accepted without dispute. "What could be less reasonable," asks Pascal, "than to choose, to govern a state, the eldest son of a queen?" We would not use such a procedure to designate holders of other authoritative posts such as captain of a ship. It is "ridiculous and unjust; but because men are these things and always will be so," to choose the eldest son becomes "reasonable and just; for who else would you choose?" If we decide to select the most virtuous or skillful, "we should immediately be reduced to bitter conflict, each one claiming to be the most virtuous or skillful." The better part then is to decide on some incontestable claim such as that of the eldest son of the reigning monarch. "That's clear, no argument about it. Reason cannot possibly do better; for civil war is the worst of evils" (Br. 320). The same holds for other ways of deciding who is to dominate, which all reduce to the original preponderance of force, perpetuated by whatever method is chosen by the forceful. "Why do we follow the majority? because they are right? no—because they have more force on their side" (Br. 301).

The absurd foundations of worldly authority and the dominance of force behind it all could be calmly contemplated by Pascal because he regarded the realm of concupiscence as a minor part of a sane human life. Like Montaigne, he asserted that critical and intelligent persons should submit to custom and pay homage to authority in order to ensure that they have space and time to devote themselves to more important things. The low estate he allocates to politics comes out clearly in his comment on Plato and Aristotle.

> When they diverted themselves by writing their *Laws* and *Politics*, they were playing games; this was the least philosophical and least serious part of their life, the most philosophical being to live simply and tranquilly. If they wrote on politics, it was to regulate a mad-

house; and if they appear to speak of this as if it were something grand, it is because they know that the madmen for whom they write imagine themselves kings and emperors. They take up their principles in order to limit their madness to as little evil as possible (Br. 331).

Thus Pascal reduces political philosophy to the regulation of a hospital of madmen. He tells us that our taste for reading such works depends on our foolish tendency to identify with the powerful figures who people their pages, unaware that this is the most effective way to moderate our own dangerous tendencies. The *Laws* and the *Politics* become a kind of political pornography written by great men in leisure moments to nourish our fantasies and keep us quiet.

Pascal defined tyranny as the desire to overreach the limits of one's order, to dominate outside one's proper realm. He regarded it as an empty threat, since those who are supreme in the realm of concupiscence ordinarily have no desire for the rewards appropriate to *la charité* or *l'esprit* (Br. 322). In his eyes, the serious threat to civil order was anarchy. In this, he shows himself, like Montaigne and Hobbes, the child of troubled times. He was convinced that if men who have probed the foundations of authority and discovered how absurd and brutal they are disclose those things to other men, they invite anarchy. Men "will throw off the yoke as soon as they see it for what it really is; and the powerful will profit from this discontent to ruin the people and along with them, the curious explorers of received customs" (Br. 294). It is therefore best to obey the laws and customs that are already established, not because they are sounder, but "because they are unique, and root out disagreement" (Br. 301). To upset them only provides the opportunity for a slightly different pattern of domination to be established. A new winning coalition will entrench itself after a period of civil anguish in which the restless men who tore apart the veil covering political reality will be the first to go under.

This position makes sense only if one is convinced that a better way cannot be found—that the whole notion of a "better way" has no meaning in this context. Pascal was convinced of this. "There is nothing else truer nor more just that could be introduced," he said. "Justice is that which is established" (Br. 312). He followed Montaigne in laughing at the gap between beautiful pronouncements about universal justice and our own human practices. "Three degrees of elevation reverse the whole of jurisprudence; a meridian determines truth; in a few years of possession, fundamental laws are transformed." What a "fine justice, bounded by a river; truth on one side of the Pyrenees, error on the other!" Almost in Montaigne's own words, Pascal asserted: "Doubtless there are natural laws; but this beautiful corrupt reason has corrupted everything" (Br. 294). "Justice and truth are two points so subtle that our blunt instruments can never touch them with precision. If we manage to get at them, we obscure them in the act of doing so and lodge all round about them, more upon the false than on the true" (Br. 82). Yet justice is a crucial symbol in human affairs, and ordinary men cannot live with the awareness that they are obeying something irrational and unjust. The wisest legislators have therefore persuaded their followers that their rules are authentic and eternal, while hiding from them the truths about civil order.[18]

Justice, in any case, will always be defined by force:

> It is just that what is just be followed, it is necessary that the strongest be obeyed. Justice without force is impotent; force without justice is tyrannical. It is necessary therefore to combine justice and force; and for this, to make justice strong, or the strong just.
>
> Justice is open to dispute; force is easily recognizable and indisputable. Thus it has been impossible to give force to justice, because force contradicts justice and says that it is unjust, that she herself is just. And so, unable to make that which is just strong, we have made the strong just.[19]

The natural human inclination to dominate is so strong that we can never hope to counteract it by preaching justice. When children cry "that cat is mine," we see there "the beginning and the image of the usurpation of the whole earth" (Br. 295). Equal distribution of goods would be abstract justice; but this could never be imposed, so we have ruled instead that it is just to obey and give more to the stronger. "Unable to fortify justice, we have justified force, so that finally force and justice are brought into harmony and we have peace, which is the sovereign good" (Br. 299).

Even more pessimistic than Montaigne about the relevance of nature and reason to worldly affairs, Pascal depicted nature as capriciously obscuring herself from our vision, showing us false rules when we

---

[18] Br. 294, as well as Br. 324,878, and 18, where Pascal asserts that "when one does not know the truth about something, it is good that there be a common error that fixes the mind of men," to ward off our "principal malady," which is "unquiet curiosity."

[19] Br. 298. This rich and subtle *pensée* provides the focus for two essays on Pascal's politics: Erich Auerbach, "On the Political Theory of Pascal," in *Scenes from the Drama of European Literature*, 101-129; and Luc Dariosecq, "La Pensée politique de Pascal."

attempt to ferret out her order.[20] In the attempt to encompass nature, we alter it by our artifice so that we can never know it as it is. Our human "nature" is more powerful, imposing its own order on whatever it confronts, finding pleasure in contemplating something that appears to reflect itself. Pascal shared the radical skepticism that accompanied the birth of modern empiricism, casting doubt on the certainty of basic sensory perceptions. And in the realm of society and behavior, he taught us to question the conventional distinction between "nature" and "custom." For, after all, he says, "What are our natural principles, except those to which we are accustomed? A different custom would give us other natural principles; this is clear from experience. . . . Custom is a second nature that destroys the former. But what is this nature? Why is not custom natural? I greatly suspect that this nature is herself only first custom, as custom is second nature" (Br. 92-93). In another *pensée*, which is placed earlier by Brunschvicg, but which once again draws conclusions from a "later" one, Pascal says: "Custom is our nature. Whoever accustoms himself to faith, believes. . . . Whoever accustoms himself to believe that the king is terrible, . . . etc." (Br. 89). He does not need to finish out the thought.

This *pensée* exemplifies one of Pascal's most distinctive principles in theology and social philosophy: the importance of *la machine*.[21] We become faithful by practicing activities associated with faith: using holy water, taking communion, kneeling before the images, and so on. We become obedient subjects through the routines of obedience, which shape our minds and will. This subtle behavioral concept is in sharp contrast to the Cartesian separation of mind and body, and to Montaigne's notion of external and internal life. In each realm of human existence, from lowly flesh through charity itself, mechanical operations and routines give shape and substance to our whole existence. One wills to believe, to know, or to obey; then one begins the simple, mechanical activities associated with faith or science or submission, and through them one *becomes* a believer, a scientist, an obedient subject.

3. PASCAL ON CONCUPISCENCE AND *Amour-propre*

In all we do, asserts Pascal, our motive is the desire for happiness. Whatever unlikely means we may employ in finding it, this is the goal

[20] Br. 91, as well as Br. 426 and 32. On the concept of nature in Pascal, see Goldmann, *The Hidden God*, pp. 213-215, 273-277.
[21] Pascal develops the concept of *la machine* most fully in Br. 247-254, and at the end of Br. 233.

we seek. "The will never takes the slightest step except in this direction. It is the motive of all human action, even of those who hang themselves" (Br. 425). Very few human beings ever attain happiness, however, because our own nature betrays us in the search for it. Our self-love or concupiscence "hoodwinks the will into choosing mere pleasure as the object of pursuit instead of true happiness," as Baird puts it.[22] Blinded by *la malice de la concupiscence* which has itself become "second nature for us," an evil nature alongside that which was originally good, we waste our lives in wretchedness (Br. 24 and 660). Deprived of their true objects, our spirit and our will attach themselves to those false and unsatisfying pleasures indicated by self-love. Because of such ignorance, we live illusory and inauthentic lives, lying to ourselves and one another to sustain the "perpetual illusion" which is *la vie humaine* (Br. 100).

In developing this somber theme, Pascal foreshadows the concept of alienation that dominates so much of modern thought:

> We are not content with the life we have within us, in our own being; we wish to live an imaginary life in the minds of others, and we force ourselves to appear other than we are in order to accomplish this. We work incessantly to embellish and maintain our imaginary being, and neglect the true one. And if we have serenity, or generosity, or fidelity, we eagerly try to make these virtues known in order to attach them to this other being; we would gladly detach them from ourselves in order to enhance it. We should happily be cowards if we could have the reputation for bravery. A splendid confirmation of the nothingness of our own being, to be unsatisfied with the one without the other, and often exchange the one for the other! (Br. 147).

The major theme in Pascal's discussion of inauthentic and alienated existence is his notion of *divertissement*.[23] He posits a fundamental human tendency to avert our eyes from our own true condition, to busy ourselves incessantly with anything at all to avoid the misery of contemplating what we really are, which threatens us when we cease

---

[22] *Studies in Pascal's Ethics*, 69; see Br. 81 and 99-100.

[23] This theme is developed in Br. 128-171; Henri Lefebvre, *Pascal*, II, 129-147, points out similarities between Pascal's *divertissement* and Hegel's *entfremdung*. The parallels with Hobbesian psychology are also striking. But perhaps it makes most sense to recall the well-documented debt to Montaigne, which comes out clearly in Br. 131: "Nothing is so insupportable to man as to be completely at rest, without passions, business, *divertissement*, purpose. Then he senses his own nothingness, his abandonment, his insufficiency, his dependence, his impotence, his emptiness. At once, there wells up from the depths of his soul boredom, blackness, sadness, chagrin, contempt, despair."

agitating and attempt repose. "Our nature is in movement; complete repose is death" (Br. 129). Any kind of repose brings us uncomfortably close to an awareness of our death, by depriving us of the frantic movements that constitute our life. But death itself is easier than meditating upon death. Alone, without occupation, we discover our own partiality, our truncatedness, our lack. Having made a whole of our own self, we learn our horrible mistake—the radical insufficiency of the single self. To avoid this discovery we fill out our selves with imagination and our lives with incessant movement.

> The sole thing that can console us for our misery is diversion, and yet this is itself the greatest of our miseries. For it is precisely this which keeps us from thinking soberly about ourselves, and which therefore makes us lose ourselves without knowing it. Without diversion we would be sunk in *ennui*, and this *ennui* would lead us to seek a firmer basis for escaping from it. But diversion amuses us, and leads us insensibly to death (Br. 171).

This holds true, affirms Pascal, even for those supposedly supremely happy beings, the kings who can command everything. "A king left to himself," without *divertissement*, is simply "a man full of misery" (Br. 142). All his glory, his satisfactions, his possessions, are forms of *divertissement*, which go no further to meeting his true human needs than those of any other man. So much for Bossuet's notion that a king who has everything has nothing left to desire, and therefore can be counted on to govern his people in justice and tranquillity.

Pascal asserts that our human morality, on which we pride ourselves so much, is based on these same noxious traits of *concupiscence* and *divertissement* that keep us from the truth about ourselves. The human animal, he observes, has an indomitable tendency to create order. Drawing on the Augustinian idea that there is justice even among robber bands, Pascal notes how men who have renounced all laws of God and nature have made their own laws, which they obey most scrupulously, including "the soldiers of Mohammed, thieves, heretics,—and the logicians, too" (Br. 393). In this connection, Pascal suggests a theme later developed productively by his friend Nicole: that men have devised a bastard morality from concupiscence itself, an inverted version of the order of charity. He marvels at "the grandeur of man in his very concupiscence, to have drawn from it an admirable regime and made of it an imitation of charity itself."[24] This false morality leads us to behave in ways very like those of charity, attend-

[24] Br. 402-403, 523, 579, 660, and 663: "Nothing is so much like *la charité* as *la cupidité*, and nothing is so contrary to it."

ing to the needs of others and appearing pious, but from the opposite motive: desire for self-aggrandizement, not love of God and neighbor. A skillful inhabitant of the earthly realm learns to get what he wants without appearing to damage others; the unjust are those who "have not yet found a way of satisfying concupiscence without harming others" (Br. 454). Quite early on, we learn that our own desires are more likely to be satisfied if we appear to be thinking of another's happiness rather than crudely and openly pursuing our own. We also need to be esteemed by others in order to esteem ourselves. We flatter others and they reciprocate, so that much of human social life consists in mutually servicing each other's *amour-propre*. Human endeavor requires the spur of competition and emulation, which rest on our hunger to be dominant and to be admired. The education of children is virtually impossible without it, says Pascal. Children at the "little schools" of Port-Royal who were not stimulated by such motives "of envy and glory, fall into indifference and lassitude" (Br. 151).

Thus our apparent "virtues" are all revealed as several guises adopted by *amour-propre*, different forms assumed by concupiscence in its endless desire to be the center of all things. However impressive it may be, our glittering morality is rotten at the core. "We have taken advantage of concupiscence as best we could to make it serve the public good," observes Pascal, but "at bottom, it is only hatred. . . . We have founded upon and drawn from concupiscence itself admirable rules of civil order, morality, and justice," but beneath it all "this villainous human foundation . . . is only covered over, not rooted out" (Br. 451-453). Our virtues are all vicious in essence, and we "cannot support ourselves in virtue by our own strength, but only by the counterweight of two opposed vices, as we stand erect between two contrary winds; if one of the vices is removed, we fall into the other" (Br. 359). Political authority, which also maintains society by fear and flattery, is part of this same network of concupiscence.[25] Great men are surrounded by swarms of adherents because a *grand seigneur* is regarded as "master of the various objects of concupiscence," and thus expected "to have the power to satisfy the needs and desires of the many." Without his command of these rewards, which rests largely on his ability to command the strength of so many who expect reward, he would simply be another little human being. Pascal advises men

[25] "Trois discours sur la condition des grandes," in Chevalier, ed., *Oeuvres complètes*, pp. 615-620, third discourse. These discourses were published by Nicole in his treatise *De l'education d'un prince* (in *Essais de morale*, ed. Despres, vol. II). They are generally accepted as Pascal's work, although Nicole may have given them their final form.

who are in such positions to find their pleasure in satisfying the desires of others, and in showing *bienfaisance*, the trait so much cherished later by the abbé de Saint-Pierre. But the better part would be to give up such glittering prizes altogether, and hope to escape damnation by aspiring to charity itself.

There might seem to be a conflict between Pascal's requirement that there be a king to maintain worldly order, and his advice to men in positions of power to give up worldly things. But the conflict is only apparent; for there will always be enough worldly men to fill the offices without ambivalence. To guide men of true charity who must, for whatever reason, hold office anyway, Pascal describes a man shipwrecked on a strange island whose inhabitants await their long-lost king.[26] Resembling that king, the man is taken for their master. He accepts the homage of the islanders, but lives a double life. In his own mind he knows he is not king, however well he plays the role. He knows that his good fortune depends on no rights or qualities of his own. Pascal advises powerful men to recognize the similarities between their situation and that of the shipwrecked king. Before their subjects, they must maintain the image of authority essential to their office; in their own minds, however, they must always conserve the thought of their innate unkingliness, their humility as miserable men before God.

4. Unity in Diversity: The Community of the Saved

The image of the schizophrenic king corresponds to a recurrent theme in the *Pensées*: the *double capacité* of men, for sin and grace, for misery and grandeur. The alternating wretchedness and glory that constitute the human condition, the heights and depths of human reach, are Pascal's most frequent themes.[27] His political theory deals, for the most part, with the role of authority in ordering the hollow lives of sinful men. But there is an alternative: the community of those who have taken the dreadful and essential step of recognizing their wretchedness, and reached out for God.

Throughout the *pensées*, Pascal's dark picture of the human condition, corrupt and wretched, is relieved in two ways. However frail and pitiful man appears by comparison with the infinite universe, he has one advantage over it—his consciousness. He can know his frailty, know that he must die, and he can know himself, which the universe

---

[26] "Trois discours," in *Oeuvres complètes*, first discourse.
[27] See especially Br. 420; Strowski, *Les Pensées de Pascal*, pp. 117-129, compares Pascal's insights on this theme with those of Bossuet, Racine, and La Rochefoucauld.

can never do. This is the true source of his grandeur—his capacity for knowing his own wretchedness. There is also another source of relief for his condition: the existence of a liberator, a *réparateur*.[28] Men can be lifted from their wretchedness; but only if they will it. They must first take the step of *willing* to be saved, and then through faith they can be. The man who commits himself to belief opens himself gradually to the blessings of *charité*.

The commitment takes the form of the *pari*, Pascal's famous wager. In the pivotal argument of the *Pensées*, Pascal appeals to the unbeliever on grounds that he can readily understand; his own urgent self-interest. Pascal shows the atheist the misery and hollowness of his earthly condition, and then invites him to consider the state of his soul during eternity. There are only two possibilities. Either God exists: in which case the commitment to believe offers eternal bliss as its reward, and the failure to believe warrants eternal damnation. Or else God does not exist, in which case the believer loses the hollow satisfaction of earthly life and gains nothing, whereas the unbeliever has at least those satisfactions to enjoy.[29] The appeal rests upon the infinite advantage offered by an eternity of bliss compared with the infinite pain of eternal damnation. Since these are at stake, no matter how small the probability of God's existence (which cannot, in any case, be estimated) the choice seems clear, according to Pascal. We cannot choose not to choose; we are already embarked, and not to choose means to choose the world. We are like a number of men in chains, condemned to death and watching some among us every day led away to slaughter. Anyone in this condition who learns that there is a way out will surely take it.

Once the unbeliever has considered what is at stake, and has willed to accept the offices of the *libérateur*, the operation of *la machine* will move him into faith itself. The patterned activities of the faithful will gradually lead him to believe whole-heartedly. Pascal puts it this way: "This will make you believe, and bestialize you." The unbeliever replies: "But this is just what I fear," and Pascal responds roughly: "And why? what have you to lose?" (Br. 233). This anti-intellectualism is an important strain in Pascal's thought. For all his interest in the workings

---

[28] In one of Pascal's sketches for ordering his *pensées* (Br. 60), we find this idea broached: "*Première partie*: Que la nature est corrompue. (Par la nature même). *Second partie*: Qu'il y a un réparateur. (Par l'Ecriture)." See also Br. 422: "It is well to be worn out by the useless search for the true good, in order to hold out our arms to the *Libérateur*."

[29] The *pari* is argued in Br. 184-241; Ian Hacking, "The Logic of Pascal's Wager," offers a good analysis of the argument.

of the mind, he insists upon keeping *l'esprit* firmly in its place. He hints at obscure similarities between the brute functions of concupiscence and the irrational mysteries of faith. Both are equally inaccessible to the intelligence. Thus Pascal congratulates ordinary men for their dimly held and irrational opinions about things, their brute habitual ways, since they make more sense in worldly activities, and in those of faith itself, than the constructions of our reason. The two extremes of human apperception meet to reject the pretensions of the intellect outside its realm.

But the routine of unthinking animal-like behaviour is not the only fate that awaits the individual who wills to believe. In the *ordre de la charité* he discovers himself as a member of a distinctive community, a "body made up of thinking members" (Br. 473-474). His self-love shrivels into appropriate insignificance as he recognizes his true condition: that of one member of an organic body moved by a single will. Pascal dwells at length upon the image of the subordination of the willing parts of a body to the more general will that governs them all: "If the feet and hands each had a *volonté particulière*, they would never be properly in order except in submitting this particular will to the *volonté première* that governs the whole body. Without this they are in disorder and misfortune; but in willing solely the good of the body they work their own good" (Br. 475). Pascal uses the analogy of a foot that had always lived in ignorance of the rest of the body, knowing and loving only its own self, failing in its function for the whole. He pictures the chagrin of the errant foot once it came to know its true condition, its deep regret and confusion at having so long been useless to the body that could have annihilated it at any moment by cutting it away. Then he describes the happy submission of the contrite member to the will that regulates the whole, thus giving us to understand that the errant member of the Christian commonwealth is as ridiculous and unhappy as a nonfunctional and solipsistic foot (Br. 476). Like the silly foot, we are born in ignorance, "born unjust, all centered on the self. This is against all order. We ought to tend toward the general; and the penchant for the self is the beginning of all disorder, in civil and economic life, in the individual human body." Pascal places our several allegiances in hierarchy of worth, as Descartes had done, arguing that "if the members of natural and civil communities ought to tend toward the good of the whole body, the communities themselves should tend toward another good, still more general, of a larger body of which they are members. The unit should look to the more general" (Br. 477). But far more vividly than Descartes, or anyone else after Saint Augustine, Pascal describes the unequaled bliss of the unit at the top of the whole hierarchy, the *république chrétienne* composed of those who have experienced redemption.

There are a number of striking similarities between Pascal's ideal community and the secular version of such blessedness held out by Rousseau in the *Contrat social*.[30] Both descriptions begin with the self —the free autonomous individual whose interests must be appealed to, the fundamental willing unit, and the value worthy of preservation in the whole. In both communities, individuals lose the narrow self to discover the true self in the whole. The individual must first of all will to give himself up to conscious participation in the larger body, convinced by the appeal to his own interest.[31] But a full understanding of what is gained and lost cannot be grasped until the wager/contract has been fulfilled; thus there is an element of absurdity in the choice. For the willing to be effective and the community to be achieved, the intervention of a suprahuman liberator is required. He takes the willing members of the community and moves them gradually, by custom and habituation (*la machine*) to a full capacity to act in their estate. In both communities there is the same stress on the intimate connection between the body and its members, the harmonious subordination of the *volonté particulière* to the *volonté général*.

The concept of the community of thinking members provides for Pascal, as the analogous idea of the community of the *Contrat social* provides for Rousseau, a resolution of the multiple tensions apparent in his thought. A number of students of Pascal have characterized his distinctive mode of thought as "tragic." They have avoided the label "dialectic" because Pascal oscillates from one part of a dichotomy to the other, never coming to a resolution in a properly "dialectical" fashion.[32] There is something to this view; Pascal himself insists upon the importance of emphasizing one extreme as soon as he feels himself (or his readers) moving too close to its opposite.[33] But in the passages on the community of thinking members, Pascal comes to rest, and pulls together the complex fragments of his thought. The *pensées* that have to do with specifically Christian matters are nowadays put last,

---

[30] A parallel between Rousseau and Pascal in suggested in passing by Broome, *Pascal*, p. 233, and by John Plamenatz in his discussion of Pascal's thought in *Man and Society*, I, 208, as well as by Bertrand de Jouvenel in the excellent introduction to his edition of Rousseau's *Contrat social*.

[31] On the intricate connection between perceiving and willing in Pascal, see Br. 99; the appeal to the interest of the independent self is discussed in the first version of Rousseau's *Contrat social*, included in his *Oeuvres complètes*, III, 281-289.

[32] This argument is made by Goldmann in *The Hidden God*, and also by Lefebvre, *Pascal*, II, 140-142.

[33] Br. 328 and 420 are striking examples of this temper.

as Pascal intended; this means that they are often ignored by readers interested in Pascal's ethics and psychology. It is in these "final" *pensées* that Pascal's thought attains its fullness, in the recurrent theme of "unity in diversity." This theme is foreshadowed earlier in his idea of unity and diversity in nature.[34] But it is worked out most fully in his discussion of the governance of the Christian community. "In considering the Church as a unity, the Pope, who is its head, is as if he were a whole. In considering it as a multitude, the Pope is only a part of it.... In establishing one of these two truths, we must not exclude the other. The multitude that does not reduce itself to unity is confusion; the unity that does not depend on the multitude is tyranny" (Br. 871). Each of the members of the multitude of the faithful is a distinct, willing, thinking unit; but they are all made whole in the greater unity of which they are a part.

In that same *pensée* in which Pascal remarks that even men who hang themselves do so to find happiness, he says that happiness cannot be found except in faith. We search for something we dimly understand, complete participation in the body of thinking members rejected by corrupt human will, which is nonetheless our true estate. Only this can satisfy our longing; but most men never find this out.

> Some seek for happiness in authority, others in curiosities and in the sciences, still others in voluptuousness. Others who are closer to the mark have seen that it is necessary that the universal good, which all men desire, cannot reside in any of those particular things that cannot be possessed except by a single man and which, being divided up, afflict their possessor more deeply by the lack of the part he does not possess, than they content him by the joy of what he has. These wise men have understood that the true good must be such that all can possess it at the same time, without diminution or envy, and that no one can lose it against his will.[35]

This suggestive notion of a happiness that can only be attained by all together, and the unhappiness inherent in things that must be enjoyed in pieces by individuals, is one of Pascal's richest social insights. It argues cogently against the view that seventeenth-century social thought was uniformly egoistic and materialist. In this passage Pascal rejects, as clearly as possible, the opinion that happiness can be obtained by

---

[34] Br. 114-121, especially no. 116: "Tout est un, tout est divers. Que de natures en celle de l'homme!"

[35] Br. 425; Albert O. Hirschman, *A Bias for Hope*, p. 7, calls Pascal "the first to note the distinction between private and public goods," with this *pensée* as his major example.

the single human self, possessing things in isolation and enjoying them alone. He suggests instead the fundamental communitarian ideal. The root of human misery is the misguided absorption in the self; and whatever counts as the good for man must be something which can be enjoyed only by all together, without dividing up or counting out. This common enjoyment is more than parallel sharing in the same good thing. It rests on and includes a full participation in the same common will. In order that members may be happy, says Pascal, "it is necessary that they have a single will and conform it to the whole" (Br. 480). The ideal is akin to that of Rousseau, once again—to show that the thinking self can be preserved in consciousness of itself and yet find itself in submission to a "moral and collective body composed of as many members as the assembly has voices, which receives from this very act its unity, its common self, its life, and its will."[36] Pascal puts it this way:

> The true and unique virtue is then to hate the self (for one is indeed worthy of hatred by reason of concupiscence), and to seek for a truly lovable being to love. But, since we cannot love that which is outside ourselves, we must love a being which will be in us and yet not us, and this is true of each and every man. There is only one universal Being which meets this stipulation. The kingdom of God is in us: the universal good is in ourselves, is ourselves, and yet is not ourselves (Br. 485).

This complex vision of unity in multiplicity, of the self which encompasses the individual self but is larger than any individual, the harmonious whole dependent on its parts, pervades Pascal's thought. His overtly political theory stresses authority, irrationality, and force; he argues for complete submission and docility before the king. But he depicts a higher irrationality beyond our critical reason where participation in a fuller community is possible, and the unity of authority springs from the plurality of the beings who compose the whole. With this vision, Pascal contributed significantly toward undermining, in the long run, the closed monarchical authority his politics upheld.

[36] Rousseau, *Du contrat social*, book I, ch. 6; in *Oeuvres complètes*, III, 361.

CHAPTER TEN

Self-Love and Society: Jansenism and the *Honnête Homme*

1. The Ideal of *l'Honnêteté*

In the years following the Fronde, the moral models of sage and hero were supplanted by a more worldly but no less demanding ideal, the *honnête homme*. This notion of *l'honnêteté*, which we have already encountered in Saint-Evremond, was closely associated with certain parts of the French aristocracy. The chevalier de Méré, who followed this ideal, pointed out with pride that neither Italian nor Spanish, and certainly neither English nor German, had an equivalent term. His explanation was that "in almost all the other courts of the world, each individual is attached to a particular profession." But at the "grandest and most beautiful of them all," the court of France, success is judged not by how well one performs in a particular *métier*, but by the sweetness of one's wit and the tenderness of one's heart. "There we find persons who are both fiery and civilized, bold and modest, neither avaricious nor ambitious; they do not strive for power or for high place, and have virtually no other goal in life than to bring enjoyment everywhere; and their greatest care is not to merit esteem, but to make themselves loved."[1]

These well-balanced persons took pride in cultivating their *honnêteté* in the last half of the seventeenth century in France. "Honesty" is surely the wrong English word to use here, although the attempt to behave "naturally" in the Epicurean sense—to eschew heroic posturing and deliberate eccentricity in favor of low-keyed enjoyment of mutual private pleasure—was part of the program of the *honnête homme*. La Rochefoucauld, whose *Maximes* are an important source for understanding *l'honnêteté*, held that the "true *honnête homme*" is frank even about his failings.[2] For most practitioners of the craft, however, frank-

---

[1] Discours premier, "De la vrai honnêteté," in Chevalier de Méré, *Oeuvres complètes*, edited by Boudhors, vol. III, p. 69.

[2] *Maxime* 202, in La Rochefoucauld, *Réflexions ou sentences et maximes morales*, edited by Paul Morand. Méré also insisted on the distinction between true and false *honnêteté* in his second discourse, "Suite de la vraie honnêteté," p. 93. As Philip Lewis points out in *La Rochefoucauld: The Art of Abstraction*, p. 116, the distinction between true *honnêtes gens* and those who attempted to copy the ideal "epitomizes the alliance of cultural perfection with social exclusivism."

ness was less important than conformity. Civility, politeness, propriety—these are the best terms for capturing the meaning of *l'honnêteté*. It was a set of values and a form of behavior that found its most comfortable setting in the salons that dominated French intellectual and social life in this era. There were *honnêtes femmes* as well as *honnêtes hommes*, and the masculine restrictiveness of the intellectual academies of the erudite libertines was replaced by a milieu in which men and women alike behaved with a studied and witty gallantry that was believed to be attractive to the other sex.

The two mottoes of the *honnête homme* were *suivre nature* and *plaire*: to follow nature, and to please. The latter clearly took precedence over the former, which was wholly unlike what Rousseau later meant by acting according to nature. The smooth, polished salon performances of *honnêteté* were based on the artifice of pleasing, and coordinating the personal search for happiness with that of one's associates to maximize the pleasure of all. The ideal arose in response to the high melodrama of the Fronde and the boorish behavior that had often been associated with rough aristocratic heroism. It was, as Krailsheimer puts it, a "social aesthetic" that "gradually became a moral anaesthetic."[3] *L'honnêteté* meant following a set of rules for civilized behavior that share certain elements of what modern-day game theorists call a "mixed-motive game."[4] Participants attempted to cooperate as well as compete, to indulge their own self-love as well as suppress it for the sake of social harmony. Several descriptions make clear that those engaged in this ritual were aware that they were allowing themselves to be duped by one another in the interests of civility and smoothness, so that everybody would be happier in the end. Molière's *Misanthrope*, Alceste, who reacts to these elaborate social maneuvers by attempting to be natural and frank, demonstrates how far the ideal of *honnêteté* is from "honesty" in the usual sense.

The subtle nuances of *l'honnêteté* defied definition, even by those who were quite sure they knew what it meant. In this respect, the ideal can be compared with modern terms of similar porosity and generality, such as "authenticity" or "quality." Most efforts at definition of *l'honnêteté* began with the human desire for happiness, and stressed the contributions of the *honnête homme* to this universal pursuit. This was true not only of Méré's oblique attempts at definition in his discourse "De la vraie honnêteté," but also of Damien Mitton's. In his

[3] Krailsheimer, *Studies in Self-Interest*, pp. 81-84, is a useful brief discussion of *l'honnêteté*. On the *honnête femme*, see Ian Maclean, *Woman Triumphant*, ch. 5.
[4] Schelling, *The Strategy of Conflict*, p. 89; this parallel is drawn by Lewis, *La Rochefoucauld*, p. 111.

Pensées sur l'honnêteté, Mitton asserted that the most certain way to achieve happiness is to seek it in such a way that others can be happy along with us. "For if one attempts to think only of oneself, one continually runs into opposition and conflict, whereas if we only wish to be happy on the condition that others are happy also, all the obstacles are removed and the whole world lends us a hand."[5] This "management of happiness for ourselves and others" is Mitton's definition of *honnêteté*, which he calls "well-regulated *amour-propre*." The *honnête homme* takes part in society not to discover himself in a larger whole, as in Pascal's blissful community, but to satisfy his own individual need for happiness most effectively by coordinating his efforts with those around him. Mitton insists that the *honnête homme* performs all his duties and is "not *interessé*," or at least does not adhere to his own interests in a rigid fashion.

Unlike most of the *honnêtes gens*, Mitton was bourgeois, which may explain his willingness to codify the craft of *honnêteté*, as well as the "embryo of the democratic and humanitarian spirit" that can be discovered in his work.[6] Mitton showed a sense of the injustice and irrationality of social distinctions, even as he enjoyed their fruits. More typical, perhaps, was the impeccably aristocratic Méré, who shared Pascal's love of mathematics. He also shared with him a famous coach ride in which Méré showed the mathematical genius Pascal the subjective, intuitive side of human psychology, the *esprit de finesse* to set alongside his *esprit de géométrie*. Méré's *honnêteté* rested on this *esprit de finesse*, and was clearly intended for a small group of specially privileged individuals. Although the virtues of the *honnête homme* were often displayed at court, Méré insisted that the "true *honnête homme*" is even more *honnête* in private than in public life. His virtues were not supposed to be mere show, nor were they reducible to gallantry. Méré distinguished between the two by speaking of Alcibiades as a *galant homme* and Epaminondas, Montaigne's favorite, as an *honnête-homme*.[7] "I know nothing under the Heavens superior to *honnêteté*; it is the quintessence of all virtues," claimed Méré. "Those who lack it are ill-received among persons of good taste; even when they discuss things of the world it is ordinarily with such bad grace

---

[5] "Pensées sur l'honnêteté," included in Henry Grubbs' study of *Damien Mitton 1618-1690: Bourgeois Honnête Homme*, pp. 55-56. Mitton's little treatise, which was erroneously attributed to Saint-Evremond, was published in 1680 in a collection of Saint-Evremond's *Oeuvres mêlées*.

[6] Grubbs, *Damien Mitton*, p. 60.

[7] Fifth discourse, "Le Commerce du monde," in *Oeuvres complètes*, vol. III, pp. 139-140. On various refinements in the notion of *honnêteté*, and its connections with "worldliness," see Peter Brooks, *The Novel of Worldliness*, ch. 2.

that one cannot bear them. This science [of *honnêteté*] is specially appropriate to man, since it consists in living and communicating in a human and reasonable way."[8] This sense of a closed elite scornful of those who did not share their secrets was similar to that found among erudite libertines earlier in the century. Indeed, the two approaches had a good deal in common, stemming from their Epicurean roots. Several *libertins* professed *honnêteté*, including Saint-Evremond himself. There was much less stress on scholarly accomplishment among the *honnêtes gens*, however; and a pleasantly optimistic skepticism replaced the corrosive cynicism of Naudé.

The moral strands of sage, saint, and hero, which had been distinct from one another in the 1630s, became hopelessly entangled in the era of *l'honnêteté*. Former heroes as well as former libertines converted to *honnêteté* in reaction to the Fronde. The most prominent among them was La Rochefoucauld, who had suffered a serious wound on the barricades at Saint-Antoine, fighting for a cause he had never been able to define. La Rochefoucauld was not only a former hero; his works can be read as an expression of *libertin* philosophy, and he was an associate and admirer of the Jansenists.[9] The concept of *amour-propre* was crucial to all moral discourse in the late seventeenth century in France. This explains why apparently disparate ideals could have so much in common. The Jansenists reacted against the appropriation of the theological concept of *amour-propre* for worldy purposes by refining the distinction between *concupiscence* and *charité*. Yet these efforts were not wholly free of the reverse influence of pervasive *honnêteté* on the Augustinians, an influence particularly apparent on Nicole. And to complete the circle, even Pascal, who was relatively untouched by *l'honnêteté* and *libertinage*, can be interpreted as transferring the grand heroic ideals of Corneille to the realm of faith instead of duels.[10]

[8] First discourse, "De la vraie honnêteté," pp. 71-72. Louise Horowitz, *Love and Language: A Study of the Classical French Moralist Writers*, ch. 1, is useful on Méré. Ira Wade deals with him more briefly in *Intellectual Origins*, pp. 293-294, describing him as the "apostle" of the *honnête homme*, who "established the principles of what was for him a new religion." On pp. 229-230, Wade argues that the ideal of the *honnête homme* was derived from Epicurus by way of Gassendi, a major influence on Saint-Evremond.

[9] Louis Hippeau, *Essai sur la morale de La Rochefoucauld*, insists on the distinction between the attitudes of Jansenism and Epicurean pessimism, and links La Rochefoucauld with the latter rather than the former.

[10] Sedgwick concludes his *Jansenism* (pp. 204-205) with the provocative assertion that "Jansenism substituted one kind of heroic ideal for another," the quest for glory in the next world instead of this one, and points out that "this inverted heroic ideal" helps explain the appeal of this austere sect to "frustrated nobles."

Méré, in a passage of splendid casuistry, attempted to break down the barriers between saint and *honnête homme* by claiming that "devotion and *honnêteté* follow almost exactly the same routes, and mutually aid one another." According to Méré, "devotion renders *l'honnêteté* more solid and worthier of confidence; *honnêteté* gives devotion a debonaire and pleasing quality." Religion, in other words, was part of the science of the true *honnête homme*, and could be counted on to improve his chances for felicity in the world. As far as the next world is concerned, Méré contended that "*honnêteté* is far from useless to salvation, and even contributes to it."[11] Such passages were no doubt welcome to those who found the austere ideals of *la charité* difficult to compass. But quite a few Frenchmen in this era continued to profess a severe devotion that included exaggerated disapproval of the worldly *honnête homme*. The angry reception of Molière's *Tartuffe* showed that this master dramatist had touched a raw nerve.[12] Would-be saints were among the favorite targets of the scorn of *honnêtes gens*, since they neither followed nature nor pleased anyone. Yet the *honnête homme* himself was always in danger of edging into caricature, through the elaborate ritual involved in the quest for the perfect solution to the social game.

Although the *honnête homme* proudly proclaimed the utility of his finesse even in matters of salvation, one thing he left pretty much alone was politics. In this again he was the heir of the libertine and the saint. The nexus between *honnêteté* and the realm of government was not any participation expected from the *honnête homme*, but the injunction on kings and their ministers to behave as *honnêtes hommes*. In insisting that the true *honnête homme* had no profession except that of *honnêteté*, Méré excepted a single *métier* as noble enough to be acceptable: that of royalty itself.[13] Jean de Silhon, who had been a member of Richelieu's entourage, produced a treatise called *De la certitude des connoissances humaines* in 1661. Silhon's goal in writing the treatise was to teach the king, to whom the treatise is dedicated, how to rule like *un honnest homme*. As the title indicates, the central argument of *La Certitude* is a Cartesian response to skeptical epistemology, in which Silhon asserts that there are truths in morals and poli-

---

A.W.S. Baird, *Studies in Pascal's Ethics*, p. 25, points out the convergence between Nicole's Jansenist ethic and *honnêteté*.

[11] Second discourse, "Suite de la vraie honnêteté," pp. 101-102.

[12] Orest Ranum, *Paris in the Age of Absolutism*, ch. XI, "A Generation of Tartuffes."

[13] Fifth discourse, "Le Commerce du monde," p. 142.

tics, as well as other things in the universe, which "present themselves immediately to our spirits." The truths are stated in a straightforwardly utilitarian fashion: sovereigns distribute benefits like fountains, and impose laws, rewards, and punishments on subjects who must obey as one of the conditions for the benefits that they enjoy.[14]

For Silhon, as for virtually all Frenchmen who wrote moral essays in this era, self-love is the primary motivating force in human behavior. Silhon insists that *l'amour-propre* is not the malignant growth some moralists had thought. It is quite natural for us to seek the good appropriate to our nature, and flee from evil. But human beings often mistake their true good to chase after shadows. This is why, asserts Silhon, *amour-propre* has gotten a bad name. This devout Catholic also champions interest, as equally natural to our species. Interest is the "faithful companion and inseparable associate" of *amour-propre*, the source of all society, the soul of economics, the root motive in the formation of a polity.[15] The "interest" Silhon has in mind here is not any "common" good in Pascal's sense, but the Hobbesian idea that each individual has a selfish interest in the maintenance of social order, since self-preservation requires the cessation of the state of war.

When monarchs mistake their true interests, the consequences for the rest of us are particularly unfortunate. This explains Silhon's concentration on the instruction of the prince. *L'honnêteté*, as the coordinated pursuit of happiness, is particularly relevant to kings, who have more power to channel interests than other men. Silhon shows Louis XIV how the enlightened pursuit of our own advantage leads us to do good to others and perform noble deeds, and knits all individuals together in mutually beneficial service. For king as well as commoners, such efforts depend not on the denial but on the expression of self-love, correctly understood. Silhon is quite comfortable with the idea that not only monarchs but even men seeking salvation are motivated by this all-pervasive stimulus. He asserts that "almost all the actions of our life are excited by some notion of Interest of whatever genre, so that we traffic perpetually for the goods of this world or of the next. To wish to ban interest entirely from our lives would be to take from a machine the springs that make it move, and destroy that part of a compound object that makes it act."[16] Only God has

---

[14] Silhon, *De la certitude des connoissances humaines . . . où sont particulièrement expliquez les principes et les fondemens de la morale et de la politique* (1661), dedication and book II, ch. 1, pp. 95-97. Like Sénault, Silhon combines the analysis of self-love with an intricate parallel between the internal "polity" and the body politic.

[15] *De la certitude*, book III, ch. 10, p. 274.

[16] *De la certitude*, book II, ch. 2, pp. 100-103; this reference to interest as the

need of nothing, and is therefore not motivated by self-interest. But human interests differ, and some are more worth following than others, such as the interests of honor, conscience, health. Silhon singles out the "interest of wealth or riches" as the hardest to contain by reason, and the most likely to lead to voracious pursuit of narrow individual happiness. Therefore the name of "interest" has become attached to this subset of a much larger category, which is tainted throughout with the scent of avarice.[17]

Many moralists of the late seventeenth century tried to construct peaceable kingdoms in which interest and *amour-propre* lie down with virtue and charity. Each of them took a slightly different tack. All, however, were convinced that human society is basically a "traffic," a commerce of goods and services, a glittering marketplace in which each individual presents his own self to best advantage. If he is enlightened, he avoids the robbery and fraud so often found in marketplaces, relying instead on intricate negotiation with occupants of neighboring stalls to seek an amicable *modus vivendi* in which all can be happy alongside one another. The forum, the monastery, and the tower library all recede from attention as spheres for moral effort in favor of the marketplace, thinly disguised as the salon.

2. THE *Maxims* OF LA ROCHEFOUCAULD

The *Maxims* of the duc de La Rochefoucauld were central in the development of seventeenth-century ethical theory in France. Like Pascal's *Pensées*, the complex and oblique fragments that compose this book lend themselves to interpretation from a number of perspectives. Though not a Jansenist himself, La Rochefoucauld was a good friend of several Jansenists, and his ideas about *amour-propre* are influenced by Augustinian motifs.[18] After his career as a noble Frondeur, he

---

spring that moves the machine of human action recalls La Mothe le Vayer, and anticipates Montesquieu's argument about honor in the *Spirit of the Laws*. Rothkrug, *Opposition to Louis XIV*, pp. 55-60, has a thoughtful discussion of Silhon.

[17] *De la certitude*, book II, ch. 2, pp. 104-105. Hirschman, *The Passions and the Interests*, p. 39, uses this passage as evidence that the notion of interest was becoming identified with economic advantage, as it moved from the international to the domestic sphere, echoing "the old association of interest and money-lending," the more ancient meaning of the word.

[18] Jean Starobinski shows persuasively in "La Rochefoucauld et les morales substitutives," that La Rochefoucauld must be understood within the context of Jansenism. See also Will G. Moore, *La Rochefoucauld: His Mind and Art*, pp. 34-36. Philippe Sellier, "La Rochefoucauld, Pascal, Saint Augustin," suggests that the *Maximes* may be "an explicitly profane book secretly linked to theology" designed to bring men to Christ without mentioning religion.

showed little interest in politics, apart from one or two trenchant maxims, such as 151: "It is more difficult to avoid being governed than to govern others." His contributions to social theory rest on his extraordinarily subtle, fluid, and precise analysis of human moral psychology, in which *amour-propre* occupies a central place. From one perspective, La Rochefoucauld's *amour-propre* appears the very core of the human self, a living, pulsating, almost mythic entity, the common denominator of interest, passion, *amour*, and will. From another perspective, the self is a moral vacuum on which strong forces impinge from all sides in a miniature Fronde, with *amour-propre* as the strongest force of all. Or *amour-propre* may be seen as the corrosive tendency that continually dissolves any tentative consistency in the self.[19]

In one of the maxims (563) that he suppressed after the first edition (perhaps because it was too lyrical and too serious to fit well with his fragmentary reflections), La Rochefoucauld depicts *amour-propre* as "the love of oneself and of all things for the self; it makes men idolators of themselves and tyrants of others," pausing outside the self only "as a bee pauses at a flower, to draw from it that which is appropriate to itself." In language that recalls the ancient notion of *fortuna*, he says: "Nothing is so impetuous as its desires, nothing so hidden as it designs, nothing so adroit as its conduct; its suppleness cannot be described, its transformations are more than metamorphoses, its refinements beyond those of chemistry." It is as though he transposes fortune from outside us to within ourselves, propelling each of us along in defiance of the notion of a conscious and well-centered "self." The "self" becomes divided up, diffused, and disappears. La Rochefoucauld has often been seen as a forerunner of modern psychoanalysis because he opens up the psyche and displays its infinite complexity. Instead of a concentrated mass neatly stratified into passion, will, and reason, he shows us an uncharted sea where powerful forces work with bewildering speed in patterns quite beyond our ability to understand. The "self" is used and dominated by passions, interests, humors, and desires that wreak havoc with our confident containment of ourselves. And "whatever discoveries have been made in the *pays* of *amour-propre*, there still remain plenty of unknown territories" (3).

The Augustinian origins of La Rochefoucauld's *amour-propre* are clearest in maxim 509: "God has permitted, in order to punish man for his original sin, that he make a God of his self-love to be tormented

---

[19] On the diverse qualities of *amour-propre*, see Donald Furber, "The Myth of *amour-propre* in La Rochefoucauld," and Philip Lewis' discussion in chapter 2 of *La Rochefoucauld*.

by it in all the actions of his life." *Amour-propre* is discovered in the least expected places, in league against itself, the better to triumph over all attempts to master it; and "at the moment when it is vanquished and one thinks it finally defeated, one finds it there triumphing at its own defeat" (563). *La charité* still exists as a counterpart to *amour-propre* for La Rochefoucauld, but he mentions it only briefly in one early draft that he discarded before publishing. He follows Montaigne closely in describing the interconnections of "vice" and "virtue." The *exergue* at the beginning of his *maxims* puts the connection baldly: "Our virtues are most often only disguised vices." In the book itself the analysis is more complex. Virtue is not just vice in disguise; it is "an assemblage of diverse actions and interests that fortune or our industry knows how to arrange" (1). The virtues of clemency, chastity, bravery, resolve into a succession of merciful or chaste or courageous behaviors normally commended to us by our desire to gain favor, follow ambition, or vent jealousy. Fidelity is a strategy for winning confidence; generosity is skillful ambition that forgoes immediate petty interests for long-run greater ones (246-247). We call such motives "vicious," forgetting how often they motivate behavior we praise as "virtuous." In a close paraphrase of a passage from Montaigne, La Rochefoucauld asserts: "Vices enter into the composition of the virtues, just as the poisons are used in making medicine. Prudence assembles and tempers them, and then makes use of them to counter the evils of our life."[20] Even in the devotion we offer to princes, says La Rochefoucauld in maxim 518, is *un second amour-propre*.

Both "vice" and "virtue" are, according to La Rochefoucauld, instruments at the service of *amour-propre* and *intérêt*, which put together the most advantageous combination of vice and virtue to achieve a goal. As he puts it in maxim 171: "The virtues lose themselves in interest as the rivers are lost in the sea." In some maxims "interest" appears the most central of all his categories, particularly in 510:

Interest is the soul of *amour-propre*, in such a fashion that just as the body deprived of its soul is sightless, ... so, separated from its interest, *amour-propre* sees, understands, feels nothing, and no longer bestirs itself at all. So it happens that a man who scours the earth and seas for his interest becomes suddenly paralyzed by the interest of others. From thence comes that sudden heaviness and death we engender in others as soon as we recount our own affairs to them,

---

[20] Maxim 182; cf. Montaigne's essay III, 1, "Of the useful and the honorable," and Augustine's *City of God*, book XI, ch. 22, which was probably Montaigne's own source. Cf. also Maxim 578, on justice, and 606.

and their prompt resurrection as soon as we mention something that has to do with them. . . . A man loses consciousness and returns to it as his own interest comes close to him or draws away from him.

Interest in this maxim is like a magnet, galvanizing *amour-propre* into action, providing it with the field for its endeavor. It is the bridge between self and the outside world, which "speaks all kinds of languages and takes on all kinds of personalities, even that of disinterestedness" (239). It blinds some of us and enlightens others (40). Less protean and mysterious than *amour-propre*, interest lends itself to ranking and ordering. We can discern and follow "greater" rather than "lesser" interests. But few of us know how to do this, for our avid desire to have everything makes us "run after so many things at the same time that, in our excessive desire for the least important, the greater ones escape us" (66).

Interest, unlike *amour-propre*, can provide a basis for action in common with others, because of its partially objective quality. La Rochefoucauld's analysis is primarily of patterns of interest in the specialized society of the salon, but much of what he says could be generalized to other patterns of social intercourse. Along with Nicole, Pascal, and Saint-Evremond, La Rochefoucauld helped make familiar the notion that worldly society is best understood as a commercial transaction.[21] We come into it to get out of it what we can and give up as little as possible. Although he, like Montaigne, held out the vision of a "true friendship" as something quite different from the relationship that ordinarily goes by that name, his own moral theory was devoted to analyzing the normal phenomenon rather than the rare pure type.[22] "What men call friendship is really only a society, a reciprocal servicing [*ménagement*] of interests, an exchange of good offices; it is finally only a commerce, in which *amour-propre* proposes to itself something to be gained" (83). To maintain society, we must hide our radical preference for the self, and strive for a situation in which each individual "finds his own pleasure in that of others, services their *amour-propre*, and does not wound them." We should attempt to smooth the rough edges of our hostile impulses so that society can endure; and "since it is unlikely that a number of persons should have the same

---

[21] Marcel Raymond, "Du Jansenisme à la morale de l'intérêt," is a useful discussion of the connections between La Rochefoucauld and the Jansenists, as well as later English thinkers.

[22] In his *Réflexions diverses*, no. 2, "De la société," p. 133, La Rochefoucauld asserts that the greatest merit of ordinary society is to resemble in some pale fashion the more elevated and worthy relationship, *l'amitié* itself. See also maxim 473: "However rare true love may be, it is less rare than true friendship."

interests, it is at least necessary for the smooth operation of society that they do not have contrary ones."[23]

La Rochefoucauld's picture of a society founded on *l'honnêteté* is not an ugly picture. It is a society without violence, with a minimum of harm to others, where trust is maintained, and the liberty to withdraw into privacy is protected. Since interests are homogenous but not identical, needs can be met in a reciprocal exchange of services. However, such a society rests not only on self-restraint, but also on cooperative delusion. We avoid telling others what we really think of them, and engage in flatery to oil the machinery of society. As La Rochefoucauld puts it in maxim 18: "Men would not live very long in society if they were not the dupes of one another." The maxims combine praise with mockery, in the face of such adroit combinations of insight and delusion among humankind. Occasionally a more critical tone creeps in, as well. La Rochefoucauld comments on human artifice, men's inability to use their own natural resources because of their anxious need to imitate other men. "Each of them wishes to be another, and no longer what he is," he asserts. "They seek a countenance outside themselves and another wit than their own."[24] In maxim 629 he asserts that "luxury and excessive *politesse* in states are a sure sign of increasing decadence, because as all individuals become attached to their private interests [*intérêts propres*] they turn away from the public good." Neither of these charges against his contemporaries was wholly novel. But La Rochefoucauld's memorable apothegms helped spur more ambitious attacks on modernity in the next century.

3. The *Essays* of Pierre Nicole

Pierre Nicole, whom Sainte-Beuve described as a "true and pure Port-Royalist," was one of the most representative Jansenist thinkers.[25] He did not match the transcendent genius of Pascal or the argumentative endurance of Arnauld. But he shared something of the qualities of both, and made available to a receptive public ideas formulated by other men. He had also a gift for language and imagery that made him an influential moralist in his own right. Nicole's *Essais de morale*, composed over several years, were largely complete by 1675, when the first edition was published. They were reissued in various editions for

---

[23] "De la société," in *Réflexions diverses*, p. 135.
[24] "De l'air et des manières," in *Réflexions diverses*, pp. 136-137.
[25] Sainte-Beuve, *Port-Royal*, I, 104; Book v, chs. 7-8 in vol. II are devoted to Nicole, whom Sainte-Beuve calls the "moraliste ordinaire de Port-Royale." E. D. James, *Pierre Nicole: Jansenist and Humanist*, is a useful general study of Nicole; see also Nigel Abercrombie, *Origins of Jansenism*, pp. 240-273.

the next century or so, and widely read. Mme. de Sévigné, Saint-Pierre, and Voltaire admired Nicole, and several of the *Essays* were translated by Locke for the countess of Shaftesbury.[26] Whereas, with Pascal, we are on weak ground in asserting influence on eighteenth-century thinkers, we can confidently assume that Nicole's version of many of the same ideas was crucial in the development of French moral and political philosophy.[27]

In his analysis of the psyche, Nicole follows Pascal fairly closely. He emphasizes *amour-propre*, the human desire to dominate and tyrannize over others, and the importance of *divertissement*. Nicole's analysis of politics incorporates several Pascalian insights, but is founded firmly on Hobbes. Nothing so well illustrates the affinities between the "underside" of Augustinian theory and the ideas of Hobbes as the way in which this devout disciple of the bishop of Hippo explored the alleys and byways of the City of the Earth with the author of *Leviathan* for a guide. Unlike Pascal or Saint Augustine, Nicole was openly fascinated by the attractions of terrestrial society, and paid little attention to the special bliss of a community of saints. He took pleasure in portraying the intricate details of human social interaction, and envisioned a rich and teeming polity, where individuals pursued the commodious life under the protection, and restraint, of an absolute monarch. At times, Nicole's delight in this complex game becomes so great that he forgets to express disapproval of it, and celebrates it with enthusiasm quite unexpected in a Jansenist.

Nicole's theory of politics rests directly upon his ideas about human psychology in much the same way as does that of Hobbes, though Nicole's picture is not so sharply drawn or coherent as Hobbes's. *Amour-propre* in Nicole's *Essays*, by contrast with that in La Rochefoucauld's *Maxims*, is potentially a moderate master in its house. It often acts irrationally or passionately, but can be made to act more reasonably and assert control of behavior. Two of Nicole's more striking images bring out this dual nature of *amour-propre* well. In one passage, he compares human life to a terrible masked ball. Super-

[26] John Locke, *Discourses*, which includes three of Nicole's essays: "On the Existence of a God," "On the Weakness of Man," and "On the Ways of Preserving Peace."

[27] Nicole was a member of the committee at Port-Royal that brought out the original edition of Pascal's *Pensées*. It is interesting to speculate about his motives in deciding on the suppression of *pensées* later adapted in his own *Essays*. Simple jealous plagiarism does not appear to fit his character. Perhaps he was overruled by other Port-Royalists, and then included the ideas in his own work to give them currency. It is more probable that he assented to the suppression of these *pensées* because he disapproved of their harsh, cynical temper, and preferred to give the same insights a more traditional Christian form in his *Essays*.

ficially, men and women appear beautiful, agreeable, enjoying themselves in each other's company; but the light of faith penetrates our masks to show as we really are—miserable, poisoned, idolatrous, inhabited by demons.[28] This is good strong Jansenist stuff, and it is a major strain in Nicole's analysis of our nature. But like the more optimistic theologians of the 1640s, he also compares human beings to little kingdoms, each man the master of his interior realm, deploying the resources of affection and esteem, which are commodities desired by other people. To be a happy citizen of one's own self is not always easy, but it is a task worth taking up. "For our diverse passions and thoughts are like a multitude of people with whom we must live; and often it is easier to live with the whole external world than with this *peuple intérieur* that we carry within ourselves."[29]

The primary obstacle to knowledge and mastery of the self, in Nicole's view, is our preference for living outside ourselves in the things we do, the things we own, and the things we want others to believe about us. This is his version of Pascal's *divertissement*. A general surrounded by many soldiers thinks of them all as portions of his own great self. A rich man does the same with his possessions, and a nobleman with the estate and servants he commands. Less powerful people identify with the prettified picture of themselves they project into the world, and with their own opinions, and are wounded if anyone questions them.[30] So many *amours-propres*, attempting to dominate one another and shape the world in their own images, provide a situation full of conflict, the natural condition of life among fallen men. Nicole explicitly accepts Hobbes's description of the state of war that derives from our human desire to tyrannize others and the world itself. He employs an image from Cartesian physics to describe the perpetual conflict among selfish men:

> Nothing is so appropriate, to represent the spiritual world formed by concupiscence, as the material world formed by nature, the assemblage of bodies that makes up the universe. For in both cases, every particle of matter tends naturally to move, extend itself, and leave its place. But being pressed in by other bodies that are also

---

[28] "De la crainte de Dieu," included in Charles Jourdain, ed., *Oeuvres philosophiques et morales de Pierre Nicole*, pp. 140-141.

[29] "Comment on doit suivre la volonté de Dieu," in Nicole, *Essais de morale*, edited by Despres, v, 129; see also Nicole's *pensée* no. xcix, "Royaume intérieur dont l'amour-propre distribue les charges," in Despres, vi, 333-336, and the essay "De la faiblesse de l'homme," included in Jourdain's selection from his works, p. 74.

[30] "De la connoissance de soi-même," and "De la faiblesse de l'homme," in Jourdain, pp. 33-35 and 70-72.

moving, it is reduced to a kind of prison from which it escapes as soon as it can command more force than its environment. This is the image of the constraint to which the *amour-propre* of each individual is subjected by all the others, not permitting it to move freely as it desires to move.[31]

In Nicole's account two factors, beyond the limit placed on the movement of *amour-propre* by the pressure of other *amours-propres*, regulate this struggle. Sophisticated practitioners of *amour-propre*, like those who attempt to live as *honnêtes gens*, soon learn that they can attain their ends more readily by disguising their selfish desire for pleasure and appearing solicitous of the needs of others, rather than attempting to tyrannize over them. Men motivated solely by the desire to maximize their own happiness do so by satisfying the needs of other men. This is, according to Nicole, the "source and foundation of all commerce among men, which diversifies itself in countless ways; for we not only make a traffic in merchandise, or money, but we also make a traffic of works, services, favors, civilities; and we exchange all these things, either for other things of the same sort, or for more solid goods."[32] In Nicole's eyes, the most fascinating thing about this busy commerce is that it allows men to live together commodiously in an efficient fashion, which even the purest charity could never duplicate. He is full of admiration for this intricate machinery of enterprise and service based on greed, so well suited to earthly intercourse. "By means of this commerce," he continues, "all the needs of life are in some way filled without the intervention of charity," so that even in societies where true religion has never been preached, men live "with as much peace, surety, and commodity as if one were in a republic of saints." In his passages in this vein, Nicole suggests ideas like those used by later thinkers in ways he could hardly have foreseen, men such as Mandeville and Adam Smith. Here, for example, is his comment upon the way cupidity takes the place of charity to fill our needs, and does the job much better:

> We find, for example, almost everywhere when we are traveling, men who are ready to serve those who pass and have lodgings ready to receive them. We dispose of their services as we wish; we command them and they obey us and make us believe that it gives them

[31] "De la charité et de l'amour propre," in Jourdain, pp. 180-182. On this aspect of Nicole's thought, see Rothkrug, *Opposition to Louis XIV*, pp. 52-54.
[32] "De la charité et de l'amour propre," in Jourdain, p. 181; see also "Des moyens de conserver la paix," Jourdain, p. 261. Jacob Viner refers to Nicole and other Jansenists in discussing the origins of "The Invisible Hand and Economic Man" in *The Role of Providence in the Social Order*, ch. 3.

pleasure to serve us. They never excuse themselves from rendering any service demanded of them. How could such behavior be more admirable if it were animated by the spirit of charity itself? It is greed which makes them act, and they do so with such good grace that one believes one does them a favor by employing their services.

Think how much charity would be required to build a whole house for another man, to furnish it completely and then hand him the key. Greed does this quite joyfully. What a degree of charity would be needed to go search for medicines in the Indies, or abase oneself to the vilest services, and the most painful? Greed does all this without complaining.[33]

Our motives are less important to Nicole in this analysis than the outcomes of our behavior. He finds, in *l'amour propre éclairé*, an instrument for social life admirably suited to our earthly needs. Instead of scorning it because it is not charity itself, he advocates its nurturance in the interests of ameliorating human life. The powerful unmasking of miserable corruption in Pascal's *Pensées* and La Rochefoucauld's sardonic mockery are both absent in Nicole. When he contemplates the products of human greed and the accommodations of self-interest, he expresses childlike wonder. The consequences of a policy of "enlightened *amour-propre* that knows its own interests and tends by reason to the end it proposes for itself" are indistinguishable from those of charity itself. Therefore, concludes Nicole, if we want to make men happier in their earthly lives, the appropriate course is to concentrate on enlightening *amour-propre*, instead of attempting to preach charity to inveterate sinners.[34] Those charged with the education of the rich and powerful are particularly urged to take this lesson to heart.

Enlightened self-interest is not sufficient to keep all these inflated self-loves from coming into conflict, however. It requires the strengthening of the gibbet and the sword to ensure that its good effects will be enjoyed. Thus, after offering his observations on the social utility of greed in the essay "De la grandeur," Nicole says:

There is nothing, then, from which one draws greater service than human greed itself. But in order that greed be disposed to render such services, it is necessary that something constrain her to it; for if left to herself she has neither limits nor measure. Instead of serving

---

[33] "De la grandeur," Jourdain, p. 398.
[34] "De la charité et de l'amour propre," p. 179, and "Des moyens de conserver la paix," p. 241.

> human society, she would destroy it. There is no excess of which she is not capable when she has no bridle.... It was therefore necessary to find an art to regulate cupidity, and that art consists in the political order which restrains it by fear of punishment, and applies it to things useful to society. It is that order which gives us merchants, doctors, artisans, and generally all those who contribute to the pleasures and provide the necessities of life. Thus we have an obligation to those who are the conservors of that order, that is to say, to those in whom resides the authority that regulates and supports the state.

Greed has beneficial effects only when a strong political power sets limits and boundaries to *amour-propre*. Rulers redirect raw human cupidity to socially useful ends, like trainers of wild beasts to human service. Although Nicole avoids any explicit notion of a contract, his explanation for the origins of government is basically that of Hobbes: men coming together to avoid the worst of fates, uniting their strength to make possible protection, security, and a more commodious life. Once it has been formed, the political union is cemented by the fear of punishment, and especially by the fear of death.[35] Nicole's sovereign, like Hobbes's, must be absolute and unlimited, to provide effective government for restless men. However, God takes a more prominent role in Nicole's founding than in Hobbes's, communicating "to the persons chosen his own power to govern those submitted to them," and demanding obedience to earthly masters as part of our duties to God Himself.[36]

Within the established civil order, men sublimate their desires for domination in socially useful patterns of competition and exchange.

> The political order is an admirable invention of men to procure to all individuals commodities that the greatest kings could never enjoy, no matter how many officers they had and how great the riches they possessed, if that order were destroyed. How much wealth,

---

[35] "Thus, by means of the wheel and the gibbet set up in common, one represses the tyrannical thoughts and designs of the *amour-propre* of each individual. The fear of death is thus the first link of civil society and the primary bridle upon *amour-propre*; and it is this that reduces men to obedience to law and makes them forget their vast dreams of domination." "De la charité et de l'amour propre," Jourdain, pp. 180-181.

[36] "De la grandeur," Jourdain, p. 390. With his penchant for making everything fit together neatly, Nicole argues in this essay that "concupiscence, reason, and religion come together in diverse ways to create that condition which we call *la grandeur*," the status of rulers and great lords. Carried away by the magnificent appropriateness of it all, Nicole asserts that the civil order is "the masterpiece of the human spirit, and the most useful thing in the world."

how many servants would be necessary for a man, without that great invention, to procure the advantages an ordinary Parisian townsman now enjoys? How many ships would be needed to send out to all parts of the world to bring him medicines, clothes, curiosities, and handicrafts? How many men would it take to bring him news regularly from all parts of Europe? How rich would he have to be to supervise and provide for that many couriers? . . . All the arts being connected, and needing one another, he would find that he would have need of all; and it would not suffice to provide for himself; he would have to do so also for his officers and for those who worked for him, which would extend indefinitely.[37]

Thus civil order makes possible the production of numberless commodities for every individual by the efficient coordination of services and the division of labor. But our *amour-propre* can be enlightened only so far, and this does not extend to a capacity to appreciate these benefits so strongly that we would maintain civil order without a strong authority over us. Stubbornly selfish men fail to recognize that goods provided in this way are as valuable as those privately commanded for their sole benefit. If force and fraud were not prevented, individuals would seize as much as possible for their own selfish use, and thereby destroy the whole intricate economy on which the benefits depend.

Few men are sufficiently moved by charity to obey a king simply because God has commanded it, or sufficiently far-sighted to obey because they profit from the social order. Relying on raw force to keep men in line, however, is both inefficient and unpleasant. So Nicole stresses the importance of glittering symbols of authority that strike awe in the hearts of worldly men and lead them to docility. The pomp and splendor of kings and magistrates may have been introduced because of the sinful pride of those who hold the offices. But such baubles elicit deference from ordinary subjects, and this means they are "useful and reasonable" in themselves, "so that if pride had not introduced them, reason would have had to invent them." Nicole, unlike other acute observers of the power of symbols, such as Montaigne, La Boétie, and Pascal, insists that *les grands* are worthy of true and sincere respect, not just external signs of honor and obedience. On this point, Nicole explicitly and ingeniously amends Pascal. He adapts Pascal's distinctive notion of *la machine* to show that if we perform the behaviors of honoring our worldly sovereigns, these acts will imprint patterns of respect upon our soul, as well. The distinction

[37] "De la grandeur," Jourdain, p. 399.

between the upright reason and the bended knee offered by Montaigne is rejected by Nicole, who points out that as we bend our knees we begin to find those to whom we kneel worthy of our honor. Pascal himself had not dealt with this dilemma, except to insist that the homage offered as we kneel to sovereigns should be of a wholly different sort from that offered as we kneel to God. Nicole says, in effect, that homage is homage, before the throne or before the altar, and that this is as it should be; sovereigns participate in God's authority, and therefore reserve our full respect.[38]

Throughout the *Essays* there are passages in which Nicole transforms Pascal, smoothing over the harsh contours of his friend's thought as he incorporates it into his own. This comes out particularly clearly in a passage in which he glosses Pascal's discussions of justice and force. The vigorous *pensée* (Br. 298) in which Pascal considers the connections between these two was left out of the Port-Royal *Pensées*; but Nicole adopts Pascal's argument as his starting point.[39] His formulation lacks the elliptical elegance that marks Pascal's thought; Nicole spells out what Pascal veils in layers of double meanings. But the substance of the argument is still there, and Nicole develops it in ways compatible with Pascal's views. For example, Nicole suggests that human beings cannot bear to think something vicious that they also regard as virtuous. They admire the impressive grandeur of force, its *virtù* in the Machiavellian sense, and to avoid cognitive dissonance (as we would say nowadays), they call the results of forceful action just. Also, since established force is the basis of all civil order, we call it justice to avoid the injustice of sedition and disorder.

Pascal's effort to force us to confront the tensions and absurdities of our condition so that we may be moved to seek for something higher, for the true peace of charity, is avoided by Nicole in favor of a more comfortable and less visionary approach. He papers over the abyss Pascal described so memorably, between the things of the earth and the things of heaven. Nicole narrows the gulf separating charity from

---

[38] "De la grandeur," Jourdain, p. 394; Nicole here refers to Pascal's distinction between the different kinds of grandeur, but does not mention him by name. See also Nicole's *pensée* no. XXI, in Despres' edition of the *Essais*, VI, 224-225, where Nicole uses Pascal's term *la grimace* to describe the ceremonies necessary to command the respect of worldly men. The behavioral insights of *la machine* are also used by Nicole in a *Traité de la comédie*, which he, like Bossuet, contributed to a dispute over the theater in the 1660s. Nicole argues that since the movements of our bodies have an important imprinting effect on our souls, comedians corrupt themselves as well as their audiences, through the systematic exciting of vicious passions in themselves to represent them on the stage.

[39] *Pensée* LXXXIII, "Le Réligion chrétienne attache sans erreur la justice à la force," in Despres, *Essais de morale*, VI, 303-306.

amour-propre, and spends a good deal of time in a pursuit Pascal dismissed as the pastime for regulating lunatics: the analysis of "the science of human utility," which means determining how we should act so as to maximize human peace and happiness on earth.[40] This science is very close to Méré's science of *honnêteté*, as well as to the enthusiastic utilitarian calculuses of Saint-Pierre and Jeremy Bentham. When Nicole advises us to study human behavior and motivation carefully, not in order to expose its corruption, but to contribute as much as possible to the peace and commodity of the earthly city, he moves far away from Augustine in the direction of utilitarianism.

Nicole's *Essays* include few passages on the community of saints. Instead, he depicts the blessings of a human religious community, marked by obedience to authority and perfect submission to the will of an earthly superior. He insists that this rule is a better way of life than liberty.[41] In Nicole's communities, unlike Pascal's communion of saints, members explicitly do not think for themselves, and this is the heart of their virtue. They have learned to be suspicious of the blandishments of "liberty," and have discovered that it is more admirable, as well as much less demanding, to subordinate one's will to that of someone else, instead of attempting to find one's own way oneself. Only a few among us, according to Nicole, have been entrusted by God with knowledge about how to guide others here on earth. The rest of us should follow them and not wander about misguided, like lost sheep. The spiritual condition of the few shepherds who bear the responsibility for exercising the liberty gratefully given up by their followers does not concern Nicole, who lacked the subtle psychology of a Dostoevsky describing the Grand Inquisitor. Nicole probably assumed that God would provide serenity to those to whom He grants authority. But a comparison between his discussion of liberty and authority, and that of Dostoevsky or Pascal, is an excellent indication of the difference between a gifted essayist in ethics and a genius describing *la condition humaine*.

Nicole offers one valuable insight into politics that makes him sound, all of a sudden, unexpectedly modern. In describing the pattern of

[40] "Des moyens de conserver la paix," in Jourdain, p. 210, a passage that advocates the importance of the science that "makes men useful" to each other.

[41] "De l'obéissance," in Despres' edition of the *Essais*, v, 1-40. Nicole argues that obedience is itself a virtue; it also removes the burden of determining whether one is truly acting virtuously or is motivated by some hidden vice. In the essay "De la soumission à la volonté de Dieu," in Jourdain, pp. 102-103, Nicole makes the explicit connection between autonomy and sin, and asserts that it is better to follow the will of another man than one's own will, since this is more like following the will of God directly.

social commerce and conflict held in place by strong political authority, Nicole outlines a theory of pluralism. Just as each individual's *amour-propre* is held in check by the pressure of the *amours-propres* of other men, so groups form through the attractions of shared benefits. These groups are themselves pressing and pressed against other groups in turn. Each group attempts to occupy as powerful a place as it possibly can, and is limited by the efforts of other groups to do the same. Nicole uses the analogy with Cartesian physics to explain his meaning here: "Just as these little imprisoned bodies [Descartes's molecules] unite their forces and their movements to form great masses of matter called whirlpools, which are like states and kingdoms, and these whirlpools are themselves pressed and imprisoned by other whirlpools, like neighboring kingdoms, so also little whirlpools form within each great whirlpool." These "little whirlpools" of molecular matter are groups made up of individuals, swirling around within the greater whirlpool of the state. In addition to "following the general movement of the great body in which they are included," they also have their own individual movements, and force other little bodies to revolve around themselves. Each little molecule always thinks first of itself and its own interest, "has its own little path which it follows around the center," while at the same time "the great and powerful men in a state follow the same kind of movement, each having his own particular interests, and forming the center of a large number of men attached to his fortunes."[42]

Nicole does not carry these thoughts very far. But they suggest patterns of connection between interested individuals in groups, and the mutually limiting effect of several groups in a struggle for power, all held together like a whirlpool around a common center. In place of the Renaissance pluralism of Seyssel, which stressed the role of estates and orders in society, Nicole's pluralism reflects the world-view of seventeenth-century science. The energy produced by multiple individual movements in pursuit of private goals is the gravitational force holding public life together. Like Bossuet, Nicole notes that men's interests unite them as well as divide them; they are sometimes led to attend to each other's needs, and at other times destroy each other to get what they want. The sovereign maintains the equilibrium of the whirlpools, ensuring that no single individual or group can amass enough force to become a tyrannical center of power detracting from that of the sovereign authority itself.

This picture of the political order as a solar system, held together

[42] "De la charité et de l'amour propre," in Jourdain, pp. 182-183.

by the centripetal patterns of the needs and fortunes of individuals, and pulled apart by the opposing patterns of hostility and competition for good things, is part of Nicole's larger vision of the world as one great city, held together by the needs and commerce of all peoples. At the beginning of his essay on "Means to conserve peace among men," he revives the Stoic image of the city of the world in a modern commercial variant that must have appealed to Voltaire and Locke:

> All the societies of which we are a part, all the things with which we have some liaison and some commerce, on which we act and which act upon us, and which are capable of altering the disposition of our soul, are the cities where we pass the time of our pilgrimage, since our soul resides in these things. Thus the whole world is our city, because in our capacity as inhabitants of the world we have connections with all men, and we can in some measure receive from any of them so much utility or so much damage. The Dutch have commerce with Japan; we have commerce with the Dutch. We are in this way connected with the peoples at the ends of the world, since the advantages which the Dutch derive from them gives us the means to profit from or be harmed by it. The same can be said of all other peoples. They touch us in some way, and all enter into the chain which links together all men, held by the reciprocal needs they have one of another.[43]

4. Jean Domat and the "Esprit des Lois"

In their political ideas, as in other respects, Jansenists differed among themselves. The Augustinian discussion of civil order among fallen men in the work of Pascal and Nicole was the most distinctively Jansenist contribution to political philosophy. But other Port-Royalists held other views. As we have seen, Arnauld d'Andilly was probably the author of several rebellious pamphlets in the Fronde. His brother, the more famous Arnauld, expressed highly conventional political ideas, derived directly from the Pauline injunctions to obey the powers that be, as did Pasquier Quesnel.[44] One of the most ambitious Jansenist treatises on political theory, Jacques-Joseph Duguet's *Institution d'un prince*, is a derivative exercise in the mirror of princes genre that stresses the religious duties of a Christian prince. Duguet's *Institution* was written in 1699, although it was not published until forty years

---

[43] "Des moyens de conserver la paix," pp. 207-208.
[44] Jean Laporte, *La Doctrine de Port-Royale*, I, ch. 7, and J.A.G. Tans, "Les Idées politiques des Jansénistes," pp. 1-18.

later. It reflects the unrest of the last decades of Louis's reign, and touches on themes of good counsel, fiscal reform, and Christian agrarianism expressed by a number of Frenchmen in those years.[45]

Quite a few Jansenists, including Arnauld and Quesnel, were influenced by theories of natural law derived from the Thomistic synthesis and from contemporary treatises such as that of Grotius. Such ideas had been almost absent from French political discourse in the first half of the seventeenth century; but they were heard with increasing frequency in the years after the Fronde. Jean de Silhon's *Certitude des connoissances humaines* relies on natural-law arguments to support the contention that relations between sovereigns and subjects are based on reciprocal duties of protection and obedience. If sovereigns become tyrants and command things that contravene the laws of God and nature, Christian subjects should not obey them. The prince cannot execute his policies alone, and "a simple cessation of obedience" on the part of all his officers will suffice.[46] If he attempts to force compliance, subjects can fall back on the natural law of self-preservation; a tyrant is no true sovereign, so the people are relieved of their duties of submission. Silhon's assertions exemplify a growing interest in natural-law argument in France.

It was a close friend of Pascal, the learned jurist Jean Domat, who wrote the treatise that most effectively combined natural-law arguments with Augustinian ideas and handed them on to the next generation. Domat was an avowed Jansenist at a time when Jansenism was very much out of favor at court. But his reputation as a jurist was so impressive that Louis XIV gave him a pension to support his project of codifying the archaic chaos of French public law. Domat was a jurist after the king's own heart. He had the same love of tidiness, capacious memory for detail, and Cartesian confidence that the innately regular order of his material would lend itself to systematic treatment. Domat restored the tradition of fruitful theorizing by jurists that had been dormant since the early decades of the century, renewing links with constitutionalists such as Seyssel, L'Hôpital, and Loyseau. His treatise on *Les Loix civiles dans leur ordre naturel* also laid the groundwork for constitutionalist argument in the eighteenth century. Montesquieu read Domat carefully, and D'Aguesseau's work has been described as "an extensive commentary on Domat."[47]

---

[45] Sedgwick, *Jansenism*, pp. 182-187.
[46] *De la certitude*, III, 6, 235-244. La Boétie uses this same phrase with the same intent in his *Voluntary Servitude*.
[47] W. F. Church, "The Decline of the French Jurists as Political Theorists," p. 24. This is among the best studies of Domat, especially on his links with past and future constitutionalists.

Unlike most earlier French jurists, Domat mixed heavy doses of abstract philosophy with his jurisprudence. He embedded discussions of specific legal practices in a series of reflections on the "spirit of the laws," so that readers would not lose sight of the grand natural and divine order of which these details were but a tiny part.[48] He was also faithful to Jansenist ethics throughout his work; his arguments rest on assumptions about human psychology and human purposes borrowed from Pascal and Nicole. In the long prefatory treatise that opens his major book (which has its own title, the *Traité des loix*), Domat elaborates the familiar argument that all human troubles stem from disobedience to the first of God's laws, which commands us to love God and through Him, our neighbors. If human beings had followed this law consistently, asserts Domat, we would all know the *souverain bien* uniquely intended for human happiness—a happiness that can only be possessed by all of us at once, and cannot be the exclusive possession of any individual: the shared love for our common Creator. But in falling away from this love, we have lost such common happiness and seek a substitute happiness to be enjoyed in isolation. "It is therefore the disorder of love that has disordered society," says Domat. "Instead of that mutual love, the character of which is to unite men in pursuit of the common good," another quite opposite love prevails, "whose character has justly given it the name of *amour-propre*, because he in whom this Love rules seeks after only those goods that he makes entirely his own, and which he loves in others only insofar as he can draw advantage from them to himself."[49]

By the poison of self-love our hearts are "benumbed and heavy," paralyzed by the particular selfish good that engages all attention. But this poison carries its own antidote, in the hands of God. "For from this very principle of division He has made a tie that binds men together in a thousand ways and supports the greater part of our engagements." After the Fall, complex new needs multiplied among selfish men, and to satisfy them, commerce with others is required despite our narrow preference for ourselves. Society founded on such ties is a pale substitute for common bliss; but it works tolerably smoothly, and even takes on the appearance of virtue, says Domat. We quickly learn to "counterfeit" integrity, fidelity, and all the other qualities of charity, to ensure that other men satisfy our needs. Thus "self-love accommodates itself to everything, so that it may reap advantage every-

[48] *Les Loix civiles dans leur ordre naturel; le droit public, et Legum delectus*, 1777 edition. The chapter "De la nature et de l'esprit des Lois" is ch. xi of the *Traité des loix*, the preface to the *Loix civiles.*
[49] *Traité des loix*, ch. ix, sec. 2. I have consulted the excellent contemporary translation by William Strahan entitled *The Civil Law in Its Natural Order*.

where."[50] Domat even asserts that *amour-propre* can incline us to feel pity and affection for other human beings. We recognize them as similar to ourselves, and since we are inclined to love the image of ourselves wherever we discover it, we extend our *amour-propre* to include concern for their suffering, desire for their company, and a willingness to embrace the golden rule. By this route, *amour-propre* comes close to charity. But it starts at the opposite pole (my love for my own narrow self), instead of beginning with the pure love of God.[51]

Besides these adaptive performances by *amour-propre*, Domat identifies several other foundations of human society. Like Nicole, he argues that God has given authority to kings, fathers, husbands, rulers of all sorts, to bear His image on earth and maintain order. Beyond this, Domat insists that even corrupt fallen man retains some glimmerings of the light of reason that illumined Adam's soul. These sparks occasionally shine out fitfully in the darkness of *amour-propre* and show how we ought to live. By revealing the rudiments of natural and divine law, they bolster civil order and supplement the machinations of *amour-propre*. Thus Domat, even more than Nicole, softens the harsh, uncompromising edge of Pascal's Jansenism.[52]

Most of Domat's theory was conventional, combining absolutist images with a few tentative constitutionalist assertions. When he touched on republican regimes, in his concern for codification of all principles of civil law, he made several points that later became commonplace. Republics are possible only in very small societies, said Domat. They tend to develop in situations of austerity rather than luxury, and have grave disadvantages in defending themselves against aggression by their larger neighbors.[53] His treatise on *Le Droit publique* includes a long discussion of municipal government, which takes for granted that "the people have common affairs, for the dispatch of which they are permitted to assemble together," and to choose representatives and officers to carry out the public business on their behalf.[54] Such arguments were part of the most ancient traditions of the French polity; but in 1690 they sounded either anachronistic or visionary. In fact, Domat was both. His discussion of this topic is a link between earlier constitutionalism and the renewed challenges to absolutism in the eighteenth century.

[50] *Traité des loix*, ch. IX, sec. 3.
[51] Preface to *Le Droit public*, which is Domat's sequel to the *Loix civiles*. Rousseau's concept of *la pitié* in the *Discourse on Inequality* is similar to Domat's.
[52] *Traité des loix*, ch. IX, sec. 4-8.
[53] *Le Droit public*, book I, title I, section 1.
[54] *Le Droit public*, book I, title XVI, sections 1-4.

5. THE DISPERSION OF JANSENIST IDEAS

In the last two decades of the seventeenth century, the ideas of the primary generation of Port-Royalists had become familiar to a great many Frenchmen. Men who were not Jansenists themselves, such as La Bruyère, Malebranche, and Jacques Abbadie, were influenced by those ideas, and developed them in new directions. These diverse uses of Jansenist themes irritated some of the Jansenists, especially when worldly figures such as La Rochefoucauld and La Bruyère discoursed about *amour-propre* without insisting on the superiority of charity and the necessity of grace. Jacques Esprit composed a ponderous treatise on *La Fausseté des vertus humaines* that was clearly written with La Rochefoucauld in mind. The frontispiece of La Rochefoucauld's *Maxims* showed Seneca, the most sublime of all secular moralists, unmasked. Esprit's frontispiece shows a man turning away from the unmasked Seneca in horror, toward a saintly figure labelled *la verité*.[55]

The purpose of Esprit's treatise, like Pascal's, was to convince his readers of the need for grace by moving them to revulsion at their own corruption, and showing God as the author of all true virtue. Esprit's strategy involved discussing each of the supposed human virtues in turn, showing that all of them (fifty-three in number) are so many disguises of self-love.[56] This rapidly becomes tedious, and yet one cannot help feeling a subversive admiration for spunky *amour-propre*, capable of presenting itself in so many seductive packages. This was hardly the effect intended by the author; but it helps explain why *amour-propre* fascinated secular as well as religious moralists.

Esprit's capacities as a vigilant unmasker of *amour-propre* are most impressive when he deals with those hallowed human virtues that seem to involve the sacrifice of self. *La bonté*, for instance, is the source of noble and apparently disinterested behavior; Esprit argues that the basis for the high esteem it enjoys is its great utility for other people. We evaluate things by how useful they are to us, and nothing is more useful than the tendency to perform grand and noble deeds for society. But when we praise Alexander for conquering the world and scorn a lowly merchant setting out to sea to enrich his family, we fail to notice that both run risks for precisely the same reason: interest. Alexander acted in the "interest of glory," and he was "incomparably more *intéressé*" than the greedy merchant. All noble acts are motivated by vanity, jealousy, or the raw taste for aggrandizement.[57] Friendship is a

[55] Louis Hippeau, *Essai sur la morale de la Rochefoucauld*, pp. 100-109.
[56] Louise Horowitz, *Love and Language*, ch. 6, is a good brief study of Esprit.
[57] Jacques Esprit, *De la fausseté des vertus humaines* (1678), ch. 17, pp. 409-412.

form of commerce designed for personal advantage; we fawn on our friends as "merchants caress and manipulate their customers."[58] Disinterestedness or impartiality only proves that interest is omnipresent in human affairs. Some ambitious men discover that the best way to advance their reputation is to appear to be above all interest (one thinks of cardinal de Retz). Other men flock to the disinterested leader in the expectation of selfish profit from his selflessness, and he can then deploy them skillfully for his own purposes, in the "ultimate strategem" of the ambitious man.[59]

When he turns to justice and other virtues relevant to politics, Esprit expresses astonishment that society was ever founded by beings so wholly lacking in cooperative qualities. His political ideas are rigorously authoritarian and not at all imaginative. But when he discusses pity, he suggests a fruitful theme. Like Domat, Esprit believes that pity is an extension of *amour-propre* arranged by a merciful God so that fallen man will not destroy himself utterly. We are naturally most interested in those who are nearest ourselves, connected to us in daily life, such as our friends and family. This is simple *amour-propre*, since these persons are essential to our own welfare and are conceived as extensions of ourselves. Pity allows us to extend this feeling beyond familiarity. We see suffering beings like ourselves, and imagine the evil happening to us; we are moved to seek remedies for the suffering of others because we want to have remedies available for ourselves.[60]

Esprit's attempt to unmask *amour-propre* and insist on the radically different quality of charity was only one way to approach these issues. In the 1680s, as in the 1630s, there was another path available: the contention that self-love can lead us either to virtue or to vice. This was the path taken by Nicolas Malebranche, a highly esteemed philosopher of the late seventeenth century. Malebranche was not a Jansenist, but a member of another religious community, the Oratory; Descartes and Leibniz were major influences on his thought.[61] Malebranche taught the supremacy of reason in the world, the Thomistic accord between nature and grace. But his moral philosophy was constructed around the analysis of different types of love; and in discuss-

---

[58] *La Fausseté*, ch. 17, 415; see also ch. 4, on friendship, in which Esprit takes Montaigne to task for his visionary and foolish ideas on this subject, pp. 147-153.

[59] *La Fausseté*, ch. 2, "Le Désintéressement," pp. 452-457.

[60] *La Fausseté*, ch. 15, "La Pitié," pp. 366-385.

[61] On Malebranche and Jansenism, see G. Rodis-Lewis, *Nicolas Malebranche*, pp. 244-254; on his moral philosophy, ch. xi of that same study, and Craig Walton, *De la Recherche du Bien*, especially chs. 7-9. Ira Wade refers to the philosophy of Malebranche often in *Intellectual Origins*, and discusses him systematically on pp. 418-436.

ing the relationship between love of self and love of God and neighbor, he contributed several thoughtful arguments to this intricate discussion.

For Malebranche, the primary love is *l'amour de l'Ordre*, the principal and unique virtue that is the source of all other virtues. Malebranche identifies the love of order with charity and grace itself. Next, he distinguishes two different types of human love: *l'amour de bienveillance*, and *l'amour d'union*.[62] The former is the love we should bear for ourselves and others, including persons in authority, according to their degrees of excellence; it is a Cartesian sentiment based on the recognition of worth. "The love of union" is the appropriate love for God Himself. We should recognize Him as the source of sovereign happiness, and seek to unite ourselves with Him. Malebranche identifies the desire for happiness as the fundamental motive of all human action, and equates this desire with *amour-propre*. In his willingness to use this term to denote the neutral desire for happiness, Malebranche departed significantly from common usage. He insisted that *amour-propre* is neither virtuous nor vicious; it is "the natural motive to virtue, which becomes in sinners the motive of vice."[63] If we love God fully, we are motivated by *amour-propre*, just as in our most selfish actions. *Amour-propre* and *l'amour d'union* with God are perfectly compatible. It is the other human love, the love of esteem or worth, that is frequently corrupted by *amour-propre*, according to Malebranche. *Amour-propre* does not readily suffer limits; thus it is easily disordered. Disorder is a crucial term for Malebranche—it is the root of all evil and vice. When our love for ourselves is no longer moderate, regulated, kept in perspective, we lose the ability to make judgments about what things are worthy of our esteem and love. We love ourselves in a sprawling and unlimited fashion, and this is the enemy of virtue and happiness itself, since earthly happiness means living an ordered life that recognizes limits.[64]

Thus Malebranche rejected the simplistic idea that all human virtue is corrupt and deceitful, in favor of a more complicated and hopeful assessment. We always love ourselves; *amour-propre* is the desire for happiness. If we are touched by grace, this self-love is well ordered, and leads to a moderate and happy life on earth; if we understand happiness aright, we will also be moved by self-love to seek union with our Creator. If self-love is disordered and irregular, we fail to

[62] Malebranche, *Traité de morale*, edited by Michel Adam, in *Oeuvres complètes*, XI; these points are from part I, chs. 2 and 3, pp. 28-42.
[63] *Traité de morale*, part II, ch. 14, p. 270.
[64] *Traité de morale*, part I, ch. 3, sec. 12-13, pp. 44-45.

esteem others or ourselves properly, and lead vicious and unhappy lives. And in the matter of order and disorder, although grace plays an important part, our will and judgment are given room for deliberate choice. Malebranche summarizes it this way:

> To seek happiness is not virtue, but necessity; for it does not depend on us to wish to be happy, whereas virtue is free. *Amour-propre*, to speak precisely, is not a quality that one can augment or diminish. One cannot cease to love oneself: but one can cease to love oneself wrongly. One cannot arrest the movement of *amour-propre*; but one can regulate it according to divine law. One can, by the movement of an *enlightened amour-propre*, an *amour-propre* sustained by faith and hope, and *animated by charity*, sacrifice present pleasures to future ones. . . . For grace does not destroy nature, which is the movement God implants in us ceaselessly for the general good. . . . Sinners and just men alike want to be happy and run toward the source of their felicity; but just men do not let themselves be deceived or corrupted by appearances.[65]

Malebranche's defense of well-ordered *amour-propre* as the source of human happiness was similar to the argument made by a Swiss Protestant named Jacques Abbadie in an influential treatise on *L'Art de se connoitre soi-même*. Abbadie lived in France until the Revocation of the Edict of Nantes in 1685; he spent the last years of his life in exile in Holland, Ireland, and Germany, working on his book, which was published in 1692. Like Malebranche, Abbadie asserts that all human action is motivated by the search for happiness, a self-love that can lead us either into virtue or (if disordered) into vice. But Abbadie's terms are different from those of Malebranche. They recall the disputes about different types of self-love among theologians in the 1630s, particularly the language of Jean-Pierre Camus. Like Camus, Abbadie separates out a "bad" from a "good" form of self-love. The former is corrupt, disorderly, *amour-propre*, the latter is *l'amour de nous-mesmes*, which is the natural and legitimate motive of all human behavior, including virtuous acts and the desire for salvation. Instead of unmasking the clever practices of disguised *amour-propre*, Abbadie attempted to advance our knowledge of our own complex motivations to teach us how to love ourselves aright.

"Interest is all-powerful over our souls," observes Abbadie with equanimity. "One searches for oneself in the object of all one's attachments; and just as there are diverse sorts of interests, so we can distin-

[65] *Traité de morale*, part II, ch. 14, pp. 269-270; emphasis added.

guish the several kinds of affection that interest engenders among men." Love affairs, political connections, business partnerships, social alliances, are all so many different forms of interested love. But this does not mean they are infected or sinful at the root. They draw us out of ourselves and make it possible for us to enter into socially useful relationships. We move from the recognition of "particular conveniences" to ourselves, services performed for us by others in which we find a direct self-interest, to an appreciation of "general conveniences" from which we derive a more diffuse benefit. Awareness of the general convenience in human relationships allows us to value things like generosity or justice in the abstract, even when we do not immediately profit from them.[66]

According to Abbadie, although we love ourselves first of all, this can lead us to love those around us. Proximity brings others to our attention and makes them familiar. We recognize them as relevant to ourselves, and love them by an extension of *l'amour de nous-mesmes*. The love of God proceeds in the same way. We love Him first as the source of our felicity, and then come to will union with him as the sovereign good in the universe. For Abbadie, human self-love and love of God are not radically disparate phenomena, but two ends of a spectrum. What begins as affection for myself proceeds, if my self-love is not disordered, through regular stages to love of family, friends, compatriots, and to the love of God Himself. To love God out of *l'amour d'intérêt*, condemned by some moralists as impure, is the beginning of an experience that conducts us eventually to love Him out of *l'amour de pure amitié*, for His own sake. Although there is nothing as striking as Pascal's wager in Abbadie's theology, the idea of an original decision made out of self-interest that can be used by grace and perfected by habit to become the basis for a more lofty love is present here, as well. And Abbadie, as well as Pascal, proved an important source for later moralists. This characteristically subtle passage from his *Art of Self-Knowledge* could easily be taken from Rousseau:

> In general, vice is a preference for the self over others, and virtue seems to be a preference for others over oneself. I say "seems to be," because in fact virtue is only one way of loving the self, much more noble and sensible than all the others.[67]

[66] *l'Art de se connoitre soy-même*, 1749 edition, part II, chs. 5-8, pp. 204-237.
[67] *L'Art de se connoitre soy-même*, part II, ch. 5, p. 204.

CHAPTER ELEVEN

The Growth of Opposition to Absolute Monarchy in France

1. The Revocation of the Edict of Nantes

> Une seule chose te manque, ô grand Estat: la connoissance de toy-mesme, et l'usage de ta force![1]

When Montchrétien wrote this in 1615, France was embarking on the course that gave her political and cultural dominance in Europe within three-quarters of a century. The achievements of Sully, Richelieu, and Colbert, of Henry IV, Louis XIII, and Louis XIV came to fruition in the early decades of Louis XIV's reign. Yet in those decades, as in the time of Montchrétien, one thing was absent: the self-knowledge that would give the state the use of its own strength. In private moralities, the theme of self-knowledge was pursued to virtual exhaustion; but in public moralities, the presentation of a splendid image, the polishing of prudence, the expansion of frontiers and concentration of power in the throne were primary concerns. Knowledge about the state itself—the actual condition of the people, the complex effects of fiscal and religious policies, the potentials and limitations of the human material—was lacking, to France's great misfortune, and with enormous costs in human suffering.

Most observers agree that the high point of the Sun King's reign was reached around 1678, after the Treaty of Nymegen settled the issues of Louis's first wars and brought temporary peace. The king turned his energies to ordering his state. Among his goals was that of reducing diversities in local government, language, law, commerce, and religion, so that the *patrie* would be united by the monarchy in fact as well as theory. The most glaring diversity was the limited set of rights and liberties granted the Huguenots by the Edict of Nantes. As Elisabeth Labrousse reminds us, religious unity was regarded in this era as essential to national cohesion, and "in the ideology of absolutism, the Edict of Nantes signified for France a humiliating weakness."[2] Persecution of the Protestants was intensified around 1680. Academies

---

[1] Antoine de Montchrétien, *Traicté de l'oeconomie politique*, p. 34.
[2] From the introduction to Labrousse' edition of Bayle's *Ce que c'est que la France toute catholique*, p. 9.

were closed, churches burned, rights withdrawn. Soldiers were quartered in Protestant homes with instructions to use whatever rough measures might aid the process of conversion. In 1685, the Edict of Fontainebleau was issued, revoking that of Nantes.[3] Obdurate Huguenots were given the choice of conversion or loss of virtually all liberties and privileges. Pastors could choose exile, but any other Huguenots who fled faced the galleys if they were caught. Nonetheless, more than two hundred thousand did flee—industrious members of the middle classes, prominent in manufacturing and business, which were the only careers open to them. These men enriched Protestant capitals with their skills and with whatever wealth they brought. They created colonies of articulate and impassioned refugees all over Europe and America.

Reaction to the Revocation was almost uniformly hostile outside France. Even the pope, whose support Louis hoped to win, was only half-hearted in his enthusiasm. Within France, adulatory subjects praised their king as conquerer of heresy and defender of the faith. Royal publicists outdid themselves in celebrating the glories of a serene, united France *toute catholique*. Within three years, however, the tenuous peace was over, and Louis had managed to unite almost the whole of Europe against France by his military adventures and his treatment of the Huguenots. From 1689 until the king died in 1715, the glories of the reign were steadily diminished.

Thus the 1680s, like the decade of the Fronde, were a watershed in French history, but a watershed of quite a different sort. Perhaps it would be more accurate to say it was the same watershed, crossed in the opposite direction. The chaos of the Fronde convinced Frenchmen of the desirability of stable repose under absolute monarchy. Between 1661 and 1685, even loyal expressions of reformist sentiment within a rigidly orthodox absolutist framework, such as Silhon's *Certitude* or Jean de Lartigue's *Politique des conquerans*, were almost unknown in France.[4] The Revocation, intended to root out the last remnants of dissent, had the opposite effect. The Protestants were dispersed, but dissent began to grow—hesitantly, loyally at first—but dissent and opposition nonetheless. Currents of dissatisfaction flowed back into

---

[3] Pierre Goubert, *Louis XIV and Twenty Million Frenchmen*, pp. 155-162, has an excellent discussion of the factors that influenced Louis's decision and its consequences.

[4] Silhon's *Certitude* is discussed in ch. 10; Rothkrug, *Opposition to Louis XIV*, ch. 2, devotes many pages to Lartigue's treatise, describing it on p. 116 as "a link between future aristocratic opposition and the complex currents of thought going back to the sixteenth century." Lartigue's *Politique*, like Silhon's last treatise, was published in 1661.

France from Protestant presses in England, Holland, and Germany. Frenchmen became more and more distressed by the devastating consequences of Louis's wars, the grave faults in the fiscal system, and the elephantiasis of the official classes. After Colbert's death in 1683, the financial and administrative geniuses who had worked wonders in the early years were gone. Their successors could not cope with the burdens created by the interminable wars, cold winters, and disastrous harvests. The myth of the king as God, the universal agreement on the superiority of absolute monarchy, began to dissipate. Social conscience and the spirit of reform were reawakened as Frenchmen in high places mulled over policies for bridling the king and assuaging the misery of the people.

Opposition to the regime took several forms after 1685. The Huguenots in exile were the most outspoken in their attacks on the Most Christian King. Even among the Huguenots, there were different patterns of criticism. Within six months after Fontainebleau, Pierre Bayle, whose brother, a Protestant pastor, died in prison in Bordeaux, published a vehement account of *Ce que c'est que la France toute catholique sous le règne de Louis le Grand*. Addressed to a canon of Notre Dame, the tract begins: "Permit me, Sir, to interrupt for a quarter of an hour your cries of joy and the universal felicitations over the total ruin of heresy." Bayle thunders against dragonnades and tortures undertaken in the name of civility and charity, justified by intricate theology. Equally powerful are the contemptuous passages describing the stupidities of the policy. "You are so inept at *la politique*," says Bayle of the French government, "that you have given out edicts that have raised all Europe against you and exposed yourself to the most odious comparisons, without having drawn from these acts the slightest profit."[5] Bayle himself was quite willing to accept the exigencies of reason of state. In one of the articles in his famous *Dictionary*, he discussed the divergence between the duties of individuals and of sovereigns, noting that "it suffices to say that in the condition in which societies find themselves, the public interest is like a sun with regard to a considerable number of the virtues. These virtues are like stars that disappear, evaporate in the presence of that interest."[6] In his attack on the Revocation, Bayle says it is generally accepted that *la politique humaine* permits dissimulation and deceit so a king can deal effectively

---

[5] Bayle, *La France toute catholique*, p. 47.
[6] From the article on *Elisabeth*, in the *Dictionnaire historique et critique*, quoted by E. Labrousse, *Pierre Bayle*, II, 497; Labrousse devotes two chapters (16 and 17) to a full account of Bayle's politics, drawn from throughout his many writings; it is by far the best available.

with powerful enemies who threaten his state. But to engage in sophisticated and sterile treachery against innocent obedient subjects who have neither the will nor the power to harm the state is simple folly. "O Molière, where are you?"[7] But Molière had died a dozen years too early to do justice to this scene.

Bayle's politics were those of the *libertins* whom he admired, La Mothe le Vayer and Naudé. In his *Dictionary*, the article on Hobbes praised the absolutist politics of the English philosopher, criticizing him only because his admirably organized system would never work in practice, given the restlessness and error of mortal men. Practicability was, in fact, Bayle's major concern when he treated political and ethical questions. In Montaigne's own words, Bayle rejected all utopian systems from Plato to Campanella as "beautiful ideas that will show themselves insufficient and defective as soon as you try to put them into practice."[8] He adds that "the passions of men, which give birth to one another in prodigious variety, would soon ruin the hopes one had for such beautiful systems." Bayle himself set great store by custom and the established order, and described men motivated by avarice and ambition, in the old familiar way.[9] His major contribution was to attempt to show that religious tolerance, instead of persecution in the interests of uniformity, was the course recommended by enlightened *raison d'état*. His condemnation of Louis XIV was not an attack on absolutism, but an account of Louis's failure to do his job as an absolutist monarch. This would-be leviathan sovereign allowed himself to be led by the nose by scheming and fanatical courtiers into a policy of consummate folly. It was Louis's weakness, not his strength, that Bayle condemned.

Other Huguenots had different ideas about Louis and the Revocation. Pastor Jurieu, who was among the most eloquent, regarded Bayle as a libertine and a Socinian.[10] His own politics were of quite another sort. Jurieu was a bitter enemy of absolutism. His pastoral letters, intended for the faithful Huguenots languishing in Babylonian captiv-

[7] *La France toute catholique*, p. 52.

[8] *Hobbes*, from the *Dictionnaire*, quoted by Labrousse, *Pierre Bayle*, II, 474; cf. Montaigne's *Essay* III, 9, "Of vanity," p. 730 in the Frame translation.

[9] Alain Niderst's edition of Bayle's *Oeuvres diverses* contains several selections that illustrate this, particularly from the *Continuation des pensées diverses sur le comète* (1704), pp. 134-137. Wade, *Intellectual Origins*, has a fine section on Bayle's philosophy that treats his skepticism and his debt to the *libertins*, pp. 542-624.

[10] Paul Hazard, *The European Mind*, ch. 5; Guy H. Dodge, *The Political Theory of the Huguenots of the Dispersion*, provides a good account of the ideas of the exiles, with special attention to Jurieu. See also W. J. Stankiewicz, *Politics and Religion in Seventeenth-Century France*, ch. 6.

ity in France, are full of the language of natural law and popular sovereignty drawn from Grotius and Locke. His exhortations found few immediate echoes in French theory, although they worried Bossuet enough to prompt a series of warnings against Jurieu's sermonizing letters. Perhaps Bossuet accepted the common attribution to Jurieu of a set of *mémoires* that circulated widely in France after 1689, and proved much more effective than Jurieu's *Lettres pastorales* in stimulating opposition to Louis XIV. If Jurieu was in fact the author, he adopted quite a different approach from the one he took in his signed letters, and helped revive historical dispute and the appeal to Gallic antiquity in France.

It was the Huguenot jurist François Hotman, in his polemic against the Valois kings, who had provided the example for those who wanted to search the distant past for the "true" constitution of France. Hotman first showed how, in the absence of reliable documents and amidst singularly fluid institutions, each man could be his own constitutional lawyer. He argued for popular sovereignty, which few later jurists did; but he also raised the issues that preoccupied numberless polemicists between 1685 and 1750—the relative position of the Franks, the Romans, and the Gauls in early French history; the manner of selection of the first kings of France, and the role of various noble assemblies in government. It is hard to tell how many Frenchmen actually read Hotman. He was not the sort of authority whom orthodox jurists or publicists would be disposed to cite by name. But his style of argument was revived in the anonymous *mémoires* called the *Soupirs de la France esclave, qui aspire après la liberté*.

The *Soupirs* was distinctive among the flood of pamphlets that followed the Revocation in that it did not depend on Calvinist and natural-law arguments that had still, for the most part, a foreign ring in French ears. Instead, the author revived the vision of the ancient constitution of the polity. Like Hotman, he asserted that the French monarchy was originally elected and limited, and that "nothing of any importance was done in the kingdom without the advice and consent of the Estates, so that the government of France was really more aristocratic than monarchic, or at least was a monarchy tempered by aristocracy, exactly like that of England."[11] Although the parlements had taken over some of those functions in more recent centuries, and then ceased

---

[11] *Soupirs de la France esclave, qui aspire après la liberté* (1690), vııe *mémoire*, pp. 95-96. The recurrent attribution to Jurieu is not entirely convincing, but there are no better candidates for authorship of these *mémoires*. Both Stankiewicz and Dodge accept the attribution, with some reservations, in their studies of this era.

to exercise them, the general assembly representing all the people was still rightfully sovereign in France by ancient prescription, and should be reinstituted in its powers, argued the *Soupirs*. Frenchmen accepted absolutism because they were deafened by the great noise made by the king's apologists (a nice variation on Priézac's theme of the stunning effects of absolutism on mortal senses). A mad jurisprudence and a madder theology had been pressed into service to instill the notion that the king is God and master of us all. Venal and corrupt lackeys filled all the offices, and the people lacked energy or courage to resist.

There had been few references to royal tyranny in French politics for many years, except to round out standard classifications of regimes. The *Soupirs* departed from such academic pigeonholing to equate French absolutism with the most cruel tyranny. The French and the Turks were lumped together as enslaved peoples, and their lot contrasted with the happy liberty of citizens of Holland, England, and the free cities of Germany, all secure under the blessings of *le gouvernement modéré*.[12] The author makes the old pseudo-semantic linkage between *Franks* and *free* to assert that the French have a basic right to liberty not destroyed by a century or two of royal usurpation. There can be no clearer evidence of the stronghold the concept of interest had come to occupy in French political discourse than the recurrent references to interest in this polemic. "It is in the interest of peoples to hold their kings to a mediocre power," asserts the *Soupirs*, "so that they cannot oppress their liberty."[13] The failure of the Fronde is laid to "the ambition of the nobles and to particular interests," and the call to action appeals to the interests of each group within the state. The interests of the dauphin, the church, the parlement, the cities, and the oppressed people are all laid before the reader in detail, and counterposed to the interests of this king, who has put his own good in the place of that of the state, and made himself everything and his people nothing.

The *Soupirs*, for all its rhetoric about popular sovereignty, is an aristocratic and conservative tract. One of the charges against Louis is that he has oppressed all Frenchmen equally, without distinction of quality or merit or birth. He has removed the privileges of the municipal corporations, and reduced the judges to begging at Versailles, rubbing shoulders with all the bastard new nobles who flock to court. "The royal authority has mounted so high that all distinctions disappear, all lights are absorbed in it. For in the elevation to which the

[12] *Soupirs*, ie *mémoire* (August 1689), pp. 3-5; ive *mémoire*, pp. 49-63; and ve *mémoire*, 63-76.
[13] *Soupirs*, iie *mémoire*, pp. 17-27.

monarch has raised himself, all men are but powder beneath his feet." The effectiveness of the *Soupirs* no doubt depended on its use of images such as this. The rhetoric of absolutism is turned against itself in the appeal to the wealthy and the aristocratic to resist the tendency of leveling within the state that lifts up the monarch by the means of abasing all other interests and powers. This is the language of Joly and of the later proponents of the *thèse nobiliaire*, not that of a natural-law democrat; and it was the language most Frenchmen were best prepared to understand.

2. DENIS VEIRAS AND THE POLITICS OF UTOPIA

The appeal of the *Soupirs* and later works in this same vein is that of a myth—a mythical version of French history designed to legitimate atrophied institutions. It proved very powerful in France between 1685 and 1750 because it assured groups best placed to work for alternatives to absolutism that they had the sanctions of the past behind them. They were not revolutionaries or usurpers, but men claiming their rightful ancient part in government. The actual origins of the regime were sufficiently confused that the elements of imagination and special pleading in the myth could conveniently be overlooked. During these same years, another sort of myth was also popular in France, one that on the face of it looks quite different from the myth of the French past. Nonetheless, the two share some interesting elements.

Seventeenth-century Frenchmen were fascinated by other cultures and exotic peoples. Traveler's tales were avidly read, and increasing knowledge of different customs and beliefs stimulated curiosity about parts yet unexplored. Men were becoming dissatisfied with social and political institutions, but discouraged by censorship from open opposition. The times were ripe for utopias. In the last decades of the century several books appeared that constitute a utopian genre called "the extraordinary voyage."[14] These novels are patterned after Cyrano de Bergerac's, although the remarkable events take place on earth. A shipwreck adventure story provides the narrative framework. Each one describes an admirable society in uncharted lands. Like most utopias, these tales describe odd forms of dress and behavior; but their authors often endowed them with verisimilitude by locating them in *la terre*

---

[14] This term was coined by Gustave Lanson and made popular by Geoffroy Atkinson; see especially his *Extraordinary Voyage in French Literature before 1700*. Other useful sources on the voyages include Daniel Mornet, *Les Origines intellectuelles de la révolution française*, pp. 19-45, and André Lichtenberger, *Le Socialisme au XVIIIe siècle*, pp. 33-60.

Australe, the huge legendary continent generally believed to await discovery in the southern seas. Many readers accepted these stories (at least the ones that lacked obvious supernatural elements such as transportation by giant birds) as genuine accounts of voyages. The regimes described were no more exotic and unexpected than the regimes of Brazil or the Iroquois. The institutions described have several things in common with the regimes idolized by noble reformers in the myth of the French past. Both myths, like most myths, derived their appeal from a peculiar mixture of fact and imagination.

Most authors of the extraordinary voyages, like the author of the *Soupirs*, were Huguenots in exile, in touch with diverse currents of ideas in Holland, England, and Germany, who stimulated the thinking of Frenchmen at home. The bizarre details and heavy doses of adventure in these tales do not obscure the intent to criticize the beliefs and institutions of France by pointing up contrasts. One of the earliest and best of them, Denis Veiras's *Histoire des Sévarambes* (published in 1675), can still be read with pleasure as a utopia. Veiras was a Protestant soldier and teacher who lived for several years in England, where he was a friend of Locke and served in Buckingham's entourage.[15] He returned to France a few years before the Revocation, and had an eclectic circle including Englishmen, Jansenists, and Huguenots. In 1685 he left for Holland. Veiras was more interested in politics than other authors of the voyages, who were often imitative and brief in discussing institutions. His Sevarambian polity is an intriguing mixture of socialism, formal absolutism, and constitutionalism.

Sevarias, a legislator of semidivine status who founded the Sevarambian state, decided on the laws and customs of his *code soleil* only after extensive reading and reflection. The institutions were designed to be consonant with Nature and Reason, as well as the tradition and character of the people. Veiras relates how Sevarias considered and discarded the notion of having seven different classes, from magistrate to laborer, distinguished by their clothes. The major sources of civil conflict, in his eyes, were pride and avarice, both nurtured by such inequalities. Each citizen worked an eight-hour day at whatever *métier* he had chosen, and took from a common stock anything he needed for work or leisure. Children were raised in age-groups in separate houses, but often had supper with their families. The authority of parents was given up when the children reached the age of seven, and

---

[15] George Ascoli gives some information about the life of Veiras (or Vairasse) in "Quelques notes biographiques sur Denis Veiras, d'Alais," as does Thomas E. Lavender in his Harvard University dissertation, "The Histoire des Sévarambes of Denis Veiras."

only love and natural respect remained. Each seven-year period in life was marked by a ritual of transition; each age cohort wore a distinct type of clothing; gold and silver cloth were reserved to those men whose merit had caused them to be raised by their compatriots to high office in the state. Young persons were encouraged to travel incognito to other parts of the world to bring back useful information, but had to leave behind at least three children as assurances of their return. Thus, the society was basically egalitarian, in that only distinctions based on age or office were allowed; but these were very marked, to reward excellence, satisfy ambition, and engender respect. All lands and goods were held in common; all citizens lived in communal houses, and private wealth was prohibited.[16]

The Sevarambian polity was absolutist in its form. The Sun was the symbolic absolute monarch; the viceroy who ruled in his name held supreme authority and was regarded as "the only master and proprietor of all the goods of the nation." Thus it was formally "monarchical, despotic, and heliocratic in its top leadership," and the viceroy was honored as the "living image of divinity."[17] This was all designed to maximize obedience and enhance the solemnity of the divine laws at the basis of the civil law. The Sun was a particularly useful symbol here. For ordinary, literal-minded Sevarambians it was a tangible and powerful element in their lives; for more sophisticated citizens it stood for the Light of Reason, the divine sustaining order of the universe. This divine reason, not the power of the specific men who governed as the Sun's lieutenants, was absolute in this polity. The mortal governors were required to share power with a number of other men and institutions, and owed their power to election by all citizens.

Thus the absolutist form veiled a participatory and constitutionalist structure. Veiras adopts Bodin's distinction between the form of the regime and the way it actually works. Although outwardly a pure monarchy, the Sevarambian state, as far as "the administration on the part of men" is concerned, was "mixed with aristocracy and democracy." The aristocratic component was the grand council drawn from all the cities of the kingdom, which elected from within its membership four candidates, one of whom became, by the casting of lots to invoke the choice of the Sun, the new viceroy. Twenty-four members

---

[16] *Histoire des Sévarambes*, edited by Garnier, pp. 230-239 and 271-295. There is a full English translation, *The History of the Sevarambians* (London, 1738), as well as an English version of the first part of the book, the *History of the Sevarites* (London, 1675), written by Veiras himself. The second volume of the *History of the Sevarites* (1679) is spurious, and does not correspond to the second part of the French edition by Veiras.

[17] *Histoire des Sévarambes*, pp. 251-263.

of the council were chosen to be senators and hold portfolios of state business; the grand council also had to approve any new laws proposed by the viceroy. The admixture of democracy in the regime came from the process by which officials were chosen. Citizens at the lowest level, in their communal houses (called *osmasies*), elected leaders on the basis of merit. The best among them had the chance to rise by further election to higher posts, even to the viceroyalty of the sun. These leaders were not, however, accountable to those who chose them. They held office for life, and could be dismissed only by the viceroy himself for grave misuse of power. While they were in power, they had absolute sway in their domains; Veiras asserted that "there is no monarch more absolute than the governors of all the towns of this nation, where all the goods and public interests are confided to their guidance and their orders are punctually observed so long as they are congruent with established law."[18]

The last phrase, "with established law," is an important indication of how Veiras expected so many holders of "absolute" power to operate in harmony. The solar ideology provided a structure of shared beliefs and unquestioned axioms that presumably guided the magistrates in their choices and prevented conflict. The legal code handed down by the founder regulated their actions and set limits to their effective power. Unlike such pluralistic systems as that of Seyssel, there was no indication that these officers kept one another in check by mutual competition; harmony derived from the enlightenment provided by divine law and the rational structure of the institutions. This also explains why the Sevarambians gave unquestioning obedience to the viceroy; "no one doubts his authority and everyone submits to it . . . for who would be so bold as to revolt against the Sun and his ministers?" The viceroy enjoys the true respect of his subjects, "for they know that all he does is for the public good and that he does nothing without the advice of his council and the order of the Sun."[19] Like other attempts in French thought to combine unitary sovereignty with widespread participation, the Sevarambian regime has an air of unreality about it. Unlike most of them, it was explicitly designed as a utopia.

Sevarambia was an unusual utopia, however, in that it had a history; it developed and matured in time. Veiras recounts the measures used

[18] *Histoire des Sévarambes*, pp. 136-138, 263-267; the quoted passage is from p. 138. St.-Pierre's electoral process (*scrutin*) is similar to this.
[19] *Histoire des Sévarambes*, p. 354. Emanuel von der Muhll, *Denis Veiras*, p. 183, suggests that what Veiras proposed was not too far removed from Colbert's ideal; "this utopia is like a beautiful model offered by the viceroy of the Sun to the glorious *Roi-soleil*."

by Sevarias at the founding to ensure the acceptance of his *code soleil*. The laws were easy to understand because they were similar to the provisions of the primitive communism that prevailed before Sevarias's arrival. The intrinsic excellence of these laws, consonant with natural reason, appealed to the more thoughtful and virtuous citizens. Superstitious Sevarambians were impressed by the fortuitous appearance of a melodious messenger from the Sun, who gave his blessing to the new institutions. More critical Sevarambians regarded this event as an admirable device to give legitimacy to the new regime. The educational system was carefully designed to instill habits of obedience and virtue in the new generations. And the force of Sevarias's armies convinced any persons not persuaded on other grounds.

When the founder felt the effects of age, he retired, refusing to violate the provisions of his own code by clinging to power or attempting to pass it on to his descendants. He admonished his subjects to obey his elected successors, insisting that even if the sovereign appeared to behave unjustly they must submit, since civil war is the greatest of follies, resulting in worse slavery after the fires of rebellion are put out. Meek submission is not only their duty, "but also their most solid interest."[20] The chronicles of his successors indicate that the grand council occasionally operated as a restraint on viceroys who attempted to abuse their power, particularly in attempts at aggrandizement abroad. This restraint appears to have been sufficient, although a further provision was built into the constitution: any viceroy who behaved as a potential tyrant would be assumed to have taken leave of his senses. A tutor appointed by the grand council would work with him in an isolated palace until the divinity gave him back his reason, when he would be reinstated with rejoicing.

In devising the political system for his utopia, it is probable that Veiras was influenced by his life in England, by Cartesian rationalism, by French jurists, and by his reading in earlier utopias, such as Campanella's *City of the Sun*. Whatever his sources, he describes a state in which heliocratic absolutism ensured efficiency and order, and merit and performance rather than birth or status were rewarded with office. Although the polity provides a large scope for action by citizens as electors and officers in governing the state, and the grand council operates to restrain misguided monarchs, we should not conclude that Veiras is a Lockean in solar clothing. The citizens were carefully indoctrinated by the solar ideology, public life completely dominated privacy, and each official had absolute power over the citizens in his

---

[20] *Histoire des Sévarambes*, pp. 225-257; the quoted passage is from p. 251.

domain. This was not a system of checks and balances, but a rational authoritative order in which everything functioned according to plan. Veiras is the intellectual ancestor of that variety of absolutism we now call "enlightened despotism." He retains an optimism about the beneficence of absolute monarchy that reflects the date of the composition of his novel, at the height of Louis's power. But his insistence on the need for enlightenment, for bridling, and for the ensurance of equally capable and active officers at every level in the state, were not common themes in 1675. They found a receptive audience a few decades later, and Veiras's utopia continued to be read well into the eighteenth century.[21]

3. LA BRUYÈRE AND THE CHARACTERS OF HIS CONTEMPORARIES

Many Frenchmen who had experienced neither exile nor extensive travel abroad, and who regarded imaginary voyages as good reading but not a source for serious political ideas, found a basis for opposition to Louis XIV in the myth of the French past. For others, however, particularly for members of the middle classes, this myth held little attraction because it put so much stress on hierarchy and noble blood. Such readers found a more sympathetic spokesman in Jean de La Bruyère, whose book *Les Caractères* was among the most popular writings of the century. This polished product of the golden age of French literature has often been admired for the delicacy of its style and the deftness of its portraits of prominent persons masked by false names. It is also, less commonly, praised for its incisive social criticism. The book was brought out in eight editions between 1688 and 1694, and the growing pessimism, originality, and independence of the author reflect the rapidly changing climate during the last decades of Louis's reign. La Bruyère's work incorporated several strands of political and social theory current at the time in France. The ways he fit these strands together, or failed to do so, make him particularly pertinent reading for anyone interested in the development of social theory.

From writers such as La Rochefoucauld and Nicole, La Bruyère adopted Jansenist assumptions about the prominence of interest and

[21] A similar hierarchical regime, with even more stress on popular power, is described in Simon Tyssot de Patot's extraordinary voyage, *Jacques Massé*, much admired by the marquis d'Argenson. Unfortunately, Tyssot gives only a sketchy description of the utopian polity, which is summarized in Aubrey Rosenberg, *Tyssot de Patot and His Work*, pp. 108-110. An overall estimate of the politics of these voyages is given by Leslie Tihany, "Utopia in Modern Western Thought: the Metamorphosis of an Idea," in Richard Herr and Harold T. Parker, ed., *Ideas in History*, pp. 20-38.

passion in human affairs, and the mixed quality of what we know as "virtue." In a series of maxims that bring La Rochefoucauld immediately to mind, La Bruyère asserted that "nothing is easier for passion than to prevail over reason; its great triumph is in prevailing over interest"; that "of all the ways to make one's fortune, the shortest and the best is to bring others to see clearly their interests in benefiting you"; and that "passions tyrannize over man, but ambitions suspend all other passions in him and give him for a time the appearance of all virtues." La Bruyère also pointed out that all men regard themselves as in some way the potential heirs of others, and cultivate, by reason of that interest, a daily desire for the death of someone else.[22] This stress upon the radical divisiveness of our interests is much more striking a trait in *Les Caractères* than the occasional assertion that our interests can lead us to behave in socially useful ways. The most vivid passages are those that demonstrate how our self-centeredness alienates us from others and closes us inexorably in on ourselves.

La Bruyère marvels that individuals characterized by pride and stubborn *amour-propre* can form social ties with other similar beings. The notion of a single universal polity (such as Saint-Pierre proposed in his *Perpetual Peace*) strikes him as ridiculous in a world where "the contrariety of spirits, tastes, and sentiments" is so extreme that it is astonishing that "seven or eight persons can assemble under one roof and compose a single family." As La Bruyère sees it, "men are so careful to advance their own affairs, so prickly about their smallest interests, so bristling with difficulties, so anxious to get the better of others and suspicious of others attempting to get the better of them, they put such a high value on what belongs to them and so little on what belongs to others, that I swear I do not understand how they can make marriages, contracts, purchases, peace, truce, or alliances."[23] This pronounced individualism, however, leads La Bruyère to a perspective on politics that was unusual in his era, one that stresses the rightful

---

[22] *Les Caractères, ou, les moeurs de ce siècle*, edited by Garapon; "Du coeur," no. 77; "Des biens de fortune," nos. 45 and 50; and "De la cour," no. 22, on pp. 150, 193-194, and 227. Good discussions of La Bruyère are available in Krailsheimer, *Studies in Self-Interest*, ch. 11; Louis van Delft, *La Bruyère: Moraliste*, and Maurice Lange, *La Bruyère: critique des conditions et des institutions sociales*. Recent studies of La Bruyère, reported by Louise Horowitz in ch. 8 of *Love and Language*, question the traditional view of his work as serenely classical, and regard La Bruyère's universe as one in which ideals have disappeared, and we are shown "the steady degradation of *l'honnête homme*" into the *habile homme*, the avaricious bourgeois accumulator who replaced Méré's gentlemanly ideal.

[23] *Les Caractères*, "De l'homme," nos. 16 and 24, pp. 307-309. See also in this same vein, "Du coeur," no. 76; "De l'homme," nos. 1 and 126; and "Des jugements," no. 9.

demands of the ordinary subject as political consumer, as well as the power and duties of the king.

No *libertin* himself, La Bruyère expressed contempt for the *esprits forts* who make much of their doubts about God and the universe.[24] He had a deep admiration for natural order and a robust faith in Providence. It was precisely *because* he was so convinced of the irreducible nit-picking selfishness of each human individual that he expressed so much admiration for a well-ordered polity, which managed somehow to capture a bit of the harmony of the universe and bring it down to earth.[25] To make an integrated structure of such unpromising material is indeed a wonderful achievement. But La Bruyère insists that we understand properly what we should admire about it. It is not the splendor of the monarch's court or the triumphs of his armies that deserve our praise, but the prince's success in providing a secure and happy life for every individual subject. La Bruyère points out that this is a far more difficult task than commanding a victorious army.

In *Les Caractères*, there are several passages that stress the awful responsibility of a monarch, the bewildering scope and detail of his *métier*. La Bruyère evokes the image of a numerous flock of sheep tranquilly munching good herbs in the sunlight, guarded by a hardworking and continuously attentive shepherd. His intent is not to point up the pastoral character of the shepherd or his superiority to his sheepish charges, but to show how much better off the subjects are. They can enjoy all kinds of comforts, while the prince is warding off wolves and searching for better pasturage. If the shepherd fails to perform satisfactorily, La Bruyère asserts that he should be brought sharply to task by suddenly unsheeplike subjects, and reminded of his job. Like Louis XIV himself, as well as many of his contemporaries, La Bruyère regards the relation between subjects and sovereign as "a commerce, or a reciprocity of duties," in which respect and obedience are exchanged for justice and protection.[26] Like Balzac, La Bruyère insists that the measure of performance in good government is the health and prosperity of ordinary subjects. What good is it for his people, asks La Bruyère straightforwardly, if a king extends his country's territories, is feared by his brother sovereigns, triumphs incessantly in battle, and assures thrones for all his family?

[24] The final section of La Bruyère's book is entitled "Des esprits forts"; see especially nos. 1, 9, 11-19, and 36-43.

[25] *Les Caractères*, section entitled "Du souverain, ou de la République," no. 32, p. 292, which echoes Nicole's phrase about political order as the "masterpiece of the human spirit."

[26] "Du souverain," nos. 28-29, p. 291.

What use is it to me, in a word, or to any other of the people, if the prince is happy and covered with glory for himself and his family, my country powerful and formidable, if, sad and anxious, I live there in oppression or in indigence; if, protected from the enemy, I am nonetheless exposed in the streets of the city to the assassin's dagger . . . ; if security, order, and property do not make life in towns delightful, and have not brought, along with abundance, sweetness in society; if, feeble and alone, I must suffer on my farm the proximity of a powerful neighbor without hope of justice in our dealings with each other; if the facility of commerce does not make it possible for me to be dressed in good stuffs, nourished with healthy foods; if finally, by the efforts of the prince, I am not just as content with my lot as he has reason to be by the attractions of his own?[27]

This attention to what each individual in the kingdom has a right to expect from his government, and the denial that the glory of the king or the power of his country serve his needs at all, is La Bruyère's most striking political argument. Other Frenchmen were attacking the king for being overly absorbed with *gloire* and too little concerned with the misery of his people. La Bruyère couched his criticism in stubbornly utilitarian and individualist language. Here is no vague exhortation to the king to pity his people, but a specific assertion about the proper benefits of government, and an individual's just claim to be ruled by someone who makes his life commodious.

Unlike Nicole, La Bruyère does not assume that people will cooperate spontaneously to provide goods and services out of self-interest as soon as the government establishes the conditions in which such business can be safely carried on. Merely having a government in place is not enough. The king is also in some measure *responsible* for the details of the commodious life within his kingdom, and for ensuring that his people are getting on as well as possible. In this La Bruyère stood apart from the growing laissez-faire tendency in French political discourse. But he shared with proponents of laissez-faire policies a focus on the individual pursuit of happiness as the basic stuff of politics, and a rejection of the sufficiency of royal splendor and the pursuit of *gloire*. Like Bossuet, he reminded the monarch that "the public is nothing but all the individuals" considered as a group.[28]

La Bruyère contributed some thoughtful passages to the analysis of

[27] "Du souverain," no. 24, pp. 288-289. Rousseau echoes this sentiment in a note to his abstract of Saint-Pierre's *Polysynodie*, in his *Oeuvres complètes*, III, 618.
[28] "Du souverain," no. 7, p. 277.

tyranny. He pointed out, for example, that "neither art nor science is needed to exercise tyranny; the policy that consists in spilling blood is very limited, and lacks any refinement." So much for any notion that tyranny is a more sophisticated variant of *raison d'état*. La Bruyère notices that regimes often resort to soporific fetes and the distribution of trinkets to keep subjects docile, and warns that this road leads easily to tyranny. He points out that "there is no such thing as the sense of *patrie* in a despotism; other things perform the same function, such as interest, glory, service to the prince."[29] But his finest contribution to the understanding of tyranny is the most famous passage in *Les Caractères*, which is a dark variation on the theme of tranquil flocks pasturing in the light of the warm sun. Here is La Bruyère's own description of an "extraordinary voyage" through the realm of France itself:

> One comes upon certain wild animals, male and female, spread out over the countryside, black and yet ashen, all burnt from the sun, attached to the ground where they rummage incessantly, and turn over the soil with invincible obstinacy; they have something like an articulate cry, and when they rise to their feet they show a human face, and in fact they are men. At night they retreat into their lairs where they live on black crusts, water, and roots; they spare other men the effort of sowing, working, and digging the earth in order to live; and thus they deserve not to lack the bread that they have sown.[30]

4. Vauban and the Self-knowledge of the "Grand Estat"

La Bruyère was no disgruntled Huguenot or disapproving Jansenist. He was an orthodox Catholic and loyal subject of his king, who lived at court. It is significant that such a man should become discontented with his government. An even more striking instance was the marshal Vauban. No one could have been more loyal or patriotic than this military engineer who fortified all France, and was ennobled for his signal services to the crown.[31] He was a bluff, straightforward man who had no taste for political discussion or theorizing. But when he became convinced of the parlous consequences of Louis's policies by his travels through the kingdom, he could not keep silent. Vauban had

---

[29] "Du souverain," nos. 2-4, pp. 275-276.
[30] *Les Caractères*, "De l'homme," no. 128, p. 339.
[31] On Vauban's life and career, consult studies by Alfred Rebelliau and Daniel Halévy, both entitled simply: *Vauban*.

no doubts about the excellence of absolutism as a form of government, and he remained deeply loyal to his king. But he was worried about specific features of the regime, particularly the taxation system and the policy against the Huguenots. He decided that information was not reaching this king, that those around him were not telling him the truth. Vauban was not afraid to tell his king hard truths. He did not consider the possibility that Louis did not want to know these truths, because they fit so badly with his own conception of his performance as a king.

It was the Revocation of the Edict of Nantes that first moved Vauban to write. He addressed to the minister Louvois a "*Mémoire* for the recall of the Huguenots."[32] This little tract was one of the few pieces of overt dissent among highly placed subjects in the wake of the glorious move against the Protestants. It sets the tone for all Vauban's criticism of the regime: common-sensical, direct, backed up with statistics. Although Vauban noted that he did not believe the king was master of the beliefs and opinions of his subjects, he did not rest his argument on the appeal to tolerance. The intentions of the king were commended as saintly and just; it was the consequences that Vauban wanted to make clear. Trade and commerce were disrupted, the forcibly converted created problems for the church itself, and good minds and bitter pens had deserted the kingdom to aid its enemies.

This appeal was not welcomed at Versailles. But Vauban did not stop writing. His own observations convinced him of the distress and exhaustion of the people. The king obviously needed to be reminded of the old dictum that the power and glory of a king rest on the health and prosperity of his subjects. The equation of the interest of king and people was, for Vauban, no comfortable tautology, but a truth that required the radical redirection of royal energies. In a *mémoire* on the war written in 1693, he put all this quite bluntly, asserting that "the king and his ministers do not seem clearly to have seen that the greatness of kings is measured by the number of their subjects. The obvious proof of this truth is that where there are no subjects there is neither prince nor state, nor any domination at all." The marshal refers to the "great and most noble kingdom of France, . . . full of the best subjects in all the world," and says that "it is necessary to pay attention to them, recall those who have been driven from the kingdom and support those who remain, instead of vexing them and tormenting them, which is happening in many provinces."[33]

---

[32] This *mémoire* is included in Rochas d'Aiglun, ed., *Vauban*, 1, 465-482. E. Esmonin, *Etudes sur la France*, warns us of the deficiencies of this edition.

[33] In d'Aiglun, ed., *Vauban*, 1, 488-489. Perhaps Vauban's awareness of the

The theme of "paying attention" to ordinary subjects, attending to their needs and miseries, is insistent throughout Vauban's *mémoires* to the government. It is also apparent in his comprehensive treatise on the *Dixme royale*. This is a proposal for abolishing the ancient, ineffective, and inequitable taxation system and replacing it with a tithe paid by all subjects, nobles and officials as well as commoners. The tenth, or a capitation tax, had been employed before, as a supplement to pay for Louis's wars. Vauban proposed entire reliance on it, as well as dismantling the noble fiction that aristocrats bore their share of the burdens of the state by participation in armies instead of paying taxes. His proposal rests on the reciprocity of kings and subjects. In Vauban's version of this utilitarian theme, the people receive an essential service, the provision of security, and must pay the costs of providing it. Those who have more to protect should pay more for the service, instead of paying little or nothing at all.[34]

In his *Dixme royale*, Vauban combines such arguments with the ancient image of the body politic. If gangrene sets in at the furthest extremity of the body and nothing is done to cure it, the body and its head are surely doomed. If other parts of the body object when surplus benefits are taken from them and given to the needy, they should be ignored as contemptible; "for it is not just that the whole body suffer in order that some of its members can be better off than others."[35] Although Vauban was proud of his nobility, he transcended the narrow interests of his class throughout his writings. Ordinary Frenchmen, and especially the poorest among them, were his prime concern. Vauban returns to this theme over and over in the *Dixme royale*:

> I find myself obliged in honor and in conscience to tell your majesty that it has seemed to me for some time that there is insufficient regard for the little people in France, and that far too little attention has been paid to their needs. This is the most ruined and miserable part of the kingdom. Yet it is the most important in numerical terms, and in terms of real and effective services performed. . . . It is, moreover, the lowest part of the people who, by their work and commerce and taxes enrich the king and all his kingdom; they furnish all the soldiers, a great number of officers, all merchants, . . .

---

distressing condition of his *patrie* rested in part, as did that of the marquis d'Argenson, on his familiarity with conditions in states on the borders of France.

[34] Vauban's *Dixme royale* is included in Eugene Daire's edition of the major works of the *Economistes-financiers du XVIIIe siècle*; these themes are developed on pp. 47-50.

[35] *Dixme royale, ibid.*, pp. 133-147.

all laborers, and this portion of the people does all the great and small works in towns and countryside alike.[36]

Vauban knew his ideas would be opposed by members of his own class who surrounded the king, and he warned his monarch not to listen. This was not just a strategic insight on his part. It reflected his belief in the opposition of interests of the king and the people, on the one hand, and a handful of privileged and powerful men, on the other. He posited a natural alliance of the French king and the ordinary people against reactionary privilege, in the best interests of the whole state. This was the antithesis of the *thèse nobilaire* that some of his colleagues were propounding, and the germ of what later came to be called the *thèse royale*.

Vauban introduced his *Dixme royale* by reporting the results of his observations of the condition of the people as a matter of statistical information, without vituperation, in a quietly urgent tone:

> As a result of all the research I have been able to do, throughout the several years I have applied myself to it, I have remarked clearly that in recent times almost a tenth of the people are reduced to begging; of the other nine-tenths, five are in no condition to give alms since they are themselves reduced virtually to the same unhappy state; of the four remaining parts, three are very badly off, entangled in debts and law-suits; in the final tenth, the nobility of the sword, the robe, the ecclesiastics, the wealthiest of the bourgeoisie, there are not more than a hundred thousand families; and I think I am not mistaken in saying that not more than ten thousand of these could be described as really well-off.[37]

But Vauban was not satisfied with his own figures. He was aware of the need for more solid information, and the dangers of relying on estimates. He broached the idea of a regular census adapted from Chinese experience, long before anybody at court took such a notion

---

[36] *Ibid.*, p. 44.
[37] *Ibid.*, pp. 34-35. For a similar set of frank and dispiriting statistics, compiled by the intendants' commission appointed for the instruction of the duke of Burgundy, see "The Condition of the Realm at Mid-Reign (1687)," included in W. F. Church, *The Impact of Absolutism in France*, pp. 96 ff. The authors of this report, D'Aguesseau and D'Ormesson, give specific information on the condition of the people; they describe houses falling into ruin, and peasants living on roots of ferns boiled with barley flour. They attribute this misery directly to the inequitable and heavy taxation system, and advise fundamental changes. Such advice had little impact on Louis's government, but it helped coalesce sentiment among the supporters of the young duke of Burgundy himself.

seriously.[38] To obtain basic information about the situation of the people throughout France was, for Vauban, the obvious first step in the desperately needed "self-knowledge" of this great state.

In addition to tax reform, Vauban proposed the rationalization of tolls, weights, and measures throughout the kingdom to reduce the disparity between the provinces that hindered commerce and justice alike. He reaffirmed mercantilist principles in an age when laissez-faire arguments were beginning to be heard, resting his case on arguments familiar since Montchrétien, including the faith in the benefits to be expected from the absolute power of a reforming and energetic king. Vauban was convinced that there were no limits to the possibilities for action "when a great king has justice on his side, joined to the evident good of his people, and two hundred thousand armed men to support it."[39] But he failed to convince Louis to behave according to this model, and his ideas were ignored.

Vauban was too loyal to join the opposition groups that began springing up between 1690 and 1710. He may well have sympathized with the work of the most prominent of these groups, the duke of Burgundy's circle, although their marked aristocratic biases were uncongenial to his own approach. Still, when he despaired of convincing the king, he could not simply keep silent while his beloved France was ruined. He resolved to obtain a wider audience, and published a small number of copies of the *Dixme royale* in 1707, to circulate among friends. His refusal to allow public sales did not prevent him from incurring the wrath of Louis's censors and police. The book was condemned, although Vauban was not named personally. Those who had published it were hunted down and punished. Such were the rewards awaiting anyone who expressed reformist notions at the end of the Sun King's reign. But the extent of the evils and the misery of the people were too great to be ignored. More and more Frenchmen began to express opposition in ways that went well beyond Vauban's staunchly monarchist proposals.

[38] *Dixme royale*, pp. 124-146; and the *mémoire* "Sur le dénombrement des peuples," in d'Aiglun, ed., *Vauban*, I, 626.
[39] *Dixme royale*, p. 130. Several of the *mémoires* in d'Aiglun, ed., *Vauban*, I, touch on these questions, including the "Intérêt present des Estats de la Chrétienté," pp. 490-496; "Sur le choix d'un bon conseil," pp. 615-626; and "Mémoire sur le canal de Languedoc," pp. 551-576.

CHAPTER TWELVE

The Conduct of a Prince and a Program for Reform

1. THE DUKE OF BURGUNDY'S CIRCLE

One consolation to Louis XIV during his last years was that the succession of his family to the French throne appeared to be assured. In 1710, his son (the grand dauphin), two grandsons (the dukes of Burgundy and Berry), and two great-grandsons were all flourishing. Around the dauphin and the duke of Burgundy two coteries had formed, waiting for power. The characteristics of the two princes matched the attitudes of those who surrounded them. The dauphin's clique, like the dauphin himself, was stolid and narrow in its views. Bossuet, his tutor, had composed magisterial treatises and histories for the young man. They excited in the dauphin only the desire never to read another book, and he gave no sign of having thought about government. The duke of Burgundy had been the pupil of the archbishop Fénelon, who had done his work so well that an intractable child given to temper tantrums had become a thoughtful, painfully conscientious prince. Fénelon had made up romances for his pupil, dialogues, travel tales, delightful pieces in which sober morals are implanted. Burgundy, like Rousseau's Emile, had been the subject of prearranged scenes in which a workman on a scaffold said something wise and puzzling, and the prince turned to his tutor for an explanation.[1] From boyhood he was surrounded by men who were critical of his grandfather's regime, who brought him information from throughout the realm, and talked about reform. The result of all this effort was a young man primed to govern according to the pattern of paternal kingship instilled in him by Fénelon.

When the grand dauphin died in 1711, a new day appeared about to dawn in France. Louis XIV was an old man, and the young duke and his clever duchess, so full of hope and promise, were next in line for the throne. The Burgundy circle was transformed from a group of dreamers united by affection for the duke and hostility to Louis's policies into a set of planners on the threshold of power. One year

[1] Paul Janet, *Fénelon: His Life and Works*, translated by V. Leuliette, pp. 41-53; M. Druon, "L'Enseignement politique donné par Bossuet et Fénelon, precepteurs."

later the duke, the duchess, and their eldest son died of measles, complicated by the attentions of their doctors. All the hopes were suddenly snuffed out, all the tutoring and planning wasted. Fénelon wrote to a friend: "Men work by their education to form a subject full of courage and ornamented by knowledge; then God comes along to destroy this house of cards. . . . His work is to annihilate ours. . . . He reduces us to believing in faith that He is all and we are nothing."[2] But Fénelon's work was not quite annihilated. Generations of Frenchmen were affected by the educational and political ideals expressed in his masterpiece, *Télémaque*.

In addition to *Télémaque*, Fénelon wrote a great many *mémoires* and letters about the appropriate conduct of a king. Unlike Vauban, Fénelon did not address the king directly. He apparently expected better results from training a new king than attempting to reform an old one. But the old king was quite aware of what he thought. *Télémaque* was published in 1699 (without Fénelon's permission), and the archbishop's disappointment with his king is apparent throughout that tale. Moreover, a set of dialogues of the dead composed for Burgundy include several dialogues among past kings of France. Louis XII and Henry IV are Fénelon's models. Other kings are excoriated in harsh terms for their Machiavellian policies of conquest. When Louis XI defends his attempts to extend monarchical authority, impose heavy taxation, and display political finesse, his successor replies: "I have shown, by the success of my maxims, that yours are false and pernicious. I have made myself loved, lived in peace without breaking my word, or spilling blood, or ruining my people. Your memory is odious; my own respected."[3] Francis I defends the brilliance of his court and the splendor of his wars; he claims to have revived the Augustan age. Louis XII replies, "I would prefer that you had been known as the father of your people instead of the father of letters."[4] It is no wonder that Louis XIV felt uncomfortable under Burgundy's disapproving scrutiny; the young duke no doubt rehearsed similar dialogues with his grandfather in his own thoughts.

In a letter to a friend, Fénelon once commented that "a king has

---

[2] Quoted in the conclusion to Emmanuel de Broglie's *Fénelon à Cambrai*.
[3] *Dialogues des morts, composés pour l'education de Mgr. le duc de Bourgogne*, in *Oeuvres* (1835), II, 637 (dialogue LXI).
[4] *Dialogues des morts, Oeuvres*, II, 640 (dialogue LXIV). See also nos. LXVIII, "Henri III et Henri IV"; LXIII, "Richelieu et Oxenstierna"; and LXXIV, "Richelieu et Mazarin." Richelieu is reproved by Oxenstierna for his willingness to sacrifice lives and happiness to his grand scheme; he condemns Mazarin in turn for his complete lack of principle and protean changes of position, calling him "un grand comédien, mais non pas un grand homme."

no other honor and no other interest than that of the nation he governs. One judges him by the government of his kingdom as one judges a watchmaker by his watches, whether they run well or badly."[5] In the eyes of the archbishop, Louis had proven inept at his *métier* because the health of the state was sacrificed to his personal and dynastic *gloire*. Fénelon spells out the consequences, in a singular letter written anonymously in 1694, addressed to Louis himself, but probably never sent. He writes as a sorrowful, loving subject, without "any interest in the world" apart from the true interest of the king. Your Majesty, he says, your ministers have kept the truth from you; you live as though with a fatal bandage over your eyes, unable to see beyond the petty daily successes reported by your aides. The truth, according to Fénelon, is that

> your people whom you ought to love as your own children, and who have until now been so devoted to you, die of hunger. The cultivation of the earth is virtually abandoned. The cities and the countryside are depopulated. All occupations languish and no longer support the workers; all commerce is destroyed. . . . The whole of France has become a great hospital, desolate and without provisions. . . . The people who loved you dearly and had such confidence in you are losing their good will, their confidence, and even their respect. Your victories and conquests no longer bring them joy; they are full of bitterness and despair. Sedition begins to glow everywhere; the people are convinced that you have no pity for their misfortunes, that you care only for your own authority and glory.[6]

In a "Mémoire sur la situation déplorable de la France en 1710," Fénelon was even more pessimistic about the condition of the realm. He concluded that things were kept from utter ruin only by a set of miracles, and that the government was like "an ancient dilapidated machine that continues to run on the impetus given it long ago, and will surely break down at the slightest shock."[7]

Fénelon's major concern, in the writings for the education of the

---

[5] Letter to the marquis de Louville, October 1710, included in Charles Urbain's edition of Fénelon's *Écrits et lettres politiques*, p. 163.

[6] Letter to Louis XIV, in Urbain, *Écrits*, pp. 144-152. Rothkrug, *Opposition to Louis XIV*, ch. v, gives lengthy excerpts from a similar anonymous *Mémoire sur les finances* submitted to the king in 1688, which he regards as the opening sally by Fénelon's group in their opposition campaign. That Fénelon apparently never sent the letter written in 1694 may have reflected his acceptance, on this issue, of the judgment of Mme. de Maintenon, who said such truths would only irritate and anger the old king. (George Havens, *The Age of Ideas*, pp. 63-65).

[7] *Oeuvres*, III, 419-424.

boy he called *le petit Prince*, was to draw very clearly the contrast between royal practices that led to such results, and those that nourished and supported all subjects. The counsels that echo so insistently through his didactic writings, made palatable only by his stylistic grace, are the reverse of the charges laid at Louis's door. The good king must seek information and shun flatterers; he must avoid interested counsellors and remember the interests of all subjects; he must eschew the search for royal *gloire*, particularly military glory, and always think first of his people. In his catechism for a king, the *Examen de conscience sur les devoirs de la royauté*, Fénelon gives his pupil a check-list of these points so that he can remind himself of them as he prepares to govern. The most insistent theme is that of obtaining information: "Do you *know*, oh king?" asks Fénelon—the condition of the kingdom, the records of your predecessors, the laws and customs of your people, the numbers of men who compose your nation, their occupations and habits, what they do for a living, how they are housed and fed?[8]

In his best-known work, *Télémaque*, an odyssey of political education, the same lessons are taught in a particularly appealing form. Burgundy must have identified very closely with the son of Odysseus traveling around the world with his Mentor, who was Minerva in disguise. The young prince is confronted with numerous examples of good and bad monarchical regimes, interspersed with miraculous episodes and romantic adventures. The excellent governments of Sesostris in Egypt, Minos in Crete, and Baleazar in Tyre are contrasted with inferior regimes. On his obligatory trip to the land of the dead to look for his father, Telemachus discovers that the darkest portions of hell are peopled by bad kings who abused their power, or simply did not put themselves out to do good. The brightest section of Elysium is reserved for truly great kings, who enjoy rewards beyond the imagination of the most virtuous of ordinary men.[9]

In Telemachus' education, several of the themes of absolutist rhetoric are adapted to the vision of ideal kingship. Sesostris, wise king of Egypt, laments to the prince that it is unfortunate to be "raised above all other men," because this means the king is not close enough to his people to see the truth with his own eyes. He is dependent on those who surround his throne to tell him the truth; and yet Mentor notes that a king must remain in this lofty position so that he can try to

[8] The *Examen* is included in Urbain, *Ecrits*, and in *Oeuvres*, III, pp. 348-365.
[9] The visit to the land of the dead is recounted in book XIV of *Les Aventures de Télémaque*; I have used the 1875 edition, although the novel is also included in *Oeuvres*, III, 1-154.

"see things whole" as far as possible.[10] It is the overall condition of the kingdom that should be his main concern, not every petty detail of government. He must get to know men well, in order to choose competent subordinates who will be truthful with him and to delegate power effectively. To feel that only he can do things as they should be done, says Fénelon, is the surest road to failure for a king. So much for the Sun King's pride in knowing everything.

Fénelon's ideas about the conduct of a king are summed up in the image of the king as architect that recurs throughout his work. The architect cannot do the whole job himself; he needs carpenters and bricklayers, carriers and suppliers. But he must know how to judge their performance and choose excellent helpers; and it is he who must keep in mind the design for the whole building and direct all efforts to that end. If there is no controlling architect, even the most competent workers cannot build. Mentor advises Telemachus that "the supreme and perfect government consists in governing those who govern," and that "true genius in conducting a state is that which, doing nothing directly, ensures that everything is done [*fait tout faire*]; which thinks, invents, sees into the future, returns into the past, arranges, sets up proportions. . . ."[11] The image of the king as God is here connected with God as divine architect of the world, or supreme watchmaker, the overseeing craftsman responsible for the workings of the whole but rarely intervening directly.

The good king imitates not only divine authority, but also God's self-restraint. He regards himself as completely bound by divine law and the laws of his own country, even though no institution or subject can call him to account for his transgressions. When Telemachus inquires, "What does a king's authority consist in?" Mentor replies: "He is all-powerful over his people, but the laws are all-powerful over him. He has absolute power to do good and his hands tied at any point he might wish to do evil."[12] According to Fénelon, self-restraint is the most economical way to tie a monarch's hands from evil. This explains his care in educating Burgundy. He insists that the power for good exercised by a conscientious king is greater than that of the unbridled tyrant. This apparently paradoxical notion—that self-limited

---

[10] *Télémaque*, book II, includes Sesostris' lament; Mentor's comment is in book XVII.

[11] *Télémaque*, book XVII, pp. 357-359.

[12] *Télémaque*, book V, in a section on Minos in Crete, p. 69. This epigram expressed elegantly and concisely a prominent strain in French thought, and was much used in the eighteenth century. Havens, *Age of Ideas*, p. 62, notes that it was uttered by Orléans upon becoming regent, by Voltaire, and by Thomas Jefferson. It was among the favorite maxims of the marquis d'Argenson, as well.

Program for Reform—337

power wisely used is more powerful than unlimited power—was developed at some length by later theorists. A king who attempts to own and control everything in fact manages only to ruin everything. When even a small misfortune arises in the state, "such monstrous power" cannot endure. Obedience melts away, and the king's power instantly collapses.[13] Political power, on this account, is a complex resource that exists only when it is used in accord with the interests of the subjects. When it is used for ill, the bases of the power are eroded, and it dissolves.

At the end of his journey, Telemachus reviews with Mentor the lessons he has learned, and comments sadly that "the lot of a king is truly unfortunate. He is the slave of all those he seems to command," made only to serve their needs and look out for them. Like La Bruyère's assiduous shepherd, Fénelon's king must "sacrifice his repose and his freedom for the liberty and happiness of the public."[14] But Mentor reminds his pupil that there is a great reward inherent in "being able to do good for so many people." The king "corrects the evildoers by punishments, encourages the good by rewards, and represents the gods in thus conducting the whole human race to virtue." These are the themes Burgundy's grandfather had expressed for his own son in the early bright years of his reign. They are repeated for the edification of his grandson, in a spirit of renewed optimism about the possibilities for monarchy focused on the person of the prince, just as they had been so many years before.

It is hard to guess what sort of government Telemachus and his Mentor would have brought to France. Their projects would have met powerful resistance, and the pious young duke might have instituted religious oppression that would have diminished the effect of any reforms he managed to accomplish. Henri Martin asserts that Burgundy would have been "Saint Louis lost in the generation of Voltaire."[15] With his mystical utopian strain, Fénelon would have made quite a different prime minister from Richelieu or Mazarin. Louis XIV referred to him as "the most intelligent and at the same time the most chimerical spirit" in his kingdom.[16] But Fénelon's extraordinary ability

[13] *Télémaque*, book x, pp. 203-204.   [14] *Télémaque*, book xviii, pp. 384.
[15] Henri Martin, *Histoire de France*, xiv, 558; for a different assessment, see Sanford B. Kanter, "Archbishop Fénelon's Political Activity: The Focal Point of Power in Dynasticism."
[16] Havens, *Age of Ideas*, p. 62; Haven's third chapter is a fine study of Fénelon. Albert Cherel, *Fénelon au XVIIIe siècle en France*, and C.-A. Sainte-Beuve, *Causeries du lundi*, ii, 1-17, and x, 16-44, attest to his reputation in the eighteenth century. Fénelon was regarded as a kindred soul by several philosophes, and the Revolution enshrined him as an early radical and foe of tyrants in the Pantheon of its

as an administrator impressed all the visitors to his diocese. He had been exiled from Versailles to his archbishopric at Cambrai in 1697, when his position on quietism displeased Bossuet, Mme. de Maintenon, and the king. He kept his lines of communication open to Versailles, but devoted himself to rebuilding churches and improving the condition of his people. His palace was a hospital for injured soldiers from both armies in the wars on the Flemish frontiers, and a source of supplies for the whole countryside. The flexible combination of idealism and practicality in his writings gives evidence that he might have been a great prime minister. But Fénelon himself died within a few months of the old monarch, of an illness contracted in a cold carriage while he was making the rounds of his diocese. Whether he would have died at sixty-four if he had been in favor at Versailles, or what kind of prime minister he would have been if Burgundy had chosen him, is a house of cards too shaky to work with any further.

2. FÉNELON'S UTOPIAS AND THE ETHIC OF *Pur Amour*

Besides providing several models of good kingship in *Télémaque*, Fénelon also describes two exemplary regimes that have come to be seen as his two utopias: Bétique and Salente. In describing these utopias, as in much else, Fénelon shows his debt to Plato. Bétique is like the simple first state of the *Republic*, the golden-age pastoral society of simple communism. Salente after Mentor's reforms is analogous to the luxurious state purged by the philosopher-king. Bétique also recalls the simple society of Montaigne's cannibals. It provides a benchmark to show us how far we have removed ourselves from simple nature in developing complex societies.

The inhabitants of Bétique, blessed with a temperate climate and rich land, live comfortably in rude huts with simple clothing. They own nothing, share lands in common, and move about to take advantage of the earth's fruits. Each father in this patriarchal society educates and controls his children, and dispenses justice. All are free and equal and respect no distinctions (beyond those of age and sex) save that of superior wisdom. They abhor conquest, refuse to engage in trade and navigation lest they be corrupted, and are admired by neighboring societies, who call on them to arbitrate disputes. Silver and gold

---

saints, alongside Voltaire and Rousseau. Fénelon's nostalgic longing for the heyday of ancient aristocracy and his intolerance for Huguenots and Jansenists fit him oddly for such a role; these factors are remarked upon by Roland Mousnier (who has little use for Fénelon) in "Les Idées politiques de Fénelon," included in *La Plume, la faucille et le marteau*, pp. 77-92.

are used interchangeably with baser metals in this contemporary survival of the golden age. Fénelon describes these people as very happy, and emphasizes that one major reason is their satisfaction with goods that are easily obtainable. There is plenty for all because they have no need for luxuries; instead of competing for scarce goods, they can live as brothers. "They have no interests to support against each other, and all love one another with an untroubled fraternal affection."[17]

When he hears about Bétique from another traveler, Telemachus rejoices that there still exists in the world "a people who, following *la droite nature*, are so wise and happy together." Such men regard civilization as a "monstrous dream." But we cannot hope to recapture their innocence. The model for his own kingship is not Bétique, but Salente, which adapts some of the same principles to a complex modern society. Fénelon shows his budding architect how such a model could become a blueprint for a reforming king. Despite his insistence that the characters in *Télémaque* were not drawn from life, Idomeneus, king of Salente, is clearly Louis XIV as Fénelon wished he would become. For all his faults, he was not an evil king; Idomeneus was misled by bad advisors, ill-informed of the correct principles of government, and ignorant of the true condition of his kingdom. But he was open to correction, and Mentor was able to wean him away from his preoccupation with false *gloire*.

When we first come upon Salente we might easily think ourselves at Versailles. The capital of Idomeneus' kingdom grows in size and splendor almost before one's eyes. But other things about the kingdom are more ominous—the impoverished countryside surrounding the impressive city, and the incessant preparations for war. The kingdom is like a "monster with a head of enormous grossness, whose body was deprived of nourishment and shrunk out of all proportion with the head."[18] When Idomeneus asks Mentor for help, he is told that the first step is to get information about his kingdom: how many people does it hold, what are their occupations and requirements, how productive is the land in various parts, what are the patterns of commerce and industry? Then, having assessed the material, Mentor shapes the society according to wise principles of political design, like a "skillful gardener" pruning away waste and corruption. Mentor stresses that radical reforms are needed, not just tinkering or face-lifting; a whole new set of laws must be instituted, and the habits of the nation must

---

[17] *Télémaque*, book VII, 128-135; cf. book II, for Telemachus' own brief experience as architect of a golden age. On Fénelon's two utopias and their influence on Rousseau, see Judith Shklar, *Men and Citizens*, ch. 1.
[18] *Télémaque*, book VIII; and book XVII, pp. 352-353.

be changed. The only man equal to such an undertaking, says Mentor to Telemachus, is a *roi philosophe*.[19]

As is true of Plato's Republic, the virtues of the political order of Salente are austerity, hierarchical order, communal happiness, and stability. Except for encouraging useful occupations (such as agriculture), regulating the traffic in luxury goods, and providing a few necessary services that private enterprise could not handle, the government of the reformed Salente refrained from interfering in commerce. The freedom of trade attracted merchants from far lands, and the economy of Salente prospered accordingly. Mentor advised the king to rely on indirect manipulation and supervision of the economy, to ensure that it would work as efficiently and productively as possible. One should lead men "without constraint, by reward and good order. Authority alone never does any good," Mentor tells the king. "Submission of inferiors does not suffice. It is necessary to win their hearts and arrange things so that men find their advantage in those areas where one wishes to profit from their industry."[20] The wise, paternal, godlike monarch was to be continually aware of the overall design, and adjust rewards and benefits to encourage subjects to move into appropriate places of their own accord, oblivious to his constraints upon their choices.

In Salente, unlike Veiras's Sevarambia, a caste system was introduced alongside elements of egalitarianism. The plan for seven ranks or classes in society distinguished by dress and housing that Sevarias had rejected as divisive was instituted by Mentor. The ancient nobility composed the first order in wealth and status, followed by those distinguished by office, and so on, down the line. Here, as elsewhere, the importance of Salente as a model for a reforming king of France is obvious; classes were not abolished, but regulated internally. Rather than taxing those who were most productive, Ideomenus fined those who were not. Odd bits of republican austerity and patriotism were interspersed with the monarchical order. Lands were divided roughly equally within each class, to ensure that all families had enough and none too much, and encourage simplicity and frugality. Magnificence could be displayed only in the public sphere, not in private show. Children be-

---

[19] *Télémaque*, book XVII, p. 353; and book X, p. 194. Françoise Gallouedec-Genuys, *La Conception du prince dans l'oeuvre de Fénelon*, emphasizes his central vision of a Christian philosopher-king.

[20] *Télémaque*, book III, on the economy of Tyre, p. 46. In this same section, principles of free trade are described as essential to prosperity. "Never attempt to meddle with commerce to make it work according to your plans," Telemachus is told. "It is much better if a prince does not touch it at all, for fear of hampering it. . . . Commerce is like certain kinds of springs; if you attempt to redirect their course, you dry them up."

longed "less to their parents than to the state," and there was public education for civic virtue. Magistrates supervised the conduct "not only of every family but of every person," and the king was reminded of his duty to maintain eternal vigilance over the morals of his subjects.[21]

Despite the differences in their economies, Bétique and Salente exemplify one of Fénelon's central principles, in theology and politics alike: the moral superiority of "pure love," selflessness and subordination of the individual to the whole. Just at the time when Pascal's sharp distinction between *concupiscence* and *charité* was blurred or denied altogether in the writings of Nicole, Malebranche, and Abbadie, Fénelon insisted on the importance of that same distinction. With his doctrine of *pur amour*, which echoed themes first broached in the controversies of the 1640s, Fénelon provided an important counterweight to the growing stress on the social utility of self-love in France. He insisted that self-love cannot provide a basis for a satisfactory human life, no matter how enlightened its interpretation of its interests. Even the interested love of God is rejected as false coin. Throughout his writings, Fénelon disagreed explicitly with those who asserted that virtue is merely *amour-propre* that sees its way more clearly. The shoddiness of such an ethic is revealed by our hesitation in admitting we are motivated by it, and our admiration for those who give of themselves for others. Enlightened *amour-propre* renders an odd homage to virtue by aping its behavior, but can never attain goodness because it is false at the core, just as Pascal had said. The man who remains centered in himself, even if he acts as though this were not the case, can never know what true love, virtue, and friendship are all about.[22]

One of Fénelon's *Dialogues des morts* makes this point quite clearly. Socrates, Timon, and Alcibiades are the participants in a discourse on virtue, in which embittered misanthropy and the ethic of *honnêteté* are both bested by Socratic virtue, pure and uncompromising. Alcibiades' *honnête* ideal is spurned by Socrates as behavior like that of

---

[21] *Télémaque*, books x-xi, pp. 193-235. On Fénelon's preoccupation with ordering the family as the cornerstone of society, see Carolyn C. Lougee, *Le Paradis des Femmes*, pp. 175-187.

[22] The theme of *pur amour* can be found in several of Fénelon's pastoral and theological writings; it is discussed most systematically in the essay "Sur le pur amour: sa possibilité, ses motifs," and subsequent shorter essays in the "Instructions et avis sur divers points de la morale," *Oeuvres*, i, 303-352. Jeanne-Lydie Goré, *L'Itinéraire de Fénelon*, part iii, ch. 5, is a thoughtful discussion of how this theme fits into Fénelon's whole life and work. On connections between Fénelon's *pur amour* and that of Camus in the 1640s, see Gabriel Joppin, *Une querelle autour de l'amour pur*, pp. 117-123.

a fisherman who throws out a baited hook; he appears to be feeding the fish, but in fact he catches them and kills them. All tyrants, magistrates, ambitious politicians appear beneficent and generous; they seem to be giving themselves in order to take in the people. . . . Such men are the pests of humanity. At least the *amour-propre* of a misanthrope is only savage and useless to the world; but that of false philanthropes is treacherous and tyrannical. They promise all the virtues of society and make of it only a traffic, in which they wish to attach everything to themselves and make all others serve them.[23]

The ethic set over against "enlightened self-interest" is Pascal's ethic of deliberate self-denial, losing oneself in the pure love of God. In Fénelon's theology, pure love is an act of pure will, rather than of sentiment, reason, or imagination.[24] Divine grace is the only force powerful enough to pull us out of our natural rootedness in ourselves; our part is to will to give in to it. Only then can we discover the bliss of true fellowship with other human beings and with God Himself.

In describing the condition of *pur amour*, Fénelon commonly uses political metaphors. He shows how "this idea of pure disinterestedness dominates the political theories of all ancient legislators." They demanded that each citizen give himself totally in love of the good order they constructed. "It was not a question of finding happiness in conforming to that order," says Fénelon, "but on the contrary, for love of that order, of devouring oneself, perishing, depriving the self of all resources."[25] The ancient polity's vision of order and justice is abstract and confused compared with the Christian love of God; but it is the nearest analogy Fénelon can find. The essential similarity is the radical denial of the self in favor of something greater than the self. In his utopias, the happiness of individuals is not the goal to be pursued, but the final by-product of a community in which justice, frugality, and union through submission to the whole are the central foci for legislative activity, just as the bliss of the saintly is not the object they pursue, but the advantage that accrues to them unsought. In both cases the starting point is loss of individuality in something greater, purer, finer—participation in a worthy whole.

[23] *Dialogues des morts*, no. XVIII, in *Oeuvres*, II, 588.
[24] "Sur la sécheresse et les distractions qui arrivent dans l'oraison," *Oeuvres*, I, 323.
[25] "Sur le pur amour," *Oeuvres*, I, 308-309. According to the archbishop, "all these legislators and philosophers who reasoned about laws supposed that the fundamental principle of political society was to prefer the public to the self, not through hope of serving one's own interests, but by the simple pure disinterested love of that political order, which is beauty, justice, and virtue itself."

Program for Reform—343

In the *Essai philosophique sur le gouvernement civil* written by Ramsay, Fénelon's admiring disciple (which is the most comprehensive and least reliable source for Fénelon's political ideas), the principle of *pur amour* is given concrete form in the Cartesian notion of a hierarchy of loves. Pondering our lowly place in this hierarchy, we should recognize that we are not "independent beings created for ourselves," but little parts of the whole republic of reasonable beings.[26] The appropriate response to such a recognition is to seek the general good in preference to our own good as individuals; this duty is particularly incumbent on those who hold power. The archbishop closes a conversation with the young pretender to the English throne by advising him that the wise ruler seeks the happiness of his country by "conserving the subordination of the several ranks, conciliating the liberty of the people with the obedience due to sovereigns, making men good citizens and faithful subjects, submissive without being slaves, free without being unrestrained. The pure love of order is the source of all political virtues, as well as of all divine virtues. The same unity of principles reigns in all his sentiments."[27]

3. A Program for Reform

The Fénelonian principles of austerity, order, hierarchy, and pure love inform a set of specific proposals for the realm of France drawn up by the Burgundy circle during that optimistic year when they prepared for power. The archbishop and two dukes—Beauvillier and Chevreuse—consulted in the town of Chaulnes and drew up a list of reforms to be put into effect as soon as *le petit prince* was on the throne. These *Plans de gouvernement* are the platform of a loyal opposition that sees victory ahead. One of the most striking things about these *Plans* (also called the *Tables de Chaulnes*) is the emphasis on the whole nation, as opposed to sole focus on the king.[28] The idea of the participation of all the people in public life, the stimulation of efforts devoted

[26] Ramsay's *Essai* is included in Fénelon's *Oeuvres*, III, 366-409; these references are from pp. 366-370. Similar ideas can be found in Fénelon's own work, as in the *Dialogues*, no. VII (Confucius and Socrates), in *Oeuvres*, II, 569-574. Ramsay's *Essai* purports to be a collection of Fénelon's ideas, and in many ways it is; but it also reflects Ramsay's own, and must be used with caution. G. D. Henderson, *Chevalier Ramsay*, p. 74 shows that he "had the editorial tendency to find more in any book of Fénelon than Fénelon ever put there."
[27] "Supplément à l'*Examen de conscience*," Urbain, *Ecrits*, pp. 95-96; *Oeuvres*, III, 364.
[28] The shift from king to nation is also apparent in a letter from Fénelon to Chevreuse in 1710 in which he asserts that the only way to end the war is for "the nation to save itself." Urbain, *Ecrits*, pp. 172-176; *Oeuvres*, III, 669-672.

to the public good, is translated from Salente to contemporary France. To adapt the ideal to a large kingdom, the Chaulnes group proposes a multilayered set of representative assemblies. The direct model for this proposal is the contemporary government of Languedoc, one of the provinces that still possessed vigorous provincial estates. But the powers proposed in the *Tables de Chaulnes* for representative assemblies, from diocesan groups to the Estates-General of the nation, are considerably broader than those enjoyed by any French assemblies in recent history. The estates at each level had an extensive role in the direction of finances, and the Estates-General were also given the right to deliberate about "all matters of justice, police, finance, war, alliances and negotiations, agriculture, commerce." The lower estates were subordinate to the Estates-General, which were to assemble every three years and remain in session as long as they thought necessary.[29]

These provisions of the *Tables de Chaulnes* represent the revival of constitutionalist ideas in France after a long dormant period, and the reemphasis on the rule of law after an era when the will of the absolute monarch was held to be sufficient guarantee of its own uprightness. The institutions designed at Chaulnes gave substance to the ideal expressed by Fénelon in the education of Burgundy: "that a people should have written laws, always constant, consecrated by the entire nation; that the laws be above everything, and that those who govern have their authority only by the laws; that they can do anything for good, following the laws; that they can do nothing to authorize evil against the laws."[30] But the theme of law "consecrated by the nation" was juxtaposed in the *Tables* with a nostalgic desire to revive the powers of the old nobility in France. The resident governors drawn from the nobility were to take powers back from the upstart intendants, and the powers of the judiciary and the magistrates were to be curtailed. The councils of the central government were to be predominantly aristocratic in composition, and the separation of the three orders in the assemblies of the Estates retained.

The administrative decentralization and revival of aristocratic power that are the most marked features of the Chaulnes proposals are found in a comparable set of proposals submitted by another of Burgundy's ducal adherents, Saint-Simon. In addition to regular meetings of the

[29] The *Tables de Chaulnes* or *Plans de gouvernement* are included in Urbain, *Ecrist*, pp. 101-129, and in *Oeuvres*, III, 446-452. The discussion of the estates is in section III. Werner Gembruch, "Reformforderungen in Frankreich um die Wende vom 17. zum 18. Jahrhundert," discusses these proposals in the context of a general analysis of ideas about reform during this period. For an overview of the situation in the *pays d'état* such as Languedoc, consult Mousnier, *Les Institutions de la France*, I, ch. XIV.

[30] *Dialogues des morts*, no. XVII (Socrates and Alcibiades); *Oeuvres*, II, 585.

estates, his *Projets de gouvernement* provide for a small council drawn from the Estates-General to remain in session permanently; and the idea broached briefly in the Chaulnes proposals for a set of aristocratic councils at the heart of the central government is developed at length by Saint-Simon, in a form that proved influential for the architects of the *polysynodie* under the Regency.[31] Saint-Simon joins the Chaulnes group in advocating full liberty of external and internal trade, thus giving evidence of the growing agreement in France on the desirability of laissez-faire. Some of the more novel aspects of the Chaulnes proposals, including sumptuary laws and regulation of occupations in the economy, pure echoes of Salente, are absent from Saint-Simon's proposals. But all Burgundy's supporters are firm in their conviction that fundamental reforms in finance and taxation are necessary to restore the kingdom to economic health.

Despite their reformist intent, however, the proposals by members of Burgundy's circle are reactionary in substance. The stress on the renewed prominence of the ancient nobility and the dismantling of various institutions devised by Richelieu and Colbert make clear the continued importance of a feudal ideal for the French nobility, which remained strong into the eighteenth century. The Burgundy group was also quite traditional in its attitude toward the monarchy. None of them supposed that they were advocating reductions in the king's power by proposing a set of assemblies and councils to help him govern well. They asserted that these measures would extend and complete the power of the king, direct and channel it for good, not limit it. We can readily predict that such assemblies would have come into sharp conflict with the king; but it is anachronistic to suppose that Fénelon and his associates foresaw and secretly hoped for such a conflict, or for a diminution of royal power. Having little experience with representative institutions, they had no reason to assume that they always tend to arrogate power to themselves. The example of England would have suggested this possibility, but that of the provincial estates in France would not. Fénelon's group expected that the members of the estates would behave just as "peaceably and affectionately" toward the king as the residents of Languedoc, and they specified that deputies must be men "interested, by their goods and their hopes, in satisfying the king," as well as being knowledgeable about their localities.[32] But the deputies were not to be vilely subservient; the elections were to be

---

[31] Saint-Simon's *Projets de gouvernement*, edited by M. P. Mesnard, are discussed by George Tréca, *Les Doctrines et les réformes de droit public en réaction contre l'absolutisme de Louis XIV*, pp. 142-149, and Henri Sée, *Les Idées politiques en France au XVIIe siècle*, pp. 236-269.

[32] *Plans de gouvernement*, in Urbain, *Ecrits*, pp. 103-104.

free from royal interference or preference, and no deputy could receive payment from the king for at least three years after his term was finished.

Thus the Burgundy circle retained the old vision of a king governing in a formally unlimited fashion, making the final decision on all issues, relying on the institutionalized help of representatives of various parts of his kingdom. Assemblies and councils were designed to give him precious information as well as salutary advice, and to bridle him if he toyed with tyranny. The scheme depended on the sincere good will of the monarch and the deference of the people, content to participate in limited ways, and not hungry for more power. Today such suppositions may appear chimerical. In 1711, with Telemachus ready for the throne, it is less apparent that they were.

4. BOULAINVILLIERS AND THE *Thèse Nobiliaire*

A number of reformist themes characteristic of the growing opposition to Louis XIV's regime are present in Fénelon's political and didactic writings. Two that proved especially important for the early eighteenth century were the call for greater economic freedom, and the claim by the nobility for a larger role in government. Both these ideas were developed more systematically by other thinkers, particularly Boulainvilliers and Boisguilbert. Both men were authors of long *mémoires*, full of ideas for reviving France, moved to write by their distress at the condition of the country and their conviction that fundamental changes were required in the regime. They were members of the small army of *donneurs d'avis* who begged the king and ministers to listen to their ideas during the last decades of the *ancien régime*. In the long run, their dissimilar proposals had similar effects in the development of political theory in France. They both contributed to arguments for more widespread participation in French life, and against control from above by absolutist power.

The comte de Boulainvilliers was the staunchest and most persistent proponent of what later historians have called the *thèse nobiliaire* in France. This term and its companion term, the *thèse royale*, were coined to help explain the complicated arguments about the true constitution of France that dominated political thought between the *Tables de Chaulnes* and the *Spirit of the Laws*.[33] Supporters of the "noble thesis" argued for a revived aristocracy and a mixed regime;

[33] Albert Mathiez, "La Place de Montesquieu dans l'histoire des doctrines politiques du XVIIIe siècle." Contemporary scholars who use the terms include Franklin L. Ford, *Robe and Sword*, and Peter Gay, *Voltaire's Politics*.

those of the "royal thesis" advocated an absolutist monarchy resting on broad popular support. The terms call attention to the markedly *historicist* temper of the debate between royalists and aristocrats, or "Romanists" and "Germanists," in these decades.[34] The two theses are part of the ancient argument between constitutionalists and absolutists that we have traced throughout this study. They describe a particular phase in the polemic, a phase in which adherents of both positions appealed primarily to French history, rather than to Scripture, juridical codes, metaphors, or abstract right, to bolster their position.

The crucial point in the argument over French history was the status of the early Frankish settlers who entered Gaul under Clovis as Roman power receded. The "Germanists," proponents of the *thèse nobilaire*, claimed that these Franks were brave free noblemen who elected their kings according to ancient Germanic custom, and were invited in as saviors by the Gauls. They and their descendents, by right of conquest or by invitation, dominated the original inhabitants. The contemporary nobility of France retained privileges dating from the conquest, including exemption from most taxes, the dispensation of justice in their seigneuries, and military leadership. Their ancient assemblies from the *champs de mars* to the Estates-General shared power with the king, especially in decisions about war and taxes. In the version of the noble thesis favorable to the *robe* nobility, the parlements were the rightful heirs of these ancient assemblies that had fallen into disuse; in the version associated with the old aristocracy, the parlements were composed of bourgeois magistrates toadying to the king.

The "Romanists," or proponents of the *thèse royale*, read French history in quite a different light. They asserted that early French kings took the place of Roman emperors in Gaul, and thus possessed absolute hereditary power, to which all inhabitants of France were equally subject. They denied that the monarchy had ever been elective, or that there was any significant distinction between Frankish "nobles" and Gallic "serfs." Romanists such as the abbé Du Bos explained feudal distinctions by asserting that counts and dukes in several provinces abused their delegated authority in a period of royal weakness and usurped power from the king. They were able to turn their posts into hereditary property and subjugate their fellow citizens. The conquest of Gaul, in this account, was not made by an army of brave nobles marching in with Clovis, but by a clutch of greedy provincial war

[34] "Germanists" and "Romanists" are distinguished by Jacques Barzun, *The French Race*; see also Augustin Thierry, *Considérations sur l'histoire de France*, and Denis Richet, "Autour des origines idéologiques lointaines de la revolution française."

lords who betrayed their king. The alliance between king and bourgeoisie, which distressed Boulainvilliers, was interpreted as a natural response by two victims of encroachment, and bourgeois rights to participation in municipal and provincial government were vindicated as part of the ancient constitution of France.[35]

Boulainvilliers's version of the *thèse nobiliaire* was based on assiduous readings of ancient chronicles and early modern jurists. His treatises were not published until after his death in 1722, but his ideas were widely known two decades earlier. The count was an eclectic freethinker, who wrote about astrology, Spinozistic philosophy, economics, and a host of other subjects.[36] His most concerted attention was devoted to the diagnosis and remedy of political ills in France. The root of these evils, in his view, lay in the exclusion of the ancient nobility from politics and the conferral of power on raw upstarts. For Boulainvilliers, the early years of the feudal period were the golden age of France. Charlemagne's novel and brilliant system of government allowed him to protect noble privileges and consolidate allegiances. This feudal structure was "the masterpiece of the human spirit" in constitution making.[37] In passages that echo a constant theme from Seyssel through Fénelon, Boulainvilliers insists that the monarch's sovereignty was not weakened or subverted by noble cooperation, but rather fully realized and made more effective throughout the kingdom.[38] All power was controlled by bonds of fealty, so that arbitrary treatment was impossible, and security assured; the people were protected by overlords who regarded them as part of their domain, and noble ambitions were channeled into socially useful pursuits.

However, despite Boulainvilliers's recital of stock phrases about noble participation extending rather than obstructing royal power, he also says something less familiar. He says that sovereign power must be limited by other powers, and introduces the temper of English constitutionalism into French thought, proposing the English system as a model for France. Like Montesquieu, who learned a good deal from his work, Boulainvilliers argues that the major threat to good govern-

[35] Jean-Baptiste Du Bos, *Histoire critique de l'établissement de la monarchie française*; I, 2-10; II, book VI.

[36] Renée Simon, *Henry de Boulainvillier*, gives full information about the count's life and work; he is mentioned several times in connection with a small group of *libres chercheurs* in Ira Wade's *Clandestine Organization and Diffusion of Ideas*.

[37] Boulainvilliers, *Histoire de l'ancien gouvernement de la France* (1727), I, 26. This edition, unlike the 1737 edition published in London, includes portions of Boulainvilliers' *Etat de la France*, a critical report of the activities of intendants drawn up for the duke of Burgundy.

[38] *Histoire*, preface, p. 2; letter I, p. 169; and letter II, pp. 218-228.

ment comes from the destruction of *les puissances particulières*, ancient power intermediate between king and people. Barbarians throughout Europe after the fall of Rome, who insisted on sharing in the government of their kings, acted not on sophisticated political philosophy but out of simple common sense. Power must be shared if it is not to be abused, says Boulainvilliers, and defies his readers to name any absolute sovereign who has governed benevolently and justly. "There can be no surety for the people," proclaims the count, "except in states governed on models given by those old destroyers of the Roman Empire, of which no trace remains today except in England."[39] He threw down the gauntlet to absolutist theorists by connecting absolute monarchy explicitly with despotism, and refusing to exempt the kings of France. Bossuet comes in for special scorn because he tried to use the Bible to "forge new chains on the natural liberty of man and augment the pomp and cruelty of kings." All the fine words in the tutorial literatures for princes about royal duties have no effect, says Boulainvilliers; the pupils pay attention only to those parts that grant them unlimited authority. Our most ancient forefathers were wiser than more recent ones, in their awareness that "the most desirable government is that where the supreme authority is tempered by a council equally wise, disinterested, and necessary."[40]

Boulainvilliers shifted French attention from harassment by numerous petty tyrants to the despotic depredations of a single all-powerful sovereign. Instead of raising up the king to protect ordinary people against the oppressions of ambitious nobles, Boulainvilliers wanted to strengthen the nobles to protect everyone against the king. He offered the feudal system as a model for contemporary reformers. The king's council would be composed of members of the old nobility, who would be responsible for governing the provinces and participating in the Estates. Boulainvilliers was contemptuous of avaricious men, and inveighed against "the unspeakable degradation of the present age, in which personal interest is the universal spring of action [*le mobile général*]."[41] But he was a sufficiently good historian to recognize that

[39] *Histoire*, letter XIV, pp. 183-186. On Boulainvilliers' role in "feudal reaction" of this period, see J.Q.C. Mackrell, *The Attack upon "Feudalism" in Eighteenth-Century France*, pp. 8-26; William Doyle, "Was There an Aristocratic Reaction in pre-Revolutionary France?" gives reason to doubt that there ever was a concerted "feudalist" movement.

[40] *Histoire*, letter III, pp. 254-255.

[41] "Mémoire sur la convocation d'une assemblée d'Etats-généraux," in *Mémoires presentés à monseigneur le duc d'Orléans*, first *mémoire*, pp. 6-7. All six of these *mémoires* are accepted by some scholars, including Renée Simon, as the work of Boulainvilliers; more recent evidence (offered by Paul Harsin, "Boulainvilliers ou Vauban?") indicates that he could not have written the fifth or sixth. Only the first has his distinctive style, and is supported by manuscript evidence.

the claims of the third estate to participate in national assemblies were sound. He even admitted that brutality and ignorance sometimes accompanied feudal control. His primary quarrel was not with the upstart clerks and merchants of the third estate, but with the domineering monarchy.

This stress on the need for a countervailing power to set up against the royal sovereignty was the real thrust of the *thèse nobiliare*. Thus, a set of writings that occasionally descends into the rankest obscurantism proved to be part of a growing movement for more participation in French politics by all portions of the state, through firmly established and regularized patterns. The Sun King's reign, which had dawned amidst universal expectations of excellent results from benevolent and conscientious absolutism, ended amidst an equally universal conviction that the salvation of the nation must be the work of many and not of one alone, and that the French monarchy had to be reorganized in fundamental ways.

5. Boisguilbert and Laissez-faire

In the last two decades of Louis XIV's reign, from 1695 until 1715, while Boulainvilliers was attacking the excessive concentration of power in the hands of the prince himself, several other Frenchmen were disturbed by another kind of concentration of power in the regime: overextended control of areas of life that would be better left alone. The advocates of the *thèse nobiliare* believed that too few Frenchmen, and generally the wrong ones, had a hand in government. They wanted political activity dispersed to other groups and persons in the state. Those who wrote in favor of laissez-faire policies proposed avoiding political activity altogether in certain spheres. Instead of constructing a countervailing power, these men advised leaving ordinary subjects alone to do things for themselves, to an extent that absolutist politics had never thought possible. Thus both sets of writers, for all their protestations of loyalty to the crown, were anti-absolutist in their intentions and their influences; and both contributed arguments for more participation in French society, despite the differences in tone and substance of their writings.

Many merchants in the last decades of Louis XIV's reign became convinced that government attempts to help them by regulating their activities were a crippling constraint. In a number of *mémoires* and petitions, they called for more freedom of action, less interference and control.[42] Among the spokesmen for laissez-faire principles against the

---

[42] Rothkrug, *Opposition to Louis XIV*, pp. 351-357, quotes from an anonymous

mercantilist mood at court was the great-grandson of the sixteenth-century chancellor de l'Hôpital, the seigneur de Belesbat. Belesbat took part in a political salon in the Luxembourg district in the 1690s, along with Fontenelle and Saint-Pierre. The meetings of this group (a prototype for later political clubs such as the *académie de l'Entresol* during the Regency) accustomed Belesbat to discussing the kingdom's ills. In 1692 he joined the *donneurs d'avis* with a set of *mémoires* offering his own suggestions for remedies. Like his spiritual descendant Fourier, Belesbat was convinced that a moment of the king's time would persuade him of the excellence of his reforming scheme.[43]

In his *mémoires*, Belesbat broached the unconventional idea that France and Holland had common interests, and should be cooperating instead of fighting over trade.[44] France was naturally fit for agriculture, Holland for commerce; the Dutch should bring the merchandise of the world to French ports in return for products of her natural fertility. In stressing agriculture against the attempt to nurture all branches of industry in France, Belesbat agreed with contemporary agrarians such as Fénelon, and foreshadowed the Physiocrats. But his description of the natural interdependence of France and Holland was only part of his celebration of the advantages of a global division of labor, in which themes familiar since Nicole's *Essays* were taken as the basis for asserting the desirability of unhampered trade. "Liberty is the soul of commerce," contended Belesbat. Natural advantages and hard work are useless without it. Not only within a nation, but between nations too, unhampered commerce is essential for the full benefits of a global economy to be obtained. The king should ensure justice and liberty for all, says Belesbat, and then leave everyone alone to pursue their own enterprises, *laissant faire le commerce que l'on voudra*.[45]

Ideas of this sort were developed by Pierre de Boisguilbert into a fairly systematic theory of laissez-faire economics. Boisguilbert sketched out the central arguments of such a system long before such English worthies as Adam Smith. It is only just to recognize such precedence, although recognition must be tempered by awareness of

---

mémoire of 1688; on pp. 392-413, he documents the extensive support for laissez-faire principles among French merchants in this period.

[43] Rothkrug, *Opposition to Louis XIV*, pp. 328-351; see also Albert Schatz and Robert Caillemer, *Le Merchantilisme libéral à la fin du XVIIe siècle*.

[44] "Mémoires presentés au Roi par Mr. de Belesbat," B.N. fds. fr. MS 1205, first *mémoire*: "Reflections sur les liaisons de la France avec la Holande"; see also the later *mémoire*, "Pour les graines."

[45] "Réflexions, sur les liaisons de la France," folio 8; the assertion *que la liberté est l'âme du commerce* is at folio 6. Other *mémoires* in this collection deal with the interests of France more generally; one is entitled "Preuves de l'union inséparable des Intérests du Roy et de ceux de ses sujets."

352—Absolute Monarchy

the innate absurdity of fixing beginnings in such matters.[46] From 1691 until his death in 1714, Boisguilbert attempted to persuade a succession of controllers general of the virtues of free trade, and the interconnectedness of the world economy. Disappointed by their rebuffs, he published two major treatises and several shorter works. In presenting his bold ideas in print, he took advantage of his position as censor in Rouen, one of several high offices he owned in that city along with a small estate outside it. But his position could not protect him indefinitely. His works were officially censured in the same year as Vauban's *Dixme*, 1707. Boisguilbert was sentenced to brief exile; he won a reprieve by flattery, the intervention of well-placed friends, and a promise to hold his peace. He did not keep his promise, but subsequently met with no more success than before.

Several of his countrymen regarded Boisguilbert as a visionary and a fool. He took pride in noting that all great innovators are so regarded. "I glory in having an unusual character," he said, "without which I should not have unusual ideas."[47] Some of his ideas were shared with others, including those concerning tax reform, where his thinking closely paralleled Vauban's. He even employed metaphors favored by the marshal, in diagnosing gangrene in the body politic.[48] But in his discussions of free trade, he used a number of novel illustrations and arguments. Against the mercantilist obsession with specie, Boisguilbert pointed out that the essence of wealth is not a stock of metal, but the possession of plenty for a pleasant life. He contended that if nature were left to herself, her intention that all men should enjoy such plenty would be realized. The government of France tried to improve on nature, and managed only to spoil her plans. The simple remedy for the evils of the kingdom was for the government to stop interfering with natural patterns of trade and commerce, and *laisser faire la nature*.[49] No superhuman effort for reform was needed, only the cessation of ill-considered effort.

[46] Franco Venturi's warning against "nostalgia for the *Ur*" should be recalled frequently by intellectual historians, who are particularly subject to this malaise. Venturi (*Utopia and Reform in the Enlightenment*, p. 3) quotes Herder on the delights of reading "a poetic account of the origin of each single thing: the first sailor, the first kiss, the first garden, the first death, the first camel."

[47] From a letter to Chamillart (1703), quoted by Hazel van Dyke Roberts, *Boisguilbert*, pp. 26-27. Roberts' book is the best account of Boisguilbert's life and writings, although her affection for her subject leads her to compare his sense of mission for saving France with that of Joan of Arc. On his contribution to the development of French economic thought, see also Charles Woolsey Cole, *French Mercantilism*, pp. 200-273.

[48] *Factum de la France* (1707), in Eugene Daire, ed., *Economistes-financiers du XVIIIe siècle*, p. 269; see also p. 336.

[49] *Factum de la France*, in Daire, ed., p. 286; see also the *Détail de la France* (1697), in Daire, ed., p. 172.

In making his case for laissez-faire, Boisguilbert drew on arguments about the power of greed and the social energy produced in the pursuit of selfish interests. Like Nicole, he was convinced that collective harmony arises from the efforts of countless individuals to advance their selfish happiness. Boisguilbert applied such arguments directly to economics, to show how interdependence requires the removal of artificial restrictions on trade, in order that selfishness may do its work. He insisted that a productive economy depends on benefits for all participants; they must have some incentive to produce. But he accepted the Jansenist notion that greed is monopolistic in its attitudes; each individual attempts to better his own position at the expense of someone else, and discounts benefits that are shared with others, because of the corrupting effects of self-love. According to Boisguilbert, the source of harmony between private greed and universal benefit is the order introduced by wise nature. So long as we do not interfere with her workings, our attempts to get as much as we can for ourselves will maximize everybody's happiness in the long run.

If human beings were clear-sighted, we would see that each of us depends on the general reciprocity of the market for our private utilities. Such enlightened self-interest might lead us to restrain selfish impulses to protect the system. Boisguilbert apparently thought human life would be more pleasant, more sociable, if men behaved in such a way. But he was confident that nature would compensate for even the blindest pursuit of selfish good by so arranging things that it served the common good. The supervision by the "superior and general authority" of Nature makes possible a smooth economy among beings who are "sufficiently inhuman to refuse to save their fellows' lives in time of need save at the price of all other worldly goods."[50] Nature is personified throughout Boisguilbert's treatises as an authoritative force combining human purposes into a harmonious whole, with which men tamper at their peril. He equates nature and providence, showing the continuity between the Christian idea of a divine directive will and the arguments of liberal economists.[51] Government can safely leave men alone because this does not mean abandoning them to their

[50] *Traité des grains*, in Daire, ed., pp. 355-356; *Factum*, p. 325, is a similar passage. The reference to "superior and general authority" setting the price of grain has been interpreted by some readers (including Albert Talbot, *Les Théories de Boisguilbert*, pp. 52-57) as inconsistency in Boisguilbert's commitment to *laissez-faire* principles; they fail to connect the "authority" with nature itself.

[51] Boisguilbert connects "nature" and "providence" in the *Traité des grains*, p. 386; *Factum*, p. 280, and *Dissertation sur la nature des richesses*, in Daire, ed., p. 409. Jacques Nagels, *Reproduction du capital selon Marx, Boisguilbert* . . . , pp. 21-22, is on weak ground in equating *laisser faire la nature* in Boisguilbert's writings with *laisser faire la bourgeoisie*.

own resources; it leaves a much more powerful and adept Authority working in the field. In its origins, at least, laissez-faire economics depended on the optimistic conviction that there is a management in the universe greater than the meager power of the state. Adam Smith's "invisible hand" is descended from the hand of Providence.

Boisguilbert asserts that "all individuals" pursuing "their own particular interest" incessantly "create at the same time, although it is the last thing on their mind, the general good, from which . . . they must always expect their private utility." Since they always seek to subvert the laws in their own favor, "and aspire incessantly to build their opulence on their neighbor's ruin," it is essential to have an overarching order (*une police*) to maintain peace and harmony. "But nature alone can introduce that order and maintain the peace. Any other authority spoils everything by trying to interfere, no matter how well-intentioned it may be." In ascribing a motive to nature for allowing herself to be upstaged by paltry human efforts, Boisguilbert uses a lofty variant of *amour-propre*: "Nature herself, jealous of her prerogatives, revenges herself on any such attempts by a general disconcerting of everything, from the instant she sees someone defying her knowledge and her wise operations by alien interference." The passage concludes with Boisguilbert's assertion that

> only Nature, or Providence if you prefer, can ensure that this justice will be observed, provided once again that no one whatsoever meddles with it. And this is how she does it. She establishes first of all an equal necessity to sell and buy in all sorts of exchanges in such a way that the pure desire for profit will be the soul of every market for seller and buyer alike; and it is with the aid of that equilibrium or balance that each partner to the transaction is equally required to listen to reason, and submit to it.[52]

Because of his conviction that the only rational course in economics is *qu'on laisse faire la nature*, Boisguilbert inveighed against attempts by the French government to deal with hunger by suppressing grain prices and directing trade.[53] Such behavior would make sense only if grain, like manna or mushrooms, sprang up without human effort, since it ignores the effects of low prices on the habits of cultivators. If government simply ceased tampering, the French economy, like a city from which a siege is lifted, would regain its health. Free to set their own price for grain, and to import grain freely throughout the

---

[52] *Dissertation sur la nature des richesses*, pp. 408-409; there is a similar passage in the *Traité*, pp. 387-392.
[53] *Factum*, p. 280.

Program for Reform—355

land, Frenchmen would be plentifully supplied with bread. In Boisguilbert's economy, nature distributes advantages and weaknesses throughout the world. Thus all men have a "solidary interest" in cooperation. If each individual, and each area of the world, concentrates on what it is best equipped to do and exchanges with others, the satisfaction of all human beings will be maximized.

To drive home his point Boisguilbert employs images dear to all authors of economics textbooks. He takes two hypothetical workers, one producing wheat, the other wool, and shows how both will perish if they do not trade; this principle is extended to workers in a comfortably sized city, and finally to the world. In language that recalls Nicole, Boisguilbert asserts that a few men in solitary possession of richly endowed land who cannot draw on the labor of others are less well-off than beggars in a wealthy country. A complex economy and its fruits depend on specialization of work and free exchange of products. For

> wealth is nothing other than a complete enjoyment, not just of the bare necessities of life, but of all that makes for delight and magnificence. To provide that wealth it is essential to have more than two hundred different professions . . . aiding each other by providing things this one has in excess and receiving in exchange those things he lacks, and this is not only from man to man, but from province to province and kingdom to kingdom. Otherwise one perishes by an abundance of some particular good while another man, or another country, is equally miserable in a completely different way.[54]

To illustrate this principle that obstacles to trade make for misery while commerce converts shortages into "perfect situations," Boisguilbert describes a tyrant who tortured his subjects by tying them up within sight of one another, and surrounding each with an abundance of one kind of good—the first has in reach all sorts of food, the second much warm clothing, the third water and liquors of all kinds. All three will perish, although taken as a whole they are quite well provided for. They could instantly be made happy if the prince removed the chains he put upon them. But if the prince responds to their pleas for freedom by demurring on the grounds that the times are not yet ripe, or says that it is necessary to wait till some far-off quarrel is settled before releasing them from chains, they can only suppose that ridicule and insult are used to compound the torture.[55]

This story of the prince with tormented subjects serves several of

[54] *Factum*, pp. 284-285; *Dissertation*, p. 394.
[55] *Dissertation*, p. 423.

Boisguilbert's purposes. It illustrates the advantages of trade, and highlights the stultifying effects of government interference. It also expresses his bitterness at royal obduracy, at the recurrent refrain that greeted all would-be reformers in these years: "We must wait for the peace." In one of his treatises, Boisguilbert composes a scathing litany on this stock response.[56] In another, he excoriates ministers for blindness in a passage that captures the reactions of those who will not see and hear, in any age:

> They take pleasure in believing that the most evident facts are falsehoods, or shut their eyes in the face of those facts. After having disposed of the evidence in this way, they contradict the most certain consequences drawn from it, to persuade themselves and others that such enlightened men, so zealous for the service of king and public, could not possibly have committed such grave errors; that they have reasons known only to themselves, that if one were privy to the whole truth one would understand.[57]

For his own part, Boisguilbert had no interest in government beyond persuading the French king and his officials of the correctness of his economics. He was not concerned with the merits or demerits of different regimes, and wasted no time celebrating the advantages of liberty in the Dutch republics. He showed no inclination to apply his arguments for freedom of action and unhampered initiative in the political sphere, to argue for participation in local government, or advise entrusting men with some measure of responsibility for their own affairs. His purpose was to influence an absolutist government, and he used conventional absolutist imagery in his treatises.[58] But his central message—that government should refrain from action that was weakening the country—had anti-absolutist connotations. Setting off large portions of human life as inappropriate for government intervention drastically reduced the scope of the royal business, compared with the conception Louis XIV had embraced. Since he set up no other power except nature herself in opposition to the king, Boisguilbert's arguments were formally compatible with absolutism. But he struck at the foundations of absolutism by claiming that even the most benevolent, omniscient, and majestic human power cannot do for ordinary

---

[56] "Supplément au *Détail de la France*," in Daire, ed., pp. 259-260.
[57] *Factum*, p. 270.
[58] See for instance *Factum*, p. 345, where he stresses the advantages to the monarchy that will attend the adoption of his ideas; he asks the king to regard France "and all her wealth as though they belonged to him alone and consider all the proprietors as his renters," to see that anything damaging to any worker is damaging to him as well.

human beings what they can do for themselves, selfishly and ignorantly pursuing what they take to be their interests. Boisguilbert implicitly put forward the counterclaim to absolutist power when he suggested that the magnificent power of the king, his sovereign will, is not what holds society together. Instead, society is held together mysteriously by natural networks of productive activity built up unwittingly by millions of self-serving men. It remained for other theorists to make this counterclaim explicit, and discover harmony between the fertile social pattern of individual activity, and the overarching sovereign will embodied in the state.

PART IV

Approaches to a Synthesis

CHAPTER THIRTEEN

A New Science of Politics in a Republic Protected by a King

1. Political Inquiry in the Regency

When Louis XIV died in 1715, the wintry numbness of the last years of his long reign was followed by the open, frenetic springtime of the Regency. In several ways, the Regency for Louis XV recalled the regency for his great-grandfather. Orléans was a more skillful governor than Anne or Mazarin, and Louis XIV had made the monarchy so secure that there was no threat of another Fronde. But the dormant parlements found their voices, and there was a resurgence of noble confidence. The air of speculation and intrigue that filled the Mississippi Bubble nurtured schemes for social and political amelioration. Cardinal Retz's *Mémoires* were published for the first time in 1717 and were immensely popular; the maneuvers of the Frondeurs fascinated their descendants. The *Persian Letters*, an excellent testimonial to the mood of gallant exhilaration that marked the Regency, include a splendid satire on Retz's strategies.[1] The political experiments of the Regency, including the system of government by multiple council known as *polysynodie*, were as ephemeral as the Bubble itself. But the atmosphere was seminal for science, literature, and social thought. Seeds of inquiry were planted that bore rich fruit in the works of Voltaire, Montesquieu, d'Argenson, and Rousseau.

Even during the Regency, royal censorship was sufficiently stringent that men rarely said in print what they said in private. However, many manuscripts circulated clandestinely, and there was a thriving traffic in treatises printed abroad and smuggled into France. Members of "the republic of letters" met regularly to discuss ideas put forward in such

[1] Montesquieu, *Lettres persanes*, no. 111; in *Oeuvres complètes*, I, 294-295. Voltaire is harsher in his *Philosophical Letters*, no. 8; he calls Retz a "rebel without a cause," his followers a "crowd of schoolboys rioting against their headmaster," and the whole thing "ridiculous." D'Argenson, *Mémoires et journal inédit*, I, 84-87, describes reactions to publications of Retz's *Mémoires* and mentions the role of his mother's family in the Fronde. On the Regency more generally, consult H. Carré, *Le Règne de Louis XV*; James Breck Perkins, *France under the Regency*; and a collection of essays on *La Regence*, published by the Centre Aixois d'études et de recherches.

362—Approaches to a Synthesis

works, and exchange their own ideas and manuscripts.[2] Discussion groups, academies, and salons proliferated. Among the most important of these groups was the club de l'Entresol, which met regularly from the last year of the Regency until its suppression by the government eight years later. It was organized by the abbé Alary and his friend Bolingbroke, a frequent visitor to France, who brought to the Entresol some of the elements of the English club. The group aspired to become a political counterpart of the Académie française, and assumed a semi-official character because of the qualifications and connections of its members. Discussions at the Entresol were known to influence decisions at Versailles. This was the reason for its downfall. Fleury, the minister who had initially protected it, was led by its increasingly bold interference in the affairs of state to require that it be disbanded.

Our best record of the Entresol is in the journals of the marquis d'Argenson, who joined the group in 1725. D'Argenson's list of members includes several impressive names, although it does not include that of Montesquieu, who may once have read a paper to the group.[3] D'Argenson's accounts of meetings of the club attest to its camaraderie, as well as a disciplined attention to history and public policy. He describes the Entresol as "a perfectly free political society, made up of men who loved to reason about what was going on and could assemble together to speak their minds openly without fear of being compromised." Each Saturday they met to read foreign newspapers and discuss essays by members on assigned topics. Early drafts of a number of treatises, including those of d'Argenson himself and of the doyen of the group, the abbé de Saint-Pierre, were read and criticized. There was a good fire in winter and a pleasant garden in the summer, along with refreshments of all sorts. D'Argenson recalled it wistfully in later years as "a café of honnêtes gens."[4]

The abbé de Saint-Pierre was a particularly enthusiastic member of the club. He dreamed of an academy of political science officially charged with thinking up useful projects and preparing young min-

[2] Ira O. Wade, *Clandestine Organization and Diffusion of Philosophic Ideas*; Antoine Adams, *Le Mouvement philosophique*; Robert Darnton, "Reading, Writing and Publishing in Eighteenth-Century France."

[3] Montesquieu's "Dialogue de Sylla et d'Eucrate" was among the papers in Alary's collection. Roger Caillois, in his edition of Montesquieu's *Oeuvres complètes* assumes that it was read before the group; see also Robert Shackleton, *Montesquieu*, pp. 63-67.

[4] The fullest version of d'Argenson's description of the club is in the edition of his *Mémoires et journal inédit* published by P. Jannet in five volumes, I, 87-110. In the *Journal et mémoires du marquis d'Argenson* edited by E.J.B. Rathery for the Société de l'histoire de France, in nine volumes, the Entresol is described in I, 91-111.

isters.⁵ He thought of himself and his colleagues in the club as contributors to *la sianse politique* (as he described it in his reformed orthography), a cumulative discipline in which each generation of laborers surpasses their forebears if they are willing to work hard. Saint-Pierre placed himself in a line of apostolic succession beginning with Plato and Aristotle, continuing through Machiavelli, Montaigne, Bodin, Hobbes, and Richelieu. In his view, political science had been allowed to atrophy in the age of Louis XIV, and he devoted his considerable energies to reviving it.⁶ He was serenely confident that *les filosofes politiques mes successeurs* would refute his errors and prove things he imperfectly sketched out.

Saint-Pierre's immediate successors, *les filosofes politiques* of the eighteenth century, laughed at the repetitive earnestness of his projects for improving everything from the condition of French roads in winter to the state-system of Europe. La Bruyère had satirized him unforgettably as Mopse, obtruding his ideas on everyone he met, sitting down where he wished without a thought for precedence, a grave unself-conscious utilitarian fool moving through the sophisticated milieu of *honnêteté*, whose mockery he never even felt. His contemporaries regarded him as a "sort of privileged nuisance."⁷ But they also admired his courage in openly criticizing the regime of Louis XIV (which led to his expulsion from the Académie française), and learned from his ideas. Saint-Pierre's dogged naive optimistic creed, shared in such simplistic form only by one or two other men, such as Condorcet, was diffused and refracted through the more complex and memorable works of the Enlightenment.⁸

⁵ *Ouvrajes de politique*, III, 11-127.

⁶ On this topic, among the abbé's favorites, see *Ouvrajes de politique*, VI, 4-23, 127-131, and XI, 276-286. Boulainvilliers was among the growing number of Frenchmen who shared Saint-Pierre's enthusiasm about political science; in the second preface to his *Etat de la France*, I, 76-77, he asserted that "all men agree that there is no science higher than that of Government, nor one in which errors have more dangerous consequences. Therefore, since it is morally impossible that the practice of Government succeed without rule or theory, we must also conclude that there is no other science that should be cultivated by citizens with so much ardor, research, work, and method."

⁷ Frederick Artz, *The Enlightenment in France*, p. 118. La Bruyère's portrait is in the *Caractères*, p. 108.

⁸ Edouard Goumy, *Etude sur la vie et les écrits de l'abbé de Saint-Pierre*, pp. 323-324, was among the first to make this point. Saint-Beuve, who could not abide Saint-Pierre because of his execrable prose, reports that Voltaire spoke of the abbé as *cet homme moitié philosophe et moitié fou*, and alternately mocked, refuted, and cited him, slipping in some of his ideas under his own name; *Causeries du lundi*, XV, 246-274. See also Carl Becker, *The Heavenly City of the Eighteenth-Century Philosophers*, p. 40. Becker exaggerates Saint-Pierre's representativeness of his century, and few scholars accept his portrait of the Enlightenment. None-

364—Approaches to a Synthesis

The eccentric abbé was a physical and spiritual link between the generation of Fénelon and Bossuet, and the generation of Helvétius and Diderot. He was born just after the Fronde had ended, and walked with Rousseau in Mme. Dupin's gardens before his death in 1743. He bridged the discussion groups of the 1690s and those of the 1720s, admired Vauban, was connected with the Burgundy circle, and had been, despite his known antipathies to Jansenist theology, a friend of Nicole's in Paris.[9] Today he is known, if at all, as a chimerical utopian, gentle creator of an international cloud-cuckoo-land, author of tedious works Rousseau had to plow through to fulfill an obligation to a misguided patroness. Chimerical he may have been, and tedious he was undoubtedly; but he contributed more than we may realize to the development of political ideas in France. The principles he preached pervaded the Enlightenment: utilitarian moral philosophy, faith in the efficacy of education, the progress of human reason, and the possibility of radical political reform engineered by fiat from above. He reflects the ideas of Bacon and Descartes, as well as other thinkers we have considered in this study; but Saint-Pierre codified those ideas, and hammered away at them at a crucial juncture in intellectual history. He professed a number of principles that fit ill with his optimistic liberalism; he was firmly authoritarian, took for granted the radical inequality of men, valued tranquillity more than truth in politics, and gave several suggestions for the manipulation of people by their educators and their rulers. Saint-Pierre's writings provoke reflections about the possible connections among these disparate ideas and the destructive seeds in the Enlightenment world-view. His work also draws out some implications of ideas about authority and utility current in the later seventeenth century. Saint-Pierre attempted the first of several syntheses of these ideas. His attempt stimulated others, whose syntheses proved more profound and durable than his own.

One of Saint-Pierre's favorite pastimes was composing avuncular letters, which had always the same message—make your work useful to mankind—and the same distinctive closing: *paradis aux bienfaizans*. Saint-Pierre did not invent the word *bienfaisance*, though he is often credited with doing so. It occurs in the work of several seventeenth-

---

theless, a kernel of truth is buried in his flamboyant generalizations. Moreover, the abbé influenced the philosophes in a number of pragmatic and less evangelistic ways, as Ira Wade points out in *The Structure and Form of the French Enlightenment*, I, 332-333.

[9] On Saint-Pierre's connections with the earlier generation, see *Ouvrajes de politique*, XII, 287-293; Albert Cherel, *De Télémaque à Candide*, pp. 155-161, and Joseph Drouet, *L'Abbé de Saint-Pierre*, pp. 19-32.

century French moralists. But it is appropriate that the word is associated with him, since his own life was so completely organized around doing good to increase well-being. Here is a characteristic paragraph, from a letter to Voltaire in 1739:

> Do not spend the rest of your life diverting witty ladies and other children. Dream instead of governing those who govern us. Give us, finally, models from history. It is true that for this task one needs great ambition and great patience and Lord knows what else, if you have enough of it. Leave your work of *gloriole* to march toward the sublimity of true glory. *Paradis aux bienfaizans*.[10]

To understand the development of social thought in the eighteenth century, we must pay some attention to this peculiar figure, at once *enfant terrible* and grand old man. Paying attention to him is not easy; as Emile Faguet once put it, "His works are unreadable; but they deserve to be read."[11] No one who has ever picked up one of Saint-Pierre's books could disagree with the first part of that statement. The second has to be demonstrated.

2. EVANGELISTIC UTILITARIANISM

Everything men value can, and should, be ranked according to comparative utility, which means the tendency to augment human happiness by increasing pleasure and reducing pain. Saint-Pierre held to this principle with singular consistency. He was one of the most thorough-going utilitarians who ever lived. His mind was of that narrow but energetic sort that regards utility as reliable and self-evident. Although he assumed that nations, cultures, and even individuals have distinctive constellations of opinions, he insisted that the basic principles of utilitarianism are "opinions of universal reason," common and evident to all. How can one doubt that "the principal goal of universal reason is the diminution or cessation of evils and of sorrows, and the multiplication and augmentation of goods and pleasures, in the present and future life?" Or that "between two possibilities the wisest is to choose the one most advantageous for oneself and others, which means the one involving fewer ills of briefer duration, which brings more

---

[10] Quoted by Ira O. Wade, *The Intellectual Development of Voltaire*, p. 314 (translation my own). In his *éloge* to the Académie française (1779), d'Alembert associated Saint-Pierre with *bienfaisance*.
[11] "L'Abbé de Saint-Pierre," p. 563, a good brief account of his importance. The best full-length study is Merle Perkins, *The Moral and Political Philosophy of the Abbé de Saint-Pierre*.

pleasures to be tasted for a longer time?"[12] Like Bentham many decades later, he drew up utility calculuses to make these truths readily applicable. Saint-Pierre counseled us to choose that course of action which increases the pleasures of the largest number of families, considering 1) the duration of the pleasures involved, 2) their intensity, 3) the intensity of pains incurred or avoided, and 4) the duration of the pains.[13] He could not see how anyone who understood these truths could contradict them. They did not need to be justified, indeed could not be justified, to a thoughtful man. All else is justified by them.

However, Saint-Pierre did not think men always behaved according to these self-evident principles. The motive of all human action is the search for happiness, but men do not always see what will make them happy. Saint-Pierre's ideas on this topic are rooted in seventeenth-century ethics. He develops arguments found in Malebranche and Abbadie, asserting that "*amour-propre* is the source of all vices and all moral virtues, according to whether it is well or badly understood."[14] He refers to prudence as "circumspect and enlightened *amour-propre*," and in an essay "Against the Opinion of Mandeville," distinguishes three sorts of *amour-propre*: innocent, virtuous, and unjust.[15] Among the virtuous parts of self-love are ambition and the wish to be esteemed by others; these impulses play a large part in Saint-Pierre's moral psychology. He also relied on the concept of interest, asserting that "the end of all men's actions is their interest, that is to say, the conservation and augmentation of their happiness." When we do not understand our true interests, we pursue ephemeral and frivolous interests; true interest in defined as "that course the wisest ordinarily pursue to augment their wealth, their reputation, and their power, to strengthen and aggrandize their family or their state."[16]

The major obstacle to our enlightened pursuit of happiness is the dominance of passion in our lives. "One passion is calmed only by another," asserts Saint-Pierre. "Reason usually comes down on the side of the stronger passion, and there is no violent passion that cannot

---

[12] *Ouvrajes de politique*, XVI, 275-279; countless instances of similar statements could be cited; for example, in III, 225-231; XI, 257-316; and XIII, 226-229.

[13] "Projet pour rendre les livres & autres monuments . . . plus utiles à la postérité," *Ouvrajes de politique*, II, 229. An alternative version of this calculus is in the *Mémoire pour diminuer le nombre des procès* (1725), pp. 66-67.

[14] Merle L. Perkins, ed., "Unpublished Maxims of the *Abbé de Saint-Pierre*" (from the bibliothèque de le ville de Neuchatel), p. 499. In *Ouvrajes de politique*, XVI, 195, a letter to the marquise de Lambert, Saint-Pierre praises Abbadie's ethics, and asserts that *l'amour propre bien antandu* [sic] is *bienfaizant* and therefore *vertueux*.

[15] *Ouvrajes de politique*, XVI, 143-151; see also "pensées diverses," *ibid*., XII, 26-30.

[16] *Projet pour rendre la paix perpétuelle en Europe* (1713), pp. 32-33.

find its reason to authorize it."[17] The gap between the happiness we intend and the evils we actually bring about is explained primarily by the strength of passion; and the effective governance of men depends on discovering passions strong enough to neutralize those that threaten to destroy us. The ultimate countervailing passion that can be relied on to goad men into happiness is the fear of hellfire and damnation. The fear of death alone is not enough, whatever Hobbes may have said. But the fear of death followed by the certainty of eternal torment should make anyone think twice; and the hope for eternal bliss can be sufficiently attractive to lead men to sacrifice their own immediate selfish pleasures to the happiness of other people. If we bring the life beyond the grace into the equation, we can expect ordinary men acting in their own self-interest to behave satisfactorily.

If such deterrence and reward is to perform its function, men must, of course, be convinced of the existence of a perfectly omniscient and exacting God who disposes of an afterlife of recompense for deeds done in this world. Saint-Pierre asserted the existence of such a God, although his *deus* had about him the suspicious odor of the *machina*. Even the abbé admitted his existence could not be proved. He adopted pieces of Pascal's wager to bolster his assertion. But unlike Pascal, Saint-Pierre's commitment to utility went deeper than his religious faith. He said that what is important about God is not whether His existence can be demonstrated, but how extraordinarily handy it is that men should believe in Him. As he put it in another context, "illusions, when they are useful to society, are illusions and errors more valuable than truths that are less useful in augmenting our happiness. If we care too much about the solidity of our pleasures and want to be rid of illusions, we risk losing an infinite number of very real advantages produced by those illusions."[18]

Thus Saint-Pierre turned Jansenism on its head—or on its feet—by firmly subordinating life after death to life here on earth. His own golden age was located at the end of human history, when men will have achieved a high level of happiness and behave much more rationally, and yet can still make incremental contributions to perfecting *la condition humaine*.[19] No static utopia would have satisfied this

[17] "Unpublished maxims," p. 499; *Ouvrajes de politique*, xi, 295-304. In the 1717 edition of his *Projet* for perpetual peace, pp. 153-154, Saint-Pierre deals with the contention that men are quite capable of acting against their own evident best interests. The abbé says that even our strong passions do not lead us to do things we can see clearly will make us worse off; but they constantly distort our perceptions, and lead us to act against our true interests.
[18] *Ouvrajes de politique*, xii, 28; see also v, 126-130, and x, 291-297.
[19] "Observations sur le progrès continuel de la Raison universelle," *Ouvrajes de politique*, xi, 257-294.

devotee of projects. He thought progress was occurring every day, and urged the government to identify and reward clever reasoners able to discern true interests, and put their findings into effect for the benefit of all. Fear of eternal torment, however effective, is a crude device for social control. Saint-Pierre wanted to encourage the development of more refined devices for manipulation and direction of men in society. He was confident that education and laws could be designed to produce docile, industrious, conscientious men.

The abbé's views on education recall those of Montaigne and Pascal, in their emphasis on the power of custom and habit to shape nature itself. He asserts that "man is nothing but a synthesis of different habits," including those of heart, which we call virtues and vices, and those of the mind, which are talents and opinions, the arts and sciences. "What makes the great difference in the worth of men is the difference in the value of their principal habits."[20] But Saint-Pierre departed sharply from his predecessors in his assurance that particular habits can be systematically inculcated by education, and his conviction that this inculcation is the business of the state. He proposed to take advantage of education "to counterpose successfully the force of habit, that is to say the force of a second nature—just, beneficent, enlightened, patient—to the force of our first nature—ignorant, imprudent, unjust."[21] Youths should be given models in life and literature to emulate, in an extensive system of public education. They should be encouraged to compete for esteem and distinction, and pressured in subtle ways to conform to accepted notions of good behavior.

Emulation, competition, and conformity—these were Saint-Pierre's basic principles in education. To ensure that men would imitate worthy models, the abbé proposed the institution of a "bureau of virtuous and knowledgeable people" to encourage the creation of the right kind of literature and art, direct the systematic revision of the great works of the past to make them serve useful purposes, and suppress unwanted books.[22] Conformity for Saint-Pierre meant conformity with good behavior, not unthinking reverence. Superstitious acceptance of the opinions of the ancients was a major impediment to the progress of human reason. Freedom of any sort must prove its utility in prac-

---

[20] *Ouvrajes de politique*, VI, 159; see also the *Projet pour perfectionner l'éducation*, in the abbé's *Oeuvres diverses* (1730), I, 15-70, 106-115; and *Ouvrajes de politique*, X, 201-202.

[21] *Les Rêves d'un homme de bien qui peuvent être réalisés*, a selection from the abbé's writings, pp. 309-310.

[22] *Ouvrajes de politique*, VII, 1-12; XIII, 114-120, and XVI, 284 ff., where the abbé illustrates this proposal by rewriting two of Plutarch's lives, those of Lycurgus and of Solon.

tice, or be ruled out. Laissez-faire notions in economics passed Saint-Pierre's test of utility, and he advocated more freedom of trade.[23] But liberty of thought that does not conduce to social improvement is useless and even dangerous. "Charity, concord, and tranquillity are greater goods than truth," he said; "and hatred, persecution, division, and civil wars are greater evils than ignorance and errors." Unlike his predecessors who had lived through civil war, Saint-Pierre's aversion was not grounded on experience, but on temperament. Conflict is messy, useless, and diverts attention from more important things. "It is good policy to snuff out by commanded silence all partisan sentiment and forbid anyone to speak for or against a faction. . . . Liberty should be augmented when it makes for good, license repressed when it leads to evil."[24]

It did not occur to the abbé that enforced silence might not provide the best atmosphere for social progress, for he assumed the hegemony of clear, distinct, and unilinear truths of universal reason. Persistent sources of conflict were ignored or discounted in his thought. He was persuaded of the fundamental harmony between the happiness of each individual and the long-run happiness of the human race. But realizing such harmony requires careful guidance and direction by those few men naturally superior to others in intellect and virtue. The second nature provided by our environment can diminish or neutralize the effects of first nature, but never wipe it out completely; authority will always be necessary among men. Like many another thinker before and after, Saint-Pierre's theory of education was indistinguishable from his theory of government. Both employ beneficent authority to guide imperfect men in the paths of happiness, and confer such authority on a self-recognizant elite who are responsible for the secular salvation of society.

3. THE MACHINE OF STATE

Among the impediments to the progress of human reason identified by Saint-Pierre are wars civil and foreign, superstition in science and religion, and false beliefs about *la sianse politique* on the part of rulers. When he finished describing what must be done to remove these obstacles and prevent their reappearance, he had sketched out a rational political machine. Although the term "enlightened despotism" was coined much later, it is appropriate to use it in discussing Saint-Pierre's

[23] "Projet pour perfectionner le commerce de France," *Ouvrajes de politique*, v, 170-183.
[24] *Ouvrajes de politique*, v, 130; vi, 83; x, 316-317; and xiii, 110, are similar.

politics. He specified that "in order to perfect the government of a state one must increase the *lumières* of those who wish to govern it well"; and he insisted that "when power is united to reason, it cannot be too great or too despotic for the greatest utility of society."[25] The Bodinian theory of sovereignty was basic to his argument; there is nothing worse, proclaimed Saint-Pierre, than "a divided authority." But neither Bodin nor anyone else before the eighteenth century had been willing to use "despotism" as a term of approbation, as Saint-Pierre did. He spoke with equanimity of France as a "despotic state," and criticized Louis XIV for stopping short of full realization of his program for rationalizing the French polity and clearing away feudal debris. Had he completed what he began, "it is true that we should be governed more despotically, but also far more tranquilly. To be assured of durable civil tranquillity is much more desirable for subjects than to have less despotism in government, but be plagued by a larger number of lesser power centers and perpetual petty despots, continually troubling the public tranquillity by their opposition and their dissident views on politics."[26] Saint-Pierre took up the old image of the monarch as protector of all people against petty tyrants, and refashioned him into the benevolent autocrat of the eighteenth century. Like Mercier de la Rivière, he associated benevolent despotism with the light of reason, and carefully differentiated it from the harsh irrational phenomenon sometimes called by the same name, or by the name "tyranny" instead.[27] But the distinction between a "royal" absolute monarchy, self-restrained and bridled by the law, and a "despotic" or seigneurial monarchy acting toward subjects with the full authority of a master over slaves, which had been retained in Bodin's *République*, was abandoned. In Saint-Pierre's theory, enlightened authority working according to evident principles of reason to maximize human happiness required no limitation.

However, Saint-Pierre also developed another familiar argument in French thought that had quite different implications. He asserted that the true goal in political science is to construct a "perpetual-motion machine" that runs smoothly on its own energy. The machine should

[25] *Ouvrajes de politique*, III, 197; see also III, 203 and IX, 280. On the general subject of "enlightened despotism," Peter Gay's bibliographical note to *The Enlightenment* II, 682-689, is useful; see also Leonard Krieger, *An Essay on the Theory of Enlightened Despotism*.
[26] *Ouvrajes de politique*, IX, 279; see also IX, 18-19; VI, 11-13; and XI, 149-150.
[27] Saint-Pierre uses *despotisme* in the derogatory sense interchangeably with *tirannie* in the *Mémoire sur la polysynodie*, pp. 114-115, and *Projet pour la paix perpetuelle*, pp. 223-229. Mercier de la Rivière praised the beneficent despotism of reason in *L'Ordre naturel et essentiel des sociétés politiques* (1767), chs. XXII-XXIV.

not depend on the accidental presence of a god-like ruler at its head. If a state is fortunate enough to have such a sovereign, he can tinker with the machine, repair it if necessary, ensure that it runs at optimal efficiency. If, as is more likely, the will of the monarch is deficient or debased, the machine should run in spite of him. The "enlightened despotic authority" described by Saint-Pierre is not necessarily associated with a single human will. Ideally, it is exercised by an impersonal political system constructed by knowledgeable experts, controlling human lives for good. The abbé occasionally spoke of the king "outside" the state, operating the springs (*ressorts*) that make the machine run.[28] More often he insisted that the true goal is to construct a machine so effective that no operator is needed. "The highest point in politics," said Saint-Pierre, "is to find or establish a form of government that will perfect itself independently of any talented or hardworking monarch. This is what I think I have discovered and demonstrated; but it is up to a wise king or prime minister to establish it."[29]

The fuel that would keep such an intricate machine running of its own accord is the interest of every person in the state, the pursuit of happiness converted into the measures that promote the public good. "The supreme political achievement," according to the abbé, would be "to construct a little society with so much artifice that it could conserve itself and grow by itself, so that in each member in working for the whole always knows that he gains more by working for others than by working for himself alone."[30] Like Bossuet before him and Rousseau after, Saint-Pierre was convinced that "it is interest that divides us but interest that unites us, too. . . . What determines our inclination is where we think our greater interest lies, on the side of division or of union."[31] Some of our interests are "particular," confined to individuals; these tend to divide us from other men. But some we have in common; and Saint-Pierre uses the term *intérêt publique* to denominate areas where particular interests converge for the common good. It is not enough to preach the common good, or even force men to act according to its dictates. Government, to be effec-

[28] This image is used, significantly enough, in the "Plan d'éducation des daufins," *Ouvrajes de politique*, VI, 162, where Saint-Pierre asserts that "a great State can be thought of as a huge machine that the king should operate [*faire mouvoir*] by means of different springs of various sorts. It is therefore necessary that he who is to become king know the principal parts of his machine, which is to say, all the different employments and the honorable and useful rewards that are distributed to all public officials." See also *Ouvrajes de politique*, III, 81-85, and *Polysynodie*, pp. 44-45.
[29] *Ouvrajes de politique*, XII, 202-203; see also III, 198-200, and VI, 33-34.
[30] *Ouvrajes de politique*, VI, 51; cf. *Polysynodie*, pp. 1-3, and *Rêves*, pp. 31-32.
[31] *Projet pour la paix perpétuelle*, p. 150.

tive, must lead them by their naturally strong passions to act in their own best interests as they serve the public purposes. Once a machine has been established that can do this effectively, it will perpetually renew itself, "because the gears are well-meshed with one another, that is, the members are sufficiently united by their particular interests to conspire together for the public interest."[32]

Constructing a well-made political machine depends on three things: making good laws, to show subjects what to do and what to avoid; creating good institutions, which means arranging for men to enforce those laws; and ensuring that those officers see their own interests in the enforcement and observation of the laws. Careful legislation manipulates the alternatives available to individuals so that decisions in calculating utility lead to behavior that tends to the public good. As Saint-Pierre put it, "it is necessary to assume that in society the interest of individuals will incessantly and strongly conflict with the public interest and often come to dominate and ruin society unless the Legislator arranges laws and regulations so that particular individuals cannot advance their selfish interests except by procuring the interest of others at the same time." He recognized that "such laws are hard to find, and even harder to establish," but was convinced that assiduous research by determined experts in the science of politics would yield good results in finding them. The goal is to create a situation in which "the penalty necessarily attached to the infringement of the law is sufficiently inevitable that no citizen is ever tempted to resist the law."[33]

Good legislation will take care of that part of the political machine that affects ordinary men most directly. To ensure that the penalty will appear "sufficiently inevitable," there must be an effective set of magistrates who can rigorously enforce those laws. Most of Saint-Pierre's efforts were devoted to describing how such magistrates should be identified, trained, and rewarded. The study of the "master-science" of politics should be diffused throughout the kingdom, by means of regular *conferences de sianse politique* in each district. These little gatherings would instill the rudiments of good government and stress obedience to law, not cultivate *un esprit frondeur*.[34] The most important purpose of the meetings would be to give talent a chance to show itself in discussions of the science of politics. Men

[32] *Ouvrajes de politique*, VI, 34; in the *Polysynodie*, pp. 102-105, Saint-Pierre specifies in more detail how ambition can be channeled for the common interest.
[33] *Polysynodie*, p. 117; *Mémoire pour diminuer le nombre des procès*, p. 22; cf. *Ouvrajes de politique*, II, 95.
[34] *Ouvrajes de politique*, IV, 82-91.

who distinguished themselves would be singled out and given responsibility for government. From this point all the way to the top of the system, Saint-Pierre proposed a pure "meritocracy," in which the only qualification for governing would be demonstrated capacity for doing so. At each level, from local assemblies through the provincial intendancies to the council of the king, officers would be selected by a process called *scrutin*, particularly dear to Saint-Pierre's heart. This was an adaptation of popular election designed to incorporate its virtues without its disadvantages. Small companies of colleagues, no more than thirty, would select three of their number as candidates for participation in government at the next higher level. Officials at that higher level would choose one among the three, and so on. Only the king himself would be appointed by the lottery of birth, to ensure the continuation of hereditary legitimacy for the throne.

Saint-Pierre gave much thought to the details of this system, to guard against bribery, cabals, and lethargy. As in Veiras's Sevarambian utopia, those best suited to rule would rise from the lowest levels of the state; but the mass of mediocre citizens had no role except starting the talented on the road to power. This was technocratic absolutism, not parliamentary constitutionalism. The rulers were not accountable to those who chose them, and had absolute authority over those from whom they had emerged. The element of responsibility in the system came from their mutual supervision of each other, and the competition of their interests. Saint-Pierre saw nothing to be gained, and much to be lost, by subjecting experts to the criticism of ordinary subjects. He called his system *aristo-monarchie*, and had no patience with democracy; for he was convinced that men "are born and develop quite unequal in wit, talent, application, work, and virtue."[35]

After his paragons were recruited, Saint-Pierre proposed to pay them well in coin and status, so that they would find personal satisfaction in their jobs and become appropriate objects for others to emulate. They should rotate jobs regularly, to avoid the institution of vested interests and to multiply perspectives. To maximize accountability, Saint-Pierre wanted the parlements retained and strengthened; this was an element of traditional constitutionalism in his thought. He specified that all decisions should be made collegially, so that each member would be ashamed to be seen trying to bend policy to his own advantage, and the expertise of all could be shared.[36] The reason that enlightens his political machine is not a god-like clarity shining

[35] The system of *scrutin* is described in *Ouvrajes de politique*, III, 128-196; the term *aristo-monarchie* appears in the *Polysynodie*, p. 45.
[36] *Polysynodie*, pp. 31-34; *Ouvrajes de politique*, VI, 94-97; and III, 174-175.

from outside the state, but the reason of the most capable men in the society put to systematic use. Their native intelligence, strengthened by the principles of *la sianse politique*, will ensure that their decisions are the most enlightened possible.

Saint-Pierre relied on interest as the most effective guarantee and stimulus of good government. He described a process in which particular interests of officers and their offices clash and neutralize one another so that the public interest can prevail. This was the basis of the *polysynodie* that he proposed—multiple interests, as well as multiple perspectives, brought to bear on any policy. The abbé indicated that he thought the way to find "our true interest" on any subject is to weigh all the different specific interests that are involved in it against each other, taking into account present and future pleasures and pains.[37] In recommending that ministers should put forward several opinions on the public interest and speak for different particular interests, as well, and in asserting that the best answer to political dilemmas will be found by such a process, Saint-Pierre sketched the elements of an argument that became central in the theory of the marquis d'Argenson, and later of Rousseau himself. It is worth pondering Rousseau's paraphrase of the passage in Saint-Pierre's "Discours sur la polysynodie" where the abbé enumerates the advantages of collegial decision making. It is a free paraphrase, which puts the matter more abstractly than Saint-Pierre's passage. The important thing is what Rousseau found in musing on it, at the time his own political ideas were just beginning to be formed:

> Let us consider now the true end of government and the obstacles that separate us from it. That end is obviously the greatest interest of the state and of the king; those obstacles are, in addition to the lack of *lumières*, the private interests of administrators. From this it follows that the more private interests find harassment and opposition, the less they will weigh against the public interest; so that if they can clash with each other and mutually destroy each other, however strong we may suppose them, they will become null in deliberation, and the public interest alone will be heard. What better way to annihilate all these private interests than to oppose them to each other by the multiplication of those expressing an opinion? That which makes interests private is that they are not in accord; for if they were they would no longer be private but common interests. If all these interests are destroyed by one another, the pub-

[37] *Mémoire pour diminuer le nombre des procès*, p. 412.

lic interest remains, and ought to gain in deliberation all that which the private interests have lost.[38]

The difference between Saint-Pierre's intricate *polysynodie* and the rule by numerous "perpetual petty despots" he condemned lies in the science of legislation and constitution making that ensures the emergence of the common interest from the clash and the convergence of private interests. The education of magistrates has something to do with this, as does the concentration of absolute decision-making power at the top. But it was Saint-Pierre's faith in the possibility of engineering the expression of private interests to make them yield the public good that was the bedrock of his system. He retained the Jansenist conviction that a harmony akin to charity can be brought out of concupiscence itself, although he relied on enlightened political men to create such a harmony rather than depending wholly on divine providence.[39] Saint-Pierre shifted discussion of individual interests from the economy and the salon to the polity itself, from the periphery to the center of domestic political concerns.

The abbé's account of the several ways private interests can be made to yield the public good was ingenious. The most direct route is when men find their own selfish interest in the common good, seeing in it "their glory, the augmentation of their income, the avoidance of some pain, or some other particular interest." A more oblique route, which fascinated Rousseau, is the route of conflict, in which competitive private interests clash with one another to allow the common good to show itself, although Saint-Pierre was not very clear about how this manifestation would occur. A third route is opened up by good laws, which require men to "take some thought for the interest of their associates," and make it in our interest to observe the golden rule. And finally, men who are enlightened enough to see where their "true interests" lie will understand that their selfish happiness—the maximum sum of long-run pleasure—is assured if they contribute to the "common good" rather than subverting it.[40]

But Saint-Pierre's conception of the "common good" or "public interest" that will emerge in all these ways was neither rich nor well

[38] Rousseau, "Polysynodie de l'abbé de Saint-Pierre," in *Oeuvres complètes*, III, 628, cf. Saint-Pierre, *Ouvrajes de politique*, VI, 361-362.

[39] *Ouvrajes de politique*, II, 107 advises statesmen to emulate the practice of God, who governs "free and immortal beings by general laws, and conducts them to their greatest happiness without diminishing any of their precious liberty," because of his understanding of their motives and their interests.

[40] *Ouvrajes de politique*, III, 131-132; *Mémoire pour diminuer le nombre des procès*, pp. 406-413.

defined. Peace, civil tranquillity, the progress of human reason, and the maintenance of a well-ordered society that allows individuals to live commodious lives—these are the things loosely associated with the "common good" in his philosophy. His ideal society is made up of individuals pursuing their own interests by means of "self-love rightly understood and well conducted." He lacked any concept of a secular analogue to *la charité*, a "common good" such as that enjoyed in the Jansenist community of saints, a good that is common by virtue of being shared by all together, which individuals intent on maximizing private happiness can never know. In all his voluminous writings, there is no sense of a community made up of parts of a larger whole, in which the self-love of individuals is extended and enriched in love of something beyond self.

4. THE MARQUIS D'ARGENSON ON INTEREST AND *Amour-propre*

In the notes to his *Contrat social*, Rousseau quotes several times from a manuscript "unknown to the public," by a man to whom he attributes "the heart of a true citizen, and correct and sane views on the government of his country."[41] The man was René-Louis de Voyer de Paulmy, marquis d'Argenson; the manuscript was entitled *Jusques où la démocratie peut être admise dans le gouvernement monarchique*. A mutilated version was published in 1764 as the *Considérations sur le gouvernement ancien et présent de la France*.[42] But the cumbersome title chosen by the author is a better indication of the contents of the book. Why, asked d'Argenson, must democracy and monarchy always be opposed to one another? Why not use the strengths of each as a cure for the defects of the other? To show how this might be done, and prove that it would support rather than subvert sovereignty, were the tasks the marquis set himself.

Like his aristocratic precursors under Louis XIV, d'Argenson was

---

[41] Rousseau, *Du contrat social*, book I, ch. 2; book II, ch. 3, book II, ch. 11, and book IV, ch. 8. Rousseau was not much given to citations; d'Alembert and Montesquieu are mentioned once, as is Bodin. Only Machiavelli and Tacitus were mentioned as frequently as d'Argenson.

[42] The title page of the *Considérations* bears the name of Rousseau's own publisher, Marc-Michel Rey of Amsterdam; it was reissued in 1765. Ira Wade, *The Intellectual Development of Voltaire*, p. 316, asserts that it was Gabriel Cramer who published it, at Voltaire's instigation. A second edition of the *Considérations*, greatly altered, was published in 1784 by d'Argenson's son, Paulmy. This edition incorporates several passages found in extant late manuscripts of the treatise, but was apparently heavily rewritten by Paulmy. For an assessment of the reliability of both editions, consult Peter Gessler, *René Louis d'Argenson*, pp. 197-199, and Nannerl O. Henry [Keohane], "Democratic Monarchy: The Political Theory of the Marquis d'Argenson," pp. 307-311.

moved to write by his distress at the consequences of the regime's misguided policies. Throughout his extensive journals, he comments on the misery of the French people, the stupidities of the fiscal system, the parasitic court, and the depopulation of the provinces. Fénelon's influence is clear in those passages where d'Argenson describes the Sun King as a *beau comédien*, attracting applause for the splendor of his court while presiding over the ruin of his country. The entire regime is so badly organized, said the marquis, that "each new remedy becomes a new evil. This evil has spread so that it undermines and ruins the interior of our provinces, which have become like a great hospital."[43] D'Argenson's goal was to "bring back true principles" to French politics, to "renew happiness and abundance," in order to ward off disaster.[44] He bent his efforts to convincing members of the government of his principles, and attempted to win power so he could put them into effect. The marquis confided to his journals a cherished fantasy that he would one day be given full power to reorder France, so that he could play Sully to Louis XV's Henry IV.

D'Argenson once said he spent his whole life studying to be prime minister.[45] This was not a completely unrealistic goal. His father was the redoubtable lieutenant of police in Paris, and there had been ministers, magistrates, ambassadors, and intendants on both sides of his family for generations. His own preparation for power probably included attendance at Torcy's Académie politique, where the curriculum focused on "interests of state."[46] Although he never became prime minister, d'Argenson did hold other offices, including counsellor to the parlement of Paris, counsellor of state, and minister of foreign affairs. However, his political effectiveness was hampered by his reputation as

[43] *Journal et mémoires du marquis d'Argenson*, edited by E.J.B. Rathery, VII, 78. Cf. II, 219; IV, 107; and VI, 271. The reference to the *beau comédien* is in another edition of the *Mémoires et journal inédit* by the marquis's great-grandnephew Charles René d'Argenson, published by Jannet, V, 277. The Rathery edition is the more scholarly and reliable, but not without its flaws; the Jannet edition includes material drawn from papers that Rathery did not use. On the difficulties with both editions and the controversies surrounding their publication, see Henry, "Democratic Monarchy," pp. 303-307.

[44] Jannet edition, V, 129 and 349; Rathery, ed., VIII, 222. D'Argenson is an exception to the generalization that opens Tocqueville's study of *L'Ancien régime*, that the Revolution was "inevitable, but completely unforeseen." In these passages he predicts the Revolution along lines very much like those it took in 1789.

[45] Rathery, ed., VII, 78; see also II, 219; IV, 107, and VI, 271.

[46] D'Argenson mentions the academy in his journals, with no indication that he was a pupil there; see Rathery, ed., I, 144, and Jannet edition, I, 101-109. On the academy itself, and evidence of René-Louis's attendance, see Joseph Klaits, "Men of Letters and Political Reform in France." Gessler, *René Louis d'Argenson*, provides a satisfactory biography, as does Arthur Ogle, *The Marquis d'Argenson*.

a blunt eccentric who lacked all courtly graces, and by his idealism. Like Fénelon, he was known to be chimerical, a citizen of the republic of Plato rather than a man of the world. He was also a free-thinker, a protégé of Saint-Pierre, and friend of Voltaire from his schooldays. Such were not the assets respected at Versailles.[47]

Like his mentor, Saint-Pierre, d'Argenson was convinced that the reformation of the government of France depended on the application of principles of political science discovered by philosophers beginning with the Greeks, and advanced by hard-working contemporaries. But the marquis thought Saint-Pierre's plans suffered from the lack of any experience in government.[48] He was optimistic about his own qualifications for governing because he combined practical experience with philosophy. By far the largest part of his journals is composed of trenchant and detailed observations of the contemporary political scene, interlaced with d'Argenson's own schemes for winning office. There are also many reports on books he read, contemporary as well as classical. Throughout his life, d'Argenson was a voracious reader. The books listed in the catalogue of his library at his death include almost all of those mentioned in this study, plus numerous works on history, theology, the theater, a sizable collection of tracts by sixteenth-century Huguenots, as well as *mazarinades* from the Fronde.[49] He also produced a small mountain of essays, *mémoires*, journals, and treatises, all written in his distinctive rough, idiosyncratic style.[50] D'Argenson published little, noting that Saint-Pierre was branded as ridiculous for publishing his schemes; he reported that when he tried to broach some of his own ideas to colleagues in government, they

[47] D'Argenson's correspondance with Voltaire is available in the Jannet edition and in standard editions of Voltaire's letters; Saint-Pierre is mentioned often in d'Argenson's journals. D'Argenson was a regular guest at the Wednesday dinners of the marquise de Lambert, who tried to persuade him to allow her to present him as a candidate for the Académie française (Rathery, ed., I, 164).

[48] Rathery, ed., I, 342-343; Jannet edition, v, 260-261, 313-314. On d'Argenson's own political science, consult Sergio Cotta, "Il problema politica" and Joseph Gallanar, "Argenson's 'Platonic Republics.'"

[49] D'Argenson observed that the lust for books is the most excusable of luxuries (Jannet edition, v, 157). Part of his library is preserved in the Bibliothèque de l'Arsenal, but much of it was sold at his death; the sale *Catalogue des livres de la bibliothèque de Monsieur **** is in the Bibliothèque nationale.

[50] A list of the works by d'Argenson in the Louvre, more than forty cartons of papers, was drawn up by his son and included in Henri Martin's *Catalogue des manuscrits* of the Bibliothèque de l'Arsenal, VIII, 74-77. Henri Lagrave, "Une Oeuvre inédité du marquis d'Argenson," p. 197, calls him a *maniaque de plume*. His homely style prompted contemporary parodies, but won the admiration of Sainte-Beuve (*Causeries du lundi*, XII, 110-111). As Grimm is supposed to have said, "It is impossible that an author so completely without affectation should not be telling the truth" (Rathery, ed., I, xiv).

yawned and closed their ears, writing him off as a man with odd ideas.[51] Most of the papers in which he developed those projects and ideas were burned in the Bibliothèque du Louvre in 1871. But enough remains to make clear why both Rousseau and Voltaire admired this *ministre-philosophe*, and prove his importance in Enlightenment political philosophy.

From the point of view of his social theory, the most important office d'Argenson held was that of intendant in the province of Hainault and Cambrésis. Living on the Flemish border gave him a firsthand opportunity to observe the contrast between the vigorous people of a free republic and the miserable, entangled citizens of an absolutist state. Like the Ohio River for Tocqueville, the border between France and Flanders proved to d'Argenson the superiority of equality and free institutions.[52] He developed contempt for venal officials and "embroidered fops" who handed down decrees in ignorance of local conditions. He discovered how effective ordinary human beings can be when they work in their interests and participate in directing their own affairs, instead of being held in leading-strings and taxed to death. "The true defect of monarchy," he argued, "is to wish to conduct everything by its own diverse agents, so that art snuffs out nature." To give free play to natural human inventiveness and the energy of individual action was the most urgent need of the French polity, in his eyes. Over and over he cried *"Laissez-faire*—that should be the motto of all public power, now that the world is civilized."[53]

A large number of d'Argenson's earliest *mémoires* develop arguments drawn up by men such as Boisguilbert and Belesbat in opposition to mercantilist policies. He recommended

> that each individual be left alone to labor on his own behalf, instead of suffering constraint and ill-conceived precautions. Then everything will go beautifully. . . . It is precisely this perfection of liberty that makes a science of commerce impossible, in the sense that our speculative thinkers understand it. They want to direct commerce by their orders and regulations; but to do this one would need to be thoroughly acquainted with the interests involved in commerce, not

[51] Jannet edition, v, 304; Rathery, ed., vii, 390-391.
[52] Rathery, ed., i, 35-46; *Considérations*, 1765 edition, p. 64; cf. Tocqueville, *Democracy in America*, i, ch. 10. Further information about d'Argenson's experiences as an intendant is provided in C. Tassin, "Un Membre de l'Académie de l'Entresol," p. 351. Tassin was working in the d'Argenson papers in the Louvre before it burned, and published several excerpts not available elsewhere.
[53] Tassin, "Un Membre de l'Académie," p. 350; Jannet edition, v, 364; Jannet, ed., iii, 394-395, 353.

only from the nation to another, but from province to province, from town to town, from one individual to another. In the absence of such knowledge, it [that is, the science of commerce] can only be a demi-science much worse than ignorance in its bad effects. . . . *Eh, qu'on laisse-faire!*[54]

D'Argenson remained interested in economics throughout his life. The only pieces he published, in fact, were several articles in the *Journal oeconomique* in the 1750s, one of which includes the first public use of the slogan *laissez-faire*.[55] But unlike Boisguilbert, d'Argenson was less interested in the economic effects of laissez-faire than its pertinence for politics. He was convinced that the potentially benevolent effects of letting men alone to pursue their impulses extended into every part of political and social life. This conviction was closely connected with the idea that interest is the mainspring of all human action, and that the prolific complexity of interest is too intricate for a single mind to encompass, let alone direct. The only reasonable course of action, therefore, is to let men alone.

D'Argenson's theory of interest, like that of his seventeenth-century predecessors, was connected with his theory of self-love. He described *amour-propre* as a necessary component of human psychology, "like bile or gall, troublesome humors but necessary ones," which should not be allowed to dominate our psychology completely, but which we cannot do without. Self-love spurs us to identify our own interests and undertake energetic and productive activities in the pursuit of happiness. These sentiments are "the source and primary engine of emulation, and even of virtue itself, unfortunately for humanity." Unlike some of his predecessors, however, d'Argenson did not think that fallen men are completely selfish. We can love ourselves well or badly, and if well, we also love something beyond ourselves. He asserted that the "second part of our affections is that which is called *amour pur*, a faculty of our soul that it would be wrong to deny, since almost all men possess it, and those who lack it entirely are monsters."[56] In the realm of religion, this sentiment is the pure disinterested love of God; in worldly things it expresses itself in a secular form of charity, a disinterested love of other men and of our country, which d'Argenson equated with *bienfaisance*. Thus d'Argenson placed self-

---

[54] Rathery, ed., IV, 455-456; cf. I, 375, and a set of *pensées* reproduced by E. Levasseur, "Le Marquis d'Argenson," pp. 80-81.

[55] *Journal oeconomique* II: 1 (April 1751), 107-117; cf. Auguste Oncken, *Die Maxime Laissez faire et laissez passer*, and Edward R. Kittrell, "'Laissez-Faire' in English Classical Economics."

[56] Rathery, ed., I, 185-187; Jannet edition, I, 224-226; *Essais dans le goût de ceux de Montaigne* (edited by d'Argenson's son in 1785), I, 152-155.

love within the context of a larger set of loves, and denied that our concern for self necessarily entails enmity to other human beings.

In d'Argenson's view, the most natural human condition is the tranquil pursuit of simple happiness, following one's *métier* in the midst of one's own family, and in so doing, serving the happiness of others primarily by refraining from harming them. In such a situation, our natural love of self is perfectly compatible with our capacity for caring about others. But civilization has ruined this equilibrium by introducing inequality and luxury, and magnifying human avarice and ambition beyond their natural extent. In modern times, prevailing *moeurs* teach us to lust for everything, and to value only those gains that involve someone else's loss, laments d'Argenson. The false morality of *la cour* suffocates the natural sentiments of *le coeur*. Whereas earlier centuries had produced virtuous men worthy of comparison with Aristides or Cato, d'Argenson saw his own era as peopled with petty, grasping, intriguing courtiers. The complicated polities we have constructed, far from encouraging us to virtue, depend on vice and promote hypocrisy.

> The general parades his willingness to sacrifice himself for his country's good. In fact his cruel ambition drives him on, and he works for the continuation of the war, so far as this is in his power. The judge says he embodies justice, and puffs himself up about this; but he encourages fraud and laughs delightedly at the sight of a fat, well-fed legal matter. The ambitious statesman destroys humanity and justice while he vaunts his midnight labors as essential to the good of the world. Thus we see everywhere the land dispeopled by avarice for wealth and power.[57]

It had been common in French social theory since the sixteenth century to condemn modern mores and juxtapose them to those of a simpler and more virtuous past. The remedy most frequently suggested was to promote purity and pleasure through philosophy for a small number of elite individuals. A few theorists, such as Montesquieu, discussed the creation of a more vigorous and generous set of *moeurs* for an entire community; but this was described as a rare and difficult process requiring a legislative genius, unusual conditions, and great sacrifices by the people. D'Argenson denied that any great sacrifices or artificial constraints are necessary to make men virtuous. All that is needed is to do away with the artificial taste for luxury, conquest, and intrigue, and give men's natural sentiments an opportunity to show themselves in simpler and more frugal pleasures. He placed his

[57] Jannet edition, v, 218-219, 242-243.

faith for the accomplishment of this clearing-away operation in an enlightened monarch, a *roi philosophe* who would enforce equality among his subjects, giving artificial sentiments no ground in which to flourish, so that they would soon die out. Such a king would initially have to act vigorously to take charge of the state and impose his vision. But that vision would not require a difficult, inhuman virtue; it would look toward the liberation of nature from artifice, and give her a chance to assert herself. Leaving men alone, in d'Argenson's philosophy, means getting rid not only of artificial constraints of state regulation on commerce, but also of the equally artificial spurs to action such as the taste for luxury emanating from a corrupt court. Men left alone would not be motivated by insatiable greed, but rather by a moderate tendency to pursue happiness for themselves and their families.

D'Argenson used the language of interest, more often than the language of self-love, to describe human motivations. Like several of his contemporaries he was fascinated by the interests of the several states of Europe; one of the alternative titles of his major treatise was *Les Intérêts de la France avec ses voisins*. However, his most important contribution lay in describing the ways in which individual interests are combined in common interests. He accepted from seventeenth-century sources the idea that "in general, the best way to judge men is by their interests; and the best method of persuading them is to make them see their own interest in what you propose to them."[58] Although he followed Fénelon in describing *pur amour* as "disinterested," to differentiate it from narrow *amour-propre*, his conviction that men are naturally capable of beneficence shaped his discussion of interest itself. Believing that man are not naturally limited by a narrow focus upon self, he was able to devise a rich notion of *shared* interests, areas of common concern discovered by cooperative human action. Several of his precursors, including the abbé de Saint-Pierre, had observed that interests bring men together as well as separate them, but no one had pursued this observation very far. The standard view was that men motivated by ambition and avarice serve one another's interests as they pursue their own. At best, particularly enlightened men can be led to see their long-run interests in beneficent behavior. D'Argenson was among the first to concern himself with the process by which men discover common worldly interests, not attributable to any individual but only to a set of individuals, as group. In his theory, the notion of interest loses its abstract and atomistic quality, its persistent overtones of selfish separatism, and becomes the fundamental basis for all social life.

[58] *Essais*, I, 7, devoted to Saint-Evremond.

5. Liberty, Equality, and Order

In one of his earliest *pensées*, d'Argenson sketched the rudiments of his theory of common interest. He called for "a return to true principles. The best arbiter of utility is the whole mass of the public, and the uniformity of suffrages of those interested in each matter. Each individual senses his own interest, each takes measures that are profitable for him. It is in this general accord that we discover truth."[59] The best policies, in other words, are discovered by allowing each individual to express his interest, expecting "truth" to be disclosed in the pattern that results. D'Argenson's description of this process of determining and harmonizing interests includes the insight that so intrigued Rousseau: "Each interest has different principles. The agreement of two particular interests is reached on grounds opposed to those of a third. It is this that makes good general laws so difficult to compose."[60] It is in contradistinction to the interests of another group that a set of individuals first discovers what they have in common. If this process is allowed to continue undisturbed, a few genuinely common interests will eventually emerge for the whole group, policies that are in the best interests of each member.

In d'Argenson's political theory, the next step in the process requires a single sovereign intelligence to discern the pattern of common interest and express it in law. The sovereign must judge when individual interests should be allowed to clash energetically "for the good of the general interests," and when they should be restrained to prevent encroachment on other individuals. He alone can decide where the preponderance of interest lies in each conflict, but he depends on information given him in manageable form, through the clash and consolidation of interests. "A king worthy of the name listens to the interests of his people and has no other organ for discovering what these are than their own voice, and no other source than their own free activity." This means, in practice, that "groups of citizens must be able to assemble together, conciliate with one another, and act with a certain independence," in local institutions that allow for "true democracy residing in the midst of monarchy."[61]

D'Argenson's major treatise was written to illustrate and defend these principles, to convince the king and his advisors to include ordinary citizens in the government of France. According to d'Argenson, the development of the monarchy from the earliest times had been accompanied by the "progress of democracy," as kings extended

[59] Jannet edition, v, 384-385. [60] *Considérations*, pp. 26-27.
[61] *Considérations*, pp. 27-28, 263.

equality and municipal liberties at the expense of feudal institutions and seigneurial power.[62] But since the Renaissance, misguided monarchs had reversed the process, withdrawing municipal liberties and creating a new feudalism through the sale of offices. As a result, eighteenth-century Frenchmen were less free than their ancestors. They had no interest in their own affairs, and their economic energies were suffocated by heavy taxation, detailed regulations, and inequalities of wealth. By contrast, in the neighboring provinces of the Netherlands, liberty and equality were effectively combined, and prosperity was the result. Dutch equality was not enforced against Dutch liberties; each citizen was equally free to pursue his own interests. As d'Argenson put it, "Each individual is perfectly free in that which brings no harm to others. From the uses of this liberty, and from the multiplicity of interests that act without combatting one another, immense consequences for commercial prosperity result."[63]

The analysis of the Netherlands is drawn from d'Argenson's careful study of nineteen contemporary European governments, which he undertook in order to extract lessons for his own polity. Among the principles suggested by his research is that small size is important to good government. The provincial governments of the Netherlands and the cantonal governments of Switzerland both demonstrate this principle. Leaders familiar with a small range of interests, and personally interested in their localities, can govern more effectively than distant ministers. In a close-knit community, "reciprocal interests can be better combined, contrary ones are less important." The examples of Holland and Switzerland demonstrate to d'Argenson "that it is useful to divide responsibilities, goods, and districts; and for each sphere of interests, the more its object is manageable, the more its sources of action are lively and durable." To know how to apply this principle judiciously is "one of the first and most essential parts of the practical science of government."[64]

When responsibilities are properly divided up, the next step is to ensure that interests within each little sphere can be freely expressed.

[62] *Considérations*, chs. iv-v. D'Argenson's definition of the democracy that progresses in history is close to that of Tocqueville: equality of all citizens, and participation in local government.

[63] *Considérations*, p. 65; this passage was among those quoted by Rousseau.

[64] *Considérations*, pp. 72, 86-87. This same principle was confirmed, for d'Argenson, by comparing Spain and Portugal. The stagnant absolutist monarchy in Spain rested on exaggerated inequalities of wealth among the people, stemming from the influx of gold from the new world. Portugal, with a similar culture, economy, and colonial experience, was healthier and more prosperous. The difference in size of the two polities was the best explanation for this, asserted d'Argenson.

The sharpest contrast with Dutch liberty was Turkish despotism, a prime example of "all the evils that follow from monarchical government without the admission of any democracy." Following the ancient recipe for despotism, the Turkish regime kept subjects isolated from each other so that "the different parts of the Turkish people" could not "become acquainted with one another, nor collect their common interests, whether of commerce or in politics, or in *moeurs*. What laws, what regulations, what cooperation can possibly result from such a great separation of the parts of the policy?" asked d'Argenson. Even in the most despotic of other European states, there was some arrangement for a "certain number of suffrages capable of representing the interests of the public," through noble councils, for example. "But in Turkey, the sole will of the monarch makes the laws and conducts everything, or rather conducts nothing"; everything "has for its sole object the interest of a greedy and barbarous chief."[65] Just as the Spartans showed their children drunken slaves to instill a horror of wine, the marquis recounted the miseries of the Turkish people to show the awful consequences of despotic monarchy, and prove the need for an infusion of democracy before France traveled too far down that same road.

D'Argenson grouped his own polity with Spain and Portugal as a "despotic monarchy," and shared Montesquieu's fear that France would become a second Spain. To remedy her political ills, and reinstitute the natural alliance of king and people, d'Argenson included at the heart of his treatise a draft constitution for France. This *plan de gouvernement* was designed to transform the regime into a set of "true republics protected by the monarchy," in a series of steps that would upset political tranquillity as little as possible. The overriding purpose was "the admission of the public into the government of the Public to the greatest extent possible."[66] In d'Argenson's plan, magistrates in each community are responsible for the everyday governing of the locality. They are selected by a system based on Saint-Pierre's *scrutin*, and must share power among themselves in groups of at least five officers. They will require no special training or wealth; the marquis

[65] *Considérations*, pp. 114-117.
[66] The plan is presented in ch. VII of the *Considérations*, 1765 edition. The reference to "republics protected by the monarchy" is from a late manuscript of d'Argenson's treatise (Arsenal ms. 2338, p. 6), which was apparently composed after his retirement and incorporates a number of revisions. The plan in the 1784 edition differs from all other versions in providing for provincial and district representative assemblies. These may have been features of one of d'Argenson's later manuscripts, or they could have been added by his son in editing the book. The several manuscripts now extant are described in Henry, "Democratic Monarchy," appendix A.

insists that "even peasants" will fill these posts. Since they are local residents, familiar with local concerns, native intelligence will suffice to qualify them for their duties. Officers of the king will oversee their activities and symbolize the sovereign, who remains the formal source of all power in the state. These intendants can dismiss any magistrate who abuses power; but they will not meddle with details of government. For they can never "know and combine the interests of all the citizens divided in so many ways, and reunite them in light of the general good," as effectively as popular representatives.[67] D'Argenson proposed to rely as much as possible on local energies and local talents for the government of France. He was convinced that people would become enthusiastic and capable governors of themselves when they were involved in matters they could comprehend, and in which they discovered their own interest. "The more the People discovers in regulations a direct and near interest," he asserted, "the less it feels distant from those laws and the more it becomes itself their advocate. And can there be any other laws over men than those that maintain themselves by the agreement and utility of the greatest number?"[68]

For all his faith in popular energies and grass-roots politics, d'Argenson was equally emphatic about the importance of hereditary monarchy to good government. In a plan proposed seriously for the government of France in 1737, this was only common sense; but d'Argenson's commitment to monarchy was principled, as well. He noted that republican government has its own defects. The Dutch regime "has many arms, but lacks a head." Democracies without a monarch lack a *point d'appui* to bring the views of all participating citizens into a coherent policy. Interests are infinitely subdivided, suffrages dissipated in combatting one another, and there is no place in the state where they can all be gathered together into law.[69] In addition to collecting interests into law, the head of state can also defend the little provinces against aggression, and protect them in a crisis. In general, "any machine so complicated, composed of so many parts," as a large modern state, needs a single controlling figure at the top. "The promptness of his orders, the force of his voice, are really necessary for success."[70]

Another argument for monarchy in d'Argenson's eyes was that men cannot manage without mysteries in politics. Convinced that "men

---

[67] *Considérations*, p. 232.   [68] *Considérations*, pp. 31-32, 274-275.
[69] The criticism of the Dutch regime in the 1765 edition is truncated; a fuller version is available in the 1784 edition and in the Arsenal ms., pp. 13-14.
[70] Jannet edition, v, 266.

are always governed by opinion," he was impressed by the tenacity of belief in the sanctity of royalty. He once reflected that it is remarkable how incompetent and contemptible a king can be and yet be obeyed and loved. "Senators who governed a republic thus would long since have been shamed, insulted, stoned to death, their bodies thrown out to the dogs." From this he concludes that "men are naturally drawn to idolatry."[71] They respect and obey a monarch enthroned by the dynastic lottery of birth more than one they have chosen through election; they can believe the former has been sent from God, whereas they know the latter is an ordinary mortal like themselves.

Beyond this, d'Argenson was convinced that the political goods he valued most—liberty and equality—depend on having a single strong individual at the head of state. Such a commitment to equality was unusual in his era, particularly for an aristocrat who took pride in noble birth. But the marquis spoke of equality as "the only legitimate good in politics," *la perfection politique*. He wanted economic equality to be approached as nearly as possible, since he regarded it as essential to political equality. Political equality should be ensured by access of all citizens to power, by making merit the sole criterion for office, and enforcing the Aristotelian principle of ruling and being ruled in turn. Each officer should return to private life as "physical bodies return to repose." All these measures were designed to enhance liberty. For d'Argenson, as for Rousseau, liberty depends upon equality. "Liberty," he asserted, "can only maintain itself in equality or near equality."[72]

The most important office of a monarch, in his theory, is thus the maintenance of equality among citizens. Only a monarch can prevent the rise of petty local tyrants, support municipal assemblies against municipal elites, preserve a healthy degree of social and economic leveling, and ensure equal justice for all citizens. Republics throughout history, noted d'Argenson, tend to dissolve into oligarchies or submit to demagogues. Contemporary Genoa attested to this tendency for republics to decay after their first "moment of heated devotion to the

[71] Jannet edition, v, 278. In an unpublished essay on "L'Etat de la tyrannie en Europe pendant le dixhuitième siècle," in the Archives des affaires etrangères (m.d.f. 502, part 2), p. 69, d'Argenson speaks of the prince as the personification of *la Patrie*, but deplores the tendency for *le symbolique* to become *la réalité* as the state absorbs the public interest.

[72] "Discours sur l'inégalité," submitted by d'Argenson in competition for the same Dijon prize that prompted Rousseau's second *Discourse*; in Roger Tisserand, ed., *Les Concurrents de J.-J. Rousseau*, pp. 118-125. See also Jannet edition, v, 188-190, 271-276, and 311-312.

common good," as "everything becomes indolent, individual interest is the sole concern, and its attacks the general interest." Monarchy is an effective antidote to this disease, for

> Monarchy can easily and promptly remedy the evils of inequality, as soon as it sees its own interest clearly. This consists, in fact, in only commanding men equal among themselves, as far as is humanly possible. . . . All the other powers, subordinate and intermediate, discover diversions from the public happiness in their particularistic views. It is this against which the sovereign must continually be on guard. If one allows this principle its full scope, perhaps it will be seen that the art of ruling consists solely in establishing approximate equality.[73]

The marriage of absolute sovereignty and extensive popular participation proposed in d'Argenson's reformist plan for France was expected to work smoothly for several reasons. Habits of deference and obedience would lead ordinary Frenchmen to accept the authority of officers of the king instead of creating obstacles to royal power. Popular power would be decentralized, and there would be safeguards against too much cooperation among the little republics throughout France. National assemblies would be avoided, to keep France from following the English route.[74] The guarantees for the good behavior of the monarch himself were variants of those suggested by Seyssel long ago. The French monarchy, asserts d'Argenson, is "tempered by *les moeurs, la raison, et la justice*. These three bridles, so sweet and amiable, when they are attended to, ceaselessly exhort the sovereign to take counsel and choose the best counsellors from all orders of his state."[75] Moreover, d'Argenson thought human social life has a natural

---

[73] "Discours sur l'inégalité," in Tisserand, pp. 131-132; cf. Arsenal ms. 2338, pp. 301-309. The discussion of Genoa is in the section on comparative politics in the *Considérations*, pp. 53-54. Genoa attracted European attention in 1746 when it experienced the "last great blaze" of the "republican and communal tradition," according to Franco Venturi, *Utopia and Reform*, p. 38.

[74] In his discussion of European regimes in ch. III of the *Considérations*, d'Argenson criticized the English for their private avarice and public corruption, and dismissed their mixed constitution as a sterile struggle between powers, one of which was bound to triumph in the end. Later in life, he came to have more respect for the English political achievement; see the *pensées* in the Jannet edition, v, 277-281.

[75] Arsenal ms. 2338, pp. 74-75; *Considérations*, p. 73. D'Argenson's insistence that the royal sovereignty would be strengthened rather than subverted by his plan was no doubt sincere; but he was also forestalling suspicion of his plan. In some notes on strategy, he reminded himself that it was necessary to proceed gradually, and "not make clear from the outset where we are headed in the end." Jannet edition, v, 261, 265.

tendency to inherent harmony when artificial constraints and artificial stimuli are removed. Therefore, his sovereign would have little to do when the plan was in working order. This would make possible the attainment of his political ideal, expressed succinctly in his story of a sovereign who loved horses. Impressed by mercantilist notions calling for state regulation of all areas of life, the king decided to make a law imposing harsh penalties against anyone who maltreated horses, to root out such practices once and for all. Unfortunately, his "lazy and arrogant ministers persecuted everyone, on the pretext that they had disobeyed the law." As a result, "the people gave up horses altogether and used only mules." The moral of the tale is that "one spoils everything by meddling too much. . . . The best government is that which governs least [*pour gouverner mieux, il faudrait gouverner moins*]."[76]

In the earlier versions of his theory, before his experiences as a minister had made him more realistic about what one can expect a king to do, d'Argenson used theological images to describe the office of the sovereign. "The whole art of government," he said, "consists in imitating absolutely that of God over men." This means giving unlimited power to the governor, "but hiding this absolute power, revealing to the governed only the idea of total liberty, as God presents things to mankind; and when this liberty becomes harmful, cutting it off clearly and precisely at this point." As a result, "the governed will believe that they govern themselves and act as masters of their lives, while in fact they will not do so at all."[77] In the later versions, d'Argenson used quite different language to describe the monarch. He borrowed from Fénelon the image of the king as gardener, and emphasized how little activity is needed in a healthy garden. "The sap will rise and the plants will flourish," all by themselves. "A single gardener will suffice to correct, on rare occasions, those few plants that degenerate or deprive their neighbors of nourishment."[78]

In the last years of his life, d'Argenson came to believe that monarchs could not be trusted to see their own interests in behaving well. He revised his draft constitution to include an element of aristocracy

[76] Jannet edition, v, 302; cf. Rathery, ed., VIII, 220. Paulmy's list of his father's writings includes an essay with this title, no. 5294.

[77] Rathery, ed., I, xl; Tassin, "Un Membre de l'Académie," p. 346. D'Argenson elsewhere repeated Bossuet's assertion that the absolute monarch who no longer has anything left to fear or desire has nothing to do but govern well; he can be "precisely like God, who, able to do anything, could do evil, but never wishes to do so." Jannet edition, V, 230, 266; *Considérations*, pp. 188-189. Voltaire, who generally admired the treatise, was provoked to a trenchant retort to this proposition: if the king has nothing left to do but govern well, let him get on with it (Voltaire's *Correspondence*, edited by T. Besterman, IX, 203).

[78] *Considérations*, pp. 22-23 and 32-34; Rathery, ed., IV, 165; cf. *Télémaque*, XVII.

for the first time. Despite his earlier identification with the *thèse royale*, the ideas he expressed in the 1750s are close to the parlementary variant of the *thèse nobiliaire*. The behavior of the judges, defending Gallican liberties against papal domination and protecting the interests of the "little people" against the crown, won his admiration in an era when the monarch and his ministers seemed bent on crushing all independent bodies in the state, democratic as well as corporate. Strong traditional institutions were the only effective bulwarks against such tendencies to royal tyranny, decided d'Argenson. Thus the final version of his plan includes a "national senate" modeled on the parlement of Paris. The judges were charged with acting as "representatives of the nation," and were given responsibility for "conserving our national constitution" against despotic encroachment. The good regime, in d'Argenson's last *pensées*, includes three elements:

1. a monarch who will only be like the father-solicitor of a convent, charged solely with protecting his people and maintaining the order of government;
2. under him, democracy, or republics in each town and borough for purposes of internal government;
3. the order of magistrates, educated men, and jurists, serving as a council to the monarch on the issue of finances demanded from the people, designed to help the king preserve himself from stupidity and passion in foreign affairs.[79]

Apart from this final turn toward constitutionalism, d'Argenson's theory is notable for the conviction that the two polar principles in politics—absolute monarchical sovereignty and vigorous participation by individual citizens—can be effectively combined, without the need for intermediaries. His ideal was a version of Bodin's model in which absolute monarchy as a form of government is combined with an administration in which democratic elements are prominent. His most important insight was that all citizens must participate equally in voicing their own interests without special privileges of wealth or blood or office, in order that the process may yield an accurate account of the general interest. D'Argenson was convinced that Nature "is divine and dictates to us only laws that are easy to execute. But it is necessary to hear her in order to follow her; and she expresses herself only among free and equal citizens. In these conditions,

---

[79] Jannet edition, v, 294-295. For d'Argenson's reactions to the conflict between king and parlement in the 1750s, see Jannet edition, IV, 116-117, 285; and Rathery, ed., VII, 450. When Adrien Lepaige's *Lettres historiques sur le Parlement* (a summary of principles from Seyssel, Pasquier, Joly, and Montesquieu) appeared in 1753, d'Argenson welcomed it as historically accurate and politically sound; Jannet edition, v, 128.

contradictory interests control and conciliate one another, sharpness is blunted, and the common good discovered. It is thus from equality alone that good laws are derived. It is through the assembly of men equal among themselves that their administration is assured."[80] Nature's dictates are revealed in the activities of communities, not lodged in the storehouse of a scholar's intellect or revealed to a single divine intelligence. Yet d'Argenson continued to assume, as had so many of his predecessors, that the formal willing of the laws discovered in this process requires a single human will.

The marquis was fond of fables. He once retold a tale from Lucian about Jupiter on his golden throne hearing the prayers of mortals wafting up through a hole in the floor of heaven. One sailor prayed for an east wind, another for a west; farmers prayed for rain, laundresses for sunshine. But Jupiter ignored all the prayers that would bring harm to another. The moral of the tale, in d'Argenson's paraphrase, is that "the father of gods and men remained deaf to all demands that could not be met without harming other mortals."[81] Jupiter's mortal counterpart depends on the same canceling out of excess and deficiency among all interests expressed before his throne. The office of the sovereign was reduced by d'Argenson to a divine clearing-house, in which such canceling could occur efficiently, so that good laws might be promulgated. It remained for Rousseau to assert that a royal clearing-house is unnecessary to this process—that the people assembled can will, on their own behalf, the general will.

[80] "Discours sur l'inégalité," in Tisserand, ed., *Les Concurrents*, pp. 130-131.
[81] Levasseur, "Le Marquis d'Argenson," p. 80. Lucian's story is from the *Icaromenippus*, II, 310-313, in the Loeb edition of his *Works*.

CHAPTER FOURTEEN

Montesquieu: Constitutionalism and Civic Virtue

1. POLITICAL SCIENCE AND THE *Spirit of the Laws*

In a discourse delivered at the autumn reconvening of the Bordeaux Academy of Sciences in 1717, Montesquieu asserted that nature, "after hiding herself for so many years, showed herself suddenly in the past century." Fortunate scientists made astounding discoveries and brought whole new systems to light. "It is left to us only to labor in the wake of these great philosophers," he said. But he counseled his colleagues not to be disheartened; "who knows what may be still reserved for us? Perhaps nature still has thousands of secrets hidden." The boundaries of the continents of knowledge are mapped; the rich interiors remain to be explored.[1] When Montesquieu spoke of the fortunate philosophers of the seventeenth century, he meant especially Descartes. Like Descartes, he began his career by exploring the physical trunk of the tree of knowledge.[2] But he moved quickly upwards to the topmost branches of moral and political philosophy, where thousands of secrets were hidden. Montesquieu devoted most of his life to mapping those branches in the *Spirit of the Laws*.

When that mammoth treatise appeared in 1748, it was heralded as a landmark in the moral sciences, and it has been so regarded ever since. To draw attention to the novelty of his enterprise, Montesquieu spoke of it as a work "without a mother," and many readers have taken him at his word.[3] But the matter of Montesquieu's originality is more complex than he makes it sound. From his extensive jottings and notebooks, we know that he read widely and depended on his reading in discovering as well as illustrating his own principles. When he ac-

---

[1] "Discours prononcé à . . . l'Académie de Bordeaux," in *Oeuvres complètes*, edited by Roger Caillois, I, 8-9.

[2] On the importance of Montesquieu's work as a physical scientist for his work as a social theorist, see Ronald Grimsley, "The Idea of Nature in Montesquieu's *Lettres Persanes*," in *From Montesquieu to Laclos*, pp. 3-14; and Colm Kiernan, *Science and Enlightenment in Eighteenth-Century France*, ch. 5.

[3] The epigram of the treatise is *Prolem sine matre creatam*. Two of the most thoughtful recent studies of Montesquieu open with an assessment of this claim: Louis Althusser, *Politics and History*, and Simone Goyard-Fabre, *Philosophie du droit de Montesquieu*.

knowledged precursors in the moral sciences, he tended to find them in antiquity. In a dossier of fragments for possible inclusion in the *Spirit of the Laws*, Montesquieu remarked that the ancient Greeks and Romans had raised the knowledge of politics "almost to the level of a cult," but since that time it had been allowed to atrophy. Contemporary philosophers, brilliant in the physical sciences, held the moral sciences in low esteem. "Among us," he said, "political good and evil are more a sentiment than an object of knowledge." He found few laborers beside him in the vineyard, and lamented that he had not been "born in the right century." He avowed himself a "votary of that excellent man the abbé de Saint Pierre, who has written so much about politics in our time," and consoled himself with the thought that "seven or eight hundred years from now there will appear some people to whom my notions will be useful."[4]

The sense of isolation that characterizes such passages was no doubt engendered by Montesquieu's absorption in his own researches in the library at La Brède. But he was not being wholly fair to his contemporaries. *The Spirit of the Laws* was only one (although by far the most impressive) product of the moral sciences between 1715 and 1748. Montesquieu may have discounted parallel efforts because they were unscientific. Most of his contemporaries mined old veins of jurisprudence, history, and political economy that he helped discredit by opening up new vistas in his own work. But several men were moving tentatively in the directions taken boldly in the *Spirit of the Laws*. Some of these works circulated only in manuscript, such as those of d'Argenson and d'Aguesseau. Others, including Mably's *Parallèle des romains et des françois*, Richer d'Aube's *Essai sur les principes du droit et de la morale*, and Le Gendre de Saint-Aubin's *Traité de l'opinion*, were published in France or abroad. Essays by Dutot and Melon on political economy, as well as Saint-Pierre's voluminous projects and several better-known works (Voltaire's *Philosophical Letters*, Montesquieu's *Persian Letters* and *Considerations on the Romans*) were all published in these years. The controversy over the early history of France was at its height. Du Bos and Boulainvilliers found numerous adherents; Montesquieu's treatise was, among many other things, a contribution to the dispute on the noble side.[5] Finally, the *Spirit of the*

---

[4] *Pensée* 1949 (198); and *pensée* 1295 (910). The first number given in citations of *pensées* in this chapter is that assigned them in the manuscript, also used in André Masson's edition of the *Oeuvres complètes*; the number in parentheses is from the more easily accessible Pléiade edition of the *Oeuvres* by Roger Caillois, where they are grouped by topic rather than chronologically.

[5] Two studies that place Montesquieu in this context are E. Carcassonne, *Montesquieu et le problème de la constitution française au XVIIIe siècle* and Albert

Laws shows that Montesquieu, like many other Frenchmen, was familiar with ideas put forward in English coffee-houses and periodicals, and with the theories of Grotius and Pufendorf popularized by Barbeyrac.

The *Spirit of the Laws* was therefore not a work without antecedents or fellows. The originality on which Montesquieu justly prided himself lies in his self-consciously scientific postulation of his principles, and in his exploration of vast areas of what we now call anthropology, sociology, and psychology that had been generally ignored by social theorists. He took as the province of the moral sciences material that had been left to fancy, or entombed in the works of classical antiquity. His contemporaries perceived his originality; they also welcomed his solutions to problems regularly raised in French social theory in the preceding decades. Montesquieu had important things to say about all three of the traditions of French thought we have traced out in this study. In his description of moderate government, he provided the fullest statement of French constitutionalist theory, combining themes familiar since Seyssel with elements drawn from reflections on English sources. He struck a mortal blow at absolutist theory by confirming the connection between despotism and absolutism toward which French jurists had been groping uncertainly since the days of Richelieu. And he provided some suggestions for resolving the dichotomy between the public and the private that had haunted French philosophy since Montaigne. In his theories of republican virtue and monarchical honor, Montesquieu offered two models for accommodating individual passions and interests in society, infusing new life into the categories of *la charité* and *l'amour-propre*.

By birth, Charles de Secondat, baron de Montesquieu, was a member of the nobility of the sword and of the robe.[6] Both lineages can be detected in his preoccupations and his preferences. Despite the scorn he sometimes showed in discussing noble honor, he clearly understood it at first hand. By training and profession, he was identified with the judiciary; he inherited the offices of counsellor and *président* of the Bordeaux parlement. But like Montaigne, he found the Bordeaux magistracy little to his liking. He sold his office in 1726, and divided his

---

Mathiez, "La Place de Montesquieu dans l'histoire des doctrines politiques du XVIIIe siècle." Brief discussions of a number of the other books mentioned above can be found in Ian Wilson, *The Influence of Hobbes and Locke*.

[6] By far the best biography is Robert Shackleton, *Montesquieu*; for Montesquieu's own attitude toward his dual lineage see the early *pensée* 5 (69), in which he shares with his son some reflections on the disparate advantages of the two nobilities.

time between Paris, Bordeaux, and La Brède. The scientific pursuits of the Bordeaux academy continued to attract him. He greatly enjoyed being lionized in the salons of Paris. But increasingly he preferred his life as master of his chateau at La Brède, where visitors discovered him tramping around his estate in rough clothes, and writing for long hours in his library. Like Descartes, he expressed ambivalence about publishing. "I suffer from the malady of making books," he said, "and being ashamed of them when they are finished."[7]

2. Social Physics and the Conservation of Complexity

In the preface to the *Spirit of the Laws*, Montesquieu professes his desire to "give every person new reasons for loving his duties, his prince, his fatherland, his laws." This is normally read as a conservative teaching, and so it is; but it is a distinctive conservatism that has much in common with that of Descartes. Here and elsewhere in his writing, Montesquieu gives patriotic duties a place in a widening series of concentric circles, moving outward from duties of the individual to himself, through duties to others and his country, to mankind and to God. As Montesquieu says of himself: "I am a good citizen; but in whatever country I had happened to be born, I would have been one all the same."[8] His is a patriotism without chauvinism. He wants to buttress existing polities not by enhancing but by destroying prejudice, which he defines as whatever makes men ignorant about themselves. If men understand their natures better, they can appreciate the importance of dutiful obedience to authority. Like Descartes, he approached this endeavor in a spirit of adventure and exploration, confident that the best way to support what exists is not to hide its foundations behind a veil of sacred mystery, but instead to comprehend why it is and must be so. The better we understand the concatenation of duties, passions, customs, and accidents that compose a state, the more we will respect its intricate accommodations, and appreciate the immensity of the task of changing it.[9]

[7] *Pensée* 837 (83).
[8] *Pensée* 1437 (27). Cf. the "Analyse du traité des devoirs," in *Oeuvres complètes*, edited by Caillois, I, 108-111; *pensée* 220 (597), 350 (10), and 741 (11).
[9] Two *pensées* strikingly reminiscent of Cartesian conservatism are 903 (1311): "It is not philosophers who trouble states, but those who are not philosophers enough to recognize their happiness and enjoy it," and 934 (632): "The best [government] of all is ordinarily that under which one lives, and a sensible man ought to love it; for, since it is impossible to change it without changing manners and *moeurs*, I do not see, given the extreme brevity of life, what utility there could be for men in departing in all respects from the bent that they have taken [*le pli qu'ils ont pris.*]"

In discussing these topics, Montesquieu assumed a principle of social physics common in seventeenth-century French thought: that the social world, like the physical universe, is composed of complex forces in opposition and attraction to one another. He described monarchical polities as like "the system of the universe, in which one force ceaselessly repels all bodies from the center, and another force, that of gravity, brings them together." He used mechanical analogies as well, praising well-constructed monarchies as "beautiful machines" in which "artifice employs the fewest possible movements, forces, and wheels" to obtain its goal.[10] Undergirding both the physical and the mechanical analogies was the ancient vision of social harmony, with its roots deep in medieval and Aristotelian theory. An eloquent passage on this topic from the *Considerations on the Romans* is reminiscent of the temper of Seyssel and Bodin:

> That which we call union in a political body is a very equivocal thing; the true unity is a union in harmony, which operates in such a fashion that all the different parts, however opposed they may appear to us to be, concur in the general good of society, as dissonances in music agree in the concord of the whole. Thus there can be union in a state where one would expect only turbulence: that is to say, a harmony that gives birth to happiness, the only true peace. It is like the parts of this universe itself, eternally linked by the action of some and the reaction of others.[11]

This conviction of the intricate forces conjoined in the harmony of a well-ordered polity explains Montesquieu's attitude toward change. He compared government to "a sum composed of many numbers. If you remove or add a single number you change the value of the whole. But since we know, in arithmetic, the value of each number and its relation to the rest, we are not deceived. It is not the same in politics: one can never know what will be the result of a change one undertakes."[12] Since the complex pattern of social forces is normally beyond our comprehension, it appeared obvious to Montesquieu that no one has any business proposing changes in a state except someone who is

---

[10] *De l'esprit des lois*, Book III, ch. 5. The best English translation of large parts of Montesquieu's *Spirit of the Laws* is Melvin Richter's *Political Theory of Montesquieu*, which supplants the heavily flawed but ubiquitous Nugent translation. On the importance of translations of Montesquieu, see Keohane, "The President's English."

[11] *Considérations sur les causes de la grandeur des Romains et de leur décadence*, ch. IX; in *Oeuvres complètes*, II, 119.

[12] *Pensée* 941 (1918); cf. 184 (1916), 603 (1917), and 1436 (1920).

"so fortunately born as to be able to penetrate with a stroke of genius the entire consitution of the state."[13]

In his awareness of the unstable character of all political accommodation, and the difficulties that beset any attempt at deliberate reform, Montesquieu followed the example of Montaigne. He bade us cherish and protect any measure of stability that we may enjoy. But unlike Montaigne, he did not think that the road ahead is only deformation and decay. Montesquieu was convinced that liberty revives after eras of stultifying docility, and then once again is threatened by aggrandizing power. His social theory emphasizes the ever-present threat of decay as well as the sources for eventual renewal; it is a theory in which flux itself is constant.[14] Rhedi's thumbnail summary of the history of Europe in the *Persian Letters* gives ground for despair as well as hope: despair, in that it shows how republics have succumbed before arbitrary power, and hope, because it also shows how the Roman empire crumbled before the inundation of Germanic nations from the north, bringing the conditions for a new liberty. In an early *pensée*, Montesquieu picks up the summary at the point where Rhedi's ended, with the establishment of the Gothic government on the ruins of the Roman empire, and continues: "It has taken nine hundred years to abolish that government in turn, and to establish in each state the rule of a single individual. Things now subsist in this fashion; and it appears that we are moving, from century to century, toward the final degree of obedience, until some accident changes the disposition of our brains and makes men as indocile as they were in the old days. Thus it has always been: a flux of domination and of liberty."[15] Thus the tendency for the tenuous equilibrium of moderate governments to be destroyed by arbitrary rule is balanced by the opposing tendency for liberty to reassert itself. Unlike his disciple Tocqueville, Montesquieu did not conceive a unilinear process of leveling of complexity; he was wary of all attempts to provide neat pattern-theories for history. But apparently he had faith in an inexhaustible supply of new social energies arising from "accidental changes in the disposition of our brains."[16]

[13] Preface to *Esprit des lois, Oeuvres complètes*, II, 230.

[14] On the theme of flux, see *pensée* 2266 (not available in Caillois's edition), as well as no. 76 (690) and Henry Vyverberg, *Historical Pessimism in the French Enlightenment*. In *pensée* 364 (1766) Montesquieu remarks that "maxims of state should be changed every twenty years, because the world itself is changing," a prescription echoed in more radical form by Thomas Jefferson.

[15] *Pensée* 100 (1475); Rhedi's summary is in letter CXXXI of the *Lettres persanes, Oeuvres complètes*, I, 327-329. On political flux, see Badreddine Kassem, *Décadence et absolutisme dans l'oeuvre de Montesquieu*.

[16] In *pensée* 291 (1463), Montesquieu criticizes pattern-theories in history;

398—Approaches to a Synthesis

Montesquieu perceived his own time as one in which moderation, and the liberty made possible by moderation, were threatened by encroaching autocratic power. He did not preach simple resignation in the face of threats to things he valued highly; although he taught that it is difficult to make deliberate changes in our institutions, he was convinced that informed human action can ward off deformation. Therefore he exhorted his contemporaries to guard the remnants of the moderating institutions still left them from the past. He taught that it is *complexity* that must be preserved, since he identified simple government with despotism. The conservation of complexity becomes the fundamental principle of his conservatism, and it is drawn directly from his hatred of despotism. Montesquieu's faith that despotism will eventually spawn new liberties was a long-term faith, not a source of comfort for his own contemporaries. He wanted them to recognize that moderate governments are fortunate exceptions to the general rule of uniform autocratic power, exceptions based on historical accidents or the rare insight of a legislative genius. Moderate polities depend on intricate patterns of mutually supportive tensions, and are not to be tampered with in the misguided hope of making them more commodious. They possess no inherent tendency to return to moderate equilibrium when they depart from it; the groundstate, the ever-present threat, is despotism.

In a passage he thought sufficiently important to rework in several versions, Montesquieu asserted that

> it should not be surprising that almost all the peoples of the world are so far from the liberty they love. Despotic government leaps immediately to the eye, so to speak, and establishes itself of its own accord. Since only the passions are required to constitute it, everyone provides material for it. But to form a moderate government, it is necessary to combine powers, temper them, make them act and regulate them; to provide, that is, ballast for the one to equip it to offer resistance to another. This is a masterpiece of legislation that chance produces only rarely, and prudence is seldom given the opportunity to create.[17]

Here Montesquieu makes several interesting assumptions beyond the

---

however, in 1917 (236), he offers his own version of a cyclical theory of development and decay.

[17] *Pensée* 892 (1794); in an earlier version, 831 (1793), Montesquieu describes a moderate government as "un système, c'est-à-dire une convention de plusieurs et une discussion d'intérêts." See also *Esprit des lois*, v, 14.

notion that power must be checked by power that is always associated with his work. He assumes that despotism is the condition toward which all polities tend unless they are pulled away from it by legislative art or happy accident. Creating a moderate government means deliberately lifting a polity out of simplicity, instituting a complexity of form where there would otherwise be pure domination. Despotism, on the other hand, constitutes itself without art out of human passion. Elsewhere in his writing, the role of passion in despotism is made more explicit, and the connection between the two is qualified significantly. He argues that moderate polities have managed to direct and channel human passion to create a supportive structure for tempered power instead of an open field for despotism; and he also points out that passions are a continual source of centrifugal tension, an element of instability that prevents despotism from perfecting itself. In despotic government, the range of human passions is distorted and truncated, and the energetic desire for self-preservation is focused in a single passion: fear. "Persons capable of esteeming themselves too much are ripe to make revolutions," observes Montesquieu. "Thus it is necessary that fear beat down all courage and extinguish it, down to the last glimmering of ambition."[18] Still, the least relaxation of vigilance allows courage and ambition to begin to flourish once again, and challenge despotic power.

The tale of the seraglio in the *Persian Letters* is Montesquieu's fullest demonstration of this truth. The seraglio initially appears serene, a rather humane and stable despotism in which strict obedience to absolute authority depends on successful arrangement of the passions. Fear attends the subordination of the women to the capricious authority of the eunuchs; but the exercise of capricious authority by the women over the eunuchs in return creates a balance of noninstitutionalized power that holds the seraglio together. The ambition of the women is channeled into competition for the favors of the master, and Usbek and his slaves are bound together by intricate ties of love and lust and duty.[19] But when Usbek leaves for Europe, this fragile stability is destroyed. The elements of complexity rooted in fundamental human passions undermine the simple despotic authority of the seraglio.

As the chief black eunuch describes it to Usbek, the core of the problem is that ambition has been loosed. No longer is feminine

[18] *Esprit des lois*, III:9; *Oeuvres complètes*, II, 258-259.
[19] The pattern of authority in the seraglio is described in letters II, IX, and XCVI.

energy channeled into pleasing the master; the women have begun to esteem themselves more highly, and compete for status and petty privileges. This leads them to challenge the allocations of the eunuchs. The eunuch advises his master that despotisms cannot be run humanely, especially in the absence of the lord and husband. The eunuchs are impotent symbols of his love and justice who cannot maintain the intricate network of passions he deployed. The only way to beat down ambition and maintain order, says the chief black eunuch, is to use the stringent measures of a perfect despotism exemplified in another seraglio in which he served, which he describes in letter LXIV. The severe eunuch in charge of that seraglio controlled the lives of the women down to the pettiest detail, and ensured that their lives were uniform and very simple. The women were isolated from one another in their cells, and guided by their slaves through regular routines each day. "Divisions and quarrels were unheard of; a profound silence reigned throughout." The women in that seraglio had no other relation to their master except availability as instruments to satisfy impersonal lust. In all else they were subordinated to the absolute authority of the chief eunuch, the grand vizier of that despotic state.

Usbek rejects such a terrible regime; but the chief eunuch's prophecy that half-way measures must fail is soon borne out. It is humanity and moderation that prove fatal to the seraglio in the end. They make it possible for the women to envision, and eventually to work for, a community in which they can fulfill their own desires and achieve some measure of autonomy, instead of remaining isolated subjects of the authoritative passions of their master and the despairing passions of his eunuchs. Their ambitions are channeled away from competition with one another into cooperation in a conspiracy to deceive the eunuchs and create a space for liberty. They find ways to satisfy their passions by taking lovers and bedding down with slaves; having known only lust and caprice, they express their desire for freedom in the only way they know, searching for love and the ordering of their lives. When the conspiracy is discovered, the chief eunuch demands authority to govern by pure fear; but it is too late. He dies before he can execute the bloody orders Usbek sends him. When a successor attempts to carry them out he triggers a revolution in the seraglio. Having experienced a measure of freedom and community, the women refuse to accept the authority of terror and caprice. Their manifesto is the eloquent closing letter written by Roxane, whose much-vaunted "virtue" is a central theme of this whole sequence. In that letter she shows herself a woman of true "virtue" in the ancient sense: a courageous, brave, resourceful leader of a revolution against arbitrary mastery. She is one of the first genuine feminist heroines in literature—an aspect of the *Letters* that too often goes unremarked.[20]

Roxane's spirited assertion that her spirit has "always been free" though she has lived in slavery, her claim that she has reformed Usbek's laws by those of nature, is a heartening affirmation of the indomitable well-springs of human liberty that recalls the eloquent passages of La Boétie. However, heartening as it may be, it is still a tragic ending. The only possible outcome is death for the women and their jailors, too. A tragic truncation of the human spirit accompanies a stable despotism, yet equally tragic difficulties attend any attempt to overthrow despotic power. Even the most benevolent despotism is a violation of the human spirit, and can maintain itself only by tending toward extreme and terrible simplicity.

3. ABSOLUTISM AND MODERATE GOVERNMENT

Why do all governments tend toward despotism? And why must power be neutralized by power? Like his counterparts across the Channel, Montesquieu was convinced that power tends to aggrandize itself unless it meets another power in its path. Power encroaches on liberty.[21] Even the English constitution, for all its capacity to rise like a phoenix free again in the midst of the fires of civil conflict, was not immune to such a threat. It was derived from a more absolutist monarchy, and the intermediate powers in the constitution have been gradually leveled over time. If the balance of power at the center, or the vigorous individualistic spirit of the people, should be weakened, Englishmen would have no protection against slavery. The regime was poised above a despotism into which it will be plunged if the peculiar sources of its liberty are ever quenched.[22]

In the *Persian Letters*, Usbek remarks that "most of the governments of Europe are monarchies, or rather are called so; for I do not know if there has ever been a true monarchy." Such a regime can hardly subsist "in all its purity," for "it is a violent state that always degenerates into despotism or a republic. Power can never be equally di-

---

[20] Roxane's letter XLCI closes the sequence of fifteen letters that describe the revolution in the seraglio. For further evidence of Montesquieu's feminist sympathies, see *pensée* 596 (1820), where he remarks that "despotic government obstructs the talents of subjects and great men, like the power of men restricts that of women," and Rica's observations in letter XXXVIII. However, some notoriously anti-feminist sentiments are also expressed in Montesquieu's work, as in *pensée* 2219 (1265).

[21] Montesquieu's familiarity with radical Whig arguments, and those of Bolingbroke as well, is apparent from his *Spicilège, Oeuvres complètes*, II, 1295 and 1358.

[22] *Esprit des lois*, II:4, and IX:27.

vided between the People and the Prince; equilibrium is difficult to maintain." Montesquieu's conception of power indicated that "power must diminish on one side as it is augmented on the other," and that "the advantage is normally on the side of the Prince, who is at the head of the armies."[23] The *Considerations on the Romans* provide other illustrations of this tendency for power to aggrandize itself. The imperial republic could not sustain its original form; the aggrandizing vigor made possible by its excellent constitution destroyed the regime. Beyond this, the overweening power of ambitious leaders proved fatal to that of the mass of the people.

This is the background against which we must understand Montesquieu's urgent warning to his countrymen. One of his major purposes was to show Frenchmen what could happen to their own monarchy if they did not protect the remnants of Gothic power in the state. Threats to moderated power identified by some of his contemporaries such as Boulainvilliers were not a peculiar or ephemeral plight of Frenchmen, said Montesquieu, but an instance of a general pattern of political development and deformation. His interest in the pattern, however, was stimulated by his concern for his own *patrie*. As with Tocqueville in America, Montesquieu discussing England or Persia or Spain was always thinking of France.

In a set of *mémoires* written in his youth, Montesquieu proposed fiscal reforms for the French state like those of Boisguilbert, Vauban, and Saint-Pierre; he also pressed for the reestablishment of vigorous communal administration and the creation of provincial estates throughout France, asserting, like d'Argenson, that "the authority of the king will in no way be weakened by such institutions." Echoing the views of noble critics of Louis XIV, he charged the old monarch with "losing the hearts of his subjects by the intolerable tributes with which he burdened them, the necessary prop for a vain war." However, Louis's "immoderate desire to augment his power over his subjects" did not surprise the *président*, who saw it as a "sentiment common to all men."[24] He placed the primary blame for attempted assault on French liberties on cardinal Richelieu. In reading Richelieu's *Testament*, he was struck by the cardinal's desire to avoid "the thorny obstacles of the companies" and to abase the ancient orders in the state. He judged that "if this man had not despotism imprinted in his heart, it would still have found a place in his head." To Montesquieu, Riche-

[23] Letter CII; cf. letter XCII, where Usbek applies the concept of absolutist deformation directly to the French monarchy, comparing the weakened parlements to ruined temples.
[24] *Pensée* 1306 (596); see also "De la politique," *Oeuvres complètes*, I, 112-119.

lieu's reliance on the personal virtues of kings and ministers and their familiarity with *raison d'état* to guarantee good government, was incredible. "He demanded so much of them that there is scarcely an angel who could be counted on to have so much attention, so much reason, firmness, knowledge; one could only with difficulty delude oneself into believing that from now until the dissolution of monarchies there could be such a prince, and ministers like that."[25]

Yet men of his own time composed books in which the same principles were put forward with equanimity. Le Gendre de Saint-Aubin's *Traité de l'opinion* contained a number of arguments on the power of *l'opinion générale*, the nature of despotism, and its foundation on fear, that were much like those of Montesquieu himself. But Saint-Aubin complacently confined despotism to Africa and Asia, and asserted that such government is fundamentally different from absolutist monarchy. In language unchanged from Bossuet's *Politique*, Saint-Aubin ascribes to the French king a *plenitudo podestas*, mastery of the lives and goods of his subjects. He makes him an image of God on the earth, accountable to God alone for what he does; there is no rightful role for "feudal institutions" in the state.[26] In Saint-Aubin's catalogue of attributes of sovereignty, the injunction that the king should not abuse his power and the feeble notion that "one cannot call power to do evil legitimate" have the effect of hollow mockery. It was against such durable, petrified absolutist dogma that Montesquieu leveled his lance so effectively. He made clear that only insofar as France retained vestiges of "Gothic government" did it deserve to be called a moderate monarchy rather than an abject despotism; and he removed despotism from the realm of oriental exotica to bring it very close to home. After he published the *Spirit of the Laws*, it was no longer possible to assume complacently that absolutism was divinely protected against the horrors of despotism by its European situation or its juristic maxims. The formulas for constitutional government took on new life in France, and efforts to salvage something from the wreckage of divine-right absolutism were required to begin with different principles.

In his chapter in the *Spirit of the Laws*, "the corruption of the prin-

[25] *Esprit des lois*, v:10; *Oeuvres complètes*, II, 289; see also *pensée* 1302 (595), "Sur l'histoire de France," and 1962 (594); Montesquieu's general opinion of *raison d'état* is expressed in *Esprit des lois* XXI:20, where he notes that his contemporaries have begun "to cure themselves of Machiavellism," so that what would once have been called *coups d'état*, would be regarded, "apart from the horror they would inspire, as imprudences" (*Oeuvres complètes*, II, 641).

[26] Gilbert-Charles Le Gendre, marquis de Saint-Aubin-sur-Loire, *Traité de l'opinion* (1735), v, 75-79 and 97-114.

ciple of monarchy," Montesquieu made his central warning quite explicit. "Monarchies are corrupted," he says, "when one gradually removes the prerogatives of the corporate bodies or the privileges of the towns." In such a case, the government moves toward "the despotism of a single man." On the basis of his research on China, Montesquieu reports that "the Tsin and Soui dynasties" had been destroyed when "instead of limiting themselves, as their ancestors had done, to a general overview of governing, the only office worthy of a sovereign, the princes attempted to govern everything directly by themselves." If any uncertainty about the implication of these principles remained, it would have been dispelled when the reader turned to a section of the treatise prefaced with the notice that "I cannot make myself understood unless the following four chapters have been read." The argument of these chapters is that the three forms of government identified by Montesquieu—republics, monarchies, and despotisms—are closely correlated with the size of different territories. When a monarchy attempts to aggrandize itself beyond a moderate extent, it commits itself to despotism. The supporting example is not faraway China or exotic Persia but Spain, the monarchy next door, ruled by the same family and originating in the same institutions as France herself. Montesquieu asserts that in its attempt to build an empire in the Americas and Europe, the Spanish monarchy was forced to use despotic methods. Despotism at home was the necessary consequence; this would have been clear to anyone familiar with the standard account of the decline of Rome. Unless the French monarchy took timely notice of such tendencies, and moved to protect ancient institutions and renounce aggrandizement, its fate, for Montesquieu, was clear. "Rivers run down to mingle with the sea; monarchies move on to lose themselves in despotism."[27]

Montesquieu recommended several courses of action to governments intent on maintaining moderate power and avoiding deformation. In the well-tempered constitutions that he praises, the executive power itself plays a moderating part. It is not simply the object of tempering or checking by other parts of the state, but has its own role in the balancing and tempering. Sometimes Montesquieu used the language of the scale, with the monarch in the center and the power of the nobles and of the people in the balances. The king can abase or raise up as necessary to prevent either from becoming dominant in the

[27] *Esprit des lois*, VIII:6-7 and 15-20. The importance of Spain as an example of monarchical decay is brought out in Mark Hulliung, *Montesquieu and the Old Regime*, pp. 46-53.

state.[28] In republics and monarchies alike, strong leaders are essential to political health as well as a source of potential deformation. In a passage that shows his affinities with d'Argenson, Montesquieu says: "If the English lacked a king, they would be less free." This is proved, he continued, by the experience of Holland, "where the people have become more enslaved since they no longer have a stadtholder; all the magistrates in each town are so many little tyrants."[29]

However, Montesquieu is as adamant as d'Argenson that the prince should not become involved in the details of his government. "He should think, and let others act, and set them into motion. He is the soul, not the arm." To meddle with details is "a *métier* he cannot do well; and if he did it well it would mean he would do all else badly."[30] One of the most important aspects of a monarch's office is delegating power, choosing good agents and ensuring that they act according to his wishes, and knowing how much power to retain in his own hands. "The authority of the sovereign ought to be communicated to as many people as necessary, and as few as possible," he says.[31] Montesquieu's model here is like that of Fénelon, Saint-Pierre, and d'Argenson: the prince as powerful overseer, animating principle in the state, acting little himself but responsible for the action of the whole. He advised the prince to give a vivacious people room, let them express their natural capacities and tendencies. "Let us be as we are," he said, rather than working against the *esprit générale* of the French nation to make them follow more sober and regular paths.[32] An appropriate balance of control and restraint on the prince's part ensures that he is more powerful than any despot, for a despot cannot possibly govern his huge territory himself, yet lacks any institutional mechanism for delegating power in an ordinary fashion. Anyone who acts in his name becomes a little despot on his own, which reduces the scope of the despot's power. "The kings of Europe govern like men, and therefore enjoy a condition as unalterable as that of gods," says Montesquieu. "The kings of Asia govern like gods and are ceaselessly exposed to the fragility of the condition of mere men."[33]

There is at least one way, however, in which "to govern like a man" means to govern like God Himself: expressing power through regulated *volonté*, in law, rather than capriciously. Montesquieu speaks of

[28] *Esprit des lois*, XIX:27; cf. III:10.
[29] *Pensée* 655 (1674); see also 1786 (207), and Jean-Jacques Granpre Molière, *La théorie de la constitution anglaise chez Montesquieu.*
[30] *Pensée* 953 (1843); see also 965 (1912).
[31] *Pensée* 1994 (659); cf. 1898 (228), and *Esprit des lois*, v:16.
[32] *Esprit des lois*, XIX:5-6. [33] *Pensée* 1889 (223).

kings as "above the law" in the sense that they establish it and are not formally subordinate to it, as are the citizens of a republic; but he also specifies that monarchs, unlike despots, govern in accordance with established laws, and obey the fundamental laws of their own state. Montesquieu takes the presence or absence of fundamental laws as the first criterion for differentiating monarchy from despotism. To such laws monarchs are indeed subordinated. Beyond this, he specifies that monarchy requires laws for the protection of the lives and property of subjects, and strong tribunals for enforcing them. When these conditions are realized, he notes in one of his most striking passages, the citizen of a moderate state who is judged according to all formalities and sentenced to be hung is freer than the Turkish sovereign.[34]

Several French absolutists had stressed the importance of governing in accordance with established law, and respecting *les lois fondamentales*. Constitutionalists were careful to specify that there must be other institutions in the state responsible for protecting and enforcing laws, in addition to the agents of the king himself. Here Montesquieu proves himself the most ardent of all French constitutionalists; for he asserts that "the intermediate, subordinate, and dependent powers constitute the nature of monarchical government, that is to say, one in which a single ruler governs by fundamental laws." The intermediate institutions in the state are not merely convenient ways to distribute power; they are fundamental to the constitution and determine the character of the regime, marking it off from despotism. "These fundamental laws necessarily suppose mediating channels along which power flows. For if there is only the ephemeral and capricious will of a single ruler in the state, nothing is fixed, and consequently there are no fundamental laws."[35]

Sometimes, particularly in his famous chapter on the English constitution, Montesquieu's language in describing the relation between institutions is that of checks and balances, mechanically acting as obstacles to one another to prevent abuse of power rather than facilitate its use.[36] In other passages his conception is more fluid, reminiscent of the Seysselian pluralism that is the hallmark of French constitutionalism. The moderation that distinguishes good government is not a blockage but a smooth flow of power from one part of a complex state to another, a harmonious tension of mutually limiting ambitions

[34] *Esprit des lois*, XII:2. Walter Kuhfuss, *Mässigung und Politik*, is a good analysis of the theme of moderation in Montesquieu's thought.
[35] *Esprit des lois*, II:4; cf. VI:5.
[36] *Esprit des lois*, XI:6: "These three powers ought to form a repose or inaction; but since, by the necessary course of things, they are required to move, they are forced to move in concert" (*Oeuvres complètes*, II, 405).

harnessed and channeled toward a single end. Montesquieu stressed the place of the nobility of robe and sword in a well-constituted monarchy "not to provide a line of demarcation between the power of the prince and the weakness of the people, but the link between the two."[37] Monarchy is defined in the *Spirit of the Laws* as government by a single man exercising power according to law rather than his own caprice, himself "the source of all political and civil power" in the state. Other powers are not only intermediate but also *subordinate*, channels along which monarchical power flows throughout the state, rather than autonomous sources of power in themselves. Montesquieu, like Seyssel, was sensitive to the importance of limiting power by opinion as well as force. Although he did not use the specific image of the bridles, his metaphors express the same attitude toward the subtle yet durable sources of power in the intermediate institutions in the French polity. "Although the French parlements have no great authority," he said, "this does not prevent them from doing good. Ministers and princes do not want to have their disapproval, since they are so much respected. Kings are like the ocean, whose impetuosity can often be arrested by seaweed or pebbles."[38]

It is clear from the chapter that immediately follows the discussion of the English constitution, and from the closing chapter of book XI, that Montesquieu regarded England as but one example of the principle that all well-constituted states distribute the several parts of sovereign power. If they do not, they degenerate into despotism. Despite the threat of despotic deformation, the French monarchy was still supported by institutions left over from "the ancient Gothic government," which Montesquieu praises as a form in which "the civil liberty of the people, the prerogatives of the nobility and the clergy, the power of the kings were so beautifully concerted that I think there has never been on earth a government so well-tempered as that found in each part of Europe while this form subsisted."[39] Intermediary powers developed under Gothic government are to some extent mutually substitutable, in his eyes. It is crucial for whatever is left of liberty in Spain, for instance, that the power of the clergy remains

---

[37] *Esprit des lois*, v:9 (*Oeuvres complètes*, II, 288).

[38] *Pensée* 589 (1962); the definition of monarchy is in *Esprit des lois* II:4 (*Oeuvres complètes*, II, 247).

[39] *Esprit des lois*, XI:8; in the manuscript copy of the treatise in the Bibliothèque nationale (*n.a.f* 12833), this chapter, at ff. 192-193, shows evidence of extensive rewriting, particularly of the last sentence, as Montesquieu attempted to ensure that he expressed his meaning here as precisely as possible; a final line is crossed out, in which he qualified his praise by noting that this was a "gouvernement qui avoit en soy la capacité de devenir meilleur."

a factor in the state when other intermediate powers and the rule of law are undermined. Contemporary France was characterized by several corporate counterweights to royal power that had managed to escape Richelieu's leveling enterprises. The *président* singles out the provincial estates and the municipal liberties as commendable on this score. But he is especially anxious to stress the power of the nobles and judges in the French monarchy. The *corps* of judicial magistrates act as a *dépôt des lois*, incessantly guarding the laws and rescuing them from the dust to which they would otherwise be relegated; held together by their training, traditions, and networks of alliances, they are centrally important to liberty in France.[40] The nobility of the sword is equally important; for the honor of the nobility is the motivating spring of monarchy as Montesquieu defines it. Both the English and the French regimes exemplify the essential character of modern monarchy for Montesquieu: the use of the unpromising raw stuff of human selfish passion to fuel the engines of society itself, the ingenious channeling of private action to create a political pattern conducive to security, liberty, and commodious life. This is a passable substitute for public life. But it should never be confused with true public life, based directly upon virtue, which is associated with the classical polities of Greece and Rome.

4. THE ANCIENTS AND THE MODERNS

The quarrel over the literary virtues of the ancients and the moderns had its counterpart in political philosophy in France. The position defended by Montesquieu in this debate was, like everything else about his work, complex. In literature and politics alike, Montesquieu held that "there are good works among the ancients and among the moderns too."[41] He admired the magnificent public life of ancient republics and the admirable efficiency of modern monarchies. The distinction between the two was not purely chronological in his eyes; he discovered a few contemporary republics and outstanding individuals who exemplified the virtues of the ancients. But he regarded monarchy as characteristic of modernity, suited to the distinctive economic and ethical dispositions of men of his own time. The difference between republics and monarchies in Montesquieu's theory rests on the configuration of passion as much as on institutional patterns of popular and monarchical rule. Like Descartes and Pascal, Montesquieu believed

[40] *Esprit des lois*, II:4; V:10; and XIII:12; cf. the "Mémoire sur les dettes de l'Etat," *Oeuvres complètes*, I, 70.
[41] *Pensée* 111 (445).

the passions were grounded in the operation of the human body, *la machine*.[42] But he was less interested in the physiology of the passions than in their psychology and sociology. In the *Spirit of the Laws*, he describes three ways of organizing passions that correspond to the three basic forms of government: despotism, monarchy, and republic.

Montesquieu describes the classical republic as an intimate community whose members are associated by a shared love of public life itself. They love the very equality of their participation in that life, and are intensely attached to *la patrie* as the symbol of the durable community that they enjoy. Members of a republican community think of "we" instead of "I." They regard the things they share in common as belonging equally to each of them, whereas in monarchy public things are treated as though they were unrelated to each individual, the property and therefore the concern of someone else.[43] Republican polities are like close-knit families with a hierarchy of paternal authority, community of goods, mediocrity of fortune, frugality, and simplicity of life. Participants in such communities realize the potential for love and justice that characterizes the species at its best. They enjoy goods that cannot be won in isolation, discovering true happiness as part of a whole. In the limiting case of the benevolent anarchy of the good Troglodytes in the *Persian Letters*, the elders continually instruct their children that "above all, the interest of individuals is always to be discovered in the common interest; that to wish to separate oneself from the whole is to will one's own destruction; that virtue is not something to be counted as costly, or regarded as a painful exercise; and that justice for others is charity for ourselves."[44]

Yet the Troglodytes proved unable to sustain such virtue. They chose a king to relieve them of the burdens of virtuous autonomy. The truth of this beautiful socializing myth was called into question in Montesquieu's own work. He never denied the sublimity of the vision, but he did deny its painlessness. Such virtue involves lifting human nature to a higher plane, transforming us from selfish individuals into something we naturally are not. It requires an austerity and singlemindedness that is difficult to maintain, however admirable and satisfying its fruits. The myth of the Troglodytes suggests that such a regime can sometimes sustain itself in extraordinary circum-

---

[42] *Pensée* 30 (549) and 2035 (183).

[43] Descriptions of virtuous republics can be found throughout Montsquieu's writings; see, for example, *Esprit des lois* III:3; v:2-3; and *pensées* 1269 (618); 1342 (1791); 1760 (232); 1854 (234); and 1891 (233).

[44] Letter XII (*Oeuvres complètes*, I, 149); the tale of the Troglodytes is given in letters XI-XIV, with a sequel in *pensée* 1616 (120).

stances for a time; but in the *Spirit of the Laws* Montesquieu stresses its exceptional demands on human beings and the difficulties of instituting it among ordinary men. He mentions the Severambian regime, along with Plato's republic, Crete, and Sparta, as specific examples of this type of polity; this indicates that he regards it as a utopian vision, although not one that is impossible to realize. A legislator of genius must create the institutional and educational frameworks that lead men to see themselves and their fellows in this way; and such a man is not to be met with every day. In modern times, the most familiar parallel to such regimes is a monastery, in which all ordinary human passions are denied, and only the obedient love of the order itself is left, partaking of the fierceness of other passions that have been channeled into this one love.[45] This analogy moves republican virtue paradoxically close to despotism, in focusing all human energy in a single direction; it also reminds us that modern men can be dealt with in this way, just as they can become the material for despotism.

Thus while Montesquieu regarded the classical republic as the site of true human virtue, he also saw that it forces men into demanding molds that thwart their most primitive desires and inclinations. In one of his earliest *pensées* he asserts the unnaturalness of such a regime:

> Just as the physical world subsists only because each portion of matter tends to flee the center, so the political world is supported only by this interior and restless desire each individual has to get out of the situation in which he finds himself. It is in vain that an overly austere morality attempts to efface these traits that the greatest of all workers has imprinted in our souls. It is up to morality, which tries to work with the human heart, to regulate these sentiments, not to destroy them.[46]

In his description of the unregenerate early Troglodytes in the *Persian Letters*, Montesquieu shows how a society of unregulated men is quickly torn apart by these centrifugal desires. Each individual follows his own interest and sees no reason to come to the aid of any of his fellows. The message of this part of the fable is that there is no innate harmony among our interests as selfish human beings. The virtuous republic seeks to induce harmony by instilling a preference for the public interest over the private from childhood, and continually rein-

---

[45] *Esprit des lois*, v:2 and iv:6. Saint-Evremond uses this same parallel in his "Réflexions sur les divers génies du peuple Romain"; according to the *Catalogue de la bibliothèque de Montesquieu*, edited by Louis Desgraves, pp. 165-166, the *président* owned several editions of Saint-Evremond's works. For Montesquieu's musings on utopias, see *pensée* 1208 (1811).

[46] *Pensée* 5 (69).

forcing this preference at every point. But there is another way, much easier and more efficient: providing a framework of laws and customs that lead individuals to serve the interest of other men as they pursue their own. In this scheme, the natural preference for the private interest is not suppressed, but made the material of public good. This is the way of modern monarchy.

The description of monarchy reflects Montesquieu's conviction that we always act according to where we think our selfish interest lies unless we are systematically taught to act otherwise. In the *Persian Letters*, Usbek insists that justice exists in the universe and does not depend on human convention or contrivance; but it is not always perceived by men, and "even when they see it they often turn away from it. For their interest is always what they see most clearly. Justice raises her voice, but can hardly be heard amidst the tumult of human passions." No one is "gratuitously unjust; there must be a reason that determines what men do, and this reason is always a reason of interest."[47] Usbek argues that the best government for men, the one "most conformable to reason," is that "which proceeds to its goal with least friction," and "guides men in a way that most closely suits their penchants and their inclinations."[48] This is the path taken by the monarchical regime described in the *Spirit of the Laws*. It requires no difficult sacrifices or artificial inculcation of virtue, only the ingenious arrangement of rules and institutions so that ambitious men are encouraged to serve the state and obey the law.

Whereas republics dissolve private interests in a public whole, monarchies assure space for pursuit of private interest within a public framework that provides for the minimal integration of those interests. The distinctive spring or motivating principle of monarchy is "honor, that is, the prejudice of each person and each rank," which takes the place of virtue in a republic and "represents it throughout." This desire to assure precedence and recognition for oneself operates "like the system of the universe, where one force ceaselessly pulls men outward from the center, and the force of gravity brings them back. Honor makes all parts of the body politic move, and links them together by its own action; and thus it happens that each individual works for the common good, while he believes himself to be pursuing his own particular interests." Montesquieu observes that "it is true, philosophically speaking, that this is a false honor that conducts all

---

[47] Letter LXXXIII. Montesquieu may well have derived this sentiment directly from cardinal de Retz, whose *Mémoires* he greatly admired; *pensée* 1203 (897).
[48] Letter LXXX; cf. *pensée* 597 (1800): "In a well-regulated monarchy, the subjects are like fish caught in a great net; they believe themselves to be free yet they are in fact constrained."

parts of the state; but this false honor is just as useful to the public as true honor would be to individuals who possess it."[49]

In the distinctive English variant of monarchy, that peculiar "mixed regime" that Montesquieu is hard put to name, avarice rather than ambition is the spring of action. Montesquieu speaks of the preoccupation with commerce as "the genius of our century," the distinguishing characteristic of modernity. He shared the common notion that noble ambition was gradually being displaced in his own time by the bourgeois passion of avarice. The English regime accommodates and thrives upon this passion. It also encourages the spirit of frugality, hard work, independence, and personal liberty with which commerce is associated.[50] However, Montesquieu is careful to point out that monarchy based on honor also gives rise to a "spirit of liberty" that is an effective substitute for liberty itself. He values liberty highly, as "that good which makes it possible to enjoy all other goods," the essential condition or ground for a happy human life.[51] But he makes clear that liberty is not uniquely associated with any form of government. It accompanies moderation; and the virtuous republic can be made as amenable to moderated power as monarchy itself. Rome and Sparta, as well as England and France, are named by Montesquieu among moderated polities, since their constitutions distribute power in complex ways. It is true that *personal independence* is closely connected with the English type of modern monarchy. But Montesquieu was ambivalent about this particular type of liberty; it isolates men from one another and leads them from honor or virtue into privatism. Liberty, in his eyes, is fundamentally identified with security; and the "political liberty" of the ancients can provide this as easily as the individualistic liberty of the moderns.[52]

Montesquieu lists many advantages of modern monarchy; yet he clearly regarded this regime as deficient, judged by the standard of

[49] *Esprit des lois* III:6-7 (*Oeuvres complètes*, II, 256-257).

[50] In *Esprit des lois*, V:6 (*Oeuvres complètes*, II, 280), Montesquieu remarks that "the spirit of commerce brings with it that of frugality, economy, moderation, work, wisdom, tranquillity, order, and rule," and thus tempers the corrupting effects of wealth so long as it prevails. This makes it possible to have commercial republics (such as Athens) as well as modern commercial mixed regimes. In XIX:27 (*Oeuvres complètes*, II, 574-579), he deals with the connections between commerce and liberty in England. The reference to commerce as the *génie particulier* of his own time is in *pensée* 810 (1228).

[51] *Pensée* 1574 (1797).

[52] *Pensées* 751 (1805), 907 (80), and 940 (1806) support this conclusion; Thomas Pangle, *Montesquieu's Philosophy of Liberalism*, is a cogent statement of an alternative reading of Montesquieu on modern liberal polities; for a fuller attempt to come to terms with his arguments, see Keohane, "The President's English," pp. 378-386.

true human excellence. His ambivalence about monarchy is apparent even in those passages in which he praises it most enthusiastically, as when he observes that in a monarchy

> policy accomplishes great things with the least possible amount of virtue, just as in the best machines, art employs the fewest possible movements, forces, gears. The state subsists independently of any love for *la patrie*, and of the desire for true glory, the renunciation of the self, the sacrifice of our dearest interests, and all those heroic virtues we discover in the ancients, known to us only by hearsay. The laws take the place of all these virtues, and there is no need of them. The state relieves you of the necessity of having them, and a private action done quietly enough is, in a sense, an action without consequence.[53]

His admiration for classical virtue was profound, although he well knew its costs. The absence of such true virtue in modern monarchy leaves a hollowness and pettiness that Montesquieu describes with uniform distaste. The ambition that undergirds modern monarchy is not even noble Corneillian heroism; in the form it takes among the denizens of Versailles, ambition degrades men into a paltry preoccupation with themselves. In describing the slothful, sly, perfidious impulses that substitute for virtue in a monarchy based on honor, Montesquieu admitted that he might be thought to be satirizing instead of praising this regime. Ambition and avarice alike encourage isolation, meanness, and triviality. Montesquieu depicts monarchy as an ambiguous bargain, and one whose terms were becoming worse in his own time. "We have left to princes the pleasures of commanding, in order to reserve to ourselves those of obedience. This means that grandeur and its perils are the lot of kings. Our own is mediocrity, security, repose. But every day they labor to make our lot less attractive. They leave us our pettiness, but work to deprive us of our tranquillity."[54]

Modernity, for Montesquieu as well as Tocqueville, means an increasing tendency toward the isolation of each individual from his fellows.[55] In the fragments of a "Treatise on duty" that Montesquieu

---

[53] *Esprit des lois*, III:5 (*Oeuvres complètes*, II, 255).

[54] *Pensée* 282 (1849); *Esprit des lois*, III:5-7, and *pensées* 998 (33) and 1272 (621), contain Montesquieu's reflections on the pettiness of his courtier contemporaries. Corrado Rosso, *Montesquieu moraliste*, pp. 100-101, remarks that this indictment of noble education and values is *une véritable autocritique* on Montesquieu's part.

[55] The comparison with Tocqueville is also made by Mark Hulliung in *Montesquieu and the Old Regime*, pp. 27-53. Montesquieu's stress on the isolation of men in modern monarchy casts doubt on Raymond Aron's conclusion in

wrote in the early 1720s, he endorses the Stoic view that the truly virtuous man "should be moved to succor the perfect stranger as much as his closest friend," so that even friendship becomes a derogation from our duty to love mankind. The man who focuses affection on a few "separates himself from the trunk and attaches himself to the branches." However, Montesquieu recognized that among imperfect men friendship is a praiseworthy extension of the self. In listing the virtues of the ancients, he remarks on the close friendship between citizens. "They were bound together by all sorts of ties," he says, whereas "today all this has been abolished. . . . Each man is isolated. It seems that the natural effect of arbitrary power is to particularize all interests. Yet the links that detach a man from himself and attach him to another lead men to undertake the most sublime actions. Without it, all is vulgar; nothing is left but the lowest interest, which is in truth only an animal instinct inherent in all men."[56]

It is not only the "false honor" of ambition that divides modern men from one another. Avarice has the same effects. In his travel notebooks, Montesquieu was vitriolic in his scorn for the Dutch passion for commerce, which he held responsible for the deformation of their public life. He was less harsh in his assessment of the same phenomenon in England, where he recognized its connections with the taste for independence. But he was careful to distinguish this sentiment that separates men from the sentiment of patriotism that unites them. He spoke of the English as "confederated" petty monarchs rather than "fellow-citizens."[57] Their focus on sturdy personal autonomy made it impossible for them to be true citizens. Their "public life" was a game of spectators and dilettantes, not the integral civic commitment of the ancient polity. Although he was willing to refer to England as "that nation where the republic hides itself under the form of a monarchy," Montesquieu never equated the English constitution with the classical republic.[58] "It was a pretty sight," he says,

---

Main Currents of Sociological Thought, I, 24, that honor shields the state "against the supreme evil of despotism," since despotism thrives on isolation.

[56] *Pensée* 1253 (604) in *Oeuvres complètes*, I, 1130; this is among a number of fragments from a lost "Traité des devoirs" summarized in *Oeuvres complètes*, I, 108-111.

[57] *Esprit des lois*, XIX:27 (*Oeuvres complètes*, II, 582); on Dutch avarice, see the "Voyage de Gratz à La Haye," *Oeuvres complètes*, I, 863-874, and *pensée* 552 (1120).

[58] *Esprit des lois*, V:19 (*Oeuvres complètes*, II, 304); judging by the handwriting in the manuscript of the treatise, this chapter was written very late. Montesquieu had a hard time deciding what to call England. It was not based on honor, virtue, or fear. In *pensée* 1744 (238) he speaks of it as a "mixed monarchy," corresponding to the mixed aristocracy of Sparta and the mixed

"in the past century, to watch the impotent efforts of the English to establish a democracy," since their politicians were wholly lacking in the virtue necessary to sustain such efforts. It was the English politicians above all whom Montesquieu had in mind in his indictment of the political culture of modernity: "Greek statesmen, who lived in a popular government, recognized no other force that could sustain them except virtue itself. Those of today speak to us only of manufactures, commerce, finances, wealth, and luxury."[59]

5. Virtue and Politics

In an *avertissement* designed to mollify critics of the *Spirit of the Laws*, Montesquieu insisted that the "virtue" he identified with classical republics and found wanting in modern monarchies was *political* virtue, not to be confused with moral or Christian virtue. The treatise contains ample evidence that he also thought "vices" in the traditional sense could be useful in politics. Book XIX is particularly full of comments on this topic; here is chapter XI of that book in its entirety:

> I have not said any of this to diminish the infinite distance between the vices and the virtues—God forbid! I have simply wished to make clear that all political vices are not moral vices, and that all moral vices are not political vices; and it is this that must not be forgotten by those who make laws that offend *l'esprit géneral*.[60]

This attitude toward the political usefulness of moral "vice" had been familiar since Machiavelli and Montaigne. Where Montesquieu differed with them both was in his conception of political *vertu*, which had nothing in common with the forceful and tortured secular morality of *raison d'état*. In identifying "love for the patrie and for equality" as the motivating principle in republican politics, Montesquieu had "new ideas, for which it was necessary to find new words, or give

---

democracy of Rome. In *Esprit des lois*, XIX:27 (*Oeuvres complètes*, II, 580), he describes it as a nation where "on the foundation of a free government one often sees the form of an absolutist regime."

[59] *Esprit des lois*, III:3 (*Oeuvres complètes*, II, 252); see also *pensée* 981 (1795). Montesquieu's most sustained discussion of English politics, touching on liberty, virtue, and corruption, is a letter to M. Domville, *pensée* 1960 (1883), *Oeuvres complètes*, I, 1447-1450.

[60] *Esprit des lois*, XI:11 (*Oeuvres complètes*, II, 563); in chapter 27 of that same book, a description of English politics, he says: "All the passions are free there—hatred, envy, jealousy, the ardor to enrich and distinguish oneself, appear in all their fullness; and if it were otherwise the state would be like a man laid low by sickness, who lacks passions because he has no strength" (*Oeuvres complètes*, II, 575).

new meanings to old ones," just as he claimed.[61] But his critics had a point; and it is not surprising that *L'Esprit des lois* soon joined Montaigne's *Essais* and Charron's *Sagesse* on the Index of forbidden books. For the political "virtue" identified by Montesquieu with classical republics, and denied to subjects of modern monarchies, was a secular version of Christian charity itself.

Montesquieu defines the "political virtue" that distinguishes republics from monarchies as "the love of the laws and of *la patrie*. This love, which demands a continual preference for public interest to one's own, gives rise to all particular virtues, which are themselves nothing but this preference." Virtue itself is defined by Montesquieu as "a general affection for the human species." He says that "nothing is closer to divine Providence than that general benevolence and grand capacity for loving that embraces all men; and nothing is closer to the instincts of beasts than the limits the heart puts upon itself when it is concerned only with its own self-interest, or with what it discovers immediately around itself."[62] The love of something beyond the self takes the specific form of love of *la patrie* and its laws in the republican polity; but the capacity to love something other than the self, to extend one's vision and affection beyond isolated individuality, is what Montesquieu means by virtue. He captured the essence of *la charité* for a particular type of *patrie*, and convicted subjects of monarchies of what Christians had always taken to be vice—ambitious, avaricious, narrow self-interest. That Montesquieu was aware of these consequences but loath to join battle on such issues is suggested by the oblique evasiveness of his replies to clerical charges that he had dishonored Christian monarchy by his notion of monarchical *honneur*.[63]

In arguing that the "spirit of commerce" unites nations but divides individuals from one another, and leads men to "make a traffic of all human actions and all moral virtues," Montesquieu summarized concisely a long tradition of argument in French moral discourse.[64] His debt to that tradition led him to take for granted the primacy of *amour-propre* in human psychology. But he contended that it expresses itself differently in different eras, societies, and individuals.

[61] "Avertissement de l'auteur," *Esprit des lois, Oeuvres complètes*, II, 227.
[62] *Pensée* 938 (1097); discourse before the Bordeaux parlement, 1725, *Oeuvres complètes*, I, 47; and *Esprit des lois*, IV:6.
[63] Andrew Lynch, "Montesquieu and the Ecclesiastical Critics of *L'Esprit des lois*."
[64] *Esprit des lois*, XX:2; Montesquieu's familiarity with Jansenist argument is clear from several references to Nicole's *Essays*; see especially *pensées* 2064 (1036), 1970 (802), and 2231 (1107); *pensée* 464 (1042) is a short statement of the ethic of *amour-propre* and *l'envie de plaire*.

In his study of the Romans, he points out that "the love of our own conservation displays itself in many ways, leading us sometimes to sacrifice ourselves for love of self."[65] It is much easier to focus *amour-propre* on narrow advancement and preservation of the individual than to turn it against itself in love for a larger whole. That is the course followed in educating the subjects of modern monarchies, who are taught a "virtue" that centers not on what we owe to others, but on duties to oneself, "not so much what calls us toward our fellow-citizens, but what sets us apart from them." This course is deficient, in Montesquieu's eyes, judged by the standard of human capacity for fellowship. He asserted that man is a social animal, in the sense that he has the capacity to enjoy things in common with other members of his species, whereas "beasts, who all have separate interests, continually harm one another."[66] Men have become more beastlike, and less godlike, in separating themselves out from one another and pursuing private interests. In ancient times, this was not so; this explains Montesquieu's tone of admiration and awe in describing the educational achievements of the Greeks and Romans, who pursued the much more difficult course of bringing men together in community. "When one ponders the pettiness of our motives, the baseness of our actions, the avarice that leads us to seek the vilest rewards, and our ambition, so different from the love of glory," says Montesquieu, "one is astounded by the difference between these two spectacles. It seems as though, since these two great ancient nations disappeared, mankind has lost at least a cubit from its stature."[67]

Yet Montesquieu did not think the species itself had altered with the centuries. In faraway Pennsylvania, among the communities established by the Jesuits in Paraguay, and in a canton hidden deep in the Swiss mountains, he found traces of civic virtue in his own times. He praised William Penn as "a true Lycurgus," forming a people worthy of Greece itself "amidst the dregs and corruptions of modern times."[68] Here was heartening evidence that modern men are not abbreviated in their moral stature. They can be led to undertake the demands and rewards of citizenship, if they are fortunate enough to find leaders of rare genius, and situations of sufficient purity and freshness. Montesquieu paid homage to the legislators who made such

[65] *Considérations sur . . . les Romains*, ch. xii (*Oeuvres complètes*, ii, 136).
[66] *Pensée* 1747 (366); *Esprit des lois*, iv:2 (*Oeuvres complètes*, ii, 262).
[67] *Pensée* 221 (598); see also *pensée* 1760 (232).
[68] *Esprit des lois*, iv:6 (*Oeuvres complètes*, ii, 268); Voltaire also refers to Penn's having brought forth the Golden Age, in *Philosophical Letters*, no. iv. Montesquieu refers to Berne in the *Considérations sur . . . les Romains*, ix (*Oeuvres complètes*, ii, 120), and to Paraguay in the passage where he praises Penn.

enclaves possible, and mused about a set of ideal institutions in which the splendors of the ancients might be recaptured among modern men. He also named a few Frenchmen who deserved to be ranked alongside the Romans for their glorious patriotism. Saint Louis and Michel de L'Hôpital were on his list, as was Henry of Navarre.[69] These men of rare civic virtue embellished his country's history and provided grounds for optimism about excellence in modern times. Montesquieu was sufficiently exhilarated by this possibility to think of ways the ideal community of classical republics might be a realistic alternative for his contemporaries. In the ninth book of the *Spirit of the Laws*, read with special interest by the legislators of the infant United States of America, he showed how a confederation of small republics might retain the blessings of intimate civic virtue, and yet also "by the strength of their association, all the advantages of large monarchies."[70]

In developing the model of modern monarchy, Montesquieu appears in his most familiar guise as the great philosopher of liberalism. His theory of the balanced constitution, and his conviction of the link between liberty and the rule of law, are the best-known aspects of his liberalism. Among other aspects, less often noticed, are Montesquieu's suspicion of direct popular power and his attitude toward property. The passages in the *Spirit of the Laws* on the advantages of representation, and the drawbacks of active involvement by all citizens in classical democracies, indicate that while Montesquieu admired the extraordinary virtue and patriotism that made self-government possible, he did not greatly admire self-government *per se*. His cavalier dismissal of the claims of a free man to govern himself makes clear that the exercise of political responsibility is not itself, for Montesquieu, a part of the good life.[71] His chapters on the connection between laws and property are among the most important in his treatise, although they are seldom read because they follow lengthy disquisitions on the details of Roman husbandry and the length of the hair of Frankish kings. In book XXVI, chapter 15, Montesquieu distinguishes political laws concerning liberty, which he describes as *l'empire de la cité*, from civil laws concerning property. His discussion recalls Bodin on the public and the private, and foreshadows Hegel on civil society and the state.

Since we encounter Montesquieu so frequently as patron saint of modern liberalism, it is easy to overlook his ambivalence about liberal politics, even in England. I have tried to bring out this ambivalence by citing passages in which he connects politics in modern monarchies, of

[69] *Pensée* 1258 (609); the sketch for ideal institutions is in *pensée* 185 (1966).
[70] *Esprit des lois*, IX:1 (*Oeuvres complètes*, II, 370).
[71] *Esprit des lois*, XI:6 (*Oeuvres complètes*, II, 399); see also VIII:2-3, and XIX:27.

both the French and English types, with hatred, envy, pettiness, isolation of all sorts. He recognized that luxury in a monarchy, where wealth is unequally distributed, has as its concomitant the misery of the poor. It is true, says Montesquieu, that "if the rich did not spend so lavishly, the poor would die of hunger"; but this is only because "in accumulating their great wealth, a few individuals have deprived a part of the citizens of physical necessities, and they must give them back."[72] He also saw threats to independence of thought entailed by the liberty the English cherished so much: "In monarchies that are extremely absolute, historians betray the truth because they lack the liberty to speak it; in states that are extremely free, they betray truth because of that very liberty, which, by producing divisions incessantly, leads each one to become as much the slave of the prejudices of his faction as he would be of a despot."[73] Such insights into dilemmas of modernity are worth noting, though they are rare. More commonly, Montesquieu criticized "liberal" practices from the standpoint of the classical ideal.

In his youth, Montesquieu cast in his lot with the Ancients against the Moderns; and he never reversed himself. His most fundamental admiration was reserved for the classical polity, the site of true human virtue. His descriptions of this alternative inspired Rousseau and others to extend his vision, and laid the foundation for modern theories of community. Montesquieu expressed deep nostalgia for the "laughing air" the world had worn in the time of Greece and Rome. He mourned the passing of the transparent simplicity and naivete that made it possible for men to "see through the eyes of others what their own *amour-propre* hid from them," rather than remaining narrowly centered and isolated in themselves. "I confess," he said, "my inclination for the ancients. Antiquity enchants me, and I am always drawn to say with Pliny: 'It is to Athens that you go. Respect her gods.' "[74]

[72] *Esprit des lois*, vii:4 (*Oeuvres complètes*, 336). In xv:9, there is an argument against slavery that depends on the notion of a lottery similar to Rawls's "veil of ignorance," as Melvin Richter points out in his note to this chapter in *The Political Theory of Montesquieu*.
[73] *Esprit des lois*, xix:27 (*Oeuvres complètes*, ii, 583).
[74] *Pensée* 110 (444); 1606 (558); and 1607 (489); and "Eloge de la sincerité," *Oeuvres complètes*, i, 99-107.

CHAPTER FIFTEEN

Rousseau: The General Interest in the General Will

1. THE MORALS OF THE AGE

In his *Reflections on Human Nature*, Arthur O. Lovejoy speaks of the "late seventeenth and early eighteenth centuries" as "the time in which the unfavorable general appraisal of man may be said to have reached, if not its climax, at any rate its most frequent and most notable expression outside the writings of theologians." This was an age in which secular as well as religious writers uncovered countless complications, hypocrisies, and stratagems in human nature, and became accustomed to assuming that overt motives and apparently virtuous acts are almost certainly a mask for something else. These authors displayed not only psychological penetration but also exceptional ingenuity in political and economic thought. Men discovered substitutes for virtue, efficient and orderly accommodations among members of a species for whom virtue itself is a rare grace. According to Lovejoy, in the eighteenth century the tide began to turn in the opposite direction, toward the optimism of the Victorian era, which he labels "the Age of Man's Good Conceit of Himself." But in 1769, Voltaire was still asserting that

> Men in general are foolish, ungrateful, jealous, covetous of their neighbor's goods; abusing their superiority when they are strong, and tricksters when they are weak. . . . Power is commonly possessed, in states and in families, by those who have the strongest arms, the most resolute minds, and the hardest hearts. From which the moralists of all ages have concluded that the human species is of little worth; and in this they have not departed widely from the truth.[1]

A number of eighteenth-century Frenchmen were fascinated by the issues in psychology and social arrangements that had been raised by seventeenth-century writers. We have seen this in the work of Saint-

[1] Voltaire, *Dieu et les hommes*, quoted by Arthur O. Lovejoy, *Reflections on Human Nature*, p. 16; the other quotations from Lovejoy's book are on pp. 7 and 15.

Pierre, d'Argenson, and Montesquieu. Of others who could be used to illustrate the point, Vauvenargues is among the most interesting.[2] In his *Introduction à la connaissance de l'esprit humain*, a good many familiar themes are evident. He asserts, for example, that "the passions oppose one another and can serve as counterweights; but the dominant passion can only conduct itself according to its own interest, true or imaginary, because it reigns despotically over the will, without which nothing can be done."[3] His pithy *Réflexions et maximes*, in the style of La Rochefoucauld, insist on the prominence of selfishness in human motivation, yet the necessity for men to aid one another to advance their purposes. Some of his maxims are cynical in the sprightly fashion of the salons. He said that "the art of pleasing is the art of deceiving," and that "interest consoles us for the death of those near us as friendship consoles us for their life"; he noted that "the utility of virtue is so obvious that knaves practice it out of interest," and that "it is a wonderful spectacle to consider men meditating in secret how to destroy one another, and nonetheless forced to aid each other against their inclination and design."[4] In a different vein, a variation on Nicole's view of life as a masked ball, Vauvenargues asserts that "we are too inattentive or too occupied with ourselves to understand one another deeply; we are like those dancers at a masked ball who hold one another by the hand affectionately without recognizing one another, and part a moment later, never to see each other again or to regret the parting." The injustices as well as the efficiencies of human society were apparent to him. "To see how men use one another," he said, "one might think of human life and the affairs of the world as a serious game where any moves are permitted to seize the goods of another at our own risk, and where the lucky players despoil, with all honor, the more unfortunate or less skilled."[5]

Vauvenargues's own conception of morality was highly social. He asserted that moral good and evil refer only to the advantage or disadvantage of an entire society, not of an individual. He defined society as "a body that subsists by the union of many members and confounds the particular interest in the general interest; this is the foundation of all morality."[6] Perhaps his most important point, for his contemporaries, was the reiteration of the distinction made by Camus and Ab-

[2] Vauvenargues' *Dialogues*, in Henry Bonnier, ed., *Oeuvres complètes*, II, 359-401, are dominated by seventeenth-century personages, and are close in style and spirit to the *Dialogues* of Fénelon.
[3] *Oeuvres complètes*, I, 239.
[4] *Oeuvres complètes*, II, nos. 312, 329, 534, and 759.
[5] *Réflexions et maximes*, *Oeuvres complètes*, II, 311.
[6] *Introduction à la connaissance de l'esprit humain*, *Oeuvres complètes*, I, 241.

badie between *l'amour-propre* and *l'amour de nous-mêmes*. A man who voluntarily dies for glory may prefer an imaginary life of fame in which he envisions himself praised by posterity, over his "real" life of physical survival; but to treat his motives as though they were equivalent to those of his neighbor who runs away from battle to save his skin, is to run everything together meaninglessly. Thus the love of self, *amour de nous-mêmes*, can lead us to actions that involve sacrifice of self, in which we "seek our happiness outside ourselves." Narrow *amour-propre*, on the other hand, "subordinates all commodities to its own well-being, is itself its only object and unique goal; so that whereas the passions that arise from *l'amour de nous-mêmes* give us to things, *amour-propre* desires things to give themselves to us, and make us the center of everything."[7]

In one of his *Réflexions* (no. 219), Vauvenargues made a particularly trenchant point about self-love:

> We love to censure human nature, to try to raise ourselves above our species and enrich ourselves with the consideration that we rob from it. We are so presumptuous that we think we can separate our personal interest in the matter from that of humanity and slander the human race without compromising ourselves. This ridiculous vanity has filled philosophy books with invectives against nature. Man is at present in disgrace among all thinking persons, and the prize goes to whoever can charge him with the most vices; but perhaps he is on the point of recovering himself and restoring to himself all his virtues; nothing is stable, and philosophy has its fashions just as much as clothes, music, architecture, etc.

Among his contemporaries, slandering human nature was a common pastime. It was rare to admit membership in the species at the same time as one indicted it. Even more common, however, was admiration for the efficient accommodations of self-love. Delisle de la Drevetière, a successful comedian who specialized in satirizing polite society and civilized mores by showing how they looked through the eyes of an innocent savage, wrote an essay on *amour-propre* in which the satirical passages are less striking than is admiration for the utility of self-love in society. It makes for an inferior sort of virtue compared with true goodness, but rescues us from the horrors of living among men whose self-love is unenlightened. Delisle describes, with tongue only occasionally in cheek, a network of reciprocal interests based on *l'amour*

[7] *Ibid.*, pp. 227-228.

propre bien entendu, capped off by a monarch who sees clearly his own interests in good government.[8]

Yet as Vauvenargues pointed out, this fashion in philosophy had reached its peak. Some writers, unsatisfied by stock recitations of depravity and complacent celebrations of its utility, were reaching for a conception of virtue that would be something other than an homage paid by vice. Montesquieu's admiration for the Greeks and Romans was shared by Henri d'Aguesseau, an exemplary man who became chancellor of France and moved his contemporaries to comparisons with L'Hôpital. D'Aguesseau condemned his contemporaries for their restlessness, their inability to live happily in themselves. "Such is the dominant character of *les moeurs de notre siècle*," he said; "a general unquietude, agitation, discontent with one's own situation." He commended the ancients for the admirable severity of their *moeurs*, without luxury or false grandeur, and attempted to instill in his own countrymen the "love for *la patrie*" that he admired in the ancients.[9] He spoke of it as a "love almost natural to man, which we know by our sentiments, praise with our reason, and should follow by our interest itself." Yet it has become an "exotic plant in monarchies," and only citizens of republics taste its fruit.

In republics, asserted d'Aguesseau in an address on "L'Amour de la patrie" in 1715, each citizen is accustomed from birth

> to regard the fortune of the state as his own individual fortune. This perfect equality, this civil fraternity, which makes of all citizens a single family, interests each of them equally in the goods and ills of their *patrie*. . . . The love of the *patrie* becomes a species of *amour-propre*. One loves oneself truly in loving the republic, and finally comes to love it more than oneself. The inflexible Roman citizen sacrificed his children for the salvation of the republic; . . . the father was absorbed and in effect annihilated in the consul. Nature is horrified by this; but *la patrie*, stronger than nature itself, gave to him as many children as the citizens he had saved by the loss of his own blood.

D'Aguesseau hotly denies that such a love is impossible in a monarchy. It should be the "sacred link between the authority of kings and the obedience of the people, uniting all their desires." But he finds none

---

[8] Delisle de la Drevetière, *Essai sur l'amour propre*; the better-known comedies are *Arlequin sauvage* (1721) and *Timon le misanthrope* (1722).

[9] Henri d'Aguesseau, *Oeuvres complètes*, edited by M. Pardessus, 1, 47-48 and 95-100; these are from d'Aguesseau's first and fifth *Mercuriales*, 1698 and 1702.

of this among his own countrymen. They think of the fortunes of France as quite alien to their own,

> and to the extent that the zeal for the public good is extinguished in our hearts, the desire for our particular interest is kindled. This becomes our law, our sovereign, our *patrie*. We know nothing of other citizens except when we wish to win their favor or fear their enmity. The rest are for us like members of a foreign nation, virtual enemies. Thus there flows into each one of us that poison fatal to society, that blind love of oneself, which, separating one's own fortune from that of the state, is always ready to sacrifice the whole state to one's own prosperity. . . . The common good is so far forgotten that there remains in the kingdom only particular interests that carry on a sort of civil war.

D'Aguesseau notices that men respond to this situation in different ways. Some become all the more avid for their own selfish advancement; others, noble enough to avoid doing evil but not strong enough to resist it, "fall into a profound indifference, and lose themselves in a round of lazy amusements. They form a kind of *patrie* apart, where, as though on an enchanted island, they drink tranquilly from those waters that make men forget the goods and ills of their former country." According to d'Aguesseau, "Those who bestow on this disgust for the *patrie* the specious title of philosophy" deserve particular censure. Men who follow this course "are insensible to the needs of their fellow citizens and deaf to the voice of society." They seek their own good in their isolated *patrie* and "find of monarchical sovereignty in the independence of their lives." Where then can the true *patrie* be found? Betrayed by laziness and interest, condemned by vain philosophy, we see "a great kingdom, and no *patrie*; a numerous people, but no citizens." D'Aguesseau exhorts his countrymen to free themselves from bondage to their individual interests and undertake the demanding but liberating tasks of public service, based on the hope of achieving public good. "It is thus that the love of *la patrie* will be rekindled in all hearts," he says; "the links of society will be tightened again, the citizens will find a fatherland and the fatherland its citizens."[10]

D'Aguesseau himself attempted throughout his life to live up to his own model. In addition to holding office, he wrote several important essays and treatises on public law, which contributed to the vigor of the eighteenth-century constitutionalist tradition. He defended the parlements as the "general council of the nation," the source of the

---

[10] D'Aguesseau, xixth *Mercuriale*, in *Oeuvres complètes*, I, 229-235.

"wise tempering" of the monarchy praised by observers from Machiavelli onwards, reining in the prince and his ministers to prevent royal power from degenerating into tyranny, as well as restraining the avidity of the rich and powerful, to protect the poor.[11] His most constant theme, however, was the necessity of combining individual and common interest; he insisted that the two are not "great enemies," as so many had said; the happiness of each individual is inextricably bound up with the fortunes of the whole. The two sorts of happiness should not be confused with one another, since they are different—"the happiness or interest of each citizen, considered separately, and the happiness or interest of all citizens considered in common, or of the entire state." The task of good government is to know how to bring them together in harmony and protect them both.[12]

There were, therefore, a few Frenchmen during this era who insisted on the distinction between an efficient social system based on coordinated *amour-propre* and a polity composed of citizens motivated by love of their fatherland. Montesquieu and d'Aguesseau were prominent among them; but the most prominent of all was a man who knew something about citizenship at first hand, the "citizen of Geneva," Jean-Jacques Rousseau.

2. The Masterpiece of Policy in Our Century

In the autumn of 1749, thirty-two years after Montesquieu delivered his discourse on bold advances in the sciences to the Bordeaux academy, another provincial academy in Dijon invited essays on the moral consequences of those advances. Rousseau won the academy's prize by answering the question "si le rétablissement des Sciences et des Arts a contribué à épurer les Moeurs" with a resounding negative. Men of the eighteenth century, including Montesquieu, as we have seen, were accustomed to saying with one breath that they were made of less sturdy moral stuff than their ancestors, and with the next that they had made enormous strides in scientific understanding and the useful arts. In his first essay in social theory, Rousseau linked science itself, as well as philosophy and literature, with luxury, vanity, and indolence. He drew specific connections between aspects of civilization and aspects of decay. Arts and letters support thrones by flattery and pretty rhetoric; they mask our chains with flowers, and thus we

[11] "Fragmens sur l'origine et l'usage des remontrances," *Oeuvres complètes*, x, 4026.
[12] *Essai d'une institution du droit public*, in *Oeuvres complètes*, xv, 164-165, 240-263.

fail to see those chains for what they are. Each science is motivated by a specific human sin. "Astronomy is born of superstition," says Rousseau; "eloquence, of ambition, hatred, flattery, lying; geometry, of avarice; physics of vain curiosity; and all, even ethics itself, of human pride. Thus the sciences and the arts owe their birth to our vices."[13] Where Montesquieu had referred to nature's sudden revelation of herself to human eyes, Rousseau speaks of men pulling themselves out of nothingness by their own efforts, dissipating by the light of their own reason the shadows in which nature had enveloped herself to prevent men from destroying themselves by means of knowledge.

Rousseau's central argument in this *Discours* is that "commerce with the muses" has infected social intercourse by focusing men's attention on winning approbation by their works. The desire for reputation distorts curiosity and talent, leading them toward corruption rather than the discovery of truth. Philosophy condones such motivations, and encourages them in its practitioners. Contemporary moralists teach the "art of pleasing," which is responsible for the vile uniformity and herd mentality that marks modern men. Men can no longer understand each other (Rousseau expresses this as *se pénétrer réciproquement*). The facility for imitation and dissimulation have covered over our rude natures. We have become adept at hypocrisy, and no longer know one another; in our furor to distinguish ourselves, our desire to be applauded, we have lost our virtue. An observer from some other world might think us very virtuous, since we appear to spend so much time obliging one another, attempting to please each other, and striving to be esteemed. He would be quite mistaken; such behavior is only a façade, and masks the most narrow and vicious preoccupation with the self. Crude xenophobia, national hatred, is unknown among us, but along with it has disappeared completely *l'amour de la patrie*. In Montesquieu's own words, Rousseau observes that "ancient statesmen spoke incessantly of *moeurs* and of virtue; our own speak of nothing but commerce and money."[14]

In response to attacks upon his *Discours*, Rousseau makes clear that it was hypocrisy, vice masquerading as virtue, that first aroused his ire. It is not science as such, but human inability to pursue science without corruption, that is his concern. "It remains an open question," he

---

[13] *Discours sur les sciences et les arts*, in Rousseau, *Oeuvres complètes*, edited by Gagnebin and Raymond, III, 17. Roger Masters, *The Political Philosophy of Rousseau*, chs. v and IX, provides a thoughtful analysis of this essay, which he calls Rousseau's "most defensible work."

[14] *Discours sur les sciences et les arts*, *Oeuvres complètes*, III, 6-9, 19.

remarks, "whether science would be advantageous to men if we could suppose that what they call by that name would actually merit the title; but it is folly to claim that the chimeras of Philosophy, the errors and lies of Philosophers can ever be good for anything."[15] Rousseau agrees with d'Alembert that now that we are corrupt it would be fruitless to thrust us back into barbarism and expect us to regain our innocence. The step we have taken is irreversible; "for when hearts have once been spoiled, they remain so always, and there is no remedy short of some great revolution almost as much to be feared as the evil it might heal, which it is blameworthy to want and impossible to foresee."[16]

In the preface to his play *Narcisse*, Rousseau redoubles his indictment against the clever moralities invented by advocates of *amour-propre*. His major quarrel is with "the taste for letters and philosophy." In addition to the charge that such pursuits "soften and enfeeble the body and the soul," Rousseau contends that they make virtue impossible by "snuffing out the love of our first duties and of true glory." The practice of philosophy isolates men from one another, says Rousseau, "relaxing all the links of esteem and benevolence that attach men to society," ensuring that each practitioner "concentrates in his own person all the interest that virtuous men share with their fellows," so that "his self-love grows in the same proportion as his indifference to the remainder of the universe." Family and *patrie* are nothing to him; "he is neither kinsman, nor citizen, nor man: he is a philosopher."[17]

These contentions disclose an aspect of the paradox of individuality and community in Rousseau's social thought quite different from the familiar picture of the solitary walker constructing social systems from the lovely stuff of reveries. Rousseau's argument here assumes that human ties of esteem, benevolence, and duty are social facts destroyed by the self-induced solitude of the philosopher. He describes virtue in terms of interests shared with other men, and its opposite as the narcissistic preoccupation with the self in the detached life of philosophy. In the next step of this same argument, when the philosopher or man of letters is drawn back into the world from his retirement into himself, he returns in such a way as to make a mockery of the virtue he has denied by his withdrawal. Instead of recognizing social ties of "esteem and benevolence" for his fellow men, the man of letters attempts to be "agreeable" to them, in order to win their admiration for

[15] "Dernière réponse," *Oeuvres complètes*, III, 73-74.
[16] "Observations," *Oeuvres complètes*, III, 56-57.
[17] Preface to *Narcisse*, *Oeuvres complètes*, II, 966-967.

himself and his accomplishments. His enjoyment of that recognition depends on ensuring that his rivals are denied it. It is not only philosophers and artists who behave this way; such conduct has become the norm for modern man. Savants who act according to these principles establish them as moral precepts in all areas of life. In fact, Rousseau says that

> of all the truths I have proposed for the consideration of the wise, here is the most astonishing and the cruelest. Our writers all regard as the masterpiece of policy in our century the sciences, the arts, luxury, commerce, the laws, and all other bonds that tighten the knots of society among men based on personal interest, placing them in mutual dependence on one another, giving them reciprocal needs and common interests, and obliging each to work for the happiness of others in order to secure his own.

Thus Rousseau connects the attitude of the artist or philosopher (who tries to be agreeable to others to gain their adulation) with a society based on the commercial model of reciprocal needs and services. Rousseau was convinced that for all its superficial plausibility, such a doctrine is responsible for the hollow unhappiness of modern man, and the radical inequalities of modern society. The central flaw in such a morality is that it assumes a natural harmony of selfish interests. Since no such harmony exists, a morality that begins by teaching us to serve the interests of others to advance our own becomes the hypocritical cover for a continual struggle among individuals attempting to make themselves happy. And so it happens that this clever morality has "made it impossible for men to live together without getting the better of each other, supplanting, deceiving, betraying, reciprocally destroying one another."

This modern morality, the "masterpiece of policy in our century" that Rousseau condemns so scornfully, teaches men to regard avarice and ambition as natural, and seek to satisfy those selfish passions by serving the needs of other men. Men are told that they will gain fortune by selling goods and services to those in need, and fame by ministering to the common good. But the motivation for such apparently non-selfish acts remains entirely selfish: I bring my bread to the marketplace not because I want to fill my neighbor's belly but because I want to fill my purse; and I serve the state not because I want to help my fellow man, but because I want to dominate him. A minimally clever reasoner discovers that he can often fill his purse more handsomely by cheating his neighbor than by giving honest service, and the man who hungers after power finds that hunger better satisfied by licensed aggression than by benevolence. As a result, modern morality continually places men in a situation in which their selfish interests in their own happiness are directly in conflict with those of other men. As Rousseau puts it:

> For any two men whose interests happen to accord with one another, there are perhaps a hundred thousand others whose interests are opposed to theirs, and there is no way to succeed in getting what they want except by deceiving or ruining all those other men. Here is the tragic source of all the violence, treacheries, perfidies, and horrors that are necessarily created by a state of things in which each individual feigns to be working for the fortune and reputation of others, and in fact seeks only to elevate his own at their expense.[18]

Rousseau's second *Discourse*, on the origins of inequality, provides an account of the genealogy of this modern morality, as the deformation of "natural man." Rousseau begins by abstracting men from all social ties to make the point that the "natural"—in the sense of healthy and appropriate—condition for a human being is an initial self-containment, a neutral *amour de soi*. Then he describes the corruption of such self-love through a complex process of fragmentation. As savage man comes into contact with other members of his species, the natural concern for self-preservation gives way to anxiety for status and recognition, a preoccupation with the advancement of the self in the eyes (and at the expense) of others, which Rousseau calls *amour-propre*. This view of the self as a type of *propriété* to be treasured and developed is profoundly different from the simple desire to satisfy basic needs and avoid extinction that constitutes *amour de soi*. It is accompanied by another erotic deformation, in the *amour* that we develop for members of the opposite sex as we begin to love ourselves corruptly. In Rousseau's account, the notion of *amour* (as opposed to simple lust) is *un sentiment factice* cultivated assiduously by women to reverse the natural sexual order of male domination in intercourse.[19] Its effect, like that of *amour-propre*, is to place a premium on individ-

---

[18] *Ibid.*, pp. 968-969; cf. also Rousseau's "Lettres morales," *Oeuvres complètes*, IV, 1089-1090.

[19] *Discours sur l'origine et les fondemens de l'inégalité parmi les hommes*, *Oeuvres complètes*, III, 158; in note xv to this discourse Rousseau describes *amour propre* as "an artificial sentiment [*sentiment factice*], relative, born in society," and *l'amour de soi-même* as "a natural sentiment" which, when "guided by reason and modified by pity, produces humanity and virtue."

ual concern with being attractive to others, so as to be admired by them, and therefore enabled to use them as a means of satisfying one's selfish desires.

Both these corrupt types of love developed by man as he becomes a social being make it impossible for him to develop any genuine sense of humanity shared with other members of his species. All his relations are dominated by the desire to make himself attractive and advance his own concerns, to validate himself by discounting his associates. When sophisticated technologies lead men to extend the notion of *propriété* from their persons and their simple huts to their tools and then to the land itself, the desire for esteem that found a comparatively innocent outlet in primitive dancing contests is channeled into advanced ambition and avarice. Yet paradoxically, as the preoccupation with the self becomes more intense, human beings develop a multitude of new and complex needs that connect them inextricably with others of their species. The satisfaction of all these artificial cravings depends on the joint efforts of many individuals, while the swollen love of self leads each to try to outstrip the others. Rousseau depicts the dilemma of man in the process of becoming civilized in striking terms:

> It was necessary that he seek incessantly to interest others in his lot, to make them find, at least apparently, their profit in working for his own. . . . In the end, devouring ambition, the ardor to raise his fortunes relatively, less out of true need than in order to set himself above others, inspired in all men a dark penchant for mutually harming one another, a secret jealousy the more dangerous because, in order to do its work more surely, it often took up the mask of benevolence; in a word, competition and rivalry on the other hand, on the other the opposition of interest, and always the hidden desire to make one's own profit at the expense of another.[20]

The most succinct and powerful statement of the antithesis between natural and civil man, and of Rousseau's scornful sorrow as he contemplates the terrible effects of a morality founded on a nonexistent harmony among conflicting selfish interests, is in note IX appended to this *Discourse*. Here he asserts:

> Admire human society as much as you like, it is no less true that it leads men to hate one another in proportion to the clashing of their

---

[20] *Discours sur l'inégalité*, Oeuvres complètes, III, 175; cf. a comparable passage in *Emile*, book IV, Oeuvres complètes, IV, 521, where Rousseau uses Fénelon's image of the falsely virtuous man as a fisherman with baited hook. Lucio Colletti, *From Rousseau to Lenin*, part III, is a useful discussion of Rousseau's rejection of modern morality.

interests, and to render one another apparent services while they in fact do all imaginable evil to each other. What can one think of a commerce where the reason of each individual dictates to him maxims directly contrary to those preached by the public reason to the body of the society, and where each finds his profit in the misfortunes of another?[21]

In laying bare the inadequacies of a pretended benevolence that in fact leads men to "do all imaginable evil to each other," Rousseau is demonstrating the inappropriateness of a model of commercial interests as a basis for construing duties. In attributing such a perverse morality to "our writers" generally (as he does in the preface to *Narcisse*), Rousseau treats it as a contemporary commonplace. The philosophic commonplaces of one age are often the cleverest discoveries of an earlier generation; and so it was with this conception of morality as a reciprocal exchange of services.

Rousseau went to some trouble to show that *amour-propre* is not the necessary condition of "fallen men," but is produced by a human enterprise, the development of a complex society and all the false needs and vain philosophy that accompany it. "It is reason that engenders *amour-propre*," says Rousseau, "and reflection that fortifies it."[22] In his indictment of philosophy for stimulating *amour-propre* and then developing the artificial morality that conserves it, Rousseau captures perfectly the tendency for the sage to dissociate himself from society that had been so highly prized by seventeenth-century philosophers such as La Mothe le Vayer. But he makes it impossible to hold any longer the comfortable conviction that such "private" behavior has no public consequences. A man who deliberately withdraws from the world to concentrate on his own thoughts and pleasures convinces himself that the hypocritical arts of pleasing, which he practices on his ventures out into the world, are an acceptable substitute for virtue. But he denies all human feeling and connection with his fellow man. If his neighbor is butchered underneath his window, he will simply cover his ears, arguing down any remaining sentiments of natural pity lest they disturb his sleep. "Perish if you will," he says. "I am secure."

Thus Rousseau shows that the links of interest and commerce designed to make virtue unnecessary are only so many methods we use to destroy one another. The personal interest of a civilized individual normally consists in trying to advance himself in comparison with other people, and thus is by definition in sharp conflict with the inter-

---

[21] *Discours sur l'inégalité, Oeuvres complètes*, III, 202.
[22] *Ibid.*, p. 156.

ests of other men. Instead of facing this conflict, philosophy tells us that hypocrisy will do quite as well as virtue if we cloak our strategies in simulated altruism. But, says Rousseau sadly, we are so thoroughly corrupted by this poisonous medicine that we have no choice but to continue to take our doses of the same brew. Philosophy, the arts and letters, human inventiveness, and creativity produced the ideas that destroyed virtue; now they provide a "public simulacrum" of the virtue they have banished, and thus deserve to be supported by well-intentioned men.[23]

3. ROUSSEAU'S ALTERNATIVE MORALITIES: *Emile*

In a footnote to the preface to *Narcisse*, Rousseau asserts that personal interest speaks equally strongly to savages and to contemporary Europeans; but it says different things. Savage men lack the sources of conflict that arise with property. No *discussion d'intérêt* divides them, and public esteem is the only good they covet. They are linked together by "the love of society and their common defense," which do not appear to them as separate from their own preservation.[24] The savage deserves to be called a good man, not because he makes strenuous efforts to be virtuous, but because he is in the fortunate position of not having to deceive anyone to advance his goals. In his mature social theory, Rousseau explored several alternatives to the deficient morality of his own century, all predicated on this idea that we must "avoid situations that set our duties in opposition to our interests and show us our good in the misfortunes of another."[25] Having rejected the route of indirect selfishness, he explores the possibility of virtue as self-abnegation, constraint of natural desires. In *La Nouvelle Héloïse*, Julie's sacrifice of her own inclinations in the service of others has overtones of saintly *charité*. But such a sacrifice proves hard for even a heroine to carry out; and in Rousseau's writings, virtue as self-denial is less important than virtue as self-extension. The enlargement of the self to embrace something larger than the self, not the repression of self, becomes the root of virtue. "The psychic energy that the will molds into virtue is always erotic," as Judith Shklar has noted. "Virtue is self-love utterly transformed."[26]

The strategies of Rousseau's major essays in prescriptive social

---

[23] Preface to *Narcisse*, *Oeuvres complètes*, II, 972.
[24] *Ibid.*, pp. 969-970.
[25] *Confessions*, book II, in *Oeuvres complètes*, I, 56; similar statements are in I, 824, and III, 202.
[26] Judith Shklar, *Men and Citizens*, p. 66; an alternative viewpoint is provided by Juliet Flower MacCannell, "Nature and Self-Love."

theory are intended to strengthen the neutral love of self, and then direct it toward good ends, so that men can go outside themselves without having continually to rush back to shore up the shaky sanctuary of self. The conclusion to the second *Discourse* suggests a course of action for well-intentioned individuals who must live in a corrupt society. Rousseau echoes Pascal's notion that the would-be believer becomes faithful by practicing the habits of belief, going through the forms of worship to prepare himself for grace. The would-be virtuous individuals, says Rousseau, "will endeavor, by the exercise of those virtues that they oblige themselves to practice in the course of learning to know them, to merit the eternal reward that they should expect from them." Such men will "respect the sacred bonds of the societies of which they are members," obey the laws and honor those rare statesmen who alleviate abuses. "But they will not have the less contempt for a constitution that can only maintain itself with the aid of so many worthy persons more sought for than discovered, and from which, despite all their efforts, more real calamities than apparent advantages always arise."[27]

Emile describes the education of a single individual to practice virtue in a deformed society, along the lines suggested in this conclusion to the *Discourse on Inequality*. The major purpose of the careful artifice devoted to bringing up Emile is to prevent the early deformation of his natural *amour de soi-même* and then direct it toward virtue.[28] All appeals to Emile in childhood must be made in terms of his personal interests or the demands of impersonal necessity, without reference to the advantage or discomfiture of any other man. Emile is not to be a solitary figure, since Rousseau is convinced that men need one another; only perfect beings can thrive in isolation.[29] But he must not be taught morality, the consciousness of his relations with other human selves, until his awareness of his own interests and their satisfactions is sufficiently clear cut and stable that pity and not self-aggrandizement can be the foundation of his first encounters. Once Emile's lessons in morality begin, the behavioral principle enunciated in Pascal's *Pensées* is drawn upon: "the exercise of the social virtues carries the love of humanity to the bottom of men's hearts; it is in doing good that one becomes good," says Rousseau.

The substance of Emile's virtue is the extension of his self-love to

[27] Note IX to the *Discours sur l'inégalité, Oeuvres complètes*, III, 207-208.
[28] Rousseau describes self-love insofar as it relates only to the individual as "always good, always in conformity with order," in *Emile*, book IV, *Oeuvres complètes*, IV, 491. Allan Bloom, "The Education of Democratic Man: *Emile*," pp. 141-147, is a useful discussion of the direction of self-love in Emile's education.
[29] *Emile*, book IV; *Oeuvres complètes*, IV, 503.

others, the more perfect as it extends beyond those persons intimately connected with himself, so that the contamination of particular interest is less threatening. This prevents pity from degenerating into feebleness, for it is extended generally over the whole species in justice rather than concentrated on those who happen to surround any particular individual. But the process of drawing Emile outside himself must begin with the phenomenon of love for another individual, his Sophie; from thence he can extend his love of self into the virtuous love of other men.[30] The fruit of Emile's education is a natural man who is ready to try his fortunes in society. He is not a savage, for he is educated to live with other men and use his reason; nor is he social man, for he has not been torn from birth in the moral duality that men inflict upon each other. Nor, it should be noted, is Emile a saint, although this alternative ideal is sketched out by the Savoyard vicar. Despite his eloquent recitation of the vicar's creed, it is clear that Rousseau takes the primacy of self-love seriously. Any workable morality for a natural man must begin with the perception of self-interest, and then extend this interest and this love to other men.[31] The saint, who truly empties and sacrifices himself for love of others and of God, is not the model for Emile. To impose such a morality on an ordinary mortal is to set the scene for the moral schizophrenia and hypocrisy from which Rousseau tries to ensure Emile's escape.

Thus he is natural man, not social man, not savage and not saint. Nor, finally, is Emile a citizen. At the beginning of the treatise, Rousseau insists upon the impossibility of training a natural man and a citizen at the same time:

> Natural man is a whole for himself; he is numerical unity, the absolute entity that relates only to himself or to his like. Civil man is only a fractional unity that depends on its denominator, whose value lies in his relation to the whole, which is the social body. Good social institutions are those that do best at denaturing man, taking from him his absolute existence to give him one that is relative, and transform the *moi* in common unity, in such a way that each person no longer thinks of himself as one, but as part of a unity, and is aware of himself only in the whole.[32]

[30] *Ibid.*, pp. 547-548.
[31] *Ibid.*, pp. 602-603; Rousseau's rejection of the saintly ethic is clear also in a letter to the abbé de Carondelet (4 March 1764), letter no. 36 in Henri Gouhier's edition of Rousseau's *Lettres philosophiques*, pp. 128-129.
[32] *Emile*, book I; *Oeuvres complètes*, IV, 241; cf. the *première version* of *Emile*, ms. Favre, *ibid.*, p. 57, where Rousseau asserts that modern men, torn by conflicting passions, rules, and axioms, "are good neither for ourselves nor for anyone else . . . —we are neither men nor citizens."

An individual and domestic education is thus necessary to produce a natural man, whereas a public and common one is required to produce a citizen. This sort of education can only be provided by a true *patrie*, a body of citizens devoted to their country with all the narrow-minded energy of patriotic love, the love of the larger whole of which the self is but a part. Emile cannot be a citizen in the true sense of the word, for he has no such *patrie*, and no such education. But he lives among men, and must perform his duties to his fellows, including those we normally think of as civic duties. He has a *pays* to which he ought to be devoted, and which he should attempt to serve as though it were a true fatherland. This "public simulacrum" of virtue within which he lives provides a minimally effective shelter against the vicious impulses of his countrymen, and a foil against which he can appreciate true virtue. Thus, says Rousseau, "what does it matter if the social contract is nowhere observed, so long as the particular interest has protected him as the general will itself would have done, public violence secures him against the violence of individuals, the evil he has seen done makes him love that which would have been good, and our institutions themselves lead him to know and hate their own iniquities?"[33]

4. Rousseau's Alternative Moralities: The *Social Contract*

For the most part, Rousseau took the course he recommended for Emile, accepting the protection of public violence and private interests even as he condemned the iniquities of institutions. In the *Social Contract* and his constitutional proposals for Corsica and Poland, however, he depicted alternative institutions designed to allow men to achieve a true community. In *Emile*, the stress is on virtue, an individual achievement made possible by independence from society. In the *Social Contract*, the language shifts to that of morality, instead, shared patterns of action that rest on the integration of individuals within society.

In a letter about a dispute over morality and interest, Rousseau asserted that men always act from what they take to be their interest: "for when we act, we must always have a motive for acting, and this motive cannot be foreign to ourselves. . . . It is absurd to think that,

[33] *Emile*, book v, *Oeuvres complètes*, IV, 858; the most commonly used translation of *Emile*, by Barbara Foxley for Everyman (1911), inexplicably refers here to protection "against the general will," p. 437. Like Montaigne, Emile is instructed to perform his political duties punctually when he is required to leave his plough, but not to worry about being called often for such burdensome duties; "so long as there are men of our own century," says his tutor, "it is not you whom they will seek to serve the State."

being myself, I might act as though I were another person. Isn't it true that if you were to say that an object had been pushed, although nothing had touched it, you would speak absurdly? It is the same thing in ethics, if someone believes he has acted without any interest." However, Rousseau emphasized that although "interest" can refer to "sensual and palpable" things, physical goods or material fortune, it can also have a more direct relation to our soul and our absolute well-being, and thus come into play in religion and morality. If we do good because we love the good, we do it because it brings us satisfaction, "a contentment without which there is no true happiness."[34]

When we do something, we always find our own good in doing it, no matter how attenuated the connection with the self may be. This is central to Rousseau's whole social theory. The first requisite for institutions that unite individuals instead of dividing them against one another and themselves is that each must discover his *own* interest there. This is the opposite of the topsy-turvy world in which "each man pretends to wish to sacrifice his own interests to those of the public, and every one of them is lying." Rousseau asserted that "no one really desires the public good except when it accords with his own; therefore this accord is the proper object of a true politics that seeks to make a people happy and good."[35]

In the opening chapters of the first draft of his *Social Contract*, Rousseau firmly rejects the idea that there is a "natural general society" among men—that our interests are naturally in harmony, our needs in consonance with one another. Such a notion had been expressed by many social theorists, including Diderot and another contemporary named Richer d'Aube, in a widely read *Essai sur les principes du droit et la morale*. Rousseau summarizes all his reasons for doubting such a notion, and concludes, "It is false that in a condition of independence reason would lead us to work for the common good with a view to our own interest; far from it being true that particular interest is allied with the general good, they are mutually exclusive in the natural order of things; and social laws are a yoke each one wants to impose on others, but not to bear himself." Rousseau hypothesizes an "independent man" who understands the idea of a "general will" instructing each individual in his duties "in the silence of his passions," but is not moved to any action by this understanding. "I quite see, I admit," says this independent man, "the rule I ought to consult; but I do not

[34] *Lettres philosophiques*, no. 18 (4 October 1761), p. 71; cf. *Considérations sur le gouvernement de Pologne, Oeuvres complètes*, III, 1005 and 1037; and *Emile*, book IV, *Oeuvres complètes*, IV, 599.
[35] "Lettre à Christophe de Beaumont," *Oeuvres complètes*, IV, 937.

see any reason why I should submit to it. It is not a question of teaching me what justice is, but rather of showing me *what interest I have in being just.*" Providing answers that will persuade this "independent man" is what the *Social Contract* is about. With his characteristic love of paradox, Rousseau determines (in language made familiar by generations of his predecessors in French thought) "to draw from the evil itself the remedy that will heal it."

> By new associations let us correct, if possible, the lack of a general association. Let our violent interlocutor himself judge our success. Show him in perfected art the reparation for the evils that art in its early stages does to nature. Clarify his reason with new understandings, warm his heart with new sentiments, that he may learn to multiply his being and his felicity in dividing them with his fellowmen. If my zeal does not blind me, there is no doubt that he . . . will learn to prefer his true interest [*intérêt bien entendu*] to his apparent interest . . . that he will become the staunchest support of a well-ordered society.[36]

In using the language of *l'intérêt bien entendu*, Rousseau comes close to recommending that very "masterpiece of policy" that he had condemned. But he also speaks of "dividing felicity" with one's fellowman in order to multiply it in new associations. His use of the language of enlightened self-interest is a ploy akin to that adopted by Pascal in his *Pensées*: enlist the interest of skeptical modern man in what you have to offer him, and by this route insensibly lead him to be receptive to grace itself. Unlike the contemporary moralists he excorciated, Rousseau was convinced that, although there is no natural harmony of selfish interests, there are such things as true *common* interests. A rational account of moral duties in society is not a fiction; the "common good" exists, when given substance through the general will. Rousseau uses an insight from the marquis d'Argenson to make this point most vividly; we recognize our individual interests in opposition to those of other men, or to the common interest, but at the same time, "the accord of all these interests is formed by opposition to those of each individual." It is this accord of interests that forms the basis for society itself; and to behave morally, according to Rousseau, means to behave in ways that are consonant with these areas of common interest. "For if the opposition of particular interests rendered the establishment of societies necessary, it was the accord of those same interests that made it possible. It is what there is in common among these different inter-

[36] *Du contrat social* (première version), *Oeuvres complètes*, III, 288-289.

ests that forms the social tie; and if there were no point where they agreed, no society could exist."[37] The difficulty is not that there is no such thing as morality and the common interest, but rather that men are not naturally motivated to behave morally. The common good has no innate attraction for them; and they tend to follow their narrow selfish interests rather than the common interests that are understood only in terms of opposition to their own.

To bridge this fatal gap between the moral good I am capable of recognizing and my natural inclination requires a political solution. Existing societies mistakenly suppose that we can simply leave men alone to pursue their own narrow interests within the framework of laws and regulations imposed upon them by a will quite alien to their own, and then expect them to behave in socially useful and harmonious ways. Rousseau's whole point is that something quite different, and far more drastic, is required. A public must be created to give substance to the common interest; and each member of that public must be taught to will his own good within that public good. To say that although individuals naturally can see the good, it does not move them to action, and has no attraction for them, is to say that they do not naturally will the good. The good itself is not a product of artifice; but the will to do it is. Emile's moral will is the product of one kind of artifice. But his lonely performance of his duty in a world where the good can be recognized only by its absence is more precarious and less satisfying than the creation of an entire society in which the good itself is given form. Since the problem is a deficient will, the solution must be the direction of the will, the creation of a general will for the general good. Since the society must be composed of individuals, the will of each must be transformed into something unnatural, a component of the general will.

This solution is even more difficult than the education of Emile. It requires a more demanding set of initial conditions, as well as the participation of a quasi-divine Legislator.[38] This Legislator employs perfected art—education, persuasion, religious symbols, carefully constructed institutions—to instill the habits and attitudes of citizenship, of being part of a public. He uses art to train men to focus on interests they can see they share, and find their satisfaction in pursuing them. These interests are not alien to individuals; each discovers his own

[37] *Du contrat social*, book II (*Oeuvres complètes*, III, 368); the reference to d'Argenson is on p. 371. Louis Althusser, *Politics and History*, part II, is a good discussion of the intricacies of Rousseau's concept of interest.

[38] *Du contrat social*, II, chs. 6-12; book IV, ch. 8; on the comparative difficulties of these enterprises, cf. Vauvenargues' *Réflexions et maximes* no. 409: "Il est quelquefois plus difficile de gouverner un seul homme qu'un grand peuple."

interest in the common interest, as well as feeling the opposition of the two, and is led to prefer the common interest that includes his own. The training of this preference is the legislator's art. It requires creating new areas of common interest not found in nature, to bolster those that are, so that the common interest can grow to a point where it holds a dominant position in men's lives.

In discussions of interest throughout his social theory, Rousseau mentions several different types of common interest, although he did not draw explicit distinctions among them. The first and simplest are what we might call "concrete" common interests—instances in which particular ends or goals of individuals happen to converge, so that they gain from cooperating with one another in the pursuit of something that will bring satisfaction to them all. In his account of the process by which savage man becomes civilized in the second *Discourse*, one of the first steps noted by Rousseau is the ability to "distinguish those rare occasions when the common interest should lead him to count on the assistance of other members of his species, and those even rarer ones when competition should make him diffident."[39] These common interests provide the basis for the first loose transient associations among human beings, which last only as long as each recognizes that the satisfaction of his needs is linked with cooperative activity.

The deer hunt is Rousseau's own instance of a concrete common interest of this sort. Note that it is indeed a *common* interest; I do not satisfy the needs of other men as I pursue my own, as would be true, for instance, if I set traps for rabbits and caught more than I needed, and left the superfluous rabbits for someone else. In the case of the deer-hunting expedition, there is a single object of the hunt that can be obtained only by the concerted activity of many individuals. However, once the deer has been caught, my enjoyment of the object of our common activity does not depend on others, since I can munch my haunch of venison in solitude. And the concerted activity is transient and fragile. Cooperation is always threatened when any member of the group discovers an easier way to satisfy his immediate interest. If a rabbit happens to run across his path, he will choose his own particular interest, which excludes the interest of the deer-hunting fraternity. Nor does the experience of the deer hunt itself lead men voluntarily to bind themselves in more lasting associations in which

---

[39] *Oeuvres complètes*, III, 166; John Charvet, *The Social Problem in the Philosophy of Rousseau*, p. 143, accuses Rousseau of running together "two very different accounts of the common interest as though they constituted one coherent position." In my view, the theory is both more complex and more coherent than Charvet indicates; but I have profited from his careful discussion.

they would regularly sacrifice their immediate interests to the pursuit of concrete common interests.

However, part of the point of Rousseau's story is that the repeated sharing of such experiences leads to the taste for more, and sets the stage for social life.[40] Men become accustomed to each other's company, and discover that a haunch of venison tastes better shared around a common fire. They find pleasure in the company of their fellows at the same time that they become competitive with them; social bonds and selfish *amour-propre* develop in close conjunction with one another. More numerous areas of concrete common interests are discovered through regular contacts and more complex needs—in the division of labor, for example. But most important, the simple fact of shared experience becomes an interest that men have in common—not a convergence of particular ends, but a common source of individual satisfaction. Echoing Pascal, Rousseau affirms that "the purest pleasures" are those enjoyed in common rather than appropriated solely to oneself.[41] This second type of common interest—the interest of many individuals in a common source of pleasure that depends on *shared* rather than parallel experience—becomes the basis of patriotism and fidelity to the community. In his discussion of the art of the Legislator in the *Social Contract*, and in his proposal for the *Government of Poland*, Rousseau stresses that full advantage must be taken of such sentiments.

Like the citizens of Lycurgus' Sparta, Polish citizens are to be shaped from youth in patriotic sentiments, instilled by children's games, by civic festivals, by participation in institutions peculiar to their country.[42] In such a fashion, Rousseau hopes that the "unthinking morality" of primitive custom can be revived to replace the corrupt "morality" of modern man. All such shared experiences are designed to ensure that love of *la patrie* will dominate all other loves. These patriotic emotions depend for their force on their exclusiveness. The general rule that interests are formed in opposition to other interests holds good even in this instance. My sense of belonging to this social group depends on my awareness that others are kept out of it; and the strength of patriotic symbols and practices rests not only on the good feeling they give to those who share in them, but on the sense that not everyone can do so. Spartans were made virtuous in their relations

---

[40] The account of this process in the second *Discourse* is elaborated in the "Fragments politiques," *Oeuvres complètes*, III, 476.

[41] *Emile*, book IV, *Oeuvres complètes*, IV, 689-690.

[42] *Considérations sur le gouvernement de Pologne*, *Oeuvres complètes*, III, 953-974.

with each other, through their all-embracing love of the community. As far as outsiders were concerned, however, they were chauvinistic, avaricious, bellicose—in general, thoroughly unpleasant.

The exclusivist patriotism recommended in Rousseau's social theory is not an end in itself, but an essential step in the formation of durable communities. For lasting human associations to be formed, men must share not only concrete common interests, but also emotional experiences of civic particularity that define the group. It is in my narrow interest to be advantaged while you suffer, to be free while you are restrained, to follow my own inclinations while you are subject to the rule of law. But if you and I are members of the same *patrie* I can come to see these things in quite another light. If I enjoy with others a community of interests, this can override my narrow sense of self. To show our hypothetical "independent man" his interest in being just, therefore, we must create for him a true *patrie*—develop strong new sentiments in his breast, give him a sense of extending himself in a true association. His natural passions are not repressed or snuffed out, but put to use. "A man who had no passions," asserts Rousseau, "would surely be a very bad citizen."[43] The citizen, like Emile, is not to be a saint; he will not sacrifice himself, but rather extend and fulfill himself. He will not cease to act from interest, but will find his satisfaction in doing good, which can only be true for a man habituated in virtue. He will vie with his fellows to win the palm of public esteem. And then, "the effervescence excited by this common emulation will give birth to that patriotic intoxication that alone can raise men above themselves, without which liberty is a hollow name, and legislation a chimera."[44]

This deliberate inducement of passionate intoxication, this highly artificial excitement and exaggeration of natural sentiments, is employed to train men to be citizens—that is, to make them able to will together the good they see as individuals. But the willing itself depends on a political commitment, a solemn engagement that creates a polity, institutes sovereignty, and gives form to the general will. Rousseau's image to describe this moment of commitment is the social contract. But this full alienation of the self in order to realize the self is more closely analogous to Pascal's wager than to the legalistic or quasi-historical device normally associated with "social contract" theory. This shared commitment creates, and has for its object, a third type

---

[43] *Discours sur l'économie politique, Oeuvres complètes*, III, 259; this entire discourse, especially pp. 252-261, is one of Rousseau's most sustained discussions of the redirection of self-love into the love of the whole community.

[44] *Pologne, Oeuvres complètes*, III, 1019; "Fragments politiques," *ibid.*, p. 494.

of common interest, resting on the other two, but more abstract and lofty. The convergence of particular ends, and the sharing of patriotic experiences, are necessary means to association; the third type of common interest is the goal. This includes those things in which citizens are most deeply interested: the enjoyment of liberty, the maintenance of equality, the institution of the rule of law. These common interests are the true stuff of virtue, the living of the moral life that justifies and gives meaning to the intricate education of the citizen.

5. Authority, Liberty, and Community

In discussing a community of citizens and the absolute sovereignty concentrated in the general will of that community, Rousseau composed some of his most famous and difficult passages. His dazzling rhetoric and fatal gift for memorable epigrams produced images that have led some readers to think of him as springing full-grown from some timeless Platonized Geneva to give birth to assorted monstrous children of the modern world. Yet many of Rousseau's authoritarian passages were restatements of hoary arguments in French absolutist thought; and several of his collectivist images echoed descriptions of saintly communities from Pascal and Fénelon. Passages which, with the dubious benefit of hindsight, read like alarming anticipations of the totalitarian evils of the twentieth century, have quite another tone when one approaches them from the opposite direction.

Of the modes of argument we have followed in this study, the only one to which Rousseau was not much indebted was constitutionalism. It is true, and easily forgotten, that he was one of the great proponents of the rule of law. But his dedication to that principle was distinct from that of French constitutionalists such as Domat or Montesquieu. In Rousseau's theory, law is identified with the sovereign will, as it was in the absolutist tradition, rather than an external bridle on that will, as it was in the constitutive laws of the French polity. His hostility to intermediate bodies in the state and scorn for representative assemblies, set him off clearly from the constitutionalist tradition. On the other hand, we have seen how his moral and social theories began as a reaction to the excesses of the individualist tradition, and incorporated important elements of that tradition in the theory of interest and self-love. And his political theory is steeped in absolutist arguments and images. The descriptions of the authority exercised by Emile's tutor, and by the Legislator in the *Social Contract*, recall the godlike absolutist monarch, controlling everything in a hidden fashion so that subjects believe themselves to be free while they are carefully manipulated. The sinister undertones so often noted in those passages are not evidence of some unprecedented boldness on Rousseau's part, but of his fidelity to past images in which those same undertones were present. The powerful effect and apparent novelty of Rousseau's assertions on this topic derive from his intense personalization of the authority, and his novelistic descriptions of scenes in which it is exercised.

The most important instance of Rousseau's indebtedness to absolutist argument is his most famous concept, *la volonté générale*. This was a phrase that Rousseau made distinctively his own, although he was not the first to use it. He was influenced by Diderot and Montesquieu, as well as by discussions of sovereignty in Hobbes and in Bodin.[45] What is striking about Rousseau's usage is his denial that the sovereign will, responsible for the general good of the community, can be permanently identified with a single individual. The consonance of absolute sovereignty with the rule of law is more convincing when the law is willed by a community of individuals to direct their own behavior, rather than by a quasi-divine human being dictating to other men. What is sacrificed is what d'Argenson called the *point d'appui*, where all these wills come together conveniently in one particular will. That Rousseau was aware of the strength of the arguments on both sides of this dilemma is clear from his identification of "the great problem of politics, comparable to squaring the circle in geometry":

> *To find a form of government that places the law above the man.* If this form is discoverable, let us seek it and work to establish it. ... But if, unfortunately, it is not to be found (and I candidly confess that I think it is not), my opinion is that it is necessary to move to the opposite extreme, and all of a sudden place the man as far above the law as possible, and thus establish the most arbitrary despotism: I would wish the despot could be God. In a word, I see no viable middle point between the most austere democracy and the most perfect Hobbism.[46]

This passage is from a letter to Mirabeau, who sent Rousseau one

---

[45] Diderot uses the term in his article for the *Encyclopédie* on "Droit naturel," in C. E. Vaughan, *Political Writings of Jean-Jacques Rousseau*, I, 422-433. Cf. Montesquieu, *Esprit des lois*, XI:6 (*Oeuvres complètes*, II, 398-399), and Hobbes, *De Cive*, VI, 1 and 13; and VII, 5. Patrick Riley, "The General Will before Rousseau," is a good account of this background that stresses the importance of theological argument, and particularly the views of Malebranche. See also J. Robert Loy, "*L'esprit générale* and *La volonte générale*," in Jean Macary, ed., *Essays ... in Honor of Ira O. Wade*, pp. 183-192.

[46] Letter to Mirabeau, 26 July 1767, in *Lettres philosophiques*, no. 47, pp. 167-168.

of the handbooks of Physiocracy, Mercier de la Rivière's *Ordre naturel et essentiel des sociétés politiques*. Rousseau linked Mercier's system with that of Saint-Pierre, putting too much faith in human reason and the accessibility of clear and distinct social truth. As Rousseau pointed out, "almost all men know their true interests, and do not follow them any better for all that." The enlightened despot advocated by Mercier, lineal descendant of the beneficent absolute monarch in French theory from Budé through Bossuet to d'Argenson, was summarily dismissed by Rousseau. "Here then is what your despot will be like," he warned: "ambitious, prodigal, avaricious, lustful, vengeful, jealous, weak. . . . Your system would be excellent for the inhabitants of Utopia. It has no value for the sons of Adam." Political sermonizers may preach to kings as much as they like that their interest lies in making their people prosperous and happy. Kings know only too well that this is not true. "Their personal interest is first of all that the People should be weak, miserable, and completely unable to resist them."[47] The reference to Hobbism, to *arbitrary* despotism, underscores Rousseau's rejection of the notion that there are clear and evident natural laws that will guide and constrain a king's performance as soon as they are recognized, a tenet dear to Physiocracy. This is a gloomy restatement of the position taken in *Emile*. If good government is unavailable, we may at least hope to be protected against private violence by forceful public violence, and take shelter with Leviathan. Any thought that Rousseau might be excited by the prospect of arbitrary despotic rule is dispelled by the next sentence in the letter to Mirabeau: "But the Caligulas, the Neros, the Tiberiuses. . . . My God, . . . I roll upon the ground, and gnash my teeth at being human."

It was this conviction that no ruler can be expected to imitate God by governing according to the precepts of universal justice that prompted Rousseau's transformation of the doctrines of absolute monarchy into those of absolute popular sovereignty. In his discussion of the formation of the *Cité* in the *Social Contract*, he revises the analysis of sovereignty provided by Bodin. The complete alienation of all rights to the community is a restatement of the absolutist tenet that sovereignty cannot be limited or divided, that nothing can in principle be held back by the subjects. The sovereign must be the judge of what it is necessary to take and use; and no independent power in the community may claim the right to limit that sovereignty. But Bodin's grave error in Rousseau's eyes (and his explanatory note makes clear that he did indeed have Bodin in mind) was to confuse

[47] *Du contrat social*, III, 6; *Oeuvres complètes*, III, 409; cf. "Discours sur l'économie politique," *ibid.*, p. 243.

the status of citizens with that of townsmen or subjects.[48] Rousseau's major point is that the citizens themselves must compose the city. They must constitute the sovereignty in every sense of the word—they cannot delegate it to anyone else and call him Sovereign. The citizens themselves, acting as members of the political body, will together for its good, and this will—which is the will of each of them as citizens—is sovereign.

In revising Bodin's account of absolute sovereignty to make the general will a collective entity, Rousseau retained an aspect of that account that readers of his treatise sometimes overlook. Individuals who are citizens are also private persons. Despite some of Rousseau's rhetoric on this subject, his theory depends on the tension between private and public wills and interests. In a well-constituted state, citizenship dominates all other aspects of men's lives; but unless they retain their individuality, unless each has his own perspective to bring to the community's deliberations, his own interest in the common interest, the intricate process Rousseau describes is void and pointless. In their capacity as citizens, a special kind of will is demanded of them, a deliberate perspective on the requirements of the common good; but this does not annihilate their private interests in their daily lives. At the end of his treatise, Rousseau quotes d'Argenson to support his assertion that "the right that the social pact gives to the Sovereign [that is, the members of the community willing together as citizens] over the subjects [that is, these same individuals as private persons] does not exceed, as I have said, the limits of public utility." The passage from d'Argenson in the footnote is his memorable statement of the central principle of liberalism: "In the Republic, each individual is perfectly free in that which does not bring harm to others."[49]

Civil liberty means for Rousseau what it did for d'Argenson—the secure ability for the individual to pursue his own happiness in his own way, protected by the general will and its laws. His *moral* liberty, distinct from civil liberty, is the liberty of the citizen, a participant in making those laws that regulate his behavior as a subject.[50] The rule of law, rather than any arbitrary human will, is the *sine qua non* for freedom in both senses; and Rousseau's great passion was for liberty. All the conditions and constraints, the artifice and education, were designed to make liberty possible. We may conclude that Rousseau underestimated the effect of these devices on individual freedom, or

---

[48] *Du contrat social*, I, 6-7; *Oeuvres complètes*, III, 360-364.
[49] *Du contrat social*, book IV; *Oeuvres complètes*, III, 467.
[50] *Du contrat social*, I, 8; *Oeuvres complètes*, III, 365. Raymond Polin, *La Politique de la solitude*, ch. 4, is an illuminating account of how Rousseau's politics joins community for citizens with liberty for individuals.

that his "moral" liberty is an odd sort of freedom. But we cannot fairly deny that his basic commitment was to liberty, not to authority or collectivity as such.

Several assurances provided by Rousseau for the sovereign's good behavior were, despite his rejection of monarchy, the same ones that had been provided for the king. The body cannot wish to harm any of its members; the general will, composed of all the wills of all the citizens, by definition cannot will their hurt.[51] In the *Discourse on Political Economy*, he asserts: "If the ruler can ensure that everybody acts rightly, then he will have nothing more to do; the masterpiece of his art is to be able to remain idle. It is certain, anyway, that the greatest talent of leaders is to disguise their power to render it less odious, and to conduct the state so peacefully that it appears to have no need of governors."[52] However, these rhetorical assurances were less important to Rousseau's theory than his insistence that equality makes authority and liberty compatible. Association in the enjoyment of the formal equality created by the contract is one of interests citizens have in common; but substantive equality is just as important. The lesson of the *Discourse on Inequality* was not forgotten: all existing governments are infected from the outset because they are premised on the protection of the privileged against the disadvantaged. In the *Social Contract*, property is not outlawed. It provides the basis of the private existence and domestic livelihood of each subject, the guarantee of his separate status as an individual, just as in Bodin's *Republic*. But the Sovereign is given full authority over property, to ensure that it contributes to rather than endangers the health of the polity. In practical terms, this means that "no citizen should be so rich as to be able to buy another, and none so poor as to be forced to sell himself."[53] Rousseau's sovereign takes on the duty assigned the monarch in absolutist thought: the equal protection of all citizens. Like d'Argenson, Rousseau was not satisfied with providing equal protection for the existing level of inequality. He condemns extreme inequal-

---

[51] *Du contrat social*, I, 7; *Oeuvres complètes*, III, 363; liberal critics such as Benjamin Constant have been quick to point out the inadequacies of this view. As soon as the sovereign "proceeds to a practical organization of its authority, which cannot by exercised by the sovereign itself, that authority is delegated, and all its preservative attributes evaporate." *Principes de politique*, ch. 1, in Constant's *Oeuvres*, edited by Alfred Roulin, p. 1106.

[52] *Oeuvres complètes*, III, 250.

[53] *Du contrat social*, II, 11; *Oeuvres complètes*, III, 391-392; book I, 9, *ibid.*, pp. 365-367. Rousseau's concept of property is discussed by James MacAdam and N. Keohane in papers for the University of Calgary workshop on *The Theory of Property in the Western Tradition*, ed. Anthony Parel and Thomas Flanagan (Wilfrid Laurier University Press, 1979).

ity of fortunes as the source of all political evils—"particular interest substituted for the common interest, mutual hate among citizens, indifference to the common cause, the corruption of the people, and the enfeeblement of all the springs of government."[54]

The heart of Rousseau's theory is what the citizens do together, on which everything else depends: the willing of the general will. The social contract creates a new body—a body of thinking members, to use Pascal's terminology—in which each individual becomes a citizen, that is, part of a larger whole. The general will for the good of this body is their deliberate intention that this good should prevail over private good. In corrupt communities, this will exists in a weak form, but cannot dominate the strong motives of selfish interest when the two are in conflict. Members of such communities are in the position of Rousseau's hypothetical independent man. They do not see why it is in their interest to be just; but they are still capable of seeing what justice would require.[55] In a community that is not corrupt, among citizens prepared by the ministrations of the great-souled Legislator, a process of mutual accommodation of perspectives on the common good yields the common interest. Rousseau indicates that whatever the outcome of the deliberations that yield this interest may look like, it is not the embodiment of clear and evident natural truth. Like Montaigne, he argues that natural laws can seem luminous and clear only when abstracted from any particular society. "In a particular government composed of so many elements, such evidentiality necessarily disappears. For the science of government is a science of combinations, applications, exceptions, according to times, places, and circumstances."[56] The common interest, which is the object of the general will, is a set of interests peculiar to a specific group of citizens, which they can understand and will only through voicing their concerns. The common good does not exist "out there" to be discovered, but as a configuration of interests revealed in the process of willing. When Rousseau first broached this idea, he assumed, like d'Argenson, that a well-intentioned ruler could discern this pattern, so that the people would not have to assemble to will

---

[54] "Discours sur l'économie politique," *Oeuvres complètes*, III, 258-259; G.D.H. Cole's familiar translation for Everyman (1950) garbles this passage, p. 307, to make it seem as though the public interest is to be avoided. Judith Shklar, "Jean-Jacques Rousseau and Equality," is a useful study of this topic.

[55] This sheds light, I think, on the difficult passage at the beginning of the fourth book of the *Contrat social*, when Rousseau speaks of the general will as "always constant, unalterable, and pure" even when it is subordinated to other wills.

[56] Letter to Mirabeau, *Lettres philosophiques*, p. 167; cf. *Contrat social*, II, 6.

the general will.[57] By the time he wrote the *Social Contract*, he was convinced that this last step, the willing of interests into law, must be taken by the people, not by someone acting on their behalf.

The distinction between the general will and will of all, upon which Rousseau insisted, sheds light on how this process works. The will of all is the fruit of parallel willing by isolated individuals stating their private interests in the matter; when they are all recorded, if we cancel out the various conflicting interests to find the solution that satisfies the largest number, we have the will of all. But if we look more closely at these expressions of "private" interest, we will see areas of overlapping interest. If the matter concerns the whole community there will be some outcome that includes that area in the interests of each individual that he shares with all. It is because our selfish interests are often opposed to those held in common with other citizens that we can recognize them as separate and distinct. In a simple community of devoted citizens, the gap between the two interests will not normally be very great, and the common interest will be fairly obvious. There will be little scope for disagreement about what the general will should will, and the preference for the common good will be sufficiently strong that each individual can will it sincerely and heartily, even though his own private interest is opposed to it. However, even among such well-intentioned men, perceptions of the common interest may differ. No outside standard of abstract right is available. But there is a "right answer," an understanding of the common interest in this situation more accurate than any other. Since each individual is as likely as any other to perceive this answer, the majority is more likely to hit upon it than any single individual. A citizen who finds himself in a minority in such instances accepts the results of the deliberations as what he actually intended, since his commitment was not to achieving the hegemony of his own perspective, but the determination of the common good.[58]

Despite the demanding conditions required for willing the general will—the specific socio-economic requisites, the training by the Legislator—Rousseau's system is not "Utopian" in his own sense of the word, because he described a polity peopled by "sons of Adam," men with strong passions and tenaciously held interests, who have a fragile capacity for community that requires artificial nourishing, men who

[57] "Discours sur l'économie politique," *Oeuvres complètes*, III, 250-251.
[58] *Du contrat social*, II, 3 and IV, 1-2. I have followed Brian Barry's interpretation of the status of the "right answer" to political questions, as given in "The Public Interest," in Anthony Quinton, ed., *Political Philosophy*, pp. 119-126. Andrew Levine, *The Politics of Autonomy*, pp. 63-66, uses this argument, as well.

need one another to fulfill their humanness and yet also need to be free of one another, and establish themselves as individuals. Rousseau had no illusions about the ease of transforming such material into the citizens of a good community. But he thought he had sketched out the requirements for doing it, if it can be done. He took elements from a number of visions from classical antiquity, and from a long tradition of social theorizing in France, and fused them together in his own theoretical imagination to produce one of the finest modern expressions of an ancient ideal: an account of what it would be like to live a fully human life.

Conclusion

1. The Individual and the Polity

In French philosophy, theology, and ideology, the individual and the polity are metaphors for one another. In Renaissance treatises the polity is a "body politic," with humors and members, controlled by a single will. In seventeenth-century theology the individual is a little republic, peopled by passions and desires, ruled by sovereign reason. More generally, the interplay between individual and polity is incessant, from the well-ordered kingdom secured by the well-ordered royal soul to the *volonté particulière* dissolved in the *volonté générale*. According to absolutist ideology, the semidivine prince incorporates within himself the entire state; in Jansenist theory, the polity is composed of numberless individuals held together by gravitational forces of their own needs and interests. Yet individual and polity are often explicitly opposed to one another. The individual sage is detached from the public realm, part of a private world of learning and liberty explicitly distinguished from the polity. The interests of all individual subjects are held, in the reasoning of reason of state, to be in conflict with those of the state as a whole.

The term "individualism" has been used in this study to identify strands of argument that differentiate the person from the polity, and focus on the needs, interests, and enjoyments of the individual rather than the demands and requisites of sovereignty. It is a rather unwieldy tradition, which brings together some unlikely bedfellows. But the epicurean sages of Montaigne and Charron are connected with Nicole's economic man, d'Argenson's interested citizen, and Rousseau's independent man, by a shared preoccupation with the self. In contrast, absolutist theory encompasses all subjects in mute subordination to the sovereign, and allows no scope for vigorous expression of individuality. Constitutionalist theory defines subjects by status or office or corporate affiliation; all are happily maintained as diverse parts of a larger whole, but integration, not individuality, is the rule. During the period we have considered, both types of theory were modified under the influence of individualist argument. Theories of interest found a place in absolutist and constitutionalist argument, and both were richer for it. Individualist argument, in turn, was transformed from the exploration of the private self set over against the polity into a theory of participation by interested individuals in the devising of the common interest.

Absolutist language, in the seventeenth century in France, was rhetorically powerful and serviceable as ideology. It was also part of a theory of politics, a distinctive conception of the way a state is constituted. Considered as a theory of politics, early absolutist argument was overly simplistic and abstract. The king was expected to be, and do, so many contradictory things. He was the abstract symbol of pure will, yet also a human figure who attracted allegiance and loyalty. He was known to be mortal, accessible to prejudice and flattery, yet expected to transcend such things, to be literally "above" everyone else. The king was called upon to provide the serene directive will that would bring other wills together into law, and to possess the vision that could discern patterns of common welfare in the whole.

It is hard to deny the attractiveness of such a simple solution to complex political problems. The appeal of absolutist argument, throughout this period, is the beauty of having a single *point d'appui* where diverse conflicting interests come together into law. If there is an obvious apex for the political pyramid, a point of sovereignty that cannot be divided or opposed, the messy and protracted disputes of multiple legislative assemblies can be avoided. The single authority charged with protecting all parts of the state equally against encroachment by any other is the apotheosis of the paternal ideal. The refutation of such a vision must come in the terms used by Montesquieu in mulling over Richelieu's description of such a sovereign: "There is scarcely an angel who could be counted on to have so much attention, so much reason, firmness, knowledge; one could only with difficulty delude oneself into believing that from now until the dissolution of monarchies there could be such a prince, and ministers like that."

Yet men did apparently, at some level of their ideological consciousness, delude themselves regularly into believing that the mystic qualities of monarchy endowed a man with enough of such divinity that he could provide an acceptable approximation to such a sovereign will. They depended heavily on education, on tutoring a prince to prepare him to be tutor to his people, ordering the sovereign will to ready an individual to give order to the state. In at least one instance, an individual came as close as one might expect any human being could to living up to the inhuman demands of the royal role. Louis XIV self-consciously undertook to be what the absolute monarch was supposed to be—brilliant, lofty, and in control of everything.

His own conception of his role was that offered by absolutist theorists for decades before; and he did his best to live up to it. The fatal flaws in his regime stemmed from deficiencies in the monarchical model itself, not from his inability to live up to it.

Publicists from the time of Richelieu onward identified the interests of the state with the interests of the prince. The aggrandizement of the territory, the cultivation of military might, the nurturing of economic prosperity, the embellishment of the court, the protection of the dynasty—all these good things were supposed to go together, and assure the welfare of the kingdom. Louis acted precisely on this model. But the aggrandizement of territory, meticulous supervision of the economy, the obsession with armies and warfare, the zealous protection of his family's interests, did not bring the welfare of the kingdom in their train. Instead they weakened it dramatically, and cost the happiness of many of his subjects. D'Argenson's description of the power of the monarchical myth over the minds of Frenchmen was accurate enough. Even the failures of Louis's regime did not efface that myth during the eighteenth century.[1] But for many thoughtful observers, the theory of absolutist monarchy was discredited by that experience. The *gloire* of the absolutist model turned out to be false *gloire*. And the idea that any individual, even the most conscientious and best prepared, could speak for the interests of all other individuals, was revealed to be a foolish fantasy.

Throughout the seventeenth century, an alternative conception of the monarch's place, less brilliant but more realistic, was available in the constitutionalist tradition. The recurrent images in this tradition are those of harmony—of treble and bass voices, high and low, orchestrated by the sovereign; and of physics—of gravity, whirlpools, the solar system, individuals pulled together and drawn apart by their own interest, pursuing their own purposes within the whole; and above all, of bridles—the energies of the sovereign reined in, controlled, and directed by institutions and patterns of political belief and action by all persons in the state. In this tradition, the king was at the center, but he did not constitute the whole. Other powers, other purposes, meshed with his own to make up the polity. Specific institutional participants in this constitution emerged and receded in the course of these centuries—estates, parlements, ministers, lesser magistrates. All were charged with protecting and preserving law, the most enduring pattern and toughest bridle on the prince, the sovereign

---

[1] N. R. Johnson, *Louis XIV and the Age of the Enlightenment*, traces the fortunes of the myth of the Sun King, and of monarchy more generally, in the eighteenth century.

expression of the sovereign will. This complex, self-sustaining order was described in the Renaissance as a body. In the seventeenth century, it was an intricate machine set in motion by a clever legislator, with multiple hidden springs driven by the energies of all parts of the state from the lowliest subject to the king himself. Great power to do good, no power to do evil—this was the concise expression of the constitutionalist ideal.

In the aftermath of Louis's *gloire*, this ideal, originally devised by Renaissance jurists, became prominent in French politics again. But much had changed in the interim. In political philosophy, the most important changes were a new understanding of the distinction between "public" and "private" spheres of human life, and a greatly enriched theory of interest. These were the contributions of the individualist tradition, with parallel developments in absolutist thought. When constitutionalism was revived in the eighteenth century, theories of interest and participation by subjects gave old arguments a new direction and enabled constitutionalism to pose effective challenges to absolutist dogma. The line between the two was blurred as theorists such as d'Argenson, Turgot, Quesnay, and Mirabeau incorporated judicial bodies and representative assemblies in reform programs that were based on the acceptance of absolute legislative and bureaucratic sovereignty in the monarchy.[2]

2. PUBLIC AND PRIVATE SPHERES

In sixteenth-century constitutionalism, exemplified by Seyssel's *Monarchie*, the line between "public" and "private" life was not sharply drawn. Economic and social activities of all subjects were parts of *la police*, the ordered pattern of the polity. *La chose publique* was not a separate sphere of activity, but a name for all common things, "divided up and distributed among all estates proportionally." In this theory, "each individual in those estates" was "maintained in his preeminence and equality" within the hierarchy. The concept of private (*privé*) occurs in Seyssel's treatise only in the context of the most familiar and intimate councils of the king, those where matters of highest policy are treated. In Commynes's *Mémoires*, the term *privé* is juxtaposed with *estrange*, to refer to the realm of France itself, "at home" contrasted with "abroad."

Thus before the late sixteenth century, "public" and "private" were

[2] Keith Baker, "French Political Thought at the Accession of Louis XVI," and Elizabeth Fox-Genovese, *The Origins of Physiocracy*, discuss these reform systems.

not opposed companion terms in French political discourse, as they are for us today. They became so for Montaigne and Bodin. Each juxtaposed public with private to make central points, and although their formulations of the dichotomy differed in certain ways, the net effect was much the same. Both authors emphasized the distinction between two spheres of life to make sense of a world ravaged by civil war, in which political life was corrupted and domestic life deformed.

In Bodin's political theory, the hierarchical division of estates within the polity, which was central to Seyssel's constitution, was overshadowed by the distinction between *res publica* and matters pertaining to the household of each citizen. Public things were defined in much the same sense as Seyssel's *chose publique*. But over against these markets, churches, roads, laws and customs, theaters and public buildings, common lands and treasures, Bodin set up a sphere of things not held in common, the affairs and possessions peculiar to each family. The two spheres are deliberately counterposed, "for nothing can be public, where nothing is private." Property was central to Bodin's privacy. It defined the space occupied by each family and gave substance to the individual citizen. The public sphere was also spatially defined as that area that each citizen entered when he went "forth out of his house . . . to negotiate and traffic with other heads of families about that which concerns them all in general." The most important public thing in Bodin's theory was shared subjection to a sovereign. But that subjection did not annihilate, or even penetrate, the private realm where each citizen was lord in his own house.

Montaigne was equally clear in his juxtaposition of public and private. But whereas for Bodin the identifying mark of privacy was property, for Montaigne it was philosophy. The exploration of the self and the world, testing one's judgment, good conversation with friends and predecessors in the philosophic life—these were activities Montaigne associated with privacy. Public life meant a different type of activity, in the affairs of the world and the business of governance, in which philosophy has little place. Occasionally Montaigne used spatial images to mark the difference. He symbolized his inner private life by the "back room" of the mind, and by his tower library. But the spatial differentiation was less important than a psychological distinction between two types of behavior, approaches to life, sets of values. Montaigne counseled his readers to retain self-centeredness and control over self even as they participated in public things. A serene internal privacy in the midst of the hustle of the public world;

a dichotomy between two aspects of the self, "the mayor" and "Montaigne"—these were the ideals presented in the *Essays*. The privacy of philosophy was the prime good to be protected. All else was "an appendage and a prop at most."

The explicit demarcation between public and private life was of great importance for seventeenth-century followers of Bodin and Montaigne. Among absolutist theorists the division between public power of the prince and private pursuits of the subjects became so pronounced that the public life of ordinary citizens was altogether atrophied, swallowed up in the great public person of the prince, whose private personality was denied any scope apart from its expression in the office of the sovereign. The only "public" dimension of a subject's life in Bossuet's theory was obedient awe, passive reception of benefits; public activity was equated with the governance of the prince. The other side of the same dichotomous perspective was expressed by individualist philosophers, especially Charron and several of the *libertins*. For these men, private philosophic pleasures of the individual were the whole focus of concern. Public life was of little relevance; it was something done by other, lesser men, that might or might not touch the philosopher tangentially. At best public life protected, at worst encroached upon, his precious privacy. The selfishness of contemporary morality that Rousseau remarked upon, and laid at the doorstep of philosophy, was rooted in the detachment of the philosopher from public life idealized in the seventeenth century. In this neat dichotomy, civic responsibility, the sense of integration of the individual within a larger whole, was eroded; and the maximizing of private happiness became the end of life.

Among the undesirable consequences of an ideology that polarized all social life into active prince and passive people, or corrupt governors and virtuous philosophers, was the mood described by Sorbière in the aftermath of the Fronde. Men who felt no direct involvement in public life, and were taught to regard it as the province of a group of specialists of no concern to them, soon came to see *la chose publique* as an opportunity for private profit at no great cost to anyone. They treated it as a "great body that cannot easily be weakened; and each individual takes thought only for the piece that he tears off." A few writers disturbed by such consequences had insisted on the interconnections between public and private life. Seventeenth-century mercantilists, especially Montchrétien, reminded the government that "private activities make up the public." The activities of all individuals and families in the society and the economy are the basis for the revenues, the armies, the dispensation of justice, and all other concerns of the crown. Balzac pointed out the other half of this same truth: that the king's glorious victories abroad, the most clearly "public" aspect of the public realm as it was then understood, have sad consequences for the lowliest peasants in their private huts. "Glory is a passion that they do not know. . . . They want more wheat and fewer laurels."

The absolute polarization of prince and people was thus called into question during the seventeenth century. In the eighteenth, it was decisively rejected. The energies of individual subjects were once more required, and so were their voices. In absolutist ideology, the presence of the prince struck his admiring subjects dumb, and blinded them with brilliant splendor. In the aftermath of the Sun King's *gloire* men found their public voices once again. The philosophers who had self-consciously withdrawn from politics were called back to civic duties in the political philosophies of the early Enlightenment. The contributions of philosophy, in the form of *la science politique*, were regarded as essential to healthy public life, in the philosophies of Saint-Pierre and d'Argenson. Philosophers were instructed to use their wisdom to counsel kings, to bend their minds as well as their knees to the service of the state, and in so doing, to shape the state itself to their design. And the mass of ordinary individuals who had been required only to suffer and produce in silence were recognized as having interests, and potentially as having voices, of their own. In the eighteenth century, on the basis of such developments, theories of general political participation were for the first time advanced in France. Yet the continued dominance of absolutist modes of thought, and the pluralist motifs available from constitutionalism, gave a distinctive and durable coloration to French discussions of participation by individuals.

3. SUBJECTS AND CITIZENS

Vigorous republican ideologies are normally associated with widespread participation in government. In France such experience was uncommon. Parish assemblies and municipal councils tended to be dominated by entrenched local oligarchies. When the monarchy began to take over these governments, there was some truth in the justification offered: that municipal governments were corrupt, indolent, or oppressive.[3] Towns with strong traditions of self-government

[3] Nora Temple, "The Control and Exploitation of French Towns during the *Ancien Régime*," *History* LI (1966), 16-35, and "Municipal Oligarchies in Eighteenth-Century France," in J. F. Bosher, ed. *French Government and Society*

bought back their privileges in order to control their own choice of officers. But these privileges, even when ancient and highly prized, rarely meant the involvement of large numbers of Frenchmen in town government. There was little basis in French life for an ideology of participant republicanism analogous to the civic humanism of the Florentine Renaissance or its offshoots among Englishmen and Americans, with their own experiences of parliamentary and local government.[4] In the mid-sixteenth century, a strain of something rather like civic humanism developed among French jurists, men such as Budé, Le Roy, and Le Caron. But the concept of citizenship associated with their work is not republican in character. The good citizen is the good subject of the prince, loyally defending and embellishing his *patrie* by his rhetoric and scholarship as much as in offices or missions he may be given by the prince. This was not a civic participatory experience, but the activist dimension of "legal humanism," the great flourishing of legal studies that distinguished the Renaissance in France.[5]

In the individualist tradition, the scholar-humanist was removed even further from involvement in civic life. Overtones of citizenship tended to be altogether lost. Yet paradoxically it was within this tradition that a theory of participation began to emerge in the late seventeenth century. Although the individual celebrated by the *libertins* and their successors had little use for politics, he developed a penchant for action in other areas—on the battlefield as well as in philosophy, literature, and science, in the economy and in society. The individual moved to accomplish great things, to vindicate his honor, appeared at Richelieu's court and in the dramas of Corneille. In a less heroic mood he adopted the values of the *honnête homme*; in the salons, his aim was to advance himself in socially acceptable ways. In the economic theory of Nicole and Boisguilbert, he became a familiar figure in the marketplace, motivated by avarice rather than ambition or honor. Then, in the eighteenth century, he went into politics. The passive subject and member of the ancient corporation were joined by a new figure: the interested individual moved to express wants and needs in the political sphere, and capable of effective participation in government.

1500-1850, 70-91; Roland Mousnier, *La Plume, la faucille et le marteau*, pp. 215-264; W. H. Lewis, *The Splendid Century*, ch. 7. J. Russell Major, "Popular Initiative in Renaissance France," in Archibald Lewis, ed., *Aspects of the Renaissance*, pp. 27-41, stresses the importance of local government and popular creative energy in France.
[4] Pocock, *Machiavellian Moment*, pp. 333-340.
[5] Donald R. Kelley, *Foundations of Modern Historical Scholarship: Language, Law and History in the French Renaissance*.

When Frenchmen looked for models of participation in political life, they found them in the robust little republics to the north, and in the history of Rome. From the mid-seventeenth century onward, subjects of absolutist monarchy were fascinated by the Netherlands. Travelers regularly praised the Dutch for their rich public life, accompanied by prosperity for all citizens. The combination of liberty and equality was particularly attractive to French admirers. The flaws in the ideal—especially the corrupting effects of avarice among a people dedicated to commerce, and the lack of a strong executive to protect the little states against aggression—were also apparent. For many observers, the political distance between these neighboring states was so vast that the Dutch example was irrelevant for France. But for some the experience of the Netherlands, and the rise and decline of republican Rome, posed an interesting challenge. Would it be possible to combine a measure of public participation, liberty, and equality, with a strong executive and the varied orders and customs that accompanied the large modern state? Saint-Evremond called for a revival of the Augustan age as the best compromise. D'Argenson proposed to move closer to republicanism, instituting little republics within the absolutist monarchy. By rejuvenating the dying local governments of his own polity, his constitution was designed to "admit the public [that is, all the citizens of the large state] into the government of the Public [*la chose publique*, the things they share in common] as far as possible."

Montesquieu took the opposite approach. He juxtaposed the two types of polity as sharply as possible, to set out the costs and benefits of each. In his view, republican and monarchical regimes require the cultivation of different aspects of the human personality. Although the first is more difficult, it lifts men to a plane they cannot otherwise experience. Self-love is systematically suppressed, all energy directed toward love of the community. This prescription depends on, and makes possible, a degree of virtue that is literally incomprehensible to those of us who have not experienced it. Yet the costs must not be forgotten in celebrating such a lofty community. The annihilation of the private self, the denial of diversity and experiment, the constricted education and concentrated passions—these are major sacrifices for human beings, who are most easily governed by a regime that goes with the grain of their ordinary inclinations.

The monarchical model in the *Spirit of the Laws* is the constitutionalist model, with roots deep in Renaissance thought. The honor of each member of each order, the relations of attraction and repulsion as each seeks to advance himself, and the resulting limits on sovereignty, as well as the focus on law, are all parts of this tradition. But Montesquieu's depiction of the advantages of such a model—civil liberty, diversity, flexibility—must be set against his distaste for narrow self-interest and petty preoccupation with status and place. In this distaste he echoes a durable theme in French social thought. From the sixteenth century onward, the simulacrum of "public life" displayed in regimes organized along these lines had moved men to scorn. Criticism of a society whose only shared activities are court flattery, salon hypocrisy, and love of luxury was commonplace.[6] Public life as a civil version of the theater, in which men play roles without any larger purposes, as they take up and cast off varied amusing masks, encountering one another but never knowing fellowship—the distinction between such a "public life" and that associated with a flourishing republican community is considerable.[7] For all his appreciation of monarchical efficiency, Montesquieu was well aware of this difference. This accounts for the ambivalence that marks even his most admiring passages on monarchy.

For Rousseau, awareness of the distinction between true and simulated public life approached obsession. In his descriptions of the requisites and temper for true public life, the associated individuals occasionally become abstract and bloodless pieces of a larger whole, and participation is reduced to virtual somnambulism. But in other passages Rousseau captures the richness of shared political experience with great clarity, and shows the participating citizens as full human individuals, each with his own wants and interests. The tensions between individual wants and interests and the requirements of the common good are fundamental to his political philosophy. In discussing such tensions, he draws on the insights of the individualist tradition, with its extensive exploration of the self, and of absolutist discourse, with its demand for unitary sovereignty. Rousseau shows how neutral love of self is transformed into self-centeredness when social life nurtures competitive passions of ambition and greed rather than compassion and autonomy. And he argues that self-centered individuals can be educated and habituated to fuse themselves in society and find their

---

[6] Pauline M. Smith, *The Anti-Courtier Trend in Sixteenth-Century French Literature*, gives ample evidence of the mood critical of luxury and court flattery in France from the early Renaissance to the seventeenth century, showing that Molière's satire of the *honnête homme* was not unprecedented.

[7] Richard Sennett, in his provocative study of *The Fall of Public Man*, ignores the contemporary sense of hollowness that accompanied the presentation of the self in streets and salons, which he identifies as public life in this era. Many of the most thoughtful Frenchmen of the seventeenth and eighteenth centuries would have been puzzled and amused by Sennett's encomium on their "public" life.

individuality in a larger whole, as self-love is redirected into patriotic zeal.

Rousseau's theory combines full popular participation in discovery of the common good with absolute sovereignty located in the will of the community as a whole. He completed the tendency in absolutist thought for the sovereign to become more and more abstract. The symbolic will of the monarch, in the theories of the early Enlightenment, was largely divorced from the mortal who wore the crown, who became less and less important. In Rousseau's thought the impersonal will is finally detached from any mortal individual. The *volonté générale* becomes general not only in its object, but also in its source. The roots of the general will lie deep in the office of the absolutist king. This helps explain some of the more puzzling aspects of that concept, which transforms the monarchical will that represents and holds together the whole polity into the absolute sovereignty of the fused individuals.

4. Interest and Community

One of the most important achievements of political philosophy in France was the refinement of the concept of "public interests." During the seventeenth century, this concept was first broached in opposition to the interests of ordinary individuals. Private interests were construed on the basis of love of self and pursuit of personal happiness; public interests demanded sacrifices from individuals, and required the subordination of private purposes to policies designed to advance the strength and grandeur of the state. By the early eighteenth century, the language for discussing these issues had shifted significantly. True "common interests," shared by all individuals, understood on the basis of what brought them together as human beings and members of communities, became the substance of the "public interest." And the self-knowledge of the great state was understood to depend not on the singular wisdom of a godlike individual, but on the voices of all members of the polity expressing their own interests in their capacities as public persons.

This generous concept of the public interest, in which individual interests are discovered and expressed rather than denied and sacrificed, was drawn from visions of a true community in which all members find their most satisfying selfhoods as parts of the larger whole. The vision was religious in origin; but even in its religious form, as in the *pensées* of Pascal and the theology of Fénelon, the language used was heavily social and political. Augustine's city of God, channeled through Jansenist treatises, gave a characteristic temper to French theories of community.

The difference between a polity composed of individuals loosely bound together by subordination to the same rules and recognition of one another's liberties, and a community of persons united by shared love of their fellowship, is reflected in Oakeshott's distinction between a *societas* and a *universitas*. These are two models for understanding the modern state. Men associated in a *societas* are joined in loyalty to one another and in obedience to rules for individual action. Each pursues his own interests, but they share no substantive commitment to any general goal. Members of a *universitas*, on the other hand, are joined by recognition of a common purpose, and think of themselves as members of a single whole.[8] This distinction sheds light on early modern political theory. But Oakeshott's assumption that strong and autonomous individuals will be associated with the former, and only those who cannot appreciate individuality will want to escape into a *universitas*, is not borne out in French philosophy. The men who formulated visions of a whole in which the isolated self would be perfected in something beyond self were the same men who preached the virtues of free robust individuality: Montaigne, Descartes, Pascal, Montesquieu, and Rousseau. The attempt by all these writers to describe a satisfying community larger than the single self was prompted by their sense of the psychological mutilation of an isolated human being with no ties of friendship or intimacy to others. The concept of *amour-propre* captures the absurdity of such a situation—the preoccupation with what is singular, unique, different about the self. For a man infected with proprietary self-love, interest in other persons comes only on the basis of what they can offer him in pleasure and enhancement. Such individuals are not robust noble adventurers but superficial, impoverished, monotonous. They are ironically incapable of self-knowledge. For self-knowledge, as Montaigne showed so well, depends on experience of something outside self.

To avoid the deficiency of the single self, Montaigne sought duplication of himself in perfect friendship. Pascal envisioned the commu-

---

[8] Oakeshott, *On Human Conduct*, pp. 196-206, 308-326. The distinction between *societas* and *universitas* is nicely captured in Montesquieu's two models, monarchical and republican. Oakeshott himself prefers *societas* to *universitas*, on the grounds that those who long for "wholeness" are feeble, frightened men, the world's second-raters, who cannot bear the isolation and responsibilities of individual freedom in a *societas*. He contrasts the bold noble adventurers along the road of a *societas* with the "individuals *manqué*" who long for community, and are susceptible to being organized into a *universitas*, like a conducted tour-group, by whatever mountebank happens to come along.

nity of saints. Descartes placed the individual in a set of concentric relationships extending from intimate family to the whole race. Montesquieu and Rousseau described the fulfillment of the self in the community as a rich political experience. The richness of all these visions rests on an equally acute understanding of the importance of the individual, in these same social philosophies. The identification of self-knowledge as the major human purpose, the conviction that duties to the self ground all other duties, and the argument that common interests must be the interests of individuals, are just as important in these theories as the search for something beyond self. The continual dialectic between these two perspectives gave rise to those aspects of French social theory that have proved most fertile and most durable. To devise a constitution for a polity in which individuality and privacy are protected, and a substantial public life is enjoyed by all citizens bound together in community, is no easy task. But it is surely a challenge worth pursuing. Those who attempt it will remain indebted to these French theorists who posed the issues with extraordinary clarity, and suggested some answers that remain worth pondering.

Bibliography

ABBREVIATIONS

AHMC   *Album Helen Maud Cam*
BHR   *Bibliothèque d'humanisme et renaissance*
FHS   *French Historical Studies*
JHI   *Journal of the History of Ideas*
JMH   *Journal of Modern History*
PMLA   *Publications of the Modern Language Association*
RHLF   *Revue d'histoire littéraire de la France*
SR   *Studies in the Renaissance*
SVEC   *Studies on Voltaire and the Eighteenth Century*

MANUSCRIPTS

Archives des affaires étrangères m.d.f. 502: d'Argenson, *Oeuvres meslées*.
Bibliothèque de l'Arsenal no. 2338: d'Argenson, *Jusques où la démocratie*. . . .
Bibliothèque nationale fonds français 1205; Belesbat, "Mémoires présentés au Roi."
Bibliothèque nationale fonds français 18472-18474: [L'Hôpital], *Traité de la Justice*.
Bibliothèque nationale, nouvelles acquisitions françaises 12833: Montesquieu, *De l'esprit des lois*.

PRIMARY SOURCES

Abbadie, Jacques. *L'Art de se connoitre soy-même*. The Hague, 1749.
Aguesseau, Henri d'. *Oeuvres complètes*. Edited by M. Pardessus. Paris, 1819.
Argenson, René Louis de Voyer d'. *Considérations sur le gouvernement ancien et présent de la France*. Amsterdam, 1765.
―――. *Considérations*. . . . Second edition by the marquis de Paulmy. Amsterdam, 1784.
―――. "Discours sur l'inégalité." In Roger Tisserand, ed., *Les Concurrents de J.-J. Rousseau à l'Académie de Dijon pour le prix de 1754*. Paris, 1936.

Argenson, René Louis de Voyer d'. *Essais dans le goût de ceux de Montaigne, ou Loisirs d'un ministre.* Edited by the Marquis de Paulmy. Amsterdam, 1785.

———. *Journal et mémoires.* Edited by E.J.B. Rathery for the Société de l'histoire de France. 9 vols. Paris, 1859-1867.

———. "Lettre à l'auteur" and "Observations sur le bien que les Seigneurs peuvent faire aux habitans de leur terres." *Journal oeconomique,* II, April and June 1751.

———. *Mémoires et journal inédit.* Edited by Charles René d'Argenson. 5 vols. Paris: Jannet, 1857-1858.

———. *Notices sur les oeuvres de théatre.* Edited by H. Lagrave. SVEC XLII-XLIII. Geneva, 1966.

Augustine. *The City of God.* Translated by Marcus Dods. New York, 1950.

Balzac, J-L. Guez de. *Oeuvres.* Edited by L. Moreau. 2 vols. Paris, 1854.

Bayle, Pierre. *Ce que c'est que la France toute catholique.* Edited by Elisabeth Labrousse. Paris, 1973.

———. *Oeuvres diverses.* Edited by Alain Niderst. Paris, 1971.

Bergerac, Cyrano de. *Oeuvres libertines.* Edited by Frédéric Lachèvre. 2 vols. Paris, 1921.

———. *Other Worlds.* Translated by Geoffrey Strachan. Oxford, 1965.

Bodin, Jean. *Colloquium of the Seven about the Secrets of the Sublime [Heptaplomeres].* Translated by Marion L. D. Kuntz. Princeton, 1975.

———. *Method for the Easy Comprehension of History.* Translated by Beatrice Reynolds. New York, 1945.

———. *La Réponse de Jean Bodin à M. de Malestroit sur les monnaies et le rencherissement.* Edited by Henri Hauser. New York, 1972.

———. *Les Six livres de la république.* Paris, 1577.

———. *The Six Bookes of a Commonweale.* Edited by Kenneth McRae. Cambridge, Mass., 1972.

———. *Six Books of the Commonwealth.* Translated and abridged by M. J. Tooley. Oxford, 1955.

Boisguilbert, Pierre le Pesant de. *Détail de la France; Dissertation sur la nature des richesses; Factum de la France; Traité des grains.* In Eugene Daire, ed., *Economistes-financiers du XVIIe siècle.* Paris, 1843.

Bossuet, Jacques-Bénigne. *Avertissements aux Protestants.* Paris, 1740.

———. *Discourse on Universal History*. Translated by Elborg Forster, edited by Orest Ranum. Chicago, 1976.
———. *Maximes et réflections sur la comédie*. Paris, 1694.
———. *Oeuvres choisies*. 5 vols. Paris, 1903-1909.
———. *Politique de Bossuet*. Edited by Jacques Truchet. Paris, 1966.
———. *Politique tirée des propres paroles de l'Ecriture sainte*. Edited by Jacques Le Brun. Geneva, 1967.
Boulainvilliers, Henri de. *Histoire de l'ancien gouvernement de la France*. The Hague and Amsterdam, 1727.
———. *Mémoires présentés à monseigneur le duc d'Orléans*. The Hague and Amsterdam, 1727.
Budé, Guillaume. *L'Institution du prince*. In Claude Bontems, et al., *Le Prince dans la France des XVIe et XVIIe siècles*. Paris, 1965.
Camus, Jean-Pierre. *La Défense du pur Amour*. Paris, 1640.
Charron, Pierre. *De la sagesse*. Edited by Amaury Duval. 3 vols. Paris, 1820.
Commynes, Philippe de. *Mémoires*. Edited by Joseph Calmette. 3 vols. Paris, 1925.
———. *The Mémoires of Philippe de Commynes*. Translated by Isabella Cazeaux, edited by Samuel Kinser. Columbia, S.C., 1949.
Constant, Benjamin. *Oeuvres*. Edited by Alfred Roulin. Paris, 1957.
Daire, Eugene, ed. *Economistes-financiers du XVIIIe siècle*. Paris, 1843.
Descartes, René. *Correspondance*. Edited by Charles Adam and Gérard Milhaud. Paris, 1936-1963.
———. *Oeuvres et lettres*. Edited by André Bridoux. Paris, 1952.
———. *The Philosophical Works of Descartes*. Edited by Elizabeth Haldane and G.R.T. Ross. Cambridge, 1931.
———. *Philosophical Writings*. Edited by Elizabeth Anscombe and Peter Geach. Edinburgh and London, 1954.
Domat, Jean. *Les Loix civiles dans leur ordre naturel; le droit public, et Legum delectus*. Paris, 1777. Translated by William Strahan as *The Civil Law in its Natural Order, together with the Public Law*. London, 1722.
Du Bos, Jean-Baptiste. *Histoire critique de l'établissement de la monarchie française dans les Gaules*. Paris, 1742.
Duclos, Charles. *Considérations sur les moeurs de ce siècle*. Paris, 1751.
Du Vair, Guillaume. *Oeuvres*. Geneva, 1970 [Paris, 1641].
Esprit, Jacques. *De la fausseté des vertus humaines*. Paris, 1678.
Fénelon, François de Salignac de La Mothe-. *Les Aventures de Télémaque*. Paris, 1875.

Fénelon, François de Salignac de La Mothe-. *Ecrits et lettres politiques*. Edited by Charles Urbain. Paris, 1920.

———. *Oeuvres*. Edited by L. Aimé-Martin. 3 vols. Paris, 1835.

Hobbes, Thomas. *Oeuvres philosophiques et politiques*. Neufchatel, 1787.

Hotman, Antoine and François. *Opuscules françoises des Hotmans*. Paris, 1616.

Hotman, François. *Francogallia*. Edited by Ralph E. Giesy and J.H.M. Salmon. Cambridge, 1972.

Joly, Claude. *Recueil des maximes véritables et importantes pour l'institution du roy*. Paris, 1653.

[Jurieu, Pierre?] *Les Soupirs de la France esclave, qui aspire après la liberté*. Amsterdam, 1690.

La Boétie, Etienne. *Oeuvres complètes*. Edited by Paul Bonnefon. Paris, 1862.

———. *The Politics of Obedience: The Discourse of Voluntary Servitude*. Edited by Murray Rothbard, translated by Harry Kurz. New York, 1965.

La Bruyère, Jean de. *Les Caractères, ou, les moeurs de ce siècle*. Edited by Robert Garapon. Paris, 1962.

La Drevetière, Delisle de. *Essai sur l'amour propre*. Paris, 1738.

La Fontaine, Jean de. *Fables*. Paris, 1974.

La Mothe le Vayer, François. *Dialogues*. 2 vols. Frankfort, 1716.

———. *Oeuvres*. Dresden, 1756.

La Perrière, Guillaume de. *Le Miroir politique*. Paris, 1567.

La Rivière, Mercier de. *L'Ordre naturel et essential des sociétés politiques*. London, 1967.

La Rochefoucauld, François, duc de. *Réflexions ou sentences et maximes morales*, including the *Réflexions diverses*. Edited by Paul Morand. Paris, 1965.

Le Caron, Loys. *Dialogues*. Paris, 1556.

Le Moyne, Pierre. *Peintures morales*. Paris, 1640.

Le Roy, Louis. *Aristotle's Politiques or Discourses of Government*. London, 1598.

———. *De la vicissitude ou variété des choses en l'univers*. Edited by Blanchard W. Bates. Princeton, 1944.

L'Hôpital, Michel de. *Oeuvres complètes de Michel de l'Hospital*. Edited by P.J.S. Duféy. 5 vols. Paris, 1824-1826.

Lipsius, Justus. *Sixe Bookes of Politickes or Civil Doctrine*. Translated by William Jones. London, 1594.

———. *Traité de la constance*. Translated by Lucien du Bois. Brussels, 1873.

Locke, John. *Discourses*. London, 1828.
Louis XIV. *Mémoires for the Instruction of the Dauphin*. Edited by Paul Sonnino. New York, 1970.
Loyseau, Charles. *Oeuvres*. Paris, 1701.
Machiavelli, Niccolò. *The Prince and the Discourses*. Edited by Max Lerner. New York, 1950.
Malebranche, Nicolas. *Oeuvres complètes*. Edited by Michel Adam. Vol. xi. Paris, 1966.
Méré, Antoine Gombaud, chevalier de. *Oeuvres complètes*. Edited by Charles H. Boudhors. 3 vols. Paris, 1930.
Montaigne, Michel de. *Complete Essays*. Translated by Donald Frame. Stanford, 1958.
———. *Oeuvres complètes*. Edited by Albert Thibaudet and Maurice Rat. Paris, 1962.
Montchrétien, Antoine de. *Traicté de l'oeconomie politique*. Edited by Théodore Funck-Brentano. Paris, 1889.
Montesquieu, Charles de Secondat, baron de. *Oeuvres complètes*. Edited by Roger Caillois. 2 vols. Paris, 1949-1951.
———. *Oeuvres completes*. Edited by André Masson. 3 vols. Paris, 1950-1955.
———. *The Spirit of the Laws*. Translated by Thomas Nugent. New York, 1949.
Naudé, Gabriel. *La Bibliographie politique contenant les livres & la méthode necessaires à estudier la politique*. Paris, 1642.
———. *Considérations politiques sur les coups d'estat*. Rome, 1639.
Nicole, Pierre. *Essais de morale*. Edited by Louis Despres. 13 vols. Paris, 1755-1757.
———. *Oeuvres philosophiques et morales*. Edited by Charles Jourdain. Paris, 1845.
———. *Traité de la comédie*. Paris, 1961.
Pascal, Blaise. *Entretien de M. Pascal et de M. de Sacy*. Edited by André Gounelle. Paris, 1966.
———. *Oeuvres complètes*. Edited by Jacques Chevalier. Paris, 1954.
———. *Pensées*. Edited by Léon Brunschvicg. Paris, 1934.
———. *Pensées*. Translated by W. F. Trotter. New York, 1931.
Pasquier, Etienne. *Ecrits politiques*. Edited by Dorothea Thickett. Geneva, 1966.
———. *Lettres familières*. Edited by D. Thickett. Paris, 1974.
———. *Oeuvres*. Amsterdam, 1723.
———. *Recherches de la France*. Paris, 1611.
Priézac, Daniel de. *Discours politiques*. Paris, 1666.

Rabelais, François. *Oeuvres complètes*. Edited by Jacques Boulenger and Lucien Scheler. Paris, 1955.
Retz, Paul de Gondi, cardinal de. *Mémoires*. Edited by Maurice Allem. Paris, 1949.
———. *Oeuvres*. Edited by Alphonse Feillet. Vol. v. Paris, 1880.
Richelieu, Armand-Jean du Plessis, cardinal de. *Mémoire . . . écrit de sa main, de l'année 1607 ou 1610*. Edited by Armand Baschet. Paris, 1880.
———. *Testament politique*. Edited by Louis André. Paris, 1947.
Rousseau, Jean-Jacques. *Lettres philosophiques*. Edited by Henri Gouhier. Paris, 1974.
———. *Oeuvres complètes*. Edited by Bernard Gagnebin and Marcel Raymond. 4 vols. Paris, 1964-1969.
———. *Social Contract*. Edited by Bertrand de Jouvenel. Geneva, 1947.
Saint-Aubin, Gilbert-Charles Le Gendre, marquis de. *Traité de l'opinion*. Paris, 1735.
Saint-Evremond, Charles de. *Oeuvres en prose*. Edited by René Ternois. 4 vols. Paris, 1962-1969.
Saint-Pierre, Charles-Irenée, abbé de. *Mémoire pour diminuer le nombre des procès*. Paris, 1725.
———. *Mémoire sur la polysynodie*. Paris, 1718.
———. *Oeuvres diverses*. Paris, 1730.
———. *Ouvrajes de politique*. 16 vols. Rotterdam, 1733-1741.
———. *Projet pour rendre la paix perpétuelle en Europe*. Utrecht, 1713 and 1717 editions.
———. *Les Rêves d'un homme de bien qui peuvent être réalisés*. Paris, 1775.
———. "Unpublished Maxims of the Abbé de Saint-Pierre." Edited by Merle Perkins. *French Review* XXXI (1958), 498-503.
Saint-Simon, Louis de Rouvroy, duc de. *Projets de gouvernement*. Edited by M. P. Mesnard. Paris, 1860.
Sales, Saint François de. *Traité de l'amour de Dieu*. Paris, 1630.
Sebond, Raimond. *Théologie naturelle*. Translated by Michel de Montaigne. Rouen, 1603.
Sénault, François. *De l'usage des passions*. Paris, 1641.
———. *Le Monarque, ou les devoirs du souverain*. Paris, 1661.
Sévigné, Marie de Rabutin-Chantal, marquise de. *Correspondance*. Edited by Roger Duchêne. Vol. III. Paris, 1978.
Seyssel, Claude de. *La Monarchie de France*. Edited by Jacques Poujol. Paris, 1961.

Silhon, Jean. *De la certitude des connoissances humaines . . . où sont particulièrement expliquez les principes et les fondemens de la morale et de la politique*. Paris, 1661.

———. *Le Ministre d'Estat*. Amsterdam, 1664.

Sorbière, Samuel. *Relations, lettres et discours sur diverses matières curieuses*. Paris, 1660.

———. "Trois discours sceptiques." In *Mémoires de Michel de Marolles*. Amsterdam, 1755.

Vauban, Sebastien Le Prestre, seigneur de. *Dixme royale*. In Eugene Daire, ed., *Economistes-financiers du XVIIIe siècle*. Paris, 1843.

Vauvenargues, Luc de Clapier, marquis de. *Oeuvres complètes*. Edited by Henry Bonnier. Paris, 1968.

Veiras, Denis. *Histoire des Sévarambes*. Vol. v of *Voyages imaginaires*. Edited by Garnier. Amsterdam, 1787.

Voltaire, François-Marie Arouet. *Voltaire's Correspondance*. Edited by Theodore Besterman. 106 vols. Geneva, 1953-1963.

———. *Philosophical Letters*. Translated by Ernest Dilworth. New York, 1961.

SECONDARY SOURCES: BOOKS

Abercrombie, Nigel. *Origins of Jansenism*. Oxford, 1936.

———. *Saint Augustine and French Classical Thought*. New York, 1972 [1938].

Adam, Antoine. *Du mysticisme à la révolte: Les jansénistes du XVIIe siècle*. Paris, 1968.

———. *Le Mouvement philosophique dans la première moitié du XVIIIe siècle*. Paris, 1967.

———, ed. *Les Libertins au XVIIe siècle*. Paris, 1964.

Aiglun, Rochas d'. *Vauban: Sa famille, ses ecrits*. Paris, 1910.

Alcover, Madeleine. *La Pensée philosophique et scientifique de Cyrano de Bergerac*. Paris and Geneva, 1970.

Althusser, Louis. *Politics and History*. Translated by Ben Brewster. London, 1972.

Anderson, Perry. *Lineages of the Absolutist State*. London, 1974.

Aron, Raymond. *Main Currents of Sociological Thought*. Vol. 1. Garden City, N.Y., 1968.

Aronson, Nicole. *Les Idées politiques de Rabelais*. Paris, 1973.

Artz, Frederick. *The Enlightenment in France*. Kent, Ohio, 1968.

Asher, Eugene L. *The Resistance to the Maritime Classes: The Survival of Feudalism in the France of Colbert*. Berkeley and Los Angeles, 1960.

Aston, Trevor, ed. *Crisis in Europe 1560-1660*. New York, 1965.
Atkinson, Geoffroy. *The Extraordinary Voyage in French Literature before 1700*. New York, 1920.
Auerbach, Erich. *Scenes from the Drama of European Literature*. Gloucester, Mass., 1973.
Baird, A.W.S. *Studies in Pascal's Ethics*. The Hague, 1975.
Barnwell, H. T. *Les Idées morales et critiques de Saint-Evremond*. Paris, 1957.
Barzun, Jacques. *The French Race*. New York, 1932.
Battista, Anna Maria. *Alle origine de pensiero politico libertino: Montaigne e Charron*. Milan, 1966.
Baudrillart, Henri. *Bodin et son temps*. Aalen, 1964 [Paris 1853].
Baumgartner, Frederic. *Radical Reactionaries: The Political Thought of the French Catholic League*. Geneva, 1976.
Becker, Carl. *The Heavenly City of the Eighteenth-Century Philosophers*. New Haven, 1932.
Bénichou, Paul. *Morales du grand siècle*. Paris, 1948.
Bickart, Roger. *Les Parlements et la notion de souveraineté nationale au XVIIIe siècle*. Paris, 1932.
Bloch, Marc. *Les Rois thaumaturges*. Paris, 1961 [Strasbourg, 1924].
Blum, Jerome. *The End of the Old Order in Rural Europe*. Princeton, 1978.
Boase, Alan. *The Fortunes of Montaigne in France*. London, 1935.
Bolgar, R. R. *Classical Influences on European Culture*. Cambridge, 1976.
Bonnefon, Paul. *Montaigne et ses amis*. Paris, 1898.
Bonney, Richard. *Political Change in France under Richelieu and Mazarin 1624-1661*. Oxford, 1978.
Bontems, Claude, et al. *Le Prince dans la France des XVIe et XVIIe siècles*. Paris, 1965.
Bosher, J. F. *French Government and Society 1500-1850*. London, 1973.
Bowen, Barbara. *The Age of Bluff*. Urbana, 1972.
Brémond, Henri. *La Querelle du pur amour au temps de Louis XIII*. Paris, 1932.
Brissaud, Jean. *Un Libéral de XVIIe siècle*. Paris, 1898.
Broglie, Emmanuel de. *Fénelon à Cambrai*. Paris, 1884.
Brooks, Peter. *The Novel of Worldliness*. Princeton, 1979.
Broome, J. H. *Pascal*. London, 1965.
Brown, Frieda. *Religious and Political Conservatism in the Essais of Montaigne*. Geneva, 1963.

Brunschvicg, Léon. *Descartes et Pascal lecteurs de Montaigne.* Paris, 1944.
Buisseret, David. *Sully and the Growth of Centralized Government in France.* London, 1968.
Carcassonne, Elie. *Montesquieu et le problème de la constitution française au XVIIIe siècle.* Paris, n.d.
Carlyle, A. J. *History of Medieval Political Theory in the West.* Vol. VI. Oxford, 1950.
Carré, H. *Le Règne de Louis XV.* Paris, 1911.
Catalogue des livres de la bibliothèque de Monsieur*** [d'Argenson]. Paris, 1755.
Centre Aixois d'études et de recherches. *La Regence.* Paris, 1970.
Charvet, John. *The Social Problem in the Philosophy of Rousseau.* Cambridge, 1974.
Cherel, Albert. *De Télémaque à Candide.* Paris, 1958.
———. *Fénelon au XVIIIe siècle en France.* Geneva, 1970 [1917].
Chinard, Gilbert. *En lisant Pascal.* Lille and Geneva, 1948.
Church, W. F. *Constitutional Thought in Sixteenth-Century France.* Cambridge, Mass., 1941.
———. *The Impact of Absolutism in France.* New York, 1969.
———. *Richelieu and Reason of State.* Princeton, 1972.
Cole, Charles Woolsey. *French Mercantilism 1683-1700.* New York, 1943.
———. *French Mercantilist Doctrines before Colbert.* New York, 1931.
Coleman, D. C., ed. *Revisions in Mercantilism.* London, 1969.
Colie, Rosalie. *Paradoxia Epidemica.* Princeton, 1966.
Colletti, Lucio. *From Rousseau to Lenin.* Translated by John Merrington and Judith White. New York, 1972.
Coltman, Irene. *Private Men and Public Causes.* London, 1962.
Coppin, Joseph. *Montaigne traducteur de Raymond Sebond.* Lille, 1925.
Coveney, P. J., ed. *France in Crisis, 1620-1675.* Totowa, N.J., 1977.
Crocker, Lester. *Rousseau's Social Contract.* Cleveland, 1968.
Croquette, Bernard. *Pascal and Montaigne.* Geneva, 1974.
Del Noce, Augusto. *Riforma cattolica et filosofia moderna.* Vol. I: *Cartesio.* Bologna, 1965.
Denzer, Horst, ed. *Jean Bodin.* International Colloquium, 1970. Munich, 1973.
Derathé, Robert. *Jean-Jacques Rousseau et la science-politique de son temps.* Paris, 1970.

Desgraves, Louis, ed. *Catalogue de la bibliothèque de Montesquieu*. Geneva, 1954.
Dodge, Guy H. *The Political Theory of the Huguenots of the Dispersion*, New York, 1947.
Dolgoff, Sam, ed. *Bakunin on Anarchy*. New York, 1971.
Doolin, Paul Rice. *The Fronde*. Cambridge, Mass., 1935.
Drouet, Joseph. *L'Abbé de Saint-Pierre, l'homme et l'oeuvre*. Paris, 1912.
Durand, Yves. *Les Républiques au temps des monarchies*. Paris, 1973.
Edwards, Tom T. "Jansenism in Church and State." Ph.D. dissertation, Harvard, 1960.
Ellul, Jacques. *Histoire des institutions de l'époque Franque à la Révolution*. Paris, 1967.
Esmonin, Edmond. *Etudes sur la France des XVIIe et XVIIIe siècles*. Paris, 1964.
Ferguson, Wallace K. *Europe in Transition: 1300-1520*. Boston, 1963.
Flammermont, Jules, ed. *Remontrances du Parlement de Paris au XVIIIe siècle*. Paris, 1888.
Ford, Franklin L. *Robe and Sword*. Cambridge, Mass., 1953.
Forster, Robert, and Jack P. Greene, eds. *Preconditions of Revolution in Early Modern Europe*. Baltimore, 1970.
Fox-Genovese, Elizabeth. *The Origins of Physiocracy*. Ithaca, N.Y., 1976.
Frame, Donald. *Montaigne: A Biography*. New York, 1956.
———. *Montaigne's Discovery of Man: The Humanization of a Humanist*. New York, 1955.
Franklin, Julian. *Constitutionalism and Resistance in the Sixteenth Century*. New York, 1969.
———. *Jean Bodin and the Rise of Absolutist Theory*. Cambridge, 1973.
———. *Jean Bodin and the Sixteenth-Century Revolution in the Methodology of Law and History*. New York, 1963.
Galloudec-Genuys, Françoise. *La Conception du prince dans l'oeuvre de Fénelon*. Paris, 1963.
Gay, Peter. *The Enlightenment*. Vol. II. New York, 1969.
———. *Voltaire's Politics: The Poet as Realist*. Princeton, 1959.
Gessler, Peter. *René Louis d'Argenson 1694-1757: Seine Ideen uber Selbtsverwaltung, Einheitstaat, Wohlfahrt und Freiheit in biographischem zusammenhang*. Basel, 1957.
Gilmore, Myron. *Argument from Roman Law in Political Thought 1200-1600*. Cambridge, Mass., 1941.

Goldmann, Lucien. *The Hidden God*. Translated by Phillip Thody. New York, 1964.
Goré, Jeanne-Lydie. *L'Itineraire du Fénelon: Humanisme et spiritualité*. Paris, 1957.
Goubert, Pierre. *L'Ancien Régime*. 2 vols. Paris, 1973.
———. *Louis XIV and Twenty Million Frenchmen*. Translated by Anne Carter. New York, 1970.
Goumy, Edouard. *Etude sur la vie et les écrits de l'abbé de Saint-Pierre*. Paris, 1859.
Goyard-Fabre, Simone. *La Philosophie du droit de Montesquieu*. Paris, 1973.
Granpre Molière, Jean-Jacques. *La Théorie de la constitution anglaise chez Montesquieu*. Leyden, 1972.
Greenleaf, W. H. *Order, Empiricism and Politics*. Oxford, 1964.
Griffiths, Richard. *The Dramatic Technique of Antoine de Montchrestien*. Oxford, 1970.
Grimsley, Ronald. *From Montesquieu to Laclos: Studies in the French Enlightenment*. Geneva, 1974.
Grubbs, Henry. *Damien Mitton 1618-1690: Bourgeois Hônnete Homme*. Princeton, 1932.
Gundersheimer, Werner. *The Life and Works of Louis Le Roy*. Geneva, 1966.
Gunn, J.A.W. *Politics and the Public Interest in the Seventeenth Century*. London and Toronto, 1969.
Halévy, Daniel. *Vauban*. Paris, 1924.
Hallie, Philip. *The Scar of Montaigne*. Middletown, Conn., 1966.
Hampson, Norman. *The Cultural History of the Enlightenment*. New York, 1968.
Harding, Robert R. *Anatomy of a Power Elite: The Provincial Governors of Early Modern France*. New Haven, 1978.
Harth, Erica. *Cyrano de Bergerac and the Polemics of Modernity*. New York, 1970.
Hatton, Ragnhild, ed. *Louis XIV and Absolutism*. Columbus, Ohio, 1976.
Havens, George R. *The Age of Ideas*. New York, 1955.
Hayden, J. Michael. *France and the Estates General of 1614*. Cambridge, 1974.
Haydn, Hiram. *The Counter-Renaissance*. New York, 1950.
Hazard, Paul. *The European Mind*. Translated by J. L. May from *La Crise de la conscience européene*. London, 1953 [1935].
Heckscher, Eli. *Mercantilism*. Translated by Mendel Shapiro. London, 1935.

Henderson, G. D. *Chevalier Ramsay*. London, 1952.
Henry, Nannerl O. "Democratic Monarchy: the Political Theory of the Marquis d'Argenson." Ph.D. dissertation, Yale, 1967.
Herr, Richard, and Harold T. Parker, eds. *Ideas in History*. Durham, N.C., 1965.
Hippeau, Louis. *Essai sur la morale de La Rochefoucauld*. Paris, 1967.
Hirschman, Albert O. *A Bias for Hope*. New Haven, 1971.
———. *The Passions and the Interests: Political Arguments for Capitalism before Its Triumph*. Princeton, 1977.
Hope, Quentin. *Saint Evremond: The Honnête Homme as Critic*. Bloomington, Ind., 1962.
Horne, Thomas A. *The Social Thought of Bernard Mandeville*. New York, 1978.
Horowitz, Louise. *Love and Language: A Study of the Classical French Moralist Writers*, Columbus, Ohio, 1977.
Hulliung, Mark, *Montesquieu and the Old Regime*. Berkeley and Los Angeles, 1976.
Huppert, George. *Les Bourgeois Gentilshommes: An Essay on the Definition of Elites in Renaissance France*. Chicago, 1977.
James, E. D. *Pierre Nicole: Jansenist and Humanist*. The Hague, 1972.
Janet, Paul. *Fénelon: His Life and Works*. Translated by Victor Leuliette, Port Washington, N.Y., 1970 [1914].
———. *Histoire de la science politique*. Paris, 1887.
Jehasse, Jean. *La Renaissance de la critique*. Saint-Etienne, 1976.
Johnson, N. R. *Louis XIV and the Age of the Enlightenment: The Myth of the Sun King from 1715 to 1789*. SVEC CLXXII. Oxford, 1978.
Joppin, Gabriel. *Une Querelle autour de l'amour pur*. Paris, 1938.
Kantorowicz, Ernst. *The King's Two Bodies: a Study in Medieval Political Theology*. Princeton, 1957.
Kassem, Badreddine. *Décadence et absolutisme dans l'oeuvre de Montesquieu*. Geneva, 1960.
Kelley, Donald R. *Foundations of Modern Historical Scholarship: Language, Law and History in the French Renaissance*. New York, 1970.
———. *François Hotman: A Revolutionary's Ordeal*. Princeton, 1973.
Kern, Fritz. *Kingship and Law in the Middle Ages*. Translated by S. B. Chrimes. Oxford, 1939.
Kettering, Sharon. *Judicial Politics and Urban Revolt in Seventeenth-Century France: The Parlement of Aix, 1629-1659*. Princeton, 1978.

Kiernan, Colm. *Science and Enlightenment in Eighteenth-Century France.* SVEC LIX. Geneva, 1968.
Kierstad, Raymond F., ed. *State and Society in Seventeenth-Century France.* New York, 1975.
King, James. *Science and Rationalism in the Government of Louis XIV.* Baltimore, 1949.
King, Preston. *The Ideology of Order.* London, 1974.
Klaits, Joseph. *Printed Propaganda under Louis XIV.* Princeton, 1976.
Knachel, Philip A. *England and the Fronde.* Ithaca, N.Y., 1967.
Knecht, R. J. *Francis I and Absolute Monarchy.* London, 1969.
Kogel, Renée. *Pierre Charron.* Geneva, 1972.
Kossman, Ernst. *La Fronde.* Leyden, 1954.
Krailsheimer, A. J. *Studies in Self-Interest from Descartes to La Bruyère.* Oxford, 1962.
Krieger, Leonard. *An Essay on the Theory of Enlightened Despotism.* Chicago, 1973.
―――, and Fritz Stern, eds. *The Responsibility of Power.* New York, 1967.
Kuhfuss, Walter. *Mässigung und Politik.* Munich, 1975.
Labrousse, Elisabeth. *Pierre Bayle.* Paris, 1973.
Lacour-Gayet, G. *L'Education politique de Louis XIV.* Paris, 1898.
Lange, Maurice. *La Bruyère: Critique des conditions et des institutions sociales.* Geneva, 1970.
Laporte, Jean. *La Doctrine de Port Royale, la Morale (d'après Arnauld).* Paris, 1951.
Lavender, Thomas E. "The *Histoire des Sévarambes* of Denis Veiras." Ph.D. dissertation, Harvard, 1937.
Lefebvre, Henri. *Descartes.* Paris, 1947.
―――. *Pascal.* Paris, 1949-1954.
Lefèvre, Roger. *L'Humanisme de Descartes.* Paris, 1957.
Lemaire, André. *Les Lois fondamentales de la monarchie française.* Paris, 1907.
Letts, J. T. *Le Cardinal de Retz, historien et moraliste du possible.* Paris, 1966.
Levi, Anthony. *French Moralists: The Theory of the Passions 1585-1659.* Oxford, 1964.
―――, ed. *Humanism in France.* Manchester, 1970.
Levine, Andrew. *The Politics of Autonomy.* Amherst, Mass., 1976.
Lewis, Archibald, ed. *Aspects of the Renaissance.* Austin, Texas, 1967.
Lewis, P. S. *Later Medieval France: The Polity.* London, 1968.
Lewis, Philip. *La Rochefoucauld: The Art of Abstraction.* Ithaca, N.Y., 1977.

Lewis, W. H. *The Splendid Century*. Garden City, N.Y., 1957.
Lichtenberger, André. *Le Socialisme au XVIIIe siècle*. Paris, 1895.
Lougee, Carolyn C. *Le Paradis des Femmes*. Princeton, 1976.
Lovejoy, Arthur O. *Reflections on Human Nature*. Baltimore, 1961.
Lublinskaya, A. D. *French Absolutism: The Crucial Phase, 1620-1629*. Translated by Brian Pearce. Cambridge, 1968.
Lukes, Steve. *Individualism*. New York, 1973.
Macary, Jean. *Essays on the Age of Enlightenment in Honor of Ira O. Wade*. Geneva, 1977.
Mackrell, J.Q.C. *The Attack upon "Feudalism" in Eighteenth-Century France*. London and Toronto, 1973.
Maclean, Ian. *Woman Triumphant: Feminism in French Literature 1610-1652*. Oxford, 1977.
Madelin, Louis. *Une Revolution manquée*. Paris, 1931.
Mahoney, Edward P., ed. *Philosophy and Humanism*. New York, 1976.
Major, J. Russell. *The Estates General of 1560*. Princeton, 1951.
———. *Representative Institutions in Renaissance France, 1421-1559*. Madison, Wisc., 1960.
Mandrou, Robert. *La France aux XVIIe et XVIIIe siècles*. Paris, 1967.
———. *Louis XIV et son temps*. Paris, 1973.
Martin, Henri. *Catalogue des mss.* [of the Bibliothèque de l'Arsenal]. Vol. VIII in the catalogues of public libraries of France.
———. *Histoire de France*. Vols. XIV, XV. Paris, 1859.
Martin, Kingsley. *French Liberal Thought in the Eighteenth Century*. New York, 1962.
Masters, Roger. *The Political Philosophy of Rousseau*. Princeton, 1968.
Maurens, Jacques. *La Tragédie sans tragique: Le néo-stoicisme dans l'oeuvre de Pierre Corneille*. Paris, 1966.
Mauzi, Robert. *L'Idée du bonheur au XVIIIe siècle*. Paris, 1960.
McGowan, Margaret. *Montaigne's Deceits*. Philadelphia, 1974.
McIlwain, C. H. *Constitutionalism Ancient and Modern*. Ithaca, N.Y., 1940.
McNeil, David O. *Guillaume Budé and Humanism in the Reign of Francis I*. Geneva, 1975.
Meinecke, Friedrich. *Machiavellism: The Doctrine of Raison d'Etat and its Place in Modern History*. Translated by Douglas Scott. New Haven, 1957.
Merlant, Joachim. *De Montaigne à Vauvenargues: Essais sur la vie intérieure et la culture du moi*. Geneva, 1969 [1914].
Mesnard, Pierre. *Essai sur la morale de Descartes*. Paris, 1936.
———. *L'Essor de la philosophie politique du XVIe siècle*. Paris, 1969.

Miloyevitch, Voukossava. *La Théorie des passions de P. Sénault*. Paris, 1934.
Molho, Anthony, and John Tedeschi, eds. *Renaissance Studies in Honor of Hans Baron*. Florence, 1970.
Moore, Will G. *French Classical Literature*. Oxford, 1961.
———. *La Rochefoucauld: His Mind and Art*. Oxford, 1969.
Moote, A. Lloyd. *The Revolt of the Judges*. Princeton, 1971.
Moreau-Reibel, Jean. *Jean Bodin et le droit public comparée*. Paris, 1933.
Mornet, Daniel. *Les Origines intellectuelles de la revolution française*. Paris, 1947.
Mousnier, Roland. *La Plume, la faucille, et le marteau*. Paris, 1970.
———. *La Venalité des offices sous Henry IV et Louis XIII*. Paris, 1971.
———. *Les XVIe et XVIIe siècles*. Vol. IV of the *Histoire générale des civilisations*, edited by Maurice Crouzet. Paris, 1954.
———. *Les Institutions de la France sous la monarchie absolue*, Vol. I. Paris, 1974.
———. *Peasant Uprisings in Seventeenth-Century France, Russia, and China*. Translated by Brian Pearce. New York, 1970.
Nagels, Jacques. *Reproduction du capital selon Marx, Boisguilbert.* . . . Brussels, 1970.
Naudeau, Olivier. *La Pensée de Montaigne et la composition des Essais*. Geneva, 1972.
Nichols, James. *Epicurean Political Philosophy: The De Rerum Naturae of Lucretius*. Ithaca, N.Y., 1976.
Oakeshott, Michael. *On Human Conduct*. Oxford, 1975.
Ogle, Arthur. *The Marquis d'Argenson*. London, 1893.
Olivier-Martin, François. *Histoire du droit français des origines à la Revolution*. Paris, 1948.
O'Loughlin, Michael. *The Garlands of Repose*. Chicago, 1978.
Oncken, Auguste. *Die Maxime Laissez faire et laissez passer*. Bern, 1886.
Orcibal, Jean. *Jean Duvergier de Hauranne abbé de Saint-Cyran et sons temps*. Vols. II and III of *Les Origines de jansenisme*. Paris, 1947.
Pagès, Georges. *La Monarchie d'Ancien Régime en France*. Paris, 1946.
Pangle, Thomas. *Montesquieu's Philosophy of Liberalism*. Chicago, 1973.
Parker, Geoffrey and Lesley Smith, eds. *The General Crisis of the Seventeenth Century*. London, 1978.

Pennock, Roland, and John Chapman, eds. *Constitutionalism*. The Yearbook of the American Society for Political and Legal Philosophy (NOMOS) xx. New York, 1979.
Perkins, James Breck. *France under the Regency*. Boston, 1892.
Perkins, Merle. *The Moral and Political Philosophy of the Abbé de Saint-Pierre*. Geneva and Paris, 1959.
Perrens, F. T. *Les Libertins en France au XVIIe siècle*. Paris, 1896.
Picot, Gilbert. *Cardin Le Bret (1558-1665) et la doctrine de la souveraineté*. Nancy, 1948.
Pintard, René. *La Libertinage érudit dans la première moitié due XVIIe siècle*. Paris, 1943.
Plamenatz, John. *Man and Society*. Vol. 1. London, 1963.
Pocock, J.G.A. *The Machiavellian Moment*. Princeton, 1975.
———. *Politics, Language and Time*. New York, 1971.
Polin, Raymond. *La Politique de la solitude*. Paris, 1971.
Popkin, Richard. *The History of Scepticism from Erasmus to Descartes*. Assen, 1960.
Porchnev, Boris. *Les Soulèvements populaires en France de 1623 à 1648*. Paris, 1963.
Post, Gaines. *Studies in Medieval Legal Thought: Public Law and the State 1100-1322*. Princeton, 1963.
Poulantzas, Nicos. *Political Power and Social Classes*. London, 1973.
Quinton, Anthony, ed. *Political Philosophy*. Oxford, 1967.
Rabb, Theodore. *The Struggle for Stability in Early Modern Europe*. Oxford, 1975.
———, and Jerrold Siegel, eds. *Action and Conviction in Early Modern Europe*. Princeton, 1969.
Ranum, Orest, ed. *National Consciousness, History, and Political Culture in Early Modern Europe*. Princeton, 1969.
———. *Paris in the Age of Absolutism*. New York, 1968.
Rebelliau, Alfred. *Vauban*. Paris, 1962.
Regosin, Richard. *The Matter of My Book: Montaigne's Essays as the Book of the Self*. Berkeley and Los Angeles, 1977.
Rice, Eugene F., Jr. *The Renaissance Idea of Wisdom*. Cambridge, Mass., 1958.
Richet, Denis. *La France moderne: L'esprit des institutions*. Paris, 1973.
Richter, Melvin. *Political Theory of Montesquieu*. Cambridge, 1977.
Rider, Frederick. *The Dialectic of Selfhood in Montaigne*. Stanford, 1973.
Rihs, Charles. *Les Philosophes utopistes*. Paris, 1970.
Roberts, Hazel van Dyke. *Boisguilbert*. New York, 1935.
Rodis-Lewis, Geneviève. *La Morale de Descartes*. Paris, 1970.

———. *Nicolas Malebranche.* Paris, 1963.
Rosenberg, Aubrey. *Tyssot de Patot and His Work.* The Hague, 1972.
Rosso, Corrado. *Montesquieu moraliste.* Translated by Marc Regaldo. Bordeaux, 1971.
Rothkrug, Lionel. *Opposition to Louis XIV: The Political and Social Origins of the French Enlightenment.* Princeton, 1965.
Rule, John C., ed. *Louis XIV and the Craft of Kingship.* Columbus, Ohio, 1970.
Sainte-Beuve, C.-A. *Causeries du lundi.* 15 vols. Paris, 1852-1862.
———. *Port-Royal.* 3 vols. Paris, 1952-1955.
Salmon, J.H.M. *Cardinal de Retz: The Anatomy of a Conspirator.* New York, 1969.
———. *The French Religious Wars in English Political Thought.* Oxford, 1959.
———. *Society in Crisis: France in the Sixteenth Century.* New York, 1975.
Saunders, Jason L. *Justus Lipsius: The Philosophy of Renaissance Stoicism.* New York, 1955.
Sayce, R. A. *Essays of Montaigne: A Critical Exploration.* London, 1972.
Sayre, Robert. *Solitude in Society.* Cambridge, Mass., 1978.
Schatz, Albert, and Robert Caillemer. *Le Mercantilisme libéral à la fin du XVIIe siècle.* Paris, 1906.
Schelling, Thomas. *The Strategy of Conflict.* Cambridge, Mass., 1960.
Schnur, Roman, ed. *Staatsräson.* Berlin, 1975. Proceedings of the International Colloquium on the Idea of Reason of State; Tübingen, 1974.
Sedgwick, Alexander. *Jansenism in Seventeenth-Century France.* Charlottesville, Va., 1977.
Sée, Henri. *Les Idées politiques en France au XVIIe siècle.* Paris, 1923.
Sennett, Richard. *The Fall of Public Man.* New York, 1974.
Shackleton, Robert. *Montesquieu: A Critical Biography.* Oxford, 1961.
Sharratt, Peter, ed. *French Renaissance Studies 1540-1570.* Totowa, N.J., 1976.
Shennan, J. H. *The Origins of the Modern European State 1450-1725.* London, 1974.
———. *The Parlement of Paris.* London, 1978.
Shklar, Judith. *Men and Citizens.* Cambridge, 1969.
Simon, Renée. *Henry de Boulainvillier.* Gap, 1940.
Simone, Franco, ed. *Culture et politique.* Turin, 1974.
Singleton, Charles S., ed. *Art, Science and History in the Renaissance.* Baltimore, 1967.

Skinner, Quentin. *The Foundations of Modern Political Thought*. 2 vols. Cambridge, 1978.
Smith, Pauline M. *The Anti-Courtier Trend in Sixteenth-Century French Literature*. Geneva, 1966.
Spink, J. H. *French Free-Thought from Gassendi to Voltaire*. London, 1960.
Stankiewicz, W. J. *Politics and Religion in Seventeenth-Century France*. Berkeley and Los Angeles, 1970.
Stegmann, André, ed. *L'Humanisme français au début de la Renaissance*. Paris, 1973.
Stepan, Alfred. *State and Society*. Princeton, 1978.
Strayer, Joseph R. *On the Medieval Origins of the Modern State*. Princeton, 1970.
———, and Charles H. Taylor. *Studies in Early French Taxation*. Cambridge, Mass., 1939.
Strowski, Fortunat. *Les Pensées de Pascal*. Paris, n.d.
Sutcliffe, F. E. *Guez de Balzac et son temps*. Paris, 1959.
———. *Politique et culture 1560-1660*. Paris, 1973.
Talbot, Albert. *Les Théories de Boisguilbert*. Paris, 1903.
Taveneaux, René. *Jansenisme et politique*. Paris, 1965.
Tawney, R. H. *Religion and the Rise of Capitalism*. London, 1926.
Thickett, Dorothea. *Bibliographie des oeuvres d'Estienne Pasquier*. Geneva, 1956.
Thierry, Augustin. *Récits des temps mérovingiens*, preceded by *Considérations sur l'histoire de France*. 2 vols. Paris, 1867.
Thireau, Jean-Louis. *Les Idées politiques de Louis XIV*. Paris, 1973.
Thuau, Etienne. *Raison d'état et pensée politique à la époque de Richelieu*. Paris, 1966.
Tocqueville, Alexis de. *L'Ancien Régime et la Révolution en France*. Paris, 1952.
Treasure, G.R.R. *Cardinal Richelieu and the Development of Absolutism*. London, 1972.
Tréca, George. *Les Doctrines et les réformes de droit public en réaction contre l'absolutisme de Louis XIV*. Paris, 1909.
Ullmann, Walter. *The Individual and Society in the Middle Ages*. Baltimore, 1966.
———. *Medieval Foundations of Renaissance Humanism*. Ithaca, 1977.
Unger, Roberto Mangabeira. *Law in Modern Society*. New York, 1976.
Vamos, Mara. *Pascal's Pensées and the Enlightenment: The Roots of a Misunderstanding*. SVEC xcvii. Geneva, 1972.
Van Delft, Louis. *La Bruyère: Moraliste*. Geneva, 1971.

Van Kley, Dale. *The Jansenists and the Expulsion of the Jesuits from France, 1757-1765.* New Haven, 1975.
Vaughan, C. E. *Political Writings of Jean-Jacques Rousseau.* New York, 1962 [1915].
Venturi, Franco. *Utopia and Reform in the Enlightenment.* Cambridge, 1971.
Villey, Pierre. *Les Sources et l'évolution des Essais de Montaigne.* Paris, 1933.
Viner, Jacob. *The Role of Providence in the Social Order.* Philadelphia, 1972.
Vinogradoff, Paul, ed. *Essays in Legal History.* London, 1913.
Von der Muhll, Emmanuel. *Denis Veiras.* Paris, 1938.
Vyverberg, Henry. *Historical Pessimism in the French Enlightenment.* Cambridge, Mass., 1958.
Wade, Ira O. *Clandestine Organization and Diffusion of Philosophic Ideas in France from 1700 to 1750.* Princeton, 1938.
———. *The Intellectual Development of Voltaire.* Princeton, 1969.
———. *The Intellectual Origins of the French Enlightenment.* Princeton, 1971.
———. *The Structure and Form of the French Enlightenment.* 2 vols. Princeton, 1977.
Wallerstein, Immanuel. *The Modern World-System.* New York, 1976.
Walton, Craig. *De la Recherche du Bien: A Study of Malebranche's Science of Ethics.* The Hague, 1972.
Westrich, Sal Alexander. *The Ormée of Bordeaux.* Baltimore, 1972.
Wilson, Ian M. *The Influence of Hobbes and Locke in the Shaping of the Concept of Sovereignty in Eighteenth Century France.* SVEC CI. Oxford, 1973.
Wolf, John B., ed. *Louis XIV: A Profile.* New York, 1972.

SECONDARY SOURCES: ARTICLES AND ESSAYS

Appolis, Emile. "La Répresentation des villes aux états généraux de Languedoc." AHMC I (Studies Presented to the International Commission for the History of Representative and Parliamentary Institutions; Louvain and Paris, 1960), 219-227.
Archambault, Paul. "The Analogy of the 'Body' in Renaissance Political Literature." BHR XXIX (1967), 21-52.
Ascoli, George. "Quelques notes biographiques sur Denis Veiras, d'Alais." In *Mélanges offerts . . . à M. Gustave Lanson.* Paris, 1922, pp. 165-177.
Baker, Keith Michael. "French Political Thought at the Accession of Louis XVI." JMH L (1978), 279-303.

Baron, Hans. "The *Querelle* of Ancients and Moderns as a Problem for Renaissance Scholarship." JHI xx (1959), 3-22.
———. "Secularization of Wisdom and Political Humanism in the Renaissance." JHI xxi (1960), 131-150.
Battista, Anna Maria. "Appunti sulla crisi della morale communitaria nel seicento francese." *Il pensiero politico* ii, (1969), 187-223.
———. "Sul rapporto tra società e stato nello Francia dell'assolutismo." *Quaderni Storici delle marche* x (1969), 85-113.
Beame, E. M. "Limits of Toleration in Sixteenth-Century France." SR xiii (1966), 250-265.
Beik, William. "Magistrates and Popular Uprisings in France before the Fronde: Toulouse." JMH xlvi (1974), 585-608.
Berlin, Isaiah. "The Question of Machiavelli." *New York Review of Books,* November 4, 1971, 20-32.
Bernard, Leon. "French Society and Popular Uprisings under Louis XIV," FHS iii (1964), 454-474.
Bloom, Allan. "The Education of Democratic Man: *Emile.*" *Daedalus* cvii (1978), 135-154.
Bonnefon, Paul. "Une Oeuvre inconnue de La Boétie: Les mémoires sur l'édit de janvier 1562," RHLF xxiv (1917), 1-33 and 307-319.
Caramaschi, Enzo. "Un Honnête homme libertin: Saint-Evremond." *Il pensiero politico* viii (1975), 160-170.
Carrier, Hubert. "Port-Royal et la Fronde: Deux mazarinades inconnues d'Arnauld d'Andilly." RHLF lxxv (1975), 3-29.
Chérel, Albert. "La Pensée de Machiavel en France au temps de la Fronde." *Revue de littérature comparée* xiii (1933), 577-587.
Church, W. F. "Cardinal Richelieu and the Social Estates of the Realm," AHMC ii, 261-272.
———. "The Decline of French Jurists as Political Theorists." FHS v (1967), 1-40.
———. "The Problem of Constitutional Thought in France." ixe International Congress of the Historical Sciences, *Etudes des . . . assemblées d'état* (1952), 173-186.
Cotta, Sergio. "Il problema politica del marchese d'Argenson." *Occidente* vii (1951), 192-220, 295-310.
Dariosecq, Luc. "La Pensée politique de Pascal." PMLA lxxvi (1961), 54-62.
Darnton, Robert. "Reading, Writing and Publishing in Eighteenth-Century France." *Daedalus* c (1971), 214-256.
Davis, Natalie Zemon. "Sixteenth-Century French Arithmetics on the Business Life." *JHI* xxi (1960), 18-48.
Del Noce, Augusto. "La crisi libertina e la ragion di stato." In Enrico

Castelli, ed., *Cristianesmo e ragion di stato* (Atti del II congresso internazionale di Studi humanistici, Rome, 1952), pp. 35-47.
Deyon, Pierre. "A propos des rapports entre la noblesse française et le monarchie absolue pendant la première moitié due XVIIe siècle." *Revue historique* CCXXXI (1964), 341-356.
Doyle, William. "Was There an Aristocratic Reaction in pre-Revolutionary France?" *Past and Present* LVII (1972), 97-117.
Dreyer, Kenneth. "Commynes and Machiavelli: A Study in Parallelism." *Symposium* V (1951), 38-61.
Druon, M. "L'Enseignement politique donné par Bossuet et Fénelon, precepteurs." *Mémoires de l'Académie de Stanislas* V (1888), 445-494.
Dumont, François. "Royauté française et monarchie absolue au XVIIe siècle." *XVIIe siècle* no. 58-59 (1963), pp. 3-29.
―――. "Recherches sur les Ordres dans l'Opinion française sous l'Ancien Régime." AHMC I, 187-201.
Euben, J. Peter. "Philosophy and Politics in Plato's *Crito*." *Political Theory* VI (1978), 149-172.
Eulau, Heinz. "The Depersonalization of the Concept of Sovereignty." *Journal of Politics* IV (1942), 3-19.
Faguet, Emile. "L'Abbé de Saint-Pierre," *Revue des deux mondes* X (1912), 559-572.
Furber, Donald. "The Myth of *amour-propre* in La Rochefoucauld." *French Review* XLIII (1969), 227-239.
Gallanar, Joseph. "Argenson's 'Platonic Republics.'" SVEC LXI (1967), 557-575.
Gembruch, Werner. "Reformforderung in Frankreich um die Wende vom 17. um 18. Jahrhundert." *Historische Zeitschrift* CCIX (1969), 265-317.
Giesey, Ralph E. "The French Estates and the Corpus Mysticum Regni." AHMC I, 153-171.
Grignashi, Mario. "Nicolas Oresme et son commentaire à la 'Politique' d'Aristote." AHMC I, 95-151.
Gunn, J.A.W., "'Interest Will Not Lie': A Seventeenth-Century Political Maxim." JHI XXIX (1968), 551-564.
Hacking, Ian. "The Logic of Pascal's Wager." *American Philosophical Quarterly* IX (1972), 186-192.
Harsin, "Boulainvilliers ou Vauban?" *Bulletin de la société d'histoire moderne*, 8th ser., no. 12 (1936).
Hartung, Fritz, and Roland Mousnier. "Quelques problèmes concernant la monarchie absolue." Proceedings of the Tenth Congress of the International Committee for the Historical Sciences, vol. IV, *Storia Moderna* (1955), 1-55.

Harvey, Howard G. "Cyrano de Bergerac and the Question of Human Liberties." *Symposium* IV (1950), 120-130.
Horowitz, Maryanne Cline. "Natural Law as the Foundation for an Autonomous Ethic: Pierre Charron's *De la sagesse*." SR XXI (1974), 204-227.
Jouvenel, Bertrand de. "Rousseau, évolutioniste pessimiste." *Annales de philosophie politique* V (Paris, 1965), 1-19.
Kanter, Sanford B. "Archbishop Fénelon's Political Activity: The Focal Point of Power in Dynasticism." FHS IV (1966), 320-334.
Kelley, Donald R. "Murd'rous Machiavel in France: A Post-Mortem." *Political Science Quarterly* LXXXV (1970), 545-559.
Keohane, Nannerl O. "The President's English: Montesquieu in America 1976." *Political Science Reviewer* VI (1976), 355-387 .
———. "The Radical Humanism of Etienne de la Boétie." JHI XXXVIII (1977), 119-130.
Kittrell, Edward R. " 'Laissez-Faire' in English Classical Economics." JHI XXVII (1966), 610-620.
Klaits, Joseph. "Men of Letters and Political Reform in France at the End of the Reign of Louis XIV." JMH XLIII (1971), 577-597.
Kristeller, Paul Oskar, "Between the Italian Renaissance and the French Enlightenment," *Renaissance Quarterly* XXXII (1979), 41-72.
Lagrave, Henri. "Une Oeuvre inédité du marquis d'Argenson." RHLF LXIII (1963), 193-206.
Lanson, Gustave. "Origines et premières manifestations de l'esprit philosophique dans la littérature française de 1675 à 1748." *Revue des cours et conférences* XVI-XVIII (1907-1910).
Le Roy Ladurie, Emmanuel. "Révoltes et contestations rurales en France de 1675 à 1788." *Annales* XXIX (1974), 6-22.
Levasseur, E. "Le Marquis d'Argenson." *Séances et travaux de l'Académie des sciences morales et politiques* LXXXVII (1869), 65-84.
Lewis, J. U. "Jean Bodin's 'Logic of Sovereignty.' " *Political Studies* XVI (1968), 206-222.
Lewis, P. S. "Jean-Juvenal des Ursins and the Common Literary Attitude towards Tyranny in Fifteenth-Century France." *Medium Aevum* XXXIV (1965), 103-121.
Limbrick, Elaine. "Montaigne et Saint Augustin." BHR XXXIV (1972), 49-64.
Little, Lester K. "Pride Goes before Avarice: Social Change and the Vices in Latin Christendom." *American Historical Review* LXXVI (1971), 16-49.
Lousse, Emile. "Absolutisme, droit divin, despotisme éclairé." *Schweizer Beitrage zur Allgemeine geschichte* XIV (1958), 91-106.

Lublinskaya, Alexandra D. "The Contemporary Bourgeois Conception of Absolute Monarchy." *Economy and Society* I (1972), 65-92.
———. "Les Etats généraux de 1614-1615 en France." AHMC I, 229-245.
Lynch, Andrew. "Montesquieu and the Ecclesiastical Critics of *L'Esprit des lois.*" JHI XXXVIII (1977), 487-500.
Lyon, Bryce. "Medieval Constitutionalism: a Balance of Power." AHMC II, 157-183.
MacCannell, Juliet Flower. "Nature and Self-love: A Reinterpretation of Rousseau's 'Passion primitive'" PMLA XCII (1977), 890-902.
MacFarlane, L. J. "Absolutism, Tyranny and the Minimum Conditions of Constitutional Rule." *Government and Opposition* XII (1977), 212-233.
McRae, Kenneth. "Ramist Tendencies in the Thought of Jean Bodin." JHI XVI (1955), 306-323.
Major, J. Russell. "The Loss of Royal Initiative and the Decay of the Estates General in France, 1421-1615." AHMC II, 245-259.
Mathiez, Albert. "La Place de Montesquieu dans l'histoire des doctrines politiques du XVIIIe siécle." *Annales historiques de la Révolution française* VII (1930), 97-112.
Mousnier, Roland. "Comment les Français du XVIIe siècle voyaient la constitution." *XVIIe siècle* no. 25-26 (1955), pp. 9-29.
———. "L'Evolution des institutions monarchiques en France et ses rélations avec l'etat social." *XVIIe siècle* no. 58-59 (1963), pp. 57-72.
———. "Monarchie contre aristocratie dans la France du XVIIe siècle." *XVIIe siècle* no. 31 (1956), pp. 377-381.
———. "Le *Testament politique* de Richelieu." *Revue historique* CCI (1949), 55-71.
Myers, A. R. "The English Parliament and the French Estates-General in the Middle Ages." AHMC II, 139-153.
Oestreich, Gerhard. "Justus Lipsius als Theoretiker." *Historische Zeitschrift* CLXXXI (1956), 31-77.
Parkin, John, "Montaigne *Essais* 3:1: The Morality of Commitment." BHR XLI (1979), 41-62.
Poujol, Jacques. "Jean Ferrault on the King's Privileges." SR V (1958), 15-26.
Ranum, Orest. "Richelieu and the Great Nobility: Some Aspects of Early Modern Political Motives." FHS III (1963), 184-209.
Raymond, Marcel. "Du Jansénisme à la morale de l'intérêt." *Mercure de France*, June 1957, pp. 238-255.

Rebhorn, Wayne. "The Burdens and Joys of Freedom." *Etudes rabelaisiennes* IX (1971), 71-90.
Regosin, Richard. "The Artist and the *Abbaye*." *Studies in Philology* LXVIII (1971), 121-129.
Richet, Denis. "Autour des origines idéologiques lointaines de la révolution française." *Annales* XXIV (1969), 1-23.
Riley, Patrick. "The General Will before Rousseau." *Political Theory* VI (1978), 485-516.
Rowen, Henry. "L'Etat c'est à moi: Louis XIV and the State." *FHS* II (1961), 83-98.
Schaefer, David L. "Montaigne's Intention and His Rhetoric." *Interpretation* V (1975), 58-90.
Screech, M. A. "Some Reflexions on the Abbey of Thelema." *Etudes rabelaisiennes* VIII (1969), 107-114.
Sellier, Philippe. "La Rochefoucauld, Pascal, St. Augustin." *RHLF* LXIX (1969), 551-575.
Shepard, Max. "Sovereignty at the Crossroads." *Political Science Quarterly* XLV (1930), 580-603.
Shklar, Judith. Review of *Jean Bodin*. *JMH* XLVII (1975), 134-141.
―――. "Jean-Jacques Rousseau and Equality." *Daedalus* CVII (1978), 13-26.
Skinner, Quentin. "Some Problems in the Analysis of Political Thought and Action." *Political Theory* II (1974), 277-303.
Soman, Albert. "Pierre Charron: A Revaluation." *BHR* XXXII (1970), 57-77.
Starobinski, Jean. "La Rochefoucauld et les morales substitutives." *La Nouvelle revue française* no. 163 (July 1966) and 164 (August 1966), pp. 16-35 and 211-229.
Stevens, Linton C. "The Contribution of French Jurists to the Humanism of the Renaissance." *SR* I (1954), 92-105.
Tans, J.A.G. "Les Idées politiques des Jansénistes." *Neophilologus* XC (1956), 1-18.
Tassin, C. "Un Membre de l'Académie de l'Entresol: Le Marquis d'Argenson." *Le Correspondant* CXXXIII (1883), 332-368.
Temple, Nora. "The Control and Exploitation of French Towns during the *Ancien Régime*." *History* LI (1966), 16-35.
Ulph, Owen. "Jean Bodin and the Estates-General of 1576." *JMH* XIX (1947), 289-296.
Watter, Pierre. "Jean Louis Guez de Balzac's *Le Prince*: A Revaluation." *Journal of the Warburg and Courtauld Institutes*, XX (1957), 216-247.

Index

Abbadie, Jacques, 307, 310-11, 341, 366, 421-22
Abercrombie, Nigel, 183, 267n, 293n
absolutism, 3-8, 15-22, 451-54, 457, 460; and reason of state, 157, 168; in eighteenth century, 373, 390, 403, 442-44; in seventeenth century, 119, 180, 282, 318; in sixteenth century, 54-71, 81-82; opposition to, 220-23, 349-50, 356-57, 394; under Louis XIV, 237, 251-52, 256-62
Académie française, 169, 362-63, 378n
Adam, Antoine, 129n, 145n, 193n, 198n, 262n, 264n, 362n
Aguesseau, Henri d', 304, 330n, 393, 423-25
Alary, Pierre-Joseph, 362
Alcover, Madeleine, 236n
Alembert, Jean Le Rond d', 365n, 376n, 427
Alexander of Macedon, 88-89, 307
Althusius, Johannes, 67
Althusser, Louis, 392n, 438n
ambition: and conflict, 29, 400, 416, 460; and corruption, 234, 381, 426-28; of monarch, 256, 389n, 444; of nobles, 200, 412-13, 458; social utility of, 21, 77, 85, 138, 151-53, 159, 366
amour de soi, 184-85, 310-11, 422, 429, 433, 460. See also self-love
amour-propre, 141, 182, 255, 324, 342, 462; and early Enlightenment, 366, 380-82, 422-23; and *honnêteté*, 285-92; and Jansenism, 184-97, 273-77, 294-302, 305-306; Montesquieu and, 394, 416-17, 419; Rousseau and, 427-32, 440. See also self-love
Anderson, Perry, 9n, 17n
Anne of Austria, 201, 361
Appian Alexandrin, 32, 34-35
Archambault, Paul, 33n
Argenson, René-Louis, marquis d', 376-91; and constitutionalism, 385-90; concept of monarchy, 81, 256, 336n, 386-90, 405, 453; contribution to Enlightenment, 361-62, 393; critic of Louis XIV, 376-79; influence on Rousseau, 374, 376, 383-84, 387, 391, 437-38, 443-47; on equality, 379, 381, 384-87, 390-91; moral psychology, 421; philosophy and public life, 378, 382, 457; theory of participation, 323n, 329n, 379, 383-91, 402, 451, 454, 459
aristocracy, as type of regime, 33-35, 76, 222, 320, 373, 389
Aristotle: and Renaissance humanism, 11, 86-87, 222n; Bodin's debt to, 13, 68-70, 76; on friendship, 106-107; philosophy and politics, 148-49, 172, 270-71, 363; theory of constitution, 40; theory of monarchy, 59
Aristotelian, 61n, 84n, 139, 148, 200, 218, 396
Arnauld, Antoine, 183, 293, 303-304
Arnauld d'Andilly, 216, 303
Aron, Raymond, 413n
Aronson, Nicole, 90n
Artz, Frederick, 363n
Ascoli, George, 319n
Asher, Eugene, 4n
assemblies, popular, 5, 30, 217-20, 247, 344, 350, 385-87, 402, 454, 457
Aston, Trevor, 124n, 236n
Atkinson, Geoffroy, 318n
Auerbach, Eric, 272n
Augustan age, 234-35, 259, 333, 459
Augustine, Saint: and French ethics, 129, 134-35, 183-84, 188-89; and Jansenism, 21, 183-84, 301; and political science, 172n, 183-84; on justice, 63, 187; on self-love, 21, 185-86, 291n; two cities, 183-86, 267, 280, 294, 461
Augustinian, 11, 22, 62-66, 135, 143, 183-87, 192-96, 200, 205, 263, 275, 286, 289-90, 294, 303-304
avarice: and conflict, 29, 319; and corruption, 234, 349, 381, 412-17, 426-28, 444, 459; social utility of, 21-22, 138, 151-53, 159, 162-68, 297, 458

Bacon, Francis, 12-13, 364
Baird, A.W.S., 266n, 274, 287n
Baker, Keith, 454n
Bakunin, Michael, 102
Balzac, J.-L. Guez de, 197-202; and Holland, 199, 242; and reason of state, 169-70, 198, 201; and Rome, 198; critic of regime, 201-202, 250, 325, 457; ethic of *la gloire*, 186, 188, 197-200; philosophy and public life, 200-201; wheat and laurels, 201, 219, 457
Barbeyrac, Jean, 11, 394
Barnwell, H. T., 230n
Baron, Hans, 12n, 136n
Barry, Brian, 448n
Barzun, Jacques, 347n
Battista, Anna Maria, 120n, 122n, 135n
Baudrillart, Henri, 67n
Baumgartner, Frederic, 52n
Bayle, Pierre, 13-14, 143, 230, 312-15
Beame, E. M., 25n
Beauvillier, Paul, duc de, 343
Becker, Carl, 363n
Beik, William, 213n
Belesbat, Charles Paul Hurault de L'Hopital, seigneur de, 351, 379
Bénichou, Paul, 129n, 134, 262n
Bentham, Jeremy, 301, 366
Bergerac, Cyrano de, 144, 229, 235-36, 243, 318
Berlin, Isaiah, 99n
Bernard, Leon, 213n
Béthune, Philippe de, 173
Beza, Theodore, 52
Bickart, Roger, 265n
bienfaisance, 277, 364-65, 380
Bignon, Jerome, 27
Bitton, Davis, 126n
Bloch, Marc, 15n
Bloom, Allan, 433n
Blum, Jerome, 5n
Boase, Alan, 98n
Bodin, Jean, 67-82; and absolutism, 16, 72-73, 370; and Aristotle, 13, 68-70, 76; and Estates-General, 67, 73-74; and mercantilism, 160-61; and religious wars, 48, 123; and Rousseau, 76, 78, 82, 443; discusses form of regime, 72, 74-77, 320, 390; influence of, 13, 67, 81-82, 87n, 123-27, 135, 141-43, 175, 222, 376n, 443, 456; method, 67-68, 74; on citizenship, 69-70, 81; on family, 68-69, 165; on pluralism, 77-79, 132, 152n, 396; on public and private, 69-70, 123, 418, 446, 455-56; science of politics, 172, 363; sovereignty, 18, 26, 58, 61-62, 67-75, 125-27, 141-43, 246, 443-45
Boisguilbert, Pierre le Pesant de, 346, 350-57, 379-80, 402, 458
Bolgar, R. R., 70n
Bolingbroke, Henry St. John, viscount, 362, 401n
Bonnefon, Paul, 94n-98n
Bonney, Richard, 3n
Bontems, Claude, 59n-61n
Bordeaux: academy of, 392, 395, 425; La Boétie and, 92, 98; Montaigne and, 99, 107; Montesquieu and, 392-95; Ormée, 10, 217-20, 260; parlement of, 92, 394
Bossuet, Jacques-Bénigne, 251-58; against Jurieu, 253-54, 316; and absolutism, 251-54, 256; attacks Fénelon, 194, 338; in seventeenth-century thought, 12, 261, 277n, 364; on constitution, 25n; on interest, 254-57, 302, 371; on monarchy, 256-57, 260-61, 275, 349, 389n, 403, 444, 456; on the people, 257, 260, 326; on the theatre, 300n; tutor of Dauphin, 332
Botero, Giovanni, 173n
Boulainvilliers, Henri, comte de, 223, 346-50, 363n, 393, 402
bourgeoisie, 9, 121-22, 128-29, 178, 263-64, 348. *See also* third estate
Bouwsma, William J., 16n
Bowen, Barbara, 101n
Brémond, Henri, 194-95n
Brissaud, Jean, 223n
Broglie, Emmanuel de, 333n
Brooks, Peter, 285n
Broome, J. H., 268n, 280n
Brown, Frieda, 108n
Brunschvicg, Léon, 102n, 111n, 265n, 268, 273
Budé, Guillaume, 58-62, 84, 86-87, 133, 222, 444, 458
Buisseret, David, 161n
Burgundy, Louis, duke of, 18, 330-38, 342-46, 348n; circle, 331, 364
Burgundy, Marie-Adelaide, duchess of, 332-33
Burke, Edmund, 106
Burlamaqui, Jean-Jacques, 11

Caillemer, Robert, 351n
Calvinist, 50, 263-64, 316
Campanella, Tommaso, 172n, 315, 322

Camus, Jean-Pierre, 194-96, 310, 341n, 421
Caramaschi, Enzo, 230n
Carcassonne, Elie, 393n
Carlyle, A. J., 6n
Carré, H., 361n
Carrier, Hubert, 216n
Cartesian, 204-206, 208, 210-11, 273, 287, 295, 302, 304, 309, 322, 343, 395. *See also* Descartes
Catholic League, 20, 28, 49, 52
charité, 21, 41, 138-41, 166, 194-96, 255, 309-10; and Jansenism, 182, 185, 291, 308; and Pascal, 266-67, 271, 277-82, 341; in the Enlightenment, 376, 394, 416, 432. *See also pur amour*; saint
Charlemagne, 46, 253, 348
Charles I, king of England, 208n, 213
Charles VI, king of France, 15
Charles VIII, king of France, 32
Charles the Bold, duke of Burgundy, 28, 31
Charron, Pierre, 135-44; and Montaigne, 135-38; debt to Lipsius, 130, 135; influence, 13, 124, 129, 135, 143-45, 416, 451; management of passions, 138-39, 151, 163; on justice, 141, 170, 172, 187; on natural law, 135-38; on prudence, 140-43; on public and private, 120, 136, 146-47, 456; sage as ideal, 137-39, 142-44
Charvet, John, 439n
Chasseneuz, Barthélemy, 55
Chavy, Paul, 32n
Cherel, Albert, 222n, 337n, 364n
Chevreuse, Charles Honoré, duc de, 343
Chinard, Gilbert, 267n
chose publique, 35, 60, 85, 87, 134, 243, 454-56, 459. *See also* common interest
Church, William Farr, 25n, 124, 179n, 244n, 304n, 330n; *Constitutional Thought*, 37n, 41n, 43n, 48n, 52n, 55n, 56n, 70n, 126n; *Richelieu*, 127n, 155n, 169n, 171n, 173n, 175n, 191n, 194n, 201n, 242n
Cicero, 11, 84
citizenship, 218, 233, 255, 257, 425, 458-59; Bodin on, 69-70, 81, 455; in heavenly city, 183-86; Rousseau on, 434-35, 442, 445, 448-49, 460
civic humanism, 83-87, 218, 458
Clovis, 347
Colbert, Jean-Baptiste, 158-59, 312-14, 321, 345

Cole, Charles Woolsey, 16n, 352n
Coleman, D. C., 158-59n
Colie, Rosalie, 101n
Colletti, Lucio, 430n
Coltman, Irene, 121n
common good, 81, 85, 219, 282, 391, 424; king as embodiment of, 54-55, 61, 75, 84-85; Rousseau on, 436-37, 447-48, 461. *See also* common interest; public good; public interest
common interest, 20-22, 65, 382-86, 390-91, 437-41, 447-48, 452. *See also* common good; public interest; *chose publique*
Commynes, Philippe, sire de, 6-7, 28-31, 46-47, 65, 73, 152n, 172n, 222, 454
Condorcet, Antoine Caritat, marquis de, 363
conservatism, 79, 109, 143, 210, 225, 271-72, 395-97
Constant, Benjamin, 446n
constitutionalism, 15-22, 442, 451, 453-55, 457, 459; in sixteenth century, 26-29, 42-43, 52-53, 220; Montesquieu and, 394, 406; revival, 344, 373, 390; submergence in seventeenth century, 119, 157, 180, 220, 223, 237
Coppin, Joseph, 188n
Coquille, Guy, 52
Corneille, Pierre, 133n, 134, 186, 197, 224, 286, 458
Corneillian, 133-34, 144, 223-24, 413
corps mystique, 15, 33, 37, 40-41, 451, 454
Cotta, Sergio, 378n
Coveney, P. J., 213n-14n
Cramer, Gabriel, 376n
Croquette, Bernard, 268n
custom: as "second nature," 106, 164, 273, 368; strength of, 105-106, 368

Daire, Eugene, 329n, 352n, 353n, 356n
Dariosecq, Luc, 272n
Darnton, Robert, 362n
dauphin, Louis (son of Louis XIV), 244, 332
Davis, Natalie Zemon, 128n
Declareuil, J., 169n
De Gaulle, Charles, 247n
del Noce, Augusto, 211n
democracy: as type of regime, 34-35, 76, 222, 320, 373, 383-87, 390, 415
Denzer, Horst, 67n-74n, 81n
Derathé, Robert, 14n, 70n
Descartes, René, 202-12; conservatism,

Descartes, René (cont.)
178, 202-203, 210, 395; generous man as ethical ideal, 133, 186, 188, 205-208, 231; individual as part of whole, 206-208, 237, 279, 462-63; influence, 13, 211-12, 308, 364, 392; on *la machine*, 408-409; philosophy and public life, 202-203, 208-12; physics, 302; reason and truth, 145, 202-203, 210-11, 246. *See also* Cartesian despotism, 349, 370-71, 385, 444; enlightened, 323, 369, 371, 444; Montesquieu on, 394, 398-408. *See also* tyranny
Diderot, Denis, 13-14, 364, 436, 443
divertissement, 88, 100, 230, 274-76, 294-95
Dodge, Guy H., 14n, 315n, 316n
Domat, Jean, 262, 303-308, 442
Doolin, Paul Rice, 214n
Dostoevsky, Fyodor, 301
Doyle, William, 349n
Dreyer, Kenneth, 31n
Drouet, Joseph, 364n
Druon, M., 332n
Du Bos, Jean-Baptiste, 347-48, 393
Du Bourg, Anne, 92
Duguet, Jacques-Joseph, 303-304
Du Haillan, Bernard de Girard, 43n, 48n
Dupin, Louise-Marie-Madeleine, 364
Du Plessis-Mornay, Philippe, 52n
Durand, Yves, 242n
Dutot, 393
Du Vair, Guillaume, 120, 130, 133-36
Duvergier de Hauranne, *see* Saint-Cyran, abbé de

Edict of Nantes, revocation of, 14, 53, 312-18, 328
Edward III, king of England, 27
Edwards, Tom T., 216n
Elizabeth, princess of Bohemia, 204-209
Ellul, Jacques, 9n, 57n
England, 345, 388, 458; and the Fronde, 213-15; and the Huguenots, 314, 318-19; claims to French throne, 6, 27; constitution of, 17, 27, 401, 406; Montesquieu on, 394, 401, 405-407, 412-15, 419; philosophical ties to France, 11-12, 362
Entresol, 351, 362
Epaminondas, 113, 285
Epicureans, 11, 101, 119, 145-46, 230, 286

Esmonin, Edmond, 175n, 328n
Esprit, Jacques, 307-308
Estates-General, 7-8, 347; Bodin and, 67, 71-73, 81; critique of, 39, 42, 46-47; defense of, 30, 65, 236, 344-45; in wars of religion, 49-51; of 1614, 128, 215; under Louis XIV, 215, 222, 236, 259
Euben, J. Peter, 110n
Eulau, Heinz, 17n
extraordinary voyage, 236, 318-19, 327

Faguet, Emile, 365
Fénelon, François Salignac de La Mothe-, 332-46; agrarianism, 351; constitutionalism, 343-46; critic of Louis XIV, 227n, 333-35; influence, 333, 364, 377, 405, 421n, 430n, 442; on justice, 63; on monarchy, 223, 335-38, 348, 389, 405; *pur amour*, 194, 341-43, 382, 461; *Télémaque*, 333-41; *thèse nobiliaire*, 18-19; tutor to Burgundy, 332-38, 343-46; utopian, 338-41, 378
Ferguson, Wallace, 5n
feudalism, 5, 126, 158, 348-49, 384
Flammermont, Jules, 265n
Fleury, André-Hercule, 362
Fontenelle, Bernard le Bovier de, 13, 145, 351
Ford, Franklin L., 346n
Forster, Robert, 122n, 213n, 220n
Fourier, Charles, 351
Fox-Genevese, Elizabeth, 454n
Frame, Donald, 93n, 98n, 188n
Francis I, king of France, 3, 9, 15-16, 32, 55-59, 121, 241, 333
Franklin, Julian, 52n, 67n, 70n-72n
Franks, 43-45, 50, 347
Freund, Julien, 170n, 172n
friendship, 106-108, 115, 161-63, 196, 292-93, 414, 462
Fronde, 7, 20, 171, 208, 213-37, 241-43, 264, 361, 378, 456
frondeur, 198, 219-20, 226, 231-32, 237, 259, 286-89, 361
fundamental laws, 4, 17, 27, 31, 73, 127, 222, 344, 406
Furber, Donald, 290n

Gallanar, Joseph, 378n
Gallicanism, 6, 14, 16, 263-64, 390
Gallouedec-Genuys, Françoise, 340n
Garasse, François, 48n
Gassendi, Pierre, 13, 145, 147, 230, 242, 287n

Gay, Peter, 346n, 370n
Genoa, 387-88
Gerhard, Dietrich, 175n
Germany, 12, 314, 317, 319
Gerson, Jean, 7n
Gessler, Peter, 376n-77n
Giesey, Ralph E., 50n-51n
Gilmore, Myron, 57n
Goldmann, Lucien, 264n, 273n, 280n
Goré, Jeanne-Lydie, 341n
Goubert, Pierre, 4n-5n, 247n, 259n, 313n
Goumy, Edouard, 363n
Goyard-Fabre, Simone, 392n
Granpre Molière, Jean-Jacques, 405n
Grassaille, Charles de, 56
great chain of being, 33, 56, 245
Greene, Jack P., 122n, 213n, 220n
Greenleaf, W. H., 56n, 68n
Griffiths, Richard, 163n
Grimm, Frédéric-Melchior, 378n
Grimsley, Ronald, 392n
Grotius, Hugo, 122, 304, 316, 394
Grubbs, Henry, 285n
Gundersheimer, Werner, 87n
Gunn, J.A.W., 154n-55n

Hacking, Ian, 269n, 278n
Halévy, Daniel, 327n
Hallie, Phillip, 99n
Hampson, Norman, 13
Harding, Robert R., 4n
Harsin, Paul, 349n
Harth, Erica, 229n, 235n
Hartung, Fritz, 4n
Harvey, Gabriel, 87n
Harvey, Howard G., 236n
Hatton, Ragnhild, 12n, 17n, 249n
Havens, George, 334n, 336n-37n
Hayden, J. Michael, 128n
Hazard, Paul, 12-13, 315n
Heckscher, Eli, 158-59n
Hegel, G.W.F., 101, 274n, 418
Helvétius, Claude-Adrien, 14, 364
Henderson, G. D., 343n
Henry, Nannerl O. [Keohane], 376n-77n, 385n
Henry IV, king of France and of Navarre, 14, 81, 119, 121, 161, 192, 236, 377; during religious wars, 99; prosperity of reign, 3, 49, 124, 333; royalist rhetoric under, 16, 27, 55, 125, 241, 253n; strong reign of, 9, 312, 418
hero, as ethical ideal, 186, 197-200, 286
Herr, Richard, 323n

Hesychius, 147-48
Hexter, J. H., 32n
Hinton, R.W.K., 74n
Hippeau, Louis, 286n, 307n
Hirschman, Albert O., 22n, 152-54, 226n, 281n, 289n
Hobbes, Thomas, 11, 153, 170n, 363, 367; and Bayle, 315; and Bodin, 67-68, 71; and Bossuet, 252-53; and Descartes, 204, 209-10; and Jansenists, 184, 294-95, 298; and Louis XIV, 248; and Montaigne, 106, 108-109; and Rousseau, 443; and Sorbière, 242-43; on civil war, 123, 271
Hobbesian, 11, 21, 208, 242, 252, 274, 288
Holland: admiration for, 198-99, 232-33, 242-43, 384-85, 459; and free trade, 351, 356; and the Huguenots, 314, 319; criticism of, 232-33, 405, 414; philosophic ties to France, 11-12, 194, 208, 459
honnêteté, 231, 283-89, 301, 341, 363, 458
Hope, Quentin, 230n
Horne, Thomas A., 12n
Horowitz, Louise, 286n, 307n, 324n
Horowitz, Maryanne Cline, 138n
Hotman, Antoine, 162-63
Hotman, François, 28, 49-53, 162, 316
Huguenots: in seventeenth century, 197, 216, 253, 312-19; La Boétie and, 92-93, 98; political theory of, 11, 14, 20, 28, 49-53, 253, 378
Hulliung, Mark, 404n, 413n
Hume, David, 78
Huppert, George, 89n

individualism, 15-22, 83-87, 451-63; in seventeenth century, 116, 119, 157, 200-201, 206-207, 230, 236-37, 279-82; Montesquieu and, 394, 409; Rousseau and, 435, 442, 462
interest, theory of, 20-22, 153-57, 223-29, 288-89, 451-54, 461-63; and Jansenism, 280-81, 307-11; and laissez-faire, 354-55, 380; and Rousseau, 427-42, 445, 448; in eighteenth century, 366, 371-75, 380-86, 410-17, 421-25; in seventeenth century, 181-82, 194-95, 231-32, 254-57, 290-93, 324. *See also* common interest; public interest
interest of state, 20, 154-56, 181, 250, 256, 453. *See also* public interest
Italy, 11, 83, 92

494—Index

James, E. D., 293n
Janet, Paul, 332n
Jansenism, 11, 21, 48, 119, 199, 207, 255, 323, 353, 416n, 451, 462; and *libertins*, 146, 187-88; and the Fronde, 216-17, 230, 303; origins and development, 125, 183-84, 192-94; political theory of, 262-66, 303-304, 307; Saint-Pierre and, 364, 367, 375-76. See also Nicole; Pascal; Port-Royal
Jansenius, Cornelius, 183, 192-94
Jefferson, Thomas, 336n, 397n
Jehasse, Jehan, 131n
Jesuits, 48, 263, 417
Johnson, N. R., 453n
Joly, Claude, 216, 220-23, 236-37, 318, 390n
Jonge, Johan Junius de, 52n
Joppin, Gabriel, 341n
Jouvenel, Bertrand de, 280n
Judges, A. V., 158
Jupiter, 59, 166, 391
Jurieu, Pierre, 14, 254, 315-18
justice, 36, 62-66, 107-109, 140-41, 275, 300, 387, 411, 437, 447; and reason of state, 170-71, 178-79; as harmonic order, 66, 80-81, 247; human and universal, 64, 172, 271-72

Kanter, Sanford B., 337n
Kantorowicz, Ernst, 15n
Kassem, Badreddine, 397n
Kelley, Donald R., 3¹n, 43n, 48n, 50n-52n, 61n, 84n, 458n
Keohane, Nannerl O., 32n, 93n, 396n, 412n, 446n
Kern, Fritz, 57
Kettering, Sharon, 214n
Kiernan, Colm, 392n
Kierstad, Raymond F., 122n
King, James, 246
King, Preston, 17n, 68n, 72n
king: as image of God, 17, 33, 56, 180, 245, 252-54, 389, 403; sacred character of, 15, 55, 96, 128
Kittrell, Edward R., 380n
Klaits, Joseph, 244n, 377n
Knachel, Phillip A., 215n
Knolles, Richard, 68n
Kogel, Renée, 135n, 144n
Kossmann, E. H., 12n, 17n, 169n, 215n, 220n-21, 223n, 228
Krailsheimer, A. J., 101n, 124n, 129n, 224n, 284n, 285, 324n
Krieger, Leonard, 175n, 370n

Kristeller, Paul O., 173n
Kuhfuss, Walter, 406n

La Boétie, Etienne de, 92-98; *Discourse on Voluntary Servitude*, 63n, 92-94, 96, 304n; Montaigne and, 92-93, 95-97, 106n; on liberty, 95-96, 401; on tyranny, 95-97, 242, 299; public and private life, 87, 97-98, 116, 146
Labrousse, Elisabeth, 312-14
La Bruyère, Jean de, 307, 323-27, 337, 363
Lachèvre, Frédéric, 229n, 235n
Lacour-Gayet, G., 248n
La Drevetière, Delisle de, 422-23
Laffemas, Barthélemy de, 161
Lagrave, Henri, 378n
laissez-faire, 10, 326, 331, 340, 350-51, 369; and mercantilism, 158-60, 164; Boisguilbert and, 350-57; d'Argenson and, 379-80
Lambert, Anne-Thérèse, marquise de, 366n, 378n
La Mothe le Vayer, François, 145-50, 173-74, 289n, 315, 431
Lange, Maurice, 324n
Lanson, Gustave, 318n
La Perrière, Guillaume de, 160n, 218
Laporte, Jean, 303n
La Rivière, Mercier de, 370, 444
La Roche-Flavin, 128
La Rochefoucauld, François, duc de, 289-93; *amour-propre* in, 224, 289-94; Augustinian ideas, 196, 289, 291; ethics of, 277n, 297, 307, 323-24, 421; in the Fronde, 286, 290; on *honnêteté*, 283, 293
Lartigue, Jean de, 313
Lavender, Thomas E., 319n
Le Bret, Cardin, 127-28
Le Caron, Louis, 84-87, 98, 133, 458
Lefebrve, Henri, 211n, 263n, 264n, 266n, 274n, 280n
Lefèvre, Roger, 211n
Lefèvre d'Etaples, Jacques, 84
legislator, 79, 211, 342, 410; in Rousseau's theory, 75, 438-39, 442, 447
Leibniz, Gottfried Wilhelm, 308
Lemaire, André, 25n, 37n, 126n, 128n
Le Moyne, Pierre, 191
Lepaige, Adrien, 390n
Le Roy, Louis, 84-87, 98, 458
Le Roy Ladurie, Emmanuel, 213n
Letts, J. T., 224n
Levasseur, E., 380n, 391n

Levi, Anthony, 84n, 119n, 129n, 135n, 185n, 193n, 194n, 196n
Levine, Andrew, 448n
Lewis, J. U., 72n
Lewis, Peter Sharvey, 6n-8n, 16n
Lewis, Philip, 283n, 284n, 290n
Lewis, W. H., 458n
L'Hôpital, Michel de, 48, 61-66, 87, 169n, 222, 304, 351, 418, 423
libertinage, 144, 177, 286
libertins, 48, 135, 143-50, 198, 204, 315, 456, 458; and Montaigne, 19, 112; and reason of state, 171-73; and the Fronde, 224, 229-37, 242-43; Jansenism and, 186-88, 286
liberty: d'Argenson on, 379-84, 387, 459; in seventeenth-century thought, 137, 144-45, 198-200, 236, 459; in sixteenth-century thought, 90-97, 102-103; Montesquieu on, 397, 400-401, 412, 418-19, 459; Rousseau on, 445-46, 460
Lichtenberger, André, 318n
Lilburne, John, 218
Limbrick, Elaine, 183n
Lipsius, Justus, 129-33, 135, 140-42, 170, 172
Little, Lester K., 22n
Livy, Titus, 32, 115
Locke, John, 11, 108, 253, 294, 303, 316, 319
Lockean, 253, 323
Lossky, Andrew, 249n, 250n
Lougee, Carolyn C., 211n, 341n
Louis IX, king of France (Saint Louis), 3, 337, 418
Louis XI, king of France, 6, 28, 31, 333
Louis XII, king of France, 32, 333
Louis XIII, king of France, 3n, 9, 121, 150n, 192, 312
Louis XIV, king of France, 244-51; age of, 121, 312; and absolutism, 4, 170, 356, 370, 452-54; and Domat, 304; Huguenots, 312-13, 328; and taxation, 30, 328; and the Fronde, 7, 214, 217, 237; as strong king, 9, 197, 244-45, 258-60; criticism of reign, 3, 166n, 256-58, 315-18, 323-39, 346, 350, 363, 376-77, 402; death of, 14, 361; education of, 173, 248, 288; royalist rhetoric under, 15-16, 170, 241, 249-52, 256-59; solar imagery, 167, 251, 260, 321; utilitarianism of, 167, 245-48
Louis XV, king of France, 361, 377
Lousse, Emile, 245n
Lovejoy, Arthur O., 163n, 420

Loy, J. Robert, 443n
Loyseau, Charles, 125-27, 222, 304
Lublinskaya, A. D., 9n
Lucian, 391n
Lucretius, 101, 112n
Lukes, Steven, 83n
Lycurgus, 368n, 417, 440
Lynch, Andrew, 416n

Mably, Gabriel Bonnot de, 393
MacAdam, James, 446n
MacCannell, Juliet Flower, 432n
MacFarlane, L. J., 18n
McGowan, Margaret, 101n
Machiavelli, Niccolò, 56, 162, 179, 200; and Bodin, 74; and Commynes, 31; and Descartes, 208-209; and Seyssel, 32, 36, 41; on faction, 132; on parlements, 425; on Rome, 32, 233; realism and obedience, 74, 222-25, 248; reason of state, 132, 169; science of politics, 172n, 363, 376n; theory of interest, 154, 175, 177; *verità effettuale*, 47, 164; vice and virtue, 99, 112-15, 415
Machiavellian, 45, 47, 78, 99, 169, 175, 226, 300, 333
Machiavellism, 144, 155n, 403n
machine: as behavioral principle, 273, 278-80, 299, 408-409, 433; state as, 174, 370-72, 386, 396, 413, 454
McIlwain, Charles H., 25n, 169n
Mackrell, J.Q.C., 349n
Maclean, Ian, 284n
McNeil, David O., 59n
McRae, Kenneth, 18n, 67n-68n
Madelin, Léon, 213n
Madison, James, 78
Mahoney, Edward P., 84n
Maintenon, Françoise d'Aubigné, marquise de, 334n, 338
Major, J. Russell, 5n, 32n, 47n, 458n
Malebranche, Nicolas, 13, 307-10, 341, 366, 443n
Mandrou, Robert, 5n, 247n
Mandeville, Bernard, 11, 12n, 112n, 296, 366
Marandé, sieur de, 263n
Marolles, Michel de, 243n
Martin, Henri, 337, 378n
Martin, Kingsley, 14n
Marxist, 18, 263-64
Masters, Roger, 426n
Mathiez, Albert, 346n, 393n, 394n
Maurens, Jacques, 129n, 133

Mazarin, Jules, cardinal de, 146, 198, 214, 216, 222, 225-26, 229, 259-60, 333n, 337, 361
mazarinades, 216-17, 227, 229, 378
Medicis, Catherine de', 62
Meinecke, Friedrich, 155n, 171n
Melon, Jean-François, 393
mercantilism, 10, 156-68, 200, 207, 331, 352-56, 379-80, 389, 456
Méré, Antoine Gombaud, chevalier de, 283-87, 301, 324n
Merlant, Joachim, 230n
Mersenne, père, 144, 203n, 242
Meslier, Jean, 144
Mesnard, Pierre, 68n, 204n
Miloyevitch, Voukossava, 196n
Mirabeau, Victor, marquis de, 443-44, 454
Mitton, Damien, 284-85
Molho, Anthony, 12n, 16n
Molière, Jean-Baptiste, 14, 284, 287, 315, 460n
monarchy, *see* absolutism; king; Renaissance
Montaigne, Michel de, 98-116; and Augustine, 183; and Charron, 135-42; and La Boétie, 92-97; and Machiavelli, 99, 112-15; and Pascal, 100-101, 107, 111n, 265, 268-74; and Pasquier, 44-45; and Raimond Sebond, 186n, 188-90, 196; and Rousseau, 104, 107, 435n, 447; Brazilian cannibals, 44, 104-105, 107-108, 243, 338; concept of justice, 64, 141, 170, 172, 271-72; conservatism, 45, 93, 97, 108-11, 178, 210, 268-71, 315, 397; *divertissement*, 88, 100, 230, 274n; individualism, source of, 19, 21, 98-102, 115-16; influence, 13, 20, 119-20, 129, 135, 144-45, 235, 363; on civil war, 87, 101, 123, 271; on custom, 105-109, 164, 178, 210, 270, 368; on freedom, 102-103; on friendship, 92, 106-108, 115-16, 292, 308n, 462; on nature, 103-105, 137-38, 272-73; on social utility of avarice, 138, 162; on obedience to monarchy, 34, 109-11, 268, 299-300; *politique*, 48; separation of public and private life, 87, 99-102, 114-16, 120, 123, 130, 135, 144, 146-47, 154, 169n, 394, 451, 455-56; vice and virtue, 111-16, 167, 189-90, 195-96, 201, 291, 415-16
Montchrétien, Antoine de, 156, 161-68, 200, 207, 312, 331, 456
Montesquieu, Charles de Secondat, baron de, 392-419; and absolutism, 394, 403-407; and England, 394, 401-402, 405-407, 412-15, 418-19; and Rousseau, 376n, 425-26, 442-43; and science, 392-95, 410, 424-25; and the Enlightenment, 13-14, 361; and the Entresol, 362; conservatism of, 45, 79, 97, 106, 108n, 178, 210, 395-98; constitutionalism, 393-94, 418, 459; debt to Bodin, 82, 418; debt to Boulainvilliers, 348; debt to Descartes, 392-95, 408; debt to Domat, 304; debt to Saint-Pierre, 393, 405; despotism, 398-403, 406-407; honor and monarchy, 178n, 289n, 411-13, 459-60; individual and community, 459-63; intermediate powers, 348-49, 390n, 406-408; moderate government, 397-99, 402-408, 412; moral psychology, 421, 425, 452; on ancients and moderns, 408-19; on France and Spain, 385, 402-404, 407; on Richelieu, 402-403, 408; on the Romans, 233, 397, 402, 419, 423; *Persian Letters*, 235, 361, 399-402, 409-11; republics and monarchies, 235, 381, 394, 404, 408-19, 425-26, 452, 459-60; *Spirit of the Laws*, 43, 67, 346, 392-94, 403-10, 415-18, 459; state as machine, 174n; *thèse nobiliaire*, 346, 393
Moore, Will G., 119n, 289n
Moote, A. Lloyd, 213n-15n, 220n, 225n, 237n
Morçaye, Raoul, 91n
More, Thomas, 172n
Moreau-Reibel, Jean, 68n
Mornet, Daniel, 318n
Mousnier, Roland, 4n, 6, 122, 126n, 220n, 236n, 264n; "Comment les français," 6n, 25n, 26n; *La Plume*, 129n, 338n, 458n; *Peasant Uprisings*, 171n, 214n; *XVIe et XVIIe*, 9n, 170n, 187n
municipal government, 5, 218, 259, 348, 384-87, 457-59

Nagels, Jacques, 353n
natural law, 11, 31, 44, 71-72, 127-28, 135, 189, 304, 316, 447
nature, 137, 272-73, 319, 339, 368, 390-92; La Boétie on, 94-95; Montaigne on, 100-105, 189; Rousseau on, 429-30, 434-36, 438; state of, in Sorbière, 243-44; the invisible hand of, 164-65, 352-54

Naudé, Gabriel, 13, 145-50, 157, 171-73, 286, 315
Naudeau, Olivier, 102n
Negri, Antonio, 122n
neo-Platonism, 185, 191
Netherlands, *see* Holland
Nicole, Pierre, 293-302; and Hobbes, 184, 294-95, 298; and *honnêteté*, 286-87, 300; and Jansenism, 293-94, 303; and laissez-faire, 296-97, 302, 351-55, 451, 458; and Pascal, 266, 275-76, 294-97, 299-303; debt to Augustine, 183-84, 294; influence, 266, 293-94, 305, 323-25, 364, 416n; moral psychology, 21, 207, 255, 275, 292, 294-95, 305, 326, 341, 421; on monarchy, 21, 262, 306
Nichols, James H., 101n
Noailles, Charles de, 171
Numa Pompilius, 36

Oakeshott, Michael, 10n, 462
Oestrich, Gerhard, 131n
Ogle, Arthur, 377n
Olivier-Martin, François, 54, 57
O'Loughlin, Michael, 100n
Oncken, Auguste, 380n
Orcibal, Jean, 125n, 193n, 199n
Orléans, Philippe, duc d', 336n, 349n, 361
Ormée, 10, 217-20, 260
Ormesson, Antoine d', 330n
Ovid, 203

Pagès, Georges, 8n
Pangle, Thomas, 412n
Parente, Margherita Isnardi, 71n
Parker, Geoffrey, 124n
Parker, Harold T., 323n
Parkin, John, 116n
parlements, 7, 26, 347; and Jansenism, 264-65; as Roman senate, 35, 49, 60; criticism of, 51, 62-65; in the Fronde, 215, 220-21, 237; Louis XIV and, 237, 259; Seyssel on, 36-37, 39, 51; support for, 42, 45-47, 373, 390, 407-408
participation: absence of, 120-24, 258-59, 457-58; advocated by reformers, 344-46, 385-91, 409, 418, 459-61; as duty, 83-87, 115-16, 134, 458; critique of, 113-14, 140, 147-50. *See also* philosophy
Pascal, Blaise, 262-82; and Augustine, 183-84, 262, 280; and Jansenism, 21, 183, 262, 265-66, 293, 303-307; and La Rochefoucauld, 289, 292; and Montaigne, 100-102, 107, 268; and Nicole, 293-303; and Rousseau, 280-82, 433, 437, 440-42, 447; community of saved, 278-82, 285, 300, 440-42, 447, 461-63; dialectic, 101, 107, 207, 265, 278-82, 462; *divertissement*, 88, 100, 230, 274-76, 294-95; moral psychology, 138, 139n, 273-77, 285-86, 294, 297, 300, 304, 368; *la machine*, 273, 278-80, 299, 407-408, 433; on justice, 63-64, 271-72, 300; symbols of monarchy, 34, 111n, 269, 299-300; three orders, 139n, 266-68, 279; vice and virtue, 275-77, 288-89, 292, 300, 341-42; wager, 278-80, 311, 367, 437, 440
Pasquier, Etienne, 28, 42-49, 87-89, 169n, 222, 231n, 390n
patriotism, 423; crown-centered, 21, 89, 124-25; Descartes on, 206-208; mercantilism and, 160-62; Montesquieu on, 395, 409, 414-15, 418; Rousseau on, 435, 440-42; self-centered, 130-31, 186
Paulmy, Antoine René de Voyer d'Argenson, marquis de, 376n, 380n, 385n, 389n
Perkins, James Breck, 361n
Perkins, Merle, 365n, 366n
Perrens, F. T., 144n
philosophy: and public life, 61, 85-88, 136-37, 208-12, 454-61; defense of privacy by, 19, 87, 91, 130-33, 144-50, 168, 177; Montaigne on, 99-101, 109-16; Rousseau on, 426-32. *See also* participation; sage
Physiocrats, 14, 351, 444
Picot, Gilbert, 127n
Pintard, René, 121n, 145n, 147n, 150, 242n
Plamenatz, John, 280n
Plato: and political science, 149, 172, 270; and Renaissance humanism, 11, 86; and seventeenth-century ethics, 129; harnessing passions, 66, 152; on justice, 66; *Republic* of, as utopia, 70, 97, 234, 243, 315, 338-40, 378, 410
Platonic, 59, 62, 66, 80, 84, 132, 185, 442
Pliny, 419
pluralism: and conflict, 29, 33, 77-78, 180-81; and constitutionalism, 16, 42; d'Argenson on, 383-84, 390-91; Nicole on, 301-302; Saint Pierre on, 369, 374-75
Plutarch, 11, 129, 224n, 368n

Pocock, J.G.A., 15n, 12 1n, 458n
Polin, Raymond, 81n, 445n
political science: critique of, 148-50, 270-71, 447; Montesquieu on, 392-93; Naudé and, 149, 172; praise of, 84-87, 127, 378, 457; Saint-Pierre on, 362-63, 369-73
politiques, 48-49, 62, 123, 144
polysynodie, 345, 361, 374-75
Popkin, Richard, 98n, 145n, 147n, 150n
Porchnev, Boris, 9n, 213n, 216n-17n
Port-Royal, 11, 21, 192-94, 259, 263-65. See also Jansenism
Post, Gaines, 156n, 169n
Poujol, Jacques, 32n-34n
Poulain de la Barre, François, 211n
Poulantzas, Nicos, 9n
Priézac, Daniel de, 142n, 157, 241-42, 252, 258, 317
property: Bodin on, 69-73, 455; consent to taxes on, 30, 47-48, 73; monarch's right to tax, 17, 55, 126, 248; Monesquieu on, 418
Providence, 354, 416; Louis XIV and, 197, 250-51
prudence, 243, 257-58, 366; and reason of state, 140-41, 169-73, 176-77; in Commynes' thought, 29-31; in sixteenth-century ethics, 85, 131-32
public good, 78-79, 112-15, 242-43, 256-57, 372-76; and republics, 234-35, 411, 424. See also *chose publique*; common good
public interest: and interest of state, 154-57, 181-82, 250; conflict with private interest, 82, 175, 181-82, 410, 436-38; theory of, 22, 146, 173-76, 228-29, 371-76, 461-63. See also common interest; interest, theory of; interest of state
Pufendorf, Samuel, 11, 394
pur amour, 185, 194, 204, 341-43, 380-82. See also *charité*

Quesnay, François, 454
Quesnel, Pasquier, 303-304

Rabb, Theodore, 32n, 36n, 124n, 126n, 213n, 236n
Rabelais, François, 87-92
Racine, Jean, 14, 169-70, 277n
raison d'état: and prudence, 112-13, 144, 146, 241-42; and the *libertins*, 144, 146; development of, 16, 20, 31, 156-57, 223-25, 451; opposition to,

80, 191-97, 219, 231, 327, 403, 415. See also Richelieu
Ramsay, chevalier, 343
Ramus, Peter, 68n
Ranum, Orest, 124n, 186n, 215n, 253n, 260, 287n
Rawls, John, 419n
Raymond, Marcel, 292n
Rebelliau, Alfred, 327n
Rebhorn, Wayne, 91n
Rebuffi, Pierre, 56
Réfuges, Eustache des, 62n
Regosin, Richard, 91n, 106n
Renaissance: doctrine of humors, 32-33, 78-79, 180, 380, 451; monarchy, 5, 9, 34, 55-56
republic, 33, 306, 458-59; as ideal, 199, 232-35, 242, 385-88; individual as, 84-85, 190-91, 450; Jansenists as, 263; Montesquieu on, 397, 408-19
Retz, Paul de Gondi, cardinal, 20, 216, 223-29, 236, 308, 361, 411
Rey, Marc-Michel, 376n
Reynolds, Beatrice, 67n
Rice, Eugene F., Jr., 84n, 133n, 136n-37n
Richelieu, Armand Jean Du Plessis de, cardinal, 174-82; and absolutist thought, 125, 127, 169-70, 179-80, 196-97, 260, 394; and Balzac, 197-98, 201; and Jansenism, 187, 191-94, 263; and Sénault, 195-96, 260; and the Fronde, 214, 216, 220, 223-26, 229; ethic of, 120, 176, 193, 197-98, 250, 458; Fénelon and, 333n, 337, 345; Huguenots and, 191, 197; *libertins* and, 146-47, 150, 177; Montesquieu and, 394, 402-403, 408, 452; on prudence, 176, 194, 241; political science and, 363; reason of state, 16, 20, 31, 154, 157, 168-71, 174-82, 191-92, 223, 229, 241, 250, 256, 403, 453; religion and politics, 176, 191-94; *Testament politique*, 175-81; theory of interest, 174-75, 181-83; transformation of regime by, 3, 213-16, 220, 225, 312, 345, 402, 408
Richer d'Aube, 393, 436
Richet, Denis, 8n, 27n, 220n, 347n
Richter, Melvin, 396n, 419n
Rider, Frederick, 102n
Riley, Patrick, 443n
Roberts, Hazel van Dyke, 352n
Rodis-Lewis, Genevieve, 203n, 206n, 308n

Rohan, Henri, duc de, 155, 174
Roman law, 16, 43-45, 57-58, 89
Rome, 32-33, 45, 459; idealized, 80, 198, 230-35, 257, 423-24; Montesquieu on, 397, 402, 404, 408, 412, 417-19
Romulus, 132
Rosenberg, Aubrey, 323n
Rosso, Corrado, 413n
Rothkrug, Lionel, 129n, 161n, 163n, 296n, 313n, 334n, 350-51n
Rousseau, Jean-Jacques, 425-45; and d'Argenson, 376, 379, 383-84, 387, 391, 445-46; and La Boétie, 95-96; and Montaigne, 104, 107, 110, 435n, 447; and Pascal, 280-82, 433, 437, 440-42, 447; and Saint-Pierre, 326n, 364, 371, 374-75, 444; and the Enlightenment, 338n, 361, 461; *Discourse on Inequality*, 96, 306n, 387n, 429-32, 439, 446; *Emile*, 332, 432-38, 442; on freedom, 95, 102, 110, 445-46; on nature, 96, 284, 429, 434-35; on philosophy, 426-28; on self-love, 194, 311, 427-35, 440, 460; Renaissance background of, 13-14, 34, 74-75, 82; *Social Contract*, 78, 280, 376, 435-49; theory of community, 107, 208, 280-82, 419, 427, 435-49, 462-63; theory of interest, 428-48, 461-63; theory of sovereignty, 246n, 444-49, 461; *volonté général*, 34, 78, 280, 391, 436, 441, 443-49, 451, 461
Rowen, Herbert H., 245n, 248n
Rule, John C., 244n-45n, 249n

sage, as ethical ideal, 143-50, 186, 286, 451. *See also* philosophy
saint, as ethical ideal, 186, 267, 286, 432-34, 441. *See also* charité
Saint-Aubin, Le Gendre de, 393, 403
Sainte-Beuve, Charles-Augustin, 265n, 293, 337n, 363n, 378n
Saint-Cyran, abbé de (Jean Duvergier de Hauranne), 125-26, 135, 192-93, 198-99, 216
Saint-Evremond, Charles de, 229-35; and Jansenists, 230, 292; and *libertins*, 230-32, 237, 286; and *raison d'état*, 231, 250n; influence, 382n, 410n; on Holland, 232-33, 242; on *honnêteté*, 231-32, 283, 285-86; on Rome, 232-35, 259, 459
Saint-Pierre, Charles-Irenée, abbé de, 362-74; and Descartes, 211, 364; and Jansenism, 294, 301, 364, 367, 376,

420; and La Bruyère, 324, 363; and Rousseau, 326n, 371, 374-75, 444; enlightened despotism, 369-71, 444; Entresol, 351, 362; influence, 363-64, 378, 385, 393, 402, 405; machine of state, 174n, 370n, 370-73, 405; on *bienfaisance*, 277, 364-65; on perpetual peace, 324, 364; political science, 362-63, 369-70, 372-73, 457; theory of interest, 366-68, 371-76, 382; utilitarianism, 301, 364-69
Saint-Simon, Louis de Rouvroy, duc de, 344-45
Sales, Saint François de, 190, 194, 196
Salmon, J.H.M., 5n, 12n, 50n, 51n, 155n, 168n, 224n, 227n
Saunders, Jason L., 130n
Sayce, R. A., 102n, 108n
Sayre, Robert, 122n, 201n
Schaefer, David L., 116n
Schatz, Albert, 351n
Schmoller, Gustav, 158
Schnur, Roman, 120n, 155n, 168n, 169n, 172n
Screech, M. A., 90n
scrutin, 321n, 373, 385
Sebond, Raimond, 186n, 188-91, 196
Sedgwick, Alexander, 191n, 193n, 216n, 262n, 266n, 304n
Sée, Henri, 127n, 345n
self-interest, 193, 353, 375, 416, 460; enlightened, 22, 165, 232, 342, 437. *See also* interest, theory of; self-love
self-love, 184-97, 422-23, 459; critique of, 253, 305-306, 341; enlightened, 21, 297, 366; Rousseau on, 432-33, 442, 460; social utility of, 288, 366, 380-82. *See also amour de soi*; *amour-propre*; self-interest
Sellier, Philippe, 289n
Sénault, François, 196-97, 206, 260, 288
Seneca, 11, 115, 129, 132, 204, 307
Sennett, Richard, 46on
Sévigné, Marie de Rabutin-Chantal, marquise de, 251, 294
Sexby, Edward, 218
Seyssel, Claude de, 32-42; influence, 16, 28, 43, 51-52, 119, 127, 172n, 222, 304, 390n, 394; on justice, 36-37, 57-58; on monarchy, 33-39, 46, 54, 60, 77-78, 348; on religion, 36, 55; on Rome, 32-33, 35; pluralism, 32-33, 39-42, 302, 321, 396; *police*, 37-38, 454; public and private, 121, 454-55; realism, 31,

Seyssel, Claude de (*cont.*)
41, 74; theory of bridles, 35-38, 42, 66, 72, 180, 222, 254, 388, 407
Seysselian, 18, 90, 128, 406
Shackleton, Robert, 362n, 394n
Sharratt, Peter, 84n
Shennan, J. H., 17n
Shepard, Max, 72n
Shklar, Judith, 67n, 338n, 432n, 447n
Siegel, Jerrold, 32n, 36n, 126n
Silhon, Jean de, 17on, 287-89, 304, 313
Simon, Renée, 348n-49n
Simone, Franco, 92n
Singleton, Charles S., 32n
Sirmond, Antoine, 194
Sirmond, Jean, 154
Skinner, Quentin, 15n, 163n
Smith, Adam, 11, 166n, 296, 351, 354
Smith, Lesley, 124n
Smith, Pauline, 46on
Socrates, 90, 100-101, 110-13, 149, 341-42
Solomon, 60-61
Soman, Albert, 140n
Sonnino, Paul, 245n
Sorbière, Samuel, 242-44, 252, 258, 456
sovereignty, 141-43, 370, 405-406, 442-48, 459-61; Bodin's theory of, 16, 67-72, 81, 125, 161, 444-45; d'Argenson on, 377, 383, 388-90; in absolutist thought, 17, 26-27, 71, 127-28, 452, 454; of the will, 186, 190-93; popular, 27, 75, 254, 316-17
Spain, 199, 384-85, 402, 404, 407
Sparta, 80, 209, 385, 410, 412, 440
Spink, J. H., 121n, 144n, 146n
Stankiewicz, W. J., 315n-16n
Starobinski, Jean, 289n
Stegmann, André, 32n, 84n
Stepan, Alfred, 18n
Stern, Fritz, 175n
Stevens, Linton C., 61n
Stoic, 100-101, 119, 132-33, 162, 183, 187-89, 204, 414
Strayer, Joseph R., 5n, 8n, 36n
Strowski, Fortunat, 266n, 277n
Sully, Maximilien de Béthune, duc de, 161, 312, 377
Sutcliffe, F. E., 170n, 198n-99n
Switzerland, 384, 417; Geneva, 425, 442
symbols, power of, 34, 95-96, 111, 141-42, 242, 299-300, 386-87, 452-53

Tacitus, 132, 156, 172n, 376n
Talbot, Albert, 353n
Talon, Omer, 220-21

Tans, J.A.G., 303n
Tassin, C., 379n, 389n
Taveneaux, René, 262n-64n
Tawney, R. H., 56
Taylor, Charles H., 8n
Tedeschi, John A., 12n, 16n
Temple, Nora, 457n
Terre-Vermeil, Jean de, 15
Thélème, abbey of, 90-92
thèse nobiliaire, 19, 223, 318, 330, 346-50, 390
thèse royale, 19, 223, 330, 346-48, 390
Thickett, Dorothea, 44n, 48n, 88n
Thierry, Augustin, 347n
third estate, 67, 165-66, 178-79, 350. *See also* bourgeoisie
Thireau, Jean-Louis, 245n
Thomas Aquinas, Saint, 156, 172n
Thomistic, 304, 308
Thuau, Etienne, 169n-73n, 176n, 198n, 250n
Thucydides, 32, 172n
Tihany, Leslie, 323n
Tisserand, Roger, 387n-91n
Tocqueville, Alexis, comte de, 232, 377n, 379, 384n, 397, 402, 413
Torcy, J. B. Colbert, marquis de, 377
Treasure, G.R.R., 161n, 170n
Tréca, George, 345n
Trevor-Roper, Hugh, 236n
Troglodytes, 409-11
Truchet, Jacques, 253n
Turgot, Anne-Robert-Jacques, baron de, 454
Turkey, 385, 406
Turquet de Mayerne, Louis, 122n, 128-29
tyranny, 30, 173, 243-44, 271, 317-18, 327, 370, 390; Bodin on, 72, 78; of overmighty subjects, 6, 33, 78, 249, 370, 375, 387; La Boétie on, 95-98; monarchy distinguished from, 3, 18, 66. *See also* despotism
Tyssot de Patot, Simon, 323n

Ullmann, Walter, 84n, 156n, 169n
Ulph, Owen, 73n
utilitarian, 11, 21, 40-41, 165, 288, 329, 383, 386; Saint-Pierre as, 363-67
utopia, 315, 367-68, 409-10; of Cyrano, 229, 235-36; of Rabelais, 90-91; of Veiras, 318-23; Rousseau on, 444, 448

Valladier, André, 253n
Vamos, Mara, 265n

Van Delft, Louis, 324n
Van Kley, Dale, 262n
Vauban, Sebastien le Prestre, seigneur de, 10, 166n, 327-33, 352, 364, 402
Vaughan, C. E., 443n
Vauvenargues, Luc de Clapier, marquis de, 421-23, 438n
Veiras (or Vairasse), Denis, 144, 318-23, 340, 373, 410
venality, of offices, 4, 126, 178, 384
Venice, 33, 48, 93
Venturi, Franco, 352n, 388n
Viau, Théophile de, 144, 198
Villey, Pierre, 101n
Vindiciae contra tyrannos, 28, 52
Viner, Jacog, 158, 296n
Vinogradoff, Paul, 57n
virtue: in politics, 113-16, 140, 235; knowledge and, 183; Montesquieu on, 394, 400, 412-19, 459; vice and, 131-33, 151-52, 167-68, 291, 311
volonté générale, 46, 279, 451. See also Rousseau
Voltaire (François-Marie Arouet), 119n, 336n, 398n; and d'Argenson, 376-79, 389n; and Nicole, 294, 303; and Saint-Pierre, 363-65; and the Enlightenment, 12-14, 337-38, 361, 393, 420; *Philosophical Letters*, 361, 393, 417n
Von der Muhll, Emanuel, 321n
Vyverberg, Henry, 397n

Wade, Ira O., 348n, 362n-65n, 376n; *Intellectual Origins*, 13n-14n, 96n, 98n, 135n, 147n, 242n, 286n, 308n, 315n
Wallerstein, Immanuel, 9n
Walton, Craig, 308n
Wartburg, Walther von, 25n
Watter, Pierre, 199n
Weber, H., 70n, 92n
Westrich, Sal Alexander, 217n-19n
Wilson, Ian, 394n
Wolf, John B., 244n, 248n
Wolfe, Martin, 159n

Young, Arthur, 25

Library of Congress Cataloging in Publication Data

Keohane, Nannerl O.   1940-
   Philosophy and the state in France.

   Bibliography: p.
   Includes index.
   1. Political science—France—History.   2. Philosophy, French—17th century.   I. Title.
JA84.F8K46   320.1'01'0944   79-3219
ISBN 0-691-07611-1
ISBN 0-691-10078-0 pbk.